Discovering Computers

FUNDAMENTALS, Second Edition

Discovering Computers

FUNDAMENTALS, Second Edition

Gary B. Shelly
Thomas J. Cashman
Misty E. Vermaat

Contributing Authors

Jeffrey J. Quasney
Susan L. Sebok
Timothy J. Walker
Jeffrey J. Webb

THOMSON
COURSE TECHNOLOGY™

COURSE TECHNOLOGY
25 THOMSON PLACE
BOSTON MA 02210

SHELLY CASHMAN SERIES®

Australia • Canada • Denmark • Japan • Mexico • New Zealand • Philippines • Puerto Rico • Singapore
South Africa • Spain • United Kingdom • United States

Discovering Computers
Fundamentals, Second Edition

Gary B. Shelly
Thomas J. Cashman
Misty E. Vermaat

Managing Editor:
Alexandra Arnold

Series Consulting Editor:
Jim Quasney

Senior Acquisitions Editor:
Dana Merk

Product Manager:
Reed Cotter

Editorial Assistant:
Selena Coppock

Print Buyer:
Laura Burns

Production Editor:
Aimee Poirier

Researcher:
F. William Vermaat

Copy Editor:
Lyn Markowitz

Proofreader:
Nancy Lamm

Interior Designer:
Pre-Press Company, Inc.

Cover Image:
Pre-Press Company, Inc.

Illustrator:
Pre-Press Company, Inc.

Compositor:
Pre-Press Company, Inc.

Indexer:
Nancy Lamm

Printer:
Banta Menasha

Discovering Computers

FUNDAMENTALS, Second Edition

Contents

CHAPTER 1

INTRODUCTION TO COMPUTERS 1

A WORLD OF COMPUTERS 2

WHAT IS A COMPUTER? 3
Data and Information 3
Advantages and Disadvantages of Using
Computers...4
Information Processing Cycle 5

THE COMPONENTS OF A COMPUTER 6
Input Devices 6
Output Devices...7
System Unit...7
Storage Devices 7
Communication Devices......................................8

NETWORKS AND THE INTERNET 8
The Internet...8

COMPUTER SOFTWARE 10
System Software..10
Application Software..11
Installing and Running Programs 11
Software Development 12

CATEGORIES OF COMPUTERS 14

PERSONAL COMPUTERS 14
Desktop Computers...14

MOBILE COMPUTERS..14
Notebook Computers 14
Mobile Devices 15

MIDRANGE SERVERS 16

MAINFRAMES 17

SUPERCOMPUTERS 17

EMBEDDED COMPUTERS 17

EXAMPLES OF COMPUTER USAGE 18
Home User 18
Small Office/Home User....................................20
Mobile User..20
Power User 21
Large Business User..21

COMPUTER APPLICATIONS IN SOCIETY 22
Education 22
Finance..23
Government 23
Health Care 23
Science 24
Publishing 25
Travel 25
Industry 25

CHAPTER SUMMARY 26

COMPANIES ON THE CUTTING EDGE.....................27
Dell 27
Apple Computer 27

TECHNOLOGY TRAILBLAZERS 27
Bill Gates 27
Carly Fiorina 27

CHAPTER REVIEW 28

KEY TERMS...29

CHECKPOINT 30

WEB RESEARCH..31

LEARN HOW TO 32

LEARN IT ONLINE...34

Special Feature

TIMELINE: MILESTONES IN
COMPUTER HISTORY   **35**

CHAPTER 2

THE INTERNET AND WORLD WIDE WEB 49

THE INTERNET 50

HOW THE INTERNET WORKS....................................51
Connecting to the Internet 51
Access Providers 52
How Data Travels the Internet.........................52
Internet Addresses 53

THE WORLD WIDE WEB...54
Browsing the Web 54
Web Addresses 56
Navigating Web Pages 57

Searching for Information on the Web 57
Types of Web Sites 61
Evaluating a Web Site 63
Multimedia on the Web 64
Web Publishing..66
E-Commerce 67

OTHER INTERNET SERVICES 68
E-Mail..69
FTP 71
Newsgroups and Message Boards 71
Mailing Lists 71
Chat Rooms..71
Instant Messaging 72
Internet Telephony 73

NETIQUETTE 73

CHAPTER SUMMARY 74

COMPANIES ON THE CUTTING EDGE.............................75
Google 75
Yahoo 75

TECHNOLOGY TRAILBLAZERS 75
Tim Berners-Lee 75
Meg Whitman 75

CHAPTER REVIEW 76

KEY TERMS..77

CHECKPOINT 78

WEB RESEARCH 79

LEARN HOW TO 80

LEARN IT ONLINE 82

Special Feature
MAKING USE OF THE WEB   83

CHAPTER 3

APPLICATION SOFTWARE 99

APPLICATION SOFTWARE 100
The Role of System Software 101
Working with Application Software 102

BUSINESS SOFTWARE 104
Word Processing Software 105
Developing a Document 106
Spreadsheet Software 107
Database Software 108
Presentation Graphics Software.................................109
Note Taking Software 110
Personal Information Manager Software 110
PDA Business Software 110
Software Suite 110
Project Management Software 111
Accounting Software 111
Enterprise Computing Software 111

GRAPHICS AND MULTIMEDIA SOFTWARE 112

Computer-Aided Design..112
Desktop Publishing Software
(for the Professional) 113
Paint/Image Editing Software
(for the Professional) 113
Video and Audio Editing Software
(for the Professional) 114
Multimedia Authoring Software 114
Web Page Authoring Software 114

SOFTWARE FOR HOME, PERSONAL, AND
EDUCATIONAL USE..115
Software Suite (for Personal Use) 116
Personal Finance Software 116
Legal Software 117
Tax Preparation Software 117
Desktop Publishing Software
(for Personal Use)..117
Paint/Image Editing Software
(for Personal Use)..118
Clip Art/Image Gallery..118
Video and Audio Editing Software
(for Personal Use)..119
Home Design/Landscaping Software..........................119
Educational and Reference Software..........................119
Entertainment Software 120

APPLICATION SOFTWARE FOR COMMUNICATIONS 120

POPULAR STAND-ALONE UTILITY PROGRAMS.....................122

LEARNING AIDS AND SUPPORT TOOLS FOR
APPLICATION SOFTWARE 122
Web-Based Training...123

CHAPTER SUMMARY 124

COMPANIES ON THE CUTTING EDGE............................125
Adobe Systems 125
Microsoft 125

TECHNOLOGY TRAILBLAZERS 125
Dan Bricklin 125
Masayoshi Son 125

CHAPTER REVIEW 126

KEY TERMS..127

CHECKPOINT 128

WEB RESEARCH 129

LEARN HOW TO 130

LEARN IT ONLINE 132

CHAPTER 4

THE COMPONENTS OF THE SYSTEM UNIT 133

THE SYSTEM UNIT 134
The Motherboard 136

PROCESSOR 137
The Control Unit 137
The Arithmetic Logic Unit 137

Machine Cycle 138
The System Clock...138
Comparison of Personal Computer Processors..........139
Buying a Personal Computer 139

DATA REPRESENTATION................................140

MEMORY...142
Bytes and Addressable Memory 142
Memory Sizes 142
Types of Memory 142
RAM 143
Cache 144
ROM 145
Flash Memory...145
CMOS..146
Memory Access Times................................146

EXPANSION SLOTS AND ADAPTER CARDS 147
PC Cards, Flash Memory Cards, and USB
Flash Drives 147

PORTS AND CONNECTORS 148
Serial Ports 149
Parallel Ports..149
USB Ports..149
FireWire Ports 150
Special Purpose Ports 150

BUSES..151

BAYS 151

POWER SUPPLY 152

MOBILE COMPUTERS AND DEVICES 152

PUTTING IT ALL TOGETHER............................154

KEEPING YOUR COMPUTER CLEAN....................155

CHAPTER SUMMARY 156

COMPANIES ON THE CUTTING EDGE.................157
AMD...157
Intel 157

TECHNOLOGY TRAILBLAZERS 157
Jack Kilby 157
Gordon Moore 157

CHAPTER REVIEW 158

KEY TERMS...159

CHECKPOINT 160

WEB RESEARCH 161

LEARN HOW TO 162

LEARN IT ONLINE 164

CHAPTER 5

INPUT AND OUTPUT **165**

WHAT IS INPUT? 166

KEYBOARD AND POINTING DEVICES...................167

The Keyboard 168
Mouse...169
Trackball 170
Touchpad 170
Pointing Stick 170
Joystick and Wheel 171
Light Pen 171
Touch Screen 171
Pen Input 172

OTHER TYPES OF INPUT 173
Voice Input 173
Input for PDAs, Smart Phones, and Tablet PCs ...174
Digital Cameras 175
Video Input 176
Scanners and Reading Devices 177
Terminals 180
Biometric Input..181

WHAT IS OUTPUT?..185

DISPLAY DEVICES 183
LCD Monitors and Screens.........................184
Plasma Monitors 185
CRT Monitors 186

PRINTERS 187
Producing Printed Output 188
Nonimpact Printers 189
Ink-Jet Printers 189
Photo Printers 190
Laser Printers 190
Thermal Printers 191
Mobile Printers 192
Plotters and Large-Format Printers...........192
Impact Printers 192

OTHER OUTPUT DEVICES................................193
Speakers and Headsets 193
Fax Machines and Fax Modems 194
MultiFunction Peripherals 194
Data Projectors 195

PUTTING IT ALL TOGETHER............................196

INPUT AND OUTPUT DEVICES FOR PHYSICALLY
CHALLENGED USERS 197

CHAPTER SUMMARY 198

COMPANIES ON THE CUTTING EDGE.................199
Logitech 199
Hewlett-Packard...199

TECHNOLOGY TRAILBLAZERS 199
Douglas Engelbart 199
Donna Dubinsky 199

CHAPTER REVIEW 200

KEY TERMS...202

CHECKPOINT 203

WEB RESEARCH 204

LEARN HOW TO 205

LEARN IT ONLINE...207

Special Feature
DIGITAL IMAGING AND
VIDEO TECHNOLOGY　　　　**208**

CHAPTER 6

STORAGE **219**

STORAGE 220

MAGNETIC DISKS 222
　Floppy Disks 223
　Zip Disks 223
　Hard Disks 224

OPTICAL DISCS 229
　CD-ROMs 231
　CD-Rs and CD-RWs 232
　DVD-ROMs...233
　Recordable and Rewritable DVDs.....................234

TAPE 234

PC CARDs 235

MINIATURE MOBILE STORAGE MEDIA 235
　Flash Memory Cards 236
　USB Flash Drives 236
　Smart Cards 237

MICROFILM AND MICROFICHE 238

ENTERPRISE STORAGE 238

PUTTING IT ALL TOGETHER 239

CHAPTER SUMMARY 240

COMPANIES ON THE CUTTING EDGE....................241
　Maxtor 241
　SanDisk Corporation 241

TECHNOLOGY TRAILBLAZERS 241
　Al Shugart 241
　Mark Dean 241

CHAPTER REVIEW 242

KEY TERMS...243

CHECKPOINT 244

WEB RESEARCH 245

LEARN HOW TO 246

LEARN IT ONLINE...248

CHAPTER 7

OPERATING SYSTEMS AND UTILITY PROGRAMS 249

SYSTEM SOFTWARE...250

OPERATING SYSTEMS 251

OPERATING SYSTEM FUNCTIONS 252
　Starting a Computer 252

Providing a User Interface 253
Managing Programs 253
Managing Memory 255
Scheduling Jobs 255
Configuring Devices 256
Establishing a Connection 256
Monitoring Performance...................................257
Providing File Management and Other
　Utilities..257
Controlling a Network 257
Administering Security 258

OPERATING SYSTEM UTILITY PROGRAMS 259
　File Manager 259
　Image Viewer 259
　Personal Firewall 260
　Uninstaller...260
　Disk Scanner 260
　Disk Defragmenter..261
　Diagnostic Utility 261
　Backup Utility 261
　Screen Saver 261

TYPES OF OPERATING SYSTEMS.........................262

STAND-ALONE OPERATING SYSTEMS...................262
　DOS 262
　Windows XP 262
　Mac OS X 264
　UNIX 264
　Linux 265

NETWORK OPERATING SYSTEMS 266

EMBEDDED OPERATING SYSTEMS 266

STAND-ALONE UTILITY PROGRAMS 267
　Antivirus Programs 267
　Spyware Removers 268
　Internet Filters 268
　File Compression 269
　File Conversion 269
　CD/DVD Burning 269
　Personal Computer Maintenance 270

CHAPTER SUMMARY 270

COMPANIES ON THE CUTTING EDGE....................271
　Red Hat 271
　Symbian...271

TECHNOLOGY TRAILBLAZERS 271
　Alan Kay 271
　Linus Torvalds 271

CHAPTER REVIEW 272

KEY TERMS...273

CHECKPOINT 274

WEB RESEARCH 275

LEARN HOW TO 276

LEARN IT ONLINE...278

Special Feature

BUYER'S GUIDE: HOW TO PURCHASE A PERSONAL COMPUTER **279**

CHAPTER 8

COMMUNICATIONS AND NETWORKS **295**

COMMUNICATIONS 296

USES OF COMPUTER COMMUNICATIONS 297
  Internet, Web, E-Mail, Instant Messaging, Chat
    Rooms, Newsgroups, Internet Telephony, FTP,
    Web Folders, Video Conferencing, and Fax 298
  Wireless Messaging Services 298
  Public Internet Access Points 300
  Global Positioning System 301
  Collaboration 302
  Groupware 302
  Voice Mail 302
  Web Services 302

NETWORKS 303
  LANs, MANs, and WANs 303
  Network Architectures 305
  Network Topologies 306
  Intranets 307
  Network Communications Standards 308

COMMUNICATIONS SOFTWARE 310

COMMUNICATIONS OVER THE TELEPHONE
  NETWORK 310
  Dial-Up Lines 311
  Dedicated Lines 311

COMMUNICATIONS DEVICES 312
  Dial-Up Modems 313
  ISDN and DSL Modems 314
  Cable Modems 314
  Wireless Modems 314
  Network Cards 315
  Wireless Access Points 315
  Routers 315

HOME NETWORKS 316
  Wired Home Networks 316
  Wireless Home Networks 316

COMMUNICATIONS CHANNEL 317

PHYSICAL TRANSMISSION MEDIA 319
  Twisted-Pair Cable 319
  Coaxial Cable 320
  Fiber-Optic Cable 320

WIRELESS TRANSMISSION MEDIA 320
  Infrared 321
  Broadcast Radio 321
  Cellular Radio 321
  Microwaves 321
  Communications Satellite 321

CHAPTER SUMMARY 322
COMPANIES ON THE CUTTING EDGE 323
  Cisco Systems 323
  Qualcomm 323

TECHNOLOGY TRAILBLAZERS 323
  Robert Metcalfe 323
  Patricia Russo 323

CHAPTER REVIEW 324

KEY TERMS 325

CHECKPOINT 326

WEB RESEARCH 327

LEARN HOW TO 328

LEARN IT ONLINE 330

CHAPTER 9

DATABASE MANAGEMENT **331**

DATABASES, DATA AND INFORMATION 332
  Data Integrity 333
  Qualities of Valuable Information 334

THE HIERARCHY OF DATA 334
  Characters 335
  Fields 335
  Records 336
  Files 336

MAINTAINING DATA 336
  Adding Records 336
  Changing Records 338
  Deleting Records 338
  Validating Data 339

FILE PROCESSING VERSUS DATABASES 341
  File Processing Systems 341
  The Database Approach 341

DATABASE MANAGEMENT SYSTEMS 343
  Data Dictionary 343
  File Retrieval and Maintenance 344
  Data Security 346
  Backup and Recovery 346

RELATIONAL, OBJECT-ORIENTED, AND
  MULTIDIMENSIONAL DATABASES 347
  Relational Databases 347
  Object-Oriented Databases 349
  Multidimensional Databases 349

WEB DATABASES 350
DATABASE ADMINISTRATION 351
  Database Design Guidelines 351
  Role of the Database Anaylsts and
    Administrators 351
  Role of the Employee as User 351

CHAPTER SUMMARY 352

COMPANIES ON THE CUTTING EDGE...........................353
   Oracle 353
   Sybase 353

TECHNOLOGY TRAILBLAZERS 353
   E. F. Codd 353
   Larry Ellison 353

CHAPTER REVIEW 354

KEY TERMS...355

CHECKPOINT 356

WEB RESEARCH 357

LEARN HOW TO 358

LEARN IT ONLINE 360

CHAPTER 10

COMPUTER SECURITY, ETHICS, AND PRIVACY 361

COMPUTER SECURITY RISKS 362

INTERNET AND NETWORK ATTACKS 364
   Computer Viruses, Worms, and Trojan Horses..........364
   Safeguards against Computer Viruses, Worms,
     and Trojan Horses 365
   Denial of Service Attacks 367
   Back Doors 367
   Spoofing..367
   Safeguards against DoS Attacks, Back Doors,
     and Spoofing..367
   Firewalls 367
   Intrusion Detection Software 368

UNAUTHORIZED ACCESS AND USE 368
   Safeguards against Unauthorized Access
     and Use 368
   Identifying and Authenticating Users 368

HARDWARE THEFT AND VANDALISM 371
   Safeguards against Hardware Theft and
     Vandalism 371

SOFTWARE THEFT 372
   Safeguards against Software Theft 372

INFORMATION THEFT 373
   Safeguards against Information Theft 373
   Encryption...373

SYSTEM FAILURE 374
   Safeguards against System Failure 374

BACKING UP — THE ULTIMATE SAFEGUARD 375

WIRELESS SECURITY...375

ETHICS AND SOCIETY 376
   Information Accuracy 377
   Intellectual Property Rights 378

INFORMATION PRIVACY...379
   Electronic Profiles 380
   Cookies 380
   Spyware and Adware 381
   Phishing 381
   Spam 382
   Privacy Laws...382
   Computer Forensics 384
   Employee Monitoring 384
   Content Filtering 384

HEALTH CONCERNS OF COMPUTER USE 385
   Computers and Health Risks................................385
   Ergonomics and Workplace Design 386
   Computer Addiction 387
   Green Computing 387

CHAPTER SUMMARY 388

COMPANIES ON THE CUTTING EDGE...........................389
   McAfee...389
   Symantec 389

TECHNOLOGY TRAILBLAZERS 389
   Donn Parker 389
   Cliff Stoll 389

CHAPTER REVIEW 390

KEY TERMS...391

CHECKPOINT 392

WEB RESEARCH 393

LEARN HOW TO 394

LEARN IT ONLINE 396

Special Feature
| DIGITAL ENTERTAINMENT   **397**

CHAPTER 11

INFORMATION SYSTEM DEVELOPMENT AND PROGRAMMING LANGUAGES 405

THE SYSTEM DEVELOPMENT CYCLE...............................406
   Who Participates in the System Development
     Cycle?..407
   Project Management 408
   Feasibility Assessment 409
   Documentation..409
   Data and Information Gathering Techniques 410
   What Initiates the System Development Cycle? 410
   Planning Phase..412
   Analysis Phase 413
   Design Phase...416
   Implementation Phase...420
   Support Phase..422
   Information System Security 422

PROGRAMMING LANGUAGES 423
   Low-Level Languages 424

Procedural Languages 425
Object-Oriented Programming Languages 427
Other Programming Languages 430
Other Program Development Tools 431
Web Page Development 433
Multimedia Program Development 437

THE PROGRAM DEVELOPMENT CYCLE 438
What Initiates the Program Development
Cycle? 439
Control Structures 440

CHAPTER SUMMARY 442

COMPANIES ON THE CUTTING EDGE 443
Computer Associates 443
Macromedia 443

TECHNOLOGY TRAILBLAZERS 443
Grace Hopper 443
James Gosling 443

CHAPTER REVIEW 444

KEY TERMS 445

CHECKPOINT 446

WEB RESEARCH 447

LEARN HOW TO 448

LEARN IT ONLINE 450

CHAPTER 12

ENTERPRISE COMPUTING 451

WHAT IS ENTERPRISE COMPUTING? 452
Organizational Structure of an Enterprise 454
Levels of Users 455
How Managers Use Information 456

INFORMATION SYSTEMS IN THE ENTERPRISE 456
Information Systems within Functional Units 457
General Purpose Information Systems 461
Integrated Information Systems 465

ENTERPRISE-WIDE TECHNOLOGIES 467
Portals 467
EDI 468
Data Warehouses 468
Extranets 469
Web Services 469
Workflow 469
Virtual Private Network 470

E-COMMERCE 470
E-Retailing 470
Finance 472
Health 472
Entertainment and Media 472
Travel 473
Other Business Services 473

ENTERPRISE HARDWARE 474
RAID 474
Network Attached Storage and Storage
Area Networks 476
Enterprise Storage Systems 476
Blade Servers 477
High-Availability Systems 477
Scalability 477
Utility and Grid Computing 478
Interoperability 478

BACKUP PROCEDURES 478
Disaster Recovery Plan 479

CHAPTER SUMMARY 480

COMPANIES ON THE CUTTING EDGE 481
SAP 481
IBM 481

TECHNOLOGY TRAILBLAZERS 481
Tom Siebel 481
Jim Clark 481

CHAPTER REVIEW 482

KEY TERMS 483

CHECKPOINT 484

WEB RESEARCH 485

LEARN HOW TO 486

LEARN IT ONLINE 488

APPENDIX A: QUIZ YOURSELF ANSWERS ....APP 1

GLOSSARY/INDEX ....IND 1

PHOTO CREDITS 000

Preface

The Shelly Cashman Series® offers the finest textbooks in computer education. This book is our answer to the many requests we have received from instructors and students for a textbook that provides a succinct, yet thorough, introduction to computers.

In *Discovering Computers: Fundamentals, Second Edition*, you will find an educationally sound, highly visual, and easy-to-follow pedagogy that presents a complete, yet to the point, treatment of introductory computer subjects. Students will finish the course with a solid understanding of computers, how to use computers, and how to access information on the World Wide Web.

OBJECTIVES OF THIS TEXTBOOK

Discovering Computers: Fundamentals, Second Edition is intended for use as a stand-alone textbook or in combination with an applications, Internet, or programming textbook in a one-quarter or one-semester introductory computer course. No experience with computers is assumed. The objectives of this book are to:

- Provide a concise, yet comprehensive, introduction to computers
- Present the most-up-to-date technology in an ever-changing discipline
- Give students an understanding of why computers are essential components in business and society
- Teach the fundamentals of computers and computer nomenclature, particularly with respect to personal computer hardware and software, the World Wide Web, and enterprise computing
- Present the material in a visually appealing and exciting manner that motivates students to learn
- Present strategies for purchasing a notebook computer, a Tablet PC, and a PDA
- Offer alternative learning techniques and reinforcement via the Web
- Offer distance-education providers a textbook with a meaningful and exercise-rich companion Web site

DISTINGUISHING FEATURES

To date, more than six million students have learned about computers using a *Discovering Computers* textbook. With the additional World Wide Web integration and interactivity, streaming up-to-date audio and video, extraordinary step-by-step visual drawings and photographs, unparalleled currency, and the Shelly and Cashman touch, this book will make your computer concepts course exciting and dynamic. Distinguishing features of this book include:

A Proven Pedagogy

Careful explanations of complex concepts, educationally-sound elements, and reinforcement highlight this proven method of presentation. A pictorial arrangement of the pedagogy can be found beginning on page xix.

Essential Computer Concepts Coverage

This book offers the same breadth of topics as our well-known *Discovering Computers 2006: Complete*, but the depth of coverage focuses on the basic knowledge required to be computer literate in today's digital world.

A Visually Appealing Book that Maintains Student Interest

The latest technology, pictures, drawings, and text are combined artfully to produce a visually appealing and easy-to-understand book. Many of the figures include a step-by-step presentation (see page 141), which simplifies the more complex computer concepts. Pictures and drawings reflect the latest trends in computer technology.

Latest Technologies and Terms

The technologies and terms your students see in this book are those they will encounter when they start using computers. Only the latest application software packages are shown throughout the book.

World Wide Web Enhanced

This book uses the World Wide Web as a major supplement. The purpose of integrating the World Wide Web into the book is to (1) offer students additional information and currency on important topics; (2) use its interactive capabilities to offer creative reinforcement and online quizzes; (3) make available alternative learning techniques with Web-based learning games, practice tests, and interactive labs; (4) underscore the relevance of the World Wide Web as a basic information tool that can be used in all facets of society; (5) introduce students to doing research on the Web; and (6) offer instructors the opportunity to organize and administer their traditional campus-based or distance-education-based courses on the Web using WebCT, Blackboard, or MyCourse 2.1. This textbook, however, does not depend on Web access to be used successfully. The Web access adds to the already complete treatment of topics within the book.

Extensive End-of-Chapter Materials

A notable strength of this book is the extensive student activities at the end of each chapter. Well-structured student activities can make the difference between students merely participating in a class and students retaining the information they learn. The activities in this book include: Chapter Review, Key Terms, Checkpoint, Web Research, Learn How To, and Learn It Online. A pictorial presentation of each end-of-chapter activities can be found beginning on page xxii.

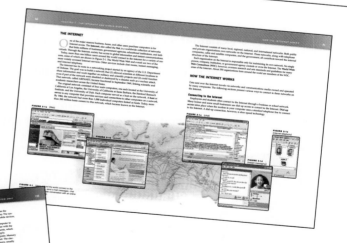

ORGANIZATION OF THIS TEXTBOOK

Discovering Computers: Fundamentals, Second Edition provides a thorough, but succinct, introduction to computers. The material is divided into twelve chapters, five special features, and a glossary/index.

Chapter 1 – Introduction to Computers   In Chapter 1, students are introduced to basic computer concepts, such as what a computer is, how it works, and what makes it a powerful tool.

Special Feature – Timeline: Milestones in Computer History   In this special feature, students learn about the major computer technology developments during the past 65 years.

Chapter 2 – The Internet and World Wide Web   In Chapter 2, students learn about the Internet, World Wide Web, browsers, e-mail, FTP, and instant messaging.

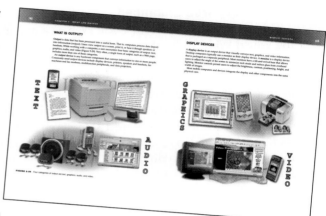

Special Feature – Making Use of the Web   In this special feature, more than 150 popular up-to-date Web sites are listed and described.

Chapter 3 – Application Software   In Chapter 3, students are introduced to a variety of business software, graphics and multimedia software, home/personal/educational software, and communications software.

Chapter 4 – The Components of the System Unit   In Chapter 4, students are introduced to the components of the system unit; how memory stores data, instructions, and information; and how the system unit executes an instruction.

Chapter 5 – Input and Output   Chapter 5 describes the various methods of input and output, and commonly used input and output devices.

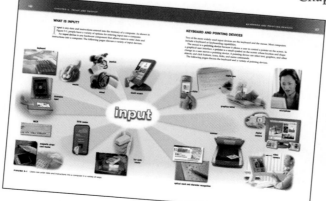

Chapter 6 – Storage   In Chapter 6, students learn about various storage media and storage devices.

Special Feature – Digital Imaging and Video Technology   In this special feature, students are introduced to using a personal computer, digital camera, and video camera to manipulate photographs and video.

Chapter 7 – Operating Systems and Utility Programs   In Chapter 7, students learn about a variety of stand-alone operating systems, network operating systems, and embedded operating systems.

Special Feature – Buyer's Guide: How to Purchase a Personal Computer   In this special feature, students are introduced to purchasing a desktop computer, notebook computer, Tablet PC, and PDA.

Chapter 8 – Communications and Networks   Chapter 8 provides students with an overview of communications technology and applications.

Chapter 9 – Database Management   Chapter 9 presents students with the advantages of organizing data in a database and describes various types of data.

Chapter 10 – Computer Security, Ethics, and Privacy   In Chapter 10, students learn about computer and Internet risks, ethical issues surrounding information accuracy, intellectual property rights, codes of conduct, information privacy, and computer-related health issues.

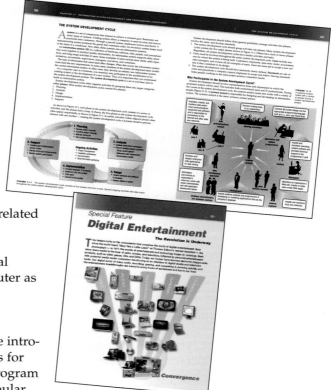

Special Feature: Digital Entertainment   In this special feature, students are introduced to the personal computer as a digital entertainment device.

Chapter 11 – Information System Development and Programming Languages   In Chapter 11, students are introduced to the system development cycle and guidelines for system development. This chapter also presents the program development cycle, program design methods, and popular programming languages.

Chapter 12 – Enterprise Computing   In Chapter 12, students learn about the special computing requirements used in an enterprise-sized organization.

Appendix A – Quiz Yourself Answers   Appendix A provides the answers for the Quiz Yourself questions in the text.

Glossary/Index   The Glossary/Index includes a definition and page references for every key term presented in the book.

SHELLY CASHMAN SERIES INSTRUCTOR RESOURCES

The Shelly Cashman Series is dedicated to providing you with all of the tools you need to make your class a success. Information on all supplementary materials is available through your Course Technology representative or by calling one of the following telephone numbers: Colleges and Universities, 1-800-648-7450; High Schools, 1-800-824-5179; Private Career Colleges, 1-800-347-7707; Canada, 1-800-268-2222; Corporations with IT Training Centers, 1-800-648-7450; and Government Agencies, Health-Care Organizations, and Correctional Facilities, 1-800-477-3692.

Instructor Resources CD-ROM

The Instructor Resources CD-ROM includes both teaching and testing aids. The contents of each item on the Instructor Resources CD-ROM (ISBN 0-619-25518-8) are described below.

Instructors Manual The Instructor's Manual is made up of Microsoft Word files, which include detailed lesson plans with page number references, lecture notes, classroom activities, discussion topics, and projects to assign.

Syllabus Sample syllabi, which can be customized easily to a course, are included. The syllabi cover policies, class and lab assignments and exams, and procedural information.

Figure Files Illustrations for every figure in the textbook are available in electronic form. Use this ancillary to present a slide show in lecture or to print transparencies for use in lecture with an overhead projector. If you have a personal computer and LCD device, this ancillary can be an effective tool for presenting lectures.

Solutions to Exercises Solutions are included for all end-of-chapter exercises.

Test Bank & Test Engine The ExamView test bank includes 110 questions for every chapter (25 multiple-choice, 50 true/false, and 35 completion) with page number references, and when appropriate, figure references. The test bank comes with a copy of the test engine, ExamView, the ultimate tool for your objective-based testing needs.

Printed Test Bank A Microsoft Word version of the test bank you can print also is included.

Data Files for Students All the files that are required by students to complete the exercises are included. You can distribute the files on the Instructor Resources CD-ROM to your students over a network, or you can have them follow the instructions on the inside back cover of this book to obtain a copy of the Data Disk.

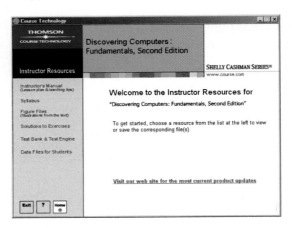

Course Presenter

Course Presenter (ISBN 0-619-25519-6) is a one-click-per-slide presentation system on CD-ROM that provides PowerPoint slides for every subject in each chapter. Use this presentation system to give interesting, well-organized, and knowledge-based lectures. Several up-to-date G4TechTV computer-related video clips are available for optional presentation. Course Presenter provides consistent coverage for multiple lecturers.

Student Edition Labs

Thirty Web-based interactive labs will help your students master hundreds of computer concepts including input and output devices, file management and desktop applications, computer privacy, virus protection, and much more. Featuring up-to-the-minute content, eye-popping graphics, and rich animation, the highly interactive Student Edition Labs offer students an alternative way to learn through dynamic observation, step-by-step practice, and challenging review questions. Access the free Student Edition Labs from the *Discovering Computers: Fundamentals, Second Edition* Web site at scsite.com/dcf2e or see the Student Edition Lab exercises on the Learn It Online pages at the end of each chapter.

Online Content

Course Technology offers textbook-based content for Blackboard, WebCT, and MyCourse 2.1.

BlackBoard and WebCT   As the leading provider of IT content for the Blackboard and WebCT platforms, Course Technology delivers rich content that enhances your textbook to give your students a unique learning experience.

MyCourse 2.1   MyCourse 2.1 is Course Technology's powerful online course management and content delivery system. MyCourse 2.1 allows nontechnical users to create, customize, and deliver Web-based courses; post content and assignments; manage student enrollment; administer exams; track results in the online grade book; and more.

SAM Computer Concepts

Add the power of assessment and detailed reporting to your Student Edition Lab assignments with SAM Computer Concepts.

SAM (Skills Assessment Manager) Computer Concepts helps you energize your training assignments by allowing students to learn and quiz on important computer skills in an active, hands-on environment. By adding SAM Computer Concepts to your curriculum, you can:

- Reinforce your students' knowledge of key computer concepts with hands-on application exercises.
- Allow your students to "learn by listening," with rich audio in their computer concepts labs.
- Build computer concepts exams from a test bank of more than 50,000 objective-based questions or create your own test questions.
- Schedule your students' computer concepts training and testing assignments with powerful administrative tools.
- Track student exam grades and training progress using more than one dozen student and classroom reports.

TO THE STUDENT...Getting the Most Out of Your Book

Welcome to *Discovering Computers: Fundamentals, Second Edition*. You can save yourself a lot of time and gain a better understanding of the computer concepts presented in this book if you spend a few minutes reviewing this section.

1   Companion Web Site

Use the Companion Web site at scsite.com/dcf2e, which includes additional information about important topics and provides unparalleled currency; and make use of online learning games, practice tests, and additional reinforcement. Gain access to this dynamic site with Course Technology's centralized login page, CoursePort.

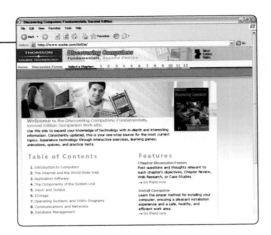

2   Chapter Objectives and Table of Contents

Before you read the chapter, carefully read through the Objectives and Contents so that you know what you should learn from the chapter.

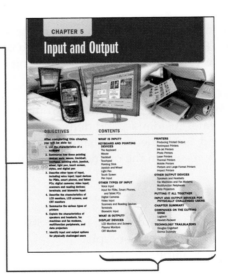

3   Initial Chapter Figure

Carefully study the first figure in each chapter because it will give you an easy-to-follow overview of the major purpose of the chapter.

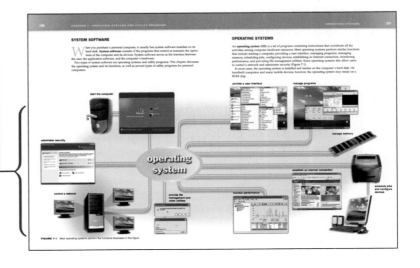

4 Web Link

Obtain current information and a different perspective about key terms and concepts by visiting the Web addresses in the Web Links found in the margins throughout the book.

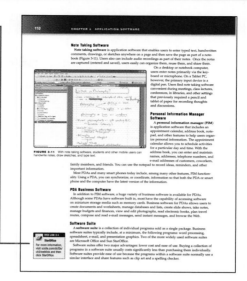

5 Step Figures

Each chapter includes numerous step figures that present the more complex computer concepts using a step-by-step pedagogy.

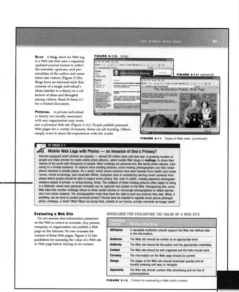

6 At Issue

At Issue boxes provide you with computer-related controversial topics of the day and stimulating questions that offer insight into the general concerns of computers in society.

7 Looking Ahead

The Looking Ahead boxes offer you a glimpse at the latest advances in computer technology that will be available, usually within five years.

8 FAQ

FAQ (frequently asked questions) boxes offer common questions and answers about subjects related to the topic at hand.

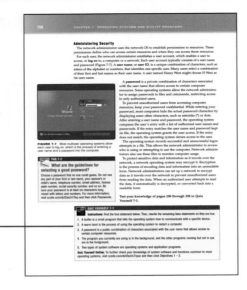

9 Quiz Yourself

Three Quiz Yourself boxes per chapter help ensure that you know the material you just read and are ready to move on in the chapter. Use the answers in Appendix A for a quick check of the answers, and take additional these quizzes on the Web for interactivity and easy use.

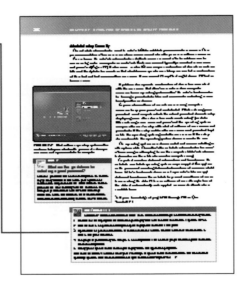

10 Career Corner

Each chapter ends with a Career Corner feature that introduces you to a computer-career opportunity relating to a topic covered in the chapter.

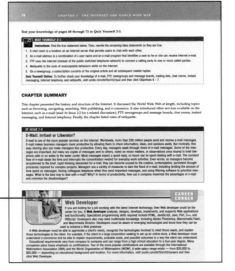

11 Companies on the Cutting Edge

Each chapter includes a profile about two key computer-related companies of which you should be aware, especially if you plan to major in the computer field.

12 Technology Trailblazers

The Technology Trailblazers page in each chapter offers a glimpse into the life and times of the more famous leaders of the computer industry.

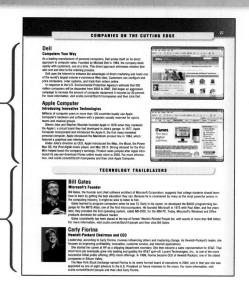

13 Chapter Review

Use the two-page Chapter Review before you take an examination to ensure that you are familiar with the computer concepts presented. This section includes each objective, followed by a one- or two-paragraph summary. Visit a Chapter Review page on the Web, and click the Audio button to listen to the Chapter Review.

14 Key Terms

Before you take a test, use the Key Terms page as a checklist of terms you should know. Visit a Key Terms page on the Web and click any term for additional information.

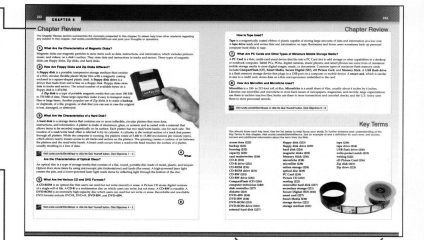

15 Checkpoint

Use these three pages of exercises to reinforce your understanding of the topics presented in the chapter.

16 Web Research

If you enjoy doing research on the Web, then you will like the Web Research exercises. Each exercise in this section references an element in the book and suggests you write a short article or do a class presentation on your findings.

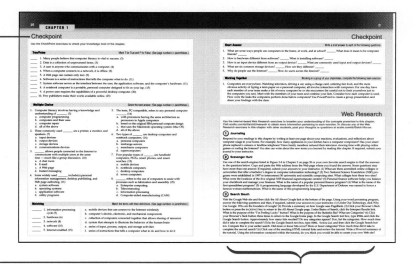

17 Learn It Online

If you prefer online reinforcement, then the Learn It Online exercises are for you. The exercises include online videos, practice tests, interactive labs, learning games, and Web-based activities.

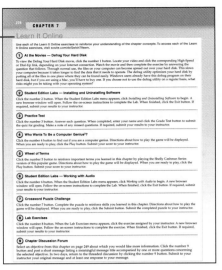

18 Glossary/Index

The Glossary Index at the back of the book not only provides page references, it also offers definitions of all the key terms included in the text and special boxed features.

SHELLY CASHMAN SERIES – TRADITIONALLY BOUND TEXTBOOKS

The Shelly Cashman Series presents the following computer subjects in a variety of traditionally bound textbooks. For more information, see your Course Technology representative or call 1-800-648-7450. For Shelly Cashman Series information, visit Shelly Cashman Online at scseries.com

COMPUTERS

Computers	Discovering Computers 2006: A Gateway to Information, Complete
	Discovering Computers 2006: A Gateway to Information, Introductory
	Discovering Computers 2006: A Gateway to Information, Brief
	Discovering Computers: Fundamentals, Second Edition
	Teachers Discovering Computers: Integrating Technology in the Classroom, Third Edition
	Essential Introduction to Computers, Sixth Edition (40-page)

WINDOWS APPLICATIONS

Microsoft Office	Microsoft Office 2003: Essential Concepts and Techniques (5 projects)
	Microsoft Office 2003: Brief Concepts and Techniques (9 projects)
	Microsoft Office 2003: Introductory Concepts and Techniques, Second Edition (15 projects)
	Microsoft Office 2003: Advanced Concepts and Techniques (12 projects)
	Microsoft Office 2003: Post Advanced Concepts and Techniques (11 projects)
	Microsoft Office XP: Essential Concepts and Techniques (5 projects)
	Microsoft Office XP: Brief Concepts and Techniques (9 projects)
	Microsoft Office XP: Introductory Concepts and Techniques, Windows XP Edition (15 projects)
	Microsoft Office XP: Introductory Concepts and Techniques, Enhanced Edition (15 projects)
	Microsoft Office XP: Advanced Concepts and Techniques (11 projects)
	Microsoft Office XP: Post Advanced Concepts and Techniques (11 projects)
Integration	Teachers Discovering and Integrating Microsoft Office: Essential Concepts and Techniques, Second Edition
	Integrating Microsoft Office XP Applications and the World Wide Web: Essential Concepts and Techniques
PIM	Microsoft Outlook 2002: Essential Concepts and Techniques • Microsoft Office Outlook 2003: Introductory Concepts and Techniques
Microsoft Works	Microsoft Works 6: Complete Concepts and Techniques[1] • Microsoft Works 2000: Complete Concepts and Techniques[1]
Microsoft Windows	Microsoft Windows XP: Comprehensive Concepts and Techniques[2]
	Microsoft Windows XP: Brief Concepts and Techniques
	Microsoft Windows 2000: Comprehensive Concepts and Techniques[2]
	Microsoft Windows 2000: Brief Concepts and Techniques
	Microsoft Windows 98: Comprehensive Concepts and Techniques[2]
	Microsoft Windows 98: Essential Concepts and Techniques
	Introduction to Microsoft Windows NT Workstation 4
Notebook Organizer	Microsoft Office OneNote 2003: Introductory Concepts and Techniques
Word Processing	Microsoft Office Word 2003: Comprehensive Concepts and Techniques[2] • Microsoft Word 2002: Comprehensive Concepts and Techniques[2]
Spreadsheets	Microsoft Office Excel 2003: Comprehensive Concepts and Techniques[2] • Microsoft Excel 2002: Comprehensive Concepts and Techniques[2]
Database	Microsoft Office Access 2003: Comprehensive Concepts and Techniques[2] • Microsoft Access 2002: Comprehensive Concepts and Techniques[2]
Presentation Graphics	Microsoft Office PowerPoint 2003: Comprehensive Concepts and Techniques[2] • Microsoft PowerPoint 2002: Comprehensive Concepts and Techniques[2]
Desktop Publishing	Microsoft Office Publisher 2003: Comprehensive Concepts and Techniques[2] • Microsoft Publisher 2002: Comprehensive Concepts and Techniques[1]

PROGRAMMING

Programming	Microsoft Visual Basic .NET: Comprehensive Concepts and Techniques[2] • Microsoft Visual Basic 6: Complete Concepts and Techniques[1] • Java Programming: Comprehensive Concepts and Techniques, Second Edition[2] • Structured COBOL Programming, Second Edition • Understanding and Troubleshooting Your PC • Programming Fundamentals Using Microsoft Visual Basic .NET

INTERNET

Concepts	Discovering the Internet: Brief Concepts and Techniques • Discovering the Internet: Complete Concepts and Techniques
Browser	Microsoft Internet Explorer 6: Introductory Concepts and Techniques, Windows XP Edition • Microsoft Internet Explorer 5: An Introduction • Netscape Navigator 6: An Introduction
Web Page Creation	Web Design: Introductory Concepts and Techniques • HTML: Comprehensive Concepts and Techniques, Third Edition[2] • Microsoft Office FrontPage 2003: Comprehensive Concepts and Techniques[2] • Microsoft FrontPage 2002: Comprehensive Concepts and Techniques[2] • Microsoft FrontPage 2002: Essential Concepts and Techniques • JavaScript: Complete Concepts and Techniques, Second Edition[1] • Macromedia Dreamweaver MX: Comprehensive Concepts and Techniques[2]

SYSTEMS ANALYSIS

Systems Analysis	Systems Analysis and Design, Sixth Edition

DATA COMMUNICATIONS

Data Communications	Business Data Communications: Introductory Concepts and Techniques, Fourth Edition

[1]Also available as an Introductory Edition, which is a shortened version of the complete book, [2]Also available as an Introductory Edition and as a Complete Edition, which are shortened versions of the comprehensive book.

Introduction to Computers

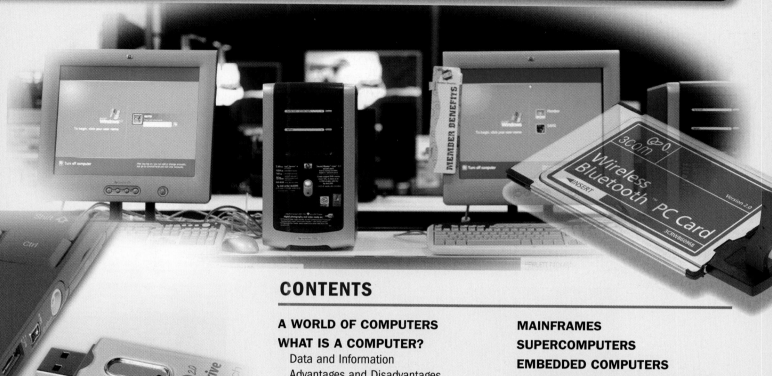

OBJECTIVES

After completing this chapter, you will be able to:

1. Recognize the importance of computer literacy
2. Identify the components of a computer
3. Discuss the uses of the Internet and World Wide Web
4. Identify the categories of software
5. Describe the categories of computers
6. Identify the types of computer users
7. Discuss various computer applications in society

CONTENTS

A WORLD OF COMPUTERS

WHAT IS A COMPUTER?
Data and Information
Advantages and Disadvantages of Using Computers
Information Processing Cycle

THE COMPONENTS OF A COMPUTER
Input Devices
Output Devices
System Unit
Storage Devices
Communications Devices

NETWORKS AND THE INTERNET
The Internet

COMPUTER SOFTWARE
System Software
Application Software
Installing and Running Programs
Software Development

CATEGORIES OF COMPUTERS

PERSONAL COMPUTERS
Desktop Computers

MOBILE COMPUTERS AND MOBILE DEVICES
Notebook Computers
Mobile Devices

MIDRANGE SERVERS

MAINFRAMES

SUPERCOMPUTERS

EMBEDDED COMPUTERS

EXAMPLES OF COMPUTER USAGE
Home User
Small Office/Home Office User
Mobile User
Power User
Large Business User

COMPUTER APPLICATIONS IN SOCIETY
Education
Finance
Government
Health Care
Science
Publishing
Travel
Industry

CHAPTER SUMMARY

COMPANIES ON THE CUTTING EDGE
Dell
Apple Computer

TECHNOLOGY TRAILBLAZERS
Bill Gates
Carly Fiorina

A WORLD OF COMPUTERS

Computers are everywhere: at work, at school, and at home (Figure 1-1). They are a primary means of communication for billions of people. Employees correspond with clients, students with teachers, and family with friends and other family members. Through computers, society has instant access to information from around the globe. Local and national news, weather reports, sports scores, airline schedules, telephone directories, maps and directions, job listings, credit reports, and countless forms of educational material always are accessible. From the computer, you can meet new friends, share photographs and videos, shop, fill prescriptions, file taxes, or take a course.

In the workplace, employees use computers to create correspondence such as e-mail messages, memos, and letters; calculate payroll; track inventory; and generate invoices. Some applications such as automotive design and weather forecasting use computers to perform complex mathematical calculations. At school, teachers use computers to assist with classroom instruction. Students use computers to complete assignments and research.

People also spend hours of leisure time on the computer. They play games, listen to music, watch videos and movies, read books and magazines, research genealogy, compose music and videos, retouch photographs, and plan vacations.

FIGURE 1-1   People use computers in their daily activities.

Many people believe that computer literacy is vital to success. **Computer literacy** involves having a knowledge and understanding of computers and their uses.

This book presents the knowledge you need to be computer literate. As you read this first chapter, keep in mind it is an overview. Many of the terms and concepts introduced in this chapter will be discussed in more depth later in the book.

WHAT IS A COMPUTER?

A **computer** is an electronic device, operating under the control of instructions stored in its own memory, that can accept data, process the data according to specified rules, produce results, and store the results for future use.

Data and Information

Computers process data into information. **Data** is a collection of unprocessed items, which can include text, numbers, images, audio, and video. **Information** conveys meaning and is useful to people.

As shown in Figure 1-2, for example, computers process several data items to print information in the form of a payroll check.

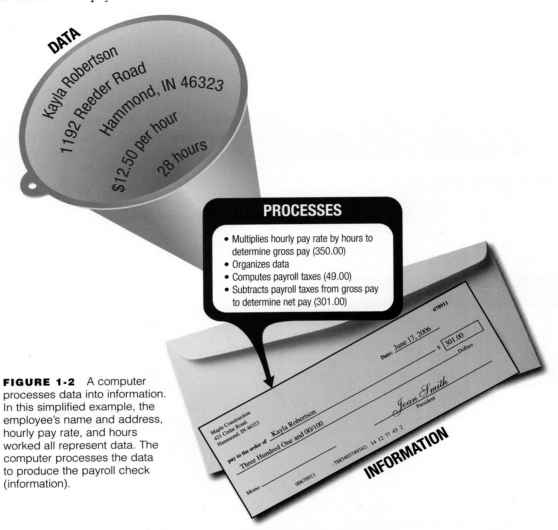

PROCESSES

- Multiplies hourly pay rate by hours to determine gross pay (350.00)
- Organizes data
- Computes payroll taxes (49.00)
- Subtracts payroll taxes from gross pay to determine net pay (301.00)

FIGURE 1-2 A computer processes data into information. In this simplified example, the employee's name and address, hourly pay rate, and hours worked all represent data. The computer processes the data to produce the payroll check (information).

FAQ 1-1

Is data a singular or plural word?

The word data is plural for datum. With respect to computers, however, it is accepted and common practice to use the word data in both the singular and plural context. For more information, visit scsite.com/dcf2e/ch1/faq and then click Data.

An **FAQ** (frequently asked question) helps you find answers to commonly asked questions. Web sites often post an FAQ section, and each chapter in this book includes FAQ boxes related to topics in the text.

Advantages and Disadvantages of Using Computers

Society has reaped many benefits from using computers. Both business and home users can make well-informed decisions because they have instant access to information from anywhere in the world. A **user** is anyone who communicates with a computer or utilizes the information it generates. Students, another type of user, have more tools to assist them in the learning process. Read Looking Ahead 1-1 for a look at the next generation of benefits from using computers.

ADVANTAGES OF USING COMPUTERS   The benefits of computers are possible because computers have the advantages of speed, reliability, consistency, storage, and communications.

- **Speed:** Computer operations occur through electronic circuits. When data, instructions, and information flow along these circuits, they travel at incredibly fast speeds. Many computers process billions or trillions of operations in a single second.
- **Reliability:** The electronic components in modern computers are dependable and reliable because they rarely break or fail.
- **Consistency:** Given the same input and processes, a computer will produce the same results — consistently. Computers generate error-free results, provided the input is correct and the instructions work.
- **Storage:** Computers store enormous amounts of data and make this data available for processing anytime it is needed.
- **Communications:** Most computers today can communicate with other computers, often wirelessly. Computers allow users to communicate with one another.

DISADVANTAGES OF USING COMPUTERS   Some disadvantages of computers relate to the violation of privacy, the impact on the labor force, health risks, and the impact on the environment.

- **Violation of Privacy:** It is crucial that personal and confidential records stored in computers be protected properly. In many instances, where these records were not properly protected, individuals have found their privacy violated and identities stolen.
- **Impact on Labor Force:** Although computers have improved productivity and created an entire industry with hundreds of thousands of new jobs, the skills of millions of employees have been replaced by computers. Thus, it is crucial that workers keep their education up-to-date. A separate impact on the labor force is that some companies are outsourcing jobs to foreign countries instead of keeping their homeland labor force employed.
- **Health Risks:** Prolonged or improper computer use can lead to health injuries or disorders. Computer users can protect themselves from health risks through proper workplace design, good posture while at the computer, and appropriately spaced work breaks.
- **Impact on Environment:** Computer manufacturing processes and computer waste are depleting natural resources and polluting the environment. Strategies that can help protect the environment include recycling, regulating manufacturing processes, extending the life of computers, and immediately donating replaced computers.

LOOKING AHEAD 1-1

Bionic People Benefit from Computer Implants

Computers eventually will become an integral part of the human body. They already are used to help some hearing-impaired people hear by stimulating the nerves within the ear and to help the vision-impaired to see by converting light into electrical impulses.

The next step will involve implanting miniature computers or computer components in the body to help it perform basic functions. A miniature computer, for example, could help release hormones. A brain computer interface may monitor and treat diseases, such as epilepsy and depression, that affect brain activity. A body-scanning machine will evaluate patients' pain when they cannot communicate.

In addition, robotic legs strapped to the body can assist people such as firefighters and soldiers who must bear heavy loads for extended periods of time. For more information, visit scsite.com/dcf2e/ch1/looking and then click Computer Implants.

Information Processing Cycle

Computers process data (input) into information (output). A computer often holds data, information, and instructions in storage for future use. Instructions are the steps that tell the computer how to perform a particular task. Some people refer to the series of input, process, output, and storage activities as the **information processing cycle**. Recently, communications also has become an essential element of the information processing cycle.

THE COMPONENTS OF A COMPUTER

A computer contains many electric, electronic, and mechanical components known as **hardware**. These components include input devices, output devices, a system unit, storage devices, and communications devices. Figure 1-3 shows some common computer hardware components.

Input Devices

An **input device** is any hardware component that allows you to enter data and instructions into a computer. Six widely used input devices are the keyboard, mouse, microphone, scanner, digital camera, and PC video camera (Figure 1-3).

A computer keyboard contains keys you press to enter data into the computer. A mouse is a small handheld device. With the mouse, you control movement of a small symbol on the screen, called the pointer, and you make selections from the screen.

A microphone allows a user to speak into the computer to enter data and instructions. A scanner converts printed material (such as text and pictures) into a form the computer can use.

With a digital camera, you take pictures and then transfer the photographed images to the computer or printer instead of storing the images on traditional film. A PC video camera is a digital video camera that allows users to create a movie or take still photographs electronically.

WEB LINK 1-1

Input Devices

For more information, visit scsite.com/dcf2e/ ch1/weblink and then click Input Devices.

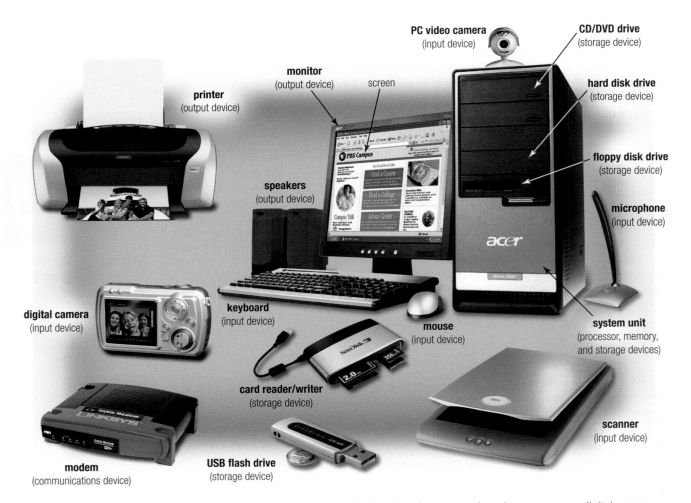

FIGURE 1-3   Common computer hardware components include the keyboard, mouse, microphone, scanner, digital camera, PC video camera, printer, monitor, speakers, system unit, disk drives, USB flash drive, card reader/writer, and modem.

Output Devices

An **output device** is any hardware component that conveys information to one or more people. Three commonly used output devices are a printer, a monitor, and speakers (Figure 1-3).

A printer produces text and graphics on a physical medium such as paper. A monitor displays text, graphics, and videos on a screen. Speakers allow you to hear music, voice, and other audio (sounds).

System Unit

The **system unit** is a case that contains electronic components of the computer that are used to process data (Figure 1-3). The circuitry of the system unit usually is part of or is connected to a circuit board called the motherboard.

Two main components on the motherboard are the processor and memory. The **processor**, also called the **central processing unit** (**CPU**), is the electronic component that interprets and carries out the basic instructions that operate the computer. **Memory** consists of electronic components that store instructions waiting to be executed and data needed by those instructions. Most memory keeps data and instructions temporarily, which means its contents are erased when the computer is shut off.

Storage Devices

Storage holds data, instructions, and information for future use. For example, computers can store hundreds or millions of customer names and addresses. Storage holds these items permanently.

A computer keeps data, instructions, and information on **storage media**. Examples of storage media are floppy disks, USB flash drives, hard disks, CDs, DVDs, and memory cards. A **storage device** records (writes) and/or retrieves (reads) items to and from storage media. Storage devices often function as a source of input because they transfer items from storage to memory.

A floppy disk consists of a thin, circular, flexible disk enclosed in a square-shaped plastic shell. A typical floppy disk stores up to about 1.4 million characters. You insert a floppy disk in and remove it from a floppy disk drive.

A USB flash drive is a portable storage device that has much more storage capacity than a floppy disk but is small and lightweight enough to be transported on a keychain or in a pocket (Figure 1-3).

A hard disk provides much greater storage capacity than a floppy disk or USB flash drive. The average hard disk can hold more than 80 billion characters. Hard disks are enclosed in an airtight, sealed case. Although some are removable, most are housed inside the system unit (Figure 1-4).

FIGURE 1-4 Most hard disks are housed inside the system unit.

A compact disc is a flat, round, portable metal disc with plastic coating. One type of compact disc is a CD-ROM, which you can access using most CD and DVD drives (Figure 1-5). Another type of compact disc is a DVD-ROM, which has enough storage capacity to store two full-length movies. To access a DVD-ROM, you need a DVD drive.

Some portable devices, such as digital cameras, use memory cards as the storage media. You can use a card reader/writer (Figure 1-3) to transfer stored items, such as electronic photographs, from the memory card to a computer or printer.

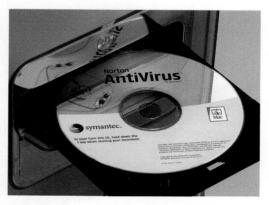

FIGURE 1-5 To use a CD or DVD, you need a CD or DVD drive.

WEB LINK 1-3

Communications Devices

For more information, visit scsite.com/dcf2e/ch1/weblink and then click Communications Devices.

Communications Devices

A **communications device** is a hardware component that enables a computer to send (transmit) and receive data, instructions, and information to and from one or more computers. A widely used communications device is a modem (Figure 1-3 on page 6).

Communications occur over cables, telephone lines, cellular radio networks, satellites, and other transmission media. Some transmission media, such as satellites and cellular radio networks, are wireless, which means they have no physical lines or wires.

Test your knowledge of pages 2 through 8 in Quiz Yourself 1-1.

 QUIZ YOURSELF 1-1

Instructions: Find the true statement below. Then, rewrite the remaining false statements so they are true.

1. A computer is a motorized device that processes output into input.

2. A storage device records (reads) and/or retrieves (writes) items to and from storage media.

3. An output device is any hardware component that allows you to enter data and instructions into a computer.

4. Computer literacy involves having a knowledge and understanding of computers and their uses.

5. Three commonly used input devices are a printer, a monitor, and speakers.

Quiz Yourself Online: To further check your knowledge of computer literacy and computer components, visit scsite.com/dcf2e/ch1/quiz and then click Objectives 1 – 2.

NETWORKS AND THE INTERNET

A **network** is a collection of computers and devices connected together via communications devices and transmission media. When a computer connects to a network, it is **online**. Networks allow computers to share resources, such as hardware, software, data, and information. Sharing resources saves time and money.

The Internet

The **Internet** is a worldwide collection of networks that connects millions of businesses, government agencies, educational institutions, and individuals (Figure 1-6).

FIGURE 1-6   The Internet is the largest computer network, connecting millions of computers around the world.

More than one billion people around the world use the Internet daily for a variety of reasons, including the following purposes:

• Communicate with and meet other people
• Access a wealth of information, news, and research findings
• Shop for goods and services
• Bank and invest
• Take a class
• Access sources of entertainment and leisure, such as online games, music, videos, books, and magazines

Figure 1-7 shows examples in each of these areas.

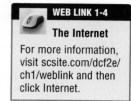

WEB LINK 1-4

The Internet
For more information, visit scsite.com/dcf2e/ch1/weblink and then click Internet.

FIGURE 1-7b (access information)

FIGURE 1-7a (communicate)

FIGURE 1-7c (shop)

FIGURE 1-7d (bank and invest)

FIGURE 1-7e (take a class)

FIGURE 1-7f (access sources of entertainment)

FIGURE 1-7 Users access the Internet for a variety of reasons: to communicate with others, to access a wealth of information, to shop for goods and services, to bank and invest, to take a class, and for entertainment.

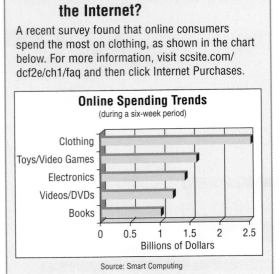
People connect to the Internet to exchange information with others around the world. E-mail allows you to send messages to other users. With instant messaging, you can have a live conversation with another connected user. In a chat room, you can communicate with multiple users at the same time — much like a group discussion.

Businesses, called access providers, offer access to the Internet free or for a fee. By subscribing to an access provider, you can use your computer and a modem to connect to the many services of the Internet.

The **Web**, short for World Wide Web, is one of the more popular services on the Internet. The Web contains billions of documents called Web pages. A **Web page** can contain text, graphics, audio, and video. The six screens shown in Figure 1-7 on the previous page are examples of Web pages.

Web pages often have built-in connections, or links, to other documents, graphics, other Web pages, or Web sites. A Web site is a collection of related Web pages. Anyone can create a Web page and then make it available, or publish it, on the Internet for others to see.

COMPUTER SOFTWARE

Software, also called a **program**, is a series of instructions that tells the computer what to do and how to do it.

You interact with a program through its user interface. Software today often has a graphical user interface. With a **graphical user interface** (**GUI** pronounced gooey), you interact with the software using text, graphics, and visual images such as icons (Figure 1-8). An icon is a miniature image that represents a program, an instruction, or some other object. You can use the mouse to select icons that perform operations such as starting a program.

The two categories of software are system software and application software. The following sections describe these categories of software.

System Software

System software consists of the programs that control or maintain the operations of the computer and its devices. System software serves as the interface between the user, the application software, and the computer's hardware. Two types of system software are the operating system and utility programs.

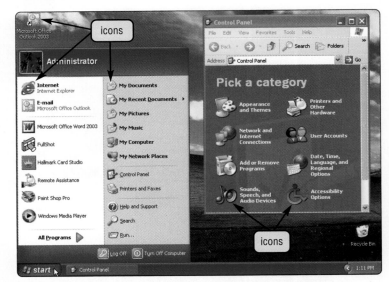

FIGURE 1-8 The graphical user interface of Windows XP.

OPERATING SYSTEM   An **operating system** is a set of programs that coordinates all the activities among computer hardware devices. It provides a means for users to communicate with the computer and other software. Many of today's computers use Microsoft's operating system, called Windows XP (Figure 1-8).

When a user starts a computer, portions of the operating system load into memory from the computer's hard disk. It remains in memory while the computer is on.

UTILITY PROGRAM   A **utility program** allows a user to perform maintenance-type tasks usually related to managing a computer, its devices, or its programs. Most operating systems include several utility programs for managing disk drives, printers, and other devices. You also can buy utility programs that allow you to perform additional computer management functions.

Application Software

Application software consists of programs designed to make users more productive and/or assist them with personal tasks. A widely used type of application software related to communications is a Web browser, which allows users with an Internet connection to access and view Web pages. Other popular application software includes word processing software, spreadsheet software, database software, and presentation graphics software.

Many other types of application software exist that enable users to perform a variety of tasks. These include personal information management, note taking, project management, accounting, computer-aided design, desktop publishing, paint/image editing, audio and video editing, multimedia authoring, Web page authoring, personal finance, legal, tax preparation, home design/landscaping, education, reference, and entertainment (e.g., games or simulations). As shown in Figure 1-9, you often purchase application software from a store that sells computer products. Read At Issue 1-1 for a related discussion.

FIGURE 1-9   Stores that sell computer products have shelves stocked with software for sale.

AT ISSUE 1-1

Can Computers Provoke Violence?

Grand Theft Auto is one of today's most popular computer games. In the game, players advance through the mafia by conveying secret packages, following alleged snitches, and planting car bombs. Since its release, shoppers have bought millions of copies of Grand Theft Auto. Purchasers praise the game's vivid graphics, edgy characters, and wide range of allowable behaviors. Some parents and politicians, however, condemn the game's explicit violence and the rewards it gives players for participating in illegal acts. They fear that games like Grand Theft Auto eventually could corrupt players, perhaps leading to antisocial or criminal behavior. Grand Theft Auto is aimed at older gamers who grew up with Mario but now are looking for something more radical. The game is rated M (for Mature, meaning it is suitable for ages 17 and older), but children as young as 12 have purchased and played with it. Even worse, critics fear that the game's popularity may influence future developers of computer games aimed at younger children. What impact, if any, do violent computer games or games that promote unacceptable acts have on individual behavior? Do these games desensitize players to violence or increase aggression? Why or why not? Should restrictions be placed on sales of computer games?

WEB LINK 1-6

Application Software

For more information, visit scsite.com/dcf2e/ch1/weblink and then click Application Software.

Installing and Running Programs

The instructions in a program are stored on storage media such as a hard disk or compact disc. When purchasing software from a computer store, you typically receive a box that includes a CD(s) or DVD(s) that contains the program. You also may receive a manual or printed instructions explaining how to install and use the software.

Installing is the process of setting up software to work with the computer, printer, and other hardware components. When you buy a computer, it usually has some software preinstalled on its hard disk. This enables you to use the computer the first time you turn it on. To begin installing additional software from a CD or DVD, insert the program disc in a CD or DVD drive. The computer then copies the program from the disc to the computer's hard disk.

Once software is installed, you can use, or **run**, it. When you instruct the computer to run an installed program, the computer loads it, which means the program is copied from storage to memory. Once in memory, the computer can carry out, or **execute**, the instructions in the program. Figure 1-10 illustrates the steps that occur when a user installs and runs a greeting card program.

FIGURE 1-10   INSTALLING AND RUNNING A COMPUTER PROGRAM

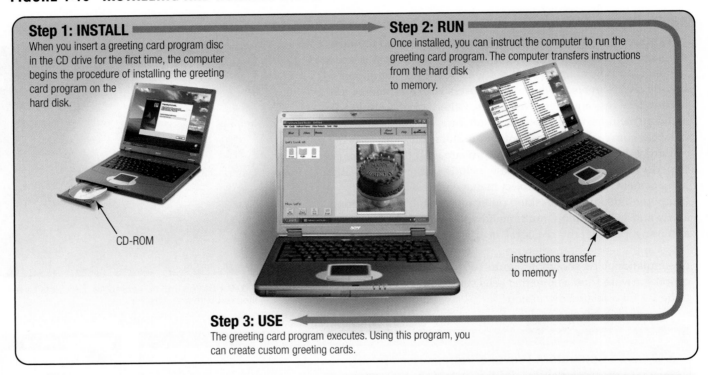

Step 1: INSTALL
When you insert a greeting card program disc in the CD drive for the first time, the computer begins the procedure of installing the greeting card program on the hard disk.

CD-ROM

Step 2: RUN
Once installed, you can instruct the computer to run the greeting card program. The computer transfers instructions from the hard disk to memory.

instructions transfer to memory

Step 3: USE
The greeting card program executes. Using this program, you can create custom greeting cards.

Software Development

A **programmer** is someone who develops software or writes the instructions that direct the computer to process data into information. Complex programs can require thousands to millions of instructions.

Programmers use a programming language or program development tool to create computer programs. Popular programming languages include C++, C#, Visual Basic .NET, JavaScript, and Java. Figure 1-11 shows part of a JavaScript program.

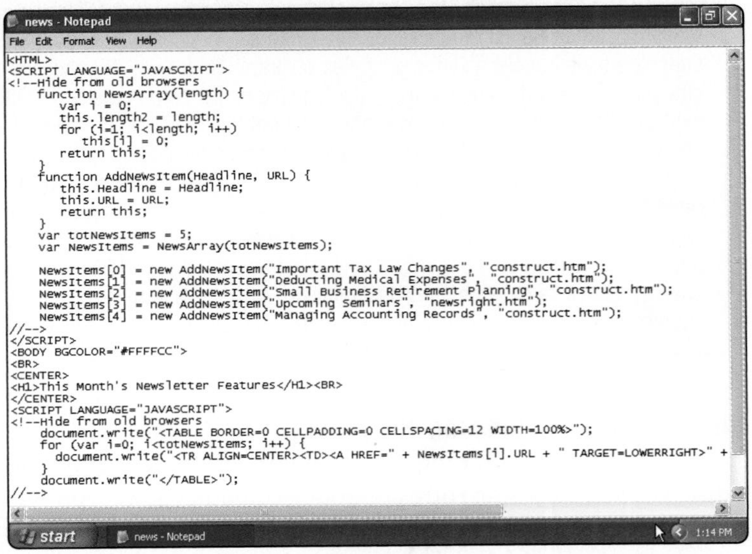

FIGURE 1-11   Some of the instructions in a JavaScript program.

Test your knowledge of pages 8 through 12 in Quiz Yourself 1-2.

QUIZ YOURSELF 1-2

Instructions: Find the true statement below. Then, rewrite the remaining false statements so they are true.

1. A resource is a collection of computers and devices connected together via communications devices and transmission media.

2. Installing is the process of setting up software to work with the computer, printer, and other hardware components.

3. Popular system software includes Web browsers, word processing software, spreadsheet software, database software, and presentation graphics software.

4. The Internet is one of the more popular services on the Web.

5. Two types of application software are the operating system and utility programs.

Quiz Yourself Online: To further check your knowledge of the Internet and software, visit scsite.com/dcf2e/ch1/quiz and then click Objectives 3 – 4.

CATEGORIES OF COMPUTERS

Industry experts typically classify computers in six categories: personal computers, mobile computers and mobile devices, midrange servers, mainframes, supercomputers, and embedded computers. A computer's size, speed, processing power, and price determine the category it best fits. Due to rapidly changing technology, however, the distinction among categories is not always clear-cut.

Figure 1-12 summarizes the six categories of computers. The following pages discuss computers and devices that fall in each category.

CATEGORIES OF COMPUTERS

Category	Physical Size	Number of Simultaneously Connected Users	General Price Range
Personal computers (desktop)	Fits on a desk	Usually one (can be more if networked)	Several hundred to several thousand dollars
Mobile computers and mobile devices	Fits on your lap or in your hand	Usually one	Less than a hundred dollars to several thousand dollars
Midrange servers	Small cabinet	Two to thousands	$1,000 to a million dollars
Mainframes	Partial room to a full room of equipment	Hundreds to thousands	$300,000 to several million dollars
Supercomputers	Full room of equipment	Hundreds to thousands	$500,000 to several billion dollars
Embedded computers	Miniature	Usually one	Embedded in the price of the product

FIGURE 1-12   This table summarizes some of the differences among the categories of computers.

PERSONAL COMPUTERS

WEB LINK 1-7

Personal Computers

For more information, visit scsite.com/dcf2e/ch1/weblink and then click Personal Computers.

A **personal computer** is a computer that can perform all of its input, processing, output, and storage activities by itself. A personal computer contains a processor, memory, and one or more input, output, and storage devices.

Two popular styles of personal computers are the PC (Figure 1-13) and the Apple (Figure 1-14). These two types of computers use different operating systems. PC and PC-compatible computers usually use the Windows operating system. Apple computers use the Macintosh operating system (Mac OS). The term, PC-compatible, refers to any personal computer based on the original IBM personal computer design. Companies such as Dell, Gateway, and Toshiba sell PC-compatible computers.

Two types of personal computers are desktop computers and notebook computers.

FIGURE 1-13
The PC and compatible computers usually use a Windows operating system.

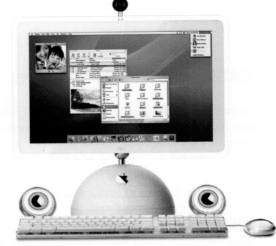

FIGURE 1-14 Apple computers, such as the iMac, use a Macintosh operating system.

Desktop Computers

A **desktop computer** is designed so the system unit, input devices, output devices, and any other devices fit entirely on or under a desk or table. In some models, the monitor sits on top of the system unit, which is placed on the desk. The more popular style of system unit is the tall and narrow tower, which can sit on the floor vertically.

MOBILE COMPUTERS AND MOBILE DEVICES

A **mobile computer** is a personal computer you can carry from place to place. Similarly, a **mobile device** is a computing device small enough to hold in your hand. The most popular type of mobile computer is the notebook computer.

Notebook Computers

WEB LINK 1-8

Notebook Computers

For more information, visit scsite.com/dcf2e/ch1/weblink and then click Notebook Computers.

A **notebook computer**, also called a **laptop computer**, is a portable, personal computer designed to fit on your lap. Notebook computers are thin and lightweight, yet can be as powerful as the average desktop computer. Notebook computers are more expensive than desktop computers with equal capabilities.

On a typical notebook computer, the keyboard is on top of the system unit, and the display attaches to the system unit with hinges (Figure 1-15). These computers weigh on average between 2.5 and 9 pounds, which allows users easily to transport the computers from place to place. Most notebook computers can operate on batteries or a power supply or both.

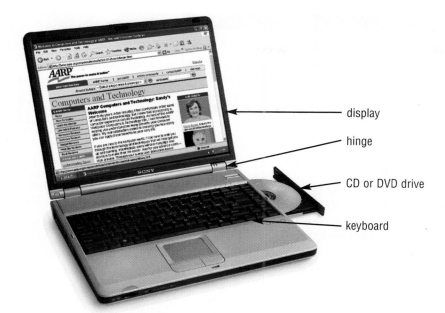

display

hinge

CD or DVD drive

keyboard

FIGURE 1-15 On a typical notebook computer, the keyboard is on top of the system unit, and the display attaches to the system unit with hinges.

TABLET PC Resembling a letter-sized slate, the **Tablet PC** is a special type of notebook computer that allows you to write or draw on the screen using a digital pen (Figure 1-16). For users who prefer typing instead of hand-writing, you can attach a keyboard to Tablet PCs that do not include one already. Tablet PCs are useful especially for taking notes in locations where the standard notebook computer is not practical.

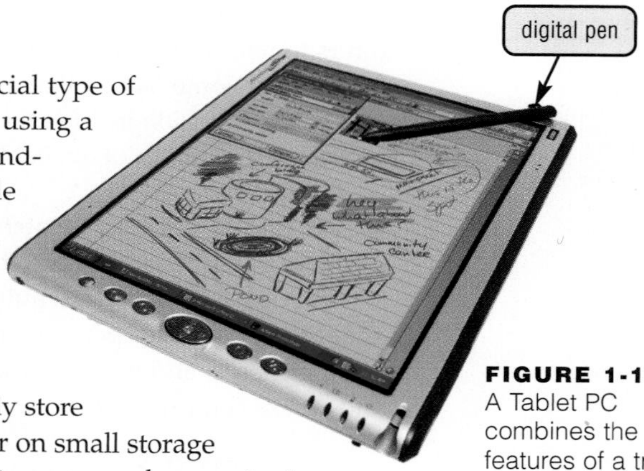

digital pen

FIGURE 1-16 A Tablet PC combines the features of a tra-ditional notebook computer with the simplicity of pencil and paper.

Mobile Devices

Mobile devices, which are small enough to carry in a pocket, usually store programs and data permanently on memory inside the system unit or on small storage media such as memory cards. You often can connect a mobile device to a personal computer to exchange information. Some mobile devices are **Internet-enabled**, meaning they can connect to the Internet wirelessly.

Four popular types of mobile devices are handheld computers, PDAs, smart phones, and smart watches.

HANDHELD COMPUTER A **handheld computer**, sometimes called a **handtop computer**, is a computer small enough to fit in one hand. Because of their reduced size, the screens on handheld computers are small. Industry-specific handheld computers serve mobile employees, such as parcel delivery people, whose jobs require them to move from place to place.

PDA A **PDA** (personal digital assistant) provides personal organizer functions such as a calendar, appointment book, address book, calculator, and notepad (Figure 1-17). Most PDAs also offer a variety of other application software such as word processing, spreadsheet, personal finance, and games.

Many PDAs are Internet-enabled so users can check e-mail and access the Web. Some also provide telephone capabilities.

The primary input device of a PDA is the **stylus**, which looks like a small ballpoint pen, but uses pressure instead of ink to write and draw.

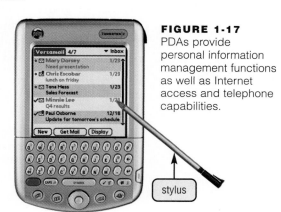

stylus

FIGURE 1-17 PDAs provide personal information management functions as well as Internet access and telephone capabilities.

FAQ 1-3

Do PDAs have industry-specific applications?

Yes. Restaurant servers use PDAs to record customer orders and transmit them to the kitchen. Doctors use PDAs to access patients' records, view laboratory results, and transmit prescriptions to the pharmacy. Law enforcement officials use PDAs to log license plate numbers, run background checks, and issue tickets. For more information, visit the scsite.com/dcf2e/ch1/faq and then click PDAs.

SMART PHONE   Offering the convenience of one-handed operation, a **smart phone** is an Internet-enabled telephone that usually also provides PDA capabilities. In addition to basic telephone capabilities, a smart phone allows you to send and receive e-mail messages, access the Web, and share photographs or videos (Figure 1-18).

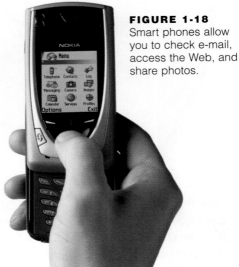

FIGURE 1-18
Smart phones allow you to check e-mail, access the Web, and share photos.

As smart phones and PDAs continue a trend of offering similar functions, it is becoming increasingly difficult to differentiate between the two devices. This trend, known as convergence, has led manufacturers to refer to PDAs and smart phones simply as **handhelds**. Some factors that affect a consumer's purchasing decision include the device's size, screen size, and capabilities of available software.

SMART WATCH   A **smart watch** is an Internet-enabled watch. In addition to basic timekeeping capabilities, a smart watch automatically adjusts to time zone changes, stores personal messages, reminds you of appointments, and wirelessly accesses news, weather, sports, and stocks (Figure 1-19).

MIDRANGE SERVERS

A **midrange server** is more powerful and larger than a desktop computer (Figure 1-20). Midrange servers typically support several hundred and sometimes up to a few thousand connected computers at the same time.

FIGURE 1-19   A smart watch.

People use personal computers or terminals to access programs on a midrange server. A terminal is a device with a monitor, keyboard, and memory. Some terminals have no processing power and must connect to a server to operate.

FIGURE 1-20   A midrange server is more powerful than a desktop computer.

MAINFRAMES

A **mainframe** is a large, expensive, powerful computer that can handle hundreds or thousands of connected users simultaneously (Figure 1-21). Mainframes store huge amounts of data, instructions, and information. Large companies such as banks and airlines use mainframes. One study reported that mainframes process more than 83 percent of transactions around the world.

Midrange servers and other mainframes can access data and information from a mainframe. People also can access programs on the mainframe using terminals or personal computers.

FIGURE 1-21 Mainframe computers can handle thousands of connected computers and process millions of instructions per second.

SUPERCOMPUTERS

A **supercomputer** is the fastest, most powerful computer — and the most expensive (Figure 1-22). The fastest supercomputers are capable of processing more than 100 trillion instructions in a single second.

Applications requiring complex, sophisticated mathematical calculations use supercomputers. Large-scale simulations and applications in medicine, aerospace, automotive design, online banking, weather forecasting, nuclear energy research, and petroleum exploration use a supercomputer.

FIGURE 1-22 This supercomputer simulates various environmental occurrences such as global climate changes, pollution, and earthquakes.

EMBEDDED COMPUTERS

An **embedded computer** is a special-purpose computer that functions as a component in a larger product. A variety of everyday products contain embedded computers:
- Consumer electronics
- Home automation devices and appliances
- Automobiles
- Process controllers and robotics
- Computer devices and office machines

Because embedded computers are components in larger products, they usually are small and have limited hardware. Embedded computers perform various functions, depending on the requirements of the product in which they reside. Embedded computers in printers, for example, monitor the amount of paper in the tray, check the ink or toner level, signal if a paper jam has occurred, and so on. Figure 1-23 shows some of the many embedded computers in cars.

Adaptive cruise control systems detect if cars in front of you are too close and, if necessary, adjust the vehicle's throttle, may apply brakes, and/or sound an alarm.

Advanced airbag systems have crash-severity sensors that determine the appropriate level to inflate the airbag, reducing the chance of airbag injury in low-speed accidents.

Tire pressure monitoring systems send warning signals if tire pressure is insufficient.

Cars equipped with wireless communications capabilities, called telematics, include such features as navigation systems and Internet access.

Drive-by-wire systems sense pressure on the gas pedal and communicate electronically to the engine how much and how fast to accelerate.

FIGURE 1-23   Some of the embedded computers designed to improve your safety, security, and performance in today's automobiles.

EXAMPLES OF COMPUTER USAGE

Every day, people around the world rely on different types of computers for a variety of applications. To illustrate the range of uses for computers, this section takes you on a visual and narrative tour of five categories of users: a home user, a small office/home office (SOHO) user, a mobile user, a power user, and a large business user.

FAQ 1-4

Can I listen to an audio CD on my computer?

Yes, in most cases. Simply insert the CD in the computer's CD or DVD drive. Within a few seconds, you should hear music from the computer's speakers or in your headset. If no music plays, it is possible you need to run a program that starts the audio CD.

For more information, visit scsite.com/dcf2e/ch1/faq and then click Audio CDs.

Home User

In an increasing number of homes, the computer is a basic necessity. Each family member, or **home user**, spends time on the computer for different reasons. These include budgeting and personal financial management, Web access, communications, and entertainment (Figure 1-24).

On the Internet, home users access a huge amount of information, take college classes, pay bills, manage investments, shop, listen to the radio, watch movies, read books, play games, file taxes, and make airline reservations. They also communicate with others around the world through e-mail, instant messaging, and chat rooms. Read At Issue 1-2 for a related discussion.

Today's homes typically have one or more desktop computers. Some home users network multiple desktop computers throughout the house, often wirelessly. These small networks allow family members to share an Internet connection and a printer.

To meet their needs, home users have a variety of software. They type letters, homework assignments, and other documents with word processing software. Personal finance software helps the home user with personal finances, investments, and family budgets. Other software assists with preparing taxes, keeping a household inventory, and setting up maintenance schedules.

Reference software, such as encyclopedias, medical dictionaries, or a road atlas, provides valuable information for everyone in the family. With entertainment software, the home user can play games, compose music, research genealogy, or create greeting cards. Educational software helps adults learn to speak a foreign language and youngsters to read, write, count, and spell.

FIGURE 1-24a (personal financial management)

FIGURE 1-24b (Web access)

FIGURE 1-24c (communications)

FIGURE 1-24 The home user spends time on a computer for a variety of reasons.

FIGURE 1-24d (entertainment)

AT ISSUE 1-2

Did You Meet Online?

Once, people met dates through family and friends, work, or community, religious, and recreational activities. These social networks sometimes resulted in a perfect match, but often time constraints, the limited pool of participants, and infrequent meetings made it difficult to find a potential partner. Today, many people are turning to another resource — online dating. Media experts forecast that 40 million people will use online dating services this year, and the market for these services has grown almost 40 percent in the past year. Online dating service members supply information about their interests and personalities and then search the service for people they might like to meet. The services are easy to use, have a large range of participants, allow relationships to develop at a comfortable pace, and usually offer advanced options such as live chat, voice mail, and computer matchmaking. On the other hand, in an online dating service it can be difficult to judge the appearance of members, obtain in-depth profiles, recognize false or exaggerated member claims, and avoid unwanted advertisements. Although introductory memberships often are free, many services require substantial fees for extended benefits. Are online dating services worth it? Why or why not? If you used an online dating service, what would you do to profit from its advantages and avoid its disadvantages?

Small Office/Home Office User

Computers assist small business and home office users in managing their resources effectively. A **small office/home office (SOHO)** includes any company with fewer than 50 employees, as well as the self-employed who work from home. Small offices include local law practices, accounting firms, travel agencies, and florists. SOHO users typically use a desktop computer. Many also use PDAs.

SOHO users access the Web — often wirelessly — to look up information such as addresses, directions (Figure 1-25a), postal codes, flights, and package shipping rates. Nearly all SOHO users communicate through e-mail. Many are entering the e-commerce arena and conduct business on the Web. Their Web sites advertise products and services and may provide a means for taking orders.

To save money on hardware and software, small offices often network their computers. For example, the small office connects one printer to a network for all employees to share.

SOHO users often have basic business software such as word processing and spreadsheet software to assist with document preparation and finances (Figure 1-25b). They are likely to use other industry-specific types of software. A candy shop, for example, will have software that allows for taking orders and payments, updating inventory, and paying vendors.

FIGURE 1-25a   (Web access)

FIGURE 1-25b   (spreadsheet program)

FIGURE 1-25 People with a home office and employees in small offices typically use a desktop personal computer.

Mobile User

Today, businesses and schools are expanding to serve people across the country and around the world. Thus, increasingly more employees and students are **mobile users**, who work on a computer while away from a main office or school (Figure 1-26). Some examples of mobile users are sales representatives, real estate agents, insurance agents, meter readers, package delivery people, journalists, and students.

notebook computer

Tablet PC

PDA

smart phone

FIGURE 1-26 Mobile users have notebook computers, Tablet PCs, PDAs, and smart phones so they can work, do homework, send messages, or connect to the Internet while away from a wired connection.

Mobile users often have a notebook computer, Internet-enabled PDA, or smart phone. With these computers and devices, the mobile user can connect to other computers on a network or the Internet. Mobile users can transfer information between their mobile devices and another computer.

The mobile user works with basic business software such as word processing and spreadsheet software. With presentation graphics software, the mobile user can create and deliver presentations to a large audience by connecting a mobile computer or device to a video projector that displays the presentation on a full screen.

Power User

Another category of user, called a **power user**, requires the capabilities of a powerful desktop computer, called a workstation (Figure 1-27). Examples of power users include engineers, scientists, architects, desktop publishers, and graphic artists. Power users typically work with multimedia, combining text, graphics, audio, and video into one application. These users need computers with extremely fast processors because of the nature of their work.

The power user's workstation contains industry-specific software. For example, engineers and architects use software to draft and design floor plans, mechanical assemblies, or vehicles. A desktop publisher uses software to prepare marketing literature such as newsletters, brochures, and annual reports. A geologist uses software to study the earth's surface. This software usually is expensive because of its specialized design.

Power users exist in all types of businesses. Some also work at home. Their computers typically have network connections and Internet access.

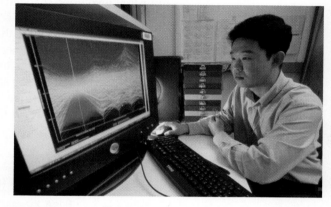

FIGURE 1-27 This scientist uses a powerful computer to study blood cells for diabetes research.

Large Business User

A large business has hundreds or thousands of employees or customers that work in or do business with offices across a region, the country, or the world. Each employee or customer who uses a computer in the large business is a **large business user** (Figure 1-28).

Many large companies use the words, **enterprise computing**, to refer to the huge network of computers that meets their diverse computing needs. The network facilitates communications among employees at all locations. Users access the network through desktop computers, mobile computers, PDAs, and smart phones.

Large businesses use computers and the computer network to process high volumes of transactions in a single day. Although they may differ in size and in the products or services offered, all generally use computers for basic business activities. For example, they bill millions of customers or prepare payroll for thousands of employees.

Large businesses typically have e-commerce Web sites, allowing customers and vendors to conduct business online. The Web site showcases products, services, and other company information. Customers, vendors, and other interested parties can access this information on the Web.

The marketing department in the large business uses desktop publishing software to prepare marketing literature. The accounting department uses software for accounts receivable, accounts payable, billing, general ledger, and payroll activities.

Large business users work with word processing, spreadsheet, database, and presentation graphics software. They also may use calendar programs to post their schedules on the network. And, they might use PDAs or smart phones to maintain contact information. E-mail and Web browsers enable communications among employees, vendors, and customers.

FIGURE 1-28 A large business can have hundreds or thousands of users in offices across a region, the country, or the world.

Many employees of large businesses today telecommute (Figure 1-29). **Telecommuting** is a work arrangement in which employees work away from a company's standard workplace and often communicate with the office through the computer. Employees who telecommute have flexible work schedules so they can combine work and personal responsibilities, such as child care.

COMPUTER APPLICATIONS IN SOCIETY

The computer has changed society today as much as the industrial revolution changed society in the eighteenth and nineteenth centuries.

People interact directly with computers in fields such as education, finance, government, health care, science, publishing, travel, and industry. In addition, they can reap the benefits from breakthroughs and advances in these fields.

FIGURE 1-29 Many employees of large businesses telecommute, which allows them to combine work and other responsibilities.

The following pages describe how computers have made a difference in people's interactions with these disciplines. Read Looking Ahead 1-2 for a look at the next generation of computer applications in society.

LOOKING AHEAD 1-2

Robots Add the Human Touch

Rosie, the robotic maid from "The Jetsons," delighted millions of television viewers with her household cleaning talents. Today's mobile, intelligent robots likewise perform tasks typically reserved for humans in a $5 billion global market.

Each day, the iRobot Roomba self-propelled vacuum cleans homes, and the da Vinci Surgical System's robotic hands drill through bones and make incisions. Sony's home robot, QRIO, responds to voices and faces, displays emotions, and walks and dances fluidly.

Tomorrow's practical and versatile robots will serve a variety of personal and industrial needs. By 2010, the expected $17 billion market should include products to care for senior citizens, transport people in major cities, and perform hundreds of thousands of mobile utility jobs, such as picking up and delivering items. For more information, visit scsite.com/dcf2e/ch1/looking and then click Robots.

Education

Education is the process of acquiring knowledge. In the traditional model, people learn from other people such as parents, teachers, and employers. Many forms of printed material such as books and manuals are used as learning tools. Today, educators also are turning to computers to assist with education (Figure 1-30).

Many schools and companies equip labs and classrooms with computers. Some schools require students to have a notebook computer or PDA, along with textbooks and other supplies.

Students use software to assist with learning or to complete assignments. To promote education by computer, many vendors offer substantial student discounts on software.

FIGURE 1-30 In some schools, students have notebook computers on their desks during classroom lectures.

Sometimes, the delivery of education occurs at one place while the learning occurs at other locations. For example, students can take a class on the Web. More than 70 percent of colleges offer some type of distance learning classes. A few even offer entire degrees online.

Finance

Many people and companies use computers to help manage their finances. Some use finance software to balance checkbooks, pay bills, track personal income and expenses, manage investments, and evaluate financial plans. This software usually includes a variety of online services. For example, computer users can track investments and do online banking (Figure 1-31). With **online banking**, users access account balances, pay bills, and copy monthly transactions from the bank's computer right into their computers.

Investors often use **online investing** to buy and sell stocks and bonds — without using a broker. With online investing, the transaction fee for each trade usually is much less than when trading through a broker.

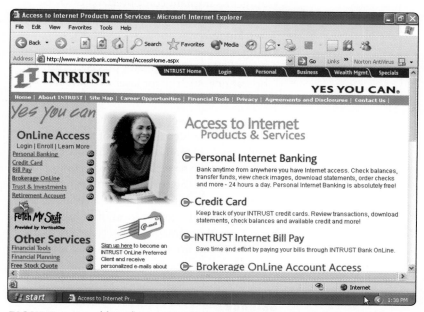

FIGURE 1-31 Many financial institutions' Web sites offer online banking.

Government

A government provides society with direction by making and administering policies. To provide citizens with up-to-date information, most government offices have Web sites. People access government Web sites to file taxes, apply for permits and licenses, pay parking tickets, buy stamps, report crimes, apply for financial aid, and renew vehicle registrations and driver's licenses.

Employees of government agencies use computers as part of their daily routine. Military and other agency officials use the U.S. Department of Homeland Security's network of information about domestic security threats to help protect our nation. Law enforcement officers have online access to the FBI's National Crime Information Center (NCIC) in police cars that have computers and fingerprint scanners or through PDAs (Figure 1-32). The NCIC contains more than 52 million missing persons and criminal records, including names, fingerprints, parole/probation records, mug shots, and other information.

FIGURE 1-32 Law enforcement officials have in-vehicle computers and PDAs to access emergency, missing person, and criminal records in computer networks in local, state, and federal agencies.

Health Care

Nearly every area of health care uses computers. Whether you are visiting a family doctor for a regular checkup, having lab work or an outpatient test, or being rushed in for emergency surgery, the medical staff around you will be using computers for various purposes:

- Hospitals and doctors use computers to maintain patient records.
- Computers monitor patients' vital signs in hospital rooms and at home.
- Doctors use the Web and medical software to assist with researching and diagnosing health conditions.
- Doctors use e-mail to correspond with patients.
- Pharmacists use computers to file insurance claims.

- Computers and computerized devices assist doctors, nurses, and technicians with medical tests (Figure 1-33).
- Surgeons implant computerized devices, such as pacemakers, that allow patients to live longer.
- Surgeons use computer-controlled devices to provide them with greater precision during operations, such as for laser eye surgery and robot-assisted heart surgery.

An exciting development in health care is telemedicine, which is a form of long-distance health care. Through **telemedicine**, health-care professionals in separate locations conduct live conferences on the computer. For example, a doctor at one location can have a conference with a doctor at another location to discuss a bone X-ray. Live images of each doctor, along with the X-ray, are displayed on each doctor's computer.

FIGURE 1-33   Doctors, nurses, technicians, and other medical staff use computers while performing tests on patients.

Science

All branches of science, from biology to astronomy to meteorology, use computers to assist them with collecting, analyzing, and modeling data. Scientists also use the Internet to communicate with colleagues around the world.

Breakthroughs in surgery, medicine, and treatments often result from scientists' use of computers. Tiny computers now imitate functions of the central nervous system, retina of the eye, and cochlea of the ear. A cochlear implant allows a deaf person to listen. Electrodes implanted in the brain stop tremors associated with Parkinson's disease. Cameras small enough to swallow — sometimes called a camera pill — take pictures inside your body to detect polyps, cancer, and other abnormalities (Figure 1-34).

FIGURE 1-34   HOW A CAMERA PILL WORKS

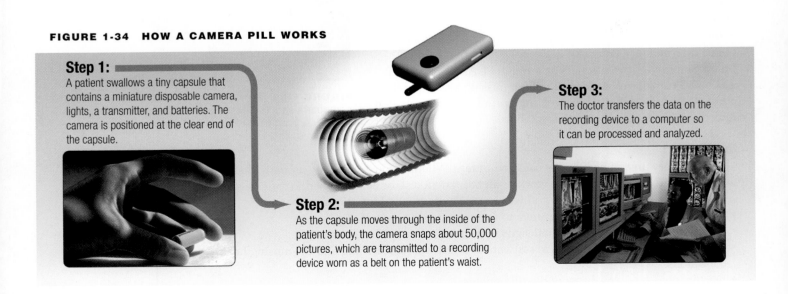

Step 1:
A patient swallows a tiny capsule that contains a miniature disposable camera, lights, a transmitter, and batteries. The camera is positioned at the clear end of the capsule.

Step 2:
As the capsule moves through the inside of the patient's body, the camera snaps about 50,000 pictures, which are transmitted to a recording device worn as a belt on the patient's waist.

Step 3:
The doctor transfers the data on the recording device to a computer so it can be processed and analyzed.

Publishing

Publishing is the process of making work available to the public. These works include books, magazines, newspapers, music, film, and video. Special software assists graphic designers in developing pages that include text, graphics, and photographs; artists in composing and enhancing songs; filmmakers in creating and editing film; and journalists and mobile users in capturing and modifying video clips.

Many publishers make their works available online (Figure 1-35). Some Web sites allow you to copy the work, such as a book or music, to your desktop computer, handheld computer, PDA, or smart phone.

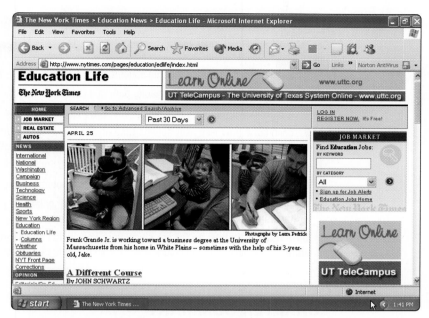

FIGURE 1-35 Many magazine and newspaper publishers make the content of their publications available online.

Travel

Many vehicles manufactured today include some type of onboard navigation system. Airlines provide online access, allowing passengers to connect a mobile computer or device to the Internet (Figure 1-36).

In preparing for a trip, you may need to reserve a car, hotel, or flight. Many Web sites offer these services to the public. For example, you can order airline tickets on the Web. If you plan to drive somewhere and are unsure of the road to take to your destination, you can print directions and a map from the Web.

FIGURE 1-36 Airlines today offer inflight Internet connections to passengers.

Industry

Computer-aided manufacturing (CAM) refers to the use of computers to assist with manufacturing processes such as fabrication and assembly. Often, robots carry out processes in a CAM environment. CAM is used by a variety of industries, including oil drilling, power generation, food production, and automobile manufacturing. Automobile plants, for example, have an entire line of industrial robots that assemble a car (Figure 1-37).

FIGURE 1-37 Automotive factories use industrial robots to weld car bodies.

Test your knowledge of pages 13 through 25 in Quiz Yourself 1-3.

QUIZ YOURSELF 1-3

Instructions: Find the true statement below. Then, rewrite the remaining false statements so they are true.

1. A desktop computer is a portable, personal computer designed to fit on your lap.

2. A personal computer contains a processor, memory, and one or more input, output, and storage devices.

3. Each large business user spends time on the computer for different reasons that include budgeting and personal financial management, Web access, communications, and entertainment.

4. A home user requires the capabilities of a workstation or other powerful computer.

5. Mainframes are the fastest, most powerful computers — and the most expensive.

6. With embedded computers, users access account balances, pay bills, and copy monthly transactions from the bank's computer right into their personal computers.

Quiz Yourself Online: To further check your knowledge of categories of computers, computer users, and computer applications in society, visit scsite.com/dcf2e/ch1/quiz and then click Objectives 5 – 7.

CHAPTER SUMMARY

Chapter 1 introduced you to basic computer concepts. You learned about the components of a computer. Next, the chapter discussed networks, the Internet, and computer software. The many different categories of computers, computer users, and computer applications in society also were presented.

This chapter is an overview. Many of the terms and concepts introduced will be discussed further in later chapters. For a history of hardware and software developments, read the Timeline that follows this chapter.

CAREER CORNER

Personal Computer Salesperson

When you decide to buy or upgrade a personal computer, the most important person with whom you interact probably will be a personal computer salesperson. This individual will be a valuable resource to you in providing the information and expertise you need to select a computer that meets your requirements.

Computer manufacturers and retailers that sell several types of personal computers need competent salespeople. A **personal computer salesperson** must be computer literate and have a specific knowledge of the computers he or she sells. In addition, a successful salesperson has a friendly, outgoing personality that helps customers feel comfortable. Through open-ended questions, the salesperson can determine a customer's needs and level of experience. With this information, the salesperson can choose the best computer for the customer and explain the features of the computer in language the customer will understand.

Most computer salespeople have at least a high school diploma. Before reaching the sales floor, however, salespeople usually complete extensive company training programs. These programs often consist of self-directed, self-paced Web-training classes. Most salespeople also participate in training updates, often on a monthly basis.

Personal computer salespeople generally earn a guaranteed amount plus a commission for each sale. A computer salesperson can earn about $40,000 a year. Top salespeople can be among a company's more highly compensated employees, earning in excess of $70,000. For more information, visit scsite.com/dcf2e/ch1/careers and then click Personal Computer Salesperson.

Dell
Computers Your Way

As a leading manufacturer of personal computers, Dell prides itself on its direct approach to computer sales. Founded by Michael Dell in 1984, the company deals openly with customers, one at a time. This direct approach eliminates retailers that add cost and time to the ordering process.

Dell uses the Internet to enhance the advantages of direct marketing and hosts one of the world's largest volume e-commerce Web sites. Customers can configure and price computers, order systems, and track their orders online.

In response to the U.S. Environmental Protection Agency's estimate that 250 million computers will be discarded from 2002 to 2007, Dell began an aggressive campaign to increase the amount of computer equipment it recycles by 50 percent. For more information, visit scsite.com/dcf2e/ch1/companies and then click Dell.

Apple Computer
Introducing Innovative Technologies

Millions of computer users in more than 120 countries loyally use Apple Computer's hardware and software with a passion usually reserved for sports teams and musical groups.

Steven Jobs and Stephen Wozniak founded Apple in 1976 when they marketed the Apple I, a circuit board they had developed in Jobs's garage. In 1977, Apple Computer incorporated and introduced the Apple II, the first mass-marketed personal computer. Apple introduced the Macintosh product line in 1984, which featured a graphical user interface.

Under Jobs's direction as CEO, Apple introduced the iMac, the iBook, the Power Mac G5, the iPod digital music player, and Mac OS X. Strong demand for the iPod Mini helped boost the company's earnings. Product sales jumped after Apple introduced its pay-per-download iTunes online music store in 2003. For more information, visit scsite.com/dcf2e/ch1/companies and then click Apple Computer.

TECHNOLOGY TRAILBLAZERS

Bill Gates
Microsoft's Founder

Bill Gates, the founder and chief software architect of Microsoft Corporation, suggests that college students should learn how to learn by getting the best education they can. Because he is considered by many as the most powerful person in the computing industry, it might be wise to listen to him.

Gates learned to program computers when he was 13. Early in his career, he developed the BASIC programming language for the MITS Altair, one of the first microcomputers. He founded Microsoft in 1975 with Paul Allen, and five years later, they provided the first operating system, called MS-DOS, for the IBM PC. Today, Microsoft's Windows and Office products dominate the software market.

Gates consistently has been placed at the top of *Forbes'* World's Richest People list, with assets of more than $46 billion. For more information, visit scsite.com/dcf2e/ch1/people and then click Bill Gates.

Carly Fiorina
Hewlett-Packard Chairman and CEO

Leadership, according to Carly Fiorina, involves influencing others and mastering change. As Hewlett-Packard's leader, she focuses on improving profitability, innovation, customer service, and Internet applications.

She started her career at HP as a shipping department secretary. She then became a sales representative for AT&T. That short-term job eventually grew into leading and guiding the AT&T spin-off, Lucent Technologies, Inc., to one of the more successful initial public offering (IPO) stock offerings. In 1999, Fiorina became CEO of Hewlett-Packard, one of the oldest companies in Silicon Valley.

The New York Stock Exchange named Fiorina to its newly formed board of executives in 2004, and in that year she was appointed as one of eight advisors to the U.S. President on future missions to the moon. For more information, visit scsite.com/dcf2e/ch1/people and then click Carly Fiorina.

CHAPTER 1

Chapter Review

The Chapter Review section summarizes the concepts presented in this chapter. To obtain help from other students regarding any subject in this chapter, visit scsite.com/dcf2e/ch1/forum and post your thoughts or questions.

(1) Why Is Computer Literacy Important?

Computer literacy involves having a knowledge and understanding of computers and their uses. As computers become an increasingly important part of daily living, many people believe that computer literacy is vital to success.

(2) What Are the Components of a Computer?

A **computer** is an electronic device, operating under the control of instructions stored in its own memory, that can accept data, process the data according to specified rules, produce results, and store the results for future use. The electric, electronic, and mechanical components of a computer, or **hardware**, include input devices, output devices, a system unit, storage devices, and communications devices. An **input device** allows you to enter data or instructions in a computer. An **output device** conveys information to one or more people. The **system unit** is a case that contains the electronic components of a computer that are used to process data. A **storage device** records and/or retrieves items to and from storage media. A **communications device** enables a computer to send and receive data, instructions, and information to and from one or more computers.

 Visit scsite.com/dcf2e/ch1/quiz or click the Quiz Yourself button. Click Objectives 1 – 2.

(3) How Are the Internet and World Wide Web Used?

The **Internet** is a worldwide collection of networks that connects millions of businesses, government agencies, educational institutions, and individuals. People use the Internet to communicate with and meet other people, access news and information, shop for goods and services, bank and invest, take classes, and access sources of entertainment and leisure. The **Web**, short for World Wide Web, is one of the more popular services on the Internet.

(4) What Are the Categories of Software?

Software, also called a **program**, is a series of instructions that tells the computer what to do and how to do it. The two categories of software are system software and application software. **System software** consists of the programs that control or maintain the operations of a computer and its devices. Two types of system software are the **operating system**, which coordinates activities among computer hardware devices, and **utility programs**, which perform maintenance-type tasks usually related to a computer, its devices, or its programs. **Application software** consists of programs designed to make users more productive and/or assist them with personal tasks. Popular application software includes Web browser, word processing software, spreadsheet software, database software, and presentation graphics software.

 Visit scsite.com/dcf2e/ch1/quiz or click the Quiz Yourself button. Click Objectives 3 – 4.

(5) What Are the Categories of Computers?

Industry experts typically classify computers into six categories: personal computers, mobile computers and mobile devices, midrange servers, mainframes, supercomputers, and embedded computers. A **personal computer** is a computer that can perform all of its input, processing, output, and storage activities by itself. A **mobile computer** is a personal computer that you can carry from place to place, and a **mobile device** is a computing device small enough to hold in your hand. A **midrange server** is a large and powerful computer that typically supports several hundred and sometimes up to a few thousand connected computers at the same time. A **mainframe** is a large, expensive, powerful computer that can handle hundreds or thousands of connected users simultaneously and can store huge amounts of data, instructions, and information. A **supercomputer** is the fastest, most powerful, and most expensive computer and is used for applications requiring complex, sophisticated mathematical calculations. An **embedded computer** is a special-purpose computer that functions as a computer in a larger product.

Chapter Review

 6 **What Are the Types of Computer Users?**

Computer users can be separated in five categories: home users, small office/home office users, mobile users, power users, and large business users. A **home user** is a family member who uses a computer for a variety of reasons, such as budgeting and personal financial management, Web access, communications, and entertainment. A **small office/home office (SOHO)** user is a small company or self-employed individual who works from home and uses basic business software and sometimes industry-specific software. **Mobile users** are employees and students who work on a computer while away from a main office or school. A **power user** can exist in all types of businesses and uses powerful computers to work with industry-specific software. A **large business user** works in a company with many employees and uses a computer and computer network to process high volumes of transactions.

 7 **What Computer Applications Are Used in Society?**

You may interact directly with computers in fields such as education, finance, government, health care, science, publishing, travel, and industry. In education, students use computers and software to assist with learning or take distance learning classes. In finance, people use computers for **online banking** to access information and **online investing** to buy and sell stocks and bonds. Government offices have Web sites to provide citizens with up-to-date information, and government employees use computers as part of their daily routines. In health care, computers are used to maintain patient records, assist doctors with medical tests and research, file insurance claims, provide greater precision during operations, and as implants. All branches of science use computers to assist with collecting, analyzing, and modeling data and to communicate with scientists around the world. Publishers use computers to assist in developing pages and make their works available online. Many vehicles use some type of online navigation system to help people travel more quickly and safely. Industries use **computer-aided manufacturing (CAM)** to assist with the manufacturing process.

 Visit scsite.com/dcf2e/ch1/quiz or click the Quiz Yourself button. Click Objectives 5 – 7.

Key Terms

You should know the Key Terms. Use the list below to help focus your study. To further enhance your understanding of the Key Terms in this chapter, visit scsite.com/dcf2e/ch1/terms. See an example of and a definition for each term, and access current and additional information about the term from the Web.

application software (11)
central processing unit (CPU) (7)
communications device (8)
computer (3)
computer literacy (3)
computer-aided manufacturing (CAM) (25)
data (3)
desktop computer (14)
embedded computer (17)
enterprise computing (21)
execute (12)
FAQ (4)
graphical user interface (GUI) (10)
handheld computer (15)

handhelds (16)
handtop computer (15)
hardware (6)
home user (18)
information (3)
information processing cycle (5)
input device (6)
installing (12)
Internet (8)
Internet-enabled (15)
laptop computer (14)
large business user (21)
mainframe (17)
memory (7)
midrange server (16)
mobile computer (14)
mobile device (14)

mobile users (20)
network (8)
notebook computer (14)
online (8)
online banking (23)
online investing (23)
operating system (11)
output device (7)
PDA (15)
personal computer (14)
personal computer salesperson (26)
power user (21)
processor (7)
program (10)
programmer (12)
run (12)

small office/home office (SOHO) (20)
smart phone (16)
smart watch (16)
software (10)
storage device (7)
storage media (7)
stylus (15)
supercomputer (17)
system software (10)
system unit (7)
Tablet PC (15)
telecommuting (22)
telemedicine (24)
user (4)
utility program (11)
Web (10)
Web page (10)

Checkpoint

Use the Checkpoint exercises to check your knowledge level of the chapter.

_____ 1. Many people believe that computer literacy is vital to success. (3)

_____ 2. Data is a collection of unprocessed items. (3)

_____ 3. A user is anyone who communicates with a computer. (4)

_____ 4. When a computer connects to a network, it is offline. (8)

_____ 5. A Web page can contain only text. (10)

_____ 6. Software is a series of instructions that tells the computer what to do. (10)

_____ 7. System software serves as the interface between the user, the application software, and the computer's hardware. (10)

_____ 8. A notebook computer is a portable, personal computer designed to fit on your lap. (14)

_____ 9. A power user requires the capabilities of a powerful desktop computer. (21)

_____ 10. Few publishers make their works available online. (25)

1. Computer literacy involves having a knowledge and understanding of _____. (3)
   a. computer programming
   b. computers and their uses
   c. computer repair
   d. all of the above

2. Three commonly used _____ are a printer, a monitor, and speakers. (7)
   a. input devices
   b. output devices
   c. storage devices
   d. communications devices

3. _____ allows people connected to the Internet to communicate with multiple users at the same time — much like a group discussion. (10)
   a. A chat room
   b. E-mail
   c. A Web page
   d. Instant messaging

4. Some widely used _____ include(s) personal information management, desktop publishing, and Web page authoring. (11)
   a. system software
   b. operating systems
   c. application software
   d. utility programs

5. The term, PC-compatible, refers to any personal computer _____. (14)
   a. with processors having the same architecture as processors in Apple computers
   b. based on the original IBM personal computer design
   c. that uses the Macintosh operating system (Mac OS)
   d. all of the above

6. Two types of _____ are desktop computers and notebook computers. (14)
   a. personal computers
   b. midrange servers
   c. mainframe computers
   d. supercomputers

7. Four popular types of _____ are handheld computers, PDAs, smart phones, and smart watches. (15)
   a. mobile devices
   b. notebook computers
   c. desktop computers
   d. tower computers

8. _____ refers to the use of computers to assist with processes such as fabrication and assembly. (25)
   a. Enterprise computing
   b. Telecommuting
   c. Information processing
   d. Computer-aided manufacturing (CAM)

_____ 1. information processing cycle (5)

_____ 2. hardware (6)

_____ 3. network (8)

_____ 4. software (10)

_____ 5. Internet-enabled (15)

a. mobile devices that can connect to the Internet wirelessly

b. computer's electric, electronic, and mechanical components

c. collection of computers connected together that allows sharing of resources

d. system that attempts to illustrate the behavior of the human brain

e. series of input, process, output, and storage activities

f. series of instructions that tells a computer what to do and how to do it

Checkpoint

Short Answer

Write a brief answer to each of the following questions.

1. What are some ways people use computers in the home, at work, and at school? _____ What does it mean to be computer literate? _____

2. How is hardware different from software? _____ What is installing software? _____

3. How is an input device different from an output device? _____ What are commonly used input and output devices? _____

4. What are six common storage devices? _____ How are they different? _____

5. Why do people use the Internet? _____ How do users access the Internet? _____

Working Together

Working in a group of your classmates, complete the following team exercise.

1. Computers are everywhere. Watching television, driving a car, using a charge card, ordering fast food, and the more obvious activity of typing a term paper on a personal computer, all involve interaction with computers. For one day, have each member of your team make a list of every computer he or she encounters (be careful not to limit yourselves just to the computers you see). Meet with the members of your team and combine your lists. Consider how each computer is used. How were the tasks the computers perform done before computers? Use PowerPoint to create a group presentation and share your findings with the class.

Web Research

Use the Internet-based Web Research exercises to broaden your understanding of the concepts presented in this chapter. Visit scsite.com/dcf2e/ch1/research to obtain more information pertaining to each exercise. To discuss any of the Web Research exercises in this chapter with other students, post your thoughts or questions at scsite.com/dcf2e/ch1/forum.

(1) Journaling Respond to your readings in this chapter by writing at least one page about your reactions, evaluations, and reflections about computer usage in your home. For example, how many appliances in your kitchen have a computer component? Has your **smart phone** replaced a camera or landline telephone? Have family members reduced their television viewing time with playing online games or surfing the Internet? You also can write about the new terms you learned by reading this chapter. If required, submit your journal to your instructor.

(2) Scavenger Hunt Use one of the **search engines** listed in Figure 2-8 in Chapter 2 on page 58 or your own favorite search engine to find the answers to the questions below. Copy and paste the Web address from the Web page where you found the answer. Some questions may have more than one answer. If required, submit your answers to your instructor. (1) What are three accredited online colleges or universities that offer a bachelor's degree in computer information technology? (2) Two National Science Foundation (NSF) programs were established in 1997 to interconnect 50 university and scientific computing sites. What colleges host these two sites? What were the locations of the five original NSF-financed supercomputer centers? (3) Personal finance software helps you balance your checkbook and manage your finances. What is the name of a popular personal finance program? (4) What is the name of the first spreadsheet program? (5) A programming language developed by the U.S. Department of Defense was named to honor a famous woman mathematician. What is the name of this programming language?

(3) Search Sleuth Visit the **Google Web site** (google.com) and then click the About Google link at the bottom of the page. Using your word processing program, answer the following questions and then, if required, submit your answers to your instructor. (1) Below Our Company, click Corporate Info. Who are the founders of Google? (2) Click the Technology link on the left side of the page. Provide a summary on how Google uses PageRank. (3) Click your browser's Back button or press the BACKSPACE key to return to the About Google page. Below Our Search, click the Google Web Search Features link. What is the purpose of the I'm Feeling Lucky button? What is the purpose of the Similar Pages link? What is Froogle? (4) Click your browser's Back button two times to return to the Google home page. In the Google Search text box, type HTML and click the Google Search button. Approximately how many hits resulted? Do any definitions appear? If so, list the definitions. How much time did it take to complete the search? (5) In the Google Search text box, type HTML Tutorial and click the Search button. Compare this to your earlier search. Are there more or fewer hits? How much time did it take to complete the second search? (6) Click one of the resulting HTML tutorial links and review the tutorial. Write a 50-word summary of the tutorial. Using the information contained within the tutorial, do you think you would be able to create your own Web site?

Learn How To

Use the Learn How To activities to learn fundamental skills when using a computer and accompanying technology. Complete the exercises and submit them to your instructor.

LEARN HOW TO 1: Start and Close an Application

An application accomplishes tasks on a computer. You can start any application by using the Start button.

Complete these steps to start the Web browser application called Internet Explorer:

1. Click the Start button (start) at the left of the Windows taskbar on the bottom of the screen. *The Start menu is displayed.*
2. Point to All Programs on the Start menu. *The All Programs submenu appears (Figure 1-38).*
3. Click the program name, Internet Explorer, on the All Programs submenu. *The Internet Explorer browser window opens (Figure 1-39).*

An item on the All Programs submenu might have a small right arrow next to it. When this occurs, point to the item and another submenu will appear. Click the application name on this submenu to start the application. Some application names might appear on the Start menu itself. If so, click any of these names to start the corresponding application.

Below the line on the left side of the Start menu, Windows displays the names of the applications recently opened on the computer. You can start any of these applications by clicking the name of the application.

To close an application, click the Close button (☒) in the upper-right corner of the window. If you have created but not saved a document, Windows will ask if you want to save the document. If you do not want to save it, click the No button in the displayed dialog box. If you want to save it, refer to Learn How To number 1 in Chapter 3 on page 130.

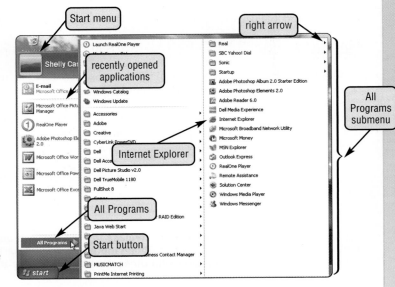

FIGURE 1-38

FIGURE 1-39

Exercise

1. Using the Start button, start the application named WordPad found on the Accessories submenu of the All Programs submenu. WordPad is a word processing application. Type the following: `To start an application, click the application name on the All Programs submenu` and then type your name. Click the Print button (🖨) on the toolbar. Submit the printout to your instructor.
2. Close the WordPad application. If you are asked if you want to save changes to the document, click the No button. Start the WordPad application again, type some new text, and then close the WordPad application. When the dialog box is displayed, click the Cancel button. What happened? Now, close the WordPad window without saving the document. Submit your answer to your instructor.
3. Using the Start button, start the e-mail program on the computer. What is the name of the e-mail program? In the program window, what menu names are displayed on the menu bar at the top of the window? Close the e-mail program. Submit your answers to your instructor.

LEARN HOW TO 2: Use the Discovering Computers Fundamentals 2e Web Site (scsite.com/dcf2e)

The Discovering Computers Fundamentals 2e Web site provides a variety of activities and exercises. To use the site, you first must register and establish a user name and password. Perform the following steps to register:

1. Find your key code on the card at the front of this book.
2. Start the Web browser.
3. Type scsite.com/dcf2e in the Address box of the Web browser. Press the ENTER key.
4. When the registration page is displayed, click the New User Registration link.
5. Enter the key code you found in Step 1.
6. Follow the on-screen instructions to complete registration.

When you first type a Web address to display a page from the dcf2e site, you must enter your user name and password to gain access to the site. When you are done using the site, close the browser so no one else can visit the site with your user name and password.

Exercise

1. Start the Web browser on your computer.
2. Type scsite.com/dcf2e/ch1/howto in the Address box of the browser and then press the ENTER key.
3. If the registration page is displayed and you have not yet registered, complete the steps above. If you are registered, click Registered User, enter your user name and password, and then click the Submit button.
4. Navigate to the Chapter 1 home page.
5. Visit each of the Exercises Web pages (Key Terms and Learn It Online). Use the navigation bar on the left of the screen to display these pages.
6. Click the browser's Close button to close the application.
7. Write a report that describes the use of each of the Exercises pages you visited. Which page do you think will prove the most valuable to you when using the book and the Web site? Why? Which will be the least useful? Why? Submit your report to your instructor.

LEARN HOW TO 3: Find Out About Your Computer

By following these steps, you can find out about the computer you are using:

1. Click the Start button on the Windows XP taskbar.
2. Point to All Programs on the Start menu, point to Accessories on the All Programs submenu, and then point to System Tools on the Accessories submenu.
3. Click System Information on the System Tools submenu. Windows displays a system summary in the right side of the window, and an index of categories in the left side of the window (Figure 1-40).

To determine more information about your computer, click any of the plus signs in the left side of the window. Then, click the item about which you want more information.

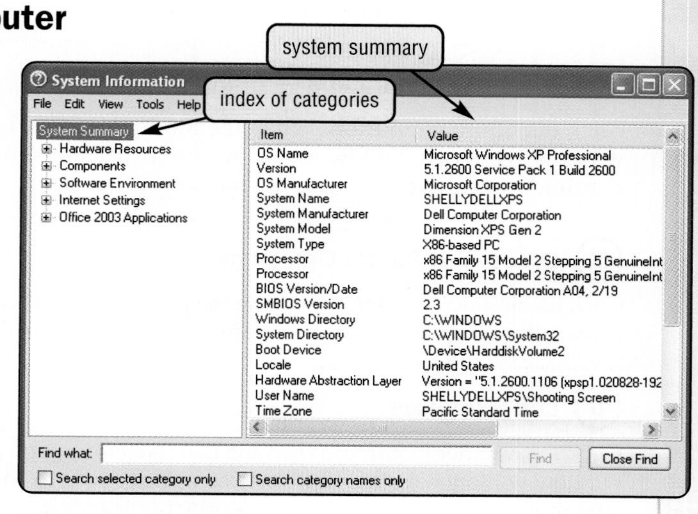

FIGURE 1-40

Exercise

1. Submit the answers to the following questions about the computer you are using:
   a. What type of operating system (OS Name) is on the computer?
   b. What company manufactured the computer?
   c. How much RAM (physical memory) is on the computer?
   d. How much data can you store on the C: drive?
   e. What is the name of a CD or DVD drive found on the computer?

Learn It Online

Use the Learn It Online exercises to reinforce your understanding of the chapter concepts. To access the Learn It Online exercises, visit scsite.com/dcf2e/ch1/learn.

(1) At the Movies — Walking the PC Pioneer Trail

To view the Walking the PC Pioneer Trail movie, click the number 1 button. Locate your video and click the corresponding High-Speed or Dial-Up link, depending on your Internet connection. Watch the movie and then complete the exercise by answering the question that follows. Many of the pioneers of the technology industry in the United States established their businesses in Silicon Valley. What explanation can you offer for why the founders of these companies all set up shop in this area?

(2) Student Edition Labs — Using Input Devices

Click the number 2 button. When the Student Edition Labs menu appears, click *Using Input Devices* to begin. A new browser window will open. Follow the on-screen instructions to complete the Lab. When finished, click the Exit button. If required, submit your results to your instructor.

(3) Practice Test

Click the number 3 button. Answer each question. When completed, enter your name and click the Grade Test button to submit the quiz for grading. Make a note of any missed questions. If required, submit your score to your instructor.

(4) Who Wants To Be a Computer Genius^2?

Click the number 4 button to find out if you are a computer genius. Directions about how to play the game will be displayed. When you are ready to play, click the Play button. Submit your score to your instructor.

(5) Wheel of Terms

Click the number 5 button to reinforce important terms you learned in this chapter by playing the Shelly Cashman Series version of this popular game. Directions about how to play the game will be displayed. When you are ready to play, click the Play button. Submit your score to your instructor.

(6) Student Edition Labs — Using Windows

Click the number 6 button. When the Student Edition Labs menu appears, click *Using Windows* to begin. A new browser window will open. Follow the on-screen instructions to complete the Lab. When finished, click the Exit button. If required, submit your results to your instructor.

(7) Crossword Puzzle Challenge

Click the number 7 button. Complete the puzzle to reinforce skills you learned in this chapter. Directions about how to play the game will be displayed. When you are ready to play, click the Play button. Submit the completed puzzle to your instructor.

(8) Lab Exercises

Click the number 8 button. When the Lab Exercises menu appears, click the exercise assigned by your instructor. A new browser window will open. Follow the on-screen instructions to complete the exercise. When finished, click the Exit button. If required, submit your results to your instructor.

(9) Chapter Discussion Forum

Select an objective from this chapter on page 1 about which you would like more information. Click the number 9 button and post a short message listing a meaningful message title accompanied by one or more questions concerning the selected objective. In two days, return to the threaded discussion by clicking the number 9 button. Submit to your instructor your original message and at least one response to your message.

Timeline

MILESTONES IN COMPUTER HISTORY

Dr. John V. Atanasoff and Clifford Berry design and build the first electronic digital computer. Their machine, the Atanasoff-Berry-Computer, or ABC, provides the foundation for advances in electronic digital computers.

John von Neumann in front of the electronic computer built at the Institute for Advanced Study. This computer and its von Neumann architecture served as the prototype for subsequent stored program computers worldwide.

William Shockley, John Bardeen, and Walter Brattain invent the transfer resistance device, eventually called the transistor. The transistor would revolutionize computers, proving much more reliable than vacuum tubes.

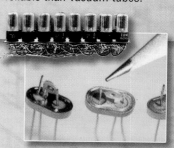

1937 **1943** **1945** **1946** **1947** **1951**

Dr. John W. Mauchly and J. Presper Eckert, Jr. complete work on the first large-scale electronic, general-purpose digital computer. The ENIAC (Electronic Numerical Integrator And Computer) weighs 30 tons, contains 18,000 vacuum tubes, occupies a 30-by-50 foot space, and consumes 160 kilowatts of power. The first time it is turned on, lights dim in an entire section of Philadelphia.

During World War II, British scientist Alan Turing designs the Colossus, an electronic computer created for the military to break German codes. The computer's existence is kept secret until the 1970s.

The first commercially available electronic digital computer, the UNIVAC I (UNIVersal Automatic Computer), is introduced by Remington Rand. Public awareness of computers increases when the UNIVAC I, after analyzing only five percent of the popular vote, correctly predicts that Dwight D. Eisenhower will win the presidential election.

Dr. Grace Hopper considers the concept of reusable software in her paper, "The Education of a Computer." The paper describes how to program a computer with symbolic notation instead of the detailed machine language that had been used.

The IBM 305 RAMAC system is the first to use magnetic disk for external storage. The system provides storage capacity similar to magnetic tape that previously was used, but offers the advantage of semi-random access capability.

More than 200 programming languages have been created.

IBM introduces two smaller, desk-sized computers: the IBM 1401 for business and the IBM 1620 for scientists. The IBM 1620 initially is called the CADET, but IBM drops the name when campus wags claim it is an acronym for, Can't Add, Doesn't Even Try.

Fortran (FORmula TRANslation), an efficient, easy-to-use programming language, is introduced by John Backus.

1952   **1953**   **1957**   **1958**   **1959**   **1960**

The IBM model 650 is one of the first widely used computers. Originally planning to produce only 50 machines, the system is so successful that eventually IBM manufactures more than 1,000. With the IBM 700 series of machines, the company will dominate the mainframe market for the next decade.

Core memory, developed in the early 1950s, provides much larger storage capacity than vacuum tube memory.

Jack Kilby of Texas Instruments invents the integrated circuit, which lays the foundation for high-speed computers and large-capacity memories. Computers built with transistors mark the beginning of the second generation of computer hardware.

COBOL, a high-level business application language, is developed by a committee headed by Dr. Grace Hopper. COBOL uses English-like phrases and runs on most business computers, making it one of the more widely used programming languages.

Dr. John Kemeny of Dartmouth leads the development of the BASIC programming language. BASIC will be widely used on personal computers.

Computer Science Corporation becomes the first software company listed on the New York Stock Exchange.

IBM

Under pressure from the industry, IBM announces that some of its software will be priced separately from the computer hardware. This unbundling allows software firms to emerge in the industry.

Digital Equipment Corporation (DEC) introduces the first minicomputer, the PDP-8. The machine is used extensively as an interface for time-sharing systems.

In a letter to the editor titled, "GO TO Statements Considered Harmful," Dr. Edsger Dijsktra introduces the concept of structured programming, developing standards for constructing computer programs.

ARPANET

The ARPANET network, a predecessor of the Internet, is established.

1964   1965   1968   1969   1970

The number of computers has grown to 18,000. Third-generation computers, with their controlling circuitry stored on chips, are introduced. The IBM System/360 computer is the first family of compatible machines, merging science and business lines.

Alan Shugart at IBM demonstrates the first regular use of an 8-inch floppy (magnetic storage) disk.

Fourth-generation computers, built with chips that use LSI (large-scale integration) arrive. While the chips used in 1965 contained as many as 1,000 circuits, the LSI chip contains as many as 15,000.

IBM introduces the term word processing for the first time with its Magnetic Tape/Selectric Typewriter (MT/ST). The MT/ST was the first reusable storage medium that allowed typed material to be edited without having to retype the document.

MITS, Inc. advertises one of the first microcomputers, the Altair. Named for the destination in an episode of *Star Trek*, the Altair is sold in kits for less than $400. Although initially it has no keyboard, no monitor, no permanent memory, and no software, 4,000 orders are taken within the first three months.

VisiCalc, a spreadsheet program written by Bob Frankston and Dan Bricklin, is introduced. Originally written to run on Apple II computers, VisiCalc will be seen as the most important reason for the acceptance of personal computers in the business world.

The IBM PC is introduced, signaling IBM's entrance into the personal computer marketplace. The IBM PC quickly garners the largest share of the personal computer market and becomes the personal computer of choice in business.

Ethernet, the first local area network (LAN), is developed at Xerox PARC (Palo Alto Research Center) by Robert Metcalf. The LAN allows computers to communicate and share software, data, and peripherals. Initially designed to link minicomputers, Ethernet will be extended to personal computers.

The first public online information services, CompuServe and the Source, are founded.

1971   1975   1976   1979   1980   1981

Dr. Ted Hoff of Intel Corporation develops a microprocessor, or microprogrammable computer chip, the Intel 4004.

IBM offers Microsoft Corporation cofounder, Bill Gates, the opportunity to develop the operating system for the soon-to-be announced IBM personal computer. With the development of MS-DOS, Microsoft achieves tremendous growth and success.

The first computer virus, Elk Cloner, is spread via Apple II floppy disks, which contained the operating system. A short rhyme would appear on the screen when the user pressed Reset after the 50th boot of an infected disk.

Steve Jobs and Steve Wozniak build the first Apple computer. A subsequent version, the Apple II, is an immediate success. Adopted by elementary schools, high schools, and colleges, for many students, the Apple II is their first contact with the world of computers.

Alan Shugart presents the Winchester hard drive, revolutionizing storage for personal computers.

3,275,000 personal computers are sold, almost 3,000,000 more than in 1981.

Apple introduces the Macintosh computer, which incorporates a unique, easy-to-learn, graphical user interface.

Compaq, Inc. is founded to develop and market IBM-compatible PCs.

Microsoft has public stock offering and raises approximately $61 million. Within 20 years, Microsoft's stock is worth nearly $350 billion or 5,735 times the amount raised in the initial public stock offering.

Hewlett-Packard announces the first LaserJet printer for personal computers.

Hayes introduces the 300 bps smart modem. The modem is an immediate success.

1982   1983   1984   1986   1988

Instead of choosing a person for its annual award, *TIME* magazine names the computer Machine of the Year for 1982, acknowledging the impact of computers on society.

Lotus Development Corporation is founded. Its spreadsheet software, Lotus 1-2-3, which combines spreadsheet, graphics, and database programs in one package, becomes the best-selling program for IBM personal computers.

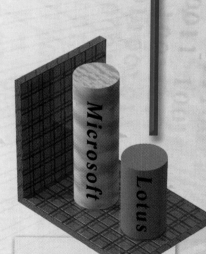

Microsoft surpasses Lotus Development Corporation to become the world's top software vendor.

World Wide Web Consortium releases standards that describe a framework for linking documents on different computers.

Several companies introduce computers using the Pentium processor from Intel. The Pentium chip is the successor to the Intel 486 processor. It contains 3.1 million transistors and is capable of performing 112,000,000 instructions per second.

While working at CERN, Switzerland, Tim Berners-Lee invents an Internet-based hypermedia enterprise for information sharing. Berners-Lee will call this innovation the World Wide Web.

Microsoft releases Microsoft Office 3 Professional, the first version of Microsoft Office.

1989 — 1991 — 1992 — 1993

The Intel 486 becomes the world's first 1,000,000 transistor microprocessor. It crams 1.2 million transistors on a .4" x .6" sliver of silicon and executes 15,000,000 instructions per second — four times as fast as its predecessor, the 80386 chip.

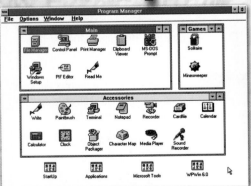

The White House launches its Web site, which includes an interactive citizens' handbook and White House history and tours.

Microsoft releases Windows 3.1, the latest version of its Windows operating system. Windows 3.1 offers improvements such as TrueType fonts, multimedia capability, and object linking and embedding (OLE). In two months, 3,000,000 copies of Windows 3.1 are sold.

U.S. Robotics introduces PalmPilot, a handheld personal organizer. The PalmPilot's user friendliness and low price make it a standout next to more expensive personal digital assistants (PDAs).

Sun Microsystems launches Java, an object-oriented programming language that allows users to write one application for a variety of computer platforms. Java becomes one of the hotter Internet technologies.

Microsoft releases Windows NT 4.0, an operating system for client-server networks. Windows NT's management tools and wizards make it easier for developers to build and deploy business applications.

Jim Clark and Marc Andreessen found Netscape and launch Netscape Navigator 1.0, a browser for the World Wide Web.

1994 1995 1996

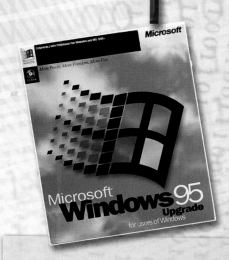

Linus Torvalds creates the Linux kernel, a UNIX-like operating system that he releases free across the Internet for further enhancement by other programmers.

Microsoft releases Windows 95, a major upgrade to its Windows operating system. Windows 95 consists of more than 10,000,000 lines of computer instructions developed by 300 person-years of effort. More than 50,000 individuals and companies test the software before it is released.

Two out of three employees in the United States have access to a personal computer, and one out of every three homes has a personal computer. Fifty million personal computers are sold worldwide and more than 250,000,000 are in use.

Apple and Microsoft sign a joint technology development agreement. Microsoft buys $150,000,000 of Apple stock.

More than 10,000,000 people take up telecommuting, which is the capability of working at home and communicating with an office via computer. Increasingly more firms embrace telecommuting to help increase productivity, reduce absenteeism, and provide greater job satisfaction.

Apple Computer introduces the iMac, the next version of its popular Macintosh computer. The iMac abandons such conventional features as a floppy disk drive but wins customers with its futuristic design, see-through case, and easy setup. Consumer demand outstrips Apple's production capabilities, and some vendors are forced to begin waiting lists.

DVD, the next generation of optical disc storage technology, is introduced. DVD can store computer, audio, and video data in a single format, with the capability of producing near-studio quality. By year's end, 500,000 DVD players are shipped worldwide.

1997

1998

Intel introduces the Pentium II processor with 7.5 million transistors. The new processor, which incorporates MMX technology, processes video, audio, and graphics data more efficiently and supports applications such as movie editing, gaming, and more.

E-commerce, or electronic commerce — the marketing of goods and services over the Internet — booms. Companies such as Dell, E*TRADE, and Amazon.com spur online shopping, allowing buyers to obtain everything from hardware and software to financial and travel services, insurance, automobiles, books, and more.

Microsoft releases Internet Explorer 4.0 and seizes a key place in the Internet arena. This new Web browser is greeted with tremendous customer demand.

Microsoft ships Windows 98, an upgrade to Windows 95. Windows 98 offers improved Internet access, better system performance, and support for a new generation of hardware and software. In six months, more than 10,000,000 copies of Windows 98 are sold worldwide.

Fifty million users are connected to the Internet and World Wide Web.

Governments and businesses frantically work to make their computers Y2K (Year 2000) compliant, spending more than $500 billion worldwide. Y2K non-compliant computers cannot distinguish whether 01/01/00 refers to 1900 or 2000, and thus may operate using a wrong date. This Y2K bug can affect any application that relies on computer chips, such as ATMs, airplanes, energy companies, and the telephone system. In the end, the Y2K bug turned out not to be a problem.

Shawn Fanning, 19, and his company, Napster, turn the music industry upside down by developing software that allows computer users to swap music files with one another without going through a centralized file server. The Recording Industry of America, on behalf of five media companies, sues Napster for copyright infringement and wins.

U.S. District Judge Thomas Penfield Jackson rules in the antitrust lawsuit brought by the Department of Justice and 19 states that Microsoft used its monopoly power to stifle competition.

1999

2000

Microsoft introduces Office 2000, its premier productivity suite, offering new tools for users to create content and save it directly to a Web site without any file conversion or special steps.

E-commerce achieves mainstream acceptance. Annual e-commerce sales exceed $100 billion, and Internet advertising expenditures reach more than $5 billion.

Open Source Code software, such as the Linux operating system and the Apache Web server created by unpaid volunteers, begin to gain wide acceptance among computer users.

Dot-com companies (Internet based) go out of business at a record pace — nearly one per day — as financial investors withhold funding due to the companies' unprofitability.

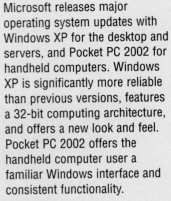

Microsoft ships Windows 2000 and Windows Me. Windows 2000 offers improved behind-the-scene security and reliability. Windows Me is designed for home users and lets them edit home movies, share digital photos, index music, and create a home network.

Intel unveils its Pentium 4 chip with clock speeds starting at 1.4 GHz. The Pentium 4 includes 42 million transistors, nearly twice as many contained on its predecessor, the Pentium III.

Microsoft releases major operating system updates with Windows XP for the desktop and servers, and Pocket PC 2002 for handheld computers. Windows XP is significantly more reliable than previous versions, features a 32-bit computing architecture, and offers a new look and feel. Pocket PC 2002 offers the handheld computer user a familiar Windows interface and consistent functionality.

According to the U.S. Department of Commerce, Internet traffic is doubling every 100 days, resulting in an annual growth rate of more than 700 percent. It has taken radio and television 30 years and 15 years, respectively, to reach 60 million people. The Internet has achieved the same audience base in 3 years.

2000

2001

Microsoft introduces Office XP, the next version of the world's leading suite of productivity software. Features include speech and handwriting recognition, smart tags, and task panes.

Telemedicine uses satellite technology and videoconferencing to broadcast consultations and to perform distant surgeries. Robots are used for complex and precise tasks. Computer-aided surgery uses virtual reality to assist with training and planning procedures.

Avid readers enjoy e-books, which are digital texts read on compact computer screens. E-books can hold the equivalent of 10 traditional books containing text and graphics. Readers can search, highlight text, and add notes.

DVD writers begin to replace CD writers (CD-RW). DVDs can store up to eight times as much data as CDs. Uses include storing home movies, music, photos, and backups. Digital cameras and video editors help the average user develop quality video to store on DVDs.

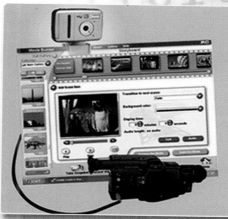

After several years of negligible sales, the Tablet PC is reintroduced as the next-generation mobile PC. The lightweight device, the size of a three-ring notebook, is ideal for people on the go. It runs Windows XP Tablet PC Edition, has wireless capabilities, and features natural input capabilities including pen and speech technologies.

Digital video cameras, DVD writers, easy-to-use video editing software, and improvements in storage capabilities allow the average computer user to create Hollywood-like videos with introductions, conclusions, scenes rearranged, music, and voice-over.

2002

Microsoft launches its .NET strategy, which is a new environment for developing and running software applications featuring ease of development of Web-based services. Users of applications immediately see the benefit of .NET as instant access to data and services in the context of their current task.

Handspring begins shipping the Treo communicator, a handheld computer with cellular telephone, e-mail, text messaging, and wireless Web capabilities.

Intel ships its revamped Pentium 4 chip with the 0.13 micron processor and Hyper-Threading (HT) Technology, operating at speeds of 3.06 GHz. This new development eventually will enable processors with a billion transistors to operate at 20 GHz.

U.S. District Judge Colleen Kollar-Kotelly rules against the nine states appealing the antitrust settlement reached between Microsoft and the Justice Department. The nine states were seeking tougher sanctions against the software giant for abusing its monopoly power. Two of the nine states, Massachusetts and West Virginia, plan to appeal the latest ruling to the U.S. District Court of Appeals.

IBM puts its weight behind On Demand computing. Its intention is to invest up to $10 billion in hardware and software, and then sell computing time and the use of applications to businesses in a manner similar to an electric utility company.

Computer manufacturers and software companies integrate high-end PCs and entertainment devices. The result is PCs with great entertainment functions that let you watch and record TV, burn CDs and DVDs, play games, and more.

Wireless computers and devices, such as keyboards, mouse devices, home networks, and public Internet access points become commonplace. Latest operating systems include support for both the Wi-Fi (wireless fidelity) and Bluetooth standards. Wireless capabilities are standard on many PDAs and Tablet PCs.

2003

In an attempt to maintain their current business model of selling songs, the Recording Industry Association of American (RIAA) files over 250 lawsuits against individual computer users who offer copyrighted music over peer-to-peer networks.

MSBlast worm and SoBig virus plague Microsoft Windows users. Microsoft Corporation responds by creating the Anti-Virus Reward Program, initially funded with $5 million, to help law enforcement agencies identify and bring to justice those who illegally release damaging worms, viruses and other types of malicious code on the Internet.

Microsoft ships Office 2003, the latest version of its flagship Office suite. New features include a consistent user interface, an overhauled Outlook, increased emphasis on task panes, improved collaboration, enhanced XML functionality, and a new application called OneNote for organizing your notes.

Flat-panel LCD monitors overtake bulky CRT monitors as the popular choice of computer users. Although flat-panel LCD monitors cost more, they offer several advantages including physical size, weight, true display size, better power consumption, and no radiation emission.

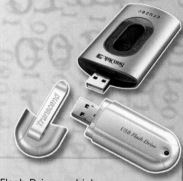

Companies such as RealNetworks, Microsoft, Sony, and Wal-Mart stake out turf in the online music store business started by Apple Computer. In the previous year, Apple's iTunes Music Store Web site sold nearly 20 million songs for 99 cents each.

USB Flash Drives, which are small enough to fit on a key chain but can store up to 4 billion characters, become a cost-effective way to transport data and information from one computer to another.

2004

Linux, the open-source operating system, makes major inroads into the server market as a viable alternative to Microsoft Windows, Sun's Solaris, and the UNIX operating systems.

Major retailers begin requiring suppliers to include Radio Frequency Identification (RFID) tags or microchips with antennas, which can be as small as 1/3 of a millimeter across, in the goods they sell. When a transponder receives a certain radio query, it responds by transmitting its unique ID code. Besides carrying out the functions of the bar code, RFIDs may eventually eliminate long checkout lines.

Apple Computer introduces the sleek iMac G5. The new computer's display device contains the system unit.

106 million, or 53 percent, of the 200 million online population in America accesses the Internet via speedy broadband.

Microsoft
Windows^{XP}
Media Center Edition 2005

Spyware
Spam
Phishing
Spim   Spit

The Mozilla Foundation, the creators of the free open source Firefox browser, predicts that by the end of 2005, it will have 10 percent of the browser market, primarily at the expense of Microsoft's Internet Explorer (IE) security-plagued browser.

Microsoft unveils Windows XP Media Center Edition 2005. This operating system allows users to access the routine capabilities of a Windows XP-based PC while focusing on delivering media content such as music, digital photography, movies, and television.

Spam, spyware, phishing, spim, and spit take center stage, along with viruses, as major nuisances to the 801 million computer users worldwide. Spam, which accounts for 45 percent of all e-mail, involves the sending of bulk e-mail that is unsolicited and masks its origin. Spyware is a program placed on the computer without the user's knowledge that secretly collects information about the user, often related to Web browsing habits. Phishing is the act of sending an e-mail to a user falsely claiming to be a legitimate enterprise in an attempt to trick the user into surrendering private information that will be used for identity theft. Spim is spam via instant messaging. Spit is spam via Internet telephony.

The OQO handheld computer is a fully-functional Windows XP computer with desktop capabilities. Just 4.9 inches long, 3.4 inches wide, .9 inch thick, and weighing only 14 ounces, the OQO fills the void between the bulk and awkwardness of a notebook computer and the limited capability of a smart phone or PDA.

2005

SP2

The smart phone overtakes the PDA as the personal mobile device of choice. A smart phone offers a cellular phone, full personal information management and e-mail functionality, a Web browser, instant message capabilities, and even the ability to listen to music, play video and games, and take pictures with its built-in camera.

To date, Microsoft has sold over 300 million copies of its Windows XP operating system. By early January, Microsoft automatically downloaded to its users' computers over 100 million copies of Service Pack 2 (SP2), its latest update to Windows XP. In addition to a new security center and firewall, SP2 adds a pop-up blocker in Internet Explorer and updated support for Wi-Fi and Bluetooth wireless technologies.

Microsoft introduces Visual Studio 2005. The product includes Visual Basic, Visual C#, Visual J#, Visual C++, and SQL Server. Microsoft also releases a Visual Studio 2005 Express Edition for hobbyists, students, and nonprofessionals.

Microsoft
Visual Studio 2005

The Internet and World Wide Web

OBJECTIVES

After completing this chapter, you will be able to:

1. Explain how to access and connect to the Internet
2. Explain how to view pages and search for information on the Web
3. Describe the types of Web sites
4. Identify the steps required for Web publishing
5. Describe the types of e-commerce
6. Explain how e-mail, FTP, newsgroups and message boards, mailing lists, chat rooms, instant messaging, and Internet telephony work
7. Identify the rules of netiquette

CONTENTS

THE INTERNET
HOW THE INTERNET WORKS
Connecting to the Internet
Access Providers
How Data Travels the Internet
Internet Addresses

THE WORLD WIDE WEB
Browsing the Web
Web Addresses
Navigating Web Pages
Searching for Information on the Web
Types of Web Sites
Evaluating a Web Site
Multimedia on the Web
Web Publishing
E-Commerce

OTHER INTERNET SERVICES
E-Mail
FTP
Newsgroups and Message Boards
Mailing Lists
Chat Rooms
Instant Messaging
Internet Telephony

NETIQUETTE
CHAPTER SUMMARY
COMPANIES ON THE CUTTING EDGE
Google
Yahoo!

TECHNOLOGY TRAILBLAZERS
Tim Berners-Lee
Meg Whitman

THE INTERNET

One of the major reasons business, home, and other users purchase computers is for Internet access. The **Internet**, also called the **Net**, is a worldwide collection of networks that links millions of businesses, government agencies, educational institutions, and individuals. Through the Internet, society has access to global information and instant communications.

Today, more than one billion users around the world connect to the Internet for a variety of reasons, some of which are shown in Figure 2-1. The World Wide Web and e-mail are two of the more widely accessed Internet services. Other services include chat rooms, instant messaging, and Internet telephony.

The Internet has its roots in a networking project started by an agency of the U.S. Department of Defense. The goal was to build a network that (1) allowed scientists at different locations to share information and work together on military and scientific projects and (2) could function even if part of the network were disabled or destroyed by a disaster such as a nuclear attack. That network, called ARPANET, became functional in September 1969, linking scientific and academic researchers across the United States.

The original network consisted of four main computers, one each located at the University of California at Los Angeles, the University of California at Santa Barbara, the Stanford Research Institute, and the University of Utah. Each computer served as a host on the network. A **host** or **server** is any computer that provides services and connections to other computers on a network. By 1984, the network had more than 1,000 individual computers linked as hosts. Today, more than 200 million hosts connect to this network, which became known as the Internet.

FIGURE 2-1a   (Web)

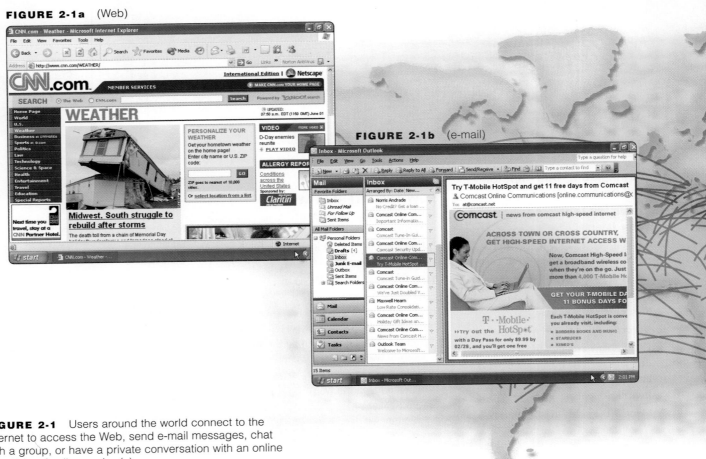

FIGURE 2-1b   (e-mail)

FIGURE 2-1   Users around the world connect to the Internet to access the Web, send e-mail messages, chat with a group, or have a private conversation with an online friend(s) or family member(s).

The Internet consists of many local, regional, national, and international networks. Both public and private organizations own networks on the Internet. These networks, along with telephone companies, cable and satellite companies, and the government, all contribute toward the internal structure of the Internet.

Each organization on the Internet is responsible only for maintaining its own network. No single person, company, institution, or government agency controls or owns the Internet. The **World Wide Web Consortium (W3C)**, however, oversees research and sets standards and guidelines for many areas of the Internet. About 350 organizations from around the world are members of the W3C.

HOW THE INTERNET WORKS

Data sent over the Internet travels via networks and communications media owned and operated by many companies. The following sections present various ways to connect to these networks on the Internet.

Connecting to the Internet

Employees and students often connect to the Internet through a business or school network. Many homes and some small businesses use dial-up access to connect to the Internet. **Dial-up access** takes place when the modem in your computer uses a standard telephone line to connect to the Internet. A dial-up connection, however, is slow-speed technology.

FIGURE 2-1c (chat)

FIGURE 2-1e
(Internet telephony)

FIGURE 2-1d
(instant messaging)

FAQ 2-1

How many people have high-speed Internet access?

According to a recent study, 55 percent of adult Americans access the Internet using high-speed connections at home or at work. About 40 percent of home users have high-speed Internet access. The main reason users switch to high-speed access is they are frustrated with the slow speeds of dial-up access. For more information, visit scsite.com/dcf2e/ch2/faq and then click High-Speed Internet.

Some home and small business users are opting for higher-speed Internet connections through DSL, cable television, radio signals, or satellite. **DSL** (digital subscriber line) is a technology that provides high-speed Internet connections using regular telephone lines. A **cable modem** allows access to high-speed Internet services through the cable television network. **Fixed wireless** high-speed Internet connections use an antenna on your house or business to communicate with a tower location via radio signals. A **satellite modem** communicates with a satellite dish to provide high-speed Internet connections via satellite.

In most cases, DSL, cable television, fixed wireless, and satellite connections are always on, that is, connected to the Internet the entire time the computer is running. With dial-up access, by contrast, you must establish the connection to the Internet.

Mobile users access the Internet using a variety of technologies. Most hotels and airports provide dial-up or high-speed Internet connections. Wireless Internet access technologies enable mobile users to connect easily to the Internet with notebook computers, Tablet PCs, PDAs, smart phones, and smart watches while away from a telephone, cable, or other wired connection.

Access Providers

An **access provider** is a business that provides individuals and companies access to the Internet free or for a fee. The most common fee arrangement for an individual account is a fixed amount, usually about $10 to $25 per month for dial-up access and $40 to $99 for higher-speed access. For this fee, many providers offer unlimited Internet access. Others specify a set number of access hours per month. With the latter arrangement, the provider charges extra for each hour of connection time that exceeds an allotted number of access hours.

Users access the Internet through ISPs, online service providers, and wireless Internet service providers. An **ISP** (**Internet service provider**) is a regional or national access provider. A regional ISP usually provides Internet access to a specific geographic area. A national ISP is a business that provides Internet access in cities and towns nationwide. National ISPs usually offer more services and have a larger technical support staff than regional ISPs. Examples of national ISPs are AT&T Worldnet Service and EarthLink.

In addition to providing Internet access, an **online service provider** (**OSP**) also has many members-only features. These features include special content and services such as news, weather, legal information, financial data, hardware and software guides, games, travel guides, e-mail, photo communities, online calendars, and instant messaging. The fees for using an OSP sometimes are slightly higher than fees for an ISP. The two more popular OSPs are AOL (America Online) and MSN (Microsoft Network).

A **wireless Internet service provider** (**WISP**) is a company that provides wireless Internet access to users with wireless modems or access devices or Internet-enabled mobile computers or devices. Internet-enabled mobile devices include PDAs, smart phones, and smart watches. Examples of wireless Internet service providers include AT&T Wireless, GoAmerica, T-Mobile, and Verizon Wireless.

WEB LINK 2-1

Internet Backbone

For more information, visit scsite.com/dcf2e/ch2/weblink and then click Internet Backbone.

How Data Travels the Internet

Computers connected to the Internet work together to transfer data and information around the world. Several main transmission media carry the heaviest amount of traffic on the Internet. These major carriers of network traffic are known collectively as the **Internet backbone**.

In the United States, the transmission media that make up the Internet backbone exchange data at several different major cities across the country. That is, they transfer data from one network to another until it reaches its final destination (Figure 2-2).

FIGURE 2-2   HOW A HOME USER'S DATA MIGHT TRAVEL THE INTERNET USING A CABLE MODEM CONNECTION

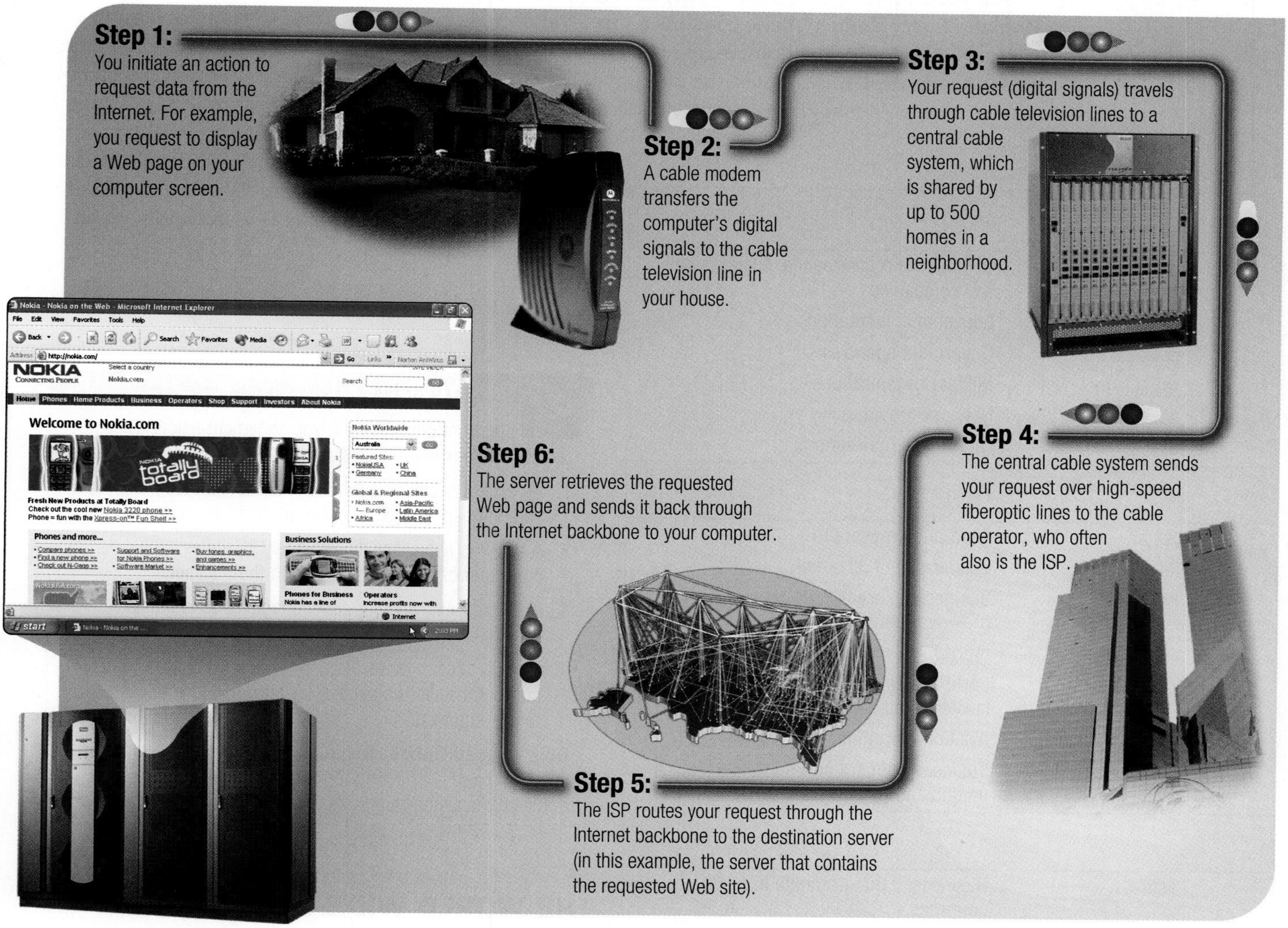

Step 1:
You initiate an action to request data from the Internet. For example, you request to display a Web page on your computer screen.

Step 2:
A cable modem transfers the computer's digital signals to the cable television line in your house.

Step 3:
Your request (digital signals) travels through cable television lines to a central cable system, which is shared by up to 500 homes in a neighborhood.

Step 4:
The central cable system sends your request over high-speed fiberoptic lines to the cable operator, who often also is the ISP.

Step 5:
The ISP routes your request through the Internet backbone to the destination server (in this example, the server that contains the requested Web site).

Step 6:
The server retrieves the requested Web page and sends it back through the Internet backbone to your computer.

Internet Addresses

The Internet relies on an addressing system much like the postal service to send data to a computer at a specific destination. An **IP address**, short for Internet Protocol address, is a number that uniquely identifies each computer or device connected to the Internet. The IP address usually consists of four groups of numbers, each separated by a period. In general, the first portion of each IP address identifies the network and the last portion identifies the specific computer.

These all-numeric IP addresses are difficult to remember and use. Thus, the Internet supports the use of a text name that represents one or more IP addresses. A **domain name** is the text version of an IP address. Figure 2-3 shows an IP address and its associated domain name. As with an IP address, the components of a domain name are separated by periods.

IP address ⟶ 216.239.39.99

Domain name ⟶ www.google.com
top-level domain

FIGURE 2-3   The IP address and domain name for the Google Web site.

In Figure 2-3 on the previous page, the com portion of the domain name is called the top-level domain. Every domain name contains a **top-level domain**, which identifies the type of organization associated with the domain. Figure 2-4 lists current top-level domains. For international Web sites outside the United States, the domain name also includes a country code. In these cases, the domain name ends with the country code, such as au for Australia or fr for France.

TOP-LEVEL DOMAINS

Original Top-Level Domains	Type of Domain
com	Commercial organizations, businesses, and companies
edu	Educational institutions
gov	Goverment agencies
mil	Military organizations
net	Network provider
org	Nonprofit organizations

Newer Top-Level Domains	Type of Domain
museum	Accredited museums
biz	Businesses of all sizes
info	Businesses, organizations, or individuals providing general information
name	Individuals or families
pro	Certified professionals such as doctors, lawyers, and accountants
aero	Aviation community members
coop	Business cooperatives such as credit unions and rural electric co-ops

Proposed Top-Level Domains	Type of Domain
asia	Businesses that originate in Asian countries
cat	Catalan cultural community
jobs	Employment or human resource businesses
mail	Registries to control spam (Internet junk mail)
mobi	Delivery and management of mobile Internet services
post	Postal service
tel	Internet communications
travel	Travel industry
xxx	Adult content

FIGURE 2-4 With the dramatic growth of the Internet during the last few years, seven new top-level domains recently have been adopted and nine additional domains are being evaluated.

When you specify a domain name, a server translates the domain name into its associated IP address so data can be routed to the correct computer. This server is an Internet server that usually is associated with an Internet access provider.

Test your knowledge of pages 50 through 54 in Quiz Yourself 2-1.

THE WORLD WIDE WEB

The **World Wide Web (WWW)**, or **Web**, a widely used service on the Internet, consists of a worldwide collection of electronic documents. Each electronic document on the Web, called a **Web page**, can contain text, graphics, audio (sound), and video. Additionally, Web pages usually have built-in connections to other documents. A **Web site** is a collection of related Web pages and associated items, such as documents and pictures, stored on a Web server. A **Web server** is a computer that delivers requested Web pages to your computer.

Browsing the Web

A **Web browser**, or **browser**, is application software that allows users to access and view Web pages. To browse the Web, you need a computer that is connected to the Internet and that has a Web browser. The more widely used Web browsers for personal computers are Internet Explorer, Netscape, Mozilla, Opera, and Safari.

With an Internet connection established, you start a Web browser. The browser retrieves and displays a starting Web page, sometimes called the browser's home page. Figure 2-5 shows how a Web browser displays a home page.

The more common usage of the term, **home page**, refers to the first page that a Web site displays. Similar to a book cover or a table of contents for a Web site, the home page provides information about the Web site's purpose and content. Often it provides connections to other documents, Web pages, or Web sites, which can be downloaded to a computer or mobile device. **Downloading** is the process of a computer receiving information, such as a Web page, from a server on the Internet. Depending on the speed of your Internet connection and the amount of graphics involved, a Web page download can take from a few seconds to several minutes.

FIGURE 2-5 HOW A WEB BROWSER DISPLAYS A HOME PAGE

Step 1:
Click the Web browser program name to start the Web browser software.

Step 2:
The Web browser looks up its home page setting, in this case, msn.com.

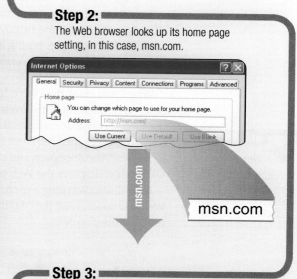

Step 3:
The Web browser communicates with a server maintained by your Internet access provider. The server translates the domain name of the home page to an IP address and then sends the IP address to your computer.

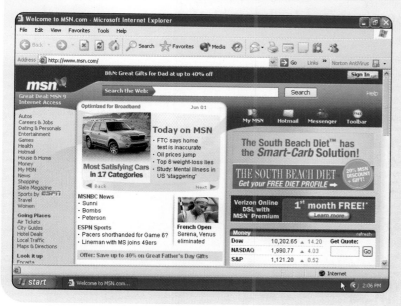

Step 4:
The Web browser uses the IP address to contact the Web server associated with the home page and then requests the home page from the server. The Web server sends the home page to the Web browser, which formats the page for display on your screen.

Web Addresses

A Web page has a unique address, which is called a **URL** (Uniform Resource Locator) or **Web address**. For example, the home page for the San Diego Zoo Web site has a Web address of http://www.sandiegozoo.org. A Web browser retrieves a Web page, such as the zoo's home page, using its Web address.

If you know the Web address of a Web page, you can type it in the Address box at the top of the browser window. If you type the Web address http://www.sandiegozoo.org/wap/condor/ home.html in the Address box and then press the ENTER key, the browser downloads and displays a Web page about condors at the San Diego Zoo (Figure 2-6).

As shown in Figure 2-6, a Web address consists of a protocol, domain name, and sometimes the path to a specific Web page or location on a Web page. Many Web page addresses begin with http://. The **http**, which stands for Hypertext Transfer Protocol, is a set of rules that defines how pages transfer on the Internet.

To help minimize errors, most current browsers and Web sites do not require the http:// and www portions of the Web address. For example, typing sandiegozoo.org/wap/condor/ home.html, instead of the entire address, still accesses the Web site.

When you enter the Web address, sandiegozoo.org/wap/ condor/home.html in the Web browser, it sends a request to the Web server that contains the www.sandiegozoo.org Web site. The server then retrieves the Web page named home.html in the wap/condor/ path and delivers it to your browser, which then displays the Web page on the screen.

For information about useful Web sites and their associated Web addresses, read the Making Use of the Web feature that follows this chapter.

FAQ 2-2

How many Web pages does the average user visit in a month?

More than one thousand. This and other interesting average Web usage statistics are in the table below. For more information, visit scsite.com/dcf2e/ch2/faq and then click Web User Statistics.

Web pages visited per month	1,036 pages
Web pages visited per Internet session	34 pages
Time spent surfing per Internet session	51 minutes
Time spent viewing a single Web page	46 seconds
Source: The ClickZ Network	

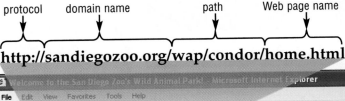

protocol   domain name   path   Web page name

http://sandiegozoo.org/wap/condor/home.html

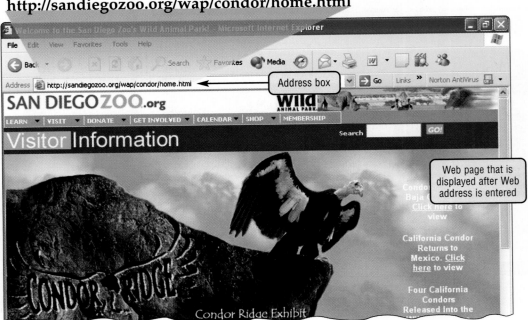

FIGURE 2-6 After entering the Web address http://www.sandiegozoo.org/ wap/condor/home.html in the Address box, this Web page at the San Diego Zoo Web site is displayed. Notice the www portion of the domain name does not appear in the Address box after the Web page downloads.

Navigating Web Pages

Most Web pages contain links. A **link**, short for **hyperlink**, is a built-in connection to another related Web page or part of a Web page. Links allow you to obtain information in a nonlinear way. That is, instead of accessing topics in a specified order, you move directly to a topic of interest.

Branching from one related topic to another in a nonlinear fashion is what makes links so powerful. Some people use the phrase, **surfing the Web**, to refer to the activity of using links to explore the Web.

On the Web, a link can be text or an image. Text links may be underlined and/or displayed in a color different from other text on the Web page. Pointing to, or positioning the pointer on, a link on the screen typically changes the shape of the pointer to a small hand with a pointing index finger. The Web page shown in Figure 2-7 contains a variety of link types, with the pointer on one of the links.

Each link on a Web page corresponds to another Web address. To activate a link, you **click** it, that is, point to the link and then press the left mouse button. Clicking a link causes the Web page associated with the link to be displayed on the screen. The linked object might be on the same Web page, a different Web page at the same Web site, or a separate Web page at a different Web site in another city or country. Read Looking Ahead 2-1 for a look at the next generation of browsing.

FIGURE 2-7   This Web page contains various types of links: text that is underlined, text in a different color, and images.

Searching for Information on the Web

The Web is a global resource of information. One primary use of the Web is to search for specific information. The first step in successful searching is to identify the main idea or concept in the topic about which you are seeking information. Determine any synonyms, alternate spellings, or variant word forms for the topic. Then, use a search tool to locate the information.

The two most commonly used search tools are subject directories and search engines. A **subject directory** classifies Web pages in an organized set of categories, such as sports or shopping, and related subcategories. A **search engine** is a program that finds Web sites and Web pages.

Some Web sites offer the functionality of both a subject directory and a search engine. Yahoo! and Google, for example, are widely used search engines that also provide a subject directory. To use Yahoo! or Google, you enter the Web address (yahoo.com or google.com) in the Address box in a browser window. The table in Figure 2-8 lists the Web addresses of several popular general-purpose subject directories and search engines.

WIDELY USED SEARCH TOOLS

Search Tool	Web Address	Subject Directory	Search Engine
A9.com	a9.com		X
AlltheWeb	alltheweb.com		X
Alta Vista	altavista.com	X	X
AOL Search	search.aol.com		X
AOMI	aomi.com		X
Ask Jeeves	askjeeves.com	X	X
Excite	excite.com	X	X
Gigablast	gigablast.com		X
Google	google.com	X	X
HotBot	hotbot.com		X
LookSmart	looksmart.com	X	X
Lycos	lycos.com	X	X
MSN Search	search.msn.com	X	X
Netscape Search	search.netscape.com	X	X
Open Directory Project	dmoz.org	X	X
Overture	overture.com		X
Teoma	teoma.com		X
WebCrawler	webcrawler.com		X
Yahoo!	yahoo.com	X	X

FIGURE 2-8 Many subject directories and search engines allow searching about any topic on the Web.

SUBJECT DIRECTORIES A subject directory provides categorized lists of links arranged by subject. Using this search tool, you can locate a particular topic by clicking links through different levels, moving from the general to the specific. Figure 2-9 shows how to use Yahoo!'s subject directory to search for information about Bob Hope.

FIGURE 2-9 HOW TO USE A SUBJECT DIRECTORY

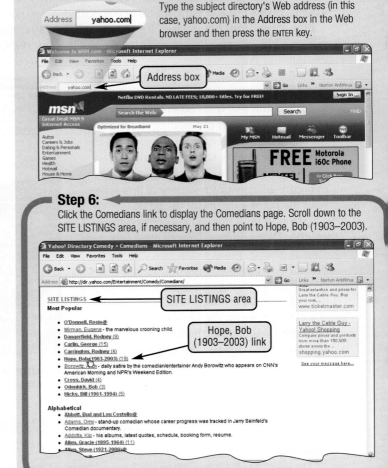

Step 1:
Type the subject directory's Web address (in this case, yahoo.com) in the Address box in the Web browser and then press the ENTER key.

Step 6:
Click the Comedians link to display the Comedians page. Scroll down to the SITE LISTINGS area, if necessary, and then point to Hope, Bob (1903–2003).

Step 7:
Click the Hope, Bob (1903–2003) link to display the Hope, Bob (1903–2003) page. Scroll down to the SITE LISTINGS area, if necessary, and then point to the Bob Hope and American Variety link.

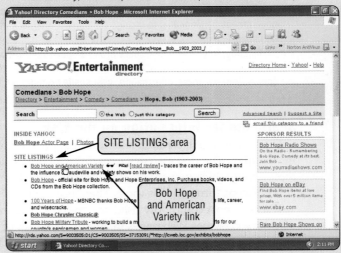

Step 2:

When the Yahoo! home page is displayed, point to the scroll box on the right side of the screen.

Step 3:

Drag the scroll box downward to display the Web Site Directory area of the Web page. Point to the Entertainment link.

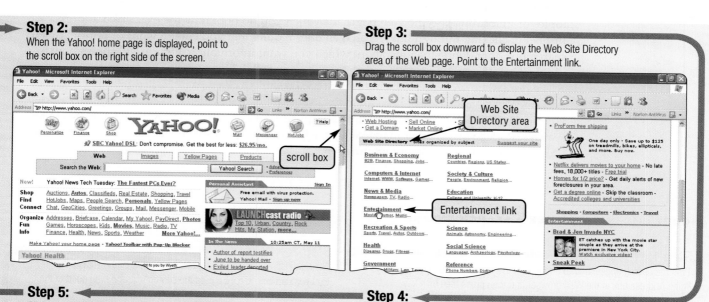

Step 5:

Click the Comedy link to display the Comedy page. In the CATEGORIES area, point to the Comedians link.

Step 4:

Click the Entertainment link to display the Entertainment page. Scroll down to the CATEGORIES area, if necessary, and then point to the Comedy link.

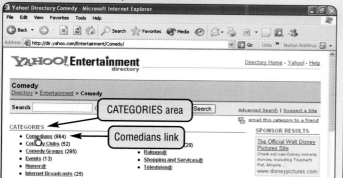

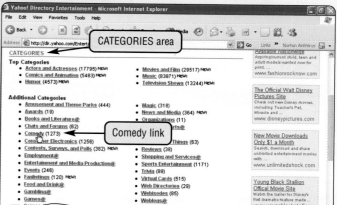

Step 8:

Click the Bob Hope and American Variety link to display the Bob Hope and American Variety Web page, which contains a variety of links to specific information about Bob Hope. After you click one of these links, click the Home button to display this home page.

SEARCH ENGINES A search engine is particularly helpful in locating Web pages about certain topics or in locating specific Web pages for which you do not know the exact Web address. Instead of clicking through links, search engines require that you enter a word or phrase, called **search text**, that define the item about which you want information. Figure 2-10 shows how to use the Google search engine to search for the phrase, Bob Hope television career.

The results shown in Step 3 include about 535,000 links to Web pages, called hits, that reference Bob Hope's television career. Each hit in the list has a link that, when clicked, displays an associated Web site or Web page. Most search engines sequence the hits based on how close the words in the search text are to one another in the Web page titles and their descriptions. Thus, the first few links probably contain more relevant information.

FIGURE 2-10 HOW TO USE A SEARCH ENGINE

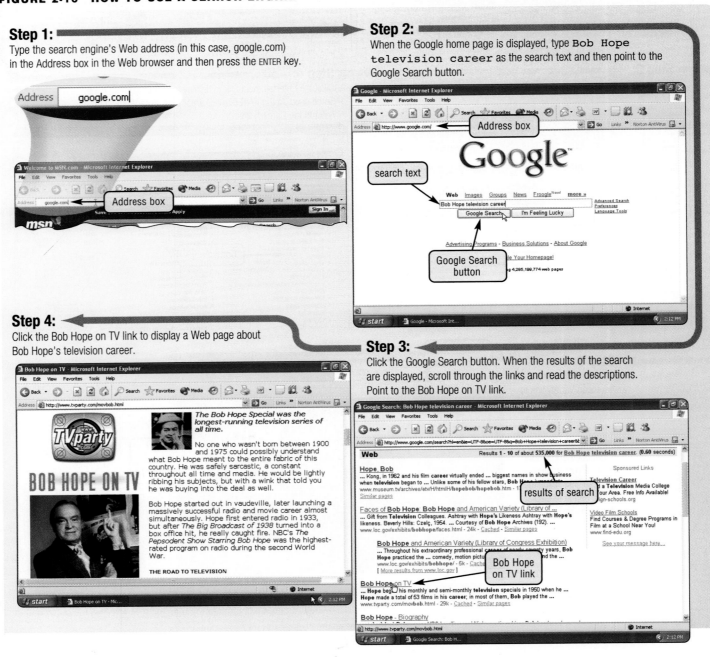

Step 1:
Type the search engine's Web address (in this case, google.com) in the Address box in the Web browser and then press the ENTER key.

Step 2:
When the Google home page is displayed, type Bob Hope television career as the search text and then point to the Google Search button.

Step 4:
Click the Bob Hope on TV link to display a Web page about Bob Hope's television career.

Step 3:
Click the Google Search button. When the results of the search are displayed, scroll through the links and read the descriptions. Point to the Bob Hope on TV link.

If you enter a phrase with spaces between the words in the search text, most search engines return links to pages that include all of the words. Techniques you can use to improve your Web searches include the following:

- Use specific nouns and put the most important terms first in the search text.
- Use the asterisk (*) to substitute characters in words. For example, retriev* returns retrieves, retrieval, retriever, and any other variation.
- Use quotation marks to create phrases so the search engine finds the exact sequence of words.
- List all possible spellings, for example, email, e-mail.
- Before using a search engine, read its Help information.
- If the search is unsuccessful with one search engine, try another.

In addition to searching for Web pages, many search engines allow you to search for images, news articles, and local businesses. Read Looking Ahead 2-2 for a look at the next generation of searching techniques.

LOOKING AHEAD 2-2

3-D Search Engines Get the Picture

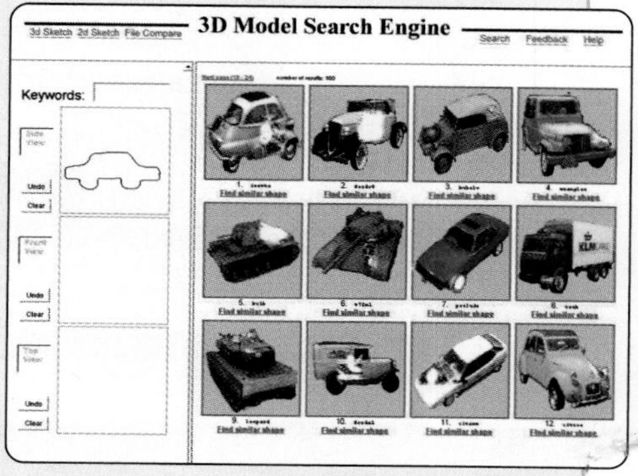

Conventional search engines, such as Google, use words to find information. But what happens when a computer user needs to locate a wing nut or camshaft based on a particular shape, not part number or model? The 3-D search engines being developed would help people who work with patterns and contours search for images. These search engines presently are being created to assist designers and engineers at large industrial companies with millions of inventoried parts, but university researchers predict image searches will be common on the Internet within 15 years.

Other search engines of the future will customize the results based on the researcher's background, include a voice interface, and use a thesaurus to keep a query in context. For more information, visit scsite.com/dcf2e/ch2/looking and then click Search Engines.

Types of Web Sites

Nine types of Web sites are portal, news, informational, business/marketing, educational, entertainment, advocacy, blog, and personal. Many Web sites fall into more than one of these categories. The following sections discuss each of these types of Web sites.

PORTAL   A **portal** is a Web site that offers a variety of Internet services from a single, convenient location (Figure 2-11a). Most portals offer the following free services: search engine and/or subject directory; news; sports and weather; free Web publishing services; reference tools such as yellow pages, stock quotes, and maps; shopping malls and auctions; and e-mail and other forms of online communications.

When you connect to the Internet, the first Web page that is displayed often is a portal. Popular portals include AltaVista, AOL, Excite, GO.com, HotBot, LookSmart, Lycos, MSN, NBCi, Netscape, and Yahoo!.

NEWS   A news Web site contains newsworthy material including stories and articles relating to current events, life, money, sports, and the weather (Figure 2-11b). Newspapers and television and radio stations are some of the media that maintain news Web sites.

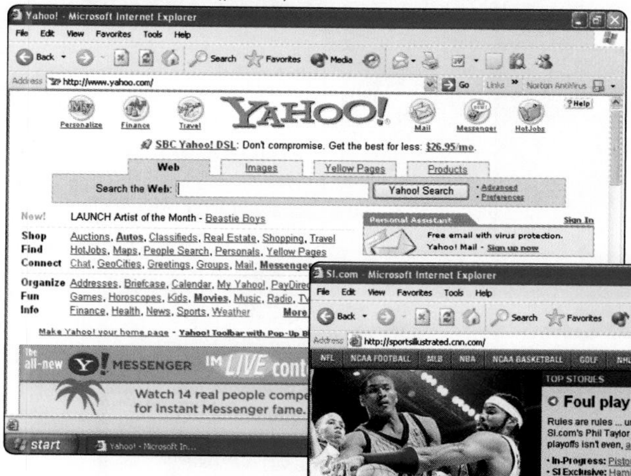

FIGURE 2-11a   (portal)

FIGURE 2-11b   (news)

FIGURE 2-11   Types of Web sites. *(continued on next page)*

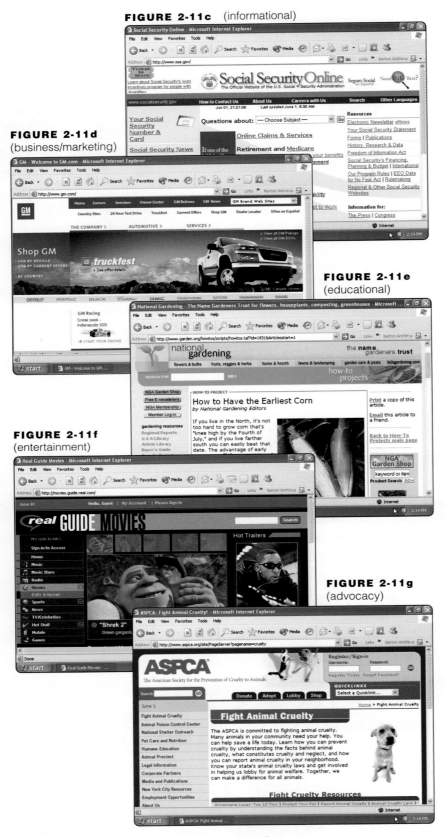

FIGURE 2-11c (informational)

FIGURE 2-11d (business/marketing)

FIGURE 2-11e (educational)

FIGURE 2-11f (entertainment)

FIGURE 2-11g (advocacy)

FIGURE 2-11 Types of Web sites. *(continued)*

INFORMATIONAL An informational Web site contains factual information (Figure 2-11c). Many United States government agencies have informational Web sites providing information such as census data, tax codes, and the congressional budget. Other organizations provide information such as public transportation schedules and published research findings.

BUSINESS/MARKETING A business/marketing Web site contains content that promotes or sells products or services (Figure 2-11d). Nearly every business has a business/marketing Web site. Many companies also allow you to purchase their products or services online.

EDUCATIONAL An educational Web site offers exciting, challenging avenues for formal and informal teaching and learning (Figure 2-11e). For a more structured learning experience, companies provide online training to employees; and colleges offer online classes and degrees. Instructors often use the Web to enhance classroom teaching by publishing course materials, grades, and other pertinent class information.

ENTERTAINMENT An entertainment Web site offers an interactive and engaging environment (Figure 2-11f). Popular entertainment Web sites offer music, videos, sports, games, ongoing Web episodes, sweepstakes, chats, and more.

ADVOCACY An advocacy Web site contains content that describes a cause, opinion, or idea (Figure 2-11g). The purpose of an advocacy Web site is to convince the reader of the validity of the cause, opinion, or idea. These Web sites usually present views of a particular group or association.

BLOG A **blog**, short for Web log, is a Web site that uses a regularly updated journal format to reflect the interests, opinions, and personalities of the author and sometimes site visitors (Figure 2-11h). Blogs have an informal style that consists of a single individual's ideas (similar to a diary) or a collection of ideas and thoughts among visitors. Read At Issue 2-1 for a related discussion.

PERSONAL A private individual or family not usually associated with any organization may maintain a personal Web site (Figure 2-11i). People publish personal Web pages for a variety of reasons. Some are job hunting. Others simply want to share life experiences with the world.

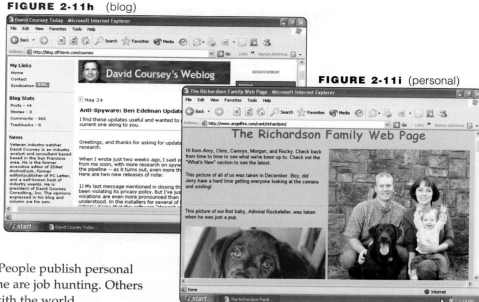

FIGURE 2-11h (blog)

FIGURE 2-11i (personal)

FIGURE 2-11 Types of Web sites. *(continued)*

AT ISSUE 2-1

Mobile Web Logs with Photos — an Invasion of One's Privacy?

Camera-equipped smart phones are popular — almost 50 million were sold last year. A growing number of people use these phones to create online photo albums, called mobile Web blogs or **moblogs**, to share their visions of the world with thousands of people. Most moblogs are personal and, like family photo albums, interesting to a limited audience. To capture more exciting pictures, some moblog photographers use their smart phone cameras in private places. As a result, smart phone cameras have been banned from health club locker rooms, movie screenings, and corporate offices. Congress even is considering barring covert cameras from places where people should be able to expect some privacy. But, even in public, moblog paparazzi photograph unaware people at private, or embarrassing, times. The subjects of these moblog pictures often object to living in a fishbowl, where even personal moments can be captured and posted on the Web. Recognizing this, some Web sites that monitor moblogs refuse to show certain photos or encourage photographers to obtain permission from photo subjects. Yet, photographers insist they have the right to post any pictures they take. What, if anything, can be done to protect personal privacy? Should laws be enacted to regulate smart phone photographers, moblogs, or both? Why? Must we accept that, outside of our homes, private moments no longer exist?

Evaluating a Web Site

Do not assume that information presented on the Web is correct or accurate. Any person, company, or organization can publish a Web page on the Internet. No one oversees the content of these Web pages. Figure 2-12 lists guidelines for assessing the value of a Web site or Web page before relying on its content.

GUIDELINES FOR EVALUATING THE VALUE OF A WEB SITE

Evaluation Criteria	Reliable Web Sites
Affiliation	A reputable institution should support the Web site without bias in the information.
Audience	The Web site should be written at an appropriate level.
Authority	The Web site should list the author and the appropriate credentials.
Content	The Web site should be well organized and the links should work.
Currency	The information on the Web page should be current.
Design	The pages at the Web site should download quickly and be visually pleasing and easy to navigate.
Objectivity	The Web site should contain little advertising and be free of preconceptions.

FIGURE 2-12 Criteria for evaluating a Web site's content.

Multimedia on the Web

Most Web pages include more than just formatted text and links. The more exciting Web pages use multimedia. **Multimedia** refers to any application that combines text with graphics, animation, audio, video, and/or virtual reality. The sections that follow discuss how the Web uses these multimedia elements.

GRAPHICS   A **graphic**, or graphical image, is a digital representation of nontext information such as a drawing, chart, or photograph. Many Web pages use colorful graphical designs and images to convey messages (Figure 2-13).

FIGURE 2-13   This Web page uses colorful graphical designs and images to convey its messages.

Of the graphics formats that exist on the Web, the two more common are JPEG and GIF formats. JPEG (pronounced JAY-peg) is a format that compresses graphics to reduce their file size, which means the file takes up less storage space. The goal with JPEG graphics is to reach a balance between image quality and file size. GIF (pronounced jiff) graphics also use compression techniques to reduce file sizes. The GIF format works best for images that have only a few distinct colors.

Some Web sites use thumbnails on their pages because graphics can be time-consuming to display. A **thumbnail** is a small version of a larger graphic. You usually can click a thumbnail to display a larger image.

ANIMATION   Many Web pages use **animation**, which is the appearance of motion created by displaying a series of still images in sequence. Animation can make Web pages more visually interesting or draw attention to important information or links.

AUDIO   On the Web, you can listen to audio clips and live audio. **Audio** includes music, speech, or any other sound. Simple applications on the Web consist of individual audio files available for downloading to a computer. Once downloaded, you can play (listen to) the contents of these files. Audio files are compressed to reduce their file sizes. For example, the **MP3** format reduces an audio file to about one-tenth its original size, while preserving much of the original quality of the sound.

Some music publishers have Web sites that allow users to download sample tracks free to persuade them to buy the entire CD. Other Web sites allow a user to purchase and download an entire CD of music tracks to the hard disk (Figure 2-14). Keep in mind that it is legal to download copyrighted music only if the song's copyright holder has granted permission for users to download and play the song.

To listen to an audio file on your computer, you need special software called a **player**. Most current operating systems contain a player. Popular players include iTunes, RealOne Player, and Windows Media Player.

Some applications on the Web use streaming audio. **Streaming** is the process of transferring data in a continuous and even flow. Streaming allows users to access and use a file while it is transmitting. For example, streaming audio enables you to listen to music as it downloads to your computer.

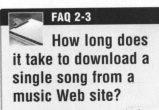

FAQ 2-3

How long does it take to download a single song from a music Web site?

Depending on the speed of your Internet connection and the size of the file, a single song can take from one to twenty minutes to download. For more information, visit scsite.com/dcf2e/ch2/faq and then click Downloading Audio Files.

FIGURE 2-14 HOW TO PURCHASE AND DOWNLOAD MUSIC

Step 1:
Display the music Web site on the screen. Search for, select, and pay for the music you want to purchase from the music Web site.

Step 2:
Download the music from the Web site's server to your computer's hard disk.

Step 3:
Listen to the music from your computer's hard disk.

VIDEO   **Video** consists of full-motion images that are played back at various speeds. Most video also has accompanying audio. Instead of turning on the television, you can use the Internet to watch live and prerecorded coverage of your favorite programs or enjoy a live performance of your favorite vocalist.

Video files often are compressed because they are quite large in size. These clips also are quite short in length, usually less than 10 minutes, because they can take a long time to download. The Moving Pictures Experts Group (MPEG) defines a popular video compression standard, a widely used one called **MPEG-4**. As with streaming audio, streaming video allows you to view longer or live video images as they download to your computer.

VIRTUAL REALITY   **Virtual reality** (**VR**) is the use of computers to simulate a real or imagined environment that appears as a three-dimensional (3-D) space. On the Web, VR involves the display of 3-D images that users explore and manipulate interactively. A VR site, for example, might show a room with furniture. Users walk through such a VR room by moving an input device forward, backward, or to the side.

PLUG-INS Most Web browsers have the capability of displaying basic multimedia elements on a Web page. Sometimes, a browser might need an additional program, called a plug-in. A **plug-in** is a program that extends the capability of a browser. You can download many plug-ins at no cost from various Web sites (Figure 2-15).

POPULAR PLUG-IN APPLICATIONS

Plug-In Application	Description	Web Address
Acrobat Reader	View, navigate, and print Portable Document Format (PDF) files — documents formatted to look just as they look in print	adobe.com
Flash Player	View dazzling graphics and animation, hear outstanding sound and music, display Web pages across an entire screen	macromedia.com
QuickTime	View animation, music, audio, video, and VR panoramas and objects directly in a Web page	apple.com
RealOne Player	Listen to live and on-demand near-CD-quality audio and newscast-quality video; stream audio and video content for faster viewing; play MP3 files; create music CDs	real.com
Shockwave Player	Experience dynamic interactive multimedia, 3-D graphics, and streaming audio	macromedia.com
Windows Media Player	Listen to live and on-demand audio; play or edit WMA and MP3 files; burn CDs, watch DVD movies	microsoft.com

WEB LINK 2-3

Plug-Ins

For more information, visit scsite.com/dcf2e/ch2/weblink and then click Plug-Ins.

FIGURE 2-15   Most plug-ins can be downloaded free from the Web.

Web Publishing

Before the World Wide Web, the means to share opinions and ideas with others easily and inexpensively was limited to the media, classroom, work, or social environments. Today, businesses and individuals convey information to millions of people by creating their own Web pages.

Web publishing is the development and maintenance of Web pages. To develop a Web page, you do not have to be a computer programmer. For the small business or home user, Web publishing is fairly easy as long as you have the proper tools.

The five major steps to Web publishing are as follows:

1. Plan a Web site
2. Analyze and design a Web site
3. Create a Web site
4. Deploy a Web site
5. Maintain a Web site

Figure 2-16 illustrates these steps with respect to a personal Web site.

FIGURE 2-16   HOW TO PUBLISH YOUR RESUME ON THE WEB

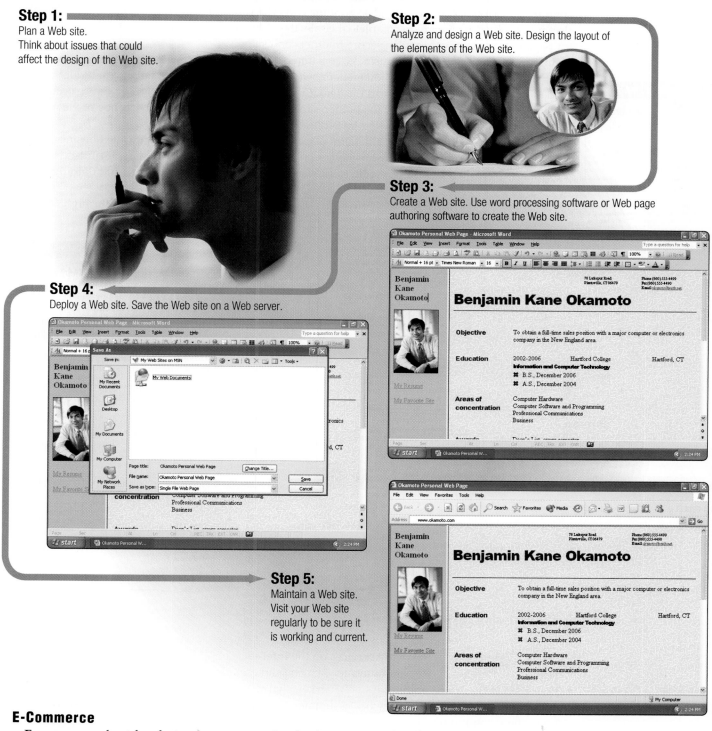

Step 1:
Plan a Web site.
Think about issues that could
affect the design of the Web site.

Step 2:
Analyze and design a Web site. Design the layout of
the elements of the Web site.

Step 3:
Create a Web site. Use word processing software or Web page
authoring software to create the Web site.

Step 4:
Deploy a Web site. Save the Web site on a Web server.

Step 5:
Maintain a Web site.
Visit your Web site
regularly to be sure it
is working and current.

E-Commerce

E-commerce, short for electronic commerce, is a business transaction that occurs over an electronic network such as the Internet. Anyone with access to a computer, an Internet connection, and a means to pay for purchased goods or services can participate in e-commerce.

Three types of e-commerce are business-to-consumer, consumer-to-consumer, and business-to-business. Business-to-consumer (B2C) e-commerce consists of the sale of goods and services to the general public. For example, Dell has a B2C Web site. Instead of visiting a computer store to purchase a computer, customers can order one directly from the Dell Web site.

A customer (consumer) visits an online business through an **electronic storefront**, which contains product descriptions, graphics, and a shopping cart. The **shopping cart** allows the customer to collect purchases. When ready to complete the sale, the customer enters personal data and the method of payment, preferably through a secure Internet connection.

Instead of purchasing from a business, consumers can purchase from each other. For example, with an **online auction**, users bid on an item being sold by someone else. The highest bidder at the end of the bidding period purchases the item. Consumer-to-consumer (C2C) e-commerce occurs when one consumer sells directly to another, such as in an online auction. eBay is one of the more popular online auction Web sites (Figure 2-17).

Most e-commerce, though, actually takes place between businesses, which is called business-to-business (B2B) e-commerce. Many businesses provide goods and services to other businesses, such as online advertising, recruiting, credit, sales, market research, technical support, and training.

WEB LINK 2-4

E-Commerce

For more information, visit scsite.com/dcf2e/ch2/weblink and then click E-Commerce.

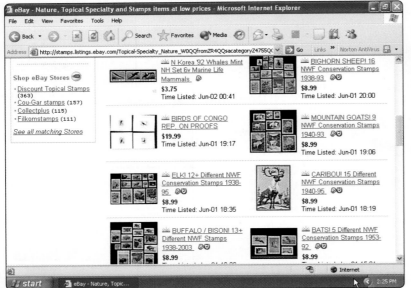

FIGURE 2-17   E-commerce activities include shopping for goods at an online auction. Shown here is an eBay auction for specialty stamps.

Test your knowledge of pages 54 through 68 in Quiz Yourself 2-2.

QUIZ YOURSELF 2-2

Instructions: Find the true statement below. Then, rewrite the remaining false statements so they are true.

1. A blog is a Web site that uses a regularly updated journal format to reflect the interests, opinions, and personalities of the author and sometimes site visitors.

2. A Web browser classifies Web pages in an organized set of categories and related subcategories.

3. Business-to-consumer e-commerce occurs when one consumer sells directly to another, such as in an online auction.

4. The more widely used search engines for personal computers are Internet Explorer, Netscape, Mozilla, Opera, and Safari.

5. To develop a Web page, you have to be a computer programmer.

Quiz Yourself Online: To further check your knowledge of Web browsers, searching, types of Web sites, Web publishing, and e-commerce, visit scsite.com/dcf2e/ch2/quiz and then click Objectives 2 – 5.

OTHER INTERNET SERVICES

The Web is only one of the many services on the Internet. The Web and other Internet services have changed the way we communicate. We can send e-mail messages to the president, have a discussion with experts about the stock market, chat with someone in another country about genealogy, and talk about homework assignments with classmates via instant messages. Many times, these communications take place completely in writing — without the parties ever meeting each other.

At home, work, and school, people use computers and Internet-enabled mobile devices so they always have instant access to e-mail, FTP (File Transfer Protocol), newsgroups and message boards, mailing lists, chat rooms, instant messaging, and Internet telephony. The following pages discuss each of these Internet services.

E-Mail

E-mail (short for electronic mail) is the transmission of messages and files via a computer network. Today, e-mail is a primary communications method for both personal and business use.

You use an **e-mail program** to create, send, receive, forward, store, print, and delete e-mail messages. Outlook and Outlook Express are two popular e-mail programs. The steps in Figure 2-18 illustrate how to send an e-mail message using Outlook. The message can be simple text or can include an attachment such as a word processing document, a graphic, an audio clip, or a video clip.

FIGURE 2-18   HOW TO SEND AN E-MAIL MESSAGE

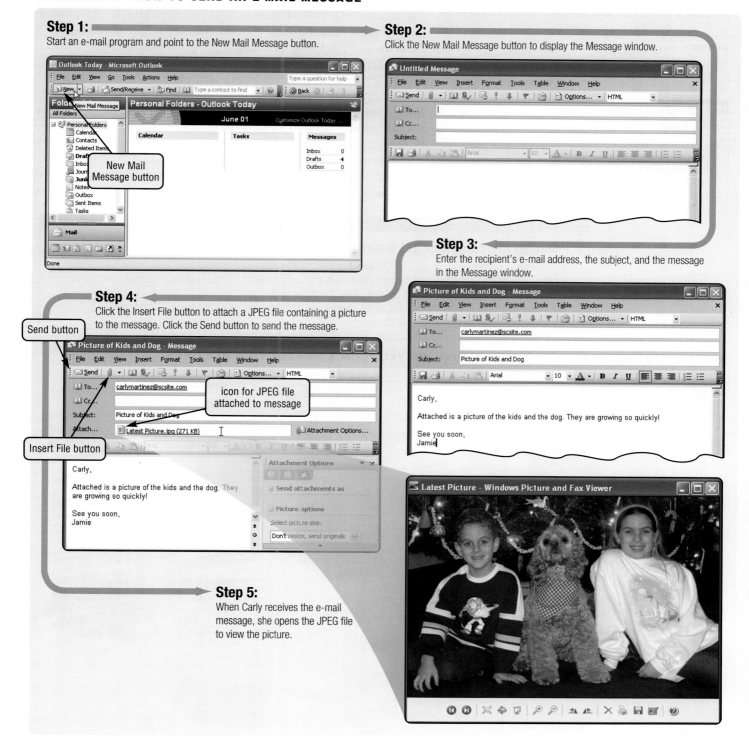

Step 1:
Start an e-mail program and point to the New Mail Message button.

Step 2:
Click the New Mail Message button to display the Message window.

Step 3:
Enter the recipient's e-mail address, the subject, and the message in the Message window.

Step 4:
Click the Insert File button to attach a JPEG file containing a picture to the message. Click the Send button to send the message.

Step 5:
When Carly receives the e-mail message, she opens the JPEG file to view the picture.

Internet access providers typically supply an e-mail program as a standard part of their Internet access services. To use these Web-based e-mail programs, you connect to the Web site and set up an e-mail account, which typically includes an e-mail address and a password.

Just as you address a letter when using the postal system, you must address an e-mail message with the e-mail address of your intended recipient. Likewise, when someone sends you a message, they must have your e-mail address. An **e-mail address** is a combination of a user name and a domain name that identifies a user so he or she can receive Internet e-mail (Figure 2-19). A **user name** is a unique combination of characters, such as letters of the alphabet and/or numbers, that identifies a specific user.

In an Internet e-mail address, an @ (pronounced at) symbol separates the user name from the domain name. Your service provider supplies the domain name. Using the example in Figure 2-19, a possible e-mail address for Carly Martinez would be carlymartinez@scsite.com, which

carlymartinez@scsite.com

FIGURE 2-19   An e-mail address is a combination of a user name and a domain name.

would be read as follows: Carly Martinez at s c site dot com. Most e-mail programs allow you to create an **address book**, which contains a list of names and e-mail addresses.

When you send an e-mail message, an outgoing mail server that is operated by your Internet access provider determines how to route the message through the Internet and then sends the message. As you receive e-mail messages, an incoming mail server — also operated by your Internet access provider — holds the messages in your mailbox until you use your e-mail program to retrieve them. Most e-mail programs have a mail notification alert that informs you via a message or sound when you receive new mail. Figure 2-20 illustrates how an e-mail message may travel from a sender to a receiver.

WEB LINK 2-5

E-Mail

For more information, visit scsite.com/dcf2e/ch2/weblink and then click E-Mail.

FAQ 2-4

Can my computer get a virus through e-mail?

Yes. A virus is a computer program that can damage files and the operating system. One way that virus authors attempt to spread a virus is by sending virus-infected e-mail attachments. If you receive an e-mail attachment, you should use an antivirus program to verify that it is virus free.

For more information, read the section about viruses and antivirus programs in Chapter 7, and visit scsite.com/dcf2e/ch2/faq and then click Viruses.

FIGURE 2-20   HOW AN E-MAIL MESSAGE MAY TRAVEL FROM A SENDER TO A RECEIVER

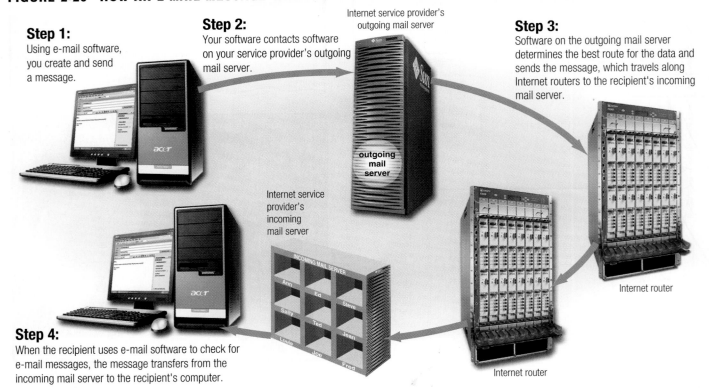

Step 1:
Using e-mail software, you create and send a message.

Step 2:
Your software contacts software on your service provider's outgoing mail server.

Internet service provider's outgoing mail server

Step 3:
Software on the outgoing mail server determines the best route for the data and sends the message, which travels along Internet routers to the recipient's incoming mail server.

outgoing mail server

Internet service provider's incoming mail server

INCOMING MAIL SERVER

Ann   Ed   Steve
Sally   Ted   Jean
Louie   Joe   Fred

Internet router

Internet router

Step 4:
When the recipient uses e-mail software to check for e-mail messages, the message transfers from the incoming mail server to the recipient's computer.

FTP

FTP (File Transfer Protocol) is an Internet standard that permits the process of file uploading and downloading (transferring) with other computers on the Internet. Uploading is the opposite of downloading; that is, **uploading** is the process of transferring documents, graphics, and other objects from your computer to a server on the Internet.

Many operating systems include FTP capabilities. An FTP site is a collection of files including text, graphics, audio clips, video clips, and program files that reside on an FTP server. Many FTP sites have anonymous FTP, whereby anyone can transfer some, if not all, available files. Some FTP sites restrict file transfers to those who have authorized accounts (user names and passwords) on the FTP server.

Newsgroups and Message Boards

A **newsgroup** is an online area in which users have written discussions about a particular subject (Figure 2-21). To participate in a discussion, a user sends a message to the newsgroup, and other users in the newsgroup read and reply to the message. Some major topic areas include news, recreation, society, business, science, and computers.

Some newsgroups require you to enter a user name and password to participate in the discussion. Only authorized members can use this type of newsgroup. For example, a newsgroup for students taking a college course may require a user name and password to access the newsgroup. This ensures that only students in the course participate in the discussion. To participate in a newsgroup, typically you use a program called a newsreader.

A popular Web-based type of discussion group that does not require a newsreader is a **message board**. Many Web sites use message boards instead of newsgroups because they are easier to use.

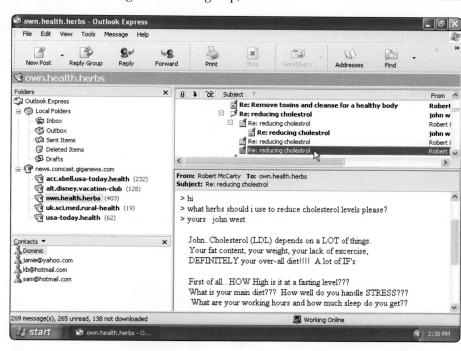

FIGURE 2-21   Users in a newsgroup read and reply to other users' messages.

Mailing Lists

A **mailing list** is a group of e-mail names and addresses given a single name. When a message is sent to a mailing list, every person on the list receives a copy of the message in his or her mailbox. To add your e-mail name and address to a mailing list, you **subscribe** to it. To remove your name, you **unsubscribe** from the mailing list.

Thousands of mailing lists exist about a variety of topics in areas of entertainment, business, computers, society, culture, health, recreation, and education. To locate a mailing list dealing with a particular topic, you can search for the search text, mailing list, in a search engine.

Chat Rooms

A **chat** is a real-time typed conversation that takes place on a computer. **Real time** means that you and the people with whom you are conversing are online at the same time. A **chat room** is a location on an Internet server that permits users to chat with each other. Anyone in the chat room can participate in the conversation, which usually is specific to a particular topic.

As you type on your keyboard, a line of characters and symbols is displayed on the computer screen. Others connected to the same chat room server also see what you type (Figure 2-22). Some chat rooms support voice chats and video chats, in which people hear or see each other as they chat.

To start a chat session, you connect to a chat server through a program called a chat client. Today's browsers usually include a chat client. If yours does not, you can download a chat client from the Web. Once you have installed a chat client, you can create or join a conversation on the chat server to which you are connected.

FIGURE 2-22   As you type, the words and symbols you enter are displayed on the computer screens of other people in the same chat room.

Instant Messaging

Instant messaging (IM) is a real-time Internet communications service that notifies you when one or more people are online and then allows you to exchange messages or files or join a private chat room with them (Figure 2-23). Some IM services support voice and video conversations. For IM to work, both parties must be online at the same time. Also, the receiver of a message must be willing to accept messages.

FIGURE 2-23   AN EXAMPLE OF INSTANT MESSAGING

Step 1:
Log in to the IM server.

Step 2:
The server determines if any of your established friends, family, or coworkers, called buddies, are online.

Step 3:
You send instant messages, voice, and/or video communications to an online buddy.

IM server

Step 4:
Your instant message, voice, and/or video travels through a messaging server and then to the online buddy's computer.

messaging server

Step 5:
Your online buddy replies.

To use IM, you may have to install instant messenger software on the computer or device, such as a smart phone, you plan to use. Some operating systems, such as Windows XP, include an instant messenger. No standards currently exist for IM. To ensure successful communications, all individuals on the notification list need to use the same or a compatible instant messenger.

WEB LINK 2-9

Instant Messaging

For more information, visit scsite.com/dcf2e/ch2/weblink and then click Instant Messaging.

Internet Telephony

Internet telephony, also called **Voice over IP** (Internet Protocol), enables users to speak to other users over the Internet (instead of the public switched telephone network) using their desktop computer, mobile computer, or mobile device.

To place an Internet telephone call, you need a high-speed Internet connection (e.g., via cable or DSL modem); Internet telephone service; a microphone or telephone, depending on the Internet telephone service; and Internet telephone software or a telephone adapter, depending on the Internet telephone service (Figure 2-24). Calls to other parties with the same Internet telephone service often are free, while calls that connect to the telephone network typically cost about $15 to $40 per month.

NETIQUETTE

Netiquette, which is short for Internet etiquette, is the code of acceptable behaviors users should follow while on the Internet; that is, it is the conduct expected of individuals while online. Netiquette includes rules for all aspects of the Internet, including the World Wide Web, e-mail, FTP, newsgroups and message boards, chat rooms, and instant messaging. Figure 2-25 outlines some of the rules of netiquette.

FIGURE 2-24 Equipment configuration for a user making a call via Internet telephony.

NETIQUETTE

Golden Rule: Treat others as you would like them to treat you.

1. In e-mail, newsgroups, and chat rooms:
   - Keep messages brief. Use proper grammar, spelling, and punctuation.
   - Be careful when using sarcasm and humor, as it might be misinterpreted.
   - Be polite. Avoid offensive language.
   - Read the message before you send it.
   - Use meaningful subject lines.
   - Avoid sending or posting flames, which are abusive or insulting messages. Do not participate in flame wars, which are exchanges of flames.
   - Avoid sending spam, which is the Internet's version of junk mail. Spam is an unsolicited e-mail message or newsgroup posting sent to many recipients or newsgroups at once.
   - Do not use all capital letters, which is the equivalent of SHOUTING!

   - Use **emoticons** to express emotion. Popular emoticons include

:) Smile	:\ Undecided	:l Indifference
:(Frown	:o Surprised	

   - Use abbreviations and acronyms for phrases:

BTW	by the way
IMHO	in my humble opinion
FYI	for your information
TTFN	ta ta for now
FWIW	for what it's worth
TYVM	thank you very much

   - Clearly identify a spoiler, which is a message that reveals a solution to a game or ending to a movie or program.

2. Read the FAQ (frequently asked questions), if one exists. Many newsgroups and Web pages have an FAQ.

3. Do not assume material is accurate or up-to-date. Be forgiving of other's mistakes.

4. Never read someone's private e-mail.

FIGURE 2-25 Some of the rules of netiquette.

Test your knowledge of pages 68 through 73 in Quiz Yourself 2-3.

 QUIZ YOURSELF 2-3

Instructions: Find the true statement below. Then, rewrite the remaining false statements so they are true.

1. A chat room is a location on an Internet server that permits users to chat with each other.

2. An e-mail address is a combination of a user name and an e-mail program that identifies a user so he or she can receive Internet e-mail.

3. FTP uses the Internet (instead of the public switched telephone network) to connect a calling party to one or more called parties.

4. Netiquette is the code of unacceptable behaviors while on the Internet.

5. On a newsgroup, a subscription consists of the original article and all subsequent related replies.

Quiz Yourself Online: To further check your knowledge of e-mail, FTP, newsgroups and message boards, mailing lists, chat rooms, instant messaging, Internet telephony, and netiquette, visit scsite.com/dcf2e/ch2/quiz and then click Objectives 6 – 7.

CHAPTER SUMMARY

This chapter presented the history and structure of the Internet. It discussed the World Wide Web at length, including topics such as browsing, navigating, searching, Web publishing, and e-commerce. It also introduced other services available on the Internet, such as e-mail (read At Issue 2-2 for a related discussion), FTP, newsgroups and message boards, chat rooms, instant messaging, and Internet telephony. Finally, the chapter listed rules of netiquette.

 AT ISSUE 2-2

E-Mail: Irritant or Liberator?

E-mail is one of the more popular services on the Internet. Worldwide, more than 230 million people send and receive e-mail messages. E-mail makes business managers more productive by allowing them to share information, ideas, and opinions easily. But ironically, this easy sharing also can make managers less productive. Every day, managers wade through rivers of e-mail messages. Some of the messages are important, but many are copies of messages sent to others, notes on minor matters, or observations once shared in brief telephone calls or on walks to the water cooler. Most messages expect a quick reply, so hours can be spent dealing with e-mail. The constant flow of e-mail steals the time and interrupts the concentration needed for everyday work activities. Even worse, as managers become accustomed to the brief, rapid thinking demanded for e-mail, they can become unused to the creative, contemplative, persistent thought processes required for complex projects. Managers use a variety of measures to dam the flood of e-mail, including limiting the amount of time spent on messages, having colleagues telephone when they send important messages, and using filtering software to prioritize messages. What is the best way to deal with e-mail? Why? In terms of productivity, how can a company maximize the advantages of e-mail and minimize the disadvantages?

CAREER CORNER

Web Developer

If you are looking for a job working with the latest Internet technology, then Web developer could be the career for you. A **Web developer** analyzes, designs, develops, implements, and supports Web applications and functionality. Specialized programming skills required include HTML, JavaScript, Java, Perl, C++, and VBScript. Developers also may need multimedia knowledge, including Adobe Photoshop, Macromedia Flash, and Macromedia Director. Developers must be aware of emerging technologies and know how they can be used to enhance a Web presence.

A Web developer must be able to appreciate a client's needs, recognize the technologies involved to meet those needs, and explain those technologies to the client. For example, if the client is a large corporation seeking to set up an online store, a Web developer must understand e-commerce and be able to explain requirements, probable costs, and possible outcomes in a way the client can understand.

Educational requirements vary from company to company and can range from a high school education to a four-year degree. Many companies place heavy emphasis on certifications. Two of the more popular certifications are available through the International Webmasters Association (IWA) and the World Organization of Webmasters (WOW). A wide salary range exists — from $35,000 to $65,000 — depending on educational background and location. For more information, visit scsite.com/dcf2e/ch2/careers and then click Web Developer.

Google
Popular Search Engine

The founders of Google, the leading Internet search engine, state that their mission is to organize the world's information. Every day, their Web site handles hundreds of millions of queries for information. In seconds, it can locate specific phrases and terms on four billion Web pages by using more than 10,000 connected computers.

Sergey Brin and Larry Page launched Google in 1998 in a friend's garage. The name is derived from "googol," which is the name of the number 1 followed by 100 zeros. Nearly 2,000 Google employees work at Googleplex, the corporate headquarters in Mountain View, California. According to Initial Public Offering documents filed in 2004, the company is worth more than $2.7 billion. For more information, visit scsite.com/dcf2e/ch2/companies and then click Google.

Yahoo!
Popular Web Portal

Yahoo!, the first navigational portal to the Web, began as a hobby for Jerry Yang and David Filo when they were doctoral candidates in electrical engineering at Stanford University. They started creating and organizing lists of their favorite Web sites in 1994. The following year, they shared their creation, named Yahoo!, with fellow students and then released their product to the Internet community.

Yahoo! is an acronym for Yet Another Hierarchical Officious Oracle. What makes Yahoo! unique is that staff members build the directory by assuming the role of a typical Web researcher. In 2004, the site enhanced its Yahoo! Messenger service with two-player games, expressive verbal animations, and the ability to listen to customized radio stations. For more information, visit scsite.com/dcf2e/ch2/companies and then click Yahoo!.

TECHNOLOGY TRAILBLAZERS

Tim Berners-Lee
Creator of the World Wide Web

The World Wide Web (WWW) has become one of the more widely used Internet services, and its roots are based on Tim Berners-Lee's work. Berners-Lee is credited with creating the first Web server, browser, and URL addresses.

He developed his ideas in 1989 while working at CERN, the European Particle Physics Laboratory in Geneva, Switzerland, and based his work on a program he had written for his own use to track random associations. Today, he works quietly in academia as director of the World Wide Web Consortium (W3C) at the Massachusetts Institute of Technology.

In 2004, Berners-Lee received the first Millennium Technology Prize, which is worth $1.2 million and recognizes technological developments that enhance the quality of life and encourage economic growth. For more information, visit scsite.com/dcf2e/ch2/people and then click Tim Berners-Lee.

Meg Whitman
eBay President and CEO

Meg Whitman joined eBay in 1998 and has been instrumental in helping the company become the world's largest online marketplace. Before that time, she was an executive for the Keds Division of the Stride Rite Corporation and general manager of Hasbro Inc.'s Preschool Division. She then served as president and CEO of Florists Transworld Delivery (FTD).

She credits her success to listening to the loyal eBay community, and she occasionally answers their e-mails personally. She holds degrees in economics from Princeton University and management from the Harvard Business School.

Fortune magazine has named Whitman one of the most powerful women in business, and *Worth* magazine has ranked her at the top of its list of most powerful business managers. For more information, visit scsite.com/dcf2e/ch2/people and then click Meg Whitman.

Chapter Review

The Chapter Review section summarizes the concepts presented in this chapter. To obtain help from other students regarding any subject in this chapter, visit scsite.com/dcf2e/ch2/forum and post your thoughts or questions.

(1) How Can You Access and Connect to the Internet?

The **Internet** is a worldwide collection of networks that links millions of businesses, government agencies, educational institutions, and individuals. Employees and students often connect to the Internet through a business or school network. Many home and small businesses connect to the Internet with **dial-up access**, which uses a modem in the computer and a standard telephone line.

Some home and small business users opt for higher-speed connections, such as DSL, cable television, radio signals, or satellite. **DSL** provides high-speed Internet connections using regular copper telephone lines. A **cable modem** allows access to high-speed Internet services through the cable television network. **Fixed wireless** high-speed Internet connections use an antenna to communicate via radio signals. A **satellite modem** communicates with a satellite dish to provide high-speed Internet connections. An **access provider** is a business that provides access to the Internet free or for a fee. An **ISP** (**Internet service provider**) is a regional or national access provider. An **online service provider** (**OSP**) provides Internet access in addition to members-only features. A **wireless Internet service provider** (**WISP**) provides wireless Internet access to users with wireless modems or Internet-enabled mobile computers or devices.

 Visit scsite.com/dcf2e/ch2/quiz or click the Quiz Yourself button. Click Objective 1.

(2) How Can You View a Web Page and Search for Information on the Web?

A **Web browser**, or **browser**, is application software that allows users to access and view Web pages. When you type a Web address in the Address box of a browser window, a computer called a **Web server** delivers the requested Web page to your computer. Most Web pages contain links. A **link** is a built-in connection that, when clicked, displays a related Web page or part of a Web page. Two commonly used search tools are subject directories and search engines. A **subject directory** classifies Web pages in an organized set of categories. A **search engine** finds Web sites and Web pages related to a word or phrase, called **search text**, that defines the item about which you want information.

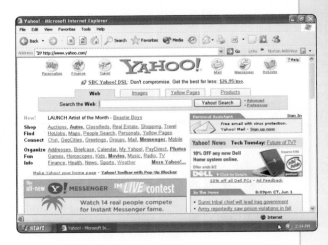

(3) What Are the Types of Web Sites?

A **portal** is a Web site that offers a variety of Internet services from a single location. A news Web site contains newsworthy material. An informational Web site contains factual information. A business/marketing Web site promotes or sells products or services. An educational Web site offers avenues for teaching and learning. An entertainment Web site offers an interactive and engaging environment. An advocacy Web site describes a cause, opinion, or idea. A **blog** is a Web site that uses a regularly updated journal format. A personal Web site is maintained by a private individual or family.

(4) What Are the Steps Required for Web Publishing?

Web publishing is the development and maintenance of Web pages. The five major steps to Web publishing are: (1) plan a Web site, (2) analyze and design a Web site, (3) create a Web site, (4) deploy a Web site, and (5) maintain a Web site.

(5) What Are the Types of E-Commerce?

E-commerce, short for electronic commerce, is a business transaction that occurs over an electronic network such as the Internet. Business-to-consumer (B2C) e-commerce consists of the sale of goods and services to the general public. Consumer-to-consumer (C2C) e-commerce occurs when one consumer sells directly to another, such as an **online auction**. Business-to-business (B2B) e-commerce takes place between businesses that exchange goods and services.

 Visit scsite.com/dcf2e/ch2/quiz or click the Quiz Yourself button. Click Objectives 2 – 5.

(6) How Do E-Mail, FTP, Newsgroups and Message Boards, Mailing Lists, Chat Rooms, Instant Messaging, and Internet Telephony Work?

E-mail (short for electronic mail) is the transmission of messages and files via a computer network. **FTP** (File Transfer Protocol) is an Internet standard that permits file uploading and downloading with other computers on the Internet. A **newsgroup** is an online area in which users have written discussions about a particular subject. A **message board** is a popular Web-based type of discussion group that is easier to use than a newsgroup. A **mailing list** is a group of e-mail names and addresses given a single name, so that everyone on the list receives a message sent to the list. A **chat room** is a location on an Internet server that permits users to **chat**, or conduct real-time typed conversations. **Instant messaging** (**IM**) is a real-time Internet communications service that notifies you when one or more people are online. **Internet telephony** enables users to speak over the Internet using a computer or mobile device.

(7) What Are the Rules of Netiquette?

Netiquette, which is short for Internet etiquette, is the code of acceptable behaviors users should follow while on the Internet. Keep messages short. Be polite. Read the FAQ if one exists. Do not assume material is accurate or up-to-date, and never read someone's private e-mail.

 Visit scsite.com/dcf2e/ch2/quiz or click the Quiz Yourself button. Click Objectives 6 – 7.

Key Terms

You should know the Key Terms. Use the list below to help focus your study. To further enhance your understanding of the Key Terms in this chapter, visit scsite.com/dcf2e/ch2/terms. See an example of and a definition for each term, and access current and additional information about the term from the Web.

access provider (52)	hyperlink (57)	shopping cart (68)
address book (70)	instant messaging (IM) (72)	streaming (64)
animation (64)	Internet (50)	subject directory (57)
audio (64)	Internet backbone (52)	subscribe (71)
blog (63)	IP address (53)	surfing the Web (57)
browser (54)	Internet telephony (73)	thumbnail (64)
cable modem (52)	ISP (Internet service provider) (52)	top-level domain (54)
chat (71)	link (57)	unsubscribe (71)
chat room (71)	mailing list (71)	uploading (71)
click (57)	message board (71)	URL (56)
dial-up access (51)	MP3 (64)	user name (70)
domain name (53)	MPEG-4 (65)	video (65)
downloading (55)	multimedia (64)	virtual reality (VR) (65)
DSL (52)	Net (50)	Voice over IP (73)
e-commerce (67)	netiquette (73)	Web (54)
electronic storefront (68)	newsgroup (71)	Web address (56)
e-mail (69)	online auction (68)	Web browser (54)
e-mail address (70)	online service provider (OSP) (52)	Web developer (74)
e-mail program (69)	player (64)	Web page (54)
emoticons (73)	plug-in (66)	Web publishing (66)
fixed wireless (52)	portal (61)	Web server (54)
FTP (71)	real time (71)	Web site (54)
graphic (64)	satellite modem (52)	wireless Internet service provider (WISP) (52)
home page (55)	search engine (57)	
host (50)	search text (60)	World Wide Web (WWW) (54)
http (56)	server (50)	World Wide Web Consortium (W3C) (51)

Checkpoint

Use the Checkpoint exercises to check your knowledge level of the chapter.

_____ 1. No single person, company, institution, or government agency controls or owns the Internet. (51)

_____ 2. An access provider is a business that provides access to the Internet for a fee. (52)

_____ 3. A domain name is the text version of an IP address. (53)

_____ 4. Each electronic document on the Web is called a Web site. (54)

_____ 5. Downloading is the process of sending information to a server on the Internet. (55)

_____ 6. A search engine is a program that finds Web sites and Web pages. (57)

_____ 7. An educational Web site contains content that describes a cause, opinion, or idea. (62)

_____ 8. Streaming is the process of transferring data in a continuous and even flow. (64)

_____ 9. Consumer-to-consumer (C2C) e-commerce consists of the sale of goods and services to the general public. (68)

_____ 10. Internet telephony is an online service in which users have written discussions. (73)

1. Although it is slow-speed technology, many homes and small businesses use _____ to connect to the Internet. (51)
   a. dial-up access
   b. a cable modem
   c. DSL
   d. a satellite modem

2. An IP address usually consists of _____. (53)
   a. two groups of numbers separated by commas
   b. two groups of numbers separated by periods
   c. four groups of numbers separated by commas
   d. four groups of numbers separated by periods

3. Many Web addresses begin with http, which is the _____. (56)
   a. path
   b. domain name
   c. protocol
   d. page name

4. The purpose of an advocacy Web site is to _____. (62)
   a. present newsworthy material related to current events
   b. contain factual information of public interest
   c. promote or sell products or services
   d. convince the reader of the validity of the cause, opinion, or idea

5. _____ format reduces the size of an audio file to about one-tenth its original size, while preserving the quality of the sound. (64)
   a. JPEG
   b. MP3
   c. MPEG-4
   d. GIF

6. _____ is the development and maintenance of Web pages. (66)
   a. Web serving
   b. Web addressing
   c. Web publishing
   d. Web browsing

7. In _____ e-commerce, a customer visits an online business through an electronic storefront. (68)
   a. consumer-to-consumer
   b. business-to-business
   c. consumer-to-business
   d. business-to-consumer

8. _____ is a rule of netiquette. (73)
   a. Use all capital letters
   b. Avoid offensive language
   c. Participate in flame wars
   d. Assume material is accurate

_____ 1. home page (55)

_____ 2. thumbnail (64)

_____ 3. streaming (64)

_____ 4. e-mail address (70)

_____ 5. uploading (71)

a. first page that a Web site displays

b. process of transferring data in a continuous and even flow

c. combination of a user name and a domain name that identifies an Internet user

d. built-in connection to a related Web page or part of a Web page

e. small version of a larger graphic

f. process of transferring documents, graphics, and other objects from your computer to an Internet server

Checkpoint

1. How is a regional ISP different from a national ISP? _____ How are an ISP, OSP, and WISP different? _____
2. How is a Web page different from a Web site? _____ How can you use a Web address to display a Web page? _____
3. How can you use a subject directory to find information? _____ What is a search engine? _____
4. What is FTP? _____ What is anonymous FTP? _____
5. What happens when you subscribe to, or unsubscribe from, a mailing list? _____ How can you locate a mailing list about a particular topic? _____

1. This chapter lists nine types of Web sites: portal, news, informational, business/marketing, educational, entertainment, advocacy, blog, and personal. Working as a team, use the Internet to find at least two examples of each type of Web site. For each Web site, identify the Web address, the multimedia elements used, the purpose of the Web site, and the type of Web site. Explain why you classified each site as you did. Then, keeping in mind the purpose of each Web site, rank the sites in terms of their effectiveness. Share your findings in a report and/or a PowerPoint presentation with the class.

Web Research

Use the Internet-based Web Research exercises to broaden your understanding of the concepts presented in this chapter. Visit scsite.com/dcf2e/ch2/research to obtain more information pertaining to each exercise. To discuss any of the Web Research exercises in this chapter with other students, post your thoughts or questions at scsite.com/dcf2e/ch2/forum.

① Journaling   Respond to your readings in this chapter by writing at least one page about your reactions, evaluations, and reflections about the first time you used the **Internet**. For example, to whom did you send your first e-mail message? Have you used chat rooms? Have you bought or sold any items through an online auction Web site? Have you shopped online? Have your instructors required you to access the Internet for class projects? You also can write about the new terms you learned by reading this chapter. If required, submit your journal to your instructor.

② Scavenger Hunt   Use one of the **search engines** listed in Figure 2-8 in Chapter 2 on page 58 or your own favorite search engine to find the answers to the questions below. Copy and paste the Web address from the Web page where you found the answer. Some questions may have more than one answer. If required, submit your answers to your instructor. (1) Microsoft Internet Explorer and Netscape Navigator are the two more popular Web browsers. What is the name of the first graphical Web browser? (2) What cable company was established in 1858 to carry instantaneous communications across the ocean that eventually would be used for Internet communications? (3) What American president in 1957 created both the interstate highway system and the Advanced Research Projects Agency (ARPA) while responding to the Soviet threat and the success of Sputnik? (4) Where is the location of Microsoft's headquarters? (5) How many Web pages is Google currently searching?

③ Search Sleuth   The Internet has provided the opportunity to access encyclopedias online. One of the more comprehensive encyclopedia research sites is **Encyclopedia.com**. Visit this Web site and then use your word processing program to answer the following questions. Then, if required, submit your answers to your instructor. (1) The site's home page provides information about who was born and died and what significant events occurred on this date. What are these facts for today? (2) Type `computer` as the keyword in the Search text box. How many articles discussing computers are found on the Encyclopedia.com Web site? (3) Click your browser's Back button or press the BACKSPACE key to return to the home page. Type `modem` as the keyword in the Search text box. How many articles discussing modems are found on this Web site? (4) In the search results list, click the modem link. What is the definition of a modem according to the first sentence of the article? What are wireless and fax modems? When were modems first used? (5) Click your browser's Back button or press the BACKSPACE key to return to the home page. Type `Bill Gates` as the keyword in the Search text box and then click the Bill Gates link and read the article. According to this source, why did the Justice Department sue Microsoft in 1997? (6) Click your browser's Back button or press the BACKSPACE key to return to the home page. Click one of the Top Searches links and review the material. Summarize the information you read and then write a 50-word summary.

Learn How To

Use the Learn How To activities to learn fundamental skills when using a computer and accompanying technology. Complete the exercises and submit them to your instructor.

LEARN HOW TO 1: Change a Web Browser's Home Page

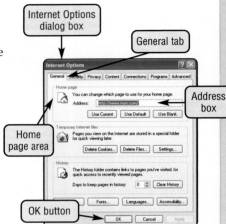

FIGURE 2-26

When you start a Web browser, a Web page is displayed. You can change the page that appears when you start a Web browser or when you click the Home button on the browser toolbar by completing the following steps:

1. With the browser running, click Tools on the menu bar and then click Internet Options on the Tools menu. *The Internet Options dialog box is displayed (Figure 2-26).*
2. If necessary, in the Home page area in the General sheet, select the Web address in the Address box.
3. Type the Web address of the page you want to display both when you start the browser and when you click the Home button.
4. Click the OK button in the Internet Options dialog box.

When you start the browser or click the Home button on the browser toolbar, the selected Web page will be displayed.

Exercise

1. Start your Web browser. Write down the address of the browser's current home page. Then, change the browser's home page to www.cnn.com. Close the browser.
2. Start your Web browser. What is the lead story on cnn.com? Use links on the page to view several stories. Which story do you find most interesting? Click the Home button on the browser toolbar. What happened? Submit these answers to your instructor.
3. Change the browser's home page to your school's home page. Click the Home button on the browser toolbar. Click the Calendar or Events link, and then locate two campus events of which you were unaware. Report these two campus events to your instructor.
4. Change the browser's home page back to the address you wrote down in Step 1.

LEARN HOW TO 2: Create and Use Your Own Web Log (Blog)

A Web log, commonly referred to as a blog, can contain any information you wish to place in it. Originally, blogs consisted of Web addresses, so that an individual or group with a specific interest could direct others to useful places on the Web. Today, blogs contain addresses, thoughts, diaries, and anything else a person or group wants to share.

Once you have created a blog, you can update it. A variety of services are available on the Web to help you create and maintain your blog. One widely used service is called Blogger. To create a blog using Blogger, complete the following steps:

1. Start your Web browser, type `www.blogger.com` in the Address box, and then press the ENTER key. *The Blogger home page is displayed (Figure 2-27).*
2. Click the CREATE YOUR BLOG NOW arrow on the Blogger home page.
3. Enter the data required on the Create an account page. Your user name and password will allow you to change and manage your blog. Your Display name is the name that will be shown on the blog as the author of the material on the blog. Many people use their own names, but others use pseudonyms as their "pen names" so they are not readily identifiable.
4. Click the Continue arrow and then enter your Blog title and Blog address. These are the names and addresses everyone will use to view your blog. By default, the blog is stored and maintained on the blogspot server.
5. Click the Continue arrow. *The Choose a template screen is displayed.*

FIGURE 2-27

6. Choose a template for your blog and then click the Continue arrow.
7. Your blog will be created for you. When you see the Your blog has been created screen, click the Start posting arrow.
8. From the screen that is displayed, you can post items for your blog, specify settings, change the template, and view your blog.
9. When you have posted all your information, click the Sign out button at the top right of the screen. You will be logged out.
10. To edit your blog and add or change information on it, visit the Blogger home page and sign in by entering your user name and password. You will be able to post to your blog.
11. Others can view your blog by entering its address in the browser's Address bar and then pressing the ENTER key.

Exercise

1. Start your Web browser and visit www.blogger.com. Click the TAKE A QUICK TOUR button and go through all the screens that explain about a blog. What did you learn that you did not know? What type of blog do you find most compelling — a group or an individual blog? Why? Turn in your answers to your instructor.
2. Optional: Create your own blog. Carefully name it and begin your posts at this time. What is your blog name and address? What is its primary purpose? Is it an individual or group blog? Write a paragraph containing the answers to these questions and any other information you feel is pertinent. Turn in this paragraph to your instructor.

LEARN HOW TO 3: Bid and Buy a Product from eBay

Online auctions have grown to be a favorite shopping space for many people. A leading online auction Web site is eBay. To submit a bid for an item on eBay, complete the following steps:

1. Type www.ebay.com in the Address box of your browser. Press the ENTER key. *The eBay home page is displayed (Figure 2-28).*
2. Pick an item you find interesting and on which you might bid.
3. Enter your item in the What are you looking for text box and then click the Find It button.
4. Scroll through the page to see the available items.
5. To bid on an item, click the Place Bid button.
6. Enter the amount of your bid. Click the Continue button.
7. You must be registered to bid on eBay. If you are registered, enter your eBay User ID and Password and then click the Submit button. If not, click the Register button and follow the instructions.
8. After registering, you will confirm your bid and receive notification about your bid.
9. You will be notified by e-mail if you won the bid. If so, you will arrange with the seller for payment and shipment.

The eBay Web site contains reminders that when you bid on an item, you are entering into a contract to purchase the item if you are the successful bidder. Bidding on eBay is serious business.

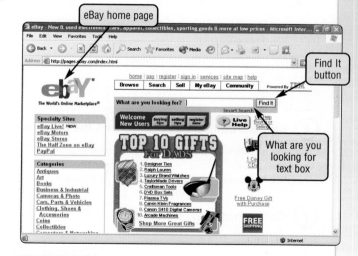

FIGURE 2-28

Exercise

1. Start your browser and display the eBay home page.
2. In the What are you looking for text box, enter the name of an upcoming sporting event you would like to attend followed by the word, tickets. For example, enter Super Bowl tickets. Click the Search button.
3. Did you find available tickets? Were there more tickets available than you expected, or fewer? Are the bid prices reasonable or ridiculous? How many bids were made for all the tickets? How much time is left to bid? What items did you find you were not expecting? Submit answers to these questions to your instructor.
4. Enter an item of your choice in the What are you looking for text box. If you feel so inclined, bid on an item. Do you think this manner of buying goods is valuable? Why? Will you visit eBay again? Why? Submit answers to these questions to your instructor.

Learn It Online

Use the Learn It Online exercises to reinforce your understanding of the chapter concepts. To access the Learn It Online exercises, visit scsite.com/dcf2e/ch2/learn.

1 At the Movies — Google Search Secrets

To view the Google Search Secrets movie, click the number 1 button. Locate your video and click the corresponding High-Speed or Dial-Up link, depending on your Internet connection. Watch the movie and then complete the exercise by answering the question that follows. Using the Internet to gather information can seem daunting. The introduction of powerful search engines has enhanced the Internet research experience. Properly utilizing a search engine can benefit almost any project. How might you go about using Google to search for information for a research paper? ....

2 Student Edition Labs — Connecting to the Internet

Click the number 2 button. When the Student Edition Labs menu appears, click *Connecting to the Internet* to begin. A new browser window will open. Follow the on-screen instructions to complete the Lab. When finished, click the Exit button. If required, submit your results to your instructor. ....

3 Practice Test

Click the number 3 button. Answer each question. When completed, enter your name and click the Grade Test button to submit the quiz for grading. Make a note of any missed questions. If required, submit your score to your instructor. ....

4 Who Wants To Be a Computer Genius^2?

Click the number 4 button to find out if you are a computer genius. Directions about how to play the game will be displayed. When you are ready to play, click the Play button. Submit your score to your instructor. ....

5 Wheel of Terms

Click the number 5 button to reinforce important terms you learned in this chapter by playing the Shelly Cashman Series version of this popular game. Directions about how to play the game will be displayed. When you are ready to play, click the Play button. Submit your score to your instructor. ....

6 Student Edition Labs — Getting the Most out of the Internet

Click the number 6 button. When the Student Edition Labs menu appears, click *Getting the Most out of the Internet* to begin. A new browser window will open. Follow the on-screen instructions to complete the Lab. When finished, click the Exit button. If required, submit your results to your instructor. ....

7 Crossword Puzzle Challenge

Click the number 7 button. Complete the puzzle to reinforce skills you learned in this chapter. Directions about how to play the game will be displayed. When you are ready to play, click the Play button. Submit the completed puzzle to your instructor. ....

8 Lab Exercises

Click the number 8 button. When the Lab Exercises menu appears, click the exercise assigned by your instructor. A new browser window will open. Follow the on-screen instructions to complete the exercise. When finished, click the Exit button. If required, submit your results to your instructor. ....

9 Chapter Discussion Forum

Select an objective from this chapter on page 49 about which you would like more information. Click the number 9 button and post a short message listing a meaningful message title accompanied by one or more questions concerning the selected objective. In two days, return to the threaded discussion by clicking the number 9 button. Submit to your instructor your original message and at least one response to your message.

Making Use of the Web

A wealth of information is available on the World Wide Web. The riches are yours if you know where to find this material. Locating useful Web sites may be profitable for your educational and professional careers, as the resources may help you research class assignments and make your life more fulfilling and manageable.

Because the World Wide Web does not have an organizational structure to assist you in locating reliable material, you need additional resources to guide you in searching. To help you find useful Web sites, this Special Feature describes specific information about a variety of Web pages, and it includes tables of Web addresses, so you can get started. The material is organized in several areas of interest.

AREAS OF INTEREST	
Fun and Entertainment	Learning
Travel	Science
Finance	Environment
Resources	Health
Auctions	Research
Government	Careers
Shopping	Arts and Literature
Weather, Sports, and News	

Web Exercises at the end of each category will reinforce the material and help you discover Web sites that may add a treasure trove of knowledge to your life.

Fun and Entertainment
THAT'S ENTERTAINMENT

Rock 'n' Roll on the Web

Consumers place great significance on buying entertainment products for fun and recreation. Nearly 10 percent of the United States's economy is spent on attending concerts and buying DVDs, CDs, reading materials, sporting goods, and toys.

Many Web sites supplement our cravings for fun and entertainment. For example, you can see and hear the musicians inducted into the Rock and Roll Hall of Fame and Museum (Figure 1). If you need an update on your favorite reality-based television program or a preview of an upcoming movie, E! Online and Entertainment Tonight provide the latest features on television and movie stars. The Internet Movie Database contains credits and reviews of more than 400,000 titles.

Watch the surfers riding the waves in Hawaii and romp with pandas at the San Diego Zoo. Web cams, which are video cameras that display their output on Web pages, take armchair travelers across the world for views of natural attractions, historical monuments, colleges, and cities. Many Web sites featuring Web cams are listed in the table in Figure 2.

FUN AND ENTERTAINMENT WEB SITES

Web Cams	URL
AfriCam Virtual Game Reserve	africam.com
Discovery Channel Cams	dsc.discovery.com/cams/cams.html
EarthCam — Webcam Network	earthcam.com
Iowa State Insect Zoo Live Camera	zoocam.ent.iastate.edu
Panda Cam San Diego Zoo	sandiegozoo.org/pandas/pandacam/index.html
The Automated Astrophysical Site-Testing Observatory (AASTO) (South Pole)	www.phys.unsw.edu.au/southpolediaries/webcam.html
Weather and Webcams from OnlineWeather.com and CamVista	onlineweather.com/v4/webcams/index.html
Wild Birds Unlimited Bird FeederCam	wbu.com/feedercam_home.htm
World Surf Cameras	surfrock.com.br/surfcam.htm
WorldLIVE	worldlive.cz/en/webcams

Entertainment	URL
AMG All Music Guide	allmusic.com
E! Online	eonline.com
Entertainment Tonight	etonline.com
Entertainment Weekly's EW.com	ew.com/ew
MSN Entertainment	entertainment.msn.com
Old Time Radio (OTR) — Radio Days: A Soundbite History	otr.com
Rock and Roll Hall of Fame and Museum	rockhall.com
The Internet Movie Database (IMDb)	imdb.com
World Radio Network (WRN)	wrn.org

For more information on fun and entertainment Web sites, visit scsite.com/dcf2e/ch2/web.

FIGURE 1 Visitors exploring the Rock and Roll Hall of Fame and Museum Web site will find history, exhibitions, programs, and the names and particulars of the latest inductees.

FIGURE 2 When you visit Web sites offering fun and entertainment resources, you can be both amused and informed.

FUN AND ENTERTAINMENT WEB EXERCISES

1 Visit the WorldLIVE site listed in Figure 2. View two of the Web cams closest to your hometown, and describe the scenes. Then, visit the Discovery Channel Cams Web site and view two of the animal cams in the Featured Cams. What do you observe? Visit another Web site listed in Figure 2 and describe the view. What are the benefits of having Web cams at these locations throughout the world?

2 What are your favorite movies? Use The Internet Movie Database Web site listed in Figure 2 to search for information about two of these films, and write a brief description of the biographies of the major stars and director for each movie. Then, visit one of the entertainment Web sites and describe three of the featured stories. At the Rock and Roll Hall of Fame and Museum Web site, view the information on Elvis and one of your favorite musicians. Write a paragraph describing the information available about these rock stars.

Travel
GET PACKING!

Explore the World without Leaving Home

When you are ready to arrange your next travel adventure or just want to explore destination possibilities, the Internet provides ample resources to set your plans in motion.

To discover exactly where your destination is on this planet, cartography Web sites, including MapQuest (Figure 3), Maps.com, and Rand McNally, allow you to pinpoint your destination. These Web pages generally are divided into geographical areas, such as North America and Europe.

Some good starting places are general travel Web sites such as Expedia Travel, Cheap Tickets, and Travelocity, which is owned by the electronic booking service travel agents use. These all-encompassing Web sites, including those in Figure 4, have tools to help you find the lowest prices and details on flights, car rentals, cruises, and hotels.

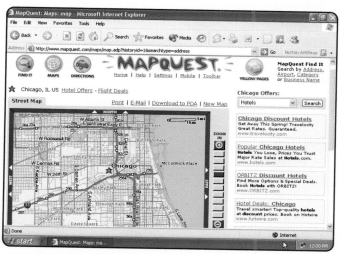

FIGURE 3 MapQuest provides directions, traffic reports, maps, and more.

TRAVEL WEB SITES

General Travel	URL
Cheap Tickets	cheaptickets.com
Expedia.com	expedia.com
Orbitz	orbitz.com
Travelocity.com	travelocity.com
Yahoo! Travel	travel.yahoo.com
Cartography	**URL**
MapQuest	mapquest.com
Maps.com	maps.com
Rand McNally	randmcnally.com
Travel and City Guides	**URL**
All the Largest Cities of the World	greatestcities.com
Frommers.com	frommers.com
U.S.-Parks.com — US National Parks Adventure Travel Guide	us-parks.com

For more information on travel Web sites, visit scsite.com/dcf2e/ch2/web.

FIGURE 4 These travel resources Web sites offer travel information to exciting destinations throughout the world.

TRAVEL WEB EXERCISES

1 Visit one of the cartography Web sites listed in Figure 4 and obtain the directions from your campus to one of these destinations: the White House in Washington, D.C.; Elvis's home in Memphis, Tennessee; Walt Disney World in Orlando, Florida; or the Grand Old Opry in Nashville, Tennessee. How many miles is it to your destination? What is the estimated driving time? Then, visit one of the general travel Web sites listed in the table and plan a flight from the nearest major airport to one of the four destinations for the week after finals and a return trip one week later. What is the lowest economy coach fare for this round-trip flight? What airline, flight numbers, and departure and arrival times did you select? Finally, explore car rental rates for a subcompact car for this one-week vacation. What rental agency and rate did you choose?

2 Visit one of the travel and city guides Web sites listed in Figure 4, and choose a destination for a getaway this coming weekend. Write a one-page paper giving details about this location, such as popular hotels and lodging, expected weather, population, local colleges and universities, parks and recreation, ancient and modern history, and tours. Include a map of this place. Why did you select this destination? How would you travel there and back? What is the breakdown of expected costs for this weekend, including travel expenditures, meals, lodging, and tickets to events and activities? What URLs did you use to complete this exercise?

Finance
MONEY MATTERS

Cashing In on Financial Advice

You can manage your money with advice from financial Web sites that offer online banking, tax help, personal finance, and small business and commercial services.

If you do not have a personal banker or a financial planner, consider a Web adviser to guide your investment decisions. The Motley Fool (Figure 5) provides commentary and education on investing strategies, financial news, and taxes.

If you are ready to ride the ups and downs of the NASDAQ and the Dow, an abundance of Web sites listed in Figure 6, including FreeEDGAR and Morningstar.com, can help you pick companies that fit your interests and financial needs.

Claiming to be the fastest, easiest tax publication on the planet, the Internal Revenue Service Web site contains procedures for filing tax appeals and contains IRS forms, publications, and legal regulations.

FINANCE WEB SITES

Advice and Education	URL
Bankrate.com	bankrate.com
LendingTree	lendingtree.com
Loan.com	loan.com
MSN Money	money.msn.com
The Motley Fool	fool.com
Wells Fargo	wellsfargo.com
Yahoo! Finance	finance.yahoo.com

Stock Market	URL
E*TRADE Financial	us.etrade.com
Financial Engines	financialengines.com
FreeEDGAR®	www.freeedgar.com
Harris*direct*	harrisdirect.com
Merrill Lynch Direct	mldirect.ml.com
Morningstar.com	www.morningstar.com
The Vanguard Group	vanguard.com

Taxes	URL
H&R Block	hrblock.com
Internal Revenue Service	www.irs.gov

For more information on finance Web sites, visit scsite.com/dcf2e/ch2/web.

FIGURE 5 The Motley Fool Web site contains strategies and news stories related to personal financing and investing.

FIGURE 6 Financial resources Web sites offer general information, stock market analyses, and tax advice, as well as guidance and money-saving tips.

FINANCE WEB EXERCISES

1 Visit three advice and education Web sites listed in Figure 6 and read their top business world reports. Write a paragraph about each, summarizing these stories. Which stocks or mutual funds do these Web sites predict as being sound investments today? What are the current market indexes for the DJIA (Dow Jones Industrial Average), S&P 500, and NASDAQ, and how do these figures compare with the previous day's numbers?

2 Using two of the stock market Web sites listed in Figure 6, search for information about Microsoft, Adobe Systems, and one other software vendor. Write a paragraph about each of these stocks describing the revenues, net incomes, total assets for the previous year, current stock price per share, highest and lowest prices of each stock during the past year, and other relevant investment information.

Resources
LOOK IT UP

Web Resources Ease Computer Concerns

From dictionaries and encyclopedias to online technical support, the Web is filled with a plethora of resources to answer your computer questions.

Keep up with the latest developments by viewing online dictionaries and encyclopedias that add to their collections of computer and product terms on a regular basis. Shopping for a new computer can be a daunting experience, but many online guides, including PCWorld.com (Figure 7), can help you select the components that best fit your needs and budget.

If you are not confident in your ability to solve a problem alone, turn to online technical support. Web sites, such as those shown in Figure 8, often provide streaming how-to video lessons, tutorials, and real-time chats with experienced technicians. Hardware and software reviews, price comparisons, shareware, technical questions and answers, and breaking technology news are found on comprehensive portals.

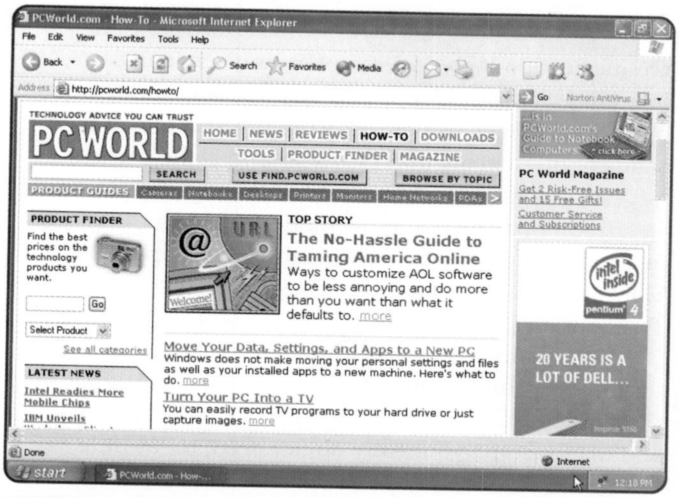

FIGURE 7 Buying and upgrading a computer is simplified with helpful Web sites such as PCWorld.com.

RESOURCES WEB SITES

Dictionaries and Encyclopedias	URL
CDT's Guide to Online Privacy	cdt.org/privacy/guide/terms
ComputerUser High-Tech Dictionary	computeruser.com/resources/dictionary
Webopedia: Online Computer Dictionary for Computer and Internet Terms	webopedia.com
whatis?com	whatis.com

Computer Shopping Guides	URL
A Computer Guide: Reviews on Software and Hardware, Software, Review and More	acomputerguide.com
The CPU Scorecard	cpuscorecard.com
The Online Computer Buying Guide™	grohol.com/computers
Viewz Desktop Computer Buying Guide	viewz.com/shoppingguide/compbuy.shtml
ZDNet	shopper-zdnet.com.com

Upgrading Guides	URL
CNET Shopper.com	shopper.cnet.com
eHow™	ehow.com
Focus on Macs	macs.about.com
PCWorld.com	pcworld.com/howto

Online Technical Support	URL
MSN Tech & Gadgets	computingcentral.msn.com
PC911	pcnineoneone.com
PC Pitstop	pcpitstop.com

Technical and Consumer Information	URL
CNET.com	cnet.com
NewsHub	newshub.com/tech
Wired News	wirednews.com

For more information on resources Web sites, visit scsite.com/dcf2e/ch2/web.

FIGURE 8 A variety of Web resources can provide information about buying, repairing, and upgrading computers.

RESOURCES WEB EXERCISES

1. Visit the dictionaries and encyclopedias Web sites listed in Figure 8. Search these resources for five terms. Create a table with two columns: one for the cyberterm and one for the Web definition. Then, create a second table listing five recently added or updated words and their definitions on these Web sites. Next, visit two of the listed computer shopping guides Web sites to choose the components you would buy if you were building a customized desktop computer and notebook computer. Create a table for both computers, listing the computer manufacturer, processor model name or number and manufacturer, clock speed, RAM, cache, number of expansion slots, and number of bays.

2. Visit three upgrading guides Web sites listed in Figure 8. Write a paragraph describing available advice for buying a motherboard. Describe the strengths and weaknesses of these Web sites, focusing on such criteria as clarity of instructions, thoroughness, and ease of navigation. Would you use these Web sites as a resource to troubleshoot computer problems? Then, view two technical and consumer information Web sites listed in the table and write a paragraph about each one, describing the top two news stories of the day.

Auctions
GOING ONCE, GOING TWICE

Rare, Common Items Flood Web Sites

Online auction Web sites can offer unusual items, including *Star Wars* props and memorabilia and a round of golf with Tiger Woods. eBay (Figure 9) is one of thousands of Internet auction Web sites and is the world's largest personal online trading community.

Traditional auction powerhouses, such as Christie's in London and Sotheby's on Manhattan's Upper East Side, are known for their big-ticket items, including a Tyrannosaurus rex fossil that sold for $8.4 million.

If those prices are a bit out of your league, you can turn to a wealth of other auction Web sites, including those listed in Figure 10, to find just the items you need, and maybe some you really do not need, for as little as $1. Categories include antiques and collectibles, automotive, computers, electronics, music, sports, sports cards and memorabilia, and toys.

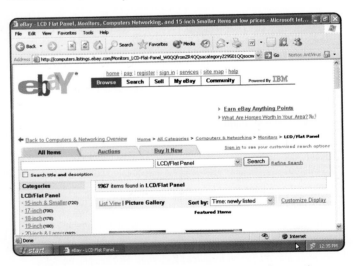

FIGURE 9 eBay is one of the world's more popular auction Web sites.

AUCTION WEB SITES

	URL
Christie's	christies.com
eBay®	ebay.com
Dargate Auction Galleries	dargate.com
musichotbid	musichotbid.com
Penbid.com	penbid.com
Sotheby's	sothebys.com
uBid™	ubid.com
Yahoo! Shopping Auctions	auctions.yahoo.com
For more information on auction Web sites, visit scsite.com/dcf2e/ch2/web.	

FIGURE 10 These auction Web sites feature a wide variety of items.

AUCTIONS WEB EXERCISES

1 Visit the Christie's and Sotheby's Web sites and read about the items that have been sold recently. Find two unusual objects and write a paragraph about each one, summarizing your discoveries. What were the opening and final bids on these objects? Then, review two of the upcoming auctions. When are the auctions' dates? What items are available? What are some of the opening bids? What are the advantages and disadvantages of bidding online?

2 Using one of the auction Web sites listed in Figure 10, search for two objects pertaining to your hobbies or interests. For example, if you are a baseball fan, you can search for a complete set of Topps cards. If you are a car buff, search for your dream car. Describe these two items. How many people have bid on these items? Who are the sellers? What are the opening and current bids?

Government
STAMP OF APPROVAL

Making a Federal Case for Useful Information

When it is time to buy stamps to mail your correspondence, you no longer need to wait in long lines at your local post office. The U.S. Postal Service has authorized several corporations to sell stamps online.

You can recognize U.S. Government Web sites on the Internet by their .gov top-level domain abbreviation. For example, The Library of Congress Web site is lcweb.loc.gov, as shown in Figure 11. Government and military Web sites offer a wide range of information, and some of the more popular sites are listed in Figure 12. The Time Service Department Web site will provide you with the correct time. If you are looking for a federal document, FedWorld lists thousands of documents distributed by the government on its Web site. For access to the names of your congressional representatives, visit the extensive Hieros Gamos Web site.

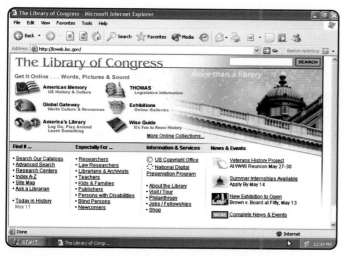

FIGURE 11 The Library of Congress Web site contains more than 119 million items written in 470 languages.

GOVERNMENT RESOURCES WEB SITES

Postage	URL
Endicia	endicia.com
Pitney Bowes	pb.com
Stamps.com	stamps.com

Government	URL
FedWorld	www.fedworld.gov
Hieros Gamos — Law and Legal Research Center	hg.org
NARA — United States National Archives and Records Administration	archives.gov
National Agricultural Library	www.nal.usda.gov
The Library of Congress	lcweb.loc.gov
THOMAS Legislative Information	thomas.loc.gov
Time Service Department	tycho.usno.navy.mil
United States Department of Education	ed.gov
United States Department of the Treasury	www.treas.gov
United States Government Printing Office	www.access.gpo.gov
United States National Library of Medicine	www.nlm.nih.gov
United States Patent and Trademark Office	www.uspto.gov
USAJOBS	www.usajobs.opm.gov
White House	whitehouse.gov

For more information on government Web sites, visit scsite.com/dcf2e/ch2/web.

FIGURE 12 These Web sites offer information about buying U.S.-approved postage online and researching federal agencies.

GOVERNMENT WEB EXERCISES

1 View the three postage Web sites listed in Figure 12. Compare and contrast the available services on each one. Consider postage cost, necessary equipment, shipping services, security techniques, and tracking capability. Explain why you would or would not like to use this service.

2 Visit the Hieros Gamos Web site listed in Figure 12. What are the names, addresses, and telephone numbers of your two state senators and your local congressional representative? On what committees do they serve? Who is the chief justice of the Supreme Court, and what has been this justice's opinion on two recently decided cases? Who are the members of the president's cabinet? Then, visit two other Web sites listed in Figure 12. Write a paragraph about each Web site describing its content and features.

Shopping
CYBERMALL MANIA

Let Your Mouse Do Your Shopping

From groceries to clothing to computers, you can buy just about everything you need with just a few clicks of your mouse. Electronic retailers (e-tailers) are cashing in on cybershoppers' purchases. Books, computer software and hardware, and music are the hottest commodities.

Holiday sales account for a large portion of Internet purchases with more than nine million households doing some of their holiday shopping online. During this season, millions of shoppers visit Web sites such as BestBuy.com (Figure 13) daily. Macy's, Bloomingdale's and other e-tailers ship more than 300,000 boxes daily out of warehouses the size of 20 football fields and stocked with five million items.

The two categories of Internet shopping Web sites are those with physical counterparts, such as Eddie Bauer, Wal-Mart, and Tower Records, and those with only a Web presence, such as Amazon.com. Popular Web shopping sites are listed in Figure 14.

SHOPPING WEB SITES

Apparel	URL
Eddie Bauer Since 1920	eddiebauer.com
J.Crew	jcrew.com
Lands' End	landsend.com
Books and Music	**URL**
Amazon.com	amazon.com
Barnes & Noble.com	bn.com
Tower Records	towerrecords.com
Computers and Electronics	**URL**
Crutchfield.com	crutchfield.com
BestBuy.com	bestbuy.com
buy.com	buy.com
Miscellaneous	**URL**
1-800-flowers.com	1800flowers.com
drugstore.com	drugstore.com
Froogle	froogle.com
The Sharper Image	sharperimage.com
Walmart.com	walmart.com
For more information on shopping Web sites, visit scsite.com/dcf2e/ch2/web.	

FIGURE 13 Shopping for popular computer equipment online eliminates waiting in lines in stores.

FIGURE 14 Making online purchases can help ease the strain of driving to and fighting the crowds in local malls.

SHOPPING WEB EXERCISES

1 Visit two of the three apparel Web sites listed in the table in Figure 14 and select a specific pair of jeans and a shirt from each one. Create a table with these headings: e-tailer, style, fabric, features, price, tax, and shipping fee. Enter details about your selections in the table. Then, visit two of the books and music Web sites and search for a CD you would consider purchasing. Create another table with the names of the Web site, artist, and CD, as well as the price, tax, and shipping fee.

2 Visit two of the computers and electronics and two of the miscellaneous Web sites listed in Figure 14. Write a paragraph describing the features these Web sites offer compared with the same offerings from stores. In another paragraph, describe any disadvantages of shopping at these Web sites instead of actually seeing the merchandise. Then, describe their policies for returning unwanted merchandise and for handling complaints.

Weather, Sports, and News
WHAT'S NEWS?

Weather, Sports, and News Web Sites Score Big Hits

Rain or sun? Hot or cold? Weather is the leading online news item, with at least 10,000 Web sites devoted to this field. The Weather Channel (Figure 15) receives more than 10 million hits each day.

Baseball may be the national pastime, but sports aficionados yearn for everything from auto racing to cricket. The Internet has more than one million pages of multimedia sports news, entertainment, and merchandise.

The Internet has emerged as a major source for news, with one-third of Americans going online at least once a week and 15 percent going online daily for reports of major news events. These viewers, who tend to be under the age of 50 and college graduates, are attracted to the Internet's flashy headline format, immediacy, and in-depth reports. Popular weather, sports, and news Web sites are listed in Figure 16.

WEATHER, SPORTS, AND NEWS WEB SITES

Weather	URL
Infoplease Weather	infoplease.com/weather.html
Intellicast.com	intellicast.com
STORMFAX®	stormfax.com
The Weather Channel	weather.com
WX.com	wx.com

Sports	URL
CBS SportsLine.com	cbs.sportsline.com
ESPN.com	espn.com
NCAAsports.com	ncaasports.com
OFFICIAL WEBSITE OF THE OLYMPIC MOVEMENT	olympic.org
SIRC — A World of Sport Information	sirc.ca
Sporting News Radio	radio.sportingnews.com

News	URL
MSNBC	msnbc.com
NYPOST.COM	nypost.com
onlinenewspapers.com	onlinenewspapers.com
Privacy.org	privacy.org
SiliconValley.com	siliconvalley.com
Starting Page Best News Sites	startingpage.com/html/news.html
USATODAY.com	usatoday.com
washingtonpost.com	washingtonpost.com

For more information on weather, sports, and news Web sites, visit scsite.com/dcf2e/ch2/web.

FIGURE 15 Local, national, and international weather conditions and details about breaking weather stories are available on The Weather Channel Web pages.

FIGURE 16 Keep informed about the latest weather, sports, and news events with these Web sites.

WEATHER, SPORTS, AND NEWS EXERCISES

1 Visit two of the weather Web sites listed in the table in Figure 16. Do they contain the same local and five-day forecasts for your city? What similarities and differences do they have in coverage of a national weather story? Next, visit two of the sports Web sites in the table and write a paragraph describing the content these Web sites provide concerning your favorite sport.

2 Visit the onlinenewspapers.com and Starting Page Best News Sites Web sites listed in Figure 16 and select two newspapers from each site. Write a paragraph describing the top national news story featured in each of these four Web pages. Then, write another paragraph describing the top international news story displayed at each Web site. In the third paragraph, discuss which of the four Web sites is the most interesting in terms of story selection, photographs, and Web page design.

Learning
YEARN TO LEARN

Discover New Worlds Online

While you may believe your education ends when you finally graduate from college, learning is a lifelong process. For example, enhancing your culinary skills can be a rewarding endeavor. No matter if you are a gourmet chef or a weekend cook, you will be cooking in style with the help of online resources, including those listed in Figure 17.

LEARNING WEB SITES

Cooking	URL
Betty Crocker	bettycrocker.com
recipecenter.com	recipecenter.com
Internet	**URL**
Learn the Net	learnthenet.com
Search Engine Watch	searchenginewatch.com
Wiredguide™	wiredguide.com
Technology and Science	**URL**
HowStuffWorks	howstuffworks.com
ScienceMaster	sciencemaster.com
General Learning	**URL**
Bartleby.com: Great Books Online	bartleby.com
Blue Web'n	www.kn.pacbell.com/wired/bluewebn
MSN Encarta	encarta.msn.com

For more information on learning Web sites, visit scsite.com/dcf2e/ch2/web.

FIGURE 17 The information gleaned from these Web sites can help you learn about many aspects of our existence.

If you would rather sit in front of the computer than stand in front of the stove, you can increase your technological knowledge by visiting several Web sites with tutorials on building your own Web sites, the latest news about the Internet, and resources for visually impaired users.

Have you ever wondered how the Global Positioning System (GPS) works? Take a look at the ScienceMaster site to find details. You might be interested in finding out about how your car's catalytic converter reduces pollution or how the Electoral College functions. Marshall Brain's HowStuffWorks Web site (Figure 18) is filled with articles and animations.

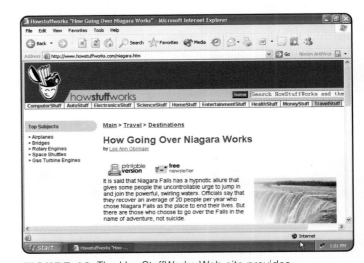

FIGURE 18 The HowStuffWorks Web site provides easy-to-understand information about technology and other facets of our lives.

LEARNING WEB EXERCISES

1 Visit one of the cooking Web sites listed in Figure 17 and find two recipes or cooking tips that you can use when preparing your next meal. Write a paragraph about each one, summarizing your discoveries. What are the advantages and disadvantages of accessing these Web sites on the new Web appliances that might someday be in your kitchen?

2 Using one of the technology and science Web sites and one of the other Web sites listed in Figure 17, search for information about communications and networks. Write a paragraph about your findings. Then, review the material in the general learning Web sites listed in Figure 18, and write a paragraph describing the content on each Web site that is pertinent to your major.

Science
E = MC²

Rocket Science on the Web

For some people, space exploration is a hobby. Building and launching model rockets allow these scientists to participate in exploring the great frontier of space. For others, space exploration is their life. Numerous Web sites, including those in Figure 19, provide in-depth information about the universe.

SCIENCE WEB SITES

Periodicals	URL
Astronomy.com	astronomy.com
Archaeology Magazine	archaeology.org
NewScientist.com	newscientist.com
OceanLink	oceanlink.island.net
Science Magazine	sciencemag.org
SCIENTIFIC AMERICAN.com	sciam.com

Resources	URL
National Science Foundation (NSF)	nsf.gov
Science.gov: FirstGov for Science	science.gov
SOFWeb	www.sofweb.vic.edu.au

Science Community	URL
American Scientist, The Magazine of Sigma Xi, The Scientific Research Society	amsci.org
Federation of American Scientists	fas.org
NASA	www.nasa.gov
Sigma Xi, The Scientific Research Society	sigmaxi.org

For more information on science Web sites, visit scsite.com/dcf2e/ch2/web.

FIGURE 19 Resources available on the Internet offer a wide range of subjects for enthusiasts who want to delve into familiar and unknown territories in the world of science.

The NASA Liftoff Web site contains information about rockets, the space shuttle, the International Space Station, space transportation, and communications. Other science resources explore space-related questions about astronomy, physics, the earth sciences, microgravity, and robotics.

Rockets and space are not the only areas to explore in the world of science. Where can you find the latest pictures taken with the Hubble Space Telescope? Do you know which cities experienced an earthquake today? Have you ever wondered what a 3-D model of the amino acid glutamine looks like? You can find the answer to these questions and many others through the Librarians' Index to the Internet (lii.org) shown in Figure 20.

FIGURE 20 Numerous science resources are organized clearly in the Librarians' Index to the Internet.

SCIENCE WEB EXERCISES

1 Visit the Liftoff to Space Exploration Web site listed in the table in Figure 19. View the links about spacecraft, the universe, or tracking satellites and spacecraft, and then write a summary of your findings.

2 Visit the Librarians' Index to the Internet shown in Figure 20. Click the Science, Computers, & Technology link and then click the Inventions topic. View the Web site for the Greatest Engineering Achievements of the Twentieth Century. Pick two achievements, read their history, and write a paragraph summarizing each of these accomplishments. Then, view two of the science Web sites listed in Figure 19 and write a paragraph about each of these Web sites describing the information each contains.

Environment
THE FATE OF THE ENVIRONMENT

Protecting the Planet's Ecosystem

From the rain forests of Africa to the marine life in the Pacific Ocean, the fragile ecosystem is under extreme stress. Many environmental groups have developed Internet sites, including those listed in Figure 21, in attempts to educate worldwide populations and to increase resource conservation.

ENVIRONMENT WEB SITES

	URL
Central African Regional Program for the Environment (CARPE)	carpe.umd.edu
Earthjustice	www.earthjustice.org
EarthTrends: The Environmental Information Portal	earthtrends.wri.org
Environmental Defense	edf.org
Environmental Sites on the Internet	www.ima.kth.se/im/envsite/envsite.htm
EPA AirData — Access to Air Pollution Data	epa.gov/air/data
Green Solitaire.org	greensolitaire.bizland.com
GreenNet	www.gn.apc.org
The Center for a New American Dream	newdream.org
The Virtual Library of Ecology & Biodiversity	conbio.org/vl
USGS Acid rain data and reports	bqs.usgs.gov/acidrain
UWM Environmental Health, Safety & Risk Management	www.uwm.edu/Dept/EHSRM/EHSLINKS

For more information on environment Web sites, visit scsite.com/dcf2e/ch2/web.

FIGURE 21 Environment Web sites provide vast resources for ecological data and action groups.

On an international scale, the Environmental Sites on the Internet Web page developed by the Royal Institute of Technology in Stockholm, Sweden, has been rated as one of the better ecological Web sites. Its comprehensive listing of environmental concerns range from aquatic ecology to wetlands.

The U.S. federal government has a number of Web sites devoted to specific environmental concerns. For example, the U.S. Environmental Protection Agency (EPA) provides pollution data, including ozone levels and air pollutants, for specific areas. Its AirData Web site, shown in Figure 22, displays air pollution emissions and monitoring data from the entire United States and is the world's most extensive collection of air pollution data.

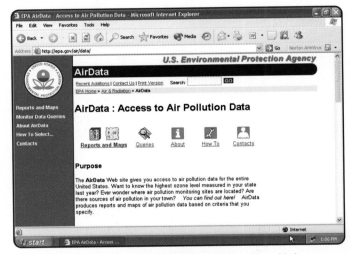

FIGURE 22 A visit to the EPA AirData Web site, with its extensive database, can assist you in checking your community's ozone and air pollutant levels.

ENVIRONMENT WEB EXERCISES

1 The Center for a New American Dream Web site encourages consumers to reduce the amount of junk mail sent to their homes. Using the table in Figure 21, visit the Web site and write a paragraph stating how many trees are leveled each year to provide paper for these mailings, how many garbage trucks are needed to haul this waste, and other statistics. Read the letters that you can use to eliminate your name from bulk mail lists. To whom would you mail these letters? How long does it take to stop these unsolicited letters?

2 Visit the EPA AirData Web site. What is the highest ozone level recorded in your state this past year? Where are the nearest air pollution monitoring Web sites, and what are their levels? Where are the nearest sources of air pollution? Read two reports about two different topics, such as acid rain and air quality, and summarize their findings. Include information on who sponsored the research, who conducted the studies, when the data was collected, and the impact of this pollution on the atmosphere, water, forests, and human health. Whom would you contact for further information regarding the data and studies?

Health
NO PAIN, ALL GAIN

Store Personal Health Records Online

More than 70 million consumers use the Internet yearly to search for health information, so using the Web to store personal medical data is a natural extension of the Internet's capabilities. Internet health services and portals are available online to store your personal health history, including prescriptions, lab test results, doctor visits, allergies, and immunizations. Web sites such as WellMed (Figure 23) are free to consumers.

In minutes, you can register with a health Web site by choosing a user name and password. Then, you create a record to enter your medical history. You also can store data for your emergency contacts, primary care physicians, specialists, blood type, cholesterol levels, blood pressure, and insurance plan. No matter where you are in the world, you and medical personnel can obtain records via the Internet or fax machine. Some popular online health database management systems are shown in Figure 24.

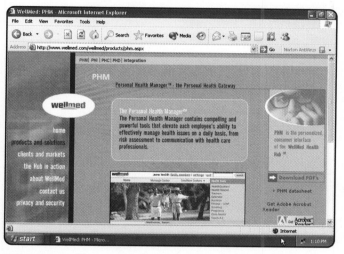

FIGURE 23 You can store health records for you and your family in the WellMed database.

HEALTH WEB SITES

	URL
AboutMyHealth	aboutmyhealth.com
Aetna InteliHealth	intelihealth.com
GlobalMedic	globalmedic.com
PersonalMD	personalmd.com
WebMD®	my.webmd.com/ my_health_record
WellMed	wellmed.com
For more information on health Web sites, visit scsite.com/dcf2e/ ch2/web.	

FIGURE 24 These Internet-based health database management systems Web sites allow you to organize your medical information and store it in an online database.

HEALTH WEB EXERCISES

1 Access one of the health Web sites listed in Figure 24. Register yourself or a family member, and then enter the full health history. Create an emergency medical card if the Web site provides the card option. Submit this record and emergency card to your instructor.

2 Visit three of the health Web sites listed in Figure 24. Describe the features of each. Which of the three is the most user-friendly? Why? Describe the privacy policies of these three Web sites. Submit your analysis of these Web sites to your instructor.

Research
SEARCH AND YE SHALL FIND

Info on the Web

A 2004 Web Usability survey conducted by the Nielsen Norman Group found that 88 percent of people log onto a computer and then use a search engine as their first action. Search engines require users to type words and phrases that characterize the information being sought. Yahoo! (Figure 25), Google, and AltaVista are some of the more popular search engines. The key to effective searching on the Web is composing search queries that narrow the search results and place the most relevant Web sites at the top of the results list.

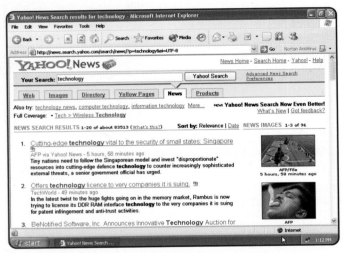

FIGURE 25 The Yahoo! News search results for the phrase, technology, lists more than 83,000 stories.

Subject directories are collections of related Web sites. Yahoo! and LookSmart have two of the more comprehensive subject directories on the Web. Their organized lists often are called trees because a few main categories, such as Entertainment, Computing, Lifestyle, and Work, branch out to more specific subtopics. Popular subject directories and search engines are listed in Figure 26.

RESEARCH WEB SITES

Search Engines	URL
AltaVista	altavista.com
Excite	excite.com
Fast Search & Transfer (FAST)	fastsearch.com
GO.com	go.com
Google	google.com
Northern Light®	northernlight.com
Yahoo!	yahoo.com
Subject Directories	**URL**
About	about.com
Librarians' Index to the Internet	lii.org
LookSmart	looksmart.com
The Internet Public Library	ipl.org
The WWW Virtual Library	vlib.org
Yahoo!	yahoo.com

For more information on research Web sites, visit scsite.com/dcf2e/ch2/web.

FIGURE 26 Web users can find information by using search engines and subject directories.

RESEARCH WEB EXERCISES

1. Use two of the search engines listed in Figure 26 to find three Web sites that review the latest digital cameras from Sony and Kodak. Make a table listing the search engines, Web site names, and the cameras' model numbers, suggested retail price, megapixels, memory, and features.

2. If money were no object, virtually everyone would have an exquisite car. On the other hand, drivers need a practical vehicle to drive around town daily. Use one of the subject directories listed in Figure 26 to research your dream car and another directory to research your practical car. Write a paragraph about each car describing the particular subject directory tree you used, the manufacturer's suggested retail price (MSRP) of the car, standard and optional equipment, engine size, miles per gallon, and safety features.

Careers
IN SEARCH OF THE PERFECT JOB

Web Helps Career Hunt

While your teachers give you valuable training to prepare you for a career, they rarely teach you how to begin that career. You can broaden your horizons by searching the Internet for career information and job openings.

First, examine some of the job search Web sites. These resources list thousands of openings in hundreds of fields, companies, and locations. For example, the Monster Web site, shown in Figure 27, allows you to choose a broad job area, narrow your search to specific fields within that area, and then search for specific salary ranges, locations, and job functions.

When a company contacts you for an interview, learn as much about it and the industry as possible before the interview. Many of the Web sites listed in Figure 28 include detailed company profiles and links to their corporate Web sites.

CAREER WEB SITES

Job Search	URL
BestJobsUSA.com	ultimatecareerfair.com
CareerBuilder	careerbuilder.com
CareerExchange.com	careerexchange.com
CareerNet	careernet.com
College Grad Job Hunter	collegegrad.com
EmploymentGuide.com	employmentguide.com
HotJobs.com	hotjobs.com
JobBankUSA.com	jobbankusa.com
JobWeb.com	www.jobweb.com
Monster	monster.com
MonsterTRAK	www.jobtrak.com
Spherion	spherion.com
USAJOBS	usajobs.opm.gov
VolunteerMatch	volunteermatch.org

Company/Industry Information	URL
Career ResourceCenter.com	www.resourcecenter.com
Forbes.com	www.forbes.com/2003/03/26/500sland.html
FORTUNE	fortune.com
Hoover's Online	hoovers.com
Occupational Outlook Handbook	stats.bls.gov/oco

For more information on career Web sites, visit scsite.com/dcf2e/ch2/web.

FIGURE 28 Career Web sites provide a variety of job openings and information about major companies worldwide.

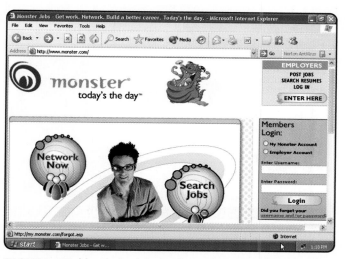

FIGURE 27 Monster's global online network connects companies with career-minded individuals.

CAREERS WEB EXERCISES

1 Use two of the job search Web sites listed in Figure 28 to find three companies with job openings in your field. Make a table listing the Web site name, position available, description, salary, location, desired education, and desired experience.

2 It is a good idea to acquire information before graduation about the industry in which you would like to work. Are you interested in the automotive manufacturing industry, the restaurant service industry, or the financial industry? Use two of the company/industry information Web sites listed in Figure 28 to research a particular career related to your major. Write a paragraph naming the Web sites and the specific information you found, such as the nature of the work, recommended training and qualifications, employment outlook, and earnings. Then, use two other Web sites to profile three companies with positions available in this field. Write a paragraph about each of these companies, describing the headquarters' location, sales and earnings for the previous year, total number of employees, working conditions, perks, and competitors.

Arts and Literature
FIND SOME CULTURE

Get Ready to Read, Paint, and Dance

Brush up your knowledge of Shakespeare, grab a canvas, and put on your dancing shoes. Visual arts and literature Web sites, including those in Figure 29, are about to sweep you off your cyberfeet.

ARTS AND LITERATURE WEB SITES

Arts	URL
Access Place Arts	accessplace.com/arts.htm
Art News – absolutearts.com	absolutearts.com
GalleryGuide.org	galleryguide.org
Louvre Museum	www.louvre.fr
Montreal Museum of Fine Arts	www.mmfa.qc.ca
The Children's Museum of Indianapolis	childrensmuseum.org
The Getty	getty.edu
The New York Times: Arts	nytimes.com/pages/arts/index.html
Virtual Library museums pages (VLmp)	vlmp.museophile.com

Literature	URL
Bartleby.com	bartleby.com
Bibliomania	bibliomania.com
Electronic Literature Directory	directory.wordcircuits.com
Fantastic Fiction Bibliographies	fantasticfiction.co.uk
Project Gutenberg	promo.net/pg
shakespeare.com	shakespeare.com
The Modern Library eBook List	randomhouse.com/modernlibrary/ebookslist.html

For more information on arts and literature Web sites, visit scsite.com/dcf2e/ch2/web.

FIGURE 29 Discover culture throughout the world by visiting these arts and literature Web sites.

The full text of hundreds of books is available online from the Bibliomania and Project Gutenberg Web sites. Shakespeare.com provides in-depth reviews and news of the world's most famous playwright and his works. The Bartleby.com Web site features biographies, definitions, quotations, dictionaries, and indexes.

When you are ready to absorb more culture, you can turn to various art Web sites. Many museums have images of their collections online. Among them are the Getty Museum in Los Angeles (Figure 30), the Montreal Museum of Fine Arts, and the Louvre Museum in Paris.

Access Place Arts and The New York Times Web sites focus on the arts and humanities and provide fascinating glimpses into the worlds of dance, music, performance, cinema, and other topics pertaining to creative expression.

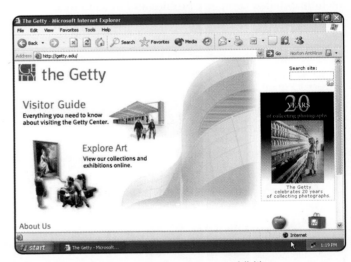

FIGURE 30 Permanent and temporary exhibitions, educational activities, and a bookstore are featured on the Getty Museum Web site.

ARTS AND LITERATURE WEB EXERCISES

1 Visit The Modern Library eBook List Web site listed in Figure 29 and view one book in the 20th CENTURY NOVELS, 19th CENTURY NOVELS, BRITISH LITERATURE, and HISTORY sections. Create a table with columns for the book name, author, cost, online store, local store, and description. Then, read the excerpt from each of the four books and write a paragraph describing which of these four books is the most interesting to you. What are the advantages and disadvantages of reading classic literature electronically?

2 Using the arts Web sites listed in Figure 29, search for three temporary exhibitions in galleries throughout the world. Describe the venues, the artists, and the works. What permanent collections are found in these museums? Some people shop for gifts in the museums' stores. View and describe three items for sale.

CHAPTER 3

Application Software

OBJECTIVES

After completing this chapter, you will be able to:

1. Identify the categories of application software
2. Explain how to work with application software
3. Identify the key features of widely used business programs
4. Identify the key features of widely used graphics and multimedia programs
5. Identify the key features of widely used home, personal, and educational programs
6. Identify the types of application software used in communications
7. Describe the function of several stand-alone utility programs
8. Describe the learning aids available for application software

CONTENTS

APPLICATION SOFTWARE
The Role of System Software
Working with Application Software

BUSINESS SOFTWARE
Word Processing Software
Developing a Document
Spreadsheet Software
Database Software
Presentation Graphics Software
Note Taking Software
Personal Information Manager Software
PDA Business Software
Software Suite
Project Management Software
Accounting Software
Enterprise Computing Software

GRAPHICS AND MULTIMEDIA SOFTWARE
Computer-Aided Design
Desktop Publishing Software (for the Professional)
Paint/Image Editing Software (for the Professional)
Video and Audio Editing Software (for the Professional)
Multimedia Authoring Software
Web Page Authoring Software

SOFTWARE FOR HOME, PERSONAL, AND EDUCATIONAL USE
Software Suite (for Personal Use)
Personal Finance Software
Legal Software
Tax Preparation Software
Desktop Publishing Software (for Personal Use)
Paint/Image Editing Software (for Personal Use)
Clip Art/Image Gallery
Video and Audio Editing Software (for Personal Use)
Home Design/Landscaping Software
Educational and Reference Software
Entertainment Software

APPLICATION SOFTWARE FOR COMMUNICATIONS

POPULAR STAND-ALONE UTILITY PROGRAMS

LEARNING AIDS AND SUPPORT TOOLS FOR APPLICATION SOFTWARE
Web-Based Training

CHAPTER SUMMARY

COMPANIES ON THE CUTTING EDGE
Adobe Systems
Microsoft

TECHNOLOGY TRAILBLAZERS
Dan Bricklin
Masayoshi Son

APPLICATION SOFTWARE

With the proper software, a computer is a valuable tool. Software allows users to create letters, reports, and other documents; design Web pages and diagrams; draw images; enhance audio and video clips; prepare taxes; play games; compose e-mail messages and instant messages; and much more. To accomplish these and many other tasks, users work with application software. **Application software** consists of programs designed to make users more productive and/or assist them with personal tasks. Application software has a variety of uses:

1. To make business activities more efficient
2. To assist with graphics and multimedia projects
3. To support home, personal, and educational tasks
4. To facilitate communications

The table in Figure 3-1 categorizes popular types of application software by their general use. Although many types of communications software exist, the ones listed in Figure 3-1 are application software oriented. Successful use of application software often requires the use of one or more of the utility programs identified in Figure 3-1. These utility programs typically are available stand-alone, that is, as separate programs that are not part of other application software.

Application software is available in a variety of forms: packaged, custom, open source, shareware, freeware, and public domain.

CATEGORIES OF APPLICATION SOFTWARE

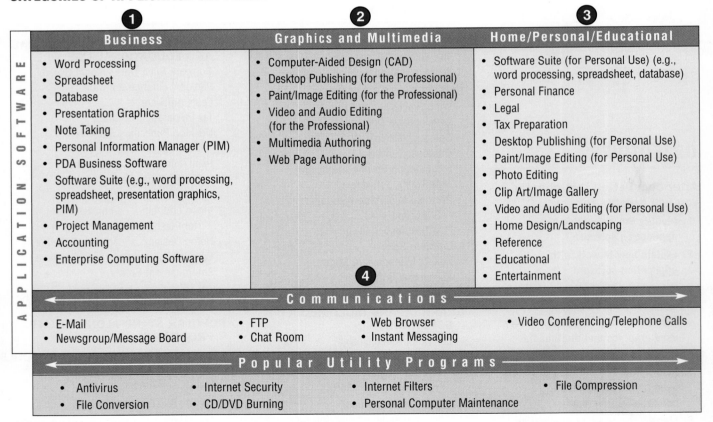

FIGURE 3-1 The four major categories of popular application software are outlined in this table. Communications software often is bundled with other application or system software. Also identified in the table are widely used stand-alone utility programs.

- **Packaged software** is mass-produced, copyrighted retail software that meets the needs of a wide variety of users, not just a single user or company. Word processing and spreadsheet software are examples of packaged software. Packaged software is available in retail stores or on the Web.
- **Custom software** performs functions specific to a business or industry. Sometimes a company cannot find packaged software that meets its unique requirements. In this case, the company may use programmers to develop tailor-made custom software.
- **Open source software** is software provided for use, modification, and redistribution. This software has no restrictions from the copyright holder regarding modification of the software's internal instructions and redistribution of the software. Open source software usually can be downloaded from the Web at no cost.
- **Shareware** is copyrighted software that is distributed at no cost for a trial period. To use a shareware program beyond that period, you send payment to the program developer.
- **Freeware** is copyrighted software provided at no cost to a user by an individual or a company that retains all rights to the software.
- **Public-domain software** has been donated for public use and has no copyright restrictions. Anyone can copy or distribute public-domain software to others at no cost.

Thousands of shareware, freeware, and public-domain programs are available on the Web for users to download. Examples include communications programs, graphics programs, and games.

The Role of System Software

System software serves as the interface between the user, the application software, and the computer's hardware (Figure 3-2). To use application software, such as a word processing program, your computer must be running system software — specifically, an operating system. Three popular personal computer operating systems are Windows XP, Linux, and Mac OS X.

Each time you start a computer, the operating system is loaded (copied) from the computer's hard disk into memory. Once the operating system is loaded, it coordinates all the activities of the computer. This includes starting application software and transferring data among input and output devices and memory. While the computer is running, the operating system remains in memory.

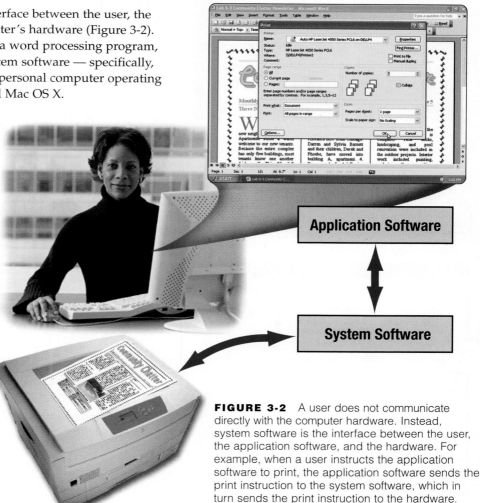

Application Software

System Software

FIGURE 3-2 A user does not communicate directly with the computer hardware. Instead, system software is the interface between the user, the application software, and the hardware. For example, when a user instructs the application software to print, the application software sends the print instruction to the system software, which in turn sends the print instruction to the hardware.

Working with Application Software

To use application software, you must instruct the operating system to start the program. The steps in Figure 3-3 illustrate how to start and interact with the Paint program. The following paragraphs explain the steps in Figure 3-3.

Personal computer operating systems often use the concept of a desktop to make the computer easier to use. The **desktop** is an on-screen work area that has a graphical user interface (read Looking Ahead 3-1 for a look at the next generation of user interfaces). Step 1 of Figure 3-3 shows icons, a button, and a pointer on the Windows XP desktop. An **icon** is a small image displayed on the screen that represents a program, a document, or some other object. A **button** is a graphical

FIGURE 3-3   HOW TO START AN APPLICATION

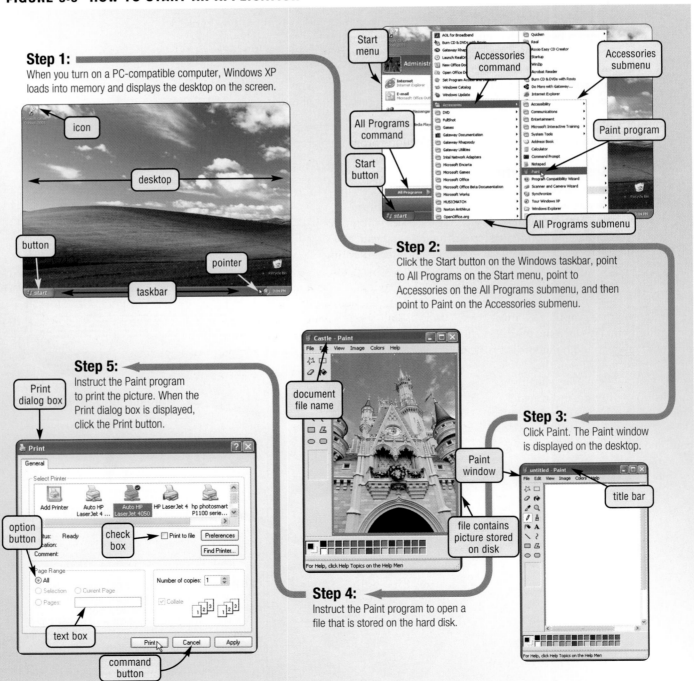

element that you activate to cause a specific action to take place. One way to activate a button is to click it. To **click** a button on the screen requires moving the pointer to the button and then pressing and releasing a button on the mouse (usually the left mouse button). The **pointer** is a small symbol displayed on the screen that moves as you move the mouse. Common pointer shapes are an I-beam ($\mathtt{I}$), a block arrow ($\,$), and a pointing hand ($\,$).

The Windows XP desktop contains a Start button on the lower-left corner of the taskbar. When you click the Start button, the Start menu is displayed on the desktop. A **menu** contains a list of commands from which you make selections. A **command** is an instruction that causes a program to perform a specific action.

The arrowhead symbol at the right edge of some menu commands indicates a submenu of additional commands is available. A submenu is a menu that is displayed when you point to a command on a previous menu. As illustrated in Step 2 of Figure 3-3, when you click the Start button and point to the All Programs command on the Start menu, the All Programs submenu is displayed. Pointing to the Accessories command on the All Programs submenu displays the Accessories submenu.

To start a program, you can click its program name on a menu or submenu. This action instructs the operating system to start the application, which means the program's instructions load from a storage medium (such as a hard disk) into memory. For example, when you click Paint on the Accessories submenu, Windows loads the Paint program instructions from the computer's hard disk into memory.

Once loaded into memory, the program is displayed in a window on the desktop (Step 3 of Figure 3-3). A **window** is a rectangular area of the screen that displays data and information. The top of a window has a **title bar**, which is a horizontal space that contains the window's name.

With the program loaded, you can create a new file or open an existing one. A **file** is a named collection of stored data, instructions, or information. A file can contain text, images, audio, and video. To distinguish among various files, each file has a file name. The title bar of the document window usually displays a document's file name. Step 4 of Figure 3-3 shows the contents of the file, Castle, displaying in the Paint window.

In some cases, when you instruct a program to perform an activity such as printing, the program displays a dialog box. A dialog box is a special window that provides information, presents available options, or requests a response. Dialog boxes, such as the one shown in Step 5 of Figure 3-3 often contain option buttons, text boxes, check boxes, and command buttons.

LOOKING AHEAD 3-1

User Interfaces of the Future

Most computers today use a graphical user interface. Next-generation user interfaces will be more natural and human-centric, meaning they will enable people to interact with a computer using human-like communication methods. Three developments in this area are gesture recognition, 3-D interfaces, and BrainGate.

With gesture recognition, the computer will detect human motions. Computers with this type of user interface will have the capability of recognizing sign language, reading lips, tracking facial movements, and following eye gazes.

Imagine rotating a window or object to read its flipside, switching from a desktop view to a panoramic view, or tacking sticky notes right on a Web screen. All these scenarios will be possible with the upcoming 3-D user interfaces.

The BrainGate neural interface may help quadriplegic people gain independence with everyday activities, such as maneuvering wheelchairs and typing. The system includes a tiny chip with 100 sensors implanted on the brain and external computers that convert brainwaves into output signals the person can control. For more information, visit scsite.com/dcf2e/ch3/looking and then click User Interfaces.

Test your knowledge of pages 100 through 103 in Quiz Yourself 3-1.

QUIZ YOURSELF 3-1

Instructions: Find the true statement below. Then, rewrite the remaining false statements so they are true.

1. Application software is used to make business activities more efficient; assist with graphics and multimedia projects; support home, personal, and educational tasks; and facilitate communications.

2. Public-domain software is mass-produced, copyrighted retail software that meets the needs of a wide variety of users, not just a single user or company.

3. To use system software, your computer must be running application software.

4. When an application is started, the program's instructions load from memory into a storage medium.

Quiz Yourself Online: To further check your knowledge of application software categories and working with application software, visit scsite.com/dcf2e/ch3/quiz and then click Objectives 1 – 2.

BUSINESS SOFTWARE

Business software is application software that assists people in becoming more effective and efficient while performing their daily business activities. Business software includes programs such as word processing, spreadsheet, database, presentation graphics, note taking, personal information manager software, PDA business software, software suites, project management, and accounting. Figure 3-4 lists popular programs for each of these categories.

POPULAR BUSINESS PROGRAMS

Application Software	Manufacturer	Program Name
Word Processing	Microsoft	Word
	Sun	StarOffice Writer
	Corel	WordPerfect
Spreadsheet	Microsoft	Excel
	Sun	StarOffice Calc
	Corel	Quattro Pro
Database	Microsoft	Access
	Sun	StarOffice Base
	Corel	Paradox
	Microsoft	Visual FoxPro
	Oracle	Oracle
	MySQL AB	MySQL
Presentation Graphics	Microsoft	PowerPoint
	Sun	StarOffice Impress
	Corel	Presentations
Note Taking	Microsoft	OneNote
	Agilix	GoBinder
	Corel	Grafigo
Personal Information Manager (PIM)	Microsoft	Outlook
	IBM	Lotus Organizer
	Palm	Desktop
PDA Business Software	CNetX	Pocket SlideShow
	Microsoft	Pocket Word
	Microsoft	Pocket Excel
	Microsoft	Pocket Outlook
	PalmOne	VersaMail
	Ultrasoft	Money Pocket Edition

Application Software	Manufacturer	Program Name
Software Suite (for the Professional)	Microsoft	Office
		Office for Mac
	Sun	StarOffice Office Suite
	Corel	WordPerfect Office
	IBM	Lotus SmartSuite
Project Management	Microsoft	Project
	Primavera	SureTrak Project Manager
Accounting	Intuit	QuickBooks
	Peachtree	Complete Accounting
Enterprise Computing Software	PeopleSoft	Enterprise Human Resources
	Best Software	MAS 500 Engineering
	MSC Software	MSC.SimManager Manufacturing
	Oracle	Oracle Manufacturing
	SmartPath	SmartPath MMS Sales
	SAP	mySAP Customer Relationship Management Distribution
	NetSuite	NetERP
	Apropos Technology	Apropos Enterprise Edition

FIGURE 3-4 Popular business software.

Word Processing Software

Word processing software, sometimes called a word processor, allows users to create and manipulate documents containing mostly text and sometimes graphics (Figure 3-5). Millions of people use word processing software every day to develop documents such as letters, memos, reports, fax cover sheets, mailing labels, newsletters, and Web pages.

Word processing software has many features to make documents look professional and visually appealing. Some of these features include the capability of changing the shape and size of characters, changing the color of characters, and organizing text in newspaper-style columns.

Most word processing software allows users to incorporate many types of graphical images in documents. One popular type of graphical image is clip art. **Clip art** is a collection of drawings, diagrams, maps, and photographs that you can insert in documents. In Figure 3-5, a user inserted a clip art image of a race car in the document.

All word processing software provides at least some basic capabilities to help users create and modify documents. Defining the size of the paper on which to print and specifying the margins are examples of some of these capabilities. If you type text that extends beyond the right page margin, the word processing software automatically positions text at the beginning of the next line. This feature, called wordwrap, allows users to type words in a paragraph continually without pressing the ENTER key at the end of each line. As you type more lines of text than can be displayed on the screen, the top portion of the document moves upward, or scrolls, off the screen.

A major advantage of using word processing software is that users easily can change what they have written. For example, a user can insert, delete, or rearrange words, sentences, paragraphs, or entire sections. Current word processing programs also have a feature that automatically corrects errors and makes word substitutions as users type text. For instance, when you type the abbreviation asap, the word processing software replaces the abbreviation with the phrase, as soon as possible.

WEB LINK 3-1

Word Processing Software

For more information, visit scsite.com/dcf2e/ch3/weblink and then click Word Processing Software.

document is displayed in window

clip art

printed document

FIGURE 3-5 Word processing software enables users to create professional and visually appealing documents.

Word processing software includes a spelling checker, which reviews the spelling of individual words, sections of a document, or the entire document. The spelling checker compares the words in the document with an electronic dictionary that is part of the word processing software.

Developing a Document

With application software, such as word processing, users create, edit, format, save, and print documents. When you **create** a document, you enter text or numbers, insert graphical images, and perform other tasks using an input device such as a keyboard, mouse, microphone, or digital pen. Most programs support voice recognition and handwriting recognition, where the computer distinguishes spoken words and handwritten text. If you are using Microsoft Office Word to design an announcement, for example, you are creating a document.

To **edit** a document means to make changes to its existing content. Common editing tasks include inserting, deleting, cutting, copying, and pasting. Inserting text involves adding text to a document. Deleting text means that you are removing text or other content.

Cutting is the process of removing a portion of the document and storing it in a temporary storage location, sometimes called a clipboard. Pasting is the process of transferring an item from a clipboard to a specific location in a document.

When users **format** a document, they change its appearance. Formatting is important because the overall look of a document significantly can affect its ability to communicate clearly. Examples of formatting tasks are changing the font, font size, or font style of text.

A **font** is a name assigned to a specific design of characters. Times New Roman and Arial are examples of fonts. **Font size** indicates the size of the characters in a particular font. Font size is gauged by a measurement system called points. A single point is about 1/72 of an inch in height. The text you are reading in this book is about 10 point. Thus, each character is about 5/36 (10/72) of an inch in height. A **font style** adds emphasis to a font. Bold, italic, and underline are examples of font styles. Figure 3-6 illustrates fonts, font sizes, and font styles.

During the process of creating, editing, and formatting a document, the computer holds it in memory. To keep the document for future use requires that you save it. When you **save** a document, the computer transfers the document from memory to a storage medium such as a floppy disk, USB flash drive, hard disk, or CD. Once saved, a document is stored permanently as a file on the storage medium.

When you **print** a document, the computer places the contents of the document on paper or some other medium. Instead of printing a document and physically distributing it, some users e-mail the document to others on a network such as the Internet.

FIGURE 3-6   The Times New Roman and Arial fonts are shown in two font sizes and a variety of font styles.

Spreadsheet Software

Spreadsheet software allows users to organize data in rows and columns and perform calculations on the data. These rows and columns collectively are called a **worksheet** (Figure 3-7). Most spreadsheet software has basic features to help users create, edit, and format worksheets. The following sections describe the features of most spreadsheet programs.

SPREADSHEET ORGANIZATION

Typically, a spreadsheet file is similar to a notebook with up to 255 related individual worksheets. Data is organized vertically in columns and horizontally in rows on each worksheet (Figure 3-7). Each worksheet typically has 256 columns and 65,536 rows. One or more letters identify each column, and a number identifies each row. Only a small fraction of these columns and rows are displayed on the screen at one time. Scrolling through the worksheet displays different parts of it on the screen.

A cell is the intersection of a column and row. The spreadsheet software identifies cells by the column and row in which they are located. For example, the intersection of column B and row 6 is referred to as cell B6. As shown in Figure 3-7, cell B6 contains the number, $40,398.00, which represents the store revenue for October.

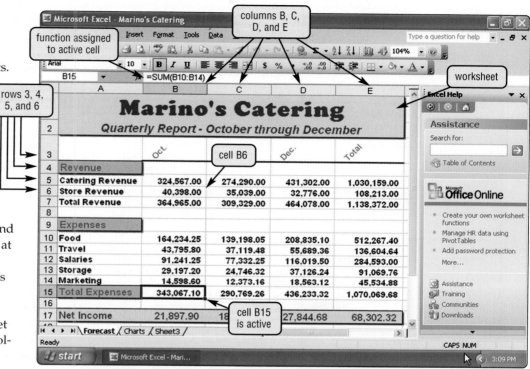

FIGURE 3-7   With spreadsheet software, you create worksheets that contain data arranged in rows and columns, and you can perform calculations on the data in the worksheet.

Cells may contain three types of data: labels, values, and formulas. The text, or label, entered in a cell identifies the worksheet data and helps organize the worksheet. Using descriptive labels, such as Total Revenue and Total Expenses, helps make a worksheet more meaningful.

CALCULATIONS   Many of the worksheet cells shown in Figure 3-7 contain a number, called a value, that can be used in a calculation. Other cells, however, contain formulas that generate values. A formula performs calculations on the data in the worksheet and displays the resulting value in a cell, usually the cell containing the formula. When creating a worksheet, you can enter your own formulas.

In many spreadsheet programs, you begin a formula with an equal sign, a plus sign, or a minus sign. Next, you enter the formula, separating cell references (e.g., B10) with operators. Common operators are + for addition, - for subtraction, * for multiplication, and / for division. In Figure 3-7, for example, cell B15 could contain the formula =B10+B11+B12+B13+B14, which would add together (sum) the contents of cells B10, B11, B12, B13, and B14. That is, this formula calculates the total expenses for October.

A function is a predefined formula that performs common calculations such as adding the values in a group of cells or generating a value such as the time or date. For example, instead of using the formula =B10+B11+B12+B13+B14 to calculate the total expenses for October, you could use the SUM function. This function requires you to identify the starting cell and the ending cell in a group to be summed, separating these two cell references with a colon. For example, the function =SUM(B10:B14) instructs the spreadsheet program to add all of the numbers in cells B10 through B14.

WEB LINK 3-2

Spreadsheet Software

For more information, visit scsite.com/dcf2e/ch3/weblink and then click Spreadsheet Software.

RECALCULATION One of the more powerful features of spreadsheet software is its capability of recalculating the rest of the worksheet when data in a worksheet changes. When you enter a new value to change data in a cell, any value affected by the change is updated automatically and instantaneously.

CHARTING Another standard feature of spreadsheet software is charting, which depicts the data in graphical form. A visual representation of data through charts often makes it easier for users to see at a glance the relationship among the numbers.

Three popular chart types are line charts, column charts, and pie charts. Figure 3-8 shows examples of these charts that were plotted from the data in Figure 3-7 on the previous page. A line chart shows a trend during a period of time, as indicated by a rising or falling line. A column chart, also called a bar chart, displays bars of various lengths to show the relationship of data. The bars can be horizontal, vertical, or stacked on top of one another. A pie chart, which has the shape of a round pie cut into slices, shows the relationship of parts to a whole.

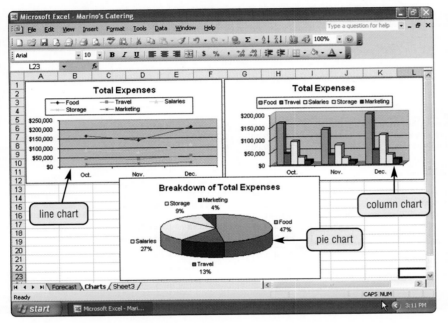

FIGURE 3-8 Three basic types of charts provided with spreadsheet software are line charts, column charts, and pie charts. The charts shown here were created from the data in the worksheet in Figure 3-7.

Database Software

A **database** is a collection of data organized in a manner that allows access, retrieval, and use of that data. In a manual database, you might record data on paper and store it in a filing cabinet. With a computerized database, such as the one shown in Figure 3-9, the computer stores the data in an electronic format on a storage medium such as a hard disk.

Database software is application software that allows users to create, access, and manage a database. Using database software, you can add, change, and delete data in a database; sort and retrieve data from the database; and create forms and reports using the data in the database.

With most popular personal computer database programs, a database consists of a collection of tables, organized in rows and columns. Each row, called a record, contains data about a given person, product, object, or event. Each column, called a field, contains a specific category of data within a record.

The Store database shown in Figure 3-9 consists of two tables: a Product table and a Supplier table. The Product table contains 10 records (rows), each storing data about one item. The product data is grouped into six fields (columns): Product ID, Description,

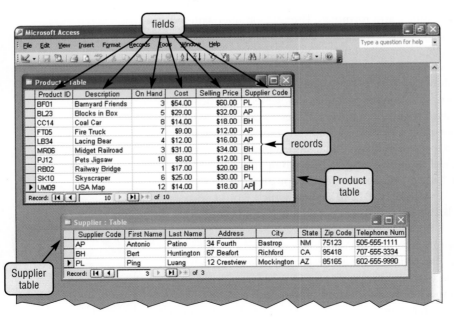

FIGURE 3-9 This database contains two tables: one for the products and one for the suppliers. The Product table has 10 records and 6 fields; the Supplier table has 3 records and 8 fields.

On Hand, Cost, Selling Price, and Supplier Code. The On Hand field, for instance, contains the quantity on hand. The Product and Supplier tables relate to one another through a common field, Supplier Code.

Users run queries to retrieve data. A query is a request for specific data from the database. For example, a query might request a list of customers that have a balance due. Database software can take the results of a query and present it in a window on the screen or send it to the printer.

Presentation Graphics Software

Presentation graphics software is application software that allows users to create visual aids for presentations to communicate ideas, messages, and other information to a group. The presentations can be viewed as slides, sometimes called a slide show, that are displayed on a large monitor or on a projection screen (Figure 3-10).

Presentation graphics software typically provides a variety of predefined presentation formats that define complementary colors for backgrounds, text, and graphical accents on the slides. This software also provides a variety of layouts for each individual slide such as a title slide, a two-column slide, and a slide with clip art, a chart, a table, or animation. In addition, you can enhance any text, charts, and graphical images on a slide with 3-D and other special effects such as shading, shadows, and textures.

When building a presentation, users can set the slide timing so the presentation automatically displays the next slide after a preset delay. Presentation graphics software allows you to apply special effects to the transition between each slide. One slide, for example, might fade away slowly as the next slide is displayed.

Presentation graphics software typically includes a clip gallery that provides images, pictures, video clips, and audio clips to enhance multimedia presentations. Users also can insert their own video, music, and audio commentary in a presentation. Presentation graphics software incorporates features such as checking spelling, formatting, recognizing voice input, research, ink input, and converting an existing slide show into a format for the World Wide Web.

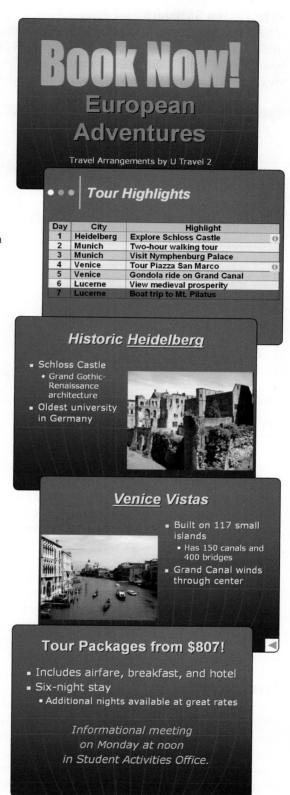

FIGURE 3-10 This presentation created with presentation graphics software consists of five slides.

WEB LINK 3-3

Presentation Graphics Software

For more information, visit scsite.com/dcf2e/ch3/weblink and then click Presentation Graphics Software.

Note Taking Software

Note taking software is application software that enables users to enter typed text, handwritten comments, drawings, or sketches anywhere on a page and then save the page as part of a notebook (Figure 3-11). Users also can include audio recordings as part of their notes. Once the notes are captured (entered and saved), users easily can organize them, reuse them, and share them.

On a desktop or notebook computer, users enter notes primarily via the keyboard or microphone. On a Tablet PC, however, the primary input device is a digital pen. Users find note taking software convenient during meetings, class lectures, conferences, in libraries, and other settings that previously required a pencil and tablet of paper for recording thoughts and discussions.

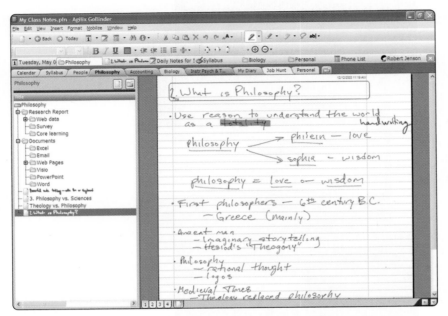

FIGURE 3-11 With note taking software, students and other mobile users can handwrite notes, draw sketches, and type text.

Personal Information Manager Software

A **personal information manager (PIM)** is application software that includes an appointment calendar, address book, notepad, and other features to help users organize personal information. The appointment calendar allows you to schedule activities for a particular day and time. With the address book, you can enter and maintain names, addresses, telephone numbers, and e-mail addresses of customers, coworkers, family members, and friends. You can use the notepad to record ideas, reminders, and other important information.

Most PDAs and many smart phones today include, among many other features, PIM functionality. Using a PDA, you can synchronize, or coordinate, information so that both the PDA or smart phone and the computer have the latest version of the information.

PDA Business Software

In addition to PIM software, a huge variety of business software is available for PDAs. Although some PDAs have software built in, most have the capability of accessing software on miniature storage media such as memory cards. Business software for PDAs allows users to create documents and worksheets, manage databases and lists, create slide shows, take notes, manage budgets and finances, view and edit photographs, read electronic books, plan travel routes, compose and read e-mail messages, send instant messages, and browse the Web.

Software Suite

A **software suite** is a collection of individual programs sold as a single package. Business software suites typically include, at a minimum, the following programs: word processing, spreadsheet, e-mail, and presentation graphics. Two of the more widely used software suites are Microsoft Office and Sun StarOffice.

Software suites offer two major advantages: lower cost and ease of use. Buying a collection of programs in a software suite usually costs significantly less than purchasing them individually. Software suites provide ease of use because the programs within a software suite normally use a similar interface and share features such as clip art and a spelling checker.

Project Management Software

Project management software allows a user to plan, schedule, track, and analyze the events, resources, and costs of a project (Figure 3-12). Project management software helps users manage project variables, allowing them to complete a project on time and within budget. An engineer, for example, might use project management software to manage new product development to schedule product screening, market evaluation, technical product evaluation, and manufacturing processes.

Accounting Software

Accounting software helps companies record and report their financial transactions (Figure 3-13). With accounting software, business users perform accounting activities related to the general ledger, accounts receivable, accounts payable, purchasing, invoicing, and payroll functions. Accounting software also enables users to write and print checks, track checking account activity, and update and reconcile balances on demand.

Newer accounting software supports online credit checks, billing, direct deposit, and payroll services. Some accounting software offers more complex features such as job costing and estimating, time tracking, multiple company reporting, foreign currency reporting, and forecasting the amount of raw materials needed for products. The cost of accounting software for small businesses ranges from less than one hundred to several thousand dollars. Accounting software for large businesses can cost several hundred thousand dollars.

Enterprise Computing Software

A large organization, commonly referred to as an enterprise, requires special computing solutions because of its size and large geographical distribution. A typical enterprise consists of a wide variety of departments, centers, and divisions — collectively known as functional units. Nearly every enterprise has the following functional units: human resources, accounting and finance, engineering or product development, manufacturing, marketing, sales, distribution, customer service, and information technology. Each of these functional units has specialized software requirements.

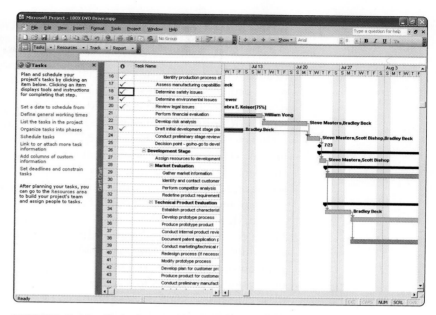

FIGURE 3-12 Project management software allows users to track, control, and manage the events, resources, and costs of a project.

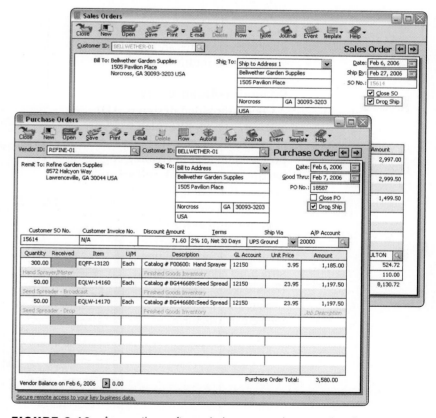

FIGURE 3-13 Accounting software helps companies record and report their financial transactions.

GRAPHICS AND MULTIMEDIA SOFTWARE

In addition to business software, many people work with software designed specifically for their field of work. Power users such as engineers, architects, desktop publishers, and graphic artists often use sophisticated software that allows them to work with graphics and multimedia. This software includes computer-aided design, desktop publishing, paint/image editing, video and audio editing, multimedia authoring, and Web page authoring. Figure 3-14 lists the more popular programs for each of these categories. Some of these programs incorporate user-friendly interfaces, or scaled-down versions, making it possible for the home and small business users to create documents using these programs. The following sections discuss the features and functions of graphics and multimedia software.

Computer-Aided Design

Computer-aided design (CAD) software is a sophisticated type of application software that assists a professional user in creating engineering, architectural, and scientific designs. For example, engineers create design plans for airplanes and security systems. Architects design building structures and floor plans (Figure 3-15). Scientists design drawings of molecular structures.

POPULAR GRAPHICS AND MULTIMEDIA SOFTWARE

Application Software	Manufacturer	Program Name
Computer-Aided Design (CAD)	Autodesk	AutoCAD
	Quality Plans	Chief Architect
	Microsoft	Visio
Desktop Publishing (for the Professional)	Adobe	InDesign
	Corel	Ventura
	Quark	QuarkXPress
Paint/Image Editing (for the Professional)	Adobe	Illustrator
		Photoshop
	Corel	Painter
	Macromedia	FreeHand
Video and Audio Editing (for the Professional)	Adobe	Audition
		Encore DVD
		Premiere Pro
	Cakewalk	SONAR
	Macromedia	SoundEdit
	Sony	ACID Pro
	Ulead	MediaStudio Pro
		DVD Workshop
Multimedia Authoring	SumTotal Systems	ToolBook Instructor
	Macromedia	Authorware
		Director
Web Page Authoring	Adobe	GoLive
	Lotus	FastSite
	Macromedia	Dreamweaver
		Fireworks
		Flash
	Microsoft	FrontPage

FIGURE 3-14 Popular graphics and multimedia programs — for the professional.

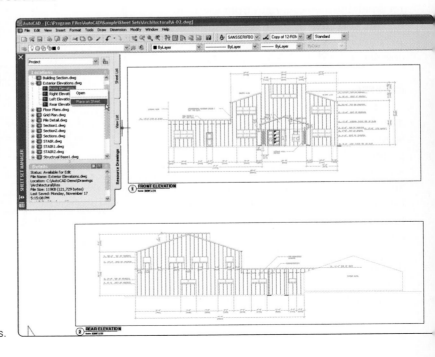

FIGURE 3-15 CAD software is sophisticated software that assists engineers, architects, and scientists in creating designs.

Desktop Publishing Software (for the Professional)

Desktop publishing (DTP) software enables professional designers to create sophisticated documents that contain text, graphics, and many colors. Professional DTP software is ideal for the production of high-quality color documents such as textbooks, corporate newsletters, marketing literature (Figure 3-16), product catalogs, and annual reports. Today's DTP software also allows designers to convert a color document into a format for use on the World Wide Web.

FAQ 3-2

Why am I not able to view some files on the Web that contain company brochures?

In many cases, you need Adobe Acrobat Reader software because some companies save documents on the Web, such as brochures, using the Adobe PDF format. To view and print a PDF file, download the free Adobe Acrobat Reader software from Adobe's Web site.

For more information, visit scsite.com/dcf2e/ch3/faq and then click Adobe Acrobat Reader.

Paint/Image Editing Software (for the Professional)

Graphic artists, multimedia professionals, technical illustrators, and desktop publishers use paint software and image editing software to create and modify graphical images such as those used in DTP documents and Web pages. **Paint software**, also called illustration software, allows users to draw pictures, shapes, and other graphical images with various on-screen tools such as a pen, brush, eyedropper, and paint bucket. **Image editing software** provides the capabilities of paint software and also includes the capability to enhance and modify existing pictures and images (Figure 3-17). Modifications can include adjusting or enhancing image colors, and adding special effects such as shadows and glows.

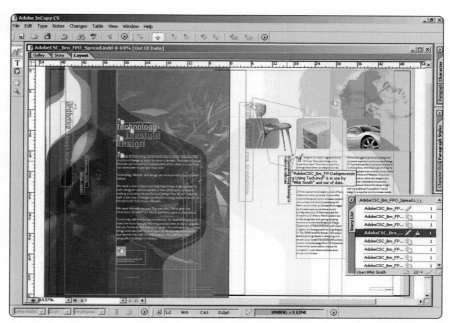

FIGURE 3-16 Professional designers and graphic artists use DTP software to produce sophisticated publications such as marketing literature.

FIGURE 3-17 With image editing software, artists create and modify any type of graphical image.

Video and Audio Editing Software (for the Professional)

Video editing software (Figure 3-18) allows professionals to modify a segment of a video, called a clip. For example, users can reduce the length of a video clip, reorder a series of clips, or add special effects such as words that move horizontally across the screen. Video editing software typically includes audio editing capabilities. **Audio editing software** lets users modify audio clips and produce studio-quality soundtracks. Read At Issue 3-1 for a related discussion.

AT ISSUE 3-1

What Should Be Done to Prevent Music and Video File Sharing?

It is illegal to use networks to share copyrighted music or video files. Despite this, a number of file-sharing networks exist, and an estimated 60 million Americans use file-sharing software to locate and download copyrighted music and videos without paying. Much of this illegal activity takes place at colleges and universities, where high-speed network connections make file sharing almost instantaneous. To combat illegal file sharing, some schools have turned to new programs that intentionally slow the performance of file-sharing software. The Recording Industry Association of America (RIAA) has gone even further, filing law suits against people suspected of downloading copyrighted music. Individuals found guilty can be liable for fines up to $150,000 for every stolen song. The RIAA maintains that downloading copyrighted music steals from both the recording artist and the recording industry. Yet, many people feel that the response to sharing copyrighted music and video files is excessive. They argue that copying music from the radio to an audio cassette is legal and insist that downloading copyrighted music is no different. Besides, someone who downloads a copyrighted song later may be inspired to purchase an artist's CD or attend a concert. Should it be illegal to share copyrighted music or video files over a network? Why or why not? Are slowing file-sharing software and filing thousand-dollar lawsuits unwarranted reactions to what some people consider a victimless violation? Why?

FIGURE 3-18 With video editing software, users modify video images.

Multimedia Authoring Software

Multimedia authoring software allows users to combine text, graphics, audio, video, and animation into an interactive application (Figure 3-19). With this software, users control the placement of text and images and the duration of sounds, video, and animation. Once created, multimedia presentations often take the form of interactive computer-based presentations or Web-based presentations designed to facilitate learning, demonstrate product functionality, and elicit direct-user participation. Training centers, educational institutions, and online magazine publishers all use multimedia authoring software to develop interactive applications. These applications may be available on a CD or DVD, over a local area network, or via the Internet.

Web Page Authoring Software

Web page authoring software helps users of all skill levels create Web pages that include graphical images, video, audio, animation, and other special effects with interactive content. In addition, many Web page authoring programs allow users to organize, manage, and maintain Web sites.

Application software, such as Word and Excel, often includes Web page authoring features. This allows home users to create basic Web pages using application software they already own. For more sophisticated Web pages, users work with Web page authoring software.

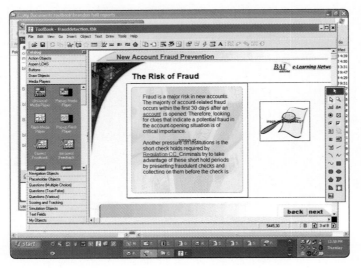

FIGURE 3-19 Multimedia authoring software allows you to create dynamic presentations that include text, graphics, video, sound, and animation.

Test your knowledge of pages 104 through 114 in Quiz Yourself 3-2.

QUIZ YOURSELF 3-2

Instructions: Find the true statement below. Then, rewrite the remaining false statements so they are true.

1. Enterprise computing software provides the capabilities of paint software and also includes the capability to modify existing images.

2. Millions of people use spreadsheet software every day to develop documents such as letters, memos, reports, fax cover sheets, mailing labels, newsletters, and Web pages.

3. Professional accounting software is ideal for the production of high-quality color documents such as textbooks, corporate newsletters, marketing literature, product catalogs, and annual reports.

4. Spreadsheet software is application software that allows users to create visual aids for presentations to communicate ideas, messages, and other information to a group.

5. Two of the more widely used CAD programs are Microsoft Office and Sun StarOffice.

6. Web page authoring software helps users of all skill levels create Web pages.

Quiz Yourself Online: To further check your knowledge of types and features of business programs and graphics/multimedia programs, visit scsite.com/dcf2e/ch3/quiz and then click Objectives 3 – 4.

SOFTWARE FOR HOME, PERSONAL, AND EDUCATIONAL USE

A large amount of application software is designed specifically for home, personal, and educational use. Most of the programs in this category are relatively inexpensive, often priced less than $100. Figure 3-20 lists popular programs for many of these categories. The following sections discuss the features and functions of this application software.

POPULAR SOFTWARE PROGRAMS FOR HOME/PERSONAL/EDUCATIONAL USE

Application Software	Manufacturer	Program Name	Application Software	Manufacturer	Program Name
Software Suite (for Personal Use)	Microsoft	Works	Photo Editing	Adobe	Photoshop Elements
	Sun	OpenOffice.org		Corel	Photobook
Personal Finance	Intuit	Quicken		Dell	Image Expert
	Microsoft	Money		Microsoft	Picture It! Photo Picture Manager
Legal	Broderbund	Family Lawyer		Roxio	PhotoSuite
	Cosmi	Perfect Attorney		Ulead	PhotoImpact Photo Express
	H&R Block Kiplinger	Home & Business Attorney WILLPower	Clip Art/Image Gallery	Broderbund	ClickArt
	Nolo	Quicken Legal Business Quicken WillMaker		Nova Development	Art Explosion
Tax Preparation	2nd Story Software	TaxACT	Video and Audio Editing (for Personal Use)	Microsoft	Movie Maker
				Pinnacle Systems	Studio Moviebox
	H&R Block Kiplinger	TaxCut		Roxio	VideoWave
	Intuit	Quicken TurboTax		Ulead	VideoStudio
Desktop Publishing (for Personal Use)	Broderbund	The Print Shop PrintMaster	Home Design/ Landscaping	ART	Home Designer Suite
				Broderbund	3D Home Architect Design Suite
	Microsoft	Publisher		Quality Plans	Home Designer Suite
Paint/Image Editing (for Personal Use)	Corel	CorelDRAW		ValuSoft	Custom LandDesigner
	Jasc	Paint Shop Pro	Reference	American Heritage	Talking Dictionary Classic
	Sun	StarOffice Draw		Microsoft	Encarta Streets & Trips
	The GIMP Team (open source software)	The Gimp		Rand McNally	StreetFinder TripMaker

FIGURE 3-20 Many popular programs are available for home, personal, and educational use.

Software Suite (for Personal Use)

A software suite (for personal use) combines application software such as word processing, spreadsheet, database, and other programs in a single, easy-to-use package. Many computer vendors install a software suite for personal use, such as Microsoft Works, on new computers sold to home users.

As mentioned earlier, the programs in a software suite use a similar interface and share some common features. For many home users, the capabilities of software suites for personal use more than meet their needs.

Personal Finance Software

Personal finance software is a simplified accounting program that helps home users and small office/home office users balance their checkbooks, pay bills, track personal income and expenses, track investments, and evaluate financial plans (Figure 3-21).

Most personal finance software includes financial planning features, such as analyzing home and personal loans, preparing income taxes, and managing retirement savings. Other features include managing home inventory and setting up budgets. Most of these programs also offer a variety of online services, such as online banking, which require access to the Internet.

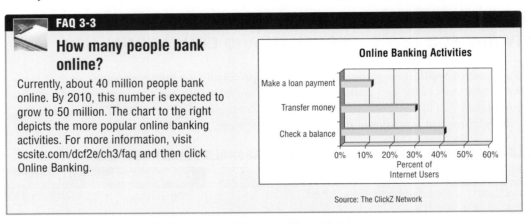

FAQ 3-3

How many people bank online?

Currently, about 40 million people bank online. By 2010, this number is expected to grow to 50 million. The chart to the right depicts the more popular online banking activities. For more information, visit scsite.com/dcf2e/ch3/faq and then click Online Banking.

Online Banking Activities

Source: The ClickZ Network

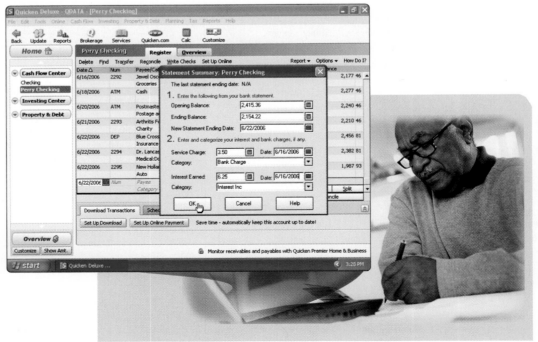

WEB LINK 3-5

Personal Finance Software

For more information, visit scsite.com/dcf2e/ch3/weblink and then click Personal Finance Software.

FIGURE 3-21   Personal finance software assists home users with balancing their checkbooks and paying bills.

Legal Software

Legal software assists in the preparation of legal documents and provides legal information to individuals, families, and small businesses (Figure 3-22). Legal software provides standard contracts and documents associated with buying, selling, and renting property; estate planning; marriage and divorce; and preparing a will or living trust. By answering a series of questions or completing a form, the legal software tailors the legal document to specific needs.

FIGURE 3-22
Legal software provides legal information to individuals, families, and small businesses and assists in record keeping and the preparation of legal documents.

Tax Preparation Software

Tax preparation software can guide individuals, families, or small businesses through the process of filing federal taxes (Figure 3-23). These programs forecast tax liability and offer money-saving tax tips, designed to lower your tax bill. After you answer a series of questions and complete basic forms, the software creates and analyzes your tax forms to search for missed potential errors and deduction opportunities.

Once the forms are complete, you can print any necessary paperwork, and then they are ready for filing. Some tax preparation programs also allow you to file your tax forms electronically.

FIGURE 3-23
Tax preparation software guides individuals, families, or small businesses through the process of filing federal taxes.

Desktop Publishing Software (for Personal Use)

Personal DTP software (Figure 3-24) helps home and small business users create newsletters, brochures, advertisements, postcards, greeting cards, letterhead, business cards, banners, calendars, logos, and Web pages.

Personal DTP programs provide hundreds of thousands of graphical images. You also can import (bring in) your own digital photographs into the documents. These programs typically guide you through the development of a document by asking a series of questions. Then, you can print a finished publication on a color printer or post it on the Web.

Many personal DTP programs also include paint/image editing software and photo editing software.

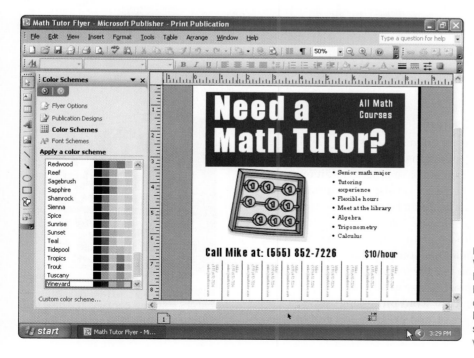

FIGURE 3-24
With Publisher, home and small business users can create professional looking publications such as this flyer with tear-offs.

WEB LINK 3-6

Personal DTP Software

For more information, visit scsite.com/dcf2e/ch3/weblink and then click Personal DTP Software.

Paint/Image Editing Software (for Personal Use)

Personal paint/image editing software provides an easy-to-use interface; includes various simplified tools that allow you to draw pictures, shapes, and other images; and provides the capability of modifying existing graphics and photos. These products also include many templates to assist you in adding an image to documents such as greeting cards (Figure 3-25), banners, calendars, signs, labels, business cards, and letterhead.

One popular type of image editing software, called **photo editing software**, allows users to edit digital photographs by removing red-eye, erasing blemishes, restoring aged photos, adding special effects, or creating electronic photo albums. When you purchase a digital camera, it usually includes photo editing software. You can print edited photographs on labels, calendars, business cards, and banners; or post them on a Web page.

FAQ 3-4

How do pictures get in the computer from a digital camera?

Most digital cameras save pictures on miniature storage media, such as a memory card. By inserting the memory card in a card reader/writer in or attached to the computer, users can access images the same way they access files on a disk drive. With some cameras, pictures also can transfer along a cable that connects the camera to the computer. For more information, visit scsite.com/dcf2e/ch3/faq and then click Digital Imaging.

FIGURE 3-25 Home users can purchase affordable paint/image editing programs that enable them to include personal pictures and graphics in many different types of documents.

Clip Art/Image Gallery

Application software often includes a **clip art/image gallery**, which is a collection of clip art and photographs. Some applications have links to additional clips available on the Web. You also can purchase clip art/image gallery software that contains hundreds of thousands of images (Figure 3-26).

In addition to clip art, many clip art/image galleries provide fonts, animations, sounds, video clips, and audio clips. You can use the images, fonts, and other items from the clip art/image gallery in all types of documents, including word processing, desktop publishing, spreadsheet, and presentation graphics.

FIGURE 3-26 Clip art/image gallery software contains hundreds of thousands of images.

Video and Audio Editing Software (for Personal Use)

Many home users work with easy-to-use video and audio editing software, which is much simpler to use than its professional counterpart, for small-scale movie making projects (Figure 3-27). With these programs, home users can edit home movies, add music or other sounds to the video, and share their movies on the Web. Some operating systems include video editing and audio editing software.

Home Design/Landscaping Software

Homeowners or potential homeowners can use **home design/landscaping software** to assist them with the design, remodeling, or improvement of a home, deck, or landscape (Figure 3-28). This software includes hundreds of predrawn plans that you can customize to meet your needs. Once designed, many home design/landscaping programs print a materials list outlining costs and quantities for the entire project.

Educational and Reference Software

Educational software is software that teaches a particular skill. Educational software exists for just about any subject, from learning how to type to learning how to cook. Preschool to high school learners use educational software to assist them with subjects such as reading and math or to prepare them for class or college entry exams. Educational software often includes games and other content to make the learning experience more fun.

Many educational programs use a computer-based training approach. **Computer-based training** (CBT) is a type of education in which students learn by using and completing exercises with instructional software. CBT typically consists of self-directed, self-paced instruction about a topic. The military and airlines use CBT simulations to train pilots to fly in various conditions and environments. Schools use CBT to teach students math, language, and software skills.

Reference software provides valuable and thorough information for all individuals (Figure 3-29). Popular reference software includes encyclopedias, dictionaries, health/medical guides, and travel directories.

FIGURE 3-27 Operating systems, such as Windows XP, include video and audio editing software so home users can create their own movies.

FIGURE 3-28 Home design/landscaping software can help you design or remodel a home, deck, or landscape.

FIGURE 3-29 This reference software shows text you can read about butterflies and moths and includes a variety of pictures, videos, and links to the Web.

Entertainment Software

Entertainment software for personal computers includes interactive games, videos, and other programs designed to support a hobby or provide amusement and enjoyment. For example, you might use entertainment software to play games (Figure 3-30), make a family tree, listen to music, or fly an aircraft.

WEB LINK 3-7

Entertainment Software

For more information, visit scsite.com/dcf2e/ch3/weblink and then click Entertainment Software.

FIGURE 3-30 Entertainment software can provide hours of recreation.

APPLICATION SOFTWARE FOR COMMUNICATIONS

One of the main reasons people use computers is to communicate and share information with others. Some communications software is considered system software because it works with hardware and transmission media. Other communications software performs specific tasks for users, and thus, is considered application software. Chapter 2 presented a variety of application software for communications, which are summarized in the table in Figure 3-31. Read At Issue 3-2 for a related discussion. Read Looking Ahead 3-2 for a look at the next generation of Web access.

AT ISSUE 3-2

Should Companies Monitor Employees' E-Mail and Web Browsing?

According to one survey, more than 75 percent of Fortune 500 companies routinely monitor employees' computer use. Employers can use software to see what is on the screen or stored on hard disks, scrutinize e-mail and Web browsing habits, and even supervise keyboard activity. About one company in four has fired an employee based on its discoveries. Companies monitor computer use to improve productivity, increase security, reduce misconduct, and control liability risks. Few laws regulate employee monitoring, and courts have given employers a great deal of leeway in watching work on company-owned computers. In one case, an employee's termination for using her office e-mail system to complain about her boss was upheld, even though the company allowed e-mail use for personal communications. The court decreed that the employee's messages were inappropriate for workplace communications. Many employees believe that monitoring software violates their privacy rights. To reduce employee anxiety about monitoring computer use, one expert suggests that companies publish written policies and accept employee feedback, provide clear descriptions of acceptable and unacceptable behavior, respect employee needs and time, and establish a balance between security and privacy. Should companies monitor how their employees use computers at work? Why or why not? How can a company balance workplace security and productivity with employee privacy? If a company monitors computer use, what guidelines should be followed to maintain worker morale? Why?

APPLICATION SOFTWARE FOR COMMUNICATIONS

E-Mail
- Messages and files sent via a network such as the Internet
- Requires an e-mail program
  - Integrated in many software suites and operating systems
  - Available free at portals on the Web
  - Included with paid Internet access service
  - Can be purchased separately from retailers

FTP
- Method of uploading and downloading files with other computers on the Internet
- Download may require an FTP program; upload usually requires an FTP program
  - Integrated in some operating systems
  - Available for download on the Web for a small fee
  - Can be purchased separately from retailers

Web Browser
- Allows users to access and view Web pages on the Internet
- Requires a Web browser program
  - Integrated in some operating systems
  - Available for download on the Web free or for a fee
  - Included with paid Internet access service

Video Conferencing/Telephone Calls
- Meeting/conversation between geographically separated people who use a network such as the Internet to transmit video/audio
- Requires a microphone, speakers, and sometimes a video camera attached to your computer
- Requires video conferencing software

Newsgroup/Message Board
- Online area where users have written discussions
- Newsgroup may require a newsreader program
  - Integrated in some operating systems, e-mail programs, and Web browsers
  - Available for download on the Web, usually at no cost
  - Included with some paid Internet access services
  - Built into some Web sites

Chat Room
- Real-time, online typed conversation
- Requires chat client software
  - Integrated in some operating systems, e-mail programs, and Web browsers
  - Available for download on the Web, usually at no cost
  - Included with some paid Internet access services
  - Built into some Web sites

Instant Messaging
- Real-time exchange of messages, files, audio, and/or video with another online user
- Requires instant messenger software
  - Integrated in some operating systems
  - Available for download on the Web, usually at no cost
  - Included with some paid Internet access services

FIGURE 3-31   A summary of application software for home and business communications.

LOOKING AHEAD 3-2

Driving Down the Web Highway

Analysts predict you will access the Internet from practically everywhere: home, office, airport, grocery store, and the local coffee shop. Why not from your car?

As it sits in your garage, your car's computer could connect to your home computer and then relay information about fluid levels and the amount of gas in the tank. It could notify you when the oil needs to be changed and when the tires should be rotated. You even could start the car remotely on chilly days by pressing a button on your notebook computer as you eat your breakfast cereal at the kitchen table.

Automobile manufacturers are touting their cyber cars of the future equipped with Internet access. They are planning in-dash screens with continuous information about traffic, weather forecasts, and restaurant guides. Their plans also call for having the Internet access disconnect when the vehicle is in motion so that drivers do not attempt to drive and surf the Web simultaneously. For more information, visit scsite.com/dcf2e/ch3/looking and then click Cyber Cars.

POPULAR STAND-ALONE UTILITY PROGRAMS

Utility programs are considered system software because they assist a user with controlling or maintaining the operation of a computer, its devices, or its software. Stand-alone utility programs typically offer features that provide an environment conducive to successful use of application software. One of the more important utility programs protects a computer against viruses. A computer virus is a potentially damaging computer program that affects, or infects, a computer negatively by altering the way the computer works without the user's knowledge or permission.

Other features of stand-alone utility programs include removing spyware, filtering e-mail and Web content, compressing files, converting files, burning (recording on) a CD or DVD, and maintaining a personal computer. The table in Figure 3-32 briefly describes several types of stand-alone utility programs.

WIDELY USED STAND-ALONE UTILITY PROGRAMS

Utility Program	Description
Antivirus Program	An antivirus program protects a computer against viruses by identifying and removing any computer viruses found in memory, on storage media, or in incoming files.
Spyware Remover	A spyware remover detects and deletes spyware on your computer.
Internet Filters • Anti-Spam Program • Web Filter • Pop-up Blocker	An anti-spam program attempts to remove spam (Internet junk mail) before it reaches your e-mail inbox. A Web filter restricts access to specified Web sites. A pop-up blocker stops advertisements from displaying on Web pages and disables pop-up windows.
File Compression	A file compression utility shrinks the size of a file(s), so the file takes up less storage space than the original file.
File Conversion	A file conversion utility transforms a file from one format to another, eliminating the need to reenter data in a new program.
CD/DVD Burning	A CD/DVD burner writes text, graphics, audio, and video files on a recordable or rewritable CD or DVD.
Personal Computer Maintenance	A personal computer maintenance utility identifies and fixes operating system problems, detects and repairs disk problems, and includes the capability of improving a computer's performance.

FIGURE 3-32   A summary of widely used stand-alone utility programs.

LEARNING AIDS AND SUPPORT TOOLS FOR APPLICATION SOFTWARE

Learning how to use application software effectively involves time and practice. To assist in the learning process, many programs provide online Help (Figure 3-33) and Web-based Help.

Online Help is the electronic equivalent of a user manual. It usually is integrated in a program. In most programs, a function key or a button on the screen starts the Help feature. When using a program, you can use the Help feature to ask a question or access the Help topics in subject or alphabetical order.

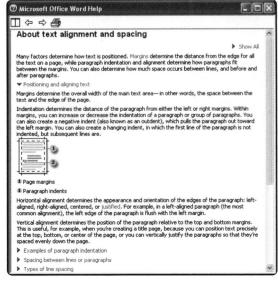

FIGURE 3-33   Many programs include online Help.

Most online Help also links to Web sites that offer Web-based help, which provides updates and more comprehensive resources to respond to technical issues about software. Some Web sites contain chat rooms, in which a user can talk directly with a technical support person or join a conversation with other users who may be able to answer questions or solve problems.

If you want to learn more about a particular program from a printed manual, many books are available to help you learn to use the features of personal computer programs. These books typically are available in bookstores and software stores (Figure 3-34).

Web-Based Training

Web-based training (WBT) is a type of CBT (computer-based training) that uses Internet technology and consists of application software on the Web. Similar to CBT, WBT typically consists of self-directed, self-paced instruction about a topic. WBT is popular in business, industry, and schools for teaching new skills or enhancing existing skills of employees, teachers, or students.

Many Web sites offer WBT to the general public (Figure 3-35). Such training covers a wide range of topics, from how to change a flat tire to creating documents in Word. Many of these Web sites are free. Others require registration and payment to take the complete Web-based course.

FIGURE 3-34 Bookstores often sell trade books to help you learn to use the features of personal computer application software.

WEB LINK 3-8

Web-Based Training

For more information, visit scsite.com/dcf2e/ch3/weblink and then click Web-Based Training.

FIGURE 3-35 At the HowStuffWorks Web-based training site, you can learn how computers, autos, electronics, and many other products work.

Test your knowledge of pages 115 through 124 in Quiz Yourself 3-3.

 QUIZ YOURSELF 3-3

Instructions: Find the true statement below. Then, rewrite the remaining false statements so they are true.

1. An anti-spam program protects a computer against viruses by identifying and removing any computer viruses found in memory, on storage media, or in incoming files.

2. Computer-based training is a type of Web-based training that uses Internet technology and consists of application software on the Web.

3. E-mail and Web browsers are examples of communications software that are considered application software.

4. Legal software is a simplified accounting program that helps home users and small office/home office users balance their checkbooks, pay bills, track investments, and evaluate financial plans.

5. Personal DTP software is a popular type of image editing software that allows users to edit digital photographs.

Quiz Yourself Online: To further check your knowledge of types and features of home, personal, educational, and communications programs, stand-alone utility programs, and software learning aids, visit scsite.com/dcf2e/ch3/quiz and then click Objectives 5 – 8.

CHAPTER SUMMARY

This chapter illustrated how to start and use application software. It then presented an overview of a variety of business software, graphics and multimedia software, home/personal/educational software, and communications software (read At Issue 3-3 for a related discussion). Finally, widely used stand-alone utility programs and learning aids for application software were presented.

 AT ISSUE 3-3

Copying Software – A Computer Crime!

Usually, when you buy software, you legally can make one copy of the software for backup purposes. Despite the law, many people make multiple copies, either to share or to sell. In one survey, more than 50 percent of respondents admitted that they had illegally copied, or would illegally copy, software. Microsoft, a leading software manufacturer, estimates that almost 25 percent of software in the United States has been copied illegally. Among small businesses, the rate may be even higher. The Business Software Alliance, an industry trade association, believes that 40 percent of small U.S. businesses use illegally copied software. Illegally copied software costs the software industry more than $13 billion a year in lost revenues. People and companies copy software illegally for a variety of reasons, insisting that software prices are too high, software manufacturers make enough money, software often is copied for educational or other altruistic purposes, copied software makes people more productive, no restrictions should be placed on the use of software after it is purchased, and everyone copies software. What should be the penalty for copying software? Why? Can you counter the reasons people give for copying software illegally? How? Would you copy software illegally? Why or why not?

Help Desk Specialist

A Help Desk specialist position is an entryway into the information technology (IT) field. A **Help Desk specialist** deals with problems in hardware, software, or communications systems. Job requirements may include the following:

- Solve procedural and software questions both in person and over the telephone
- Develop and maintain Help Desk operations manuals
- Assist in training new Help Desk personnel

Usually, a Help Desk specialist must be knowledgeable about the major programs in use. Entry-level positions primarily involve answering calls from people with questions. Other positions provide additional assistance and assume further responsibilities, often demanding greater knowledge and problem-solving skills that can lead to more advanced positions in the IT field. Help Desk specialist is an ideal position for people who must work irregular hours, because many companies need support people to work evenings, weekends, or part-time.

Educational requirements are less stringent than they are for other jobs in the computer field. In some cases, a high school diploma is sufficient. Advancement requires a minimum of a two-year degree, while management generally requires a bachelor's degree in IT or a related field. Certification is another way Help Desk specialists can increase their attractiveness in the marketplace. Entry-level salaries range from $27,500 to $56,500 per year. Managers range from $49,000 to $72,500. For more information, visit scsite.com/dcf2e/ch3/careers and then click Help Desk Specialist.

Adobe Systems
Digital Imaging Leader

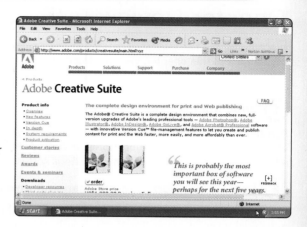

Practically every image seen on a computer and in print has been shaped by software developed by Adobe Systems, Inc. The company, based in San Jose, California, is one of the world's largest application software corporations and is committed to helping people communicate effectively.

Adobe Photoshop and Photoshop Album have set the industry standard for digital imaging and digital video software, while Creative Suite is used for design and publishing. The company's Portable Document Format (PDF) and Adobe Reader are used to share documents among users electronically. More than 600 million copies of the free Adobe Reader have been downloaded.

Fortune magazine named Adobe as the best high-tech company to work for in America in 2004. For more information, visit scsite.com/dcf2e/ch3/companies and then click Adobe.

Microsoft
Realizing Potential with Business Software

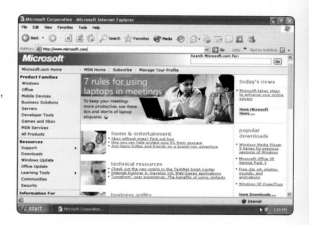

Microsoft's mission is "to enable people and businesses throughout the world to realize their potential." As the largest software company in the world, Microsoft has indeed helped computer users in every field reach their goals.

When Microsoft was incorporated in 1975, the company had three programmers, one product, and revenues of $16,000. Thirty years later, the company employs more than 56,000 people, produces scores of software titles with Office and Windows leading the industry, and has annual revenue of more than $32 billion.

The company's recent efforts have focused on developing the next version of its operating system, which is named Longhorn, and the Smart Personal Objects Technology (SPOT), which brings computing power into everyday objects, such as wristwatches. For more information, visit scsite.com/dcf2e/ch3/companies and then click Microsoft.

TECHNOLOGY TRAILBLAZERS

Dan Bricklin
VisiCalc Developer

When Dan Bricklin was enrolled at the Harvard Business School in the 1970s, he often used his calculator to determine the effect of changing one value on a balance sheet. He recognized the need to develop a program that would perform a series of calculations automatically when the first number was entered.

He named his creation VisiCalc, short for Visible Calculator. He and a friend formed a company called Software Arts and programmed the VisiCalc prototype using Apple Basic on an Apple II computer. The small program was the first piece of application software that provided a reason for businesses to buy Apple computers. It laid the foundation for the development of other spreadsheets and included many of the features found in today's spreadsheet software.

His current venture is Trellix, which lets people turn everyday documents into Web pages with colors, graphics, and links. For more information, visit scsite.com/dcf2e/ch3/people and then click Dan Bricklin.

Masayoshi Son
Softbank President and CEO

Many students carry photographs of family and friends in their wallets and book bags. As a 16-year-old student in the 1970s, Masayoshi Son carried a picture of a microchip. He predicted that the microchip was going to change people's lives, and he wanted to be part of that trend.

While majoring in economics at the University of California, Berkeley, he earned his first million dollars by importing arcade games from Japan to the campus, developing new computer games, and selling a patent for a multilingual pocket translator to Sharp Corporation.

At age 23 he founded Softbank, which is Japan's foremost software distributor and publisher and the country's largest broadband Internet service provider. Today, he is one of the world's wealthiest entrepreneurs. For more information, visit scsite.com/dcf2e/ch3/people and then click Masayoshi Son.

Chapter Review

The Chapter Review section summarizes the concepts presented in this chapter. To obtain help from other students regarding any subject in this chapter, visit scsite.com/dcf2e/ch3/forum and post your thoughts or questions.

(1) What Are the Categories of Application Software?

Application software consists of programs designed to make users more productive and/or assist them with personal tasks. The major categories of application software are business software; graphics and multimedia software; home, personal, and educational software; and communications software.

(2) How Do You Work with Application Software?

Personal computer operating systems often use the concept of a **desktop**, which is an on-screen work area that has a graphical user interface. To start an application in Windows XP, move the **pointer** to the Start **button** in the corner of the desktop and **click** the Start button by pressing and releasing a button on the mouse. Then, click the program name on the Start **menu** or on the submenu that displays when you point to a **command**. Once loaded in memory, the program is displayed in a **window** on the desktop.

 Visit scsite.com/dcf2e/ch3/quiz or click the Quiz Yourself button. Click Objectives 1 – 2.

(3) What Are the Key Features of Widely Used Business Programs?

Business software is application software that assists people in becoming more effective and efficient while performing daily business activities. Business software includes the following programs. **Word processing software** allows users to **create** a document by entering text or numbers and inserting graphical images, **edit** the document by making changes to its existing content, and **format** the document by altering its appearance. **Spreadsheet software** allows users to organize data in rows and columns, perform calculations, recalculate when data changes, and chart the data in graphical form. **Database software** allows users to create a **database**, which is a collection of data organized in a manner that allows access, retrieval, and use of that data. **Presentation graphics software** allows users to create slides that are displayed on a monitor or on a projection screen. **Note taking software** enables users to enter typed text, handwritten comments, drawings, and sketches. A **personal information manager** (PIM) is software that includes an appointment calendar, address book, notepad, and other features to help users organize personal information. A **software suite** is a collection of individual programs sold as a single package. **Project management software** allows users to plan, schedule, track, and analyze the events, resources, and costs of a project. **Accounting software** helps companies record and report their financial transactions.

(4) What Are the Key Features of Widely Used Graphics and Multimedia Programs?

Graphics and multimedia software includes the following. **Computer-aided design (CAD) software** assists a professional user in creating engineering, architectural, and scientific designs. **Desktop publishing (DTP) software** enables professional designers to create sophisticated documents that contain text, graphics, and colors. **Paint software** allows users to draw pictures, shapes, and other graphical images with various on-screen tools. **Image editing software** provides the capabilities of paint software and also includes the capability to modify existing images. **Video editing software** allows professionals to modify a segment of a video, called a clip. **Audio editing software** lets users modify audio clips and produce studio-quality soundtracks. **Multimedia authoring software** allows users to combine text, graphics, audio, video, and animation into an interactive application. **Web page authoring software** helps users of all skill levels create Web pages that include graphical images, video, audio, animation, and other special effects.

 Visit scsite.com/dcf2e/ch3/quiz or click the Quiz Yourself button. Click Objectives 3 – 4.

(5) What Are the Key Features of Widely Used Home, Personal, and Educational Programs?

Software for home, personal, and educational use includes the following. A software suite (for personal use) combines application software such as word processing, spreadsheet, and database into a single, easy-to-use package. **Personal finance software** is a simplified accounting program that helps users balance their checkbooks, pay bills, track personal income and expenses, track investments, and evaluate financial plans. **Legal software** assists in the preparation of legal documents and provides legal information. **Tax preparation software** guides users through the process of filing federal taxes. **Personal DTP software** helps home and small business users create newsletters, brochures, advertisements, postcards, greeting cards, letterhead, business cards, banners, calendars, logos, and Web pages. **Paint/image editing software** for personal use provides an easy-to-use interface, and includes various simplified tools that allow you to draw pictures, shapes, and other images and to modify existing graphics and photos. Application software often includes a **clip art/image gallery**, which is a collection of clip art and photographs. **Home design/landscaping software** assists users with the design, remodeling, or improvement of a home, deck, or landscape. **Educational software** teaches a particular skill. **Reference software** provides valuable and thorough information for all individuals. **Entertainment software** for personal computers includes interactive games, videos, and other programs to support hobbies or provide amusement and enjoyment.

 6 **What Are the Types of Application Software Used in Communications?**

Application software for communications includes e-mail programs to transmit messages via a network, FTP programs to upload and download files on the Internet, Web browser programs to access and view Web pages, video conferencing/telephone call software for meetings or conversations on a network between geographically separated people, newsreader/message board programs that allow online written discussions with other users, chat room software to have real-time, online typed conversations, and instant messaging software for real-time exchange of messages or files.

 7 **What Are the Functions of Stand-Alone Utility Programs?**

Stand-alone utility programs support the successful use of application software. An antivirus program protects a computer against a computer virus, which is a potentially damaging computer program. A spyware remover detects and deletes spyware. An anti-spam program removes spam (Internet junk-mail). A Web filter restricts access to specified Web sites. A pop-up blocker disables pop-up windows. A file compression utility shrinks the size of a file. A file conversion utility transforms a file from one format to another. A CD/DVD burner writes files to a recordable CD or DVD. A personal computer maintenance utility fixes operating system and disk problems.

 8 **What Learning Aids Are Available for Application Software?**

To assist in the learning process, many programs provide a variety of Help features. **Online Help** is the electronic equivalent of a user manual. Most online Help also links to Web-based help, which provides updates and more comprehensive resources to respond to technical issues about software.

 Visit scsite.com/dcf2e/ch3/quiz or click the Quiz Yourself button. Click Objectives 5 – 8.

You should know the Key Terms. Use the list below to help focus your study. To further enhance your understanding of the Key Terms in this chapter, visit scsite.com/dcf2e/ch3/terms. See an example of and a definition for each term, and access current and additional information about the term from the Web.

accounting software (111)
application software (100)
audio editing software (114)
business software (104)
button (103)
click (103)
clip art (105)
clip art/image gallery (118)
command (103)
computer-aided design (CAD) software (112)
computer-based training (CBT) (119)
create (106)
custom software (101)
database (108)
database software (108)
desktop (102)

desktop publishing (DTP) software (113)
edit (106)
educational software (119)
entertainment software (120)
file (103)
font (106)
font size (106)
font style (106)
format (106)
freeware (101)
Help Desk specialist (124)
home design/ landscaping software (119)
icon (102)
image editing software (113)
legal software (117)
menu (103)

multimedia authoring software (114)
note taking software (110)
online Help (122)
open source software (101)
packaged software (101)
paint software (113)
personal DTP software (117)
personal finance software (116)
personal information manager (PIM) (110)
personal paint/image editing software (118)
photo editing software (118)
pointer (103)
presentation graphics software (109)
print (106)

project management software (111)
public-domain software (101)
reference software (119)
save (106)
shareware (101)
software suite (110)
spreadsheet software (106)
system software (101)
tax preparation software (117)
title bar (103)
video editing software (114)
Web page authoring software (114)
Web-based training (WBT) (123)
window (103)
word processing software (105)
worksheet (106)

Checkpoint

Use the Checkpoint exercises to check your knowledge level of the chapter.

_____ 1. Open source software has restrictions from the copyright holder regarding modification of the software's internal instructions and redistribution of the software. (101)

_____ 2. Shareware, freeware, and public-domain programs usually are not available on the Web for users to download. (101)

_____ 3. The desktop is an on-screen work area that has a graphical user interface. (102)

_____ 4. A button is a small image displayed on the screen that represents a program, a document, or some other object. (102)

_____ 5. Business software includes programs such as word processing, spreadsheet, and presentation graphics. (104)

_____ 6. Font size is gauged by a measurement system called points. (106)

_____ 7. The programs in a software suite use a similar interface and share some common features. (116)

_____ 8. Educational software is software that assists instructors in planning a course. (119)

_____ 9. All communications software is considered to be application software. (120)

_____ 10. When using a program, you can use the Help feature to ask a question or access the Help topics in subject or alphabetical order. (122)

1. Presentation graphics software, project management software, accounting software, and enterprise computing software are examples of _____ software. (100)
   a. graphics and multimedia
   b. communications
   c. home/personal/educational
   d. business

2. The title bar of a document window usually displays the document's _____. (103)
   a. file name   b. file size
   c. file path   d. all of the above

3. A feature, called _____, allows users of word processing software to type words continually without pressing the ENTER key at the end of each line. (105)
   a. AutoCorrect   b. wordwrap
   c. AutoFormat   d. clipboard

4. When using spreadsheet software, a function _____. (107)
   a. depicts data in graphical form
   b. changes certain values to reveal the effects of the changes
   c. is a predefined formula that performs common calculations
   d. contains the formatting necessary for a specific worksheet type

5. With database software, users can run a _____ to request specific data from the database. (109)
   a. query   b. record
   c. field   d. form

6. Training centers, educational institutions, and online magazine publishers all use _____ software to develop interactive applications. (114)
   a. multimedia authoring
   b. desktop publishing
   c. computer-aided design
   d. image editing

7. _____ typically consists of self-directed, self-paced instruction about a topic. (119)
   a. CBT (computer-based training)
   b. DTP (desktop publishing)
   c. CAD (computer-aided design)
   d. PIM (personal information manager)

8. A(n) _____, which can be used to upload and download files with other computers and on the Internet, is integrated in some operating systems. (121)
   a. chat client
   b. e-mail program
   c. Web browser
   d. FTP program

_____ 1. clip art (105)

_____ 2. clipboard (106)

_____ 3. font (106)

_____ 4. cell (107)

_____ 5. record (108)

a. name assigned to a specific design of characters

b. row in a database table that contains data about a given item

c. collection of drawings, diagrams, maps, and photographs

d. intersection of a row and column in a worksheet

e. delivers applications to meet a specific business need

f. temporary storage location that contains items cut from a document

Checkpoint

Short Answer

Write a brief answer to each of the following questions.

1. What is charting? _____ How are line charts, column charts, and pie charts different? _____
2. What is a software suite? _____ What are the major advantages of using a software suite? _____
3. How do professional designers use DTP software? _____ What is computer-aided design (CAD) software? _____
4. What is computer-based training (CBT)? _____ How is CBT used? _____
5. What is online Help? _____ How can Web-based Help assist software users? _____

Working Together

Working in a group of your classmates, complete the following team exercise.

1. In any software application, each program is not exactly the same. Different spreadsheet programs, for example, may have different methods to enter formulas, use functions, and draw charts. Have each member of your team interview someone who works with an application described in this chapter. What specific program is used? Why? For what purpose is the program used? What does the interviewee like, or dislike, about the program? Would the interviewee recommend this program? Why? Meet with the members of your team to discuss the results of your interviews. Then, use PowerPoint to create a group presentation and share your findings with the class.

Web Research

Use the Internet-based Web Research exercises to broaden your understanding of the concepts presented in this chapter. Visit scsite.com/dcf2e/ch3/research to obtain more information pertaining to each exercise. To discuss any of the Web Research exercises in this chapter with other students, post your thoughts or questions at scsite.com/dcf2e/ch3/forum.

① Journaling Respond to your readings in this chapter by writing at least one page about your reactions, evaluations, and reflections about the first time you used word processing software. For example, what word processing software did you use? What was the first document you created? Have your instructors required you to use word processing software for class projects? How did you edit and format your document? Did you back up your file? You also can write about the new terms you learned by reading this chapter. If required, submit your journal to your instructor.

② Scavenger Hunt Use one of the search engines listed in Figure 2-8 in Chapter 2 on page 58 or your own favorite search engine to find the answers to the questions below. Copy and paste the Web address from the Web page where you found the answer. Some questions may have more than one answer. If required, submit your answers to your instructor. (1) What is the name of the curves Adobe Systems uses to define shapes in its PostScript programming language? (2) Microsoft developed what popular entertainment software in 1983 in cooperation with Bruce Artwick of SubLogic? (3) What application software company did Microsoft acquire in 1987 that developed and marketed PowerPoint? (4) What software was provided on a free floppy disk inserted in *PC World* magazine's special Software Review in 1983? (5) What is the name of the first successful spreadsheet program? (6) How many Americans filed their federal income taxes electronically this past year?

③ Search Sleuth A virus is a potentially damaging computer program that can harm files and the operating system. The National Institute of Standards and Technology Computer Security Resource Center (csrc.nist.gov/virus/) is one of the more comprehensive Web sites discussing viruses. Visit this Web site and then use your word processing program to answer the following questions. Then, if required, submit your answers to your instructor. (1) The Virus Information page provides general information about viruses and links to various resources that provide more specific details. What two steps does the National Institute recommend to detect and prevent viruses from spreading? (2) Click the Symantec link in the Virus Resources & Other Areas of Interest section. What viruses are the latest threats, and when were they discovered? (3) Click Search at the top of the page and then type "Sasser worm" as the keyword in the Search text box. How many articles discuss the Sasser worm on the Symantec Web site? What three functions does the Sasser Removal Tool perform? (4) Click your browser's Back button or press the BACKSPACE key to return to the National Institute of Standards and Technology Virus Information page. Click the F-Secure link in the Virus Resources & Other Areas of Interest section. (5) What are three viruses listed in the Latest Threats section? (6) Click one of the Latest News links and review the material. Summarize the information you read and then write a 50-word summary.

Learn How To

Use the Learn How To activities to learn fundamental skills when using a computer and accompanying technology. Complete the exercises and submit them to your instructor.

LEARN HOW TO 1: Save a File in Application Software

When you use application software, most of the time you either will be creating a new file or modifying an existing file. For example, if you are using a word processor, when you create a new document, the document is a file.

When you create or modify a file, it is contained in RAM. If you turn off your computer or lose electrical power, the file will not be retained. In order to retain the file, you must save it on disk or other permanent storage, such as a USB drive.

As you create the file, you should save the file often. To save a new file, you must complete several tasks:

1. Initiate an action indicating you want to save the file, such as clicking the Save button on the Standard toolbar.
2. Designate where the file should be stored. This includes identifying both the device (such as drive C) and the folder (such as My Documents).
3. Specify the name of the file, using the file name rules as specified by the application or operating system.
4. Click the Save button to save the file.

Tasks 2 through 4 normally can be completed using a dialog box such as shown in Figure 3-36.

If you use application software to create or modify a file and attempt to close the program prior to saving the new or modified file, the program will display a dialog box that asks if you want to save the file. If you click the Yes button, a modified file will be saved using the same file name in the same location from which it was retrieved. Saving a new file requires that you complete tasks 2 through 4.

FIGURE 3-36

Exercise

1. Start the WordPad program from the Accessories submenu on the All Programs submenu.
2. Type Saving a file is the best insurance against losing work.
3. Click the Save button on the WordPad toolbar. What dialog box is displayed? Where will the file be saved? What is the default file name? If you wanted to save the file on the desktop, what would you do? (*Hint:* Look in the left margin of the dialog box.) Click the Cancel button in the dialog box. Submit your answers to your instructor.
4. Click the Close button in the upper-right corner of the WordPad window. What happened? Click the Yes button in the WordPad dialog box. What happened? Place either a floppy disk in drive A or a USB drive in a USB port. Select either the floppy disk or the USB drive as the location for saving the file. Name the file, Chapter 3 How To 1. Save the file. What happened when you clicked the Save button? Submit your answers to your instructor.

LEARN HOW TO 2: Install and Uninstall Application Software

When you purchase application software, you must install the software on the computer where you want to run it. The exact installation process varies with each program, but generally you must complete the following steps:

1. Insert the CD-ROM containing the application software into a drive.
2. The opening window will appear. If the CD-ROM contains more than one program, choose the program you want to install. Click the Continue or Next button.
3. Some file extractions will occur and then an Install Wizard will begin. The method for using this wizard will vary, but you normally must accomplish the following steps by completing the directions within the wizard:
   a. Accept the terms of the license agreement.
   b. Identify where on your computer the software will be stored. The software usually selects a default location on drive C, and you normally will accept the default location.
   c. Select any default options for the software.
   d. Click a button to install the software.
4. A Welcome/Help screen often will be displayed. It might provide help or documentation. Click a button to finish the installation process.

After you have installed software, use it in the manner you require. At some point, you may want to remove software from your computer. Most application software includes uninstall programming that will remove the program and all its software components from the computer. To uninstall a program, complete the following steps:

1. Click the Start button on the Windows taskbar.
2. Click Control Panel on the Start menu.
3. Click or double-click Add or Remove Programs. *The Add or Remove Programs window will open (Figure 3-37).*
4. Select the program you wish to remove. *In Figure 3-37, Macromedia Dreamweaver is selected as the program to remove.*
5. Click the Change/Remove button.
6. A dialog box will be displayed informing you that the software is being prepared for uninstall. You then will be informed that the process you are following will remove the program. You will be asked if you want to continue. To uninstall the program, click the Yes button.

The program will be removed from the computer. Sometimes, all the shortcut icons for the program might not be removed. If you discover a shortcut icon after a program has been removed, delete the shortcut icon.

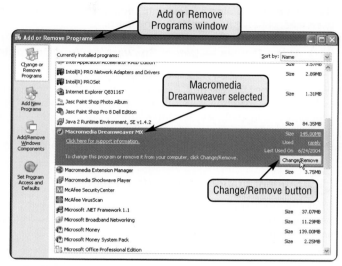

FIGURE 3-37

Exercise

1. Optional: Insert the CD-ROM containing the software you want to install into a drive and follow the instructions for installing the software. **Warning: If you are using a computer other than your own, particularly in a school laboratory, do not perform this exercise unless you have specific permission from your instructor.**
2. Optional: Follow the steps above to uninstall software you want to remove. Be aware that if you uninstall software, the software will not be available for use until you reinstall it. **Warning: If you are using a computer other than your own, particularly in a school laboratory, do not perform this exercise unless you have specific permission from your instructor.**

LEARN HOW TO 3: Check Application Software Version

Most application software will be modified from time to time by its developer to enable it to work better and faster or to correct errors. Each time the software is changed, it acquires a new version number and sometimes an entirely new name. To determine what version of software you have available on a computer, perform the following steps:

1. Start the application program.
2. Click Help on the menu bar and then click About on the Help menu (the program name often follows the word, About). *The program displays the About window (Figure 3-38). This window specifies the name of the software (Microsoft Paint in the example), the version of the software (Version 5.1), and the person to whom the software is licensed.*
3. To close the About window, click the OK button.

Depending on the software, in the About window you also might be able to determine further copyright or patent protection for the software, people who developed the software, registration and serial number information, and other facts.

Exercise

1. Start your Web browser and display the About window for the browser. What is the name of the browser? What version of the browser are you using? What is the product ID? What does the copyright notice say? Submit your answers to your instructor.
2. Start any other application software on the computer you are using. Display the About window. What is the name of the application software? What is the version of the software? What information do you find that you did not see in Exercise 1? What did you find in Exercise 1 that you do not see now? Which window do you find more useful? Why? Submit your answers to your instructor.

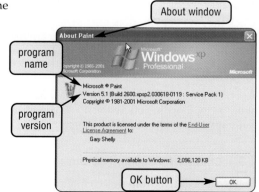

FIGURE 3-38

Learn It Online

Use the Learn It Online exercises to reinforce your understanding of the chapter concepts. To access the Learn It Online exercises, visit scsite.com/dcf2e/ch3/learn.

(1) At the Movies — Detect Spyware on Your Computer

To view the Detect Spyware on Your Computer movie, click the number 1 button. Locate your video and click the corresponding High-Speed or Dial-Up link, depending on your Internet connection. Watch the movie and then complete the exercise by answering the question that follows. Many of the programs installed on your computer also installed spyware along with the program you loaded. Several different types of spyware exist, two of which are keystroke recorders and advertising spyware. Spyware either collects information and sends it over the Internet to whoever installed it or stores it for later retrieval. Why might you want to detect and delete a keystroke recorder from your computer?

(2) Student Edition Labs — Word Processing

Click the number 2 button. When the Student Edition Labs menu appears, click *Word Processing* to begin. A new browser window will open. Follow the on-screen instructions to complete the Lab. When finished, click the Exit button. If required, submit your results to your instructor.

(3) Practice Test

Click the number 3 button. Answer each question. When completed, enter your name and click the Grade Test button to submit the quiz for grading. Make a note of any missed questions. If required, submit your score to your instructor.

(4) Who Wants To Be a Computer Genius²?

Click the number 4 button to find out if you are a computer genius. Directions about how to play the game will be displayed. When you are ready to play, click the Play button. Submit your score to your instructor.

(5) Wheel of Terms

Click the number 5 button to reinforce important terms you learned in this chapter by playing the Shelly Cashman Series version of this popular game. Directions about how to play the game will be displayed. When you are ready to play, click the Play button. Submit your score to your instructor.

(6) Student Edition Labs — Spreadsheets

Click the number 6 button. When the Student Edition Labs menu appears, click *Spreadsheets* to begin. A new browser window will open. Follow the on-screen instructions to complete the Lab. When finished, click the Exit button. If required, submit your score to your instructor.

(7) Crossword Puzzle Challenge

Click the number 7 button. Complete the puzzle to reinforce skills you learned in this chapter. Directions about how to play the game will be displayed. When you are ready to play, click the Play button. Submit the completed puzzle to your instructor.

(8) Lab Exercises

Click the number 8 button. When the Lab Exercises menu appears, click the exercise assigned by your instructor. A new browser window will open. Follow the on-screen instructions to complete the exercise. When finished, click the Exit button. If required, submit your results to your instructor.

(9) Chapter Discussion Forum

Select an objective from this chapter on page 99 about which you would like more information. Click the number 9 button and post a short message listing a meaningful message title accompanied by one or more questions concerning the selected objective. In two days, return to the threaded discussion by clicking the number 9 button. Submit to your instructor your original message and at least one response to your message.

CHAPTER 4

The Components of the System Unit

CONTENTS

OBJECTIVES

After completing this chapter, you will be able to:

1. Differentiate among various styles of system units
2. Describe the components of a processor and how they complete a machine cycle
3. Define a bit and describe how a series of bits represents data
4. Differentiate among the various types of memory
5. Describe the types of expansion slots and adapter cards
6. Explain the differences among a serial port, a parallel port, a USB port, and other ports
7. Describe how buses contribute to a computer's processing speed
8. Identify components in mobile computers and mobile devices
9. Understand how to clean a system unit

THE SYSTEM UNIT
The Motherboard

PROCESSOR
The Control Unit
The Arithmetic Logic Unit
Machine Cycle
The System Clock
Comparison of Personal Computer Processors
Buying a Personal Computer

DATA REPRESENTATION

MEMORY
Bytes and Addressable Memory
Memory Sizes
Types of Memory
RAM
Cache
ROM
Flash Memory
CMOS
Memory Access Times

EXPANSION SLOTS AND ADAPTER CARDS
PC Cards, Flash Memory Cards, and USB Flash Drives

PORTS AND CONNECTORS
Serial Ports
Parallel Ports
USB Ports
FireWire Ports
Special-Purpose Ports

BUSES

BAYS

POWER SUPPLY

MOBILE COMPUTERS AND DEVICES

PUTTING IT ALL TOGETHER

KEEPING YOUR COMPUTER CLEAN

COMPANIES ON THE CUTTING EDGE
AMD
Intel

TECHNOLOGY TRAILBLAZERS
Jack Kilby
Gordon Moore

THE SYSTEM UNIT

Whether you are a home user or a business user, you most likely will make the decision to purchase a new computer or upgrade an existing computer within the next several years. Thus, you should understand the purpose of each component in a computer. As Chapter 1 discussed, a computer includes devices used for input, processing, output, storage, and communications. Many of these components are part of the system unit.

The **system unit** is a case that contains electronic components of the computer used to process data. System units are available in a variety of shapes and sizes. The case of the system unit is made of metal or plastic and protects the internal electronic components from damage. All computers have a system unit (Figure 4-1).

On desktop personal computers, the electronic components and most storage devices are part of the system unit. Other devices, such as the keyboard, mouse, microphone, monitor, printer, scanner, PC video camera, and speakers, normally occupy space outside the system unit. On notebook computers, the keyboard and pointing device often occupy the area on the top of the system unit, and the display attaches to the system unit by hinges. The location of the system unit

FIGURE 4-1   All sizes of computers have a system unit.

on a Tablet PC varies, depending on the design of the Tablet PC. Some models position the system unit below the keyboard, while others build the system unit behind the display. The system unit on a PDA and smart phone usually consumes the entire device. On these mobile devices, the display often is built into the system unit.

At some point, you might have to open the system unit on a desktop personal computer to replace or install a new electronic component. For this reason, you should be familiar with the electronic components of a system unit. Figure 4-2 identifies some of these components, which include the processor, memory, adapter cards, ports, drive bays, and the power supply.

The processor interprets and carries out the basic instructions that operate a computer. Memory typically holds data waiting to be processed and instructions waiting to be executed. The electronic components and circuitry of the system unit, such as the processor and memory, usually are part of or are connected to a circuit board called the motherboard. Many motherboards also integrate modem and networking capabilities.

Adapter cards are circuit boards that provide connections and functions not built into the motherboard. Two adapter cards found in some desktop personal computers today are a sound card and a video card.

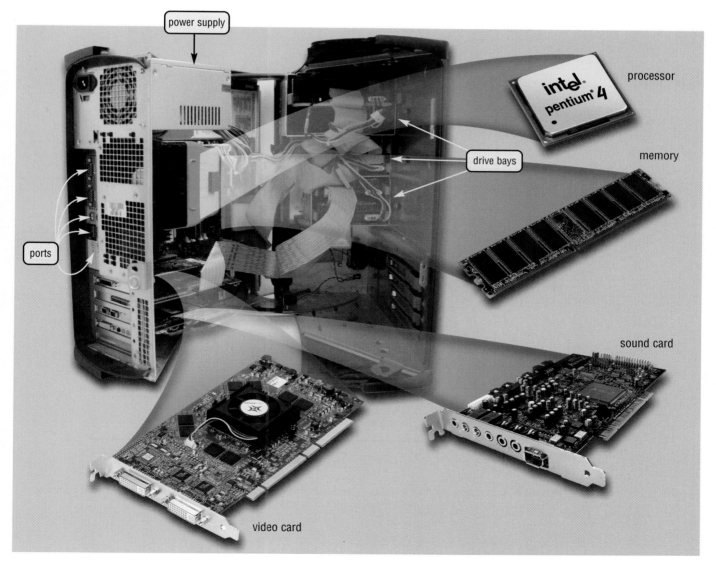

FIGURE 4-2   The system unit on a typical personal computer consists of numerous electronic components, some of which are shown in this figure. The sound card and video card are two types of adapter cards.

Devices outside the system unit often attach to ports on the system unit by a connector on a cable. These devices may include a keyboard, mouse, microphone, monitor, printer, scanner, card reader/writer, digital camera, PC video camera, and speakers. A drive bay holds one or more disk drives. The power supply allows electricity to travel through a power cord from a wall outlet into a computer.

The Motherboard

The **motherboard**, sometimes called a system board, is the main circuit board of the system unit. Many electronic components attach to the motherboard; others are built into it. Figure 4-3 shows a photograph of a current desktop personal computer motherboard and identifies some components that attach to it, including adapter cards, a processor chip, and a memory module. Memory chips are installed on memory cards (modules) that fit in a slot on the motherboard.

A computer **chip** is a small piece of semiconducting material, usually silicon, on which integrated circuits are etched. An integrated circuit contains many microscopic pathways capable of carrying electrical current. Each integrated circuit can contain millions of elements such as resistors, capacitors, and transistors.

WEB LINK 4-1

Motherboards

For more information, visit scsite.com/dcf2e/ch4/weblink and then click Motherboards.

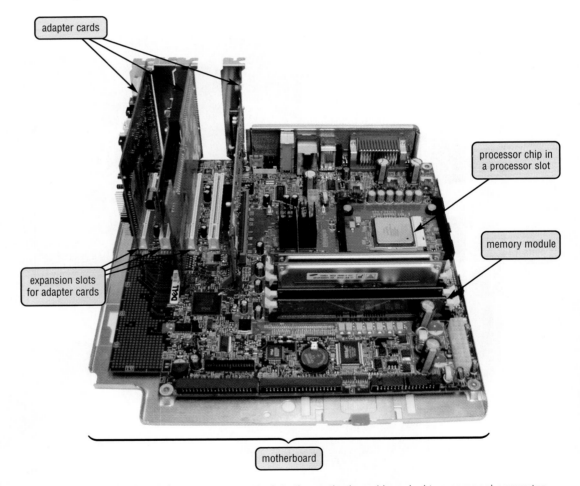

FIGURE 4-3   Many electronic components attach to the motherboard in a desktop personal computer, including a processor chip, memory module, and adapter cards.

PROCESSOR

The **processor**, also called the **central processing unit** (**CPU**), interprets and carries out the basic instructions that operate a computer. The processor significantly impacts overall computing power and manages most of a computer's operations. On a personal computer, all functions of the processor usually are on a single chip. Some computer and chip manufacturers use the term **microprocessor** to refer to a personal computer processor chip.

Processors contain a control unit and an arithmetic logic unit (ALU). These two components work together to perform processing operations. Figure 4-4 illustrates how other devices that are connected to the computer communicate with the processor to carry out a task.

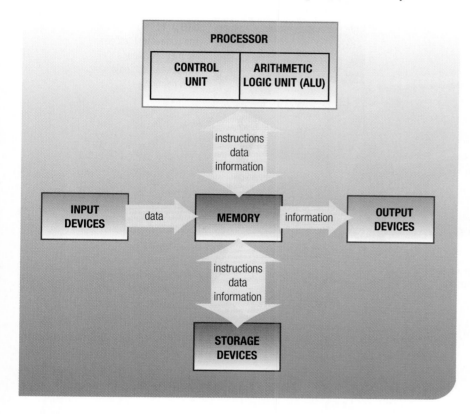

FIGURE 4-4 Most devices connected to the computer communicate with the processor to carry out a task. When a user starts a program, for example, its instructions transfer from a storage device to memory. Data needed by programs enters memory from either an input device or a storage device. The control unit interprets and executes instructions in memory, and the ALU performs calculations on the data in memory. Resulting information is stored in memory, from which it can be sent to an output device or a storage device for future access, as needed.

The Control Unit

The **control unit** is the component of the processor that directs and coordinates most of the operations in the computer. The control unit has a role much like a traffic cop: it interprets each instruction issued by a program and then initiates the appropriate action to carry out the instruction.

The Arithmetic Logic Unit

The **arithmetic logic unit** (ALU), another component of the processor, performs arithmetic, comparison, and other operations. Arithmetic operations include basic calculations such as addition, subtraction, multiplication, and division. Comparison operations involve comparing one data item with another to determine whether the first item is greater than, equal to, or less than the other item. Depending on the result of the comparison, different actions may occur.

Machine Cycle

For every instruction, a processor repeats a set of four basic operations, which comprise a machine cycle (Figure 4-5): (1) fetching, (2) decoding, (3) executing, and, if necessary, (4) storing. Fetching is the process of obtaining a program instruction or data item from memory. The term decoding refers to the process of translating the instruction into signals the computer can execute. Executing is the process of carrying out the commands. Storing, in this context, means writing the result to memory (not to a storage medium).

FIGURE 4-5   THE STEPS IN A MACHINE CYCLE

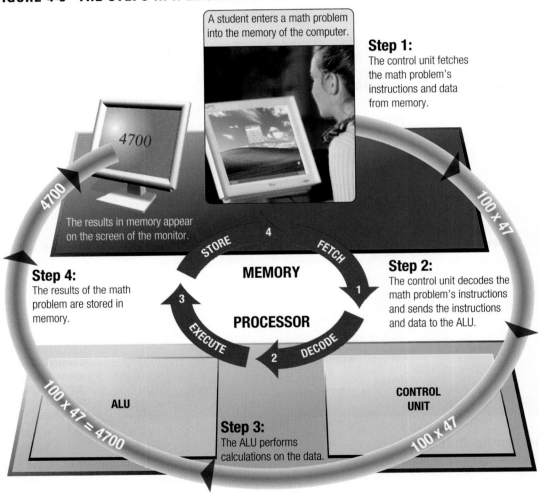

A student enters a math problem into the memory of the computer.

Step 1: The control unit fetches the math problem's instructions and data from memory.

Step 2: The control unit decodes the math problem's instructions and sends the instructions and data to the ALU.

Step 3: The ALU performs calculations on the data.

Step 4: The results of the math problem are stored in memory.

The results in memory appear on the screen of the monitor.

The System Clock

The processor relies on a small quartz crystal circuit called the **system clock** to control the timing of all computer operations. Just as your heart beats at a regular rate to keep your body functioning, the system clock generates regular electronic pulses, or ticks, that set the operating pace of components of the system unit.

The pace of the system clock, called the **clock speed**, is measured by the number of ticks per second. Current personal computer processors have clock speeds in the gigahertz range. Giga is a prefix that stands for billion, and a hertz is one cycle per second. Thus, one **gigahertz (GHz)** equals one billion ticks of the system clock per second. A computer that operates at 3.2 GHz has 3.2 billion (giga) clock cycles in one second (hertz). The system clock is one of the major factors that influence a computer's speed. The faster the clock speed, the more instructions the processor can execute per second. Read Looking Ahead 4-1 for a look at the next generation of processing speeds.

WEB LINK 4-2

Clock Speed

For more information, visit scsite.com/ dcf2e/ch4/weblink and then click Clock Speed.

LOOKING AHEAD 4-1

U.S. Plans World's Fastest Computer

Nine of the world's ten fastest computers are located in the United States. The fastest computer is located in Japan, according to the Top500 Project, a group that monitors supercomputers throughout the world.

The U.S. Department of Energy is planning to have the United States regain the record as having the world's fastest civilian computer. It is helping to fund a new supercomputer at a research laboratory in Oak Ridge, Tennessee, with $50 million in federal grants and assistance from Cray Corp., IBM Corp., and Silicon Graphics Inc.

Oak Ridge scientists predict the new computer will be able to perform 50 trillion calculations per second. The Japanese computer sustains 36 trillion calculations per second. For more information, visit scsite.com/dcf2e/ch4/looking and then click Fastest Computer.

Comparison of Personal Computer Processors

The leading processor chip manufacturers for personal computers are Intel, AMD (Advanced Micro Devices), IBM, Motorola, and Transmeta. These manufacturers often identify their processor chips by a model name or model number.

With its earlier processors, Intel used a model number to identify the various chips. After learning that processor model numbers could not be trademarked and protected from use by competitors, Intel began identifying its processors with names — thus emerged the series of processors known as the Pentium. Most high-performance PCs use some type of Pentium processor. Many notebook computers and Tablet PCs use a Pentium M processor. Less expensive, basic PCs use a brand of Intel processor called the Celeron. Two more brands, called the Xeon and Itanium processors, are ideal for workstations and low-end servers.

AMD is the leading manufacturer of Intel-compatible processors, which have an internal design similar to Intel processors, perform the same functions, and can be as powerful, but often are less expensive. Transmeta, also a manufacturer of Intel-compatible processors, specializes in processors for mobile computers and devices. Intel and Intel-compatible processors are used in PCs.

Apple computers use an IBM processor or a Motorola processor, which has a design different from the Intel-style processor. The PowerPC processor has a new architecture that increased the speed of the lastest Apple computers.

In the past, chip manufacturers listed a processor's clock speed in marketing literature and advertisements. Today, however, clock speed is only one factor that impacts processing speed. To help consumers evaluate various processors, manufacturers such as Intel and AMD now use a numbering scheme that more accurately reflects the processing speed of their chips.

Buying a Personal Computer

If you are ready to buy a new computer, the processor you select should depend on how you plan to use the computer. If you purchase an IBM-compatible PC, you will choose an Intel processor or an Intel-compatible processor. Apple Macintosh and Power Macintosh computers have a Motorola or IBM processor. Current Apple processors include the PowerPC G4 and PowerPC G5.

Your intended use also will determine the clock speed you need. A home user surfing the Web, for example, may need only a 2 GHz processor, while an artist working with graphics or applications requiring multimedia capabilities such as full-motion video, may require at least a 3 GHz processor.

For detailed computer purchasing guidelines, read the Buyer's Guide feature that follows Chapter 7. Read At Issue 4-1 for a related discussion.

AT ISSUE 4-1

Computer Waste and the Environment: Whose Problem Is It?

Experts estimate that about 1 billion computers will be discarded by 2010. As technology advances and prices fall, many people think of computers as disposable items. But, disposing of old system units, monitors, and other computer components is a major problem. Computers contain several toxic elements, including lead, mercury, and barium. Computers thrown into landfills or burned in incinerators can pollute the ground and the air. One solution is to recycle old computers. Computers for Schools refurbishes donated computers and makes them available to schools and students at very low prices, and donors earn tax breaks. Some lawmakers prefer a more aggressive approach, such as setting up a recycling program that would be paid for by adding a $10 fee to a computer's purchase price, or forcing computer makers to be responsible for collecting and recycling their products. Manufacturers already have taken steps. Several have reduced the amount of toxic material in their products, and some have set up their own recycling programs, for which users pay a fee. One manufacturer admits, however, that only seven percent of the computers it has sold have been recycled. What can be done to ensure that computers are disposed of safely? Should government, manufacturers, or users be responsible for safe disposal? Why? How can computer users be motivated to recycle obsolete equipment?

Test your knowledge of pages 134 through 139 in Quiz Yourself 4-1.

QUIZ YOURSELF 4-1

Instructions: Find the true statement below. Then, rewrite the remaining false statements so they are true.

1. A computer chip is a small piece of semiconducting material, usually silicon, on which integrated circuits are etched.

2. Four basic operations in a machine cycle are: (1) comparing, (2) decoding, (3) executing, and, if necessary, (4) pipelining.

3. Processors contain a motherboard and an arithmetic logic unit (ALU).

4. The central processing unit, sometimes called a system board, is the main circuit board of the system unit.

5. The leading processor chip manufacturers for personal computers are Microsoft, AMD, IBM, Motorola, and Transmeta.

6. The system unit is a case that contains mechanical components of the computer used to process data.

Quiz Yourself Online: To further check your knowledge of system unit styles, processor components, and machine cycles, visit scsite.com/dcf2e/ch4/quiz and then click Objectives 1 – 2.

DATA REPRESENTATION

To understand fully the way a computer processes data, you should know how a computer represents data. Most computers are **digital**. They recognize only two discrete states: on and off. The two digits, 0 and 1, easily can represent these two states (Figure 4-6). The digit 0 represents the electronic state of off (absence of an electronic charge). The digit 1 represents the electronic state of on (presence of an electronic charge).

The computer uses a binary system because it recognizes only two states. The **binary system** is a number system that has just two unique digits, 0 and 1, called bits. A **bit** (short for binary digit) is the smallest unit of data the computer can process. By itself, a bit is not very informative.

When 8 bits are grouped together as a unit, they form a **byte**. A byte provides enough different combinations of 0s and 1s to represent 256 individual characters. These characters include numbers, uppercase and lowercase letters of the alphabet, punctuation marks, and others, such as the letters of the Greek alphabet.

The combinations of 0s and 1s that represent characters are defined by patterns called a coding scheme. In one coding scheme, the number 4 is represented as 00110100, the number 6 as 00110110, and the capital letter E as 01000101 (Figure 4-7). Two popular coding schemes are ASCII and EBCDIC (Figure 4-8). The American Standard Code for Information Interchange (ASCII pronounced ASK-ee) scheme is the most widely used coding system to represent data. Most personal computers and midrange servers use the ASCII coding scheme. The Extended Binary Coded Decimal Interchange Code (EBCDIC pronounced EB-see-dik) scheme is used primarily on mainframe computers and high-end servers.

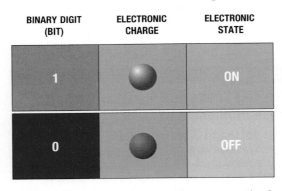

FIGURE 4-6 A computer circuit represents the 0 or the 1 electronically by the presence or absence of an electronic charge.

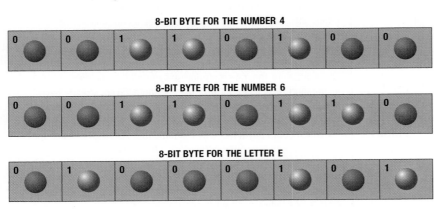

8-BIT BYTE FOR THE NUMBER 4

8-BIT BYTE FOR THE NUMBER 6

8-BIT BYTE FOR THE LETTER E

FIGURE 4-7 Eight bits grouped together as a unit are called a byte. A byte represents a single character in the computer.

ASCII	SYMBOL	EBCDIC
00110000	0	11110000
00110001	1	11110001
00110010	2	11110010
00110011	3	11110011
00110100	4	11110100
00110101	5	11110101
00110110	6	11110110
00110111	7	11110111
00111000	8	11111000
00111001	9	11111001
01000001	A	11000001
01000010	B	11000010
01000011	C	11000011
01000100	D	11000100
01000101	E	11000101
01000110	F	11000110
01000111	G	11000111
01001000	H	11001000
01001001	I	11001001
01001010	J	11010001
01001011	K	11010010
01001100	L	11010011
01001101	M	11010100
01001110	N	11010101
01001111	O	11010110
01010000	P	11010111
01010001	Q	11011000
01010010	R	11011001
01010011	S	11100010
01010100	T	11100011
01010101	U	11100100
01010110	V	11100101
01010111	W	11100110
01011000	X	11100111
01011001	Y	11101000
01011010	Z	11101001
00100001	!	01011010
00100010	"	01111111
00100011	#	01111011
00100100	$	01011011
00100101	%	01101100
00100110	&	01010000
00101000	(	01001101
00101001	)	01011101
00101010	*	01011100
00101011	+	01001110

FIGURE 4-8 Two popular coding schemes are ASCII and EBCDIC.

Coding schemes such as ASCII make it possible for humans to interact with a digital computer that processes only bits. When you press a key on a keyboard, a chip in the keyboard converts the key's electronic signal into a scan code that is sent to the system unit. Then, the system unit converts the scan code into a binary form the computer can process and is stored in memory. Every character is converted to its corresponding byte. The computer then processes the data as bytes, which actually is a series of on/off electrical states. When processing is finished, software converts the byte into a human-recognizable number, letter of the alphabet, or special character that is displayed on a screen or is printed (Figure 4-9). All of these conversions take place so quickly that you do not realize they are occurring.

Standards, such as those defined by ASCII and EBCDIC, also make it possible for components in computers to communicate successfully with each other.

FIGURE 4-9 HOW A LETTER IS CONVERTED TO BINARY FORM AND BACK

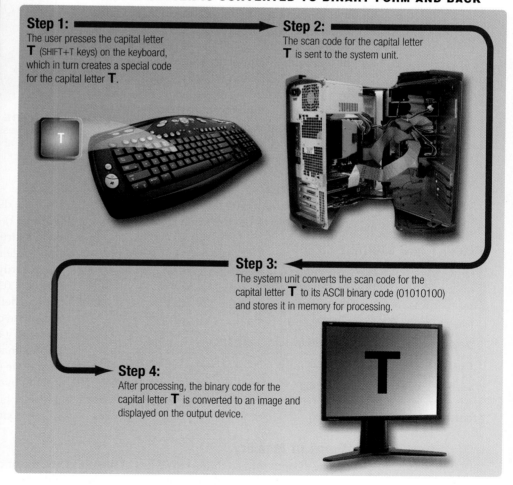

Step 1:
The user presses the capital letter **T** (SHIFT+T keys) on the keyboard, which in turn creates a special code for the capital letter **T**.

Step 2:
The scan code for the capital letter **T** is sent to the system unit.

Step 3:
The system unit converts the scan code for the capital letter **T** to its ASCII binary code (01010100) and stores it in memory for processing.

Step 4:
After processing, the binary code for the capital letter **T** is converted to an image and displayed on the output device.

MEMORY

Memory consists of electronic components that store instructions waiting to be executed by the processor, data needed by those instructions, and the results of processed data (information). Memory usually consists of one or more chips on the motherboard or some other circuit board in the computer.

Memory stores three basic categories of items: (1) the operating system and other system software that control or maintain the computer and its devices; (2) application programs that carry out a specific task such as word processing; and (3) the data being processed by the application programs and resulting information. This role of memory to store both data and programs is known as the stored program concept.

Bytes and Addressable Memory

A byte (character) is the basic storage unit in memory. When application program instructions and data are transferred to memory from storage devices, the instructions and data exist as bytes. Each byte resides temporarily in a location in memory that has an address. An address simply is a unique number that identifies the location of the byte in memory. The illustration in Figure 4-10 shows how seats in a concert hall are similar to addresses in memory: (1) a seat, which is identified by a unique seat number, holds one person at a time, and a location in memory, which is identified by a unique address, holds a single byte; and (2) both a seat, identified by a seat number, and a byte, identified by an address, can be empty. To access data or instructions in memory, the computer references the addresses that contain bytes of data.

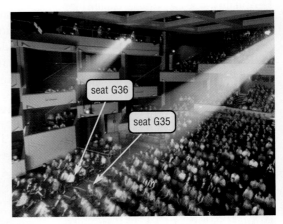
seat G36

seat G35

FIGURE 4-10   Seats in a concert hall are similar to addresses in memory: a seat holds one person at a time, and a location in memory holds a single byte; and both a seat and a byte can be empty.

Memory Sizes

Manufacturers state the size of memory chips and storage devices in terms of the number of bytes the chip or device has available for storage (Figure 4-11). Recall that storage devices hold data, instructions, and information for future use, while most memory holds these items temporarily. A **kilobyte** (**KB** or **K**) is equal to exactly 1,024 bytes. To simplify memory and storage definitions, computer users often round a kilobyte down to 1,000 bytes. For example, if a memory chip can store 100 KB, it can hold approximately 100,000 bytes (characters). A **megabyte** (**MB**) is equal to approximately 1 million bytes. A **gigabyte** (**GB**) equals approximately 1 billion bytes. A **terabyte** (**TB**) is equal to approximately 1 trillion bytes.

MEMORY AND STORAGE SIZES

Term	Abbreviation	Approximate Number of Bytes	Exact Amount of Bytes	Approximate Number of Pages of Text
Kilobyte	KB or K	1 thousand	1,024	1/2
Megabyte	MB	1 million	1,048,576	500
Gigabyte	GB	1 billion	1,073,741,824	500,000
Terabyte	TB	1 trillion	1,099,511,627,776	500,000,000

FIGURE 4-11   Terms commonly used to define memory and storage sizes.

Types of Memory

The system unit contains two types of memory: volatile and nonvolatile. When the computer's power is turned off, **volatile memory** loses its contents. **Nonvolatile memory**, by contrast, does not lose its contents when power is removed from the computer. Thus, volatile memory is temporary and nonvolatile memory is permanent. RAM is the most common type of volatile memory. Examples of nonvolatile memory include ROM, flash memory, and CMOS. The following sections discuss these types of memory.

RAM

Users typically are referring to RAM when discussing computer memory. **RAM** (random access memory), also called main memory, consists of memory chips that can be read from and written to by the processor and other devices. When you turn on power to a computer, certain operating system files (such as the files that determine how the Windows XP desktop appears) load into RAM from a storage device such as a hard disk. These files remain in RAM as long as the computer has continuous power. As additional programs and data are requested, they also load into RAM from storage.

The processor interprets and executes a program's instructions while the program is in RAM. During this time, the contents of RAM may change (Figure 4-12). RAM can hold multiple programs simultaneously, provided the computer has enough RAM to accommodate all the programs.

Most RAM is volatile, which means it loses its contents when the power is removed from the computer. For this reason, you must save any items you may need in the future. Saving is the process of copying items from RAM to a storage device such as a hard disk.

FIGURE 4-12   HOW PROGRAM INSTRUCTIONS TRANSFER IN AND OUT OF RAM

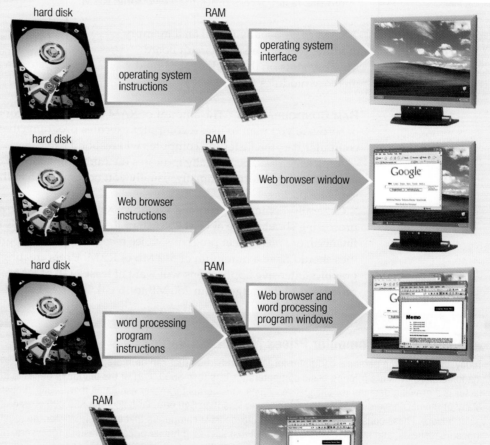

Step 1:
When you start the computer, certain operating system files are loaded into RAM from the hard disk. The operating system displays the user interface on the screen.

Step 2:
When you start a Web browser, the program's instructions are loaded into RAM from the hard disk. The Web browser and certain operating system instructions are in RAM. The Web browser window is displayed on the screen.

Step 3:
When you start a word processing program, the program's instructions are loaded into RAM from the hard disk. The word processing program, along with the Web browser and certain operating system instructions, are in RAM. The word processing program window is displayed on the screen.

Step 4:
When you quit a program, such as the Web browser, its program instructions are removed from RAM. The Web browser no longer is displayed on the screen.

Three basic types of RAM chips exist: dynamic RAM, static RAM, and magnetoresistive RAM.

- Dynamic RAM (DRAM pronounced DEE-ram) chips must be re-energized constantly or they lose their contents.
- Static RAM (SRAM pronounced ESS-ram) chips are faster and more reliable than any variation of DRAM chips. These chips do not have to be re-energized as often as DRAM chips, thus, the term static.
- A newer type of RAM, called magnetoresistive RAM (MRAM pronounced EM-ram), stores data using magnetic charges instead of electrical charges. Manufacturers claim that MRAM has greater storage capacity, consumes less power, and has faster access times than electronic RAM.

RAM chips usually reside on a **memory module**, which is a small circuit board. **Memory slots** on the motherboard hold memory modules (Figure 4-13).

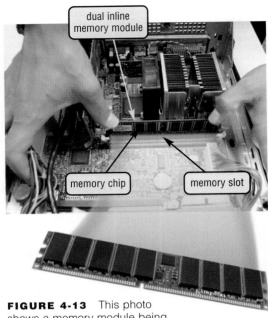

FIGURE 4-13   This photo shows a memory module being inserted in a motherboard.

WEB LINK 4-3

RAM

For more information, visit scsite.com/ dcf2e/ch4/weblink and then click RAM.

RAM CONFIGURATIONS   The amount of RAM necessary in a computer often depends on the types of software you plan to use. A computer executes programs that are in RAM. The more RAM a computer has, the faster the computer will respond.

A software package typically indicates the minimum amount of RAM it requires. If you want the application to perform optimally, usually you need more than the minimum specifications on the software package.

Generally, home users running Windows XP and using basic application software such as word processing should have at least 256 MB of RAM. Most business users who work with accounting, financial, or spreadsheet programs, voice recognition, and programs requiring multimedia capabilities should have a minimum of 512 MB of RAM. Users creating professional Web sites or using graphics-intensive applications will want at least 2 GB of RAM. The amount of RAM in computers purchased today ranges from 256 MB to 16 GB. Read At Issue 4-2 for a related discussion.

AT ISSUE 4-2

Do Lower Computer Prices Mean Less Value?

Today, you can buy a personal computer for less than $1,000 that can do more than one sold at nearly twice its cost three years ago. Some manufacturers even are offering basic computers for less than $500. Part of the plunge in prices is lower-cost components, but another factor is a growing demand for cheaper machines. One computer maker estimates that it sells almost 3,500 sub-$500 computers a month. Many of the new buyers are from families earning less than $40,000, far below the $50,000 average that once characterized typical computer buyers. These consumers are looking for inexpensive computers that are adequate for the most popular tasks, such as word processing, spreadsheets, and Internet access. They feel that spending higher prices for faster processors, more memory, 3-D graphics cards, higher-quality sound cards, more hard disk space, and other extras is an unnecessary, frivolous expense. As one industry analyst asks, "Why buy a Porsche when you are going to drive only 55 miles per hour?" How might a greater availability of lower costing personal computers change the way people, schools, and businesses buy and use them? With respect to computers, does a higher price always mean greater usefulness? Why or why not? Who might be satisfied with less than the latest and greatest computer technology? Why?

WEB LINK 4-4

Cache

For more information, visit scsite.com/dcf2e/ ch4/weblink and then click Cache.

Cache

Most of today's computers improve processing times with **cache** (pronounced cash). Two types of cache are memory cache and disk cache. This chapter discusses memory cache.

Memory cache helps speed the processes of the computer because it stores frequently used instructions and data. Most personal computers today have two types of memory cache: L1 cache and L2 cache.

- **L1 cache** is built directly in the processor chip. L1 cache usually has a very small capacity, ranging from 8 KB to 128 KB.
- **L2 cache** is slightly slower than L1 cache but has a much larger capacity, ranging from 64 KB to 16 MB. Current processors include **advanced transfer cache**, a type of L2 cache built directly on the processor chip. Processors that use advanced transfer cache perform at much faster rates than those that do not use it. Personal computers today typically have from 512 KB to 2 MB of advanced transfer cache.

Cache speeds up processing time because it stores frequently used instructions and data. When the processor needs an instruction or data, it searches memory in this order: L1 cache, then L2 cache, then RAM — with a greater delay in processing for each level of memory it must search. If the instruction or data is not found in memory, then it must search a slower speed storage medium such as a hard disk, CD, or DVD.

ROM

Read-only memory (**ROM** pronounced rahm) refers to memory chips storing permanent data and instructions. The data on most ROM chips cannot be modified — hence, the name read-only. ROM is nonvolatile, which means its contents are not lost when power is removed from the computer.

Manufacturers of ROM chips often record data, instructions, or information on the chips when they manufacture the chips. These ROM chips, called **firmware**, contain permanently written data, instructions, or information.

Flash Memory

Flash memory is a type of nonvolatile memory that can be erased electronically and rewritten. Most computers use flash memory to hold their startup instructions because it allows the computer easily to update its contents. For example, when the computer changes from standard time to daylight savings time, the contents of a flash memory chip (and the real-time clock chip) change to reflect the new time.

Flash memory chips also store data and programs on many mobile computers and devices, such as PDAs, smart phones, printers, digital cameras, automotive devices, music players, digital voice recorders, and pagers. Some MP3 players store music on flash memory chips (Figure 4-14). Others store music on tiny hard disks or flash memory cards. A later section in this chapter discusses flash memory cards, which contain flash memory on a removable device instead of a chip.

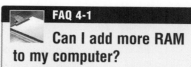

FAQ 4-1

Can I add more RAM to my computer?

Check your computer documentation to see how much RAM you can add. RAM modules are relatively inexpensive and usually include easy-to-follow installation instructions. Be sure to purchase RAM compatible with your brand and model of computer. For more information, visit scsite.com/dcf2e/ch4/faq and then click Upgrading RAM.

FAQ 4-2

How much music can I store on an MP3 player?

MP3 players that store music on flash memory chips can hold up to 8 or 9 hours of music, which is about 120 songs in the WMA format or 60 songs in the MP3 format. MP3 players with tiny hard disks have a much greater storage capacity — from 1,000 to 10,000 songs. For more information, visit scsite.com/dcf2e/ch4/faq and then click MP3 Players.

FIGURE 4-14 HOW AN MP3 MUSIC PLAYER MIGHT STORE MUSIC ON FLASH MEMORY

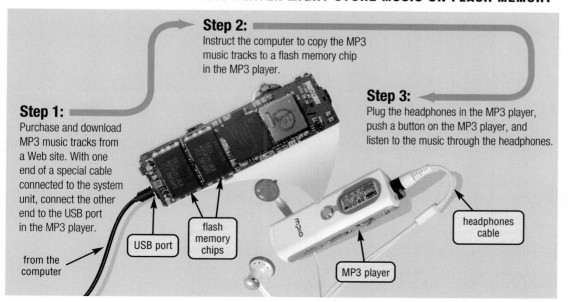

Step 1:
Purchase and download MP3 music tracks from a Web site. With one end of a special cable connected to the system unit, connect the other end to the USB port in the MP3 player.

Step 2:
Instruct the computer to copy the MP3 music tracks to a flash memory chip in the MP3 player.

Step 3:
Plug the headphones in the MP3 player, push a button on the MP3 player, and listen to the music through the headphones.

from the computer

USB port

flash memory chips

MP3 player

headphones cable

WEB LINK 4-5

Flash Memory

For more information, visit scsite.com/dcf2e/ch4/weblink and then click Flash Memory.

CMOS

Some RAM chips, flash memory chips, and other types of memory chips use complementary metal-oxide semiconductor (**CMOS** pronounced SEE-moss) technology because it provides high speeds and consumes little power. CMOS technology uses battery power to retain information even when the power to the computer is off. Battery-backed CMOS memory chips, for example, can keep the calendar, date, and time current even when the computer is off. The flash memory chips that store a computer's startup information often use CMOS technology.

FAQ 4-3

What should I do if my computer's date and time are wrong?

First, try resetting the date and time. To do this in Windows XP, double-click the time on the taskbar. If the computer continues to lose time or display an incorrect date, you may need to replace the CMOS battery on the motherboard that powers the system clock. For more information, visit scsite.com/dcf2e/ch4/faq and then click CMOS Battery.

Memory Access Times

Access time is the amount of time it takes the processor to read data, instructions, and information from memory. A computer's access time directly affects how fast the computer processes data. Accessing data in memory can be more than 200,000 times faster than accessing data on a hard disk because of the mechanical motion of the hard disk.

Today's manufacturers use a variety of terminology to state access times (Figure 4-15). Some use fractions of a second, which for memory occurs in nanoseconds. A **nanosecond** (abbreviated ns) is one billionth of a second. A nanosecond is extremely fast (Figure 4-16). Other manufacturers state access times in MHz; for example, 133 MHz RAM.

While access times of memory greatly affect overall computer performance, manufacturers and retailers usually list a computer's memory in terms of its size, not its access time.

ACCESS TIME TERMINOLOGY

Term	Abbreviation	Speed
Millisecond	ms	One-thousandth of a second
Microsecond	µs	One-millionth of a second
Nanosecond	ns	One-billionth of a second
Picosecond	ps	One-trillionth of a second

FIGURE 4-15   Access times are measured in fractions of a second. This table lists the terms used to define access times.

10 million operations = 1 blink

FIGURE 4-16   It takes about one-tenth of a second to blink your eye, which is the equivalent of 100 million nanoseconds. In the time it takes to blink your eye, a computer can perform some operations 10 million times.

Test your knowledge of pages 140 through 146 in Quiz Yourself 4-2.

QUIZ YOURSELF 4-2

Instructions: Find the true statement below. Then, rewrite the remaining false statements so they are true.

1. A computer's memory access time directly affects how fast the computer processes data.
2. A gigabyte (GB) equals approximately 1 trillion bytes.
3. Memory cache helps speed the processes of the computer because it stores seldom used instructions and data.
4. Most computers are analog, which means they recognize only two discrete states: on and off.
5. Most RAM retains its contents when the power is removed from the computer.
6. Read-only memory (ROM) refers to memory chips storing temporary data and instructions.

Quiz Yourself Online: To further check your knowledge of bits, bytes, data representation, and types of memory, visit scsite.com/dcf2e/ch4/quiz and then click Objectives 3 – 4.

EXPANSION SLOTS AND ADAPTER CARDS

An **expansion slot** is a socket on the motherboard that can hold an adapter card. An **adapter card**, sometimes called an **expansion card**, is a circuit board that enhances functions of a component of the system unit and/or provides connections to peripherals. A **peripheral** is a device that connects to the system unit and is controlled by the processor in the computer. Examples of peripherals are modems, disk drives, printers, scanners, and keyboards.

Figure 4-17 lists a variety of types of adapter cards. Sometimes, all functionality is built into the adapter card. With others, a cable connects the adapter card to a peripheral, such as a scanner, outside the system unit. Figure 4-18 shows an adapter card being inserted in an expansion slot on a personal computer motherboard.

Some motherboards include all necessary capabilities and do not require adapter cards. Other motherboards may require adapter cards to provide capabilities such as sound and video. A **sound card** enhances the sound-generating capabilities of a personal computer by allowing sound to be input through a microphone and output through external speakers or headset. A **video card**, also called a **graphics card**, converts computer output into a video signal that travels through a cable to the monitor, which displays an image on the screen.

WEB LINK 4-6

Adapter Cards
For more information, visit scsite.com/dcf2e/ch4/weblink and then click Adapter Cards.

TYPES OF ADAPTER CARDS

Adapter Card	Purpose
Disk controller	Connects disk drives
FireWire	Connects to FireWire devices
Graphics accelerator	Increases the speed at which graphics are displayed
MIDI	Connects musical instruments
Modem	Connects other computers through telephone or cable television lines
Network	Connects other computers and peripherals
PC-to-TV converter	Connects a television
Sound	Connects speakers or a microphone
TV tuner	Allows viewing of television channels on the monitor
USB 2.0	Connects to USB 2.0 devices
Video	Connects a monitor
Video capture	Connects a camcorder

FIGURE 4-17 Currently used adapter cards and their functions.

FIGURE 4-18 An adapter card being inserted in an expansion slot on the motherboard of a personal computer.

PC Cards, Flash Memory Cards, and USB Flash Drives

Notebook and other mobile computers have at least one **PC Card slot**, which is a special type of expansion slot that holds a PC Card. A **PC Card** is a thin, credit card-sized device that adds memory, storage, sound, fax/modem, network, and other capabilities to mobile computers (Figure 4-19).

All PC Cards conform to standards developed by the Personal Computer Memory Card International Association (these cards originally were called PCMCIA cards). These standards help to ensure the interchangeability of PC Cards among mobile computers. Although some PC Cards contain tiny hard disks, many PC Cards are a type of flash memory card.

PC Card

FIGURE 4-19 A PC Card slides in a PC Card slot on a notebook computer.

A **flash memory card** is a removable flash memory device that allows users to transfer data and information conveniently from mobile devices to their desktop computers. Many mobile and consumer devices, such as PDAs, smart phones, digital cameras, and digital music players use these memory cards. Some printers and computers have built-in card readers/writers or slots that read flash memory cards. In addition, you can purchase an external card reader/writer that attaches to any computer. The type of flash memory card you have will determine the type of card reader/writer you need. Storage capacities of flash memory cards range from 64 MB to 5 GB.

Another widely used type of removable flash memory is the USB flash drive. A **USB flash drive** is a flash memory storage device that plugs in a USB port on a computer or portable device. (The next section discusses USB ports.) Storage capacities of USB flash drives range from 64 MB to 1 GB.

Figure 4-20 shows a variety of removable flash memory devices.

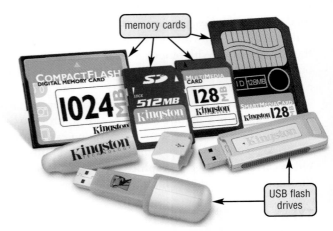

FIGURE 4-20 Removable flash memory devices are available in a range of sizes.

PORTS AND CONNECTORS

A **port** is the point at which a peripheral attaches to a system unit so the peripheral can send data to or receive information from the computer. An external device, such as a keyboard, monitor, printer, mouse, and microphone, often attaches by a cable to a port on the system unit. Instead of port, the term jack sometimes is used to identify audio and video ports. The back of the system unit contains many ports; some newer personal computers also have ports on the front of the system unit (Figure 4-21).

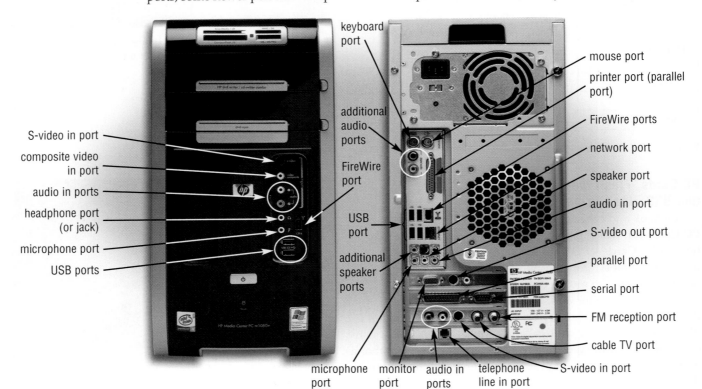

FIGURE 4-21 The back of a system unit has many ports. Most computers have ports on the front of the system unit, also.

Ports have different types of connectors. A **connector** joins a cable to a peripheral. One end of a cable attaches to the connector on the system unit, and the other end of the cable attaches to a connector on the peripheral.

Most desktop personal computers have at least one serial port, one parallel port, several USB ports, and a FireWire port. The next section discusses these and other ports.

Serial Ports

A **serial port** is a type of interface that connects a device to the system unit by transmitting data one bit at a time (Figure 4-22). Serial ports usually connect devices that do not require fast data transmission rates, such as a mouse, keyboard, or modem. The COM port (short for communications port) on the system unit is one type of serial port.

Parallel Ports

Unlike a serial port, a **parallel port** is an interface that connects devices by transferring more than one bit at a time (Figure 4-23). Parallel ports originally were developed as an alternative to the slower speed serial ports. Many printers connect to the system unit using a parallel port. This parallel port can transfer eight bits of data (one byte) simultaneously through eight separate lines in a single cable.

USB Ports

A **USB port**, short for universal serial bus port, can connect up to 127 different peripherals together with a single connector type. Devices that connect to a USB port include the following: mouse, printer, digital camera, scanner, speakers, MP3 music player, CD, DVD, and removable hard disk. Personal computers typically have six to eight USB ports either on the front or back of the system unit (Figure 4-21). The latest version of USB, called USB 2.0, is a more advanced and faster USB, with speeds 40 times higher than that of its predecessor.

To attach multiple peripherals using a single port, you can use a USB hub. A **USB hub** is a device that plugs in a USB port on

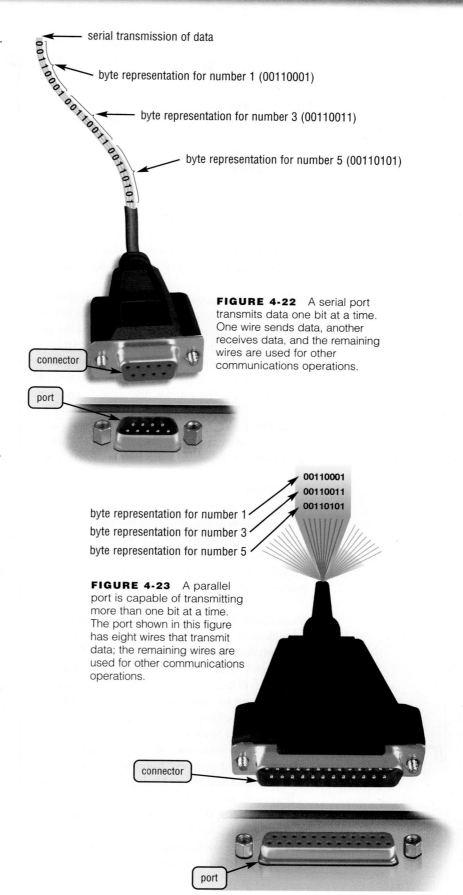

serial transmission of data

byte representation for number 1 (00110001)

byte representation for number 3 (00110011)

byte representation for number 5 (00110101)

connector

port

FIGURE 4-22 A serial port transmits data one bit at a time. One wire sends data, another receives data, and the remaining wires are used for other communications operations.

00110001
00110011
00110101

byte representation for number 1
byte representation for number 3
byte representation for number 5

FIGURE 4-23 A parallel port is capable of transmitting more than one bit at a time. The port shown in this figure has eight wires that transmit data; the remaining wires are used for other communications operations.

connector

port

the system unit and contains multiple USB ports in which you plug cables from USB devices. Some newer peripherals may attach only to a USB port. Others attach to either a serial or parallel port, as well as a USB port.

FireWire Ports

Previously called an IEEE 1394 port, a **FireWire port** is similar to a USB port in that it can connect multiple types of devices that require faster data transmission speeds, such as digital video cameras, digital VCRs, color printers, scanners, digital cameras, and DVD drives, to a single connector. A FireWire port allows you to connect up to 63 devices together. Ports such as USB and FireWire are replacing all other types of ports.

Special-Purpose Ports

Four special-purpose ports are MIDI, SCSI, IrDA, and Bluetooth. These ports are not included in typical computers. For a computer to have these ports, you must customize the computer purchase order. The following sections discuss each of these ports.

MIDI PORT   A special type of serial port that connects the system unit to a musical instrument, such as an electronic keyboard, is called a **MIDI port**. Short for Musical Instrument Digital Interface, MIDI (pronounced MID-dee) is the electronic music industry's standard that defines how devices, such as sound cards and synthesizers, represent sounds electronically. A synthesizer, which can be a peripheral or a chip, creates sound from digital instructions. A system unit with a MIDI port has the capability of recording sounds that have been created by a synthesizer and then processing the sounds (the data) to create new sounds.

SCSI PORT   A special high-speed parallel port, called a **SCSI port**, allows you to attach SCSI (pronounced skuzzy) peripherals such as disk drives and printers. Some computers include a SCSI port. Others have a slot that supports a SCSI card.

IrDA PORT   Some devices can transmit data via infrared light waves. For these wireless devices to transmit signals to a computer, both the computer and the device must have an **IrDA port**.

To ensure nothing obstructs the path of the infrared light wave, you must align the IrDA port on the device with the IrDA port on the computer, similarly to the way you operate a television remote control. Devices that use IrDA ports include a PDA, smart phone, keyboard, mouse, printer, and pager.

BLUETOOTH PORT   An alternative to IrDA, **Bluetooth** technology uses radio waves to transmit data between two devices. Unlike IrDA, the Bluetooth devices do not have to be aligned with each other. Many computers, peripherals, PDAs, smart phones, cars, and other consumer electronics are Bluetooth-enabled, which means they contain a small chip that allows them to communicate with other Bluetooth-enabled computers and devices. If you have a computer that is not Bluetooth enabled, you can purchase a Bluetooth wireless port adapter that will convert an existing USB port or serial port into a Bluetooth port. Also available are Bluetooth PC Cards for notebook computers and Bluetooth cards for PDAs and smart phones.

WEB LINK 4-8

Ports and Connectors

For more information, visit scsite.com/ dcf2e/ch4/weblink and then click Ports and Connectors.

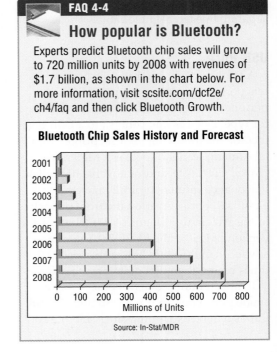

FAQ 4-4

How popular is Bluetooth?

Experts predict Bluetooth chip sales will grow to 720 million units by 2008 with revenues of $1.7 billion, as shown in the chart below. For more information, visit scsite.com/dcf2e/ ch4/faq and then click Bluetooth Growth.

Bluetooth Chip Sales History and Forecast

Source: In-Stat/MDR

WEB LINK 4-9

Buses

For more information, visit scsite.com/dcf2e/ch4/weblink and then click Buses.

BUSES

As explained earlier in this chapter, a computer processes and stores data as a series of electronic bits. These bits transfer internally within the circuitry of the computer along electrical channels. Each channel, called a **bus**, allows the various devices both inside and attached to the system unit to communicate with each other. Just as vehicles travel on a highway to move from one destination to another, bits travel on a bus (Figure 4-24).

Buses transfer bits from input devices to memory, from memory to the processor, from the processor to memory, and from memory to output or storage devices. Buses consist of two parts: a data bus and an address bus. The data bus transfers actual data and the address bus transfers information about where the data should reside in memory.

The size of a bus, called the bus width, determines the number of bits that the computer can transmit at one time. For example, a 32-bit bus can transmit 32 bits (4 bytes) at a time. On a 64-bit bus, bits transmit from one location to another 64 bits (8 bytes) at a time. The larger the number of bits handled by the bus, the faster the computer transfers data. Most personal computers today use a 64-bit bus.

Every bus also has a clock speed. Just like the processor, manufacturers state the clock speed for a bus in hertz. Recall that one megahertz (MHz) is equal to one million ticks per second. Most of today's processors have a bus clock speed of 400, 533, or 800 MHz. The higher the bus clock speed, the faster the transmission of data, which results in applications running faster.

A computer has two basic types of buses: a system bus and an expansion bus. A **system bus** is part of the motherboard and connects the processor to main memory. When computer professionals use the term bus by itself, they usually are referring to the system bus.

An **expansion bus** allows the processor to communicate with peripherals. Some peripherals outside the system unit connect to a port on an adapter card, which is inserted in an expansion slot on the motherboard. This expansion slot connects to the expansion bus, which allows the processor to communicate with the peripheral attached to the adapter card.

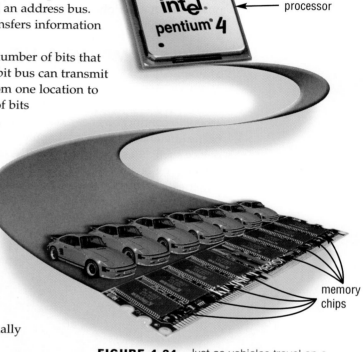

FIGURE 4-24 Just as vehicles travel on a highway, bits travel on a bus. Buses transfer bits from input devices to memory, from memory to the processor, from the processor to memory, and from memory to output or storage devices.

BAYS

After you purchase a computer, you may want to install an additional storage device such as a disk drive in the system unit. A **bay** is an opening inside the system unit in which you can install additional equipment. A bay is different from a slot, which is used for the installation of adapter cards. Rectangular openings, called **drive bays**, typically hold disk drives.

Two types of drive bays exist: external and internal. An external drive bay allows a user to access the drive from outside the system unit (Figure 4-25). Floppy disk drives, CD drives, DVD drives, Zip drives, and tape drives are examples of devices installed in external drive bays. An internal drive bay is concealed entirely within the system unit. Hard disk drives are installed in internal bays.

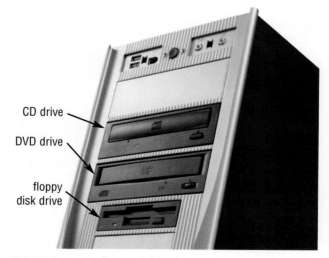

FIGURE 4-25 External drive bays usually are located beside or on top of one another.

POWER SUPPLY

Many personal computers plug in standard wall outlets, which supply an alternating current (AC) of 115 to 120 volts. This type of power is unsuitable for use with a computer, which requires a direct current (DC) ranging from 5 to 12 volts. The **power supply** is the component of the system unit that converts the wall outlet AC power into DC power.

Some external peripherals such as an external modem, speakers, or a tape drive have an **AC adapter**, which is an external power supply. One end of the AC adapter plugs in the wall outlet and the other end attaches to the peripheral. The AC adapter converts the AC power into DC power that the peripheral requires.

MOBILE COMPUTERS AND DEVICES

As businesses and schools expand to serve people across the country and around the world, increasingly more people need to use a computer while traveling to and from a main office or school to conduct business, communicate, or do homework. Users with such mobile computing needs often have a mobile computer, such as a notebook computer or Tablet PC, or a mobile device such as a smart phone or PDA (Figure 4-26).

Weighing on average between 2.5 and 8 pounds, notebook computers can run either using batteries or using a standard power supply. Smaller PDAs and smart phones run strictly on batteries. Like their desktop counterparts, mobile computers and devices have a motherboard that contains electronic components that process data.

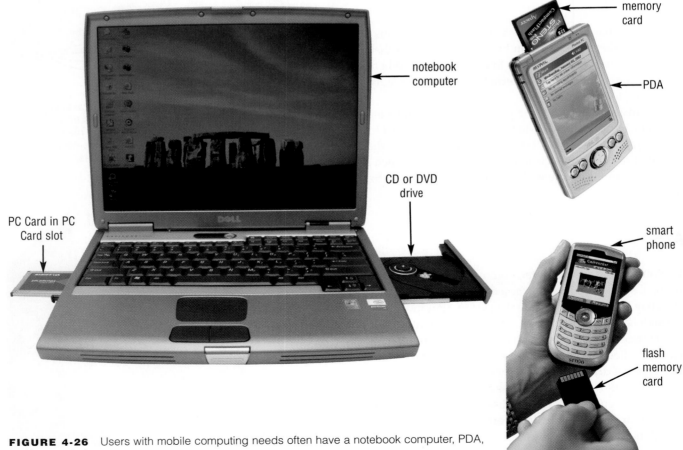

FIGURE 4-26   Users with mobile computing needs often have a notebook computer, PDA, and/or smart phone.

A notebook computer usually is more expensive than a desktop computer with the same capabilities because it is more costly to miniaturize the components. The typical notebook computer often has video, serial, parallel, modem, network, FireWire, USB, headphones, and microphone ports (Figure 4-27).

Two basic designs of Tablet PC are available: slate and convertible. With the slate Tablet PC (shown in Figure 4-1 on page 134), all hardware is behind the display — much like a PDA. Users can attach a removable keyboard to the slate Tablet PC. The display on the convertible Tablet PC, which is attached to a keyboard, can be rotated 180 degrees and folded down over the keyboard. Thus, the convertible Tablet PC can be repositioned to look like either a notebook computer or a slate Tablet PC. Tablet PCs usually include several slots and ports (Figure 4-28).

PDAs and smart phones are quite affordable, usually priced at a few hundred dollars or less. These mobile devices often have an IrDA port or are Bluetooth enabled so users can communicate wirelessly with other computers or devices such as a printer. Read Looking Ahead 4-2 for a look at the next generation of mobile computer.

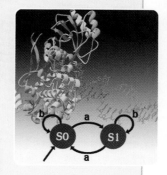

LOOKING AHEAD 4-2

DNA Computer Works to Fight Cancer

One of the newest computers is so tiny that one trillion of them can fit inside a drop of water. The hardware of this biological invention is composed of enzymes that manipulate DNA, and the software is composed of actual DNA.

The concept for this computer had been proposed in 1936, but the actual computer was developed at the Weizmann Institute in Israel in 2001. Today, researchers at the Weizmann Institute are developing applications that process biological information. Their most current success is being able to program the computer to diagnose and treat cancer.

The researchers are hopeful they will be able to have the medical computer function inside a human cell. For more information, visit scsite.com/dcf2e/ch4/looking and then click DNA Computer.

video port   serial port   parallel port   network port   USB ports   microphone port

FIGURE 4-27   Ports on a typical notebook computer.   modem port   FireWire port   headphones port

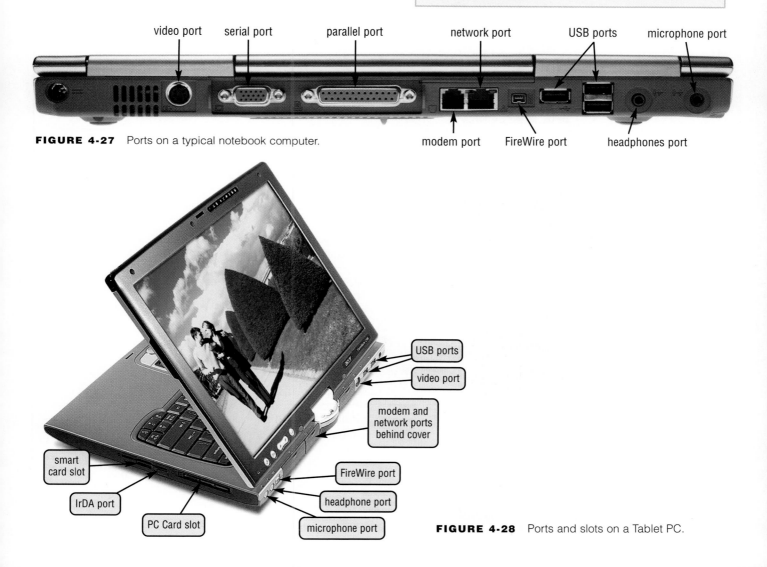

USB ports

video port

modem and network ports behind cover

smart card slot

FireWire port

IrDA port

headphone port

PC Card slot

microphone port

FIGURE 4-28   Ports and slots on a Tablet PC.

PUTTING IT ALL TOGETHER

When you purchase a computer, it is important to understand how the components of the system unit work. Many components of the system unit influence the speed and power of a computer. These include the type of processor, the clock speed of the processor, the amount of RAM, bus width, and the clock speed of the bus. The configuration you require depends on your intended use.

The table in Figure 4-29 lists the suggested minimum processor, clock speed, and RAM requirements based on the needs of various types of computer users.

SUGGESTED MINIMUM CONFIGURATIONS BY USER

User	Processor, Clock Speed, and RAM
HOME 	Celeron (3 GHz or higher) or Sempron (2 GHz or higher) or Pentium 4 (2.8 GHz or higher) or Athlon 64 (2 GHz or higher) Minimum RAM: 256 MB
SMALL OFFICE/HOME OFFICE 	Pentium 4 (3 GHz or higher) or Athlon 64 (2.4 GHz or higher) Minimum RAM: 512 MB
MOBILE 	Celeron M (1.5 GHz or higher) or Pentium M (2 GHz or higher) or Mobile Sempron (1.8 GHz or higher) Minimum RAM: 512 MB
POWER 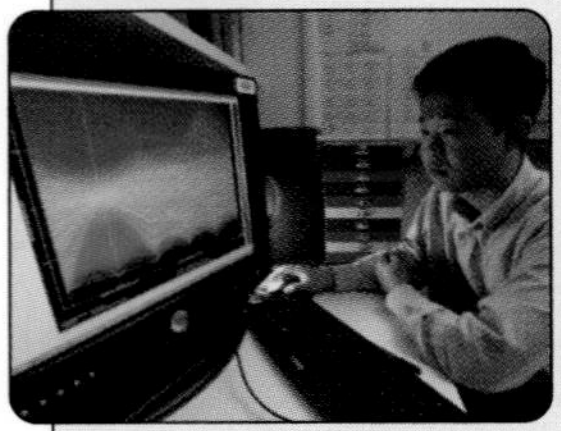	Itanium 2 (1.6 GHz or higher) or Opteron (2.4 GHz or higher) or Xeon MP (3 GHz or higher) or Athlon MP (2.25 GHz or higher) Minimum RAM: 2 GB
LARGE BUSINESS 	Pentium 4 (3.4 GHz or higher) or Athlon 64 (2.4 GHz or higher) Minimum RAM: 1 GB

FIGURE 4-29
Suggested processor, clock speed, and RAM configurations by user.

KEEPING YOUR COMPUTER CLEAN

Over time, the system unit collects dust — even in a clean environment. Built up dust can block airflow in the computer, which can cause it to overheat, corrode, or even stop working. By cleaning your computer once or twice a year, you can help extend its life. This preventive maintenance requires a few basic products (Figure 4-30):

• can of compressed air — removes dust and lint from difficult-to-reach areas
• lint-free antistatic wipes and swabs
• bottle of rubbing alcohol
• small computer vacuum (or small attachments on your house vacuum)
• antistatic wristband — to avoid damaging internal components with static electricity
• small screwdriver (may be required to open the case or remove adapter cards)

Before cleaning the computer, turn it off, unplug it from the electrical outlet, and unplug all cables from the ports. Blow away any dust from all openings on the computer case, such as drives, slots, and ports. Vacuum the power supply fan on the back of the computer case to remove any dust that has accumulated on it. Next, release short blasts of compressed air on the power supply fan. Then, use an antistatic wipe to clean the exterior of the case.

If you need assistance opening the computer case, refer to the instructions that came with the computer. Once the case is open, put the antistatic wristband on your wrist and attach its clip to the case of the computer. Use the antistatic wipes to clean dust and grime inside the walls of the computer case. Vacuum as much dust as possible from the interior of the case, including the wires, chips, adapter cards, and fan blades. Next, release short blasts of compressed air in areas the vacuum cannot reach. If the motherboard and adapter cards still look dirty, gently clean them with lint-free wipes or swabs lightly dampened with alcohol.

When finished, be sure all adapter cards are tightly in their expansion slots. Then close the case, plug in all cables, and attach the power cord. Write down the date you cleaned the computer so you have a record for your next cleaning.

If you do not feel comfortable cleaning the system unit yourself, have a local computer company clean it for you.

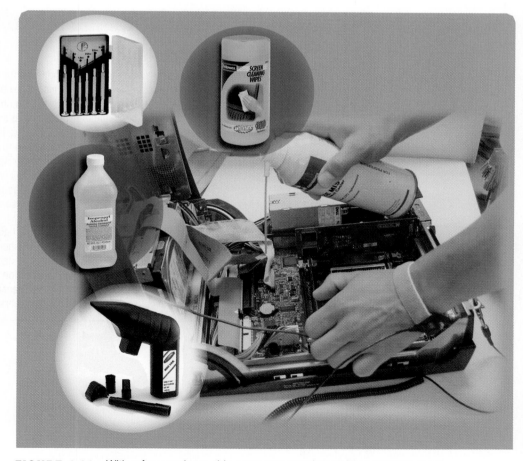

FIGURE 4-30 With a few products, this computer user keeps his computer clean.

Test your knowledge of pages 147 through 155 in Quiz Yourself 4-3.

QUIZ YOURSELF 4-3

Instructions: Find the true statement below. Then, rewrite the remaining false statements so they are true.

1. A bus is the point at which a peripheral attaches to a system unit so the peripheral can send data to or receive information from the computer.

2. An AC adapter is a socket on the motherboard that can hold an adapter card.

3. Serial ports can connect up to 127 different peripherals together with a single connector type.

4. The higher the bus clock speed, the slower the transmission of data.

5. When cleaning the inside of the system unit, wear an antistatic wristband to avoid damaging internal components with static electricity.

Quiz Yourself Online: To further check your knowledge of expansion slots, adapter cards, ports, buses, components of mobile computers and devices, and cleaning a computer, visit scsite.com/dcf2e/ch4/quiz and then click Objectives 5 – 9.

CHAPTER SUMMARY

Chapter 4 presented the components of the system unit; described how memory stores data, instructions, and information; and discussed the sequence of operations that occur when a computer executes an instruction. The chapter included a comparison of various personal computer processors on the market today. It also discussed how to clean a system unit.

CAREER CORNER

Computer Engineer

A **computer engineer** designs and develops the electronic components found in computers and peripheral devices. They also can work as researchers, theorists, and inventors. Companies may hire computer engineers for permanent positions or as consultants, with jobs that extend from a few months to a few years, depending on the project. Engineers in research and development often work on projects that will not be released to the general public for two years.

Responsibilities vary from company to company. All computer engineering work, however, demands problem-solving skills and the ability to create and use new technologies. The ability to handle multiple tasks and concentrate on detail is a key component. Assignments often are taken on as part of a team. Therefore, computer engineers must be able to communicate clearly with both computer personnel and computer users, who may have little technical knowledge.

Before taking in-depth computer engineering design and development classes, students usually take mathematics, physics, and basic engineering. Computer engineering degrees include B.S., M.S., and Ph.D. Because computer engineers employed in private industry often advance into managerial positions, many computer engineering graduates obtain a master's degree in business administration (M.B.A.). Most computer engineers earn between $56,000 and $92,000 annually, depending on their experience and employer, but salaries can exceed $115,000. For more information, visit scsite.com/dcf2e/ch4/careers and then click Computer Engineer.

AMD
PC Processor Supplier

Customer needs influence the integrated circuits Advanced Micro Devices (AMD) develops for the computing, communications, and consumer electronics industries. AMD calls this philosophy "customer-centric innovation."

As a global supplier of PC processors, AMD engineers its technologies at its Submicron Development Center (SDC) in Sunnyvale, California. The technologies are put into production at manufacturing facilities in the United States, Europe, Asia, and Japan.

Among the company's most recent products are the AMD Athlon 64 processor for desktop and personal computers and the AMD Opteron processor for servers and workstations. The company also is working with personal computer manufacturers to develop media-center computers based on its Athlon 64 chips for playing and distributing music and video throughout a home. For more information, visit scsite.com/dcf2e/ch4/companies and then click AMD.

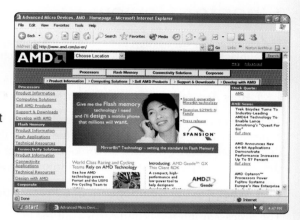

Intel
Chip Maker Dominates the Computer Market

When Gordon Moore and Robert Noyce started Intel in 1968, their goal was to replace magnetic core memory with semiconductor memory. Noyce and Moore, together with Andy Grove, refined the process of placing thousands of tiny electronic devices on a silicon chip. In 1971, the company introduced the Intel 4004, the first single-chip microprocessor.

When IBM chose the Intel 8008 chip for its new personal computer in 1980, Intel chips became standard for all IBM-compatible personal computers. Today, Intel's microprocessors are the building blocks in countless personal computers, servers, networks, and communications devices. In 2003, Intel developed its Centrino mobile technology, which integrates wireless capabilities in notebook computers and Tablet PCs. For more information, visit scsite.com/dcf2e/ch4/companies and then click Intel.

TECHNOLOGY TRAILBLAZERS

Jack Kilby
Integrated Circuit Inventor

Jack Kilby holds more than 60 patents, but one has changed the world. His integrated circuit, or microchip, invention made microprocessors possible.

Kilby started his work with miniature electrical components at Centralab, where he developed transistors for hearing aids. He then took a research position with Texas Instruments and developed a working model of the first integrated circuit, which was patented in 1959. Kilby applied this invention to various industrial, military, and commercial applications, including the first pocket calculator, called the Pocketronic.

Kilby is retired from Texas Instruments and works as a consultant and teacher. He was awarded the Nobel Prize in physics in 2000 for his invention of the integrated circuit, an invention he believes will continue to change the world. For more information, visit scsite.com/dcf2e/ch4/people and then click Jack Kilby.

Gordon Moore
Intel Cofounder

More than 40 years ago, Gordon Moore predicted that the number of transistors and resistors placed on computer chips would double every year, with a proportional increase in computing power and decrease in cost. This bold forecast, now known as Moore's Law, proved amazingly accurate for 10 years. Then, Moore revised the estimate to doubling every two years.

Convinced of the future of silicon chips, Moore founded Intel in 1968. Moore's lifelong interest in technology was kindled at an early age when he experimented with a neighbor's chemistry set. Even then, he displayed the passion for practical outcomes that has typified his work as a scientist and engineer.

Moore says that the semiconductor industry's progress will far surpass that of nearly all other industries. For more information, visit scsite.com/dcf2e/ch4/people and then click Gordon Moore.

Chapter Review

The Chapter Review section summarizes the concepts presented in this chapter. To obtain help from other students regarding any subject in this chapter, visit scsite.com/dcf2e/ch4/forum and post your thoughts or questions.

① How Are Various Styles of System Units Different?

The **system unit** is a case that contains electronic components of the computer used to process data. On desktop personal computers, most storage devices also are part of the system unit. On notebook computers, the keyboard and pointing device often occupy the area on top of the system unit, and the display attaches to the system unit by hinges. On mobile devices, the display frequently is built into the system unit.

② What Are the Components of a Processor, and How Do They Complete a Machine Cycle?

The **processor** interprets and carries out the basic instructions that operate a computer. Processors contain a **control unit** that directs and coordinates most of the operations in the computer and an **arithmetic logic unit** (ALU) that performs arithmetic, comparison, and other operations. The machine cycle is a set of four basic operations — fetching, decoding, executing, and storing — that the processor repeats for every instruction. The control unit fetches program instructions and data from memory and decodes the instructions into commands the computer can execute. The ALU executes the commands, and the results are stored in memory.

 Visit scsite.com/dcf2e/ch4/quiz or click the Quiz Yourself button. Click Objectives 1 – 2.

③ What Is a Bit, and How Does a Series of Bits Represent Data?

Most computers are **digital** and recognize only two discrete states: off and on. To represent these two states, computers use the **binary system**, which is a number system that has just two unique digits — 0 (for off) and 1 (for on) — called bits. A **bit** is the smallest unit of data a computer can process. Grouped together as a unit, 8 bits form a **byte**, which provides enough different combinations of 0s and 1s to represent 256 individual characters. The combinations are defined by patterns, called coding schemes, such as ASCII and EBCDIC.

④ What Are the Various Types of Memory?

The system unit contains volatile and nonvolatile memory. **Volatile memory** loses its contents when the computer's power is turned off. **Nonvolatile memory** does not lose its contents when the computer's power is turned off. RAM is the most common type of volatile memory. ROM, flash memory, and CMOS are examples of nonvolatile memory. **RAM** consists of memory chips that can be read from and written to by the processor and other devices. **ROM** refers to memory chips storing permanent data and instructions that usually cannot be modified. **Flash memory** can be erased electronically and rewritten. **CMOS** technology uses battery power to retain information even when the power to the computer is turned off.

 Visit scsite.com/dcf2e/ch4/quiz or click the Quiz Yourself button. Click Objectives 3 – 4.

⑤ What Are the Types of Expansion Slots and Adapter Cards?

An **expansion slot** is a socket on the motherboard that can hold an adapter card. An **adapter card** is a circuit board that enhances functions of a component of the system unit and/or provides a connection to a **peripheral** such as a modem, disk drive, printer, scanner, or keyboard. Several types of adapter cards exist. A **sound card** enhances the sound-generating capabilities of a personal computer. A **video card** converts computer output into a video signal that displays an image on the screen.

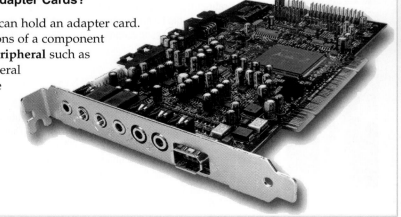

Chapter Review

 6 **How Are a Serial Port, a Parallel Port, a USB Port, and Other Ports Different?**

A **port** is the point at which a peripheral attaches to a system unit so the peripheral can send data to or receive information from the computer. A **serial port**, which transmits data one bit at a time, usually connects devices that do not require fast data transmission, such as a mouse, keyboard, or modem. A **parallel port**, which transfers more than one bit at a time, often connects a printer to the system unit. A **USB port** can connect up to 127 different peripherals together with a single connector type. A **FireWire port** can connect multiple types of devices that require faster data transmission speeds. Four special-purpose ports are MIDI, SCSI, IrDA, and Bluetooth. A **MIDI port** connects the system unit to a musical instrument. A **SCSI port** attaches the system unit to SCSI peripherals, such as disk drives. An **IrDA port** and **Bluetooth** technology allow wireless devices to transmit signals to a computer via infrared light waves or radio waves.

 7 **How Do Buses Contribute to a Computer's Processing Speed?**

A **bus** is an electrical channel along which bits transfer within the circuitry of a computer, allowing devices both inside and attached to the system unit to communicate. The size of a bus, called the bus width, determines the number of bits that the computer can transmit at one time. The larger the bus width, the faster the computer transfers data.

 8 **What Are the Components in Mobile Computers and Mobile Devices?**

Mobile computers and devices have a motherboard that contains electronic components that process data. The system unit for a typical notebook computer often has video, serial, parallel, modem, network, FireWire, USB, headphones, and microphone ports. Tablet PCs usually include several slots and ports. PDAs and smart phones often have an IrDA port or are Bluetooth enabled so users can communicate wirelessly.

 9 **How Do You Clean a System Unit?**

Before cleaning a system unit, turn off the computer and unplug it from the wall. Use a small vacuum and a can of compressed air to remove external dust. After opening the case, wear an antistatic wristband and vacuum the interior. Wipe away dust and grime using lint-free antistatic wipes and rubbing alcohol.

 Visit scsite.com/dcf2e/ch4/quiz or click the Quiz Yourself button. Click Objectives 5 – 9.

Key Terms

You should know each key term. Use the list below to help focus your study. To further enhance your understanding of the Key Terms in this chapter, visit scsite.com/dcf2e/ch4/terms. See an example of and a definition for each term, and access current and additional information about the term from the Web.

AC adapter (152)
access time (146)
adapter card (147)
advanced transfer cache (145)
arithmetic logic unit (137)
bay (151)
binary system (140)
bit (140)
Bluetooth (150)
bus (151)
byte (140)
cache (144)
central processing unit (CPU) (137)
chip (136)
clock speed (138)
CMOS (146)

connector (149)
control unit (137)
digital (140)
drive bays (151)
expansion bus (151)
expansion card (147)
expansion slot (147)
FireWire port (150)
firmware (145)
flash memory (145)
flash memory card (148)
gigabyte (GB) (142)
gigahertz (GHz) (138)
graphics card (147)
IrDA port (150)
kilobyte (KB or K) (142)
L1 cache (145)

L2 cache (145)
megabyte (MB) (142)
memory (142)
memory cache (144)
memory module (144)
memory slots (144)
microprocessor (137)
MIDI port (150)
motherboard (136)
nanosecond (146)
nonvolatile memory (142)
parallel port (149)
PC Card (147)
PC Card slot (147)
peripheral (147)
port (148)
power supply (152)

processor (137)
RAM (143)
read-only memory (ROM) (145)
SCSI port (150)
serial port (149)
sound card (147)
system bus (151)
system clock (138)
system unit (134)
terabyte (TB) (142)
USB flash drive (148)
USB hub (149)
USB port (149)
video card (147)
volatile memory (142)

Checkpoint

Use the Checkpoint exercises to check your knowledge level of the chapter.

True/False

Mark T for True and F for False. (See page numbers in parentheses.)

_____ 1. On desktop personal computers, the electronic components and most of the storage devices normally occupy space outside of the system unit. (134)

_____ 2. The motherboard is the main circuit board of the system unit. (136)

_____ 3. The arithmetic logic unit directs and coordinates most of the operations in the computer. (137)

_____ 4. The system clock generates regular electronic pulses, or ticks, that set the operating pace of components of the system unit. (138)

_____ 5. A bit is the smallest unit of data the computer can process. (140)

_____ 6. A gigabyte equals approximately 1 million bytes. (142)

_____ 7. RAM can hold only one program at a time. (143)

_____ 8. Read-only memory (ROM) refers to memory chips storing permanent data and instructions. (145)

_____ 9. A sound card converts computer output into a video signal, which displays a message on the screen. (147)

_____ 10. Serial ports usually connect devices that require fast transmission rates, such as printers. (149)

_____ 11. A bay is an opening inside the system unit in which you can install additional equipment. (151)

Multiple Choice

Select the best answer. (See page numbers in parentheses.)

1. On _____, the display often is built into the system unit. (135)
   a. desktop personal computers
   b. notebook computers
   c. mobile devices
   d. all of the above

2. An integrated circuit _____. (136)
   a. contains microscopic pathways capable of carrying electrical current
   b. acts as an electronic switch that opens or closes a circuit for electrical charges
   c. cools the processor in notebook computers
   d. speeds the processes of a computer by storing frequently used instructions

3. The term decoding refers to the process of _____. (138)
   a. obtaining a program instruction or data item from memory
   b. translating an instruction into signals a computer can execute
   c. carrying out commands
   d. writing a result to memory

4. Less expensive, basic PCs use a brand of Intel processor called the _____. (139)
   a. Pentium   b. Celeron
   c. Xeon   d. Itanium

5. _____ is the most widely used coding scheme and is used by most personal computers and midrange servers. (140)
   a. ASCII
   b. Unicode
   c. EBCDIC
   d. Microcode

6. Memory stores _____. (142)
   a. the operating system and other system software
   b. application programs that carry out specific tasks
   c. the data being processed by the application programs
   d. all of the above

7. Nonvolatile memory _____. (142)
   a. loses its contents when the computer's power is turned off
   b. does not lose its contents when the computer's power is turned off
   c. includes RAM
   d. both a and c

8. A type of RAM called _____ stores data using magnetic charges instead of electrical charges. (144)
   a. DRAM
   b. SRAM
   c. ERAM
   d. magnetoresistive RAM

Matching

Match the terms with their definitions. (See page numbers in parentheses.)

_____ 1. microprocessor (137)

_____ 2. memory module (144)

_____ 3. USB flash drive (148)

_____ 4. synthesizer (150)

_____ 5. expansion bus (151)

_____ 6. bay (151)

a. small circuit board on which RAM chips usually reside

b. allows the processor to communicate with peripherals

c. term used by some manufacturers to refer to a personal computer processor chip

d. peripheral or chip that creates sound from digital instructions

e. opening inside the system unit in which additional equipment can be installed

f. small ceramic or metal component that absorbs and ventilates heat

g. memory storage device that plugs in a port on a computer or portable device

Checkpoint

Short Answer

Write a brief answer to each of the following questions.

1. What is the system clock? _____ How does clock speed affect a computer's speed? _____
2. How is dynamic RAM different from static RAM? _____ On what does the amount of necessary RAM in a computer depend? _____
3. What is memory cache? _____ How are the two types of cache (L1 cache and L2 cache) different? _____
4. What is a port? _____ How are a serial port, a parallel port, a USB port, and a FireWire port different? _____
5. What is a bus? _____ How does bus width affect a computer's data transfer speed? _____

Working Together

Working in a group of your classmates, complete the following team exercise.

1. Prepare a report on the different types of ports and the way you connect peripheral devices to a computer. As part of your report, include the following subheadings and an overview of each subheading topic: (1) What is a port? (2) What is a connector? (3) What is a serial port and how does it work? (4) What is a parallel port and how does it work? (5) What is a USB port and how does it work? Expand your report so that it includes information beyond that in your textbook. Create a PowerPoint presentation from your report. Share your presentation with your class.

Web Research

Use the Internet-based Web Research exercises to broaden your understanding of the concepts presented in this chapter. Visit scsite.com/dcf2e/ch4/research to obtain more information pertaining to each exercise. To discuss any of the Web Research exercises in this chapter with other students, post your thoughts or questions at scsite.com/dcf2e/ch4/forum.

① Journaling Respond to your readings in this chapter by writing at least one page containing your reactions, evaluations, and reflections about when you have considered buying a computer. For example, did you shop online, at a local computer dealer, at a local large retail store, or your school bookstore? What type of processor did you contemplate? How much memory? Desktop or mobile? Apple or PC? What type of ports did the computer have? How many bays? You also can write about the new terms you learned by reading this chapter. If required, submit your journal to your instructor.

② Scavenger Hunt Use one of the search engines listed in Figure 2-8 in Chapter 2 on page 58 or your own favorite search engine to find the answers to the questions below. Copy and paste the Web address from the Web page where you found the answer. Some questions may have more than one answer. If required, submit your answers to your instructor. (1) Which Microsoft Windows operating systems support USB? (2) The USB port supports hot plugging or hot swapping. What is "hot plugging"? (3) What is the name of the suit that people wear when they work in chip manufacturing clean rooms? (4) What is the name of the group of integrated circuits designed to perform one or more related functions that orchestrate the flow of data to and from key components of a personal computer? (5) What is the name of the type of memory that retains its contents until it is exposed to ultraviolet light?

③ Search Sleuth Ask Jeeves (ask.com) is one of the faster growing research Web sites. The search engine uses natural language, which allows researchers to type millions of questions each day using words a human would use rather than words a computer understands. This enables you to ask a question just like you would ask your instructor a question during class. Visit this Web site and then use your word processing program to answer the following questions. Then, if required, submit your answers to your instructor. (1) Click the P.G. Wodehouse link at the bottom of the home page. Who are P.G. Wodehouse and Bertie Wooster? (2) Click your browser's Back button or press the BACKSPACE key to return to the Ask Jeeves home page. Click the Search text box and then type What were the top grossing films this weekend? as the keywords in the Search text box. (3) Scroll through the links Ask Jeeves returns and then click one that provides the information requested. What three films grossed the most money this weekend? How much did the top film gross? (4) Click your browser's Back button or press the BACKSPACE key to return to the Ask Jeeves home page. Click the News Search link at the bottom of the page. (5) Click one of the Top Stories links and review the material. Review the information you read and then write a 50-word summary.

Learn How To

Use the Learn How To activities to learn fundamental skills when using a computer and accompanying technology. Complete the exercises and submit them to your instructor.

LEARN HOW TO 1: Purchase and Install Memory in a Computer

One of the less expensive and more effective ways to speed up a computer, make it capable of processing more programs at the same time, and enable it to handle graphics, gaming, and other high-level programs is to increase the amount of memory. The process of increasing memory is accomplished in two phases — purchasing the memory and installing the memory. To purchase memory for a computer, complete the following steps:

1. Determine the amount of memory currently in the computer. For a method to do this, see Learn How To number 3 in Chapter 1.
2. Determine the maximum amount of memory your computer can contain. This value can change for different computers, based primarily on the number of slots on the motherboard available for memory and the size of the memory modules you can place in each slot. On most computers, different size memory modules can be inserted in slots. A computer, therefore, might allow a 128 MB, 256 MB, or 512 MB memory module to be inserted in each slot. To determine the maximum memory for a computer, multiply the number of memory slots on the computer by the maximum size memory module that can be inserted in each slot.

   For example, if a computer contains four memory slots and is able to accept memory modules of 128 MB, 256 MB, or 512 MB in each of its memory slots, the maximum amount of memory the computer can contain is 2 GB (4 x 512 MB).

   You can find the number of slots and the allowable sizes of each memory module by contacting the computer manufacturer, looking in the computer's documentation, or contacting sellers of memory such as Kingston (www.kingston.com) or Crucial (www.crucial.com) on the Web. These sellers have documentation for most computers, and even programs you can download to run on your computer that will specify how much memory your computer currently has and how much you can add.
3. Determine how much memory you want to add, which will be somewhere between the current memory and the maximum memory allowed on the computer.
4. Determine the current configuration of memory on the computer. For example, if a computer with four memory slots contains 512 MB of memory, it could be using one memory module of 512 MB in a single slot and the other three slots would be empty; two memory modules of 256 MB each in two slots with two slots empty; one memory module of 256 MB and two memory modules of 128 MB each in three slots with one slot empty; or four memory modules of 128 MB each in four slots with no slots empty. You may be required to look inside the system unit to make this determination. The current memory configuration on a computer will determine what new memory modules you should buy to increase the memory to the amount determined in Step 3.

   You also should be aware that a few computers require memory to be installed in the computer in matching pairs. This means that a computer with four slots could obtain 512 MB of memory with two memory modules of 256 MB each in two slots, or four memory modules of 128 MB each in four slots.
5. Determine the number of available memory slots on your computer and the number and size memory modules you must buy to fulfill your requirement. Several scenarios can occur (in the following examples, assume you can install memory one module at a time).
   a. Scenario 1: The computer has one or more open slots. In this case, you might be able to purchase a memory module that matches the amount of memory increase you desire. For example, if you want to increase memory by 256 MB, you should purchase a 256 MB memory module for insertion in the open slot. Generally, you should buy the maximum size module you can for an open slot. So, if you find two empty slots and wish to increase memory by 256 MB, it is smarter to buy one 256 MB module and leave one empty slot rather than buy two 128 MB memory modules and use both slots. This allows you to increase memory again without removing currently used modules.
   b. Scenario 2: The computer has no open slots. For example, a computer containing 512 MB of memory could have four slots each containing 128 MB memory modules. If you want to increase the memory on the computer to 1 GB, you will have to remove some of the 128 MB memory modules and replace them with the new memory modules you purchase. In this example, you want to increase the memory by 512 MB. You would have several options: (1) You could replace all four 128 MB memory modules with 256 MB memory modules; (2) You could replace all four 128 MB memory modules with two 512 MB memory modules; (3) You could replace one 128 MB memory module with a 512 MB memory module, and replace a second 128 MB module with a 256 MB memory module. Each of these options results in a total memory of 1 GB. The best option will depend on the price of memory and whether you anticipate increasing the memory size at a later time. The least expensive option probably would be number 3.

Learn How To

c. Scenario 3: Many other combinations can occur. You may have to perform arithmetic calculations to decide the combination of memory modules that will work for the number of slots on the computer and the desired additional memory.

6. Determine the type of memory to buy for the computer. Computer memory has many types and configurations, and it is critical that you buy the kind of memory for which the computer was designed. It is preferable to buy the same type of memory that currently is found in the computer. That is, if the memory is DDR SDRAM with a certain clock speed, then that is the type of additional memory you should place in the computer. The documentation for the computer should specify the memory type. In addition, the Web sites cited above, and others as well, will present a list of memory modules that will work with your computer. Enough emphasis cannot be placed on the fact that the memory you buy must be compatible with the type of memory usable on your computer. Because there are so many types and configurations, you must be especially diligent to ensure you purchase the proper memory for your computer.

7. Once you have determined the type and size of memory to purchase, buy it from a reputable dealer. Buying poor or mismatched memory is a major reason for a computer's erratic performance and is one of the more difficult problems to troubleshoot.

After purchasing the memory, you must install it on your computer. Complete the following steps to install memory on a computer:

1. Unplug the computer, and remove all electrical cords and device cables from the ports on the computer. Open the case of the system unit. You may want to consult the computer's documentation to determine the exact procedure for opening the system unit.

2. Ground yourself so you do not generate static electricity that can cause memory or other components within the system unit to be damaged. To do this, wear an antistatic wristband you can purchase inexpensively in a computer or electronics store; or, before you touch any component within the system unit, touch an unpainted metal surface such as the metal on the back of the computer. If you are not wearing an antistatic wristband, periodically touch an unpainted metal surface to dissipate any static electricity.

3. Within the system unit, find the memory slots on the motherboard. The easiest way to do this is look for memory modules that are similar to those you purchased. The memory slots often are located near the processor. If you cannot find the slots, consult the documentation. A diagram often is available to help you spot the memory slots.

4. Insert the memory module in the next empty slot. Orient the memory module in the slot to match the modules currently installed. A notch or notches on the memory module will ensure you do not install the module backwards. If your memory module is a DIMM, insert the module straight down into grooves on the clips and then apply gentle pressure to seat the modules properly (see Figure 4-13 on page 144). If your memory is SIMM, which is used on older computers, insert the module at a 45 degree angle and then rotate it to a vertical position until the module snaps into place.

5. If you must remove one or more memory modules before inserting the new memory, carefully release the clips before lifting the memory module out of the memory slot.

6. Plug in the machine and replace all the device cables without replacing the cover.

7. Start the computer. In most cases, the new memory will be recognized and the computer will run normally. If an error message appears, determine the cause of the error. In most cases, if you turn off the computer, remove the chords and cables, ground yourself, and then reinstall the memory, everything will be fine.

8. Replace the computer cover.

Adding memory to a computer can extend its usefulness and increase its processing power.

Exercise

1. Assume you have a computer that contains 256 MB of memory. It contains four memory slots. Each slot can contain 128 MB or 256 MB memory modules. Two of the slots contain 128 MB memory modules. What memory chip(s) would you buy to increase the memory on the computer to 512 MB? What is the maximum memory on the computer? Submit your answers to your instructor.

2. Assume you have a computer that contains 1 GB of memory. It contains four memory slots. Each slot can contain 128 MB, 256 MB, 512 MB, or 1 GB memory modules. Currently, the four slots each contain a 256 MB memory module. What combinations of memory modules will satisfy your memory upgrade to 2 GB? Visit an appropriate Web site to determine which of these combinations is the least expensive. What is your recommendation? Submit your answers to your instructor.

Learn It Online

Use the Learn It Online exercises to reinforce your understanding of the chapter concepts. To access the Learn It Online exercises, visit scsite.com/dcf2e/ch4/learn.

(1) At the Movies — Computing Clusters

To view the Computing Clusters movie, click the number 1 button. Locate your video and click the corresponding High-Speed or Dial-Up link, depending on your Internet connection. Watch the movie, and then complete the exercise by answering the questions below. Many graphics and animation programs have heavy data loads. When using a processing cluster, these difficult memory-intensive tasks can be divided over several different computers linked through a network. Using multiple computers to do a big job means it gets done faster. What types of tasks are best accomplished by a cluster? How would you handle a large, time-consuming project?

(2) Student Edition Labs — Understanding the Motherboard

Click the number 2 button. When the Student Edition Labs menu appears, click *Understanding the Motherboard* to begin. A new browser window will open. Follow the on-screen instructions to complete the Lab. When finished, click the Exit button. If required, submit your results to your instructor.

(3) Practice Test

Click the number 3 button. Answer each question. When completed, enter your name and click the Grade Test button to submit the quiz for grading. Make a note of any missed questions. If required, submit your score to your instructor.

(4) Who Wants To Be a Computer Genius²?

Click the number 4 button to find out if you are a computer genius. Directions about how to play the game will be displayed. When you are ready to play, click the Play button. Submit your score to your instructor.

(5) Wheel of Terms

Click the number 5 button to reinforce important terms you learned in this chapter by playing the Shelly Cashman Series version of this popular game. Directions about how to play the game will be displayed. When you are ready to play, click the Play button. Submit your score to your instructor.

(6) Student Edition Labs — Binary Numbers

Click the number 6 button. When the Student Edition Labs menu appears, click *Binary Numbers* to begin. A new browser window will open. Follow the on-screen instructions to complete the Lab. When finished, click the Exit button. If required, submit your results to your instructor.

(7) Crossword Puzzle Challenge

Click the number 7 button. Complete the puzzle to reinforce skills you learned in this chapter. Directions about how to play the game will be displayed. When you are ready to play, click the Play button. Submit the completed puzzle to your instructor.

(8) Lab Exercises

Click the number 8 button. When the Lab Exercises menu appears, click the exercise assigned by your instructor. A new browser window will open. Follow the on-screen instructions to complete the exercise. When finished, click the Exit button. If required, submit your results to your instructor.

(9) Chapter Discussion Forum

Select an objective from this chapter on page 133 about which you would like more information. Click the number 9 button and post a short message listing a meaningful message title accompanied by one or more questions concerning the selected objective. In two days, return to the threaded discussion by clicking the number 9 button. Submit to your instructor your original message and at least one response to your message.

CHAPTER 5

Input and Output

OBJECTIVES

After completing this chapter, you will be able to:

1. List the characteristics of a keyboard

2. Summarize how these pointing devices work: mouse, trackball, touchpad, pointing stick, joystick, wheel, light pen, touch screen, stylus, and digital pen

3. Describe other types of input, including voice input; input devices for PDAs, smart phones, and Tablet PCs; digital cameras; video input; scanners and reading devices; terminals; and biometric input

4. Describe the characteristics of LCD monitors, LCD screens, and CRT monitors

5. Summarize the various types of printers

6. Explain the characteristics of speakers and headsets, fax machines and fax modems, multifunction peripherals, and data projectors

7. Identify input and output options for physically challenged users

CONTENTS

WHAT IS INPUT?

KEYBOARD AND POINTING DEVICES
The Keyboard
Mouse
Trackball
Touchpad
Pointing Stick
Joystick and Wheel
Light Pen
Touch Screen
Pen Input

OTHER TYPES OF INPUT
Voice Input
Input for PDAs, Smart Phones, and Tablet PCs
Digital Cameras
Video Input
Scanners and Reading Devices
Terminals
Biometric Input

WHAT IS OUTPUT?

DISPLAY DEVICES
LCD Monitors and Screens
Plasma Monitors
CRT Monitors

PRINTERS
Producing Printed Output
Nonimpact Printers
Ink-Jet Printers
Photo Printers
Laser Printers
Thermal Printers
Mobile Printers
Plotters and Large-Format Printers
Impact Printers

OTHER OUTPUT DEVICES
Speakers and Headsets
Fax Machines and Fax Modems
Multifunction Peripherals
Data Projectors

PUTTING IT ALL TOGETHER

INPUT AND OUTPUT DEVICES FOR PHYSICALLY CHALLENGED USERS

CHAPTER SUMMARY

COMPANIES ON THE CUTTING EDGE
Logitech
Hewlett-Packard

TECHNOLOGY TRAILBLAZERS
Douglas Engelbart
Donna Dubinsky

WHAT IS INPUT?

Input is any data and instructions entered into the memory of a computer. As shown in Figure 5-1, people have a variety of options for entering input into a computer.

An **input device** is any hardware component that allows users to enter data and instructions into a computer. The following pages discuss a variety of input devices.

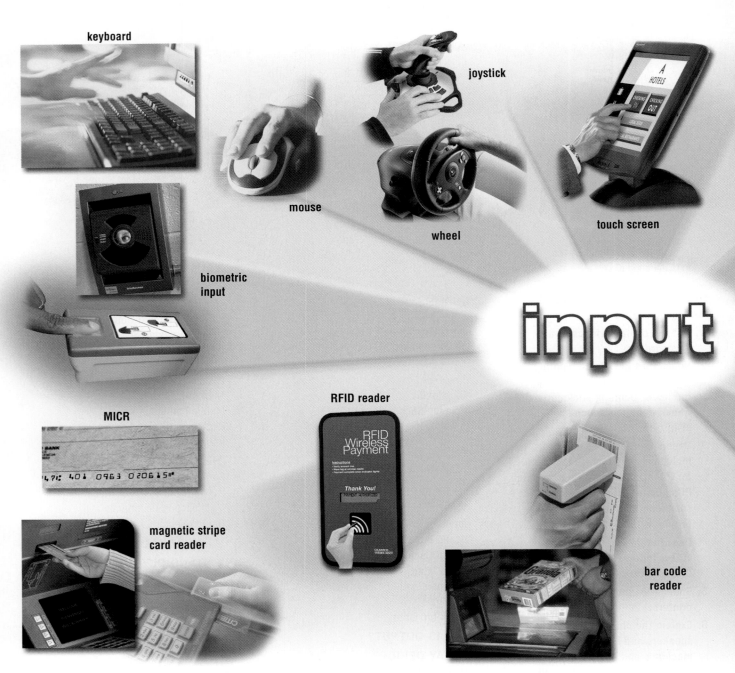

keyboard

joystick

mouse

wheel

touch screen

biometric input

input

MICR

RFID reader

magnetic stripe card reader

bar code reader

FIGURE 5-1   Users can enter data and instructions into a computer in a variety of ways.

KEYBOARD AND POINTING DEVICES

Two of the more widely used input devices are the keyboard and the mouse. Most computers include a keyboard or keyboarding capabilities.

The mouse is a **pointing device** because it allows a user to control a pointer on the screen. In a graphical user interface, a **pointer** is a small symbol on the screen whose location and shape change as a user moves a pointing device. A pointing device can select text, graphics, and other objects; and click buttons, icons, links, and menu commands.

The following pages discuss the keyboard and a variety of pointing devices.

stylus

digital pen

graphics tablet

microphone

scanner

digital camera

video camera

optical mark and character recognition

The Keyboard

Many people use a keyboard as one of their input devices. A **keyboard** is an input device that contains keys users press to enter data and instructions into a computer (Figure 5-2).

All computer keyboards have a typing area that includes the letters of the alphabet, numbers, punctuation marks, and other basic keys. Many desktop computer keyboards also have a numeric keypad on the right side of the keyboard.

Most of today's desktop computer keyboards are enhanced keyboards. An enhanced keyboard has twelve function keys along the top and a set of arrow and additional keys between the typing area and the numeric keypad (Figure 5-2). Function keys are special keys programmed to issue commands to a computer. Many keyboards also have a WINDOWS key(s) and an APPLICATION key. When pressed, the WINDOWS key displays the Start menu, and the APPLICATION key displays an item's shortcut menu.

Newer keyboards also include media control buttons that allow you to access the computer's CD/DVD drive and adjust speaker volume, and Internet controls that allow you to open an e-mail program, start a Web browser, and search the Internet.

Desktop computer keyboards often attach via a cable to a serial port, a keyboard port, or a USB port on the system unit. Some keyboards, however, do not use wires at all. A wireless keyboard, or cordless keyboard, is a battery-powered device that transmits data using wireless technology, such as radio waves or infrared light waves. Wireless keyboards often communicate with a receiver attached to a port on the system unit.

On notebook and some handheld computers, PDAs, and smart phones, the keyboard is built in the top of the system unit. To fit in these smaller computers, the keyboards usually are smaller and have fewer keys.

Regardless of size, many keyboards have a rectangular shape with the keys aligned in straight, horizontal rows. Users who spend a lot of time typing on these keyboards sometimes experience repetitive strain injuries (RSI) of their wrists and hands. For this reason, some manufacturers offer ergonomic keyboards. An ergonomic keyboard has a design that reduces the chance of wrist and hand injuries.

The goal of **ergonomics** is to incorporate comfort, efficiency, and safety in the design of the workplace. Employees can be injured or develop disorders of the muscles, nerves, tendons, ligaments, and joints from working in an area that is not ergonomically designed.

FAQ 5-1

What can I do to reduce chances of experiencing repetitive strain injuries?

Do not rest your wrist on the edge of a desk; use a wrist rest. Keep your forearm and wrist level so your wrist does not bend. Do hand exercises every 15 minutes. Keep your shoulders, arms, hands, and wrists relaxed while you work. Maintain good posture. Keep feet flat on the floor, with one foot slightly in front of the other. For more information, visit scsite.com/dcf2e/ch5/faq and then click Repetitive Strain Injuries.

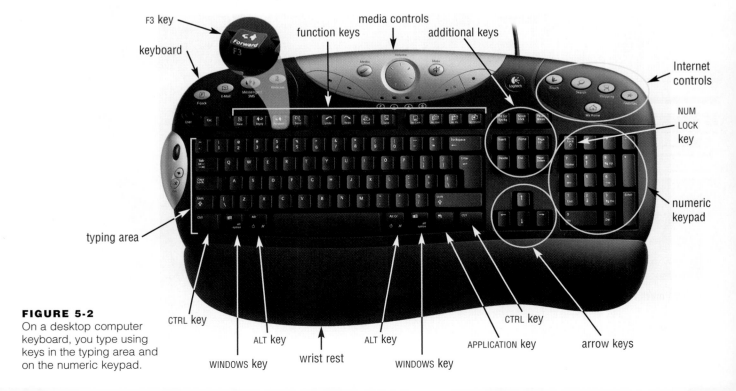

FIGURE 5-2
On a desktop computer keyboard, you type using keys in the typing area and on the numeric keypad.

Mouse

A **mouse** is a pointing device that fits comfortably under the palm of your hand. With a mouse, users control the movement of the pointer. As you move a mouse, the pointer on the screen also moves. Generally, you use the mouse to move the pointer on the screen to an object such as a button, a menu, an icon, a link, or text. Then, you press a mouse button to perform a certain action associated with that object.

A **mechanical mouse** has a rubber or metal ball on its underside (Figure 5-3a). When the ball rolls in a certain direction, electronic circuits in the mouse translate the movement of the mouse into signals the computer can process. You should place a mechanical mouse on a mouse pad. A **mouse pad** is a rectangular rubber or foam pad that provides better traction than the top of a desk.

An optical mouse, by contrast, has no moving mechanical parts inside. Instead, an **optical mouse** uses devices that emit and sense light to detect the mouse's movement. Some use optical sensors (Figure 5-3b); others use laser (Figure 5-3c). An optical mouse is more precise than a mechanical mouse and does not require cleaning as does a mechanical mouse, but it also is more expensive.

A mouse connects to a computer in several ways. Many types connect with a cable that attaches to a serial port, mouse port, or USB port on the system unit. A wireless mouse, or cordless mouse, is a battery-powered device that transmits data using wireless technology, such as radio waves or infrared light waves. Read At Issue 5-1 for a related discussion.

WEB LINK 5-1

Mouse

For more information, visit scsite.com/dcf2e/ch5/weblink and then click Mouse.

FIGURE 5-3a (mechanical mouse) **FIGURE 5-3b** (optical mouse that uses optical sensor) **FIGURE 5-3c** (optical mouse that uses laser)

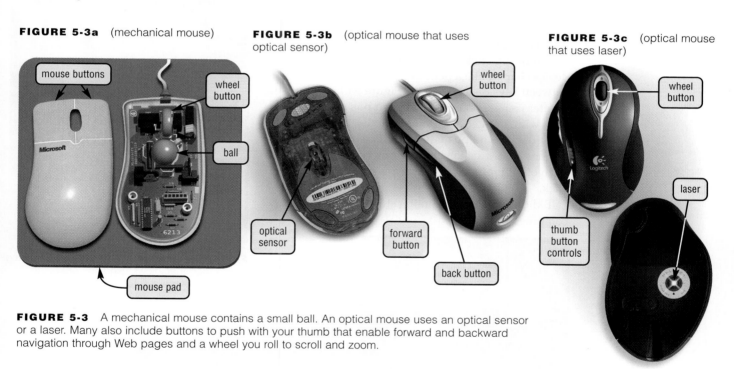

FIGURE 5-3 A mechanical mouse contains a small ball. An optical mouse uses an optical sensor or a laser. Many also include buttons to push with your thumb that enable forward and backward navigation through Web pages and a wheel you roll to scroll and zoom.

 AT ISSUE 5-1

Should the Government Set Computer Use Standards?

When you consider the causes of workplace injuries, you might not put clicking a mouse in the same category with lifting a bag of concrete, but perhaps you should. According to the chairman of a National Academy of Sciences panel that investigated workplace injuries, every year one million Americans lose workdays because of repetitive strain injuries. Repetitive strain injuries are caused when muscle groups perform the same actions over and over again. Once, repetitive strain injuries were common among factory workers who performed the same tasks on an assembly line for hours a day. Today, these injuries, which often result from prolonged use of a computer mouse and keyboard, are the largest job-related injury and illness problem in the United States. OSHA proposed standards whereby employers would have to establish programs to prevent workplace injuries with respect to computer use. Yet, congress rejected the standards, accepting the argument that the cost to employers would be prohibitive and unfair, because no proof exists that the injuries are caused exclusively by office work. Should the government establish laws regarding computer use? Why or why not? Who is responsible for this type of workplace injury? Why?

Trackball

Similar to a mechanical mouse that has a ball on the bottom, a **trackball** is a stationary pointing device with a ball on its top or side (Figure 5-4).

To move the pointer using a trackball, you rotate the ball with your thumb, fingers, or the palm of your hand. In addition to the ball, a trackball usually has one or more buttons that work just like mouse buttons.

Touchpad

A **touchpad** is a small, flat, rectangular pointing device that is sensitive to pressure and motion (Figure 5-5). To move the pointer using a touchpad, slide your fingertip across the surface of the pad. Some touchpads have one or more buttons around the edge of the pad that work like mouse buttons. On most touchpads, you also can tap the pad's surface to imitate mouse operations such as clicking. Touchpads are found most often on notebook computers.

Pointing Stick

A **pointing stick** is a pressure-sensitive pointing device shaped like a pencil eraser that is positioned between keys on a keyboard (Figure 5-6). To move the pointer using a pointing stick, you push the pointing stick with a finger. The pointer on the screen moves in the direction you push the pointing stick. By pressing buttons below the keyboard, users can click and perform other mouse-type operations with a pointing stick.

IBM developed the pointing stick for its notebook computers.

FIGURE 5-4 A trackball is like an upside-down mouse.

FIGURE 5-5 Most notebook computers have a touchpad that allows users to control the movement of the pointer.

FIGURE 5-6 Some notebook computers include a pointing stick to allow a user to control the movement of the pointer.

Joystick and Wheel

Users running game software or flight and driving simulation software often use a joystick or wheel as a pointing device (Figure 5-7). A **joystick** is a vertical lever mounted on a base. You move the lever in different directions to control the actions of the simulated vehicle or player. The lever usually includes buttons called triggers that you press to activate certain events.

A **wheel** is a steering-wheel-type input device. Users turn the wheel to simulate driving a car, truck, or other vehicle. Most wheels also include foot pedals for braking and acceleration actions.

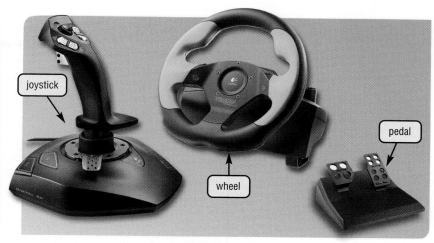

FIGURE 5-7 Joysticks and wheels help a user control the actions of players and vehicles in game and simulation software.

Light Pen

A **light pen** is a handheld input device that can detect the presence of light. Some light pens require a specially designed monitor, while others work with a standard monitor (Figure 5-8). To select objects on the screen, a user presses the light pen against the surface of the screen or points the light pen at the screen and then presses a button on the pen.

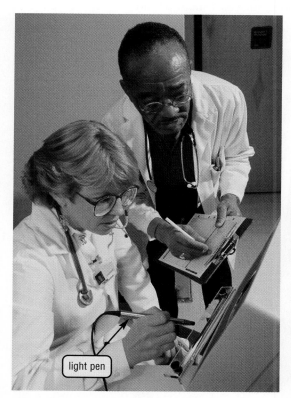

FIGURE 5-8 To use a light pen, you press the pen against the screen or press a button on the pen while pointing the pen toward an object on the screen.

Touch Screen

A **touch screen** is a touch-sensitive display device. Users can interact with these devices by touching areas of the screen. Because touch screens require a lot of arm movements, you do not enter large amounts of data using a touch screen. Instead, users touch words, pictures, numbers, letters, or locations identified on the screen. Kiosks, which are freestanding computers, often have touch screens (Figure 5-9).

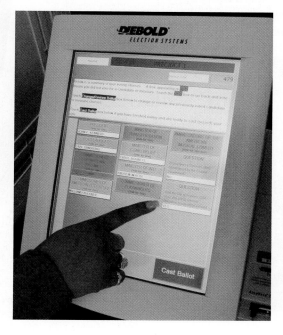

FIGURE 5-9
A voter uses a kiosk touch screen to cast ballots in an election.

Pen Input

Mobile users often enter data and instructions with a pen-type device. With **pen input**, users write, draw, and tap on a flat surface to enter input. The surface may be a monitor, a screen, or a special type of paper. Two devices used for pen input are the stylus and digital pen. A **stylus** is a small metal or plastic device that looks like a tiny ink pen but uses pressure instead of ink. A **digital pen**, which is slightly larger than a stylus, is available in two forms: some are pressure-sensitive; others have built-in digital cameras.

Some mobile computers and nearly all mobile devices have touch screens. Instead of using a finger to enter data and instructions, most of these devices include a pressure-sensitive digital pen or stylus. You write, draw, or make selections on the computer screen by touching the screen with the pen or stylus. For example, Tablet PCs use a pressure-sensitive digital pen (Figure 5-10) and PDAs use a stylus. Pressure-sensitive digital pens, often simply called pens, typically provide more functionality than a stylus, featuring electronic erasers and programmable buttons.

Pen input is possible on computers without touch screens by attaching a graphics tablet to the computer. A **graphics tablet** is a flat, rectangular, electronic, plastic board. Architects, mapmakers, designers, artists, and home users create drawings and sketches by using a pressure-sensitive pen on a graphics tablet (Figure 5-11).

Digital pens that have built-in digital cameras work differently from pressure-sensitive digital pens. These pens look very much like a ballpoint pen and typically do not contain any additional buttons. As you write or draw on special digital paper with the pen, it captures every handwritten mark and then stores the images in the pen's memory. You then can transfer the images from the pen to a computer (Figure 5-12) or mobile device, such as a smart phone.

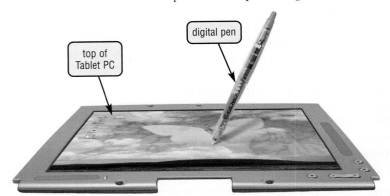

FIGURE 5-10   Tablet PCs use a pressure-sensitive pen.

FIGURE 5-11   Artist using a pen.

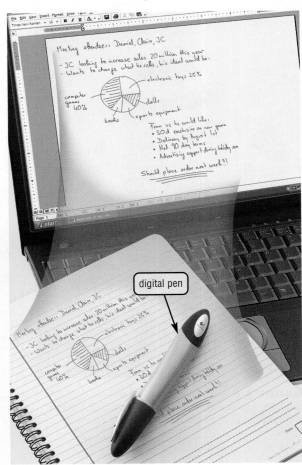

FIGURE 5-12   Some digital pens have built-in digital cameras that store handwritten marks and allow you to transfer your handwriting to a computer.

Test your knowledge of pages 166 through 172 in Quiz Yourself 5-1.

OTHER TYPES OF INPUT

In addition to the keyboard, mouse, and pointing devices just discussed, users have a variety of other options available to enter data and instructions into a computer. These include voice input; input for PDAs, smart phones, and Tablet PCs; digital cameras; video input; scanners and reading devices; terminals; and biometric input. Read Looking Ahead 5-1 for a look at the next generation of input devices.

Voice Input

Voice input is the process of entering input by speaking into a microphone. **Voice recognition**, also called **speech recognition**, is the computer's capability of distinguishing spoken words. Voice recognition programs recognize a vocabulary of preprogrammed words. The vocabulary of voice recognition programs can range from two words to millions of words. Some business software, such as word processing and spreadsheet, includes voice recognition as part of the program. For example, users can dictate memos and letters into a word processing program instead of typing them.

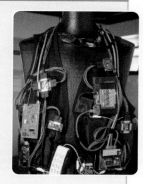
AUDIO INPUT   Voice input is part of a larger category of input called audio input. **Audio input** is the process of entering any sound into the computer such as speech, music, and sound effects. To enter high-quality sound into a personal computer, the computer must have a sound card. Users enter sound into a computer via devices such as microphones, tape players, CD/DVD players, or radios, each of which plugs in a port on the sound card.

Some users also enter music and other sound effects using external MIDI devices such as an electronic piano keyboard (Figure 5-13). MIDI (musical instrument digital interface) is the electronic music industry's standard that defines how digital musical devices represent sounds electronically. Software that conforms to the MIDI standard allows users to compose and edit music and many other sounds.

FIGURE 5-13
An electronic piano keyboard is an external MIDI device that allows users to record music, which can be stored in the computer.

Input for PDAs, Smart Phones, and Tablet PCs

Mobile devices, such as the PDA and smart phone, and mobile computers, such as the Tablet PC, offer convenience for the mobile user. A variety of alternatives for entering data and instructions is available for these devices and computers.

PDAs   A user enters data and instructions into a PDA in many ways (Figure 5-14). PDAs ship with a basic stylus, which is the primary input device. With the stylus, you enter data in two ways: using an on-screen keyboard or using handwriting recognition software. With a specialized pen and data reader, you also can transfer notes as you write them on a pad of paper.

For users who prefer typing to handwriting, some PDAs have a built-in mini keyboard. For PDAs without a keyboard, users can purchase a keyboard that snaps on the bottom of the device. Other users type on a desktop computer or notebook computer keyboard and transfer the data to the PDA. To take photographs and view them on a PDA, simply attach a digital camera directly to the PDA.

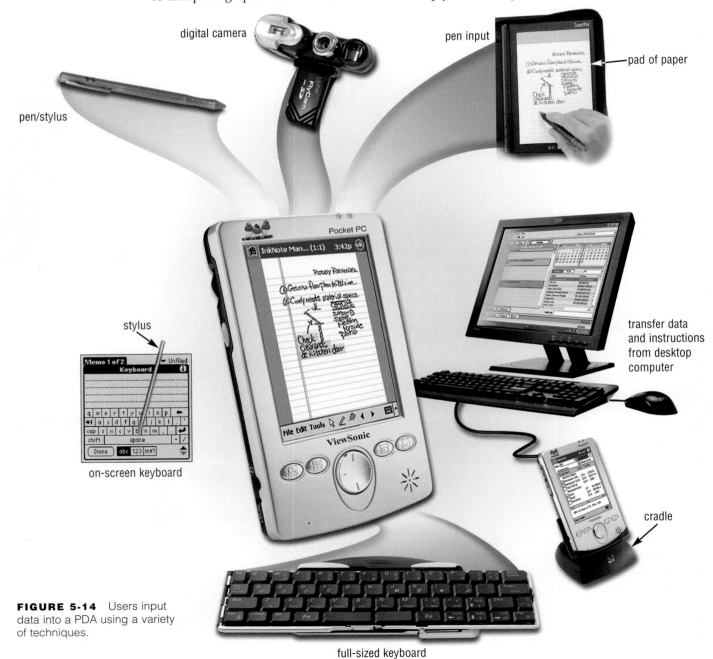

digital camera

pen input

pad of paper

pen/stylus

stylus

on-screen keyboard

Pocket PC

transfer data and instructions from desktop computer

cradle

FIGURE 5-14 Users input data into a PDA using a variety of techniques.

full-sized keyboard

SMART PHONES   Voice is the traditional method of input for smart phones. That is, a user speaks into the phone. Today, however, text messaging, instant messaging, and picture messaging have become popular means of entering data and instructions into a smart phone. With text messaging, you type and send a short message to another smart phone by pressing buttons on the telephone's keypad. Some wireless Internet service providers (WISPs) partner with IM (instant messaging) services so you can use your smart phone to communicate via text with other smart phone or computer users with the same IM service. Users can send graphics, pictures, video clips, and sound files, as well as short text messages with picture messaging, to another smart phone with a compatible picture messaging service.

Most smart phones include PDA capabilities. Thus, input devices used with PDAs typically also are available for smart phones.

TABLET PCs   The primary input device for a Tablet PC is a pressure-sensitive digital pen, which allows users to write on the device's screen. Both the slate and convertible designs of Tablet PC provide a means for keyboard input.

To access peripherals at their home or office, users can slide their Tablet PC in a docking station. A docking station, which is an external device that attaches to a mobile computer, contains a power connection and provides connections to peripherals (Figure 5-15). The design of docking stations varies depending on the type of mobile computer or device to which they attach.

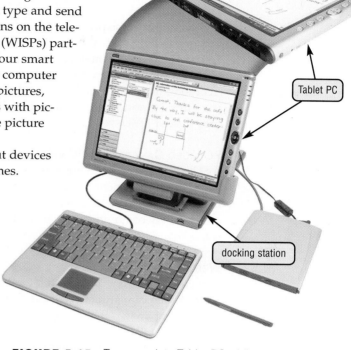

Tablet PC

docking station

FIGURE 5-15   To use a slate Tablet PC while working at a desk, simply insert the Tablet PC in a docking station. Devices such as a keyboard and CD drive can be plugged in the docking station.

Digital Cameras

A **digital camera** allows users to take pictures and store the photographed images digitally, instead of on traditional film (Figure 5-16). Some digital cameras use internal flash memory to store images. Others store images on mobile storage media, including a flash memory card, memory stick, and mini-CD/DVD.

Digital cameras typically allow users to review, and sometimes edit, images while they are in the camera. Some digital cameras can connect to or communicate wirelessly with a printer or television, allowing users to print or view images directly from the camera.

Often users prefer to download, or transfer a copy of, the images from the digital camera to the computer's hard disk, where the images are available for editing with photo editing software, printing, faxing, sending via e-mail, including in another document, or posting to a Web site or photo community for everyone to see.

A digital camera often features flash, zoom, automatic focus, and special effects. Some allow users to record short audio narrations for photographed images. Others even record short video clips in addition to still images.

One factor that affects the quality of a digital camera is its resolution. **Resolution** is the number of horizontal and vertical pixels in a display device. A digital camera's resolution is defined in pixels. A **pixel** (short for picture element) is the smallest element in an electronic image. The greater the number of pixels the camera uses to capture an image, the better the quality of the image. Digital camera resolutions range from about 1 million to more than 8 million pixels (MP).

FIGURE 5-16   With a digital camera, users can view photographed images immediately through a small screen on the camera to see if the picture is worth keeping.

For additional information about digital cameras, read the Digital Imaging and Video Technology feature that follows this chapter.

Video Input

Video input is the process of capturing full-motion images and storing them on a computer's storage medium such as a hard disk or DVD. Some video devices use analog video signals. A **digital video (DV) camera**, by contrast, records video as digital signals instead of analog signals. Many DV cameras have the capability of capturing still frames, as well as motion. To transfer recorded images to a hard disk or CD or DVD, users connect DV cameras directly to a USB port or a FireWire port on the system unit. After saving the video on a storage medium, such as a hard disk or DVD, you can play it or edit it using video editing software on a computer.

PC VIDEO CAMERAS A **PC video camera**, or **PC camera**, is a type of digital video camera that enables a home or small business user to capture video and still images, send e-mail messages with video attachments, add live images to instant messages, broadcast live images over the Internet, and make video telephone calls. During a **video telephone call**, both parties see each other as they communicate over the Internet (Figure 5-17). The cost of PC video cameras usually is less than $100.

WEB CAMS A **Web cam** is any video camera that displays its output on a Web page. A Web cam attracts Web site visitors by showing images that change regularly. Home or small business users might use Web cams to show a work in progress, weather and traffic information, employees at work, photographs of a vacation, and countless other images.

PC video camera

FIGURE 5-17 Using a PC video camera, home users can see each other as they communicate over the Internet.

VIDEO CONFERENCING A **video conference** is a meeting between two or more geographically separated people who use a network or the Internet to transmit audio and video data (Figure 5-18). To participate in a video conference, you need video conferencing software along with a microphone, speakers, and a video camera attached to a computer. As you speak, members of the meeting hear your voice on their speakers. Any image in front of the video camera, such as a person's face, appears in a window on each participant's screen.

As the costs of video conferencing hardware and software decrease, increasingly more business meetings, corporate training, and educational classes will be conducted as video conferences.

FIGURE 5-18 To save on travel expenses, many large businesses are turning to video conferencing.

Scanners and Reading Devices

Some input devices save users time by capturing data directly from a source document, which is the original form of the data. Examples of source documents include time cards, order forms, invoices, paychecks, advertisements, brochures, photographs, inventory tags, or any other document that contains data to be processed.

Devices that can capture data directly from a source document include optical scanners, optical readers, bar code readers, RFID readers, magnetic stripe card readers, and magnetic-ink character recognition readers.

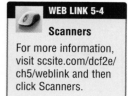

OPTICAL SCANNERS   An optical scanner, usually called a **scanner**, is a light-sensing input device that reads printed text and graphics and then translates the results into a form the computer can process. A **flatbed scanner** works in a manner similar to a copy machine except it creates a file of the document in memory instead of a paper copy (Figure 5-19). Once you scan a picture or document, you can display the scanned object on the screen, store it on a storage medium, print it, fax it, attach it to an e-mail message, include it in another document, or post it to a Web site or photo community for everyone to see.

Many scanners include OCR (optical character recognition) software, which can read and convert text documents into electronic files. OCR software converts a scanned image into a text file that can be edited, for example, with a word processing program.

FIGURE 5-19
A flatbed scanner.

OPTICAL READERS   An optical reader is a device that uses a light source to read characters, marks, and codes and then converts them into digital data that a computer can process. Two technologies used by optical readers are optical character recognition and optical mark recognition.

- **Optical character recognition** (**OCR**) involves reading typewritten, computer-printed, or hand-printed characters from ordinary documents and translating the images into a form the computer can process. Most **OCR devices** include a small optical scanner for reading characters and sophisticated software to analyze what is read. OCR devices range from large machines that can read thousands of documents per minute to handheld wands that read one document at a time.

Many companies use OCR characters on turnaround documents. A **turnaround document** is a document that you return (turn around) to the company that creates and sends it. For example, when consumers receive a bill, they often tear off a portion of the bill and send it back to the company with their payment (Figure 5-20). The portion of the bill they return usually has their payment amount, account number, and other information printed in OCR characters.

- **Optical mark recognition** (**OMR**) devices read hand-drawn marks such as small circles or rectangles. A person places these marks on a form, such as a test, survey, or questionnaire answer sheet.

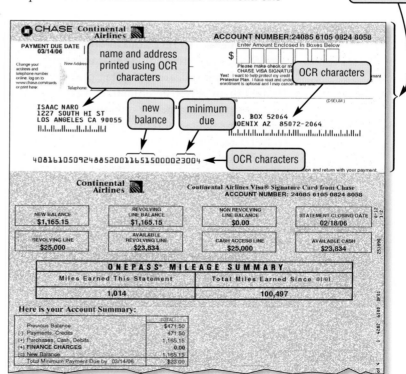

FIGURE 5-20   OCR characters frequently are used with turnaround documents. With this bill, you tear off the top portion and return it with a payment.

BAR CODE READERS A **bar code reader**, also called a bar code scanner, is an optical reader that uses laser beams to read bar codes (Figure 5-21). A **bar code** is an identification code that consists of a set of vertical lines and spaces of different widths. The bar code represents data that identifies the manufacturer and the item.

Manufacturers print a bar code either on a product's package or on a label that is affixed to a product. Read At Issue 5-2 for a related discussion.

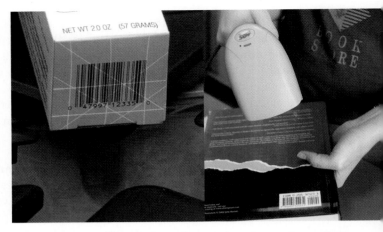

FIGURE 5-21 A bar code reader uses laser beams to read bar codes on products such as groceries and books.

AT ISSUE 5-2

Scanner Errors at the Checkout Counter?

Have you ever taken an item to a store's check-out and discovered that the price displayed when the item's bar code was scanned was different from the price shown on a shelf tag, sign, or advertisement? If you have, you are not alone. A government survey found that eight percent of the time, an item's scanned price is different from the price presented elsewhere. When an item is scanned at a store's checkout counter, a computer finds the item's price in the store's database. Store owners claim that discrepancies between the scanned price and a listed price are the result of human error — either failure to update the store's price database or incorrect shelf tags, signs, or advertisements. Yet, some consumer advocates claim that the discrepancy is intentional. They accuse stores of scanner fraud, insisting that some stores advertise one price and then charge another, hoping buyers will not recognize the difference. Even if consumers identify a pricing error, they may not bring the mistake to the store's attention, especially if the discrepancy is detected after the item is purchased or if the amount at issue is small. Who do you think is responsible for differences between scanned prices and posted costs? Why? Should stores be responsible for pricing errors? Why or why not?

RFID READERS RFID (radio frequency identification) is a technology that uses radio signals to communicate with a tag placed in or attached to an object, an animal, or a person. RFID tags, which contain a memory chip and an antenna, are available in many shapes and sizes. An **RFID reader** reads information on the tag via radio waves. RFID readers can be handheld devices or mounted in a stationary object such as a doorway.

Many retailers see RFID as an alternative to bar code identification because it does not require direct contact or line-of-site transmission. Each product in a store would contain a tag that identifies the product (Figure 5-22). As consumers remove products from the store shelves and walk through a checkout area, an RFID reader reads the tag(s) and communicates with a computer that calculates the amount due.

Other uses of RFID include tracking times of runners in a marathon; tracking location of soldiers, employee wardrobes, and airline baggage; checking

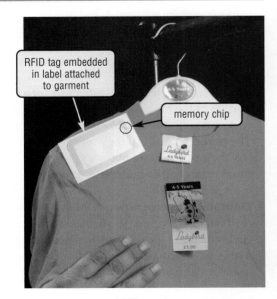

FIGURE 5-22 RFID readers read information stored on an RFID tag and then communicate this information to computers, which instantaneously compute payments and update inventory records. In this example, the RFID tag is embedded in a label attached to the garment.

lift tickets of skiers; gauging pressure and temperature of tires on a vehicle; checking out library books; and tracking payment as vehicles pass through booths on tollway systems. Read Looking Ahead 5-2 for a look at the next generation of tracking devices.

LOOKING AHEAD 5-2

Smart Dust Monitors the Environment

If you are too hot at work while your office mate is too cold, smart dust may one day solve the problem. Researchers at the University of California at Berkeley are testing tiny airborne devices called smart dust or dust motes, which combine sensors and communication components. Eventually the smart dust will be the size of a grain of sand.

Many uses for the ubiquitous smart dust are planned. The sensors could measure the temperature and humidity in various areas of a room and then send readings to a central computer that can regulate the air flow. In the warehouse, they could help track packages by sensing and transmitting product locations. In the battlefield, they could sense vehicle and missile movement. For more information, visit scsite.com/dcf2e/ch5/looking and then click Smart Dust.

MAGNETIC STRIPE CARD READERS   A **magnetic stripe card reader**, often called a magstripe reader, reads the magnetic stripe on the back of credit cards, entertainment cards, bank cards, and other similar cards. The stripe contains information identifying you and the card issuer (Figure 5-23). Some information stored in the stripe includes your name, account number, the card's expiration date, and a country code.

When a consumer swipes a credit card through the magstripe reader, it reads the information stored on the magnetic stripe on the card. If the magstripe reader rejects your card, it is possible that the magnetic stripe is scratched, dirty, or erased. Exposure to a magnet or magnetic field can erase the contents of a card's magnetic stripe.

FIGURE 5-23   A magnetic stripe card reader reads information encoded on the stripe on the back of your credit card.

MICR READERS   MICR (magnetic-ink character recognition) devices read text printed with magnetized ink. An **MICR reader** converts MICR characters into a form the computer can process. The banking industry almost exclusively uses MICR for check processing. Each check in your checkbook has precoded MICR characters beginning at the lower-left edge (Figure 5-24).

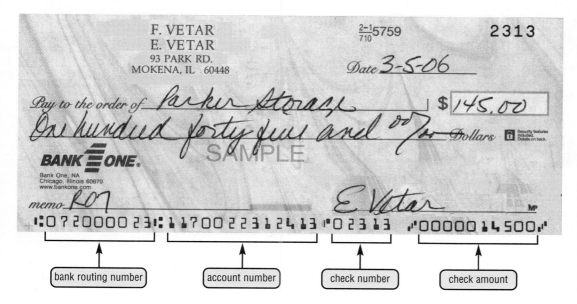

bank routing number   account number   check number   check amount

FIGURE 5-24
The MICR characters preprinted on the check represent the bank routing number, the customer account number, and the check number. The amount of the check in the lower-right corner is added after the check is cashed.

When a bank receives a check for payment, it uses an MICR inscriber to print the amount of the check in MICR characters in the lower-right corner. The check then is sorted or routed to the customer's bank, along with thousands of others. Each check is inserted in an MICR reader, which sends the check information — including the amount of the check — to a computer for processing.

Terminals

A **terminal** consists of a keyboard, a monitor, a video card, and memory. These components often are housed in a single unit. Users enter data and instructions into a terminal and then transmit some or all of the data over a network to a host computer.

Special-purpose terminals perform specific tasks and contain features uniquely designed for use in a particular industry. Two special-purpose terminals are point-of-sale (POS) terminals and automated teller machines.

- **Point-of-Sale (POS) Terminals** — The location in a retail or grocery store where a consumer pays for goods or services is the point of sale (POS). Most retail stores use a **POS terminal** to record purchases, process credit or debit cards, and update inventory.

  Many POS terminals handle credit card or debit card payments and thus also include a magstripe reader. Once the transaction is approved, the terminal prints a receipt for the customer. A self-service POS terminal allows consumers to perform all checkout-related activities (Figure 5-25). That is, they scan the items, bag the items, and pay for the items themselves.

- **Automated Teller Machines** — An **automated teller machine** (ATM) is a self-service banking machine that connects to a host computer through a network (Figure 5-26). Banks place ATMs in convenient locations, including grocery stores, convenience stores, retail outlets, shopping malls, and gas stations.

  Using an ATM, people withdraw cash, deposit money, transfer funds, or inquire about an account balance. Some ATMs have a touch screen; others have special buttons or keypads for entering input. To access a bank account, you insert a plastic bankcard in the ATM's magstripe reader. The ATM asks you to enter a password, called a personal identification number (PIN), which verifies that you are the holder of the bankcard. When your transaction is complete, the ATM prints a receipt for your records.

FIGURE 5-25 Some grocery stores offer self-serve checkouts, where the consumers themselves use the POS terminals to scan purchases, scan their store saver card and coupons, and then pay for the goods. This POS terminal prints a receipt for the customer.

FIGURE 5-26 An ATM is a self-service banking terminal that allows customers to access their bank accounts.

Biometric Input

Biometrics is the technology of authenticating a person's identity by verifying a personal characteristic. Biometric devices grant users access to programs, systems, or rooms by analyzing some physiological (related to physical or chemical activities in the body) or behavioral characteristic. Examples include fingerprints, hand geometry, facial features, voice, signatures, and eye patterns.

The most widely used biometric device today is a fingerprint scanner. A **fingerprint scanner** captures curves and indentations of a fingerprint. With the cost of fingerprint scanners dropping to less than $100, many homes and small businesses install fingerprint scanners to authenticate users before they can access a personal computer. Instead of lunch money, grade schools use fingerprint scanners to identify students in the cafeteria and adjust account balances for each lunch purchased (Figure 5-27).

A face recognition system captures a live face image and compares it with a stored image to determine if the person is a legitimate user. Some buildings use face recognition systems to secure access to rooms. Law enforcement, surveillance systems, and airports use face recognition to protect the public.

Biometric devices measure the shape and size of a person's hand using a hand geometry system. Because their cost is more than $1,000, larger companies typically use these systems as time and attendance devices or as security devices.

A voice verification system compares a person's live speech with their stored voice pattern. Larger organizations sometimes use voice verification systems as time and attendance devices. Many companies also use this technology for access to sensitive files and networks.

A signature verification system recognizes the shape of your handwritten signature, as well as measures the pressure exerted and the motion used to write the signature. Signature verification systems use a specialized pen and tablet.

High security areas use iris recognition systems. The camera in an iris recognition system uses iris recognition technology to read patterns in the iris of the eye (Figure 5-28). These patterns are as unique as a fingerprint. Iris recognition systems are quite expensive and are used by government security organizations, the military, and financial institutions that deal with highly sensitive data.

Sometimes, fingerprint, iris, and other biometric data are stored on a smart card. A **smart card**, which is comparable in size to a credit card or ATM card, stores the personal data on a thin microprocessor that is embedded in the card.

Test your knowledge of pages 173 through 181 in Quiz Yourself 5-2.

WEB LINK 5-5

Biometric Input
For more information, visit scsite.com/dcf2e/ch5/weblink and then click Biometric Input.

FIGURE 5-27 This elementary school student pays for lunch by placing his finger on a fingerprint scanner.

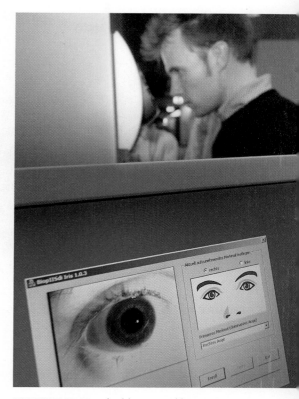

FIGURE 5-28 An iris recognition system.

QUIZ YOURSELF 5-2

Instructions: Find the true statement below. Then, rewrite the remaining false statements so they are true.

1. A digital camera allows users to take pictures and store the photographed images digitally, instead of on traditional film.
2. A fingerprint scanner captures curves and indentations of a signature.
3. After swiping a credit card through an MICR reader, it reads the information stored on the magnetic stripe on the card.
4. Instant messaging is the computer's capability of distinguishing spoken words.
5. Many smart phones today have POS capabilities.
6. RFID is a technology that uses laser signals to communicate with a tag placed in an object, an animal, or a person.

Quiz Yourself Online: To further check your knowledge of voice input; input devices for PDAs, smart phones, and Tablet PCs; digital cameras; video input; scanners and reading devices; terminals; and biometric devices, visit scsite.com/dcf2e/ch5/quiz and then click Objective 3.

WHAT IS OUTPUT?

Output is data that has been processed into a useful form. That is, computers process data (input) into information (output). Users view output on a screen, print it, or hear it through speakers or headsets. While working with a computer, a user encounters four basic categories of output: text, graphics, audio, and video (Figure 5-29). Very often, a single form of output, such as a Web page, includes more than one of these categories.

An **output device** is any hardware component that conveys information to one or more people. Commonly used output devices include display devices, printers, speakers and headsets, fax machines and fax modems, multifunction peripherals, and data projectors.

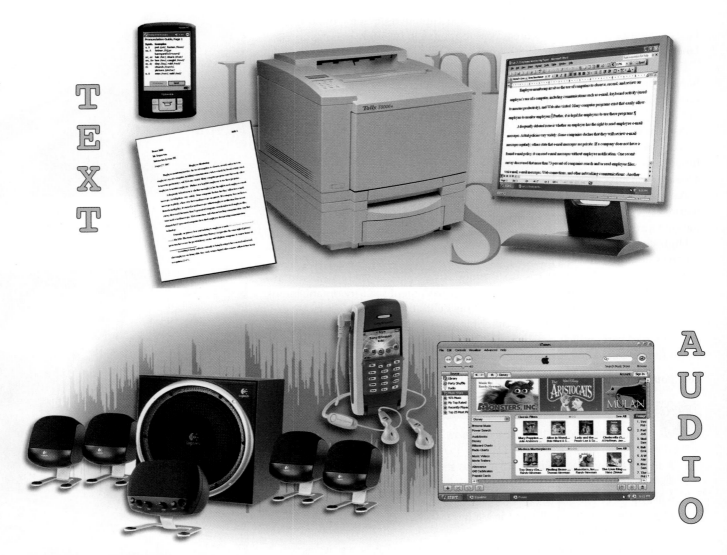

FIGURE 5-29   Four categories of output are text, graphics, audio, and video.

DISPLAY DEVICES

A **display device** is an output device that visually conveys text, graphics, and video information. Desktop computers typically use a monitor as their display device. A **monitor** is a display device that is packaged as a separate peripheral. Most monitors have a tilt-and-swivel base that allows users to adjust the angle of the screen to minimize neck strain and reduce glare from overhead lighting. Monitor controls permit users to adjust the brightness, contrast, positioning, height, and width of images.

Most mobile computers and devices integrate the display and other components into the same physical case.

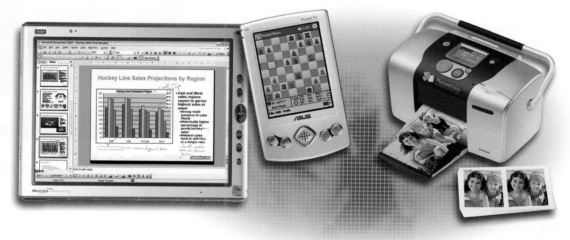

Display devices usually show text, graphics, and video information in color. Some, however, are monochrome. Monochrome means the information appears in one color (such as white, amber, green, black, blue, or gray) on a different color background (such as black or grayish-white). Some PDAs and other mobile devices use monochrome displays to save battery power.

Types of display devices include LCD monitors and screens, plasma monitors, and CRT monitors. The following pages discuss each of these display devices.

LCD Monitors and Screens

An **LCD monitor**, also called a flat panel monitor, is a desktop monitor that uses a liquid crystal display to produce images (Figure 5-30). These monitors produce sharp, flicker-free images. LCD monitors have a small footprint; that is, they do not take up much desk space. LCD monitors are available in a variety of sizes, with the more common being 15, 17, 18, 19, 20, 21, and 23 inches — some are 30 or 40 inches. You measure a monitor the same way you measure a television, that is, diagonally from one corner to the other.

Mobile computers, such as notebook computers and Tablet PCs, and mobile devices, such as PDAs and smart phones, often have built-in LCD screens (Figure 5-31). Notebook computer screens are available in a variety of sizes, with the more common being 14.1, 15.4, and 17.1 inches. Tablet PC screens range from 10.4 inches to 15 inches. PDA screens average 3.5 inches. On smart phones, screen sizes range from 2.5 to 3.5 inches.

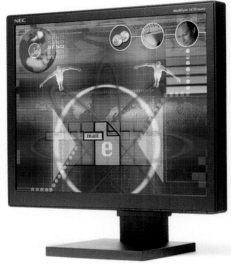

FIGURE 5-30 An LCD monitor is thin and lightweight.

notebook computer

Tablet PC

PDA

smart phone

FIGURE 5-31 Notebook computers and Tablet PCs have color LCD screens. Many PDAs and smart phones also have color displays.

LCD Technology and Quality   A **liquid crystal display** (**LCD**) uses a liquid compound to present information on a display device. Computer LCDs typically contain fluorescent tubes that emit light waves toward the liquid-crystal cells, which are sandwiched between two sheets of material.

The quality of an LCD monitor or LCD screen depends primarily on its resolution, response time, brightness, and pixel pitch.

- Resolution is the number of horizontal and vertical pixels in a display device. For example, a monitor that has a 1600 × 1200 resolution displays up to 1600 pixels per horizontal row and 1200 pixels per vertical row, for a total of 1,920,000 pixels to create a screen image. A higher resolution uses a greater number of pixels and thus provides a smoother, sharper, and clearer image. As the resolution increases, however, some items on the screen appear smaller, such as menu bars, toolbars, and rulers.

  With LCD monitors and screens, resolution generally is proportional to the size of the device. That is, the resolution increases for larger monitors and screens. For example, a 17-inch LCD monitor typically has a resolution of 1280 × 1024, while a 20-inch LCD monitor has a resolution of 1600 × 1200. LCDs are geared for a specific resolution.

- Response time of an LCD monitor or screen is the time in milliseconds (ms) that it takes to turn a pixel on or off. LCD monitors' and screens' response times range from 16 to 25 ms. The lower the number, the faster the response time.

- Brightness of an LCD monitor or LCD screen is measured in nits. A nit is a unit of visible light intensity. The higher the nits, the brighter the images.

- Pixel pitch, sometimes called dot pitch, is the distance in millimeters between pixels on a display device. Average pixel pitch on LCD monitors and screens should be .28 mm or lower. The lower the number, the sharper the image.

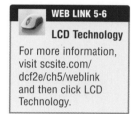

WEB LINK 5-6

LCD Technology

For more information, visit scsite.com/ dcf2e/ch5/weblink and then click LCD Technology.

Ports and LCD Monitors   A cable on a monitor plugs in a port on the system unit. LCD monitors use a digital signal to produce a picture. To display the highest quality images, an LCD monitor should plug in a DVI (Digital Video Interface) port, which enables digital signals to transmit directly to an LCD monitor.

Plasma Monitors

Large business users or power users sometimes have plasma monitors, which often measure more than 60 inches wide (Figure 5-32). A **plasma monitor** is a display device that uses gas plasma technology, which sandwiches a layer of gas between two glass plates.

Plasma monitors offer larger screen sizes and higher display quality than LCD monitors but are more expensive. These monitors also can hang directly on a wall.

FIGURE 5-32 Large plasma monitors can measure more than 60 inches wide.

CRT Monitors

A **CRT monitor** is a desktop monitor that contains a cathode-ray tube (Figure 5-33). A cathode-ray tube (CRT) is a large, sealed glass tube. The front of the tube is the screen.

CRT monitors for desktop computers are available in various sizes, with the more common being 15, 17, 19, 21, and 22 inches. In addition to monitor size, advertisements also list a CRT monitor's viewable size. The viewable size is the diagonal measurement of the actual viewing area provided by the screen in the CRT monitor. A 21-inch monitor, for example, may have a viewable size of 20 inches.

A CRT monitor costs less than an LCD monitor but also generates more heat and

FIGURE 5-33   The core of a CRT monitor is a cathode-ray tube.

uses more power than an LCD monitor. To help reduce the amount of electricity used by monitors and other computer components, the United States Department of Energy (DOE) and the United States Environmental Protection Agency (EPA) developed the **ENERGY STAR program**. This program encourages manufacturers to create energy-efficient devices that require little power when the devices are not in use. Monitors and devices that meet ENERGY STAR guidelines display an ENERGY STAR label.

CRT monitors produce a small amount of electromagnetic radiation. Electromagnetic radiation (EMR) is a magnetic field that travels at the speed of light. Excessive amounts of EMR can pose a health risk. To be safe, all high-quality CRT monitors comply with a set of standards that defines acceptable levels of EMR for a monitor. To protect yourself even further, sit at arm's length from the CRT monitor because EMR travels only a short distance.

QUALITY OF A CRT MONITOR   The quality of a CRT monitor depends largely on its resolution, dot pitch, and refresh rate.

- Most CRT monitors support a variety of screen resolutions. Standard CRT monitors today usually display up to a maximum of 1800 × 1440 pixels, with 1280 × 1024 often the norm. High-end CRT monitors (for the power user) can display 2048 × 1536 pixels or more.
- As with LCD monitors, text created with a smaller dot pitch, or pixel pitch, is easier to read. To minimize eye fatigue, use a CRT monitor with a dot pitch of .27 millimeters or lower.
- Electron beams inside a CRT monitor "draw" an image on the entire screen many times per second so the image does not fade. The number of times the image is drawn per second is called the refresh rate. A CRT monitor's refresh rate, which is expressed in hertz (Hz), should be fast enough to maintain a constant, flicker-free image. A high-quality CRT monitor will provide a vertical refresh rate of at least 68 Hz. This means the image on the screen redraws itself vertically 68 times in a second.

GRAPHIC CHIPS AND CRT MONITORS   Many CRT monitors use an analog signal to produce an image. A cable on the CRT monitor plugs in a port on the system unit, which enables communications from a graphics chip. If the graphics chip resides on a video card, the video card converts digital output from the computer into an analog video signal and sends the signal through the cable to the monitor, which displays output on the screen.

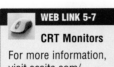

FAQ 5-2

What type of video content do users view on display devices?

Music videos and newscasts are the most widely viewed video content on display devices, as shown in the chart to the right. For more information, visit scsite.com/dcf2e/ch5/faq and then click Video Output Content.

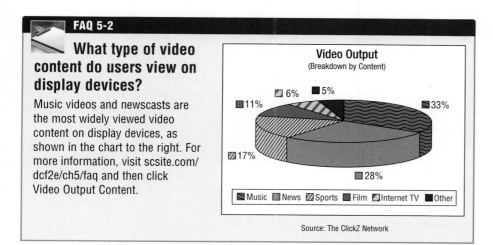

Video Output
(Breakdown by Content)

6% · 5% · 33% · 11% · 17% · 28%

Music · News · Sports · Film · Internet TV · Other

Source: The ClickZ Network

Test your knowledge of pages 182 through 187 in Quiz Yourself 5-3.

QUIZ YOURSELF 5-3

Instructions: Find the true statement below. Then, rewrite the remaining false statements so they are true.

1. A lower resolution uses a greater number of pixels and thus provides a smoother image.
2. An output device is any type of software component that conveys information to one or more people.
3. LCD monitors have a larger footprint than CRT monitors.
4. You measure a monitor diagonally from one corner to the other.

Quiz Yourself Online: To further check your knowledge of LCD monitors, LCD screens, and CRT monitors, visit scsite.com/dcf2e/ch5/quiz and then click Objective 4.

PRINTERS

A **printer** is an output device that produces text and graphics on a physical medium such as paper or transparency film. Many different printers exist with varying speeds, capabilities, and printing methods. Figure 5-34 presents a list of questions to help you decide on the printer best suited to your needs.

The following pages discuss producing printed output and the various printer types including ink-jet printers, photo printers, laser printers, thermal printers, mobile printers, plotters, and large format printers.

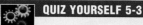

1. What is my budget?
2. How fast must my printer print?
3. Do I need a color printer?
4. What is the cost per page for printing?
5. Do I need multiple copies of documents?
6. Will I print graphics?
7. Do I want to print photographs?
8. Do I want to print directly from a memory card or other type of miniature storage media?
9. What types of paper does the printer use?
10. What sizes of paper does the printer accept?
11. Do I want to print on both sides of the paper?
12. How much paper can the printer tray hold?
13. Will the printer work with my computer and software?
14. How much do supplies such as ink and paper cost?
15. Can the printer print on envelopes and transparencies?
16. How many envelopes can the printer print at a time?
17. How much do I print now, and how much will I be printing in a year or two?
18. Will the printer be connected to a network?
19. Do I want wireless printing capability?

FIGURE 5-34 Questions to ask when purchasing a printer.

Producing Printed Output

Although many users today print by connecting a computer to a printer with a cable, a variety of printing options are available as shown in Figure 5-35.

Today, wireless printing technology makes the task of printing from a notebook computer, Tablet PC, PDA, or smart phone much easier. Two wireless technologies for printing are Bluetooth and infrared. With Bluetooth printing, a device transmits output to a printer via radio waves. With infrared printing, a printer communicates with a device using infrared light waves.

Instead of downloading images from a digital camera to a computer, users can print images using a variety of other techniques. Some cameras connect directly to a printer via a cable. Others store images on media cards that can be removed and inserted in the printer. Some printers have a docking station, into which the user inserts the camera to print pictures stored in the camera.

Finally, many home and business users print to a central printer on a network. Their computer may communicate with the network printer via cables or wirelessly.

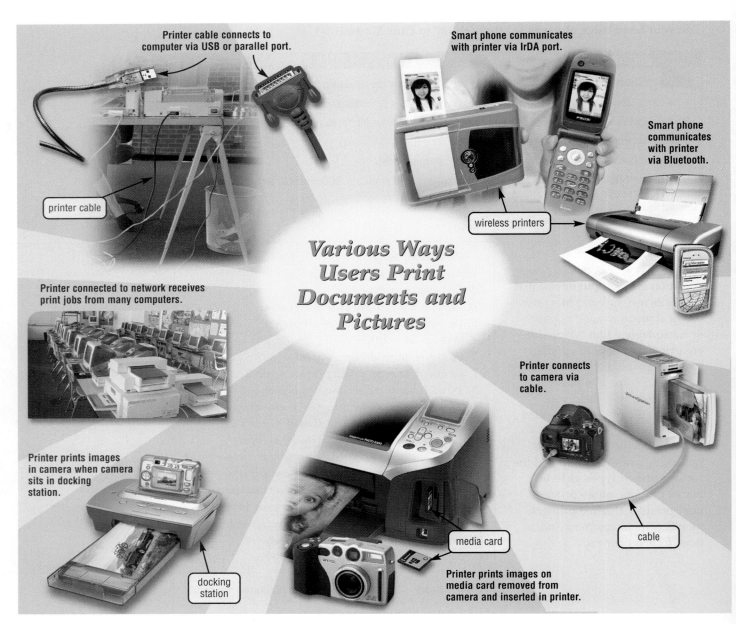

FIGURE 5-35 Users print documents and pictures using a variety of printing methods.

Nonimpact Printers

A **nonimpact printer** forms characters and graphics on a piece of paper without actually striking the paper. Some nonimpact printers spray ink, while others use heat or pressure to create images. Commonly used nonimpact printers are ink-jet printers, photo printers, laser printers, thermal printers, mobile printers, plotters, and large-format printers.

Ink-Jet Printers

An **ink-jet printer** is a type of nonimpact printer that forms characters and graphics by spraying tiny drops of liquid ink onto a piece of paper. Ink-jet printers have become a popular type of color printer for use in the home. Ink-jet printers produce text and graphics in both black-and-white and color on a variety of paper types (Figure 5-36). A reasonable quality ink-jet printer costs less than $100.

As with many other input and output devices, one factor that determines the quality of an ink-jet printer is its resolution. Printer resolution is measured by the number of dots per inch (dpi) a printer can print. Most ink-jet printers can print from 600 to 4800 dpi.

The speed of an ink-jet printer is measured by the number of pages per minute (ppm) it can print. Most ink-jet printers print from 3 to 26 ppm. Graphics and colors print at a slower rate.

FIGURE 5-36   Ink-jet printers are a popular type of color printer used in the home.

The print head mechanism in an ink-jet printer contains ink-filled print cartridges. Each cartridge has fifty to several hundred small ink holes, or nozzles. The ink propels through any combination of the nozzles to form a character or image on the paper. When the print cartridge runs out of ink, you simply replace the cartridge. Most ink-jet printers have at least two print cartridges: one containing black ink and the other(s) containing colors. Read At Issue 5-3 for a related discussion.

AT ISSUE 5-3

Ink-Jet Ink Wars?

In 1903, King Camp Gillette introduced an innovative product — a safety razor with disposable blades. Gillette accompanied his product with an even more innovative idea — sell the razor, which was purchased once, at or below cost, and rely on sales of the razor blades, which were purchased repeatedly, for profit. The idea made Gillette a millionaire. Manufacturers of ink-jet printers use a similar approach. The printers are inexpensive, often less than $200. The ink cartridges the printers use, however, can cost from $30 to $50 each time they are replaced. To avoid the high cost of cartridges, some people use ink refill kits. These kits, which are far less expensive than a new cartridge, typically include several vials of ink and a syringe-like tool used to inject the ink into existing ink cartridges. To counter the kits, some printer manufacturers have inserted special chips that keep a cartridge from being refilled and, some claim, shut down a cartridge before it really is out of ink. Ink refill kits cost much less than a new cartridge, but the kits can be messy, contain low-quality ink, and even damage a print head if used improperly. Should manufacturers be allowed to prevent people from refilling ink cartridges? Why? Would you use an ink refill kit? Why or why not?

Photo Printers

A **photo printer** is a color printer that produces photo-lab-quality pictures (Figure 5-37). Some photo printers print just one or two sizes of images, for example, 3 × 5 inches and 4 × 6 inches. Others print up to letter size, legal size, or even larger. Many photo printers use ink-jet technology. With models that can print letter-sized documents, users connect the photo printer to their computer and use it for all their printing needs.

Many photo printers have a built-in card slot so the printer can print digital photographs directly from a media card. That is, you do not need to transfer the images from the media card to the computer to print them. Some photo printers have built-in LCD color screens, allowing users to view and enhance the pictures before printing them.

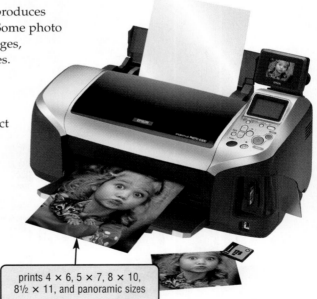

prints 4 × 6, 5 × 7, 8 × 10, 8½ × 11, and panoramic sizes

FIGURE 5-37   Photo printers print in a range of sizes.

Laser Printers

A **laser printer** is a high-speed, high-quality nonimpact printer (Figure 5-38). Laser printers for personal computers ordinarily use individual sheets of paper stored in one or more removable trays that slide in the printer case.

Laser printers print text and graphics in high-quality resolutions, usually ranging from 1200 to 2400 dpi. While laser printers usually cost more than ink-jet printers, they also are much faster. A laser printer for the home and small office user typically prints black-and-white text at speeds of 15 to 50 ppm. Color laser printers print 4 to 24 ppm. Laser printers for large business users print more than 150 ppm.

Depending on the quality, speed, and type of laser printer, the cost ranges from a few hundred to several thousand dollars for the home and small office user, and several hundred thousand dollars for the large business user. Color laser printers are slightly higher priced than otherwise equivalent black-and-white laser printers.

Operating in a manner similar to a copy machine, a laser printer creates images using a laser beam and powdered ink, called toner. When the toner runs out, you replace the toner cartridge.

WEB LINK 5-9

Laser Printers

For more information, visit scsite.com/dcf2e/ch5/weblink and then click Laser Printers.

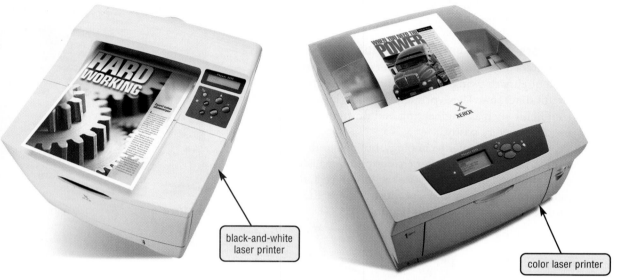

black-and-white laser printer

color laser printer

FIGURE 5-38   Laser printers are available in both black-and-white and color models.

FAQ 5-3

How do I dispose of toner cartridges?

Do not throw them in the garbage. The housing contains iron, metal, and aluminum that is not biodegradable. The ink toner inside the cartridges contains toxic chemicals that pollute water and soil if discarded in dumps. Instead, recycle empty toner cartridges. Contact your printer manufacturer to see if it has a recycling program. For more information, visit scsite.com/dcf2e/ch5/faq and then click Recycling Toner Cartridges.

Thermal Printers

A **thermal printer** generates images by pushing electrically heated pins against heat-sensitive paper. Basic thermal printers are inexpensive, but the print quality is low and the images tend to fade over time. Self-service gas pumps often print gas receipts using a built-in lower-quality thermal printer.

Some thermal printers have high print quality. A dye-sublimation printer, sometimes called a digital photo printer, uses heat to transfer colored dye to specially coated paper. Professional applications requiring high image quality, such as photography studios, medical labs, and security identification systems, use dye-sublimation printers. These high-end printers cost thousands of dollars and print images in a wide range of sizes.

Dye-sublimation printers for the home or small business user, by contrast, typically print images in only one or two sizes and are much slower than their professional counterparts. These lower-end dye-sublimation printers are comparable in cost to a photo printer based on ink-jet technology (Figure 5-39).

FIGURE 5-39   The printer shown in this figure uses dye-sublimation technology to create photographic-quality output for the home or small office user.

Mobile Printers

A **mobile printer** is a small, lightweight, battery-powered printer that allows a mobile user to print from a notebook computer, Tablet PC, PDA, or smart phone while traveling (Figure 5-40). Barely wider than the paper on which they print, mobile printers fit easily in a briefcase alongside a notebook computer. Mobile printers mainly use ink-jet or thermal technology.

Plotters and Large-Format Printers

Plotters are sophisticated printers used to produce high-quality drawings such as blueprints, maps, and circuit diagrams. These printers are used in specialized fields such as engineering and drafting and usually are very costly.

Using ink-jet printer technology, but on a much larger scale, a **large-format printer** creates photo-realistic-quality color prints. Graphic artists use these high-cost, high-performance printers for signs, posters, and other professional quality displays (Figure 5-41).

FIGURE 5-40   A mobile printer.

FIGURE 5-41   Graphic artists use large-format printers to print signs, posters, and other professional quality displays.

Impact Printers

An **impact printer** forms characters and graphics on a piece of paper by striking a mechanism against an inked ribbon that physically contacts the paper. Impact printers are ideal for printing multipart forms because they easily print through many layers of paper. Two commonly used types of impact printers are dot-matrix printers and line printers.

A **dot-matrix printer** is an impact printer that produces printed images when tiny wire pins on a print head mechanism strike an inked ribbon (Figure 5-42). When the ribbon presses against the paper, it creates dots that form characters and graphics.

Dot-matrix printers typically use continuous-form paper, in which thousands of sheets of paper are connected together end to end. The pages have holes along the sides to help feed the paper through the printer. The speed of most dot-matrix printers ranges from 400 to 1100 characters per second (cps), depending on the desired print quality.

A **line printer** is a high-speed impact printer that prints an entire line at a time. The speed of a line printer is measured by the number of lines per minute (lpm) it can print. Some line printers print as many as 3,000 lpm.

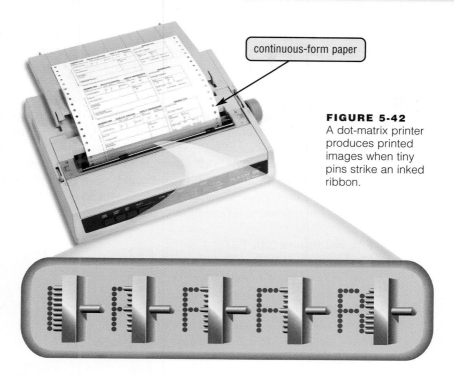

continuous-form paper

FIGURE 5-42
A dot-matrix printer produces printed images when tiny pins strike an inked ribbon.

OTHER OUTPUT DEVICES

In addition to monitors and printers, other output devices are available for specific uses and applications. These include speakers and headsets, fax machines and fax modems, multifunction peripherals, and data projectors.

Speakers and Headsets

An **audio output device** is a component of a computer that produces music, speech, or other sounds, such as beeps. Two commonly used audio output devices are speakers and headsets.

Most personal computers have a small internal speaker that usually emits only low-quality sound. Thus, many personal computer users add surround sound **speakers** to their computers to generate a higher-quality sound (Figure 5-43). Most surround sound computer speaker systems include one or two center speakers and two or more satellite speakers that are positioned so sound emits from all directions. Speakers typically have tone and volume controls, allowing users to adjust settings. To boost the low bass sounds, surround sound speaker systems also include a subwoofer. Users connect the speakers and subwoofer to ports on the sound card.

satellite speakers

subwoofer

center speaker

satellite speakers

FIGURE 5-43   Most personal computer users add high-quality surround sound speaker systems to their computers.

In a computer laboratory or other crowded environment, speakers might not be practical. Instead, users can plug a headset in a port on the sound card, in a speaker, or in the front of the system unit. With the **headset**, only the individual wearing the headset hears the sound from the computer.

Electronically produced voice output is growing in popularity. **Voice output** occurs when you hear a person's voice or when the computer talks to you through the speakers on the computer. In some software applications, the computer can speak the contents of a document through voice output. On the Web, you can listen to (or download and then listen to) interviews, talk shows, sporting events, news, recorded music, and live concerts from many radio and television stations. Some Web sites dedicate themselves to providing voice output, where you can hear songs, quotes, historical lectures, speeches, and books. Internet telephony allows users to speak to other users over the Internet using their computer or mobile device.

WEB LINK 5-10

Speakers and Headsets

For more information, visit scsite.com/ dcf2e/ch5/weblink and then click Speakers and Headsets.

Fax Machines and Fax Modems

A **fax machine** is a device that codes and encodes documents so they can be transmitted over telephone lines (Figure 5-44). The documents can contain text, drawings, or photographs, or can be handwritten. The term fax refers to a document that you send or receive via a fax machine.

Many computers include fax capability by using a fax modem. A fax modem transmits computer-prepared documents, such as a word processing letter, or documents that have been digitized with a scanner or digital camera. A fax modem transmits these faxes to a fax machine or to another fax modem.

FIGURE 5-44   A stand-alone fax machine.

Multifunction Peripherals

A **multifunction peripheral** is a single device that looks like a copy machine but provides the functionality of a printer, scanner, copy machine, and perhaps a fax machine (Figure 5-45). Some use color ink-jet printer technology, while others include a black-and-white laser printer. An advantage of these devices is they are significantly less expensive than if you purchase each device separately. If the device breaks down, however, you lose all four functions, which is the primary disadvantage.

FIGURE 5-45   This multifunction peripheral is a color printer, scanner, copy machine, and fax machine all-in-one device.

Data Projectors

A **data projector** is a device that takes the text and images displaying on a computer screen and projects them on a larger screen so an audience can see the image clearly. Some data projectors are large devices that attach to a ceiling or wall in an auditorium. Others are small portable devices (Figure 5-46). Read Looking Ahead 5-3 for a look at the next generation of digital cinema projectors.

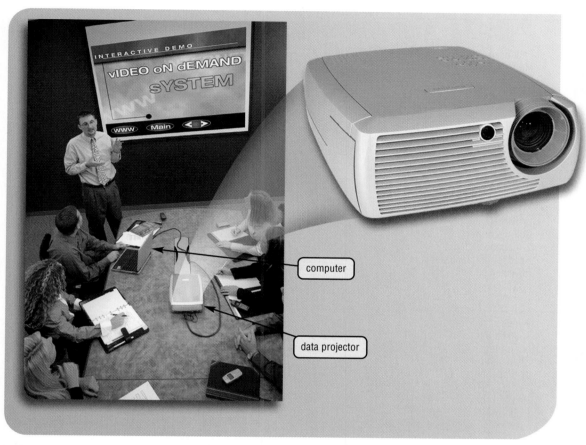

computer

data projector

FIGURE 5-46　Data projectors can produce sharp, bright images.

 LOOKING AHEAD 5-3

Digital Cinema Just the Right Picture

Computers have influenced the motion picture business by modifying how movies are produced, distributed, and exhibited. Digital technology is expected to replace film by 2007, and the new technology's superior sound and visual clarity have been heralded as the greatest innovations since talkies replaced silent movies 80 years ago.

The seven larger Hollywood movie studios have cleared the final hurdle in the digital cinema process: agreeing on a compression scheme to deliver the movies to theaters. Called JPG 2000, this image coding system will allow the studios to distribute the movies without having to make thousands of prints, thus saving millions of dollars annually.

With the compression standard in place, manufacturers now can intensify their efforts to develop digital cinema projectors. For more information, visit scsite.com/dcf2e/ch5/looking and then click Digital Cinema.

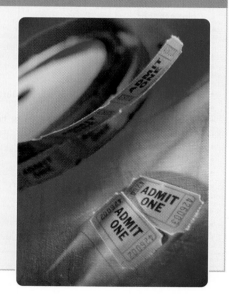

PUTTING IT ALL TOGETHER

Many factors influence the type of input and output devices you should use: the type of input and output desired, the hardware and software in use, and the anticipated cost. Figure 5-47 outlines several suggested input and output devices for various types of computer users.

SUGGESTED INPUT AND OUTPUT DEVICES BY USER

User	Input Device	Output Device
HOME 	• Enhanced keyboard or ergonomic keyboard • Mouse • Stylus for PDA or smart phone • Joystick or wheel • Color scanner • 2-megapixel digital camera • Headset that includes a microphone • PC video camera	• 17- or 19-inch color LCD monitor • Ink-jet color printer; or • Photo printer • Speakers • Headset
SMALL OFFICE/ HOME OFFICE 	• Enhanced keyboard or ergonomic keyboard • Mouse • Stylus and portable keyboard for PDA or smart phone, or digital pen for Tablet PC • Color scanner • 2-megapixel digital camera • Headset that includes a microphone • PC video camera	• 19- or 21-inch LCD monitor • Color LCD screen on Tablet PC, PDA, or smart phone • Multifunction peripheral; or • Ink-jet color printer; or • Laser printer • Fax machine • Speakers
MOBILE 	• Wireless mouse for notebook computer • Trackball, touchpad, or pointing stick on notebook computer • Stylus and portable keyboard for PDA or smart phone, or digital pen for Tablet PC • 2- or 3-megapixel digital camera • Headset that includes a microphone • Fingerprint scanner for notebook computer	• 15.7-inch LCD screen on notebook computer • Color LCD screen on PDA or smart phone • Mobile color printer • Ink-jet color printer; or • Laser printer, for in-office use • Photo printer • Fax modem • Headset • Data projector
POWER 	• Enhanced keyboard or ergonomic keyboard • Mouse • Stylus and portable keyboard for PDA or smart phone • Pen for graphics tablet • Color scanner • 8-megapixel digital camera • Headset that includes a microphone • PC video camera	• 23-inch LCD monitor • Laser printer • Plotter or large-format printer; or • Photo printer; or • Dye-sublimation printer • Fax machine or fax modem • Speakers • Headset
LARGE BUSINESS	• Enhanced keyboard or ergonomic keyboard • Mouse • Stylus and portable keyboard for PDA or smart phone, or digital pen for Tablet PC • Touch screen • Light pen • Color scanner • OCR/OMR readers, bar code readers, or MICR reader data collection devices • Microphone • Video camera for video conferences • Fingerprint scanner or other biometric device	• 19- or 21-inch LCD monitor • Color LCD screen on Tablet PC, PDA, or smart phone • High-speed laser printer • Laser printer, color • Line printer (for large reports from a mainframe) • Fax machine or fax modem • Speakers • Headset • Data projector

FIGURE 5-47   This table recommends suggested input and output devices for various types of users.

INPUT AND OUTPUT DEVICES FOR PHYSICALLY CHALLENGED USERS

The ever-increasing presence of computers in everyone's lives has generated an awareness of the need to address computing requirements for those who have or may develop physical limitations. The **Americans with Disabilities Act (ADA)** requires any company with 15 or more employees to make reasonable attempts to accommodate the needs of physically challenged workers. Read At Issue 5-4 for a related discussion.

Besides voice recognition, which is ideal for blind or visually impaired users, several other input devices are available. Users with limited hand mobility who want to use a keyboard have several options. Keyboards with larger keys are available. Still another option is the on-screen keyboard, in which a graphic of a standard keyboard is displayed on the user's screen. As the user clicks letters on the on-screen keyboard, they appear in the document at the location of the insertion point. An option for people with limited hand movement is a head-mounted pointer to control the pointer or insertion point (Figure 5-48). To simulate the functions of a mouse button, a user works with switches that control the pointer. The switch might be a hand pad, a foot pedal, a receptor that detects facial motions, or a pneumatic instrument controlled by puffs of air.

For users with mobility, hearing, or vision disabilities, many different types of output devices are available. Hearing-impaired users, for example, can instruct programs to display words instead of sounds.

Visually impaired users can change Windows XP settings, such as increasing the size or changing the color of the text to make the words easier to read. Instead of using a monitor, blind users can work with voice output. That is, the computer reads the information that appears on the screen. Another alternative is a Braille printer, which outputs information on paper in Braille (Figure 5-49).

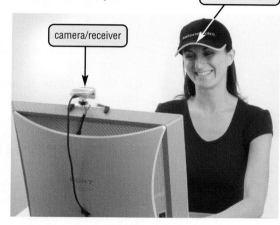

FIGURE 5-48 A camera/receiver mounted on the monitor tracks the position of the head-mounted pointer, which is reflective material that this user is wearing on brim of her hat. As the user moves her head, the pointer on the screen also moves.

reflective tracking surface attached to brim of hat

camera/receiver

AT ISSUE 5-4

Should Web Sites Geared for Physically Challenged People Be Held Accountable for Accessibility Levels?

The World Wide Web Consortium (W3C) has published accessibility guidelines for Web sites. The guidelines specify measures that Web site designers can take to increase accessibility for physically challenged users. Among its guidelines, the W3C urges Web site designers to provide equivalent text for audio or visual content, include features that allow elements to be activated and understood using a variety of input and output devices, and make the user interface follow principles of accessible design. A recent report found that most Web sites do not meet all of the W3C guidelines. This failure is disappointing, because many physically challenged users could benefit from the Web's capability to bring products and services into the home. Ironically, a survey discovered that more than 50 percent of the Web sites run by disability organizations also fail to meet the W3C guidelines. Critics contend that these Web sites neglect the needs of their users and fail to lead by example. Web site apologists contend, however, that many sponsoring organizations lack the funding necessary to comply with the guidelines. Should all Web sites meet the W3C accessibility guidelines? Why or why not? Do Web sites run by disability organizations have a moral obligation to meet the guidelines? Why? What can be done to encourage sponsors to make their Web sites more accessible?

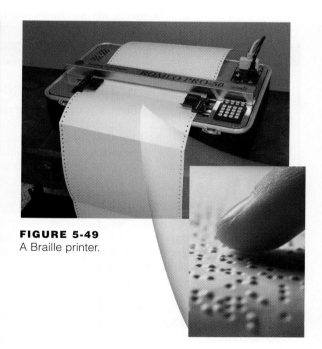

FIGURE 5-49
A Braille printer.

Test your knowledge of pages 187 through 197 in Quiz Yourself 5-4.

QUIZ YOURSELF 5-4

Instructions: Find the true statement below. Then, rewrite the remaining false statements so they are true.

1. A laser printer generates images by pushing electrically heated pins against heat-sensitive paper.
2. A photo printer creates images using a laser beam and powdered ink, called toner.
3. An ink-jet printer is a type of impact printer that forms characters and graphics by spraying tiny drops of liquid nitrogen onto a piece of paper.
4. Many personal computer users add surround sound printer systems to their computers to generate a higher-quality sound.
5. Multifunction peripherals require more space than having a separate printer, scanner, copy machine, and fax machine.
6. The Americans with Disabilities Act (ADA) requires any company with 15 or more employees to make reasonable attempts to accommodate the needs of physically challenged workers.

Quiz Yourself Online: To further check your knowledge of types of printers, other output devices, and input and output options for physically challenged users, visit scsite.com/dcf2e/ch5/quiz and then click Objectives 5 – 7.

CHAPTER SUMMARY

Input is any data and instructions you enter into the memory of a computer. This chapter described the various techniques of entering input and several commonly used input devices. Topics included the keyboard; mouse and other pointing devices; voice input; input for PDAs, smart phones, and Tablet PCs; digital cameras; video input; scanners and reading devices; terminals; and biometric input.

Computers process and organize data (input) into information (output). This chapter also described the various methods of output and several commonly used output devices. Output devices presented included CRT monitors, LCD monitors and screens, printers, speakers and headsets, fax machines and fax modems, multifunction peripherals, and data projectors.

CAREER CORNER

Graphic Designer/Illustrator

Graphic designers and **graphic illustrators** are artists, but many do not create original works. Instead, they portray visually the ideas of their clients. Illustrators create pictures for books and other publications and sometimes for commercial products, such as greeting cards. They work in fields such as fashion, technology, medicine, animation, or even cartoons. Illustrators often prepare their images on a computer. Designers combine practical skills with artistic talent to convert abstract concepts into designs for products and advertisements. Many use computer-aided design (CAD) tools to create, visualize, and modify designs. Designer careers usually are specialized in particular areas, such as:

- Graphic designers — book covers, stationery, and CD covers
- Commercial and industrial designers — products and equipment
- Costume and theater designers — costumes and settings for theater and television
- Interior designers — layout, decor, and furnishings of homes and buildings
- Merchandise displayers — commercial displays
- Fashion designers — clothing, shoes, and other fashion accessories

Certificate, two-year, four-year, and masters-level educational programs are available within design areas. About 30 percent of graphic illustrators/designers choose to freelance, while others work with advertising agencies, publishing companies, design studios, or specialized departments within large companies. Salaries range from $25,000 to $80,000-plus, based on experience and educational background. For more information, visit scsite.com/dcf2e/ch5/careers and then click Graphic Designer/Illustrator.

Logitech
Personal Interface Products Leader

The average Internet user has more than 40 inches of cords on his desktop, according to a Logitech survey. This company is working to reduce desktop clutter with a variety of cordless peripherals, including mouse devices, keyboards, mobile headsets, and game controllers.

A market leader, Logitech has sold more than 45 million wireless devices. It also designs, manufactures, and markets corded devices. The company's retail sales account for more than 80 percent of its revenue.

Two engineering students from Stanford University, Italian-born Pierluigi Zappacosta and Swiss-born Daniel Borel, launched Logitech in 1981. Today, the corporation is the world's largest manufacturer of the mouse, having sold more than 500 million since the company's founding. For more information, visit scsite.com/dcf2e/ch5/companies and then click Logitech.

Hewlett-Packard
Technology for Business and Life

If you have printed a document recently, chances are the printer manufacturer was Hewlett-Packard (HP). Market analysts estimate that 60 percent of printers sold today bear the HP logo, and HP says it ships one million printers each week.

HP is noted for a range of high-quality printers, disk storage systems, UNIX and Windows servers, and notebook, desktop, and handheld computers. In 2002, HP enlarged its presence in the computer market with a $25 billion buyout of Compaq Computer Corporation.

William Hewlett and David Packard started the company in a one-car garage in 1939 with the goal of manufacturing test and measurement equipment. HP has been developing personal information devices, including calculators and computers, for the past 30 years. For more information, visit scsite.com/dcf2e/ch5/companies and then click Hewlett-Packard.

TECHNOLOGY TRAILBLAZERS

Douglas Engelbart
Creator of the Mouse

The phrase "point and click" might not be part of every computer user's vocabulary if Douglas Engelbart had not pursued his engineering dreams. In 1964, he developed the first prototype computer mouse with the goal of making it easier to move a cursor around a computer screen.

Ten years later, engineers at Xerox refined Engelbart's prototype and showed the redesigned product to Apple's Steve Jobs, who applied the concept to his graphical Macintosh computer. The mouse was mass produced in the mid-1980s, and today it is the most widely used pointing device.

Engelbart currently serves as director of the Bootstrap Institute, a company he founded with his daughter to form strategic alliances and consequently improve corporations' performances. For more information, visit scsite.com/dcf2e/ch5/people and then click Douglas Engelbart.

Donna Dubinsky
palmOne Director

PDAs are ubiquitous, partly due to the efforts of Donna Dubinsky. In the mid-1990s, she sensed that people wanted to own an electronic version of their paper appointment books. She and Jeff Hawkins introduced the original Palm Pilot prototype made of mahogany and cardboard at Palm Computing in 1996. Sales of more than two million units made the Palm Pilot the most rapidly adopted new computing product ever manufactured.

Dubinsky and Hawkins left Palm in 1998 to cofound Handspring, where they introduced several successful products, including the Treo smart phone. In 2003, Handspring merged with the Palm hardware group to create palmOne.

Dubinsky currently serves as a director of palmOne and of Intuit Corporation. For more information, visit scsite.com/dcf2e/ch5/people and then click Donna Dubinsky.

Chapter Review

The Chapter Review section summarizes the concepts presented in this chapter. To obtain help from other students regarding any subject in this chapter, visit scsite.com/dcf2e/ch5/forum and post your thoughts or questions.

① What Are the Characteristics of a Keyboard?

Any hardware component that allows users to enter data and instructions is an **input device**. A **keyboard** is an input device that contains keys users press to enter data and instructions into a computer. Computer keyboards have a typing area that includes letters of the alphabet, numbers, punctuation marks, and other basic keys. An enhanced keyboard also has function keys programmed to issue commands, a numeric keypad, arrow keys, and additional keys and buttons.

② How Do Pointing Devices Work?

A **pointing device** allows users to control a small symbol, called a **pointer**, on the computer screen. A **mouse** is a pointing device that fits under the palm of your hand. As you move the mouse, the pointer on the screen also moves. A **trackball** is a stationary pointing device with a ball that you rotate to move the pointer. A **touchpad** is a flat, pressure-sensitive device that you slide your finger across to move the pointer. A **pointing stick** is a pointing device positioned on the keyboard that you push to move the pointer. A **joystick** is a vertical lever that you move to control a simulated vehicle or player. A **wheel** is a steering-wheel-type device that you turn to simulate driving a vehicle. A **light pen** is a light-sensitive device that you press against or point at the screen to select objects. A **touch screen** is a touch-sensitive display device that you interact with by touching areas of the screen. A **stylus** and **digital pen** use pressure to write text and draw lines.

 Visit scsite.com/dcf2e/ch5/quiz or click the Quiz Yourself button. Click Objectives 1 – 2.

③ What Are Other Types of Input?

Voice input is the process of entering input by speaking into a microphone. Mobile users employ a basic stylus to enter data and instructions into a PDA, or sometimes use a built-in keyboard or snap-on keyboard. The primary input device for a Tablet PC is a digital pen. A **digital camera** allows users to take pictures, store the images digitally, and download the images to a computer's hard disk. **Video input** is the process of capturing full-motion pictures and storing them on a computer's storage medium. A **digital video (DV) camera**, a **PC video camera**, and a **Web cam** are used for video input. A **scanner** is a light-sensing input device that reads printed text and graphics and translates the results into a form a computer can process. Reading devices use a light source to read characters, marks, and codes and convert them into digital data. **OCR (optical character recognition)** devices use a small optical scanner and software to analyze characters from ordinary documents. **OMR (optical mark recognition)** devices read hand-drawn marks on a form. A **bar code reader** uses laser beams to read bar codes. An **RFID reader** reads information on an embedded tag via radio waves. A **magnetic stripe card reader** reads the magnetic stripe on the back of credit, entertainment, bank, and other similar cards. A **MICR** (magnetic-ink character recognition) **reader** reads text printed in magnetized ink. A **terminal** consists of a keyboard, a monitor, a video card, and memory and often is used to perform specific tasks for a particular industry. **Biometrics** is the technology of authenticating a person's identity by verifying a physical characteristic. Biometric input can include fingerprints, hand geometry, facial features, voice, signatures, and eye patterns.

 Visit scsite.com/dcf2e/ch5/quiz or click the Quiz Yourself button. Click Objective 3.

Chapter Review

 4 What Are the Characteristics of LCD Monitors, LCD Screens, and CRT Monitors?

Any hardware component that conveys information to one or more people is an **output device**. A **display device** is a commonly used output device that visually conveys text, graphics, and video information. An **LCD monitor**, also called a flat panel monitor, is a desktop display that uses a liquid crystal display. A **liquid crystal display (LCD)** uses a liquid compound to present information on the screen. A **CRT monitor** is a desktop display device that contains a cathode-ray tube.

 Visit scsite.com/dcf2e/ch5/quiz or click the Quiz Yourself button. Click Objective 4.

 5 What Are Various Types of Printers?

A **printer** is an output device that produces text and graphics on a physical medium. A **nonimpact printer** forms characters and graphics without striking the paper. Several types of nonimpact printers are available. An **ink-jet printer** forms characters and graphics by spraying tiny drops of ink onto paper. A **photo printer** produces lab-quality pictures. A **laser printer** is a high-speed, high-quality printer that operates in a manner similar to a copy machine. A **thermal printer** generates images by pushing electrically heated pins against heat-sensitive paper. A **mobile printer** is a small, battery-powered printer used to print from a notebook computer, Tablet PC, PDA, or smart phone. **Plotters** are used to produce high-quality drawings in specialized fields. A **large-format printer** creates large, photo-realistic-quality color prints. An **impact printer** forms characters and graphics by striking a mechanism against an inked ribbon that physically contacts the paper. A **dot-matrix printer** is an impact printer that produces an image when tiny wire pins on a print head strike an inked ribbon. A **line printer** is an impact printer that prints an entire line at a time.

 6 What Are the Characteristics of Speakers and Headsets, Fax Machines and Fax Modems, Multifunction Peripherals, and Data Projectors?

Speakers are an **audio output device** added to computers to generate higher-quality sound. With a **headset**, only the individual wearing the headset hears the sound from the computer. A **fax machine** is a device that codes and encodes documents so they can be transmitted over telephone lines. Many computers have a fax modem that transmits computer-prepared documents. A **multifunction peripheral** is a single device that provides the functionality of a printer, scanner, copy machine, and perhaps a fax machine. A **data projector** is a device that takes the text and images displaying on a computer screen and projects them onto a larger screen for an audience.

7 What Are Input and Output Options for Physically Challenged Users?

Voice recognition, which is the computer's capability of distinguishing spoken words, is an ideal input option for visually impaired users. Input options for people with limited hand mobility include keyboards with larger keys, on-screen keyboards, and head-mounted pointers. Hearing-impaired users can instruct programs to display words instead of sound. Visually impaired users can change Windows XP settings such as the size and color of text to make words easier to use. Instead of a monitor, blind users can use voice output and a Braille printer.

 Visit scsite.com/dcf2e/ch5/quiz or click the Quiz Yourself button. Click Objectives 5 – 7.

Key Terms

You should know each key term. Use the list below to help focus your study. To further enhance your understanding of the Key Terms in this chapter, visit scsite.com/dcf2e/ch5/terms. See an example of and a definition for each term, and access current and additional information about the term from the Web.

Americans with Disabilities Act (ADA) (197)
audio input (173)
audio output device (193)
automated teller machine (ATM) (180)
bar code (178)
bar code reader (178)
biometrics (181)
CRT monitor (186)
data projector (195)
digital camera (175)
digital pen (172)
digital video (DV) camera (176)
display device (183)
dot-matrix printer (192)
ENERGY STAR program (186)
ergonomics (168)
fax machine (194)
fingerprint scanner (181)
flatbed scanner (177)
graphic designers (198)
graphic illustrators (198)
graphics tablet (172)
headset (194)
impact printer (192)
ink-jet printer (189)
input (166)
input device (166)
joystick (171)
keyboard (168)

large-format printer (192)
laser printer (190)
LCD monitor (184)
light pen (171)
line printer (193)
liquid crystal display (LCD) (185)
magnetic stripe card reader (179)
mechanical mouse (169)
MICR (179)
MICR reader (179)
mobile printer (192)
monitor (183)
mouse (169)
mouse pad (169)
multifunction peripheral (194)
nonimpact printer (189)
OCR devices (177)
optical character recognition (OCR) (177)
optical mark recognition (OMR) (177)
optical mouse (169)
output (182)
output device (182)
PC camera (176)
PC video camera (176)
pen input (172)
photo printer (190)
pixel (175)
plasma monitor (185)
plotters (192)

pointer (167)
pointing device (167)
pointing stick (170)
POS terminal (180)
printer (187)
resolution (175)
RFID (178)
RFID reader (178)
scanner (177)
smart card (181)
speakers (193)
speech recognition (173)
stylus (172)
terminal (180)
thermal printer (191)
touch screen (171)
touchpad (170)
trackball (170)
turnaround document (177)
video conference (176)
video input (176)
video telephone call (176)
voice input (173)
voice output (194)
voice recognition (173)
Web cam (176)
wheel (171)

Checkpoint

Use the Checkpoint exercises to check your knowledge level of the chapter.

True/False

Mark T for True and F for False. (See page numbers in parentheses.)

_____ 1. To fit notebook and many handheld computers, keyboards usually are larger and have more keys. (168)

_____ 2. Touchpads are found most often on mainframe computers. (170)

_____ 3. Resolution is the number of horizontal and vertical pixels in a display device. (175)

_____ 4. A turnaround document is a document that is returned to the company that creates and sends it. (177)

_____ 5. Plasma monitors offer larger screen sizes and higher display quality than LCD monitors. (185)

_____ 6. While laser printers usually cost less than ink-jet printers, they also are much slower. (190)

_____ 7. The disadvantage of a multifunction peripheral is that it is significantly more expensive than if you purchase each device separately. (194)

_____ 8. Visually impaired users can change Windows XP settings to change the color of text in order to make words easier to read. (197)

Multiple Choice

Select the best answer. (See page numbers in parentheses.)

1. An ergonomic keyboard _____. (168)
   a. is used to enter data into a biometric device
   b. transmits data using wireless technology
   c. has a design that reduces wrist and hand injuries
   d. is built into the top of a handheld computer

2. To move the pointer using a pointing stick, you _____. (170)
   a. move the pointing stick across a desktop
   b. rotate the pointing stick with your thumb
   c. slide a fingertip across the surface of the pointing stick
   d. push the pointing stick with a finger

3. Two types of pen input are _____. (172)
   a. digital pen and touch screen
   b. trackball and stylus
   c. digital pen and stylus
   d. pointing stick and digital pen

4. Most retail stores use a(n) _____ to record purchases, process credit or debit cards, and update inventory. (180)
   a. smart display
   b. POS terminal
   c. biometric device
   d. ATM machine

5. Display devices, printers, speakers and headsets, fax machines and fax modems, and multifunction peripherals are examples of commonly used _____ devices. (182)
   a. output
   b. digital
   c. input
   d. POS terminals

6. The speed of an ink-jet printer is measured by the number of _____ it can print. (189)
   a. pages per minute (ppm)
   b. dots per inch (dpi)
   c. characters per second (cps)
   d. lines per page (lpp)

7. A multifunction peripheral provides the functionality of a _____. (194)
   a. printer
   b. scanner
   c. copy machine
   d. all of the above

8. A(n) _____ is an output device for blind users. (197)
   a. Braille printer
   b. head-mounted pointer
   c. on-screen keyboard
   d. all of the above

Matching

Match the terms with their definitions. (See page numbers in parentheses.)

_____ 1. graphics tablet (172)

_____ 2. bar code (178)

_____ 3. magnetic stripe card reader (179)

_____ 4. smart card (181)

_____ 5. plasma monitor (185)

a. identification that consists of a set of vertical lines and spaces of different widths

b. flat, rectangular, electronic plastic board used by architects and artists

c. substitutes a layer of gas for the liquid crystal material in a flat panel monitor

d. reads information on back of credit cards, entertainment cards, bank cards, and other similar cards

e. stores data on a thin microprocessor that is embedded in a credit-card-sized card

f. self-service banking machine that connects to a host computer through a network

CHAPTER 5

Checkpoint

Short Answer

Write a brief answer to each of the following questions.

1. How are a mechanical mouse, an optical mouse, and a wireless mouse different? _____ What is a mouse pad? _____

2. What is a video conference? _____ What is needed to participate in a video conference? _____

3. How are optical character recognition (OCR), optical mark recognition (OMR), and magnetic ink character recognition (MICR) different? _____ How is an RFID reader used? _____

4. What factors determine the quality of a CRT monitor? _____ What is the ENERGY STAR program? _____

5. What is continuous-form paper? _____ How is infrared printing different from Bluetooth printing? _____

Working Together

Working in a group of your classmates, complete the following team exercise.

1. Stores, libraries, parcel carriers, and other organizations use optical codes. Some people mistakenly believe that an optical code contains the name of a product or its price, but the codes are only a link to a database in which this information, and more, is stored. Have each member of your team visit an organization that uses optical codes. How are the optical codes read? What information is obtained when the code is read? What information is recorded? How is the information used? Meet with the members of your team to discuss the results of your investigations. Then, use PowerPoint to create a group presentation and share your findings with the class.

Web Research

Use the Internet-based Web Research exercises to broaden your understanding of the concepts presented in this chapter. Visit scsite.com/dcf2e/ch5/research to obtain more information pertaining to each exercise. To discuss any of the Web Research exercises in this chapter with other students, post your thoughts or questions at scsite.com/dcf2e/ch5/forum.

① **Journaling** Respond to your readings in this chapter by writing at least one page about your reactions, evaluations, and reflections about using **input devices**. For example, do you recall the first time you used a mouse? What experiences have you had with voice recognition? Do you own a PDA or Tablet PC, digital camera, or smart phone? Have you ever suffered from repetitive strain injuries from using a mouse or keyboard? What do you do to reduce the chances of experiencing repetitive strain injuries? You also can write about the new terms you learned by reading this chapter. If required, submit your journal to your instructor.

② **Scavenger Hunt** Use one of the **search engines** listed in Figure 2-8 in Chapter 2 on page 58 or your own favorite search engine to find the answers to the questions below. Copy and paste the Web address from the Web page where you found the answer. Some questions may have more than one answer. If required, submit your answers to your instructor. (1) The primary inventor of the first commercial typewriter wanted to persuade people to buy and use the device, so he ordered the keys to allow users to type as quickly as possible. Who was the QWERTY keyboard's primary inventor? (2) Many of the new handheld devices, including PDAs, allow you to input data through the use of handwriting software. What are the three more popular handwriting/input programs? (3) Find two Web sites that sell these programs, and create a table listing the cost of each of these programs on each Web site.

③ **Search Sleuth** Typical search Web sites, such as Google and Ask Jeeves, maintain their own internal databases of links to Web pages. **MetaCrawler** (metacrawler.com) is a different type of search Web site because it returns combined results from these and other leading search engines. Visit this Web site and then use your word processing program to answer the following questions. Then, if required, submit your answers to your instructor. (1) Click the Tools and Tips link at the top of the page. Browse and then explore some of the tools, such as MiniCrawler and MetaSpy. (2) Scroll down and then read some of the information contained in the Basic Searching section. Make notes of two new things you learned. (3) Click your browser's Back button or press the BACKSPACE key to return to the MetaCrawler home page. What are the six most popular searches today? Click a link for one of these popular searches and scroll through the results MetaCrawler returns. (4) Click your browser's Back button or press the BACKSPACE key to return to the MetaCrawler home page. Click the Search text box and then type What is the top selling SUV? as the keywords in the Search text box. (5) Scroll through the links MetaCrawler returns and then click one that provides the information requested. What are the three most popular SUVs? Read the information and then write a 50-word summary.

Learn How To

Use the Learn How To activities to learn fundamental skills when using a computer and accompanying technology. Complete the exercises and submit them to your instructor.

LEARN HOW TO 1: Adjust the Sound on a Computer

Every computer today contains a sound card and associated hardware and software that allow you to play and record sound. You can adjust the sound by completing the following steps:

1. Click the Start button on the Windows taskbar and then click Control Panel on the Start menu.
2. When the Control Panel window opens, click Sounds, Speech, and Audio Devices and then click Adjust the system volume; or double-click Sounds and Audio Devices. *The Sounds and Audio Devices Properties dialog box is displayed (Figure 5-50).*
3. To adjust the volume for all devices connected to the sound card, drag the Device volume slider left or right to decrease or increase the volume.
4. If you want to mute the sound on the computer, click the Mute check box so it contains a check mark, and then click the OK button or the Apply button.
5. To place the volume icon on the Windows taskbar, click the Place volume icon in the taskbar check box so it contains a check mark, and then click the OK button or the Apply button. You can click the icon on the taskbar to set the volume level or mute the sound.
6. To make sound and other adjustments for each device on the computer, click the Advanced button in the Device volume area. *The Play Control or Recording Control window opens, depending on prior choices for this window (Figure 5-51).*
7. If the Recording Control window is opened, click Options on the window menu bar, click Properties on the Options menu, click the Playback option button, and then click the OK button.
8. In the Play Control window, Play Control volume is the same as the volume adjusted in the Sounds and Audio Devices Properties dialog box. The other columns in the Play Control window refer to devices found on the computer. To select the columns that are displayed, click Options on the menu bar and then click Properties. With Playback selected, place checks in the check boxes for those devices you want to be displayed in the Control window.
9. To adjust volumes, drag the Volume sliders. To adjust speaker balance, drag the Balance sliders.
10. If the Advanced button is not displayed in the Play Control window, click Options on the menu bar and then click Advanced Controls on the Options menu. Click the Advanced button. You can control the Bass and Treble settings by using the sliders in the Tone Controls area of the Advanced Controls for Play Control dialog box.

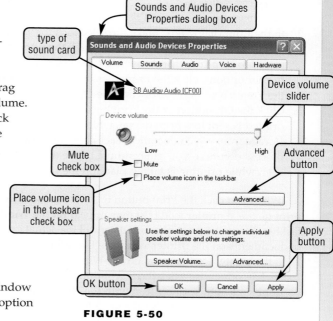

FIGURE 5-50

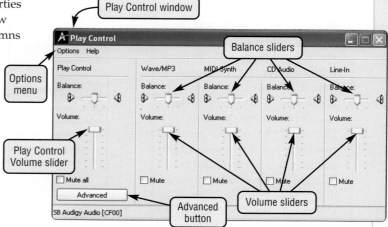

FIGURE 5-51

Exercise

1. Open the Control Panel window and then display the Sounds and Audio Devices Properties dialog box. What kind of sound card is on the computer? Click the Place volume icon in the taskbar check box and then click the Apply button. What change did you notice on the Windows taskbar? Do the same thing again. What change occurred on the Windows taskbar? Click the Advanced button in the Device volume area. Ensure the Play Control window is open. What devices are chosen for control in the Play Control window? How would you change what devices are chosen? Submit your answers to your instructor.

Learn How To

LEARN HOW TO 2: Control Printing on Your Computer

When you print using a computer, you control printing at two different points: first, before the printing actually begins, and second, after the document has been sent to the printer and either is physically printing or is waiting to be printed. To set the parameters for printing and then print the document, complete the following steps:

1. Click File on the menu bar of the program that will be used for printing and then click Print on the File menu. *The Print dialog box is displayed (Figure 5-52). The Print dialog box will vary somewhat depending on the program used.*

2. In the Print dialog box, make the selections for what printer will be used, what pages will be printed, the number of copies to be printed, and any other choices available. For further options, click the Properties button (or, sometimes, the Preferences button), or click the Options button.

3. Click the OK button or the Print button. The document being printed is sent to a print queue, which is an area on disk storage from which documents actually are printed. This process occurs so you can continue to use the program even while printing is taking place on the printer.

When you click the Print button to send the document to the print queue, a printer icon [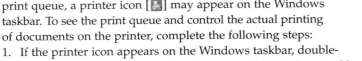] may appear on the Windows taskbar. To see the print queue and control the actual printing of documents on the printer, complete the following steps:

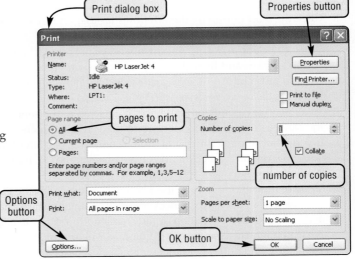

FIGURE 5-52

1. If the printer icon appears on the Windows taskbar, double-click it; otherwise, click the Start button on the Windows taskbar, click Printers and Faxes on the Start menu, and then double-click the printer icon with the check mark. The check mark indicates the default printer. *A window opens with the name of the printer on the title bar (Figure 5-53). All the documents either printing or waiting to be printed are listed in the window. The Status column indicates whether the document is printing or waiting. In addition, the owner of the file, number of pages, size, date and time submitted, and printer port are listed.*

2. If you click Printer on the menu bar in the printer window, you can set printing preferences from the Printer menu. In addition, you can pause all printing and cancel all printing jobs from the Printer menu.

3. If you select a document in the document list and then click Document on the menu bar, you can cancel the selected document for printing, or you can pause the printing for the selected document. To continue printing for the selected document, click Document on the menu bar and then click Resume on the Document menu.

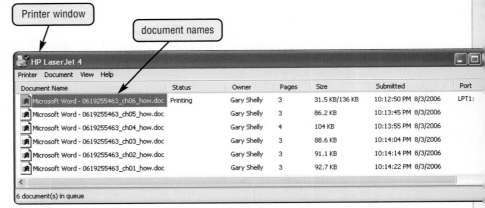

FIGURE 5-53

Exercise

1. Start WordPad from the Accessories submenu. Type `The Print dialog box is displayed by clicking Print on the File menu`.

2. Display the Print dialog box and then click the Preferences button. When the Printing Preferences dialog box appears, click the Layout tab. What choices do you have in the Layout sheet? Close the Printing Preferences dialog box. How do you select the number of copies you want to print? How would you print pages 25–35 of a document? Submit your answers to your instructor.

Learn It Online

Use the Learn It Online exercises to reinforce your understanding of the chapter concepts. To access the Learn It Online exercises, visit scsite.com/dcf2e/ch5/learn.

(1) At the Movies — Get the Best of Both Worlds with a Convertible Tablet PC

To view the Get the Best of Both Worlds with a Convertible Tablet PC movie, click the number 1 button. Locate your video and click the corresponding High-Speed or Dial-Up link, depending on your Internet connection. Watch the movie and then complete the exercise by answering the questions that follow. Taking classroom notes with pen and paper may be a thing of the past if the Tablet PC continues its rise in popularity. Switching to a Tablet PC can offer you some options that are not available on a regular notebook or desktop computer. What are some of the drawbacks to using a Tablet PC? What are some of the benefits?

(2) Student Edition Labs — Peripheral Devices

Click the number 2 button. When the Student Edition Labs menu appears, click *Peripheral Devices* to begin. A new browser window will open. Follow the on-screen instructions to complete the Lab. When finished, click the Exit button. If required, submit your results to your instructor.

(3) Practice Test

Click the number 3 button. Answer each question. When completed, enter your name and click the Grade Test button to submit the quiz for grading. Make a note of any missed questions. If required, submit your results to your instructor.

(4) Who Wants To Be a Computer Genius^2?

Click the number 4 button to find out if you are a computer genius. Directions about how to play the game will be displayed. When you are ready to play, click the Play button. Submit your score to your instructor.

(5) Wheel of Terms

Click the number 5 button to reinforce important terms you learned in this chapter by playing the Shelly Cashman Series version of this popular game. Directions about how to play the game will be displayed. When you are ready to play, click the Play button. Submit your score to your instructor.

(6) Student Edition Labs — Working with Graphics

Click the number 6 button. When the Student Edition Labs menu appears, click *Working with Graphics* to begin. A new browser window will open. Follow the on-screen instructions to complete the Lab. When finished, click the Exit button. If required, submit your results to your instructor.

(7) Crossword Puzzle Challenge

Click the number 7 button. Complete the puzzle to reinforce skills you learned in this chapter. Directions about how to play the game will be displayed. When you are ready to play, click the Submit button. Submit the completed puzzle to your instructor.

(8) Lab Exercises

Click the number 8 button. When the Lab Exercises menu appears, click the exercise assigned by your instructor. A new browser window will open. Follow the on-screen instructions to complete the exercise. When finished, click the Exit button. If required, submit your results to your instructor.

(9) Chapter Discussion Forum

Select an objective from this chapter on page 165 about which you would like more information. Click the number 9 button and post a short message listing a meaningful message title accompanied by one or more questions concerning the selected objective. In two days, return to the threaded discussion by clicking the number 9 button. Submit to your instructor your original message and at least one response to your message.

Digital Imaging and Video Technology

Everywhere you look, people are capturing moments they want to remember. They take pictures or make movies of their vacations, birthday parties, activities, accomplishments, sporting events, weddings, and more. Because of the popularity of digital cameras and digital video cameras, increasingly more people desire to capture their memories digitally, instead of on film. With digital technology, photographers have the ability to modify and share the digital images and videos they create. When you use special hardware and/or software, you can copy, manipulate, print, and distribute digital images and videos using your personal computer and the Internet. Amateurs can create professional quality results by using more sophisticated hardware and software.

digital camera (input)

digital video camera (input)

FireWire or USB 2.0

television (output)

FIGURE 1   The top portion of the figure shows a typical home digital imaging setup, and the lower portion of the figure shows a typical home setup for editing personal video.

Digital photography and recordings deliver significant benefits over film-based photography and movie making. With digital cameras, no developing is needed. Instead, the images reside on storage media such as a hard disk, DVD, or flash memory card. Unlike film, storage media can be reused, which reduces costs, saves time, and provides immediate results. Digital technology allows greater control over the creative process, both while taking pictures and video and in the editing process. You can check results immediately after capturing a picture or video to determine whether it meets your expectations. If you are dissatisfied with a picture or video, you can erase it and recapture it, again and again.

As shown in the top portion of Figure 1, a digital camera functions as an input device when it transmits pictures through a cable to a personal computer via a USB port or FireWire port. Using a digital camera in this way allows you to edit the pictures, save them on storage media, and print them on a photographic-quality printer via a parallel port or USB port.

The lower portion of Figure 1 illustrates how you might use a digital video camera with a personal computer. The process typically is the same for most digital video cameras. You capture the images or video with the video camera. Next, you connect the video camera to your personal computer using a FireWire or USB 2.0 port, or you place the storage media used on the camera in the computer. The video then is copied or downloaded to the computer's hard disk. Then, you can edit the video using video editing software. If desired, you can preview the video during the editing process on a television. Finally, you save the finished result to the desired media, such as a VHS tape or DVD+RW or, perhaps, e-mail the edited video. In this example, a VCR and a DVD player also can be used to input video from a VHS tape or a DVD.

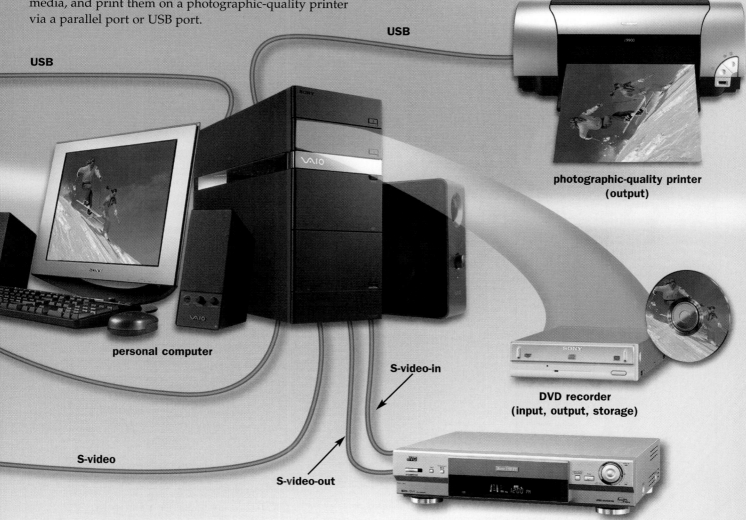

USB

USB

photographic-quality printer
(output)

personal computer

S-video-in

DVD recorder
(input, output, storage)

S-video

S-video-out

VCR (input, output, storage)

DIGITAL IMAGING TECHNOLOGY

Digital imaging technology involves capturing and manipulating still photographic images in an electronic format. The following sections outline the steps involved in the process of using digital imaging technology.

1 Select a Digital Camera

A **digital camera** is a type of camera that stores photographed images electronically instead of on traditional film. Digital cameras are divided into three categories (Figure 2) based mainly on image resolution, features, and of course, price. The image resolution is measured in pixels (short for picture element). The image quality increases with the number of pixels. The image resolution usually is measured in **megapixels** (million of pixels), often abbreviated as **MP**. Features of digital cameras include red-eye reduction, zoom, autofocus, flash, self-timer, and manual mode for fine-tuning settings. Figure 3 summarizes the three categories of digital cameras.

TYPES OF DIGITAL CAMERAS

Type	Resolution Range	Features			Price
Point and shoot	Less than 6 MP	Fully automatic; fits in your pocket; easy to use; ideal for average consumer usage.			Less than $600
Field cameras	Greater than 5 MP	Used by photojournalists; portable but flexible; provides ability to change lenses and use other attachments; great deal of control over exposure and other photo settings.			$800 to $2,000
Studio cameras	Greater than 5 MP	Stationary camera used for professional studio work; flexible; widest range of lenses and settings.			$1,500 and up

FIGURE 3 Digital cameras often are categorized by image resolution, features, and price.

(a) point-and-shoot

(b) field

(c) studio

FIGURE 2 The point-and-shoot digital camera (a) requires no adjustments before shooting. The field digital camera (b) offers improved quality and features that allow you to make manual adjustments before shooting and use a variety of lenses. The studio digital camera (c) offers better color and resolution and greater control over exposure and lenses.

2 Take Pictures

Digital cameras provide you with several options that are set before a picture is taken. Three of the more important options are the resolution, compression, and image file format in which the camera should save the picture. While a camera may allow for a very high resolution for a large print, you may choose to take a picture at a lower resolution if the image does not require great detail or must be a small size. For example, you may want to use the image on a Web page where smaller image file sizes are beneficial.

Compression results in smaller image file sizes. Figure 4 illustrates the image file sizes for varying resolutions and compressions under standard photographic conditions using a 4 megapixel digital camera. Figure 4 also shows the average picture size for a given resolution. The camera may take more time to save an image at lower compression, resulting in a longer delay before the camera is ready to take another picture. A higher compression, however, may result in some loss of image quality. If a camera has a 16 MB flash memory card, you can determine the number of pictures the card can hold by dividing 16 MB by the file size. Flash memory cards are available in sizes from 16 MB to 8 GB.

Most digital cameras also allow you to choose an image file format. Two popular file formats are TIFF and JPEG. The **TIFF** file format saves the image uncompressed. All of the image detail is captured and stored, but the file sizes can be large. The **JPEG** file format is compressed. The resolution of the image may be the same as a TIFF file, but some detail may be lost in the image.

Finally, before you take the photograph, you should choose the type of media on which to store the resulting image file. Some cameras allow for a choice of media to which you can store the image, such as a CompactFlash card or Memory Stick, while others allow for only one type of storage media. One major advantage of a digital camera is that you easily can erase pictures from its media, freeing up space for new pictures.

IMAGE FILE SIZE WITH A FOUR MEGAPIXEL DIGITAL CAMERA

Resolution in Pixels	COMPRESSION			Picture Size in Inches
	Low	Medium	High	
	Resulting Image File Size			
2272 × 1704	2 MB	1.1 MB	556 KB	11 by 17
1600 × 1200	1 MB	558 KB	278 KB	8 by 10
1024 × 768	570 KB	320 KB	170 KB	4 by 6
640 × 480	249 KB	150 KB	84 KB	3 by 5

FIGURE 4 Image file sizes for varying resolutions and compressions under standard photographic conditions using a 4 megapixel digital camera.

③ Transfer and Manage Image Files

The method of transferring images from the camera to the personal computer differs greatly depending on the capabilities of both. Digital cameras use a variety of storage media (Figure 5). If your camera uses a flash memory card such as a CompactFlash, Memory Stick, SmartMedia, or Secure Digital (SD), you can remove the media from the camera and place it in a slot on the personal computer or in a device, such as a card reader, connected to the personal computer. The Microdrive media shown in Figure 5 is a type of CompactFlash media. Your camera or card reader also may connect to the personal computer using a USB, USB 2.0, or FireWire (Figure 6) port. When you insert the memory card or connect the camera, software on the personal computer guides you through the process of transferring the images to the hard disk. Some operating systems and software recognize a memory card or camera as though it is another hard disk on the computer. This feature allows you to access the files, navigate them, and then copy, delete, or rename the files while the media still is in the camera.

After you transfer the files to the hard disk on your personal computer, you should organize the files by sorting them or renaming them so that information, such as the subject, date, time, and purpose, is saved along with the image. Finally, before altering the images digitally or using the images for other purposes, you should back up the images to another location, such as a CD or DVD, so the original image is recoverable.

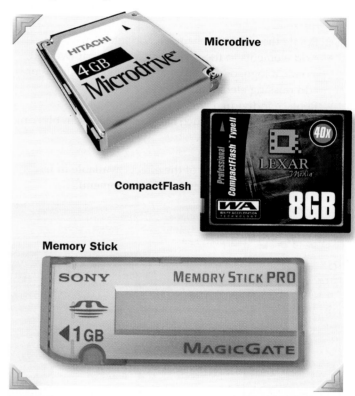

FIGURE 5 Microdrives, CompactFlash, and Memory Sticks are popular storage devices for digital cameras.

FIGURE 6 Using a USB or FireWire connection, you can add a card reader to your personal computer.

4 Edit Images

Image editing software allows you to edit digital images. The following list summarizes the more common image enhancements or alterations:

- Adjust the contrast and brightness; correct lighting problems; or help give the photograph a particular feeling, such as warm or stark.
- Remove red-eye.
- Crop an image to remove unnecessary elements and resize it.
- Rotate the image to change its orientation.
- Add elements to the image, such as descriptive text, a date, a logo, or decorative items; create collages or add missing elements.
- Replace individual colors with a new color.
- Add special effects, such as texture or motion blurring to enhance the image.

Figure 7 shows some of the effects available in Jasc's Paint Shop Pro on the Artistic Effects submenu.

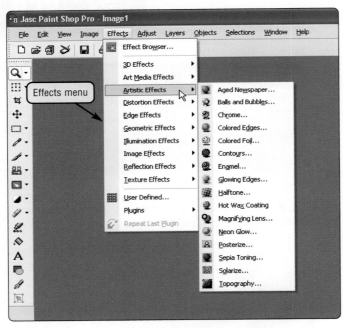

FIGURE 7 The capability of applying effects separates digital photography from film photography.

5 Print Images

Once an image is digitally altered, it is ready to be printed. You can print images on a personal color printer or send them to a professional service that specializes in digital photo printing.

When printing the images yourself, make sure that the resolution used to create the image was high enough for the size of the print you want to create. For example, if the camera used a resolution of 640 × 480 pixels, then the ideal print size is a wallet size. If you print such an image at a size of 8-by-10 inches, then the image will appear **pixilated**, or blurry. Use high-quality photo paper for the best results. A photo printer gives the best results when printing digital photography.

Many services print digital images, either over the Internet or through traditional photo developing locations and kiosks (Figure 8), such as those found in drug stores or shopping marts. Some services allow you to e-mail or upload the files to the service, specify the size, quality, and quantity of print; and then receive the finished prints via the postal service. Other services allow you to drop off flash memory cards, CD-ROMs, or floppy disks at a photo shop and later pick up the prints, just as you do with traditional photo developing shops.

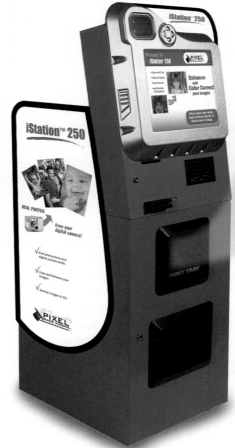

FIGURE 8
A Pixel Magic Imaging Photo Ditto kiosk allows you to print digital images in high resolution on photo paper.

6 Distribute Images Electronically

Rather than printing images, you often need to use the images electronically. Depending on the electronic use of the image, the image may require additional processing. If you use the images on a Web site or want to e-mail a photo, you probably want to send a lower-resolution image. Image editing software allows you to lower the resolution of the image, resulting in a smaller file size. You also should use standard file formats when distributing an electronic photo. The JPEG format is viewable using most personal computers or Web browsers.

You can store very high resolution photos on a DVD or a CD. **DVD and CD mastering software** (Figure 9) allows you to create slide show presentations on a recordable DVD or CD that can play in many home DVD players or personal computer DVD drives.

Finally, you should back up and store images that you distribute electronically with the same care as you store your traditional film negatives.

FIGURE 9 Nero PhotoShow Elite and similar software applications allow you to create your own photo slide show on DVD or CD.

DIGITAL VIDEO TECHNOLOGY

Digital video technology allows you to input, edit, manage, publish, and share your videos using a personal computer. With digital video technology, you can transform home videos into Hollywood-style movies by enhancing the videos with scrolling titles and transitions, cutting out or adding scenes, and adding background music and voice-over narration. The following sections outline the steps involved in the process of using digital video technology.

1 Select a Video Camera

Video cameras record in either analog or digital format. **Analog formats** include 8mm, Hi8, VHS, VHS-C, and Super VHS-C. The last three formats use the types of tapes similar to those used in a standard VCR. **Digital formats** include Mini-DV, MICROMV, Digital8, and DVD. Consumer digital video cameras are by far the most popular type among consumers. They fall into three general categories: high-end consumer, consumer, and webcasting and monitoring (Figure 10). Digital video cameras provide more features than analog video cameras, such as a higher level of zoom, better sound, or greater control over color and lighting.

2 Record a Video

Most video cameras provide you with a choice of recording programs, which sometimes are called automatic settings. Each recording program includes a different combination of camera settings, so you can adjust the exposure and other functions to match the recording environment. Usually, several different programs are available, such as point and shoot, point and shoot with manual adjustment, sports, portrait, spotlit scenes, and low light. You also have the ability to select special digital effects, such as fade, wipe, and black and white. If you are shooting outside on a windy day, then you can enable the wind screen to prevent wind noise. If you are shooting home videos, then the point-and-shoot recording program is sufficient.

3 Transfer and Manage Videos

After recording the video, the next step is to transfer the video to your personal computer. Most video cameras connect directly to a USB 2.0 or FireWire port on your personal computer (Figure 11). Transferring video with a digital camera is easy, because the video already is in a digital format that the computer can understand.

(a) high-end consumer

(b) consumer

(c) webcasting and monitoring

FIGURE 10 The high-end consumer digital video camera (a) can produce professional-grade results. The consumer digital video camera (b) produces amateur-grade results. The webcasting and monitoring digital video camera (c) is appropriate for webcasting and security monitoring.

An analog camcorder or VCR requires additional hardware to convert the analog signals to a digital format before the video can be manipulated on a personal computer. The additional hardware includes a special video capture card using a standard RCA video cable or an S-video cable (Figure 12). *S-video* cables provide sharper images and greater overall quality. When you use video capture hardware with an analog video, be sure to close all open programs on your computer because capturing video requires a great deal of processing power.

When transferring video, plan to use approximately 15 to 30 gigabytes of hard disk storage space per hour of digital video. A typical video project requires about four times the amount of raw footage as the final product. Therefore, at the high end, a video that lasts an hour may require up to 120 gigabytes of storage for the raw footage, editing process, and final video. This storage requirement can vary depending on the software you use to copy the video from the video camera to the hard disk and the format you select to save the video. For example, Microsoft claims that the latest version of its Windows Movie Maker can save 15 hours of video in 10 gigabytes when creating video for playback on a computer, but saves only 1 hour of video in 10 gigabytes when creating video for playback on a DVD or VCR.

FIGURE 11   A digital video camera is connected to the personal computer via a FireWire or USB 2.0 port. No additional hardware is needed.

FIGURE 12   An analog camcorder or VCR is connected to the personal computer via an S-video port on a video capture card.

The video transfer requires application software on the personal computer (Figure 13). Windows XP includes the Windows Movie Maker software that allows you to transfer the video from your video camera. Depending on the length of video and the type of connection used, the video may take a long time to download. Make certain that no other programs are running on your personal computer while transferring the video.

When transferring video, the software may allow you to choose a file format and a codec to store the video. A video **file format** holds the video information in a manner specified by a vendor, such as Apple or Microsoft. Three of the more popular file formats are listed in Figure 14.

File formats support codecs to encode the audio and video into the file formats. A particular file format may be able to store audio and video in a number of different codecs. A **codec** specifies how the audio and video is compressed and stored within the file. Figure 15 shows some options available for specifying a file format and codec in a video capture application. The dialog box in Figure 15 allows the user to determine whether the video is smoother in playback or if the video is more crisp, meaning that it includes more detail. The file format and codec you choose often is based on what you plan to do with the movie. For example, if you plan to stream video over the Web using RealNetworks software, the best choice for the file format is the RealMedia format, which uses the RealVideo codec.

After transferring the video to a personal computer, and before manipulating the video, you should store the video files in appropriate folders, named correctly, and backed up. Most video transfer application software helps manage these tasks.

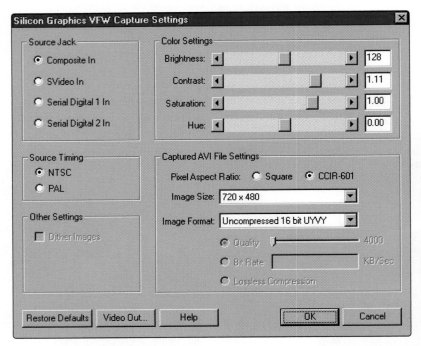

FIGURE 13 Some video editing software allows you to transfer your video from any video source to a hard disk. This dialog box allows the user to set various video parameters for capturing video from a camera or other device.

POPULAR VIDEO FILE FORMATS

File Format	File Extensions
Apple QuickTime	.MOV or .QT
Microsoft Windows Media Video	.WMV or .ASF
RealNetworks RealMedia	.RM or .RAM

FIGURE 14 Apple, Microsoft, and RealNetworks offer the more popular video file formats.

FIGURE 15 Video editing software applications allow you to specify a combination of file format and codec when saving a video.

4 Edit a Video

Once the video is stored on your hard disk, the next step is to edit, or manipulate, the video. If you used a video capture card to transfer analog video to your computer (Figure 12 on page 215), the files may require extra initial processing. When you use a video capture card, some of the video frames may be lost in the transfer process. Some video editing programs allow you to fix this problem with **frame rate correction** tools.

The first step in the editing process is to split the video into smaller pieces, or *scenes*, that you can manipulate more easily. This process is called *splitting*. Most video software automatically splits the video into scenes, thus sparing you the task. After splitting, you should cut out unwanted scenes or portions of scenes. This process is called *pruning*.

After you create the scenes you want to use in your final production, you edit each individual scene. You can *crop*, or change the size of, scenes. That is, you may want to cut out the top or a side of a scene that is irrelevant. You also can resize the scene. For example, you may be creating a video that will be displayed in a Web browser.

Making a smaller video, such as 320 × 200 pixels instead of 640 × 480 pixels, results in a smaller file that transmits faster over the Internet.

If video has been recorded over a long period, using different cameras or under different lighting conditions, the video may need color correction. *Color correction tools* (Figure 16) analyze your video and match brightness, colors, and other attributes of video clips to ensure a smooth look to the video.

You can add logos, special effects, or titles to scenes. You can place a company logo or personal logo in a video to identify yourself or the company producing the video. Logos often are added on the lower-right corner of a video and remain for the duration of the video. Special effects include warping, changing from color to black and white, morphing, or zoom motion. *Morphing* is a special effect in which one video image is transformed into another image over the course of several frames of video, creating the illusion of metamorphosis. You usually add titles at the beginning and end of a video to give the video context. A training video may have titles throughout the video to label a particular scene, or each scene may begin with a title.

FIGURE 16 Color correction tools in video editing software allow a great deal of control over the mood of your video creation.

The next step in editing a video is to add audio effects, including voice-over narration and background music. Many video editing programs allow you to add additional tracks, or *layers*, of sound to a video in addition to the sound that was recorded on the video camera. You also can add special audio effects.

The final step in editing a video is to combine the scenes into a complete video (Figure 17). This process involves ordering scenes and adding transition effects between scenes (Figure 18). Video editing software allows you to combine scenes and separate each scene with a transition. *Transitions* include fading, wiping, blurry, bursts, ruptures, erosions, and more.

FIGURE 17 In Windows Movie Maker 2, scenes, shown on the top, are combined into a sequence on the bottom of the screen.

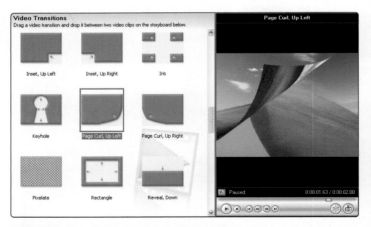

FIGURE 18 Smooth and dynamic transitions eliminate the hard cuts between scenes typically found in raw footage.

⑤ Distribute the Video

After editing the video, the final step is to distribute it or save it on an appropriate medium. You can save video in a variety of formats. Using special hardware, you can save the video on standard video tape. *A digital-to-analog converter* is necessary to allow your personal computer to transmit video to a VCR. A digital-to-analog converter may be an external device that connects to both the computer and input device, or may be a video capture card inside the computer.

Video also can be stored in digital formats in any of several DVD formats, on CD-R, or on video CD (VCD). *DVD* or *CD creation software*, which often is packaged with video editing software, allows you to create, or *master*, DVDs and CDs. You can add interactivity to your DVDs. For example, you can allow viewers to jump to certain scenes using a menu (Figure 19). A *video CD (VCD)* is a CD format that stores video on a CD-R that can be played in many DVD players.

You also can save your video creation in electronic format for distribution over the Web or via e-mail. Your video editing software must support the file format and codec you want to use. For example, RealNetworks's Helix media delivery system allows you to save media files in the RealVideo file formats.

Professionals use hardware and software that allow them to create a film version of digital video that can be played in movie theaters. This technology is becoming increasingly popular and has been used in such movies as the recent *Lord of the Rings* movies. Some Hollywood directors believe that eventually, all movies will be recorded and edited digitally.

After creating your final video for distribution or your personal video collection, you should backup the final video file. You can save your scenes for inclusion in other video creations or create new masters using different effects, transitions, and ordering of scenes.

FIGURE 19 DVD mastering software allows you to create interactive menus on your DVD.

OBJECTIVES

After completing this chapter, you will be able to:

1. Describe the characteristics of magnetic disks
2. Differentiate between floppy disks and Zip disks
3. Describe the characteristics of a hard disk
4. Describe the characteristics of optical discs
5. Differentiate among various CD and DVD formats
6. Identify the uses of tape
7. Discuss PC Cards and the various types of miniature mobile storage media
8. Identify uses of microfilm and microfiche

CONTENTS

STORAGE

MAGNETIC DISKS
Floppy Disks
Zip Disks
Hard Disks

OPTICAL DISCS
CD-ROMs
CD-Rs and CD-RWs
DVD-ROMs
Recordable and Rewritable DVDs

TAPE

PC CARDS

MINIATURE MOBILE STORAGE MEDIA
Flash Memory Cards
USB Flash Drives
Smart Cards

MICROFILM AND MICROFICHE

ENTERPRISE STORAGE

PUTTING IT ALL TOGETHER

CHAPTER SUMMARY

COMPANIES ON THE CUTTING EDGE
Maxtor
SanDisk Corporation

TECHNOLOGY TRAILBLAZERS
Al Shugart
Mark Dean

STORAGE

Storage holds data, instructions, and information for future use. For example, the home user might store letters, budgets, bank statements, a household inventory, records of stock purchases, tax data, addresses of friends and relatives, daily schedules, e-mail messages, homework assignments, recipes, digital photographs, music, and videos. A business user accesses many stored items, including customer orders and invoices, vendor payments, payroll records, tax data, inventory records, presentations, digital photographs, contracts, marketing literature, contacts, appointments, schedules, e-mail messages, and Web pages. Other users store diagrams, drawings, blueprints, designs, marketing literature, corporate newsletters, product catalogs,

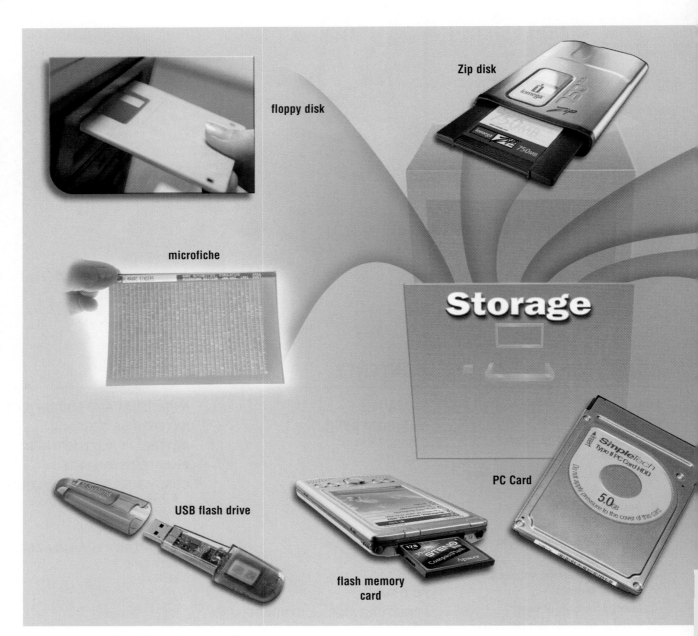

FIGURE 6-1   A variety of storage media.

videos, audio recordings, multimedia presentations, and digital photographs. All computers also use storage to hold system and application software.

Storage requirements among users vary greatly. Home users typically have much smaller storage requirements than business users. For example, a home user may need 80 billion bytes of storage, while large businesses may require 50 trillion bytes of storage.

A **storage medium** (media is the plural), also called **secondary storage**, is the physical material on which a computer keeps data, instructions, and information. Examples of storage media are floppy disks, Zip disks, hard disks, CDs and DVDs, tape, PC Cards, flash memory cards, USB flash drives, and microfiche (Figure 6-1).

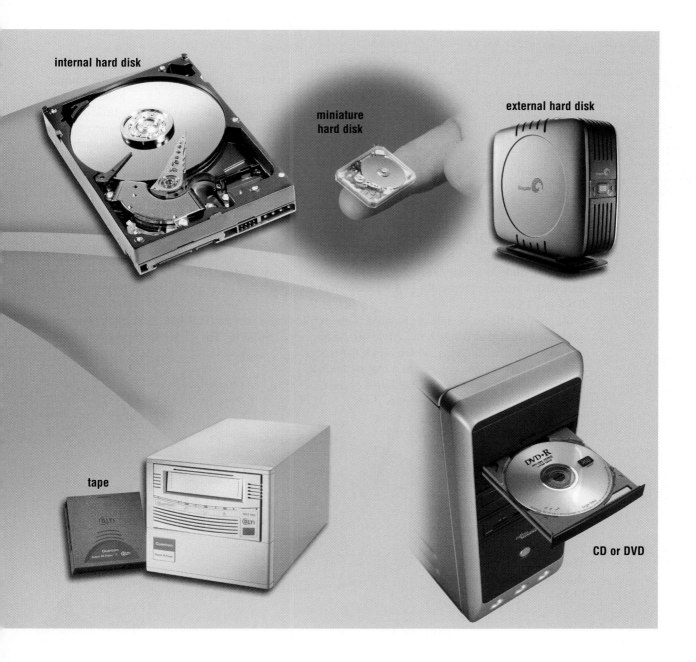

internal hard disk

miniature hard disk

external hard disk

tape

CD or DVD

Capacity is the number of bytes (characters) a storage medium can hold. Figure 6-2 identifies the terms manufacturers use to define the capacity of storage media. For example, a typical floppy disk can store up to 1.44 MB of data (approximately 1.4 million bytes) and a typical hard disk has 80 GB (approximately 80 billion bytes) of storage capacity.

A **storage device** is the computer hardware that records and/or retrieves items to and from storage media. **Writing** is the process of transferring data, instructions, and information from memory to a storage medium. **Reading** is the process of transferring these items from a storage medium into memory. When storage devices write data on storage media, they are creating output. Similarly, when storage devices read from storage media, they function as a source of input. Nevertheless, they are categorized as storage devices, not as input or output devices.

The speed of storage devices is defined by access time. **Access time** measures the amount of time it takes a storage device to locate an item on a storage medium. The access time of storage devices is slow, compared with the access time of memory. Memory (chips) accesses items in billionths of a second (nanoseconds). Storage devices, by contrast, access items in thousandths of a second (milliseconds).

STORAGE TERMS

Storage Term	Approximate Number of Bytes	Exact Number of Bytes
Kilobyte (KB)	1 thousand	2^{10} or 1,024
Megabyte (MB)	1 million	2^{20} or 1,048,576
Gigabyte (GB)	1 billion	2^{30} or 1,073,741,824
Terabyte (TB)	1 trillion	2^{40} or 1,099,511,627,776
Petabyte (PB)	1 quadrillion	2^{50} or 1,125,899,906,842,624
Exabyte (EB)	1 quintillion	2^{60} or 1,152,921,504,606,846,976
Zettabyte (ZB)	1 sextillion	2^{70} or 1,180,591,620,717,411,303,424
Yottabyte (YB)	1 septillion	2^{80} or 1,208,925,819,614,629,174,706,176

FIGURE 6-2   The capacity of a storage medium is measured by the amount of bytes it can hold.

MAGNETIC DISKS

Magnetic disks use magnetic particles to store items such as data, instructions, and information on a disk's surface. Depending on how the magnetic particles are aligned, they represent either a 0 bit or a 1 bit.

Magnetic disks store data and instructions in tracks and sectors (Figure 6-3). A track is a narrow recording band that forms a full circle on the surface of the disk. The disk's storage locations consist of pie-shaped sections, which break the tracks into small arcs called sectors. On a magnetic disk, a sector typically stores up to 512 bytes of data.

Three types of magnetic disks are floppy disks, Zip disks, and hard disks. Some of these disks are portable; others are not. With respect to a storage medium, the term portable means you can remove the medium from one computer and carry it to another computer. The following sections discuss types of magnetic disks.

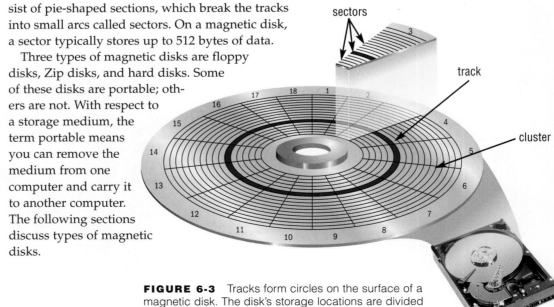

FIGURE 6-3   Tracks form circles on the surface of a magnetic disk. The disk's storage locations are divided into pie-shaped sections, which break the tracks into small arcs called sectors.

Floppy Disks

A **floppy disk**, also called a **diskette**, is a portable, inexpensive storage medium that consists of a thin, circular, flexible plastic Mylar film with a magnetic coating enclosed in a square-shaped plastic shell. A typical floppy disk is 3.5 inches wide and can store up to 500 double-spaced pages of text, several digital photographs, or a small audio file. Floppy disks are not as widely used as they were 15 years ago because of their low storage capacity. They are used, however, for specific applications. Some users work with floppy disks to transport small files to and from nonnetworked personal computers, such as from school or work to home.

A **floppy disk drive** is a device that reads from and writes on a floppy disk. A user inserts a floppy disk in and removes it from a floppy disk drive. Desktop personal computers and notebook computers may have a floppy disk drive installed inside the system unit (Figure 6-4a).

Some users purchase an external floppy disk drive, in which the drive is a separate device with a cable that plugs in a port on the system unit (Figure 6-4b). These external drives are attached to the computer only when the user needs to access items on a floppy disk.

You can read from and write on a floppy disk any number of times. To protect a floppy disk from accidentally being erased, the plastic outer shell on the disk contains a write-protect notch in its corner. A **write-protect notch** is a small opening that has a tab you slide to cover or expose the notch. If the write-protect notch is open, the drive cannot write on the floppy disk. If the write-protect notch is covered, or closed, the drive can write on the floppy disk. A floppy disk drive can read from a floppy disk whether the write-protect notch is open or closed.

WEB LINK 6-1

Floppy Disks

For more information, visit scsite.com/dcf2e/ch6/weblink and then click Floppy Disks.

As mentioned earlier, a floppy disk stores data in tracks and sectors. A typical floppy disk stores data on both sides of the disk, has 80 tracks on each side of the recording surface, and has 18 sectors per track. The actual number of available bytes on a floppy disk is 1,474,560.

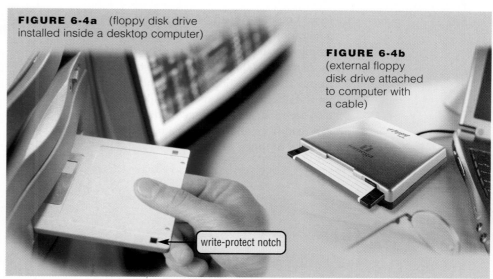

FIGURE 6-4a (floppy disk drive installed inside a desktop computer)

FIGURE 6-4b (external floppy disk drive attached to computer with a cable)

write-protect notch

FIGURE 6-4 Two types of floppy disk drives.

Zip Disks

A **Zip disk** is a type of portable magnetic media that can store from 100 MB to 750 MB of data. The larger capacity Zip disks hold about 500 times more than a standard floppy disk. These large capacities make it easy to transport many files or large items such as graphics, audio, or video files. Another popular use of Zip disks is to back up important data and information. A **backup** is a duplicate of a file, program, or disk that you can use in case the original is lost, damaged, or destroyed. A **Zip drive** is a high-capacity disk drive developed by Iomega Corporation that reads from and writes on a Zip disk (Figure 6-5).

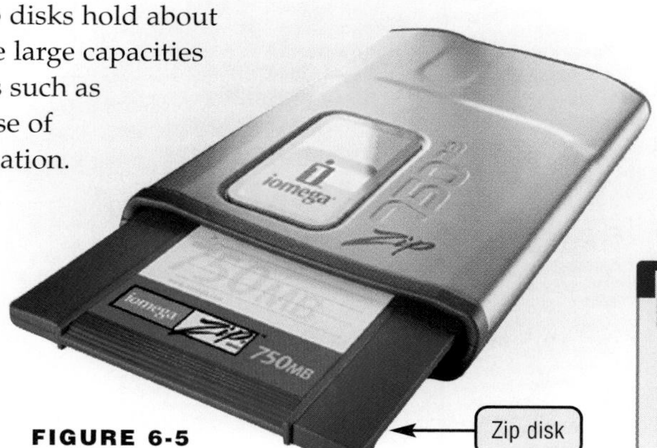

FIGURE 6-5
An external Zip drive.

Zip disk

WEB LINK 6-2

Zip Disks

For more information, visit scsite.com/dcf2e/ch6/weblink and then click Zip Disks.

Hard Disks

A **hard disk** is a storage device that contains one or more inflexible, circular platters that store data, instructions, and information. People use hard disks to store all types of documents, spreadsheets, presentations, databases, e-mail messages, Web pages, digital photographs, music, videos, and software. Businesses use hard disks to store correspondence, reports, financial records, e-mail messages, customer orders and invoices, payroll records, inventory records, presentations, contracts, marketing literature, schedules, and Web sites.

The system unit on most desktop and note-book computers contains at least one hard disk. The entire device is enclosed in an airtight, sealed case to protect it from contamination. A hard disk that is mounted inside the system unit sometimes is called a fixed disk because it is not portable (Figure 6-6).

Current personal computer hard disks have storage capacities from 40 to 300 GB and more (read Looking Ahead 6-1 for a look at the next generation of hard disk storage capacities). The storage capacity of the average hard disk is more than 40,000 times that of a standard floppy disk. Like floppy disks and Zip disks, hard disks store data magnetically. Hard disks also are read/write storage media. That is, you can read from and write on a hard disk any number of times.

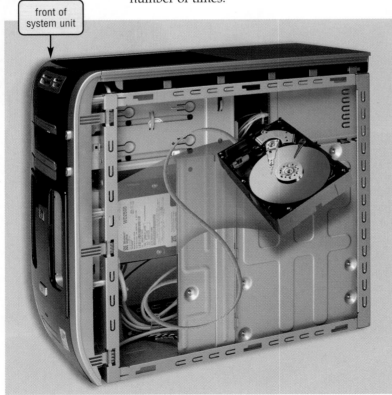

front of system unit

FIGURE 6-6 The hard disk in a desktop computer is enclosed inside an airtight, sealed case inside the system unit.

FAQ 6-1

Have personal computer hard disk capacities grown much since their inception?

Yes, hard disk capacities have grown phenomenally over the past several years, as shown in the chart below. This trend is expected to continue at a rate of 60 percent annually. For more information, visit scsite.com/dcf2e/ch6/faq and then click Hard Disk Capacities.

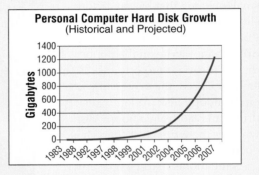

Personal Computer Hard Disk Growth
(Historical and Projected)

LOOKING AHEAD 6-1

Heat Increases Disk Capacity

Things are heating up in the data storage industry. Engineers at IBM Research are testing the use of heat to record data inexpensively on magnetic media, such as hard disks.

Within the next ten years, the researchers predict that this new technique will allow storage of more than one terabit per square inch; today's magnetic media can store approximately 60 giga-bits per square inch.  With this capacity, a hard disk drive that can store seven terabits will be commonplace.

IBM calls this new storage system Millipede. It uses heated tips mounted on the ends of canti-levers, in a fashion similar to the way the stylus on an old phonograph sat on the grooves of vinyl records. For more information, visit scsite.com/dcf2e/ch6/looking and then click Heated Storage.

CHARACTERISTICS OF A HARD DISK   Characteristics of a hard disk include capacity, platters, read/write heads, cylinders, sectors and tracks, revolutions per minute, transfer rate, and access time. Figure 6-7 shows sample characteristics of a 120 GB hard disk. The following paragraphs discuss each of these characteristics.

The capacity of a hard disk is determined from the number of platters it contains, together with composition of the magnetic coating on the platters. A platter is made of aluminum, glass, or ceramic and is coated with an alloy material that allows items to be recorded magnetically on its surface. The coating usually is three millionths of an inch thick.

On desktop computers, platters most often have a size of approximately 3.5 inches in diameter. A typical hard disk has multiple platters stacked on top of one another. Each platter has two read/write heads, one for each side. The hard disk has arms that move the read/write heads to the proper location on the platter (Figure 6-8).

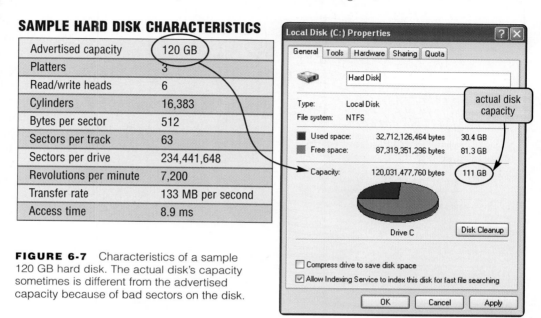

SAMPLE HARD DISK CHARACTERISTICS

Advertised capacity	120 GB
Platters	3
Read/write heads	6
Cylinders	16,383
Bytes per sector	512
Sectors per track	63
Sectors per drive	234,441,648
Revolutions per minute	7,200
Transfer rate	133 MB per second
Access time	8.9 ms

FIGURE 6-7   Characteristics of a sample 120 GB hard disk. The actual disk's capacity sometimes is different from the advertised capacity because of bad sectors on the disk.

FIGURE 6-8   HOW A HARD DISK WORKS

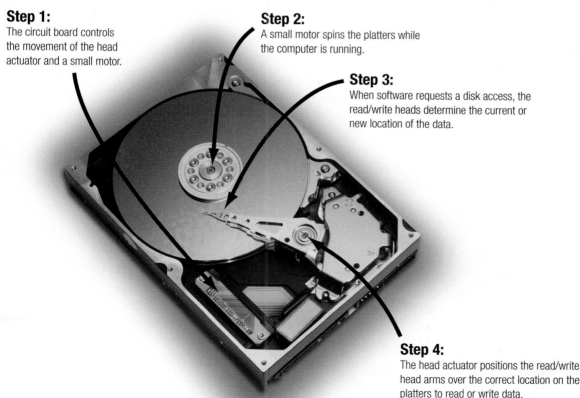

Step 1:
The circuit board controls the movement of the head actuator and a small motor.

Step 2:
A small motor spins the platters while the computer is running.

Step 3:
When software requests a disk access, the read/write heads determine the current or new location of the data.

Step 4:
The head actuator positions the read/write head arms over the correct location on the platters to read or write data.

The location of the read/write heads often is referred to by its cylinder. A cylinder is the vertical section of a track that passes through all platters (Figure 6-9). A single movement of the read/write head arms accesses all the platters in a cylinder. If a hard disk has two platters (four sides), each with 1,000 tracks, then it will have 1,000 cylinders with each cylinder consisting of 4 tracks (2 tracks for each platter).

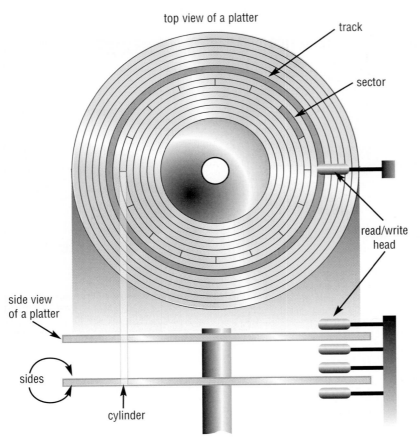

top view of a platter

track

sector

read/write head

side view of a platter

sides

cylinder

FIGURE 6-9   A cylinder is the vertical section of track through all platters on a hard disk.

While the computer is running, the platters in the hard disk rotate at a high rate of speed. This spinning, which usually is 5,400 to 15,000 revolutions per minute (rpm), allows nearly instant access to all tracks and sectors on the platters. The platters typically continue to spin until power is removed from the computer. (On many computers, the hard disk stops spinning after a specified time to save power.) The spinning motion creates a cushion of air between the platter and its read/write head. This cushion ensures that the read/write head floats above the platter instead of making direct contact with the platter surface. The distance between the read/write head and the platter is about two millionths of one inch.

As shown in Figure 6-10, this close clearance leaves no room for any type of contamination. Dirt, hair, dust, smoke, and other particles could cause the hard disk to have a head crash. A head crash occurs when a read/write head touches the surface of a platter, usually resulting in a loss of data or sometimes loss of the entire drive. Access time for today's hard disks ranges from approximately 3 to 12 ms (milliseconds). The average hard disk access time is at least seven times faster than the average floppy disk drive.

hair

read/write head

dust

smoke

clearance

platter

FIGURE 6-10   The clearance between a disk read/write head and the platter is about two millionths of an inch. A smoke particle, dust particle, human hair, or other contaminant could render the drive unusable.

MINIATURE HARD DISKS Many mobile devices and consumer electronics include miniature hard disks to provide users with greater storage capacities than flash memory. These tiny hard disks (Figure 6-11) are found in devices such as music players, digital cameras, smart phones, and PDAs. Miniature hard disks have storage capacities that range from 2 GB to 100 GB.

PORTABLE HARD DISKS Portable hard disks either are external or removable and have storage capacities up to 250 GB or higher.

An **external hard disk**, shown in the upper-left picture in Figure 6-12, is a separate free-standing hard disk that connects with a cable to a USB port or FireWire port on the system unit. As with the internal hard disk, the entire hard disk is enclosed in an airtight, sealed case.

FIGURE 6-11 This hard disk has a form factor of 0.85 inch and storage capacities up to 4 GB.

A **removable hard disk** is a hard disk that you insert and remove from either a dock or a drive. Removable hard disks that insert in a dock are self-contained units. Removable hard disks that insert in a drive, shown in the bottom-right picture in Figure 6-12, operate in a manner similar to a floppy disk drive, reading from and writing on the removable hard disk.

Portable hard disks offer the following advantages over internal hard disks (fixed disks):

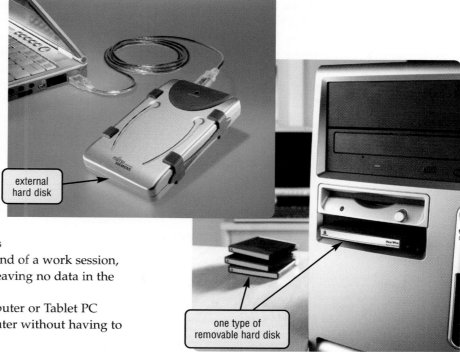

external hard disk

one type of removable hard disk

- Transport a large number of files
- Back up important files or an entire internal hard disk
- Easily store large audio and video files
- Secure your data; for example, at the end of a work session, remove the hard disk and lock it up, leaving no data in the computer
- Add storage space to a notebook computer or Tablet PC
- Add storage space to a desktop computer without having to open the system unit
- Share a drive with multiple computers

FIGURE 6-12 Examples of portable hard disks.

As the prices of portable hard disks drop, increasingly more users will purchase one to supplement a home or office internal hard disk.

HARD DISK CONTROLLERS A **disk controller** consists of a special-purpose chip and electronic circuits that control the transfer of data, instructions, and information from a disk to and from the system bus and other components in the computer. That is, it controls the interface between the hard disk and the system bus. A disk controller for a hard disk, called the hard disk controller, may be part of a hard disk or the motherboard, or it may be a separate adapter card inside in the system unit.

In their personal computer advertisements, vendors usually state the type of hard disk interface supported by the hard disk controller. Thus, you should understand the types of available hard disk interfaces. In addition to USB and FireWire (external hard disk interfaces), three other types of hard disk interfaces for internal use in personal computers are SATA, EIDE, and SCSI.

- SATA (Serial Advanced Technology Attachment), the newest type of hard disk interface, uses serial signals to transfer data, instructions, and information. The primary advantage of SATA interfaces is their cables are thinner, longer, more flexible, and less susceptible to interference than cables used by hard disks that use parallel signals. SATA interfaces also support connections to CD and DVD drives.
- EIDE (Enhanced Integrated Drive Electronics) is a hard disk interface that uses parallel signals to transfer data, instructions, and information. EIDE interfaces can support up to four hard disks at 137 GB per disk. EIDE interfaces also provide connections for CD and DVD drives and tape drives.
- SCSI interfaces, which also use parallel signals, can support up to eight or fifteen peripheral devices. Supported devices include hard disks, CD and DVD drives, tape drives, printers, scanners, network cards, and much more. Some computers have a built-in SCSI interface, while others use an adapter card to add a SCSI interface.

ONLINE STORAGE   Some users choose online storage instead of storing data locally on a hard disk. **Online storage** is a service on the Web that provides hard disk storage to computer users, usually for a minimal monthly fee (Figure 6-13). Fee arrangements vary. For example, one online storage service charges $10 per month for 5 GB of storage.

Users subscribe to an online storage service for a variety of reasons:
- To access files on the Internet hard disk from any computer or device that has Internet access
- To allow others to access files on their Internet hard disk so others can listen to an audio file, watch a video clip, or view a picture — instead of e-mailing the file to them
- To view time-critical data and images immediately while away from the main office or location; for example, doctors can view x-ray images from another hospital, home, or office
- To store offsite backups of data

Once users subscribe to the online storage service, they can save on the Internet hard disk in the same manner they save on their local hard disk.

FIGURE 6-13   An example of one Web site advertising its online storage service.

Test your knowledge of pages 220 through 228 in Quiz Yourself 6-1.

QUIZ YOURSELF 6-1

Instructions: Find the true statement below. Then, rewrite the remaining false statements so they are true.

1. Hard disks contain one or more inflexible, circular platters that magnetically store data, instructions, and information.

2. SATA is a hard disk interface that uses parallel signals to transfer data, instructions, and information.

3. Storage media is the computer hardware that records and/or retrieves items to and from a storage device.

4. Three types of manual disks are floppy disks, Zip disks, and hard disks.

Quiz Yourself Online: To further check your knowledge of magnetic disks, floppy disks, Zip disks, and hard disks, visit scsite.com/dcf2e/ch6/quiz and then click Objectives 1 – 3.

OPTICAL DISCS

An **optical disc** is a type of optical storage media that consists of a flat, round, portable, disc made of metal, plastic, and lacquer. These discs usually are 4.75 inches in diameter and less than one-twentieth of an inch thick.

Optical discs primarily store software, data, digital photographs, movies, and music. Some optical disc formats are read only, meaning users cannot write (save) on the media. Others are read/write, which allows users to save on the disc just as they save on a hard disk.

Nearly every personal computer today includes some type of optical disc drive installed in a drive bay. On these drives, you push a button to slide out a tray, insert the disc, and then push the same button to close the tray (Figure 6-14). Other convenient features on most of these drives include a volume control button and a headphone port (or jack) so you can use headphones to listen to audio without disturbing others nearby.

With some discs, you can read and/or write on one side only. Manufacturers usually place a silk-screened label on the top layer of these single-sided discs. You insert a single-sided disc in the drive with the label side up. Other discs are double-sided. Simply remove the disc from the drive, flip it over, and reinsert it in the drive to use the other side of the disc. Double-sided discs often have no label; instead each side of the disc is identified with small writing around the center of the disc.

Optical discs store items by using microscopic pits (indentations) and lands (flat areas) that are in the middle layer of the disc. A high-powered laser light creates the pits. A lower-powered laser light reads items from the disc by reflecting light through the bottom of the disc, which usually is either solid gold or silver in color. The reflected light is converted into a series of bits the computer can process.

Push the button to slide out the tray.

Insert the disc, label side up.

Push the same button to close the tray.

FIGURE 6-14 On optical disc drives, you push a button to slide out a tray, insert the disc with the label side up, and then push the same button to close the tray.

Manufacturers guarantee that a properly cared for high-quality optical disc will last 5 years but could last up to 100 years. Figure 6-15 offers some guidelines for the proper care of optical discs.

Many different formats of optical discs exist today. Two general categories are CDs and DVDs, with DVDs having a much greater storage capacity than CDs. Specific formats include CD-ROM, CD-R, CD-RW, DVD-ROM, DVD-R, DVD+R, DVD-RW, DVD+RW, and DVD+RAM. Figure 6-16 identifies each of these optical disc formats and specifies whether a user can read from the disc, write to the disc, and/or erase the disc. The following sections describe characteristics unique to each of these disc formats.

OPTICAL DISC FORMATS

Optical Disc	Read	Write	Erase
CD-ROM	Y	N	N
CD-R	Y	Y	N
CD-RW	Y	Y	Y
DVD-ROM	Y	N	N
DVD-R DVD+R	Y	Y	N
DVD-RW DVD+RW DVD+RAM	Y	Y	Y

FIGURE 6-16 Manufacturers sell CD-ROM and DVD-ROM media prerecorded (written) with audio, video, and software. Users cannot change the contents of these discs. Users, however, can purchase the other formats of CDs and DVDs as blank media and record (write) their own data, instructions, and information on these discs.

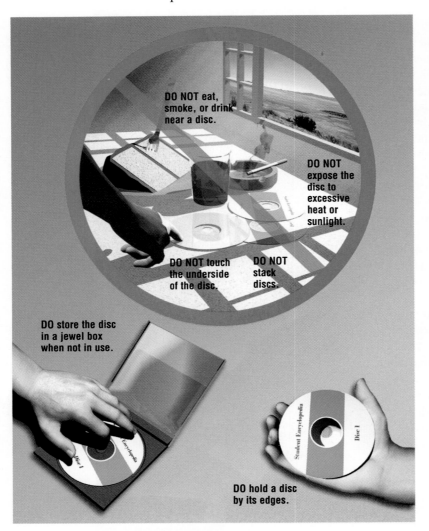

DO NOT eat, smoke, or drink near a disc.

DO NOT expose the disc to excessive heat or sunlight.

DO NOT touch the underside of the disc.

DO NOT stack discs.

DO store the disc in a jewel box when not in use.

DO hold a disc by its edges.

FIGURE 6-15 Some guidelines for the proper care of optical discs.

CD-ROMs

A **CD-ROM** (pronounced SEE-DEE-rom), or compact disc read-only memory, is a type of optical disc that users can read but not write (record) or erase — hence, the name read-only. Manufacturers write the contents of standard CD-ROMs. A standard CD-ROM is called a single-session disc because manufacturers write all items on the disc at one time. Software manufacturers often distribute programs using CD-ROMs (Figure 6-17).

A typical CD-ROM holds from 650 MB to 1 GB of data, instructions, and information. This is equivalent to about 450 standard 3.5-inch floppy disks. To read a CD-ROM, insert the disc in a **CD-ROM drive** or a CD-ROM player. Because audio CDs and CD-ROMs use the same laser technology, you may be able to use a CD-ROM drive to listen to an audio CD while working on the computer.

FAQ 6-2

Can I clean a disc?

Yes, you can remove dust, dirt, smudges, and fingerprints from the bottom surface of a CD or DVD. Moisten a soft cloth with warm water or rubbing alcohol and then wipe the disc in straight lines from the center outward. You also can repair scratches on the bottom surface with a specialized disc repair kit. For more information, visit scsite.com/dcf2e/ch6/faq and then click Cleaning and Repairing Discs.

FIGURE 6-17 Encyclopedias, games, simulations, and many other programs are distributed on CD-ROM.

WEB LINK 6-4

CD-ROMs

For more information, visit scsite.com/dcf2e/ch6/weblink and then click CD-ROMs.

PICTURE CDs   A Kodak **Picture CD** is a type of single-session disc that stores digital versions of a single roll of film using a jpg file format. Many film developers offer Picture CD service for consumers when they drop off film to be developed. That is, in addition to printed photographs and negatives, you also receive a Picture CD containing the film's pictures. The additional cost for a Picture CD is about $10 per roll of film.

Most optical disc drives can read a Picture CD. A Picture CD allows you to print copies of the photographs on paper with an ink-jet printer. If you do not have a printer to print the images, many stores have kiosks at which you can print pictures from a Picture CD (Figure 6-18).

FIGURE 6-18   HOW A PICTURE CD WORKS

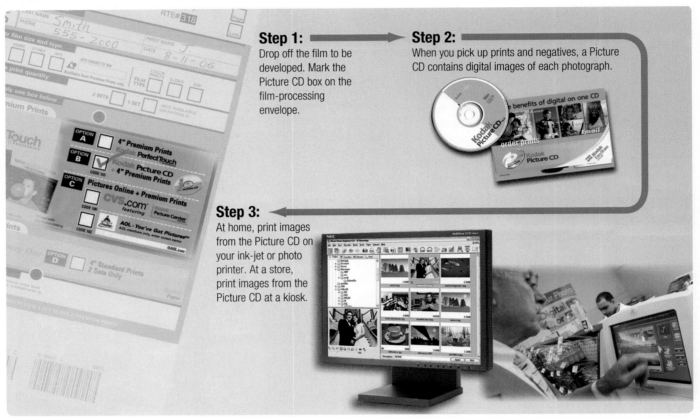

Step 1:
Drop off the film to be developed. Mark the Picture CD box on the film-processing envelope.

Step 2:
When you pick up prints and negatives, a Picture CD contains digital images of each photograph.

Step 3:
At home, print images from the Picture CD on your ink-jet or photo printer. At a store, print images from the Picture CD at a kiosk.

CD-Rs and CD-RWs

Many personal computers today include either a CD-R or CD-RW drive as a standard feature. Unlike standard CD-ROM drives, users record, or write, their own data on a disc with a CD-R or CD-RW drive. The process of writing on an optical disc is called **burning**.

A **CD-R** (compact disc-recordable) is a multisession optical disc on which users can write, but not erase, their own items such as text, graphics, and audio. Multisession means you can write on part of the disc at one time and another part at a later time. Each part of a CD-R can be written on only one time, and the disc's contents cannot be erased. Writing on the CD-R requires a CD recorder or a **CD-R drive**. A CD-R drive usually can read both audio CDs and standard CD-ROMs.

A **CD-RW** (compact disc-rewritable) is an erasable multisession disc you can write on multiple times. To write on a CD-RW disc, you must have CD-RW software and a **CD-RW drive**. Using a CD-RW disc, users easily back up large files from a hard disk. Another popular use of CD-RW and CD-R discs is to create audio CDs. For example, users can record their own music and save it on a CD, purchase and download songs from the Web, or rearrange tracks on a purchased music CD. The process of copying an individual song from a purchased audio CD and converting it to a digital format is called ripping. Read At Issue 6-1 for a related discussion.

DVD-ROMs

A **DVD-ROM** (digital versatile disc-read-only memory or digital video disc-read-only memory) is an extremely high-capacity optical disc on which users can read but not write or erase. Manufacturers write the contents of DVD-ROMs and distribute them to consumers. DVD-ROMs store movies, music, huge databases, and complex software (Figure 6-19).

To read a DVD-ROM, you must have a **DVD-ROM drive** or DVD player. Most DVD-ROM drives also can read audio CDs, CD-ROMs, CD-Rs, and CD-RWs.

A DVD-ROM uses one of three storage techniques. The first involves making the disc denser by packing the pits closer together. The second involves using two layers of pits. For this technique to work, the lower layer of pits is semitransparent so the laser can read through it to the upper layer. This technique doubles the capacity of the disc. Finally, some DVD-ROMs are double-sided. The storage capacities of various types of widely used DVD-ROMs are shown in the table in Figure 6-20. For a look at the next generation of disc storage, read Looking Ahead 6-2.

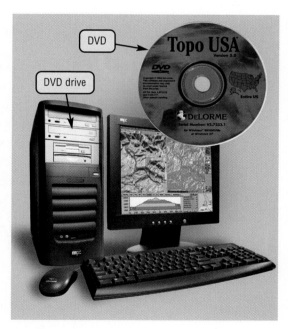

FIGURE 6-19 A DVD-ROM is an extremely high-capacity optical disc.

DVD-ROM STORAGE CAPACITIES

Sides	Layers	Storage Capacity
1	1	4.7 GB
1	2	8.5 GB
2	1	9.4 GB
2	2	17 GB

FIGURE 6-20 Storage capacities of DVD-ROMs.

LOOKING AHEAD 6-2

Paper Discs Offer Increased Capacity

The next generation high-capacity optical storage media will be composed of 51 percent paper and will hold as much as 50 GB of data. These discs will store more than 13 hours of video, which is more than five times the 8.5 GB capacity of current DVD discs. This recording capacity will become increasingly important as consumers purchase more high-definition television products and desire to record and view movies, photos, and other digital content on these devices.

The products are expected to cost no more than a currently priced DVD disc when produced in mass quantities and will be based on Blu-Ray disc technology. Destroying unwanted or sensitive data will be easy: just cut the disc with scissors. For more information, visit scsite.com/dcf2e/ch6/looking and then click Paper Discs.

Recordable and Rewritable DVDs

Many types of recordable and rewritable DVD formats are available. DVD-R and DVD+R (DVD-recordable) allow users to write on the disc once and read (play) it many times. DVD-RW, DVD+RW, and DVD+RAM are three competing rewritable DVD formats. With **DVD-RW** and **DVD+RW** discs, a user can erase and record more than 1,000 times. To write on these discs, you must have a DVD-RW drive, a DVD+RW drive, or a DVD recorder.

DVD+RAM (DVD+random access memory) allows users to erase and record on a DVD+RAM disc more than 100,000 times. These discs can be read by DVD+RAM drives and some DVD-ROM drives and players.

As the cost of DVD technologies becomes more reasonable, many industry professionals expect that DVD eventually will replace all CD media.

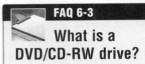

FAQ 6-3

What is a DVD/CD-RW drive?

It is a combination drive that reads DVD and CD media; it also writes to CD-RW media. This drive allows you to watch a DVD or burn a CD. For more information, visit scsite.com/dcf2e/ch6/faq and then click DVD/CD-RW Drives.

WEB LINK 6-6

DVDs

For more information, visit scsite.com/dcf2e/ch6/weblink and then click DVDs.

Test your knowledge of pages 229 through 234 in Quiz Yourself 6-2.

QUIZ YOURSELF 6-2

Instructions: Find the true statement below. Then, rewrite the remaining false statements so they are true.

1. A CD-RW is a type of optical disc on which users can read but not write (record) or erase.

2. A DVD-RAM is a single-session disc that stores digital versions of a single roll of film using a jpg file format.

3. DVDs have the same storage capacities as CDs.

4. Optical discs are written and read by mirrors.

5. Three competing rewritable DVD formats are DVD-RW, DVD+RW, and DVD+RAM.

Quiz Yourself Online: To further check your knowledge of optical discs and various optical disc formats, visit scsite.com/dcf2e/ch6/quiz and then click Objectives 4 – 5.

TAPE

One of the first storage media used with mainframe computers was tape. **Tape** is a magnetically coated ribbon of plastic capable of storing large amounts of data and information at a low cost. Tape no longer is used as a primary method of storage. Instead, business and home users utilize tape most often for long-term storage and backup.

A **tape drive** reads and writes data and information on a tape. Although older computers used reel-to-reel tape drives, today's tape drives use tape cartridges. A tape cartridge is a small, rectangular, plastic housing for tape (Figure 6-21). Tape cartridges that contain quarter-inch-wide tape are slightly larger than audiocassette tapes. Business and home users sometimes back up personal computer hard disks to tape.

Some personal computers have external tape units. Others have the tape drive built into the system unit. On larger computers, tape cartridges are mounted in a separate cabinet called a tape library.

FIGURE 6-21   A tape drive and a tape cartridge.

Tape storage requires sequential access, which refers to reading or writing data consecutively. As with a music tape, you must forward or rewind the tape to a specific point to access a specific piece of data.

Floppy disks, Zip disks, hard disks, CDs, and DVDs all use direct access. Direct access means that the device can locate a particular data item or file immediately, without having to move consecutively through items stored in front of the desired data item or file. When writing or reading specific data, direct access is much faster than sequential access.

PC CARDS

A **PC Card** is a thin, credit-card-sized device that fits into a PC Card slot. Different types and sizes of PC Cards add storage, additional memory, fax/modem, networking, sound, and other capabilities to a desktop or notebook computer. PC Cards commonly are used in notebook computers (Figure 6-22).

Three kinds of PC Cards are available: Type I, Type II, and Type III (Figure 6-23). The advantage of a PC Card for storage is portability. You easily can transport large amounts of data, instructions, and information from one computer to another using a PC Card.

FIGURE 6-22 A PC Card in a notebook computer.

PC CARDS

Category	Thickness	Use
Type I	3.3 mm	RAM, SRAM, flash memory
Type II	5.0 mm	Modem, LAN, SCSI, sound, TV tuner, hard disk, or other storage
Type III	10.5 mm	Rotating storage such as a hard disk

FIGURE 6-23 Various uses of PC Cards.

MINIATURE MOBILE STORAGE MEDIA

Miniature mobile storage media allow mobile users easily to transport digital images, music, or documents to and from computers and other devices. Many desktop computers, notebook computers, Tablet PCs, PDAs, digital cameras, music players, and smart phones have built-in ports or slots to hold miniature mobile storage media. For computers or devices without built-in slots, users insert the media in separate peripherals such as card reader/writers, which typically plug in a USB port, or devices such as digital photo viewers, which connect to a television port for on-screen picture viewing. Three types of miniature mobile storage media include flash memory cards, USB flash drives, and smart cards.

Flash Memory Cards

Common types of flash memory cards include **CompactFlash (CF)**, **SmartMedia**, **Secure Digital (SD)**, **xD Picture Card**, and **Memory Stick**. The table in Figure 6-24 compares storage capacities and uses of these miniature mobile storage media. Depending on the device, manufacturers claim miniature mobile storage media can last from 10 to 100 years.

To view, edit, or print images and information stored on miniature mobile storage media, you transfer the contents to your desktop computer or other device such as a digital photo viewer. Some printers have slots to read PC Cards and flash memory cards. If your computer or printer does not have a built-in slot, you can purchase a **card reader/writer**, which is a device that reads and writes data, instructions, and information stored on PC Cards or flash memory cards. Card reader/writers usually connect to the USB port, FireWire port, or parallel port on the system unit. The type of card you have will determine the type of card reader/writer needed.

VARIOUS FLASH MEMORY CARDS

Media Name		Storage Capacity	Use
CompactFlash		32 MB to 4 GB	Digital cameras, PDAs, smart phones, photo printers, music players, notebook computers, desktop computers
SmartMedia		32 MB to 128 MB	Digital cameras, PDAs, smart phones, photo printers, music players
Secure Digital		64 MB to 1 GB	Digital cameras, digital video cameras, PDAs, smart phones, photo printers, music players
xD Picture Card		64 MB to 512 MB	Digital cameras, photo printers
Memory Stick		256 MB to 2 GB	Digital cameras, digital video cameras, PDAs, photo printers, smart phones, notebook computers

FIGURE 6-24   A variety of flash memory cards.

USB Flash Drives

A **USB flash drive**, sometimes called a pen drive, is a flash memory storage device that plugs in a USB port on a computer or mobile device (Figure 6-25). USB flash drives are convenient for mobile users because they are small and lightweight enough to be transported on a keychain or in a pocket. Experts predict that USB flash drives will become the mobile user's primary storage device, eventually making the floppy disk obsolete because they have much greater storage capacities and are much more convenient to carry. Current USB flash drives have storage capacities up to 4 GB.

FIGURE 6-25   A USB flash drive.

Smart Cards

A **smart card**, which is similar in size to a credit card or ATM card (Figure 6-26), stores data on a thin microprocessor embedded in the card. Smart cards contain a processor and have input, process, output, and storage capabilities. When you insert the smart card in a specialized card reader, the information on the smart card is read and, if necessary, updated. Uses of smart cards include storing medical records, vaccination data, and other health-care or identification information; tracking information such as customer purchases or employee attendance; storing a prepaid amount of money; and authenticating users such as for Internet purchases. Read At Issue 6-2 for a related discussion.

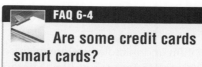

FAQ 6-4

Are some credit cards smart cards?

Yes. More than 60 million people around the world have the smart Visa card, which contains a microchip filled with their personal information. Credit card smart cards offer the consumer the convenience of using the card to make purchases in stores and online. In both cases, users simply swipe the card in a card reader. At home, the card reader is attached to the home computer. For more information, visit scsite.com/dcf2e/ch6/faq and then click Credit Card Smart Cards.

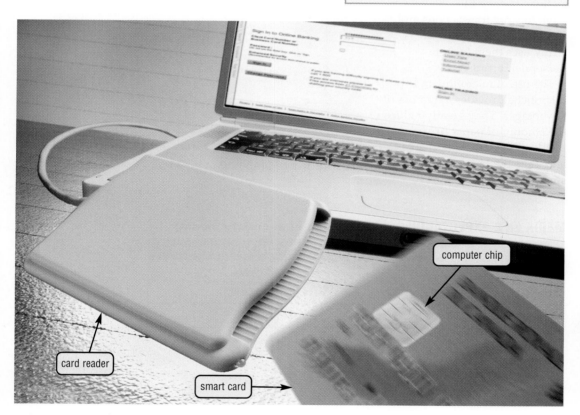

computer chip

card reader

smart card

WEB LINK 6-8

Smart Cards

For more information, visit scsite.com/dcf2e/ch6/weblink and then click Smart Cards.

FIGURE 6-26 A smart card and smart card reader.

AT ISSUE 6-2

Should the World Become a Cashless Society?

Do you toss your loose change in a jar with the hopes of making a special purchase with the savings someday? Futurists predict that this practice may one day go the way of making purchases with silver and gold. Some forecasters say that the world is moving toward a cashless society. One form of payment that could end the need for cash is the smart card, which can store a dollar amount on a thin microprocessor and update the amount whenever a transaction is made. Advocates claim that smart cards would eliminate muggings and robberies, make it difficult to purchase illegal goods, and reduce taxes by identifying tax cheats. Smart cards already are common in Europe, but many Americans cite privacy concerns as reasons to avoid them. In a recent survey, most Americans said that they would not use a smart card even if privacy was guaranteed. A cash purchase usually is anonymous. Yet, a smart card purchase preserves a record of the transaction that could become available to other merchants, advertisers, government agencies, or hackers. Considering the advantages and disadvantages, should the world become a cashless society? Why or why not? Would you be comfortable using a smart card instead of cash? Why?

MICROFILM AND MICROFICHE

Microfilm and microfiche store microscopic images of documents on roll or sheet film. **Microfilm** is a 100- to 215-foot roll of film. **Microfiche** is a small sheet of film, usually about 4 inches by 6 inches. A computer output microfilm recorder is the device that records the images on the film. The stored images are so small that you can read them only with a microfilm or microfiche reader (Figure 6-27).

Applications of microfilm and microfiche are widespread. Libraries use these media to store back issues of newspapers, magazines, and genealogy records. Large organizations use microfilm and microfiche to archive inactive files. Banks use them to store transactions and canceled checks. The U.S. Army uses them to store personnel records.

The use of microfilm and microfiche provides a number of advantages. They greatly reduce the amount of paper firms must handle. They are inexpensive and have the longest life of any storage media (Figure 6-28).

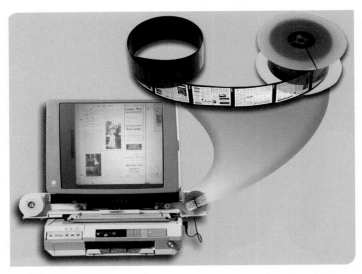

FIGURE 6-27   Images on microfilm can be read only with a microfilm reader.

MEDIA LIFE EXPECTANCIES (when using high-quality media)

Media Type	Guaranteed Life Expectancy	Potential Life Expectancy
Magnetic disks	3 to 5 years	20 to 30 years
Optical discs	5 to 10 years	50 to 100 years
Microfilm	100 years	500 years

FIGURE 6-28   Microfilm is the medium with the longest life.

ENTERPRISE STORAGE

A large business, commonly referred to as an enterprise, has hundreds or thousands of employees in offices across the country or around the world. Enterprises use computers and computer networks to manage and store huge volumes of data and information about customers, suppliers, and employees.

To meet their large-scale needs, enterprises use special hardware geared for heavy use, maximum availability, and maximum efficiency. One or more servers on the network have the sole purpose of providing storage to connected users. For high-speed storage access, entire networks are dedicated exclusively to connecting devices that provide storage to other servers. In an enterprise, some storage systems can provide more than 185 terabytes (trillion bytes) of storage capacity. CD-ROM servers and DVD-ROM servers hold hundreds of CD-ROMs or DVD-ROMs.

An enterprise's storage needs usually grow daily. Thus, the storage solutions an enterprise chooses must be able to store its data and information requirements today and tomorrow. Read At Issue 6-3 for a related discussion.

AT ISSUE 6-3

Who Is Looking at Your Medical Records?

A medical transcriber based in Pakistan and hired by a U.S. medical center threatened to post private medical records to the Internet if she was not paid more. With the widespread use of computers and an explosion in data storage capacity around the world, private information, such as medical records, requires increased diligence by companies, governments, and individuals to maintain this privacy. Updates to the Health Insurance Portability and Accountability Act (HIPAA) effective in 2003 set rigorous standards for medical record privacy. The law, however, still leaves much of your medical information at risk. The law does not cover financial records, education records, or employment records — each of which may contain medical information about you. Your medical information also may be examined by insurance companies, government agencies, the Medical Information Bureau (MIB), employers, and the courts. You also inadvertently may pass on medical information to direct marketers when you participate in informal health screenings or surveys. Some people have found that discussing medical conditions via Internet chat rooms or newsgroups has resulted in unwanted attention, and they later regret the disclosures. You can limit the amount of information available about you by discussing confidentiality with your medical providers and by requesting additional restrictions when you sign waivers to release your medical records, such as when applying for a job or applying for insurance. Should more limits be placed on what other people can do with your medical information? Why or why not? What are the advantages of increased access to medical records? What are the disadvantages?

PUTTING IT ALL TOGETHER

Many factors influence the type of storage devices you should use: the amount of data, instructions, and information to be stored; the hardware and software in use; and the desired cost. The table in Figure 6-29 outlines several suggested storage devices for various types of computer users.

CATEGORIES OF USERS

User	Typical Storage Devices
HOME 	• 80 GB hard disk • Online storage • CD or DVD drive • Card reader/writer • USB flash drive and/or 3.5-inch floppy disk drive
SMALL OFFICE/ HOME OFFICE 	• 750 MB Zip drive • 120 GB hard disk • Online storage • CD or DVD drive • External hard disk for backup • USB flash drive and/or 3.5-inch floppy disk drive
MOBILE 	• 80 GB hard disk • Online storage • CD or DVD drive • Card reader/writer • Portable hard disk for backup • USB flash drive, and/or 2 GB PC Card hard disk, and/or 3.5-inch floppy disk drive
POWER 	• CD or DVD drive • 300 GB hard disk • Online storage • Portable hard disk for backup • USB flash drive and/or 3.5-inch floppy disk drive
LARGE BUSINESS 	• Desktop Computer - 160 GB hard disk - CD or DVD drive - Smart card reader - Tape drive - USB flash drive and/or 3.5-inch floppy disk drive • Server or Mainframe - Network storage server - 40 TB hard disk system - CD-ROM or DVD-ROM server - Microfilm or microfiche

FIGURE 6-29 Recommended storage devices for various users.

Test your knowledge of pages 234 through 239 in Quiz Yourself 6-3.

QUIZ YOURSELF 6-3

Instructions: Find the true statement below. Then, rewrite the remaining false statements so they are true.

1. A USB flash drive is a flash memory storage device that plugs in a parallel port on a computer or mobile device.

2. CompactFlash and Memory Sticks are two types of flash memory cards.

3. Microfilm and microfiche have the shortest life of any storage media.

4. Tape storage requires direct access, which refers to reading or writing data consecutively.

Quiz Yourself Online: To further check your knowledge of tape, PC Cards, miniature mobile storage media, and microfilm and microfiche, visit scsite.com/dcf2e/ch6/quiz and then click Objectives 6 – 8.

CHAPTER SUMMARY

Storage holds data, instructions, and information, which includes pictures, music, and videos, for future use. Users depend on storage devices to provide access to their storage media for years and decades to come.

This chapter identified and discussed various storage media and storage devices. Storage media covered included floppy disks, Zip disks, internal hard disks, portable hard disks, CD-ROMs, recordable and rewritable CDs, DVD-ROMs, recordable and rewritable DVDs, tape, PC Cards, flash memory cards, USB flash drives, smart cards, and microfilm and microfiche.

CAREER CORNER

Computer Technician

The demand for computer technicians is growing in every organization and industry. For many, this is the entry point for a career in the computer/ information technology field. The responsibilities of a **computer technician**, also called a computer service technician, include a variety of duties. Most companies that employ someone with this title expect the technician to have basic across-the-board knowledge of concepts in the computer electronics field. Some of the tasks are hardware repair and installation; software installation, upgrade, and configuration; and troubleshooting client and/or server problems. Because the computer field is rapidly changing, technicians must work to remain abreast of current technology and become aware of future developments. Computer technicians generally work with a variety of users, which requires expert people skills, especially the ability to work with groups of nontechnical users.

Most entry-level computer technicians possess the A+ certification. This certification attests that a computer technician has demonstrated knowledge of core hardware and operating system technology including installation, configuration, diagnosing, preventive maintenance and basic networking that meets industry standards and has at least six months of experience in the field. The Electronics Technicians Association also provides a Computer Service Technician (CST) certification program.

Because this is an entry-level position, the pay scale is not as high as other more demanding and skilled positions. Individuals can expect an average annual starting salary of around $28,000 to $42,000. Companies pay more for computer technicians with experience and certification. For more information, visit scsite.com/ dcf2e/ch6/careers and then click Computer Technician.

Maxtor
Information Storage Supplier

Computer-industry experts predict that 68 million hard disks will be needed for consumer electronic applications by 2007. Maxtor is poised to meet the demands of this rapidly growing market with its hard disks manufactured for the digital video recorder/personal video recorder (DVR/PVR) market.

Maxtor is a leading manufacturer of hard disks and storage solutions for desktop computers, high-performance servers, and consumer electronics, including digital video recorders and game consoles. Its wholly owned subsidiary, MMC Technology, manufactures nearly 50 million disks each year.

Maxtor's 250 GB OneTouch external hard disk was honored as the "Product of the Year" by *CRN* magazine and received a World Class Award from *PC World* in 2004. For more information, visit scsite.com/dcf2e/ch6/companies and then click Maxtor.

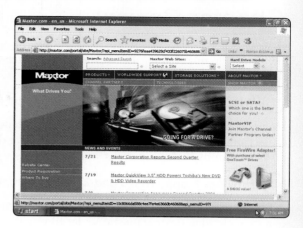

SanDisk Corporation
World's Largest Flash Memory Card Supplier

The next time you buy milk at the grocery store or shampoo at the drug store, you might want to purchase a flash memory card for your digital camera, too. SanDisk Corporation products can be found in more than 10,000 retail stores across the United States, including Rite Aid and Kmart.

With retail sales of flash memory cards soaring, SanDisk executives believe consumers buy multiple flash memory cards to store their digital photographs in much the same manner as they formerly stored film negatives in shoe boxes. They also prefer to take a separate flash memory card to digital photo processing centers, which produce high-quality prints.

SanDisk also designs, develops, and manufactures USB flash drives and readers, Memory Sticks, and Wi-Fi cards. For more information, visit scsite.com/dcf2e/ch6/companies and then click SanDisk.

TECHNOLOGY TRAILBLAZERS

Al Shugart
Storage Expert

Al Shugart enjoys fixing broken items and developing new technology. The day after receiving his bachelor's degree in 1951, he went to work at IBM to repair broken machines. IBM then promoted him to supervisor of the product development team that developed the first removable rigid read/write disk drive.

He left IBM in 1969 and went to work as vice president of product development for Memorex. In 1973, he started Shugart Associates, a pioneer in the manufacture of floppy disks. Six years later he and some associates founded Seagate Technology, Inc., which is a leader in designing and manufacturing storage products.

Today he serves as president, chairman, and CEO of Al Shugart International, a venture capital firm in California. For more information, visit scsite.com/dcf2e/ch6/people and then click Al Shugart.

Mark Dean
IBM Inventor

The next generation of IBM's hardware and software might be the work of Mark Dean. As vice president of IBM's Almaden Research Center lab in California, Dean is responsible for developing innovative products.

His designs are used in more than 40 million personal computers manufactured each year. He has more than 40 patents or patents pending, including four of the original seven for the architecture of the original personal computer.

Dean joined IBM in 1979 after graduating at the top of his class at the University of Tennessee. Dean earned his Ph.D. degree at Stanford, and he headed a team at IBM that invented the first CMOS microprocessor to operate at 1 gigahertz (1,000 MHz). For more information, visit scsite.com/dcf2e/ch6/people and then click Mark Dean.

Chapter Review

The Chapter Review section summarizes the concepts presented in this chapter. To obtain help from other students regarding any subject in this chapter, visit scsite.com/dcf2e/ch6/forum and post your thoughts or questions.

(1) What Are the Characteristics of Magnetic Disks?

Magnetic disks use magnetic particles to store items such as data, instructions, and information, which includes pictures, music, and videos, on a disk's surface. They store data and instructions in tracks and sectors. Three types of magnetic disks are floppy disks, Zip disks, and hard disks.

(2) How Are Floppy Disks and Zip Disks Different?

A **floppy disk** is a portable, inexpensive storage medium that consists of a thin, circular, flexible plastic Mylar film with a magnetic coating enclosed in a square-shaped plastic shell. A **floppy disk drive** is a device that reads from and writes on a floppy disk. Floppy disks store data in tracks and sectors. The actual number of available bytes on a floppy disk is 1,474,560.

A **Zip disk** is a type of portable magnetic media that can store 100 MB to 750 MB of data. These large capacities make it easy to transport many files or large items. Another popular use of Zip disks is to make a **backup**, or duplicate, of a file, program, or disk that you can use in case the original is lost, damaged, or destroyed.

(3) What Are the Characteristics of a Hard Disk?

A **hard disk** is a storage device that contains one or more inflexible, circular platters that store data, instructions, and information. A platter is made of aluminum, glass, or ceramic and is coated with a material that allows items to be recorded magnetically on its surface. Each platter has two read/write heads, one for each side. The location of a read/write head often is referred to by its cylinder. A cylinder is the vertical section of a track that passes through all platters. While the computer is running, the platters rotate at 5,400 to 15,000 revolutions per minute (rpm), which allows nearly instant access to all tracks and sectors on the platters. The spinning creates a cushion of air between the platters and the read/write heads. A head crash occurs when a read/write head touches the surface of a platter, usually resulting in a loss of data.

 Visit scsite.com/dcf2e/ch6/quiz or click the Quiz Yourself button. Click Objectives 1 – 3.

(4) What Are the Characteristics of Optical Discs?

An optical disc is a type of storage media that consists of a flat, round, portable disc made of metal, plastic, and lacquer. Optical discs store items by using microscopic pits (indentations) and lands (flat areas). A high-powered laser light creates the pits, and a lower-powered laser light reads items by reflecting light through the bottom of the disc.

(5) What Are the Various CD and DVD Formats?

A **CD-ROM** is an optical disc that users can read but not write (record) or erase. A Picture CD stores digital versions of a single roll of film. A **CD-R** is a multisession disc on which users can write, but not erase. A **CD-RW** is erasable. A **DVD-ROM** is an extremely high-capacity disc which users can read but not write or erase. Recordable and rewritable DVD formats include DVD-R, DVD+R, **DVD-RW**, and **DVD+RW.**

 Visit scsite.com/dcf2e/ch6/quiz or click the Quiz Yourself button. Click Objectives 4 – 5.

Chapter Review

(6) How Is Tape Used?

Tape is a magnetically coated ribbon of plastic capable of storing large amounts of data and information at a low cost. A **tape drive** reads and writes data and information on tape. Businesses and home users sometimes back up personal computer hard disks to tape.

(7) What Are PC Cards and Other Types of Miniature Mobile Storage Media?

A **PC Card** is a thin, credit-card-sized device that fits into a PC Card slot to add storage or other capabilities to a desktop or notebook computer. Tablet PCs, PDAs, digital cameras, music players, and smart phones use some form of miniature mobile storage media to store digital images, music, or documents. Common types of miniature flash memory cards include **CompactFlash (CF)**, **SmartMedia**, **Secure Digital (SD)**, **xD Picture Card**, and **Memory Stick**. A **USB flash drive** is a flash memory storage device that plugs in a USB port on a computer or mobile device. A **smart card**, which is similar in size to a credit card, stores data on a thin microprocessor embedded in the card.

(8) How Are Microfilm and Microfiche Used?

Microfilm is a 100- to 215-foot roll of film. **Microfiche** is a small sheet of film, usually about 4 inches by 6 inches. Libraries use microfilm and microfiche to store back issues of newspapers, magazines, and records; large organizations use them to archive inactive files; banks use them to store transactions and canceled checks; and the U.S. Army uses them to store personnel records.

 Visit scsite.com/dcf2e/ch6/quiz or click the Quiz Yourself button. Click Objectives 6 – 8.

Key Terms

 You should know each key term. Use the list below to help focus your study. To further enhance your understanding of the Key Terms in this chapter, visit scsite.com/dcf2e/ch6/terms. See an example of and a definition for each term, and access current and additional information about the term from the Web.

access time (222)
backup (223)
burning (232)
capacity (222)
card reader/writer (236)
CD-R (232)
CD-R drive (232)
CD-ROM (231)
CD-ROM drive (231)
CD-RW (232)
CD-RW drive (232)
CompactFlash (CF) (236)
computer technician (240)
disk controller (227)
diskette (223)
DVD+RW (234)
DVD-ROM (233)
DVD-ROM drive (233)
DVD-RW (234)
external hard disk (227)

floppy disk (223)
floppy disk drive (223)
hard disk (224)
magnetic disks (222)
Memory Stick (236)
microfiche (238)
microfilm (238)
online storage (228)
optical disc (229)
PC Card (235)
Picture CD (232)
reading (222)
removable hard disk (227)
secondary storage (221)
Secure Digital (SD) (236)
smart card (237)
SmartMedia (236)
storage device (222)
storage medium (221)

tape (234)
tape drive (234)
USB flash drive (236)
write-protect notch (223)
writing (222)
xD Picture Card (236)
Zip disk (223)
Zip drive (223)

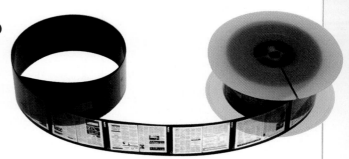

Checkpoint

Use the Checkpoint exercises to check your knowledge level of the chapter.

True/False

_____ 1. Storage holds data, instructions, and information for future use. (220)

_____ 2. A storage medium is the physical material on which a computer keeps data, instructions, and information. (221)

_____ 3. A sector is a narrow recording band that forms a full circle on the surface of the disk. (222)

_____ 4. A floppy disk is a portable storage medium. (223)

_____ 5. On a floppy disk, if the write-protect notch is open, the drive can write on the floppy disk. (223)

_____ 6. A typical hard disk contains only one platter. (225)

_____ 7. An external hard disk is a separate, free-standing hard disk that connects with a cable to a port on the system unit. (227)

_____ 8. A CD-ROM can be read from and written to any number of times. (231)

_____ 9. Ripping is the process of copying a song from an audio CD and converting it to a digital format. (232)

_____ 10. Direct access means that the device locates a particular data item by moving consecutively through the items stored. (235)

Multiple Choice

1. On a floppy disk, if the write-protect notch is closed, the floppy disk drive _____. (223)
   a. can write on but cannot read from the floppy disk
   b. can write on and read from the floppy disk
   c. can read from but cannot write on the floppy disk
   d. cannot read from or write on the floppy disk

2. A Zip disk can store from _____ of data. (223)
   a. 10 MB to 75 MB
   b. 100 MB to 750 MB
   c. 10 GB to 75 GB
   d. 100 GB to 750 GB

3. The storage capacity of the average hard disk is _____ that of a standard floppy disk. (224)
   a. less than half
   b. about the same as
   c. more than 40,000 times
   d. more than 400,000 times

4. Users subscribe to an online storage service to _____. (228)
   a. access files from any computer that has Internet access
   b. allow others to access files
   c. store offsite backups of data
   d. all of the above

5. A storage technique that a DVD-ROM uses to achieve a higher storage capacity than a CD-ROM is _____. (233)
   a. making the disc denser by packing the pits closer together
   b. using two layers of pits
   c. using both sides of the disc
   d. all of the above

6. _____ storage requires sequential access. (235)
   a. Hard disk
   b. Tape
   c. Floppy disk
   d. CD

7. A _____ is a memory storage device that plugs in a USB port on a computer or mobile device. (236)
   a. PC Card
   b. USB flash drive
   c. card reader/writer
   d. Memory Stick

8. Microfilm and microfiche _____. (238)
   a. greatly increase the amount of paper firms must handle
   b. are expensive
   c. have the longest life of any storage media
   d. all of the above

Matching

_____ 1. online storage (228)

_____ 2. CD-ROM (231)

_____ 3. PC Card (235)

_____ 4. smart card (237)

_____ 5. microfilm (238)

a. Web service that provides storage to computer users for a monthly fee
b. 100- to 215-foot roll of film that stores microscopic images of documents
c. thin, credit-card sized device that fits into a PC Card slot
d. portable, large-capacity magnetic medium that can store from 100 MB to 750 MB of data
e. stores data on an embedded microprocessor with input, process, and output capabilities
f. optical disc that stores data, instructions, and information

Checkpoint

Short Answer

Write a brief answer to each of the following questions.

1. What is access time? _____ How does the access time of storage devices compare with access time of memory? _____

2. Why is a floppy disk considered a portable storage medium? _____ What is a floppy disk drive? _____

3. Why is a hard disk inside the system unit sometimes called a fixed disk? _____ What are the different types of portable hard disks? _____

4. How is a single-session disc different from a multisession disc? _____ What is a CD-RW? _____

5. How is sequential access different from direct access? _____ When reading or writing specific data, which type of access is faster? _____

Working Together

Working in a group of your classmates, complete the following team exercise.

1. Data and information backup is as important for people with personal computers as it is for companies. Develop a report detailing what your group would consider to be the ideal backup system and required devices for the following scenarios: (1) a home computer for personal use, (2) a computer used in a home-based business, (3) a small business with 6 to 8 computers, (4) a business or organization with up to 100 computers, and (5) a business or organization with more than 100 computers. Include information that supports why you selected the particular options. Develop a PowerPoint presentation to share the information with your class.

Web Research

Use the Internet-based Web Research exercises to broaden your understanding of the concepts presented in this chapter. Visit scsite.com/dcf2e/ch6/research to obtain more information pertaining to each exercise. To discuss any of the Web Research exercises in this chapter with other students, post your thoughts or questions at scsite.com/dcf2e/ch6/forum.

① Journaling Respond to your readings in this chapter by writing at least one page about your reactions, evaluations, and reflections about using storage devices. For example, have you used USB flash drives, smart cards, or Zip disks? How do you care for your floppy disks? Have you ever encountered a corrupt floppy disk? What is the storage capacity of your school, office, or home computer's hard disk? Do you clean your CDs and DVDs? Have you copied a CD or DVD? You also can write about the new terms you learned by reading this chapter. If required, submit your journal to your instructor.

② Scavenger Hunt Use one of the search engines listed in Figure 2-8 in Chapter 2 on page 58 or your own favorite search engine to find the answers to the questions that follow. Copy and paste the Web address from the Web page where you found the answer. Some questions may have more than one answer. If required, submit your answers to your instructor. (1) What are the three different laser powers used in a CD-rewritable recorder? How do two of the powers affect the recording layer? During writing, to what temperature does the laser beam selectively heat areas of the recording material? (2) Daniel Bernoulli's principle has many practical applications. Describe two of them, and then explain how Iomega used the principle in its Bernoulli drive. (3) What is the Red Book standard? (4) What is the function of a hard disk's actuator? (5) What is areal density? What unit of measurement is used to describe this density?

③ Search Sleuth Many computer users search the World Wide Web by typing words in the search text box, and often they are overwhelmed when the search engine returns thousands of possible Web sites. You can narrow your search by typing quotation marks around phrases and by adding words that give details about the phrase. Go.com is a Web portal developed by the Walt Disney Internet Group. It features a search engine, the latest ABC news and ESPN sports stories, stock market quotes, weather forecasts, maps, and games. Visit this Web site and then use your word processing program to answer the following questions. Then, if required, submit your answers to your instructor. (1) Click the Search for text box at the top of the page. Type hard disk in the box. How many search results are returned that are not sponsored links? (2) Type "hard disk" in the Search for box. How many search results are returned that are not sponsored links? (3) Scroll down to the bottom of the page and then type "access time" in the text box to search within the "hard disk" results and narrow your results. How many search results are returned that are not sponsored links? (4) Review the Hard Disks section of your textbook for additional words that give details about this device. Perform two more searches with these words. Review your search results and then write a 50-word summary of your findings.

Learn How To

Use the Learn How To exercises to learn fundamental skills when using a computer and accompanying technology. Complete the exercises and submit them to your instructor.

LEARN HOW TO 1: Maintain a Hard Disk

A computer's hard disk is used for the majority of storage requirements. It is important, therefore, to ensure that each hard disk on a computer is operating at peak efficiency, both to effectively use the storage space available and to make disk operations as fast as possible.

Three tasks that maximize disk operations are detecting and repairing disk errors by using the Check Disk utility program; removing unused or unnecessary files and folders by using the Disk Cleanup utility program; and, consolidating files and folders into contiguous storage areas using the Disk Defragmenter utility program. Defragmenting allows your system to access stored files and folders more efficiently.

A. Check Disk

To detect and repair disk errors using the Check Disk utility program, complete the following steps:

1. Click the Start button on the Windows taskbar and then click My Computer on the Start menu.
2. When the My Computer window opens, right-click the hard disk icon for drive C (or any other hard disk you want to select), and then click Properties on the shortcut menu.
3. In the Properties dialog box, if necessary click the Tools tab. *The Tools sheet contains buttons to start the Check Disk program, the Defragment program, and the Backup program (Figure 6-30).*
4. Click the Check Now button. *The Check Disk dialog box is displayed.*
5. To do a complete scan of the disk and correct any errors that are found, place a check mark in the Scan for and attempt recovery for bad sectors check box, and then click the Start button. Four phases of checking the disk will occur. While the checking is in progress, the disk being checked cannot be used for any purpose whatsoever; furthermore, once it has started, the process cannot be stopped.
6. When the four phases are complete (this may take more than one-half hour, depending on the size of the hard disk and how many corrections must occur), a dialog box is displayed with the message, Disk Check Complete. Click the OK button in the dialog box to complete the disk check.

B. Cleanup Disk

After checking the disk, your next step can be to clean up the disk by removing any programs and data that are not required for the computer. To do so, complete the following steps:

1. Click the General tab (Figure 6-30) in the disk drive Properties dialog box to display the General sheet.
2. Click the Disk Cleanup button in the General sheet.
3. The Disk Cleanup dialog box is displayed and contains a message that indicates the amount of space that can be freed up is being calculated.
4. After the calculation is complete, the Disk Cleanup dialog box specifies the amount of space that can be freed up and the files to delete, some of which are checked automatically (Figure 6-31). Select those items from which you wish to delete files.
5. Click the OK button in the Disk Cleanup dialog box.
6. A dialog box asks if you are sure you want to perform these actions. Click the Yes button. The Disk Cleanup dialog box illustrates the progress of the cleanup. When the cleanup is complete, the dialog box closes.

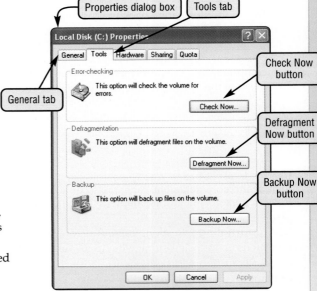

FIGURE 6-30

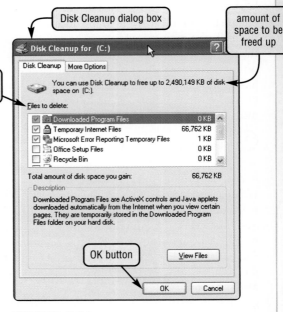

FIGURE 6-31

Learn How To

C. Defragment Disk

After removing all the unnecessary files from the hard disk, the next step in disk maintenance is to defragment all the files on the disk. When a file is stored on disk, the data in the file sometimes is stored contiguously, and other times is stored in a noncontiguous manner. The greater the amount of data on a disk, the more likely files will be stored noncontiguously. When a file is stored in a noncontiguous manner, it can take significantly longer to find and retrieve data from the file. Therefore, one of the more useful utilities to speed up disk operations is the defragmentation program, which combines all files so that no files are stored in a noncontiguous manner. To use the defragmentation program, complete the following steps:

1. If necessary, click the Tools tab in the Properties dialog box for the hard disk to be defragmented.
2. Click the Defragment Now button in the Tools sheet. *The Disk Defragmenter window opens (Figure 6-32). This window displays the hard disks on the computer and shows the size and amount of free space for each disk. During defragmentation, the Estimated disk usage before defragmentation area and the Estimated disk usage after defragmentation area display the layout of the data on the disk. If you click the Analyze button, the disk will be analyzed for its data layout but defragmentation will not occur.*
3. Click the Defragment button. The defragmentation process begins. The amount of processing completed is shown on the status bar at the bottom of the window. The defragmentation process can consume more than one hour in some cases, depending on the size of the hard disk and the amount of processing that must occur. You can pause or stop the operation at any time by clicking the Pause or Stop button in the Disk Defragmenter window.
4. When the process is complete, the Disk Defragmenter dialog box displays the message, Defragmentation is complete for (C:). Click the View Report button to see a complete report about the hard disk, including items such as size, used space, free space, number of files and folders on the disk, and other information.
5. Click the Close button to close the Disk Defragmenter dialog box.

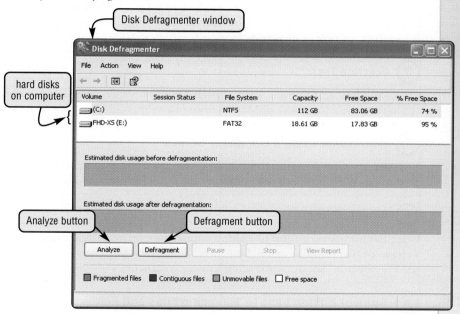

FIGURE 6-32

Proper disk maintenance is critically important so disk operation is as efficient as possible.

Exercise

Caution: The exercises for this chapter that require the actual disk maintenance are optional. If you are performing these exercises on a computer that is not your own, obtain explicit permission to complete these exercises. Keep in mind that these exercises can require significant computer time and the computer may be unusable during this time.

1. Display the Properties dialog box for a hard disk found on the computer. Display the Tools sheet. Click the Check Now button and then place a check mark in the Scan for and attempt recovery for bad sectors check box. Click the Start button. How long did it take to complete the check of the hard disk? Were any errors discovered and corrected? Submit your answers to your instructor.
2. Display the Properties dialog box for a hard disk found on the computer. Display the General sheet. What is the capacity of the hard disk? How much space is used? How much free space is available? Click the Disk Cleanup button. How much space can be freed up if you use the Disk Cleanup program? Click the OK button to clean up the disk. How long did it take to perform the disk cleanup? Submit your answers to your instructor.
3. Display the Properties dialog box for a hard disk found on the computer. Display the Tools sheet. Click the Defragment Now button. In the Disk Defragmenter window, click the Analyze button. Does the hard disk need to be defragmented? Click the View Report button. How many files are stored on the disk? What is the average size of the files stored on the disk? If necessary, click the Defragment button in the Analysis Report window. How long did defragmentation require? Submit your answers to your instructor.

Learn It Online

Use the Learn It Online exercises to reinforce your understanding of the chapter concepts. To access the Learn It Online exercises, visit scsite.com/dcf2e/ch6/learn.

(1) At the Movies — Repair Your CD Scratches

To view the Repair Your CD Scratches movie, click the number 1 button. Locate your video and click the corresponding High-Speed or Dial-Up link, depending on your Internet connection. Watch the movie and then complete the exercise by answering the questions that follow. Just because your favorite CD has a few scratches is no reason to toss it. There are a few options to help you keep those scratched CDs playing longer and smoothly. How does resurfacing work to restore your scratched CDs? What common household product can be used to repair a CD?

(2) Student Edition Labs — Maintaining a Hard Drive

Click the number 2 button. When the Student Edition Labs menu appears, click *Maintaining a Hard Drive* to begin. A new browser window will open. Follow the on-screen instructions to complete the Lab. When finished, click the Exit button. If required, submit your results to your instructor.

(3) Practice Test

Click the number 3 button. Answer each question. When completed, enter your name and click the Grade Test button to submit the quiz for grading. Make a note of any missed questions. If required, submit your results to your instructor.

(4) Who Wants To Be a Computer Genius²?

Click the number 4 button to find out if you are a computer genius. Directions about how to play the game will be displayed. When you are ready to play, click the Play button. Submit your score to your instructor.

(5) Wheel of Terms

Click the number 5 button to reinforce important terms you learned in this chapter by playing the Shelly Cashman Series version of this popular game. Directions about how to play the game will be displayed. When you are ready to play, click the Play button. Submit your score to your instructor.

(6) Student Edition Labs — Managing Files and Folders

Click the number 6 button. When the Student Edition Labs menu appears, click *Managing Files and Folders* to begin. A new browser window will open. Follow the on-screen instructions to complete the Lab. When finished, click the Exit button. If required, submit your results to your instructor.

(7) Crossword Puzzle Challenge

Click the number 7 button. Complete the puzzle to reinforce skills you learned in this chapter. Directions about how to play the game will be displayed. When you are ready to play, click the Submit button. Submit the completed puzzle to your instructor.

(8) Lab Exercises

Click the number 8 button. When the Lab Exercises menu appears, click the exercise assigned by your instructor. A new browser window will open. Follow the on-screen instructions to complete the exercise. When finished, click the Exit button. If required, submit your results to your instructor.

(9) Chapter Discussion Forum

Select an objective from this chapter on page 219 about which you would like more information. Click the number 9 button and post a short message listing a meaningful message title accompanied by one or more questions concerning the selected objective. In two days, return to the threaded discussion by clicking the number 9 button. Submit to your instructor your original message and at least one response to your message.

CHAPTER 7

Operating Systems and Utility Programs

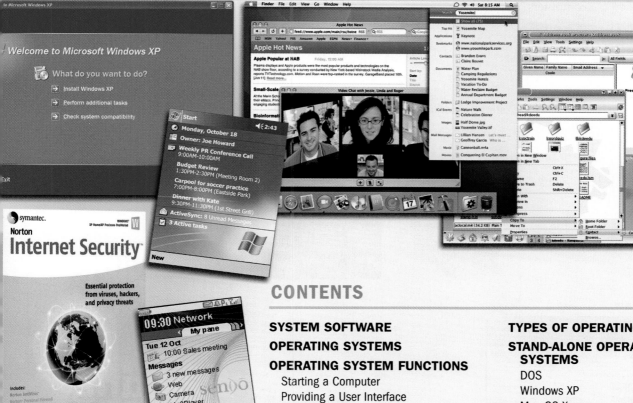

OBJECTIVES

After completing this chapter, you will be able to:

1. Identify the types of system software
2. Describe the functions of an operating system
3. Explain the purpose of the utilities included with most operating systems
4. Summarize the features of several stand-alone operating systems
5. Identify devices that use embedded operating systems
6. Explain the purpose of several stand-alone utility programs

CONTENTS

SYSTEM SOFTWARE

OPERATING SYSTEMS

OPERATING SYSTEM FUNCTIONS
Starting a Computer
Providing a User Interface
Managing Programs
Managing Memory
Scheduling Jobs
Configuring Devices
Establishing an Internet Connection
Monitoring Performance
Providing File Management
  and Other Utilities
Controlling a Network
Administering Security

OPERATING SYSTEM UTILITY PROGRAMS
File Manager
Image Viewer
Personal Firewall
Uninstaller
Disk Scanner
Disk Defragmenter
Diagnostic Utility
Backup Utility
Screen Saver

TYPES OF OPERATING SYSTEMS

STAND-ALONE OPERATING SYSTEMS
DOS
Windows XP
Mac OS X
UNIX
Linux

NETWORK OPERATING SYSTEMS

EMBEDDED OPERATING SYSTEMS

STAND-ALONE UTILITY PROGRAMS
Antivirus Programs
Spyware Removers
Internet Filters
File Compression
File Conversion
CD/DVD Burning
Personal Computer Maintenance

CHAPTER SUMMARY

COMPANIES ON THE CUTTING EDGE
Red Hat
Symbian

TECHNOLOGY TRAILBLAZERS
Alan Kay
Linus Torvalds

SYSTEM SOFTWARE

When you purchase a personal computer, it usually has system software installed on its hard disk. **System software** consists of the programs that control or maintain the operations of the computer and its devices. System software serves as the interface between the user, the application software, and the computer's hardware.

Two types of system software are operating systems and utility programs. This chapter discusses the operating system and its functions, as well as several types of utility programs for personal computers.

FIGURE 7-1   Most operating systems perform the functions illustrated in this figure.

OPERATING SYSTEMS

An **operating system** (OS) is a set of programs containing instructions that coordinate all the activities among computer hardware resources. Most operating systems perform similar functions that include starting a computer, providing a user interface, managing programs, managing memory, scheduling jobs, configuring devices, establishing an Internet connection, monitoring performance, and providing file management utilities. Some operating systems also allow users to control a network and administer security (Figure 7-1).

In most cases, the operating system is installed and resides on the computer's hard disk. On handheld computers and many mobile devices, however, the operating system may reside on a ROM chip.

provide a user interface

manage programs

manage memory

monitor performance

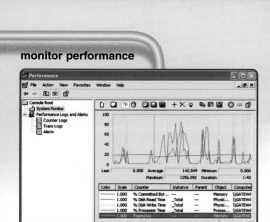

establish an Internet connection

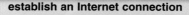

schedule jobs and configure devices

Different sizes of computers typically use different operating systems. For example, a mainframe computer does not use the same operating system as a personal computer. Even the same types of computers, such as desktop computers, may not use the same operating system. Furthermore, the application software designed for a specific operating system may not run when using another operating system. For example, PCs often use Windows XP, and iMacs use Mac OS X. When purchasing application software, you must ensure that it works with the operating system installed on your computer.

The operating system that a computer uses sometimes is called the platform. On purchased application software, the package identifies the required platform (operating system). A cross-platform program is one that has multiple versions, and each version runs identically on multiple operating systems.

OPERATING SYSTEM FUNCTIONS

Many different operating systems exist; however, most operating systems provide similar functions. The following sections discuss functions common to most operating systems. The operating system handles many of these functions automatically, without requiring any instruction from a user.

Starting a Computer

Booting is the process of starting or restarting a computer. When turning on a computer that has been powered off completely, you are performing a **cold boot**. A **warm boot**, by contrast, is the process of using the operating system to restart a computer. With Windows XP, for example, you can perform a warm boot by selecting a button in a dialog box (Figure 7-2). Some computers have a reset button that when pressed restarts the computer as if it had been powered off.

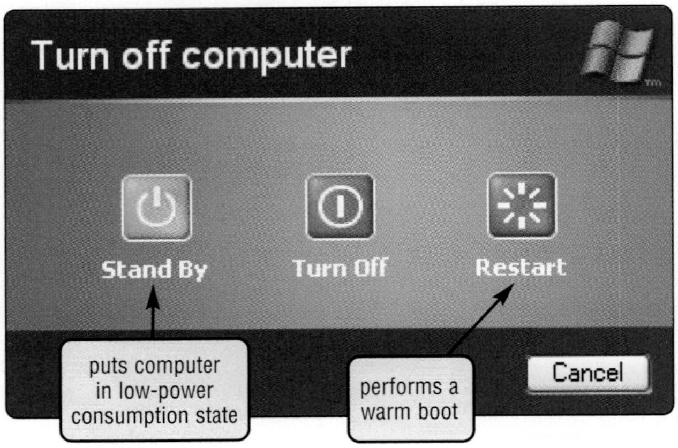

When you install new software, often an on-screen prompt instructs you to restart the computer. In this case, a warm boot is appropriate.

Each time you boot a computer, the kernel and other frequently used operating system instructions are loaded, or copied, from the hard disk (storage) into the computer's memory (RAM). The kernel is the core of an operating system that manages memory and devices, maintains the computer's clock, starts applications, and assigns the computer's resources, such as devices, programs, data, and information. The kernel is memory resident, which means it remains in memory while the computer is running. Other parts of the operating system are nonresident, that is, these instructions remain on the hard disk until they are needed.

When you boot a computer, a series of messages may be displayed on the screen. The actual information displayed varies depending on the make and type of the computer and the equipment installed. The boot process, however, is similar for large and small computers.

Turn off computer

Stand By   Turn Off   Restart

puts computer in low-power consumption state

performs a warm boot

Cancel

FIGURE 7-2   To reboot a running computer, click the Restart button in the Turn off computer dialog box.

FAQ 7-1

When I am finished using the computer, can I simply turn it off?

No! You must use the operating system's shut-down procedure so various processes are closed in sequence and items in memory released properly. Depending on the computer, several shut-down options exist. The Turn Off command removes power from the computer. Restart does a warm boot. Hibernate saves all documents in memory and then turns off the computer. Stand By places the entire computer in a low-power state but does not turn it off. With the Hibernate and Stand By options, the next time you resume work on the computer, the desktop is restored to exactly how you left it. For more information, visit scsite.com/dcf2e/ch7/faq and then click Shut-Down Options.

Providing a User Interface

You interact with software through its user interface. That is, a **user interface** controls how you enter data and instructions and how information is displayed on the screen. Two types of user interfaces are command-line and graphical. Operating systems sometimes use a combination of these interfaces to define how a user interacts with a computer.

COMMAND-LINE INTERFACE   To configure devices, manage system resources, and troubleshoot network connections, network administrators and other advanced users work with a command-line interface. In a **command-line interface**, a user types commands or presses special keys on the keyboard to enter data and instructions (Figure 7-3a). Command-line interfaces often are difficult to use because they require exact spelling, grammar, and punctuation. Minor errors, such as a missing period, generate an error message. Command-line interfaces, however, give a user more control to manage detailed settings.

GRAPHICAL USER INTERFACE   Most users today work with a graphical user interface. With a **graphical user interface** (GUI), you interact with menus and visual images such as buttons and other graphical objects to issue commands (Figure 7-3b). Many current GUI operating systems incorporate features similar to those of a Web browser.

FIGURE 7-3a   (command-line interface)

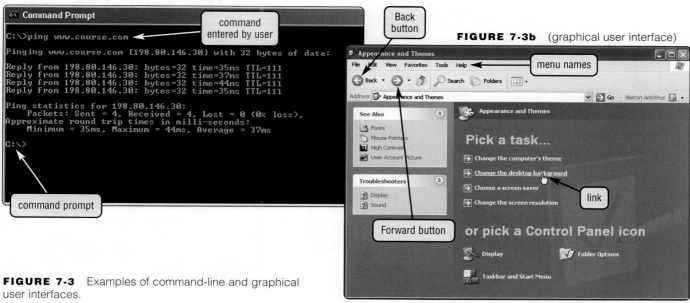

FIGURE 7-3b   (graphical user interface)

FIGURE 7-3   Examples of command-line and graphical user interfaces.

Managing Programs

Some operating systems support a single user and only one running program at a time. Others support thousands of users running multiple programs. How an operating system handles programs directly affects your productivity.

A single user/single tasking operating system allows only one user to run one program at a time. PDAs, smart phones, and other small computing devices often use a single user/single tasking operating system.

A single user/multitasking operating system allows a single user to work on two or more programs that reside in memory at the same time. Users today typically run multiple programs concurrently. It is common to have an e-mail program and Web browser open at all times, while working with application programs such as word processing or graphics.

When a computer is running multiple programs concurrently, one program is in the foreground and the others are in the background. The one in the foreground is the active program, that is, the one you currently are using. The other programs running but not in use are in the background. In Figure 7-4, the PowerPoint program, which is showing a slide show, is in the foreground, and three other programs are running in the background (Paint Shop Pro, Encarta Encyclopedia, and iTunes).

FIGURE 7-4   The foreground program, PowerPoint, is displayed on the desktop. The other programs (Paint Shop Pro, Encarta Encyclopedia, and iTunes) are in the background.

The foreground program typically is displayed on the desktop but the background programs often are partially or completely hidden behind the foreground program. You easily can switch between foreground and background programs. To make a program active (in the foreground) in Windows XP, click its program button on the taskbar. This causes the operating system to place all other programs in the background.

A multiuser operating system enables two or more users to run programs simultaneously. Networks, midrange servers, mainframes, and supercomputers allow hundreds to thousands of users to connect at the same time, and thus are multiuser.

A multiprocessing operating system supports two or more processors running programs at the same time. Multiprocessing involves the coordinated processing of programs by more than one processor. Multiprocessing increases a computer's processing speed.

A computer with separate processors also can serve as a fault-tolerant computer. A **fault-tolerant computer** continues to operate when one of its components fails, ensuring that no data is lost. Fault-tolerant computers have duplicate components such as processors, memory, and disk drives. If any one of these components fails, the computer switches to the duplicate component and continues to operate. Airline reservation systems, communications networks, automated teller machines, and other systems that must be operational at all times use fault-tolerant computers.

Managing Memory

The purpose of **memory management** is to optimize the use of random access memory (RAM). RAM consists of one or more chips on the motherboard that hold items such as data and instructions while the processor interprets and executes them. The operating system allocates, or assigns, data and instructions to an area of memory while they are being processed. Then, it carefully monitors the contents of memory. Finally, the operating system releases these items from being monitored in memory when the processor no longer requires them.

Virtual memory is a concept in which the operating system allocates a portion of a storage medium, usually the hard disk, to function as additional RAM. As you interact with a program, part of it may be in physical RAM, while the rest of the program is on the hard disk as virtual memory. Because virtual memory is slower than RAM, users may notice the computer slowing down while it uses virtual memory.

The operating system uses an area of the hard disk for virtual memory, in which it swaps (exchanges) data, information, and instructions between memory and storage. The technique of swapping items between memory and storage is called paging. When an operating system spends much of its time paging, instead of executing application software, it is said to be thrashing. If application software, such as a Web browser, has stopped responding and the hard disk's LED blinks repeatedly, the operating system probably is thrashing.

Scheduling Jobs

The operating system determines the order in which jobs are processed. A **job** is an operation the processor manages. Jobs include receiving data from an input device, processing instructions, sending information to an output device, and transferring items from storage to memory and from memory to storage.

A multiuser operating system does not always process jobs on a first-come, first-served basis. Sometimes, one user may have a higher priority than other users. In this case, the operating system adjusts the schedule of jobs.

Sometimes, a device already may be busy processing one job when it receives a second job. This occurs because the processor operates at a much faster rate of speed than peripheral devices. For example, if the processor sends five print jobs to a printer, the printer can print only one document at a time.

While waiting for devices to become idle, the operating system places items in buffers. A **buffer** is a segment of memory or storage in which items are placed while waiting to be transferred from an input device or to an output device.

The operating system commonly uses buffers with print jobs. This process, called **spooling**, sends print jobs to a buffer instead of sending them immediately to the printer. The buffer holds the information waiting to print while the printer prints from the buffer at its own rate of speed. By spooling print jobs to a buffer, the processor can continue interpreting and executing instructions while the printer prints. This allows users to work on the computer for other tasks while a printer is printing. Multiple print jobs line up in a **queue** (pronounced Q) in the buffer. A program, called a print spooler, intercepts print jobs from the operating system and places them in the queue (Figure 7-5).

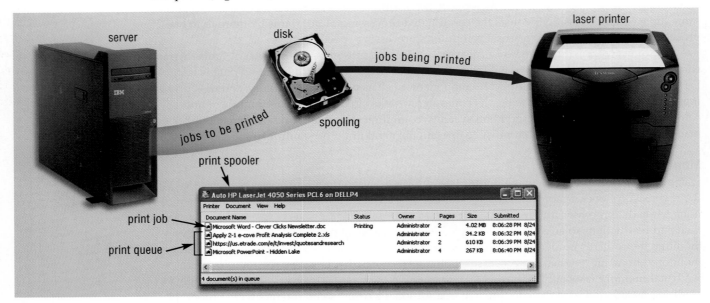

FIGURE 7-5 Spooling increases both processor and printer efficiency by placing print jobs in a buffer on disk before they are printed. This figure illustrates three jobs in the queue with one job printing.

Configuring Devices

A **driver** is a small program that tells the operating system how to communicate with a specific device. Each device on a computer, such as the mouse, keyboard, monitor, printer, and scanner, has its own specialized set of commands and thus requires its own specific driver. When you boot a computer, the operating system loads each device's driver.

If you attach a new device to a computer, such as a printer or scanner, its driver must be installed before you can use the device. For many devices, the computer's operating system may include the necessary drivers. If it does not, you can install the drivers from the CD or disk provided with the purchased device.

Today, many devices and operating systems support Plug and Play. **Plug and Play** means the operating system automatically configures new devices as you install them. With Plug and Play, a user can plug in a device, turn on the computer, and then use the device without having to configure the system manually.

Establishing an Internet Connection

Operating systems typically provide a means to establish Internet connections. For example, Windows XP includes a New Connection Wizard that guides users through the process of setting up a connection between a computer and an Internet service provider (Figure 7-6).

Some operating systems also include a Web browser and an e-mail program, enabling you to begin using the Web and communicate with others as soon as you set up the Internet connection. Some also include a built-in firewall to protect computers from unauthorized intrusions.

WEB LINK 7-1

Plug and Play

For more information, visit scsite.com/dcf2e/ch7/weblink and then click Plug and Play.

FIGURE 7-6 To display the New Connection Wizard in Windows XP, click the Start button, point to All Programs, point to Accessories, point to Communications, and then click New Connection Wizard on the Communications submenu.

Monitoring Performance

Operating systems typically contain a performance monitor. A **performance monitor** is a program that assesses and reports information about various computer resources and devices.

The information in performance reports helps users and administrators identify a problem with resources so they can try to resolve any problems. If a computer is running extremely slow, for example, the performance monitor may determine that the computer's memory is being used to its maximum. Thus, you might consider installing additional memory in the computer.

Providing File Management and Other Utilities

Operating systems often provide users with the capability of managing files, viewing images, securing a computer from unauthorized access, uninstalling programs, scanning disks, defragmenting disks, diagnosing problems, backing up files and disks, and setting up screen savers. A later section in the chapter discusses these utilities in depth. Read At Issue 7-1 for a related discussion.

Controlling a Network

Some operating systems are network operating systems. A **network operating system**, or **network OS**, is an operating system that organizes and coordinates how multiple users access and share resources on a network. Resources include hardware, software, data, and information. For example, a network OS allows multiple users to share a printer, Internet access, files, and programs.

Some operating systems have network features built into them. In other cases, the network OS is a set of programs separate from the operating system on the client computers that access the network. When not connected to the network, the client computers use their own operating system. When connected to the network, the network OS may assume some of the operating system functions.

The **network administrator**, the person overseeing network operations, uses the network OS to add and remove users, computers, and other devices to and from the network. The network administrator also uses the network operating system to install software and administer network security.

AT ISSUE 7-1

Who Is Responsible for Operating System Security?

A few years ago, the Sasser worm infected almost one million computers in the stretch of a weekend. Surprisingly, most computer users already had the necessary means to stop this worm before it even got started. The Windows XP operating system comes equipped with built-in firewall protection, but, by default, the feature was turned off. Microsoft later released a service pack, or update, for the operating system in which the feature was turned on by default. Most operating system manufacturers allow users automatically to download and install up-to-date security patches. It is up to the users to make use of this service properly and make certain that their operating system software is up-to-date. Sometimes, as was the case with the Sasser worm, the updates come too late. Often, users are not technically savvy enough to keep up with the security updates or to configure a network connection with a firewall properly. Who should be responsible for operating system security? Why? Should operating system manufacturers be required to send security updates to computer users? Why or why not? Should users be required to take responsibility for worms and viruses that they spread to others due to lax security? Why or why not?

Administering Security

The network administrator uses the network OS to establish permissions to resources. These permissions define who can access certain resources and when they can access those resources.

For each user, the network administrator establishes a user account, which enables a user to access, or **log on** to, a computer or a network. Each user account typically consists of a user name and password (Figure 7-7). A **user name**, or **user ID**, is a unique combination of characters, such as letters of the alphabet or numbers, that identifies one specific user. Many users select a combination of their first and last names as their user name. A user named Henry West might choose H West as his user name.

FIGURE 7-7 Most multiuser operating systems allow each user to log on, which is the process of entering a user name and a password into the computer.

A **password** is a private combination of characters associated with the user name that allows access to certain computer resources. Some operating systems allow the network administrator to assign passwords to files and commands, restricting access to only authorized users.

To prevent unauthorized users from accessing computer resources, keep your password confidential. While entering your password, most computers hide the actual password characters by displaying some other characters, such as asterisks (*) or dots. After entering a user name and password, the operating system compares the user's entry with a list of authorized user names and passwords. If the entry matches the user name and password kept on file, the operating system grants the user access. If the entry does not match, the operating system denies access to the user.

The operating system records successful and unsuccessful logon attempts in a file. This allows the network administrator to review who is using or attempting to use the computer. Network administrators also use these files to monitor computer usage.

To protect sensitive data and information as it travels over the network, a network operating system may encrypt it. Encryption is the process of encoding data and information into an unreadable form. Network administrators can set up a network to encrypt data as it travels over the network to prevent unauthorized users from reading the data. When an authorized user attempts to read the data, it automatically is decrypted, or converted back into a readable form.

Test your knowledge of pages 250 through 258 in Quiz Yourself 7-1.

FAQ 7-2

What are the guidelines for selecting a good password?

Choose a password that no one could guess. Do not use any part of your first or last name, your spouse's or child's name, telephone number, street address, license plate number, Social Security number, and so on. Be sure your password is at least six characters long, mixed with letters and numbers. For more information, visit scsite.com/dcf2e/ch7/faq and then click Passwords.

QUIZ YOURSELF 7-1

Instructions: Find the true statement below. Then, rewrite the remaining false statements so they are true.

1. A buffer is a small program that tells the operating system how to communicate with a specific device.

2. A warm boot is the process of using the operating system to restart a computer.

3. A password is a public combination of characters associated with the user name that allows access to certain computer resources.

4. The program you currently are using is in the background, and the other programs running but not in use are in the foreground.

5. Two types of system software are operating systems and application programs.

Quiz Yourself Online: To further check your knowledge of system software and functions common to most operating systems, visit scsite.com/dcf2e/ch7/quiz and then click Objectives 1 – 2.

OPERATING SYSTEM UTILITY PROGRAMS

A **utility program**, also called a **utility**, is a type of system software that allows a user to perform maintenance-type tasks, usually related to managing a computer, its devices, or its programs. Most operating systems include several built-in utility programs (Figure 7-8). Users often buy stand-alone utilities, however, because they offer improvements over those included with the operating system.

Utility programs included with most operating systems provide the following functions: managing files, viewing images, securing a computer from unauthorized access, uninstalling programs, scanning disks, defragmenting disks, diagnosing problems, backing up files and disks, and setting up screen savers. The following sections briefly discuss each of these utilities.

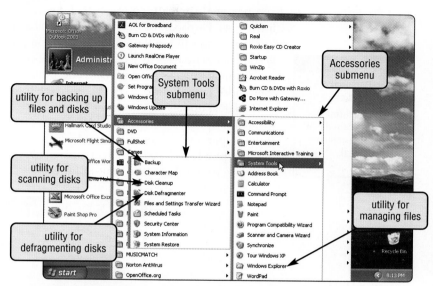

FIGURE 7-8 Many utilities available in Windows XP are accessible through the Accessories and System Tools submenus.

File Manager

A **file manager** is a utility that performs functions related to file management. Some of the file management functions that a file manager performs are formatting and copying disks; displaying a list of files on a storage medium (Figure 7-9); checking the amount of used or free space on a storage medium; and organizing, copying, renaming, deleting, moving, and sorting files.

Formatting is the process of preparing a disk for reading and writing. Most floppy and hard disk manufacturers preformat their disks. If you must format a floppy disk or other media, you can do so using the file manager.

Image Viewer

An **image viewer** is a utility that allows users to display, copy, and print the contents of a graphics file. With an image viewer, users can see images without having to open them in a paint or image editing program. Windows XP includes an image viewer called Windows Picture and Fax Viewer (Figure 7-10). To display a file in this image viewer, simply double-click the thumbnail of the image in the file manager, such as the one shown in Figure 7-9.

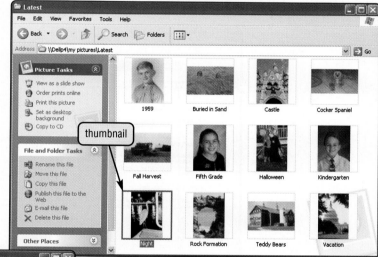

FIGURE 7-9 With Windows Explorer, which is the file manager included with Windows XP, users can display a list of graphics files on a disk. In this case, thumbnails of the files are displayed.

FIGURE 7-10 Windows Picture and Fax Viewer allows users to see the contents of a graphics file.

Personal Firewall

A **personal firewall** is a utility that detects and protects a personal computer from unauthorized intrusions. Personal firewalls constantly monitor all transmissions to and from a computer.

When connected to the Internet, your computer is vulnerable to attacks from a hacker. A hacker is someone who tries to access a computer or network illegally. Users with broadband Internet connections, such as through DSL and Internet cable television service, are even more susceptible than those with dial-up access because the Internet connection is always on.

The latest update to Windows XP automatically enables the built-in personal firewall upon installation. This firewall, called Windows Firewall, is easy to access and configure (Figure 7-11). If your operating system does not include a personal firewall or you want additional protection, you can purchase a stand-alone personal firewall utility or a hardware firewall, which is a device such as a router that has a built-in firewall.

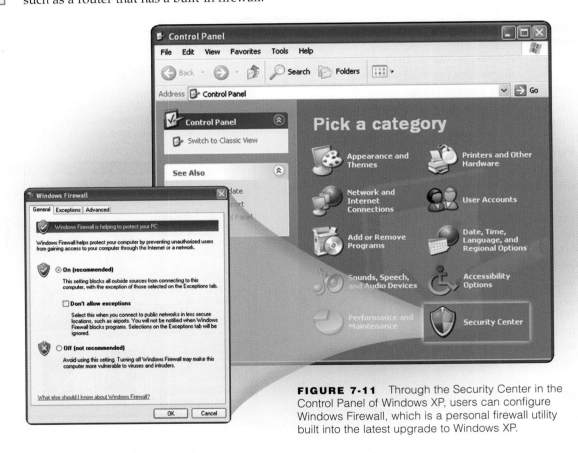

FIGURE 7-11 Through the Security Center in the Control Panel of Windows XP, users can configure Windows Firewall, which is a personal firewall utility built into the latest upgrade to Windows XP.

Uninstaller

An **uninstaller** is a utility that removes a program, as well as any associated entries in the system files. When you install a program, the operating system records the information it uses to run the software in the system files. The uninstaller deletes files and folders from the hard disk, as well as removes program entries from the system files.

Disk Scanner

A **disk scanner** is a utility that (1) detects and corrects both physical and logical problems on a hard disk and (2) searches for and removes unnecessary files. A physical disk problem is a problem with the media such as a scratch on the surface of the disk. A logical disk problem is a problem with the data, such as a corrupt file.

Disk Defragmenter

A **disk defragmenter** is a utility that reorganizes the files and unused space on a computer's hard disk so the operating system accesses data more quickly and programs run faster. When an operating system stores data on a disk, it places the data in the first available sector on the disk. It attempts to place data in sectors that are contiguous (next to each other), but this is not always possible. When the contents of a file are scattered across two or more noncontiguous sectors, the file is fragmented.

Fragmentation slows down disk access and thus the performance of the entire computer. **Defragmenting** the disk, or reorganizing it so the files are stored in contiguous sectors, solves this problem (Figure 7-12). Windows XP includes a disk defragmenter available on the System Tools submenu.

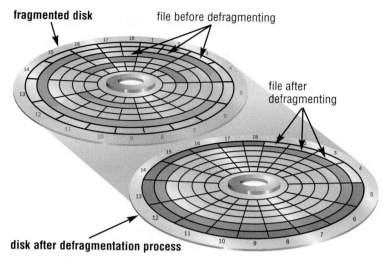

FIGURE 7-12 A fragmented disk has many files stored in noncontiguous sectors. Defragmenting reorganizes the files, so they are located in contiguous sectors, which speeds access time.

Diagnostic Utility

A **diagnostic utility** compiles technical information about your computer's hardware and certain system software programs and then prepares a report outlining any identified problems. Information in the report assists technical support staff in remedying any problems.

Backup Utility

A **backup utility** allows users to copy, or back up, selected files or an entire hard disk to another storage medium. During the backup process, the backup utility monitors progress and alerts you if it needs additional discs or tapes. Many backup programs compress, or shrink the size of, files during the backup process. By compressing the files, the backup program requires less storage space for the backup files than for the original files.

Because they are compressed, you usually cannot use backup files in their backed up form. In the event you need to use a backup file, a **restore program** reverses the process and returns backed up files to their original form. Backup utilities include restore programs.

You should back up files and disks regularly in the event your originals are lost, damaged, or destroyed. Instead of backing up to a local disk storage device, some users opt to use online storage to back up their files. Online storage is a service on the Web that provides hard disk storage to computer users, usually for a minimal monthly fee.

WEB LINK 7-3

Screen Savers

For more information, visit scsite.com/dcf2e/ch7/weblink and then click Screen Savers.

Screen Saver

A **screen saver** is a utility that causes a display device's screen to show a moving image or blank screen if no keyboard or mouse activity occurs for a specified time (Figure 7-13). When you press a key on the keyboard or move the mouse, the screen saver disappears and the screen returns to the previous state.

Screen savers originally were developed to prevent a problem called ghosting, in which images could be permanently etched on a monitor's screen. Although ghosting is not as severe of a problem with today's displays, manufacturers continue to recommend that users install screen savers for this reason. Screen savers also are popular for security, business, and entertainment purposes. To secure a computer, users configure their screen saver to require a password to deactivate. In addition to those included with the operating system, many screen savers are available for a minimal fee in stores and on the Web.

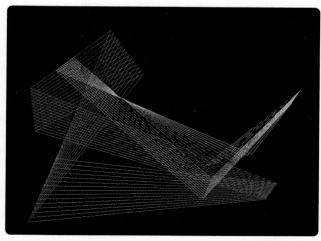

FIGURE 7-13 A Windows XP screen saver.

TYPES OF OPERATING SYSTEMS

When you purchase a new computer, it typically has an operating system preinstalled. As new versions of the operating system are released, users upgrade their existing computers to incorporate features of the new version. An upgrade usually costs less than purchasing the entire operating system.

New versions of an operating system usually are downward compatible. That is, they recognize and work with application software written for an earlier version of the operating system (or platform). The application software, by contrast, is said to be upward compatible, meaning it will run on new versions of the operating system.

The three basic categories of operating systems that exist today are stand-alone, network, and embedded. The table in Figure 7-14 lists names of operating systems in each category. The following pages discuss the operating systems listed in the table.

CATEGORIES OF OPERATING SYSTEMS

Category	Operating System Name
Stand-alone	• DOS • Early Windows versions (Windows 3.x, Windows 95, Windows NT Workstation, Windows 98, Windows 2000 Professional, Windows Millennium Edition) • Windows XP • Mac OS X • UNIX • Linux
Network	• NetWare • Early Windows Server versions (Windows NT Server, Windows 2000 Server) • Windows Server 2003 • UNIX • Linux • Solaris
Embedded	• Windows CE • Windows Mobile • Palm OS • Embedded Linux • Symbian OS

FIGURE 7-14   Examples of stand-alone, network, and embedded operating systems. Some stand-alone operating systems include the capability of configuring small home or office networks.

STAND-ALONE OPERATING SYSTEMS

A **stand-alone operating system** is a complete operating system that works on a desktop computer, notebook computer, or mobile computing device. Some stand-alone operating systems are called client operating systems because they also work in conjunction with a network operating system. Client operating systems can operate with or without a network. Other stand-alone operating systems include networking capabilities, allowing the home and small business user to set up a small network. Examples of stand-alone operating systems are DOS, Windows XP, Mac OS X, UNIX, and Linux.

DOS

The term **DOS** (Disk Operating System) refers to several single user operating systems developed in the early 1980s for personal computers. The two more widely used versions of DOS were PC-DOS and MS-DOS.

DOS used a command-line interface when Microsoft first developed it. Later versions included both command-line and menu-driven user interfaces. DOS hardly is used today because it does not offer a graphical user interface and it cannot take full advantage of modern 32-bit personal computer processors.

Windows XP

In the mid-1980s, Microsoft developed its first version of Windows, which provided a graphical user interface (GUI). Since then, Microsoft continually has updated its Windows operating system, incorporating innovative features and functions with each new version. **Windows XP** is Microsoft's fastest, most reliable Windows operating system yet, providing quicker startup,

WEB LINK 7-4

Windows XP

For more information, visit scsite.com/dcf2e/ch7/weblink and then click Windows XP.

better performance, and a simplified visual look (Figure 7-15). Windows XP is available in five editions: Home Edition, Professional, Media Center Edition, Tablet PC Edition, and 64-bit Edition.

With Windows XP Home Edition, users easily can organize and share digital pictures, download and listen to music, create and edit videos, network home computers, and communicate with instant messaging. Windows XP Professional includes all the capabilities of Windows XP Home Edition and also offers greater data security, remote access to a computer, simpler administration of groups of users, and support for a wireless network. Windows XP Media Center Edition includes all features of Windows XP Professional and provides additional features for the personal computer used as a home entertainment computer (Figure 7-16). Windows XP Tablet PC Edition includes all features of Windows XP Professional and provides additional features designed to make users more productive while working on their Tablet PC. Windows XP 64-bit Edition is designed for workstations that use an Itanium 2 processor. Read Looking Ahead 7-1 for a look at the next generation of the Windows operating system.

FIGURE 7-15 Windows XP, with its simplified look, is the fastest and most reliable Windows operating system to date.

LOOKING AHEAD 7-1

The Future of Windows

Searching for computer files can be a frustrating experience. Microsoft, however, plans to simplify the process with an eventual add-on to its next version of the Windows operating system, currently code-named Longhorn.

With this search feature, called WinFS (Windows Future Storage), users will be able to locate e-mail messages, documents, and multimedia images, no matter what their format, on a stand-alone computer and on a network.

Longhorn is being developed as a consumer-friendly product with a completely object-oriented interface. When this major update to Windows XP is released in 2006 or later, it will recognize users and tailor the systems for their specific needs. It also will feature new security technology called Palladium, an antivirus program, and recordable DVD capabilities. For more information, visit scsite.com/dcf2e/ch7/looking and then click Longhorn.

FIGURE 7-16 With Windows XP Media Center Edition, users access recorded videos, pictures, music, television programs, radio stations, or movies via a remote control device.

Mac OS X

Since it was released with Macintosh computers in 1984, Apple's **Macintosh operating system** has set the standard for operating system ease of use and has been the model for most of the new GUIs developed for non-Macintosh systems. The latest version, **Mac OS X**, is a multitasking operating system available only for computers manufactured by Apple (Figure 7-17).

WEB LINK 7-5

Mac OS X

For more information, visit scsite.com/ dcf2e/ch7/weblink and then click Mac OS X.

FIGURE 7-17 Mac OS X is the operating system used with Apple Macintosh computers.

UNIX

UNIX (pronounced YOU-nix) is a multitasking operating system. Several versions of this operating system exist, each slightly different. Although some versions of UNIX have a command-line interface, most versions of UNIX offer a graphical user interface (Figure 7-18). Today, a version of UNIX is available for most computers of all sizes. Power users often work with UNIX because of its flexibility and power.

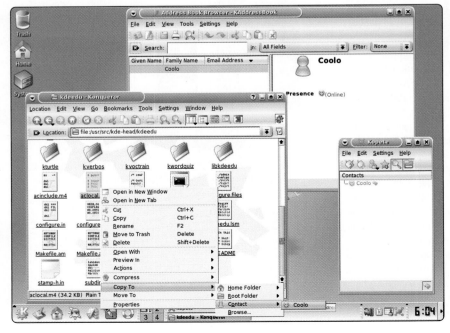

WEB LINK 7-6

UNIX

For more information, visit scsite.com/dcf2e/ ch7/weblink and then click UNIX.

FIGURE 7-18 Some versions of UNIX have a graphical user interface.

Linux

Linux is one of the faster growing operating systems. **Linux** (pronounced LINN-uks) is a popular, multitasking UNIX-type operating system. In addition to the basic operating system, Linux also includes many free programming languages and utility programs. Linux is not proprietary software like the operating systems discussed thus far. Instead, Linux is open source software, which means its code is available to the public for use, modification, and redistribution. Read At Issue 7-2 for a related discussion.

Some versions of Linux are command-line. Others are GUI (Figure 7-19). Users obtain Linux in a variety of ways. Some people download it free from the Web. Others purchase it from vendors, who bundle their own software with the operating system. Linux CD-ROMs are included in many Linux books and also are available for purchase from vendors. For purchasers of new personal computers, some retailers such as Dell will preinstall Linux on the hard disk on request. Read Looking Ahead 7-2 for a look at the next generation of Linux.

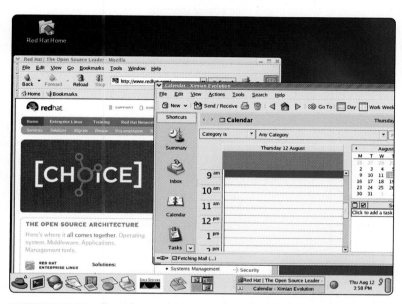

FIGURE 7-19   Red Hat provides a version of Linux called Red Hat Linux.

LOOKING AHEAD 7-2
The Future of Linux

The Linux operating system has been altered and enhanced since Linus Torvalds wrote the initial source code in 1991. With hundreds of programmers donating their time to make Linux the best possible version of UNIX, the software literally has changed on a daily basis.

As these developers work to improve Linux, their efforts are helping to shape the software's future. Experts predict the operating system may change by establishing a consistent desktop environment that is easy for all computer users to use. They also believe that hardware manufacturers will promote Linux-approved systems that maximize the software's features. Others forecast that a few major distributors will issue the software, in contrast to the hundreds of independent distributors that now exist. For more information, visit scsite.com/dcf2e/ch7/looking and then click Linux Future.

AT ISSUE 7-2
Closed Source vs. Open Source Software

Linux is a fast-growing, innovative operating system. One of the features that make it different from other operating systems is that Linux is open source and its source code, along with any changes, remains public. Since its introduction in 1991, Linux has been altered, adapted, and improved by hundreds of programmers. Unlike Linux, most operating systems are proprietary, and their program code often is a zealously guarded secret. At one large software developer, an employee reported that application programmers had little opportunity to contribute to operating system programs because they had no access to the operating system program source code. Supporters of open source maintain that source code should be open to the public so that it can be scrutinized, corrected, and enhanced. In light of concerns about security and fears of possible virus problems, however, some people are not sure open source software is a good idea. Besides, they argue, programmers should be able to control, and profit from, the operating systems they create. On the other hand, open source software can be scrutinized for errors by a much larger group of people and changes can be made immediately. Is open source software a good idea? Why or why not? Can the concerns about open source software be addressed? How? What are the advantages and disadvantages of open versus closed source software? Does open source software lead to better software?

Test your knowledge of pages 259 through 265 in Quiz Yourself 7-2.

QUIZ YOURSELF 7-2

Instructions: Find the true statement below. Then, rewrite the remaining false statements so they are true.

1. A file manager is a utility that detects and protects a personal computer from unauthorized intrusions.
2. Fragmenting a disk is the process of reorganizing it so the files are stored in contiguous sectors.
3. Linux is available in five editions: Home Edition, Professional, Media Center Edition, Tablet PC Edition, and 64-bit Edition.
4. Mac OS X is a multitasking operating system available only for computers manufactured by Apple.
5. Windows XP is a UNIX-type operating system that is open source software.

Quiz Yourself Online: To further check your knowledge of utilities included with most operating systems and stand-alone operating systems, visit scsite.com/dcf2e/ch7/quiz and then click Objectives 3 – 4.

NETWORK OPERATING SYSTEMS

As discussed earlier in this chapter, a network operating system is an operating system that is designed specifically to support a network. A network operating system typically resides on a server. The client computers on the network rely on the server(s) for resources. Many of the client operating systems discussed in the previous section work in conjunction with a network operating system.

Some of the stand-alone operating systems discussed in the previous section include networking capability; however, network operating systems are designed specifically to support all sizes of networks, including medium to large-sized businesses and Web servers.

Examples of network operating systems include NetWare, Windows Server 2003, UNIX, Linux, and Solaris.

- Novell's Netware is a network operating system designed for client/server networks.
- Windows Server 2003 is an upgrade to Windows 2000 Server, which was an upgrade to Windows NT Server.
- UNIX and Linux often are called multipurpose operating systems because they are both stand-alone and network operating systems.
- Solaris, a version of UNIX developed by Sun Microsystems, is a network operating system designed specifically for e-commerce applications.

EMBEDDED OPERATING SYSTEMS

The operating system on most PDAs and small devices, called an **embedded operating system**, resides on a ROM chip. Popular embedded operating systems include Windows CE, Windows Mobile, Palm OS (Figure 7-20), embedded Linux, and Symbian OS.

- Windows CE is a scaled-down Windows operating system designed for use on communications, entertainment, and computing devices with limited functionality. It supports color, sound, multitasking, multimedia, e-mail, Internet access, and Web browsing.
- Windows Mobile is built on Windows CE and works on a specific type of PDA, called a Pocket PC, and smart phones. With this operating system and a Pocket PC or smart phone, users have access to the basic PIM (personal information manager) functions such as contact lists, schedules, tasks, calendars, and notes.
- Palm OS, which is a competing operating system to Windows Mobile, runs on PDAs and smart phones. With Palm OS and a compatible PDA, users manage schedules and contacts, telephone messages, project notes, reminders, tasks and address lists, and important dates and appointments.

Palm OS PDA

FIGURE 7-20 Many mobile devices use Palm OS.

WEB LINK 7-7

Palm OS

For more information, visit scsite.com/dcf2e/ch7/weblink and then click Palm OS.

- Embedded Linux is a scaled-down Linux operating system designed for PDAs, smart phones, smart watches, set-top boxes, Internet telephones, and many other types of devices and computers requiring an embedded operating system. PDAs and smart phones with embedded Linux offer calendar and address book and other PIM functions, touch screens, and handwriting recognition.
- Symbian OS is an open source multitasking operating system designed for smart phones. Users enter data by pressing keys on the keypad or keyboard, touching the screen, and writing on the screen with a stylus.

STAND-ALONE UTILITY PROGRAMS

Although operating systems typically include some built-in utilities, many stand-alone utility programs are available for purchase. For example, you can purchase personal firewalls, backup utilities, and screen savers. These stand-alone utilities typically offer improvements over those features built into the operating system or provide features not included in an operating system.

Other functions provided by stand-alone utilities include protecting against viruses, removing spyware, filtering Internet content, compressing files, converting files, burning CDs and DVDs, and maintaining a personal computer. The following sections discuss each of these utilities.

Antivirus Programs

The term, computer **virus**, describes a potentially damaging computer program that affects, or infects, a computer negatively by altering the way the computer works without the user's knowledge or permission. More specifically, a computer virus is a segment of program code from some outside source that implants itself in a computer. Once the virus is in a computer, it can spread throughout and may damage your files and operating system.

Currently, more than 81,000 known virus programs exist with an estimated 6 new virus programs discovered each day. Computer viruses do not generate by chance. The programmer of a virus, known as a virus author, intentionally writes a virus program. Some virus authors find writing viruses a challenge. Others write them to cause destruction. Writing a virus program usually requires significant programming skills.

Some viruses are harmless pranks that simply freeze a computer temporarily or display sounds or messages. The Music Bug virus, for example, instructs the computer to play a few chords of music. Other viruses destroy or corrupt data stored on the hard disk of the infected computer. If you notice any unusual changes in your computer's performance, it may be infected with a virus. Figure 7-21 outlines some common symptoms of virus infection.

A **worm** copies itself repeatedly, for example, in memory or over a network, using up system resources and possibly shutting the system down. A **Trojan horse** hides within or looks like a legitimate program such as a screen saver. A certain condition or action usually triggers the Trojan horse. Unlike a virus or worm, a Trojan horse does not replicate itself to other computers.

SIGNS OF VIRUS INFECTION
• An unusual message or image is displayed on the computer screen
• An unusual sound or music plays randomly
• The available memory is less than what should be available
• A program or file suddenly is missing
• An unknown program or file mysteriously appears
• The size of a file changes without explanation
• A file becomes corrupted
• A program or file does not work properly
• System properties change

FIGURE 7-21 Viruses attack computers in a variety of ways. This list indicates some of the more common signs of virus infection.

To protect a computer from virus attacks, users should install an antivirus program and update it frequently. An **antivirus program** protects a computer against viruses by identifying and removing any computer viruses found in memory, on storage media, or on incoming files (Figure 7-22). Most antivirus programs also protect against worms and Trojan horses. When you purchase a new computer, it often includes antivirus software.

The two more popular antivirus programs are McAfee VirusScan and Norton AntiVirus. As an alternative to purchasing these products on CD, both McAfee and Norton offer Web-based antivirus programs. That is, during your paid subscription period, the program continuously protects the computer against viruses.

Spyware Removers

Spyware is a program placed on a computer without the user's knowledge that secretly collects information about the user, often related to Web browsing habits. The spyware program communicates information it collects to some outside source while you are online. A **spyware remover** is a program that detects and deletes spyware. Most spyware removers cost less than $50; some are available on the Web at no cost.

Internet Filters

Filters are programs that remove or block certain items from being displayed. Three widely used Internet filters are anti-spam programs, Web filters, and pop-up blockers.

ANTI-SPAM PROGRAMS   Spam is an unsolicited e-mail message or newsgroup posting sent to many recipients or newsgroups at once. Spam is Internet junk mail. An **anti-spam program** is a filtering program that attempts to remove spam before it reaches your inbox. If your e-mail program does not include an anti-spam program, many anti-spam programs are available at no cost on the Web.

WEB FILTERS   **Web filtering software** is a program that restricts access to certain material on the Web. Some restrict access to specific Web sites; others filter sites that use certain words or phrases. Many businesses use Web filtering software to limit employee's Web access. Some schools, libraries, and parents use this software to restrict access to minors.

FAQ 7-3

What steps should I take to prevent virus infections on my computer?

Set up the antivirus software to scan on a regular basis. Never open an e-mail attachment unless you are expecting the attachment and it is from a trusted source. Set macro security in programs such as word processing and spreadsheet so you can enable or disable macros. Write-protect your recovery disk. Back up files regularly. For more information, visit scsite.com/dcf2e/ch7/faq and then click Virus Infections.

FIGURE 7-22   An antivirus program scans memory, disks, and incoming e-mail messages and attachments for viruses and attempts to remove any viruses it finds.

FAQ 7-4

Should anti-spam programs be installed on home computers?

Yes. With more than 65 percent of all e-mail categorized as spam, home and business users could lose valuable time sifting through messages related to the variety of subjects shown in the chart below. For more information, visit scsite.com/dcf2e/ch7/faq and then click Anti-Spam Programs.

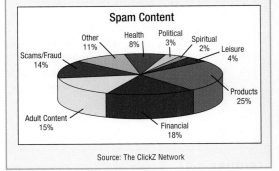

Spam Content

Other 11%
Health 8%
Political 3%
Spiritual 2%
Leisure 4%
Products 25%
Financial 18%
Adult Content 15%
Scams/Fraud 14%

Source: The ClickZ Network

POP-UP BLOCKERS A pop-up ad is an Internet advertisement that appears in a new window in the foreground of a Web page displayed in your browser. A **pop-up blocker** is a filtering program that stops pop-up ads from displaying on Web pages. If your operating system does not block pop-up ads, many pop-up blockers can be downloaded from the Web at no cost.

File Compression

A **file compression utility** shrinks the size of a file(s). A compressed file takes up less storage space than the original file (Figure 7-23). Compressing files frees up room on the storage media and improves system performance. Attaching a compressed file to an e-mail message, for example, reduces the time needed for file transmission. Uploading and downloading compressed files to and from the Internet reduces the file transmission time.

Compressed files sometimes are called **zipped files**. When you receive or download a compressed file, you must uncompress it. To **uncompress**, or unzip, a file, you restore it to its original form. Some operating systems such as Windows XP include uncompress capabilities. To compress a file, however, you need a stand-alone file compression utility. Two popular stand-alone file compression utilities are PKZIP and WinZip.

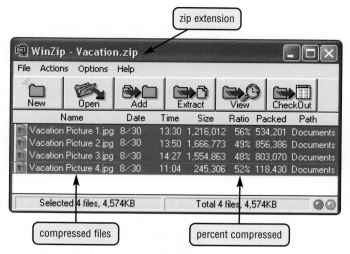

FIGURE 7-23 This file (Vacation) contains four compressed files. Without being compressed, these files consume 4,574 KB. Compressing them reduced the amount of storage by about 50 percent.

File Conversion

A **file conversion utility** transforms the contents of a file or data from one format to another. When a business develops a new system, often the data in the current system is not in the correct format for the new system. Thus, part of the system development process is to convert data — instead of having users re-enter all the existing data in the new system. On a smaller scale, when home users purchase new software, they may need to convert files so the files will be displayed properly in the new software.

CD/DVD Burning

CD/DVD burning software writes text, graphics, audio, and video files on a recordable or rewritable CD or DVD. This software enables the home user easily to back up contents of their hard disk on a CD/DVD and make duplicates of uncopyrighted music or movies. CD/DVD burning software usually also includes photo editing, audio editing, and video editing capabilities (Figure 7-24).

When you buy a recordable or rewritable CD or DVD, it typically includes CD/DVD burning software. You also can buy CD/DVD burning software for a cost of less than $100.

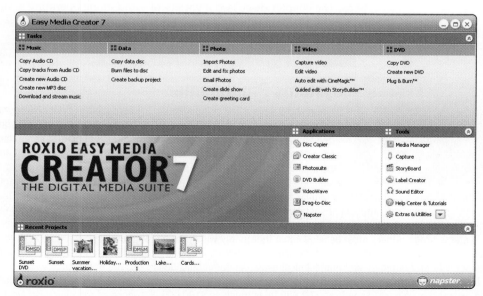

FIGURE 7-24 Using CD/DVD burning software, you can copy text, graphics, audio, and video files on a CD or DVD, if you have the correct type of CD/DVD drive and media.

Personal Computer Maintenance

Operating systems typically include a diagnostic utility that diagnoses computer problems but does not repair them. A **personal computer maintenance utility** identifies and fixes operating system problems, detects and repairs disk problems, and includes the capability of improving a computer's performance. Additionally, some personal computer maintenance utilities continuously monitor a computer while you use it to identify and repair problems before they occur. Norton SystemWorks is a popular personal computer maintenance utility designed for Windows operating systems (Figure 7-25).

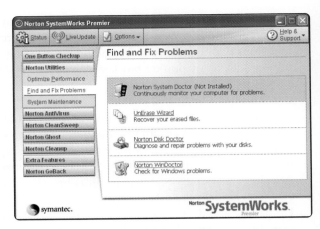

FIGURE 7-25 A popular maintenance program for Windows users.

Test your knowledge of pages 266 through 270 in Quiz Yourself 7-3.

QUIZ YOURSELF 7-3

Instructions: Find the true statement below. Then, rewrite the remaining false statements so they are true.

1. A pop-up blocker shrinks the size of a file(s).
2. An anti-spam program protects a computer against viruses.
3. Examples of network operating systems include NetWare, Windows Server 2003, UNIX, Linux, and Solaris.
4. Pocket PCs use Palm OS as their operating system.
5. Web filtering software writes text, graphics, audio, and video files to a recordable or rewritable CD or DVD.

Quiz Yourself Online: To further check your knowledge of embedded operating systems and stand-alone utility programs, visit scsite.com/dcf2e/ch7/quiz and then click Objectives 5 – 6.

CHAPTER SUMMARY

This chapter defined an operating system and then discussed the functions common to most operating systems. Next, it introduced several utility programs commonly found in operating systems. The chapter discussed a variety of stand-alone operating systems, network operating systems, and embedded operating systems. Finally, the chapter described several stand-alone utility programs.

CAREER CORNER

Systems Programmer

System software is a key component in any computer. A **systems programmer** evaluates, installs, and maintains system software and provides technical support to the programming staff.

Systems programmers work with the programs that control computers, such as operating systems, network operating systems, and database systems. They identify current and future processing needs and then recommend the software and hardware necessary to meet those needs. In addition to selecting and installing system software, systems programmers must be able to adapt system software to the requirements of an organization, provide regular maintenance, measure system performance, determine the impact of new or updated software on the system, design and implement special software, and provide documentation. Because they are familiar with the entire system, systems programmers often help application programmers to diagnose technical problems.

Systems programmers must be acquainted thoroughly with a variety of operating systems. They must be able to think logically, pay attention to detail, work with abstract concepts, and devise solutions to complex problems. Systems programmers often work in teams and interact with programmers and nontechnical users, so communications skills are important.

Most systems programmers have a four-year B.S. degree in Computer Science or Information Technology. Depending on responsibilities and experience, salaries range from $53,000 to as much as $100,000. For more information, visit scsite.com/dcf2e/ch7/careers and then click Systems Programmer.

Red Hat
Sharing Open Source Software

When you were young, you were taught to share. University professors share their research with colleagues throughout the world; and Red Hat shares software code, or instructions, with computer users.

Red Hat is the largest supplier of open source software, which allows buyers to view, modify, and perhaps improve, the software. The company delivers the software improvements to customers through the Red Hat Network, the company's Internet service.

Bob Young and Marc Ewing founded Red Hat in 1994 and started distributing a version of the Red Hat Linux operating system complete with documentation and support. Today, Linux is Red Hat's most well-known product. In addition, its open source Apache Web server commands 67 percent of the market, according to E-Soft, a consulting firm that tracks online services. For more information, visit scsite.com/dcf2e/ch7/companies and then click Red Hat.

Symbian
Handheld Computing Devices Manufacturer

The next time you send a text message using your smart phone, you may be using an operating system developed by Symbian. This British company's operating system is the global industry standard and is licensed to leading cellular telephone manufacturers, including Ericsson, Matsushita (Panasonic), Motorola, Nokia, and Psion, which account for more than 80 percent of annual worldwide mobile phone sales.

In 1994, former CEO Colly Myers began experimenting with his programming expertise with the goal of developing a full operating system for a handset rivaling that found on a mainframe computer. Four years later, he convinced Ericsson, Motorola, and Nokia to invest in his product.

The Symbian open standards allow manufacturers to customize services and user interfaces, including graphics, e-mail, and touch screens. For more information, visit scsite.com/dcf2e/ch7/companies and then click Symbian.

TECHNOLOGY TRAILBLAZERS

Alan Kay
Computer Pioneer

Chances are that every time you use your computer you use one of Alan Kay's ideas. More than 35 years ago — long before the personal computer became ubiquitous — he was developing a notebook computer complete with a flat screen, wireless network, and storage. More than 20 years ago, he engineered a graphical user interface, object-oriented languages, and personal computer networks.

Kay did much of his early work at the U.S. Defense Department's Advance Research Project Agency (DARPA) and Xerox's Palo Alto Research Center (PARC). Today he is a senior fellow at HP Labs and a computer science professor at UCLA. In 2004, he won three major awards for his breakthrough inventions that have enhanced society scientifically, culturally, and spiritually. For more information, visit scsite.com/dcf2e/ch7/people and then click Alan Kay.

Linus Torvalds
Linux Creator

When Linus Torvalds developed a new operating system in 1991, he announced his project in an Internet newsgroup, made the source code available, and asked for suggestions. Computer users responded by reviewing the system and offering enhancements. Three years later, Torvalds released a much-enhanced version of open source operating system he called Linux.

Torvalds decided to create the innovative operating system when he was a 21-year-old computer science student in Finland. Today, Linux is estimated to be running on at least 10 percent of computers and is Microsoft's main competitor. Torvalds leads the development of Linux as a fellow at OSDL (Open Source Development Labs), a not-for-profit consortium of companies dedicated to developing and promoting the operating system. For more information, visit scsite.com/dcf2e/ch7/people and then click Linus Torvalds.

Chapter Review

The Chapter Review section summarizes the concepts presented in this chapter. To obtain help from other students regarding any subject in this chapter, visit scsite.com/dcf2e/ch7/forum and post your thoughts or questions.

① What Are the Types of System Software?

System software consists of the programs that control or maintain the operations of a computer and its devices. Two types of system software are operating systems and utility programs. An **operating system (OS)** contains instructions that coordinate all the activities among computer hardware resources. A **utility program** performs maintenance-type tasks, usually related to managing a computer, its devices, or its programs.

② What Are the Functions of an Operating System?

The operating system provides a user interface, manages programs, manages memory, schedules jobs, configures devices, establishes an Internet connection, and monitors performance. The **user interface** controls how data and instructions are entered and how information is displayed. Two types of user interfaces are a **command-line interface** and a **graphical user interface (GUI)**. Managing programs refers to how many users, and how many programs, an operating system can support at one time. An operating system can be single user/single tasking, single user/multitasking, multiuser, or multi-processing. **Memory management** optimizes the use of random access memory (RAM). **Virtual memory** allocates a portion of a storage medium to function as additional RAM. Scheduling jobs determines the order in which jobs are processed. A **job** is an operation the processor manages. Configuring devices involves loading each device's driver when a user boots the computer. A **driver** is a program that tells the operating system how to communicate with a specific device. Establishing an Internet connection sets up a connection between a computer and an Internet service provider. A **performance monitor** is an operating system program that assesses and reports information about computer resources and devices.

 Visit scsite.com/dcf2e/ch7/quiz or click the Quiz Yourself button. Click Objectives 1 – 2.

③ What Is the Purpose of the Utilities Included with Most Operating Systems?

Most operating systems include several built-in utility programs. A **file manager** performs functions related to file management. An **image viewer** displays, copies, and prints the contents of a graphics file. A **personal firewall** detects and protects a personal computer from unauthorized intrusions. An **uninstaller** removes a program and any associated entries in the system files. A **disk scanner** detects and corrects problems on a disk and searches for and removes unnecessary files. A **disk defragmenter** reorganizes the files and unused space on a computer's hard disk. A **diagnostic utility** compiles and reports technical information about a computer's hardware and certain system software programs. A **backup utility** is used to copy, or back up, selected files or an entire hard disk. A **screen saver** displays a moving image or blank screen if no keyboard or mouse activity occurs for a specified time.

④ What Are Features of Several Stand-Alone Operating Systems?

A **stand-alone operating system** is a complete operating system that works on a desktop computer, notebook computer, or mobile computing device. Stand-alone operating systems include DOS, Windows XP, Mac OS X, UNIX, and Linux. **DOS (Disk Operating System)** refers to several single user, command-line operating systems developed for personal computers. **Windows XP** is Microsoft's fastest, most reliable Windows operating system, providing better performance and a simplified look. **Mac OS X** is a multitasking GUI operating system available only for Apple computers. **UNIX** is a multitasking operating system that is flexible and powerful. **Linux** is a popular, multitasking UNIX-type operating system that is open source software, which means its code is available to the public.

 Visit scsite.com/dcf2e/ch7/quiz or click the Quiz Yourself button. Click Objectives 3 – 4.

5 **What Devices Use Embedded Operating Systems?**

Most PDAs and smart phones have an **embedded operating system** that resides on a ROM chip. Popular embedded operating systems include Windows CE, Windows Mobile, Palm OS, embedded Linux, and Symbian OS. Windows CE is a scaled-down Windows operating system designed for use on communications, entertainment, and computing devices with limited functionality. Windows Mobile is built on Windows CE and works on a specific type of PDA, called a Pocket PC, and smart phones. Palm OS is an operating system used on PDAs and smart phones. Embedded Linux is a scaled-down Linux operating system for PDAs, smart phones and watches, and other devices. Symbian OS is an open source multitasking operating system designed for smart phones.

 6 **What Is the Purpose of Several Stand-Alone Utility Programs?**

Stand-alone utility programs offer improvements over features built into the operating system or provide features not included in the operating system. An **antivirus program** protects computers against a **virus**, or potentially damaging computer program, by identifying and removing any computer viruses. A **spyware remover** detects and deletes spyware. An **anti-spam program** attempts to remove **spam** before it reaches your inbox. **Web filtering software** restricts access to certain material on the Web. A **pop-up blocker** stops pop-up ads from displaying on Web pages. A **file compression utility** shrinks the size of a file. A **file conversion utility** transforms the contents of a file from one format to another. **CD/DVD burning software** writes to a recordable or rewritable CD or DVD. A **personal computer maintenance utility** identifies and repairs operating system or disk problems and improves a computer's performance.

 Visit scsite.com/dcf2e/ch7/quiz or click the Quiz Yourself button. Click Objectives 5 – 6.

Key Terms

You should know each key term. Use the list below to help focus your study. To further enhance your understanding of the Key Terms in this chapter, visit scsite.com/dcf2e/ch7/terms. See an example of and a definition for each term, and access current and additional information about the term from the Web.

anti-spam program (268)
antivirus program (268)
backup utility (261)
booting (252)
buffer (255)
CD/DVD burning
   software (269)
cold boot (252)
command-line interface
   (253)
defragmenting (261)
diagnostic utility (261)
disk defragmenter (261)
disk scanner (260)
DOS (262)
driver (256)
embedded operating
   system (266)
fault-tolerant computer
   (255)

file compression utility
   (269)
file conversion utility (269)
file manager (259)
graphical user interface
   (GUI) (253)
image viewer (259)
job (255)
Linux (265)
log on (258)
Mac OS X (264)
Macintosh operating
   system (264)
memory management (255)
network administrator
   (257)
network operating system
   (257)
network OS (257)

operating system (OS)
   (251)
password (258)
performance monitor (257)
personal computer
   maintenance utility (270)
personal firewall (260)
Plug and Play (256)
pop-up blocker (269)
queue (256)
restore program (261)
screen saver (261)
spam (268)
spooling (256)
spyware remover (268)
stand-alone operating
   system (262)
system software (250)
systems programmer (270)

Trojan horse (267)
uncompress (269)
uninstaller (260)
UNIX (264)
user ID (258)
user interface (253)
user name (258)
utility (259)
utility program (259)
virtual memory (255)
virus (267)
warm boot (252)
Web filtering software
   (268)
Windows XP (262)
worm (267)
zipped files (269)

Checkpoint

Use the Checkpoint exercises to check your knowledge level of the chapter.

True/False

Mark T for True and F for False. (See page numbers in parentheses.)

_____ 1. The operating system that a computer uses sometimes is called the level. (252)

_____ 2. Booting is the process of starting or restarting a computer. (252)

_____ 3. A user interface controls how you enter data and instructions and how information is displayed on the screen. (253)

_____ 4. A buffer is a segment of memory or storage in which items are placed while waiting to be transferred from an input device or to an output device. (255)

_____ 5. A utility program is a program that assesses and reports information about various computer resources and devices. (257)

_____ 6. A personal firewall is a utility program that detects and protects a personal computer from unauthorized intrusions. (260)

_____ 7. A disk defragmenter is a utility that reorganizes the files and unused space on a computer's hard disk so the operating system accesses data more quickly and programs run faster. (261)

_____ 8. A stand-alone operating system is a complete operating system that works on a desktop computer, notebook computer, or mobile computing device. (262)

_____ 9. Most antivirus programs do not protect against worms or Trojan horses. (268)

_____ 10. Web filtering software is a program that secretly collects information about a user, often related to the user's Web browsing habits. (268)

Multiple Choice

Select the best answer. (See page numbers in parentheses.)

1. Many current _____ operating systems incorporate features similar to those of a Web browser. (253)
   a. command-line interface
   b. menu-driven interface
   c. graphical user interface
   d. all of the above

2. A process called _____ sends print jobs to a buffer instead of sending them immediately to the printer. (256)
   a. booting   b. thrashing
   c. spooling   d. formatting

3. Encryption is the process of _____. (258)
   a. encoding data and information into an unreadable form
   b. recording successful and unsuccessful logon attempts in a file
   c. establishing a user account that allows a user to log on to a network
   d. entering a user name and password

4. Defragmenting reorganizes the files on a disk so they are located in _____ access time. (261)
   a. noncontiguous sectors, which slows
   b. noncontiguous sectors, which speeds
   c. contiguous sectors, which slows
   d. contiguous sectors, which speeds

5. Apple's _____ has set the standard for operating system ease of use and has been the model for most of the new GUIs. (264)
   a. UNIX operating system
   b. Macintosh operating system
   c. Windows XP operating system
   d. Linux operating system

6. In addition to being a stand-alone operating system, _____ also is a network operating system. (266)
   a. DOS   b. UNIX
   c. NetWare   d. Windows XP

7. Personal firewalls, backup utilities, and screen savers are examples of _____. (267)
   a. stand-alone operating systems
   b. network operating systems
   c. stand-alone utility programs
   d. antivirus programs

8. Two popular stand-alone _____ are PKZIP and WinZip. (269)
   a. antivirus programs
   b. personal computer maintenance utilities
   c. personal firewalls
   d. file compression utilities

Matching

Match the terms with their definitions. (See page numbers in parentheses.)

_____ 1. fault-tolerant computer (255)

_____ 2. buffer (255)

_____ 3. password (258)

_____ 4. restore program (261)

_____ 5. uncompress (269)

a. continues to operate when one of its components fails

b. private combination of characters associated with a user name

c. reverses the backup process and restores backed up files

d. restore a zipped file to its original form

e. segment of memory or storage in which items are placed while waiting to be transferred

f. contains a list of programs that open when a computer boots up

Checkpoint

Short Answer
Write a brief answer to each of the following questions.

1. How is a cold boot different from a warm boot? _____ How is a memory-resident part of an operating system different from a nonresident part of an operating system? _____

2. What is a user interface? _____ How are a command-line interface and a graphical user interface different? _____

3. How is a single user/single tasking operating system different from a single user/multitasking operating system? _____ What is a multiuser operating system? _____

4. What is a computer virus? _____ How is a worm different from a Trojan horse? _____

5. What is spyware? _____ What are some examples of Internet filters? _____

Working Together
Working in a group of your classmates, complete the following team exercise.

1. The Buyer's Guide on page 279 offers tips on buying a computer. Have each member of your team answer the four questions presented in the Buyer's Guide to determine the type of computer he or she needs. Then, each team member should visit one or more computer vendors and, using the guidelines and tools presented in the Buyer's Guide, find the "perfect" computer. Later, meet with the members of your team and compare your results. How are the computers similar? How are they different? Use PowerPoint to create a group presentation and share your findings with the class.

Web Research

Use the Internet-based Web Research exercises to broaden your understanding of the concepts presented in this chapter. Visit scsite.com/dcf2e/ch7/research to obtain more information pertaining to each exercise. To discuss any of the Web Research exercises in this chapter with other students, post your thoughts or questions at scsite.com/dcf2e/ch7/forum.

(1) Journaling

Respond to your readings in this chapter by writing at least one page about your reactions, evaluations, and reflections about using **stand-alone utility programs**. For example, does your computer have an antivirus program? If so, how often do you check for new virus definition updates? Has a virus ever infected one of your files or your computer? Do you have a backup of your hard disk? Do you have a recovery disk? Do you have a personal firewall? You also can write about the new terms you learned by reading this chapter. If required, submit your journal to your instructor.

(2) Scavenger Hunt

Use one of the **search engines** listed in Figure 2-8 in Chapter 2 on page 58 or your own favorite search engine to find the answers to the questions below. Copy and paste the Web address from the Web page where you found the answer. Some questions may have more than one answer. If required, submit your answers to your instructor. (1) What are the three file systems for disk partitions on a computer running the Windows XP operating system? Which of the three does Microsoft recommend using? Why? (2) If you use Microsoft Office on a computer running Windows XP, can you use the same software on a computer running the UNIX or Linux operating system? Why or why not? (3) What did Gary Kildall develop in 1974 while working for Intel? What is the basis of the lawsuit Caldera Inc. filed against Microsoft in 1996?

(3) Search Sleuth

A search engine using a **concept-based search system** seeks Web sites containing a search term along with related concepts. For example, if you search for "operating systems," this type of search engine also returns links to books, professional organizations, and other operating system-related topics. Many researchers consider Excite (excite.com) the best concept-based search engine. Visit this Web site and then use your word processing program to answer the following questions. Then, if required, submit your answers to your instructor. (1) Click the Member Info link at the bottom of the page. What are the benefits of free membership? (2) Click the Web search text box and type "utility programs" in the box. How many search results are returned that are not sponsored links? (3) Click the View By Search Engine option button near the top of the page. What are three search engines Excite used to return results? Which search engine returned the most links? (4) Click two of the unsponsored links discussing backing up and recovering files. Review these articles and then write a 50-word summary of your findings.

Learn How To

Use the Learn How To activities to learn fundamental skills when using a computer and accompanying technology. Complete the exercises and submit them to your instructor.

LEARN HOW TO 1: Install a Computer

Once you have purchased a computer, you must install it for use. Based on years of experience, a set of guidelines for installing and using your computer has been developed. To examine these guidelines, complete the following steps:

1. Start the browser on your computer.
2. Type the Web address scsite.com/dcf2e in the Address box and then press the ENTER key.
3. Click the Chapter 7 link in the top navigation bar.
4. Click Install Computer in the left sidebar below the heading, Beyond the Book.
5. Read the material presented about how to install a computer.

Exercise

1. Using your Web search skills, research the latest recommendations with respect to proper ergonomics for using a computer. What information did you find that you did not know before? What changes would you make to your current computer setup that might make you more productive? Submit your answers to your instructor.
2. Many people report illnesses or injuries from using computers. Perform research in a library or on the Web to discover the five most common ailments associated with using a computer. Determine the actions people can take to minimize or eliminate these ailments. Submit a report to your instructor describing your findings.
3. Your computer lab at school contains multiple computers for student use. Using the knowledge you have obtained from this Learn How To activity, evaluate the computer installation in your school lab. In a report to your instructor, specify those items you think can be improved in the lab.

LEARN HOW TO 2: Maintain a Computer

While computers are amazingly resilient and reliable, you still should perform certain activities to ensure they maintain peak performance. To learn about these activities, complete the following steps:

1. Start the browser on your computer.
2. Type the Web address scsite.com/dcf2e in the Address box and then press the ENTER key.
3. Click the Chapter 7 link in the top navigation bar.
4. Click Maintain Computer in the left sidebar below the heading, Beyond the Book.
5. Read the material presented about how to maintain a computer.

Exercise

1. On either your computer or the computer on which you are working, perform a hardware and software inventory of at least five hardware devices and five application programs on the computer. List the vendor, product, vendor Web address, vendor e-mail address, and vendor support telephone number. Submit your inventory to your instructor.
2. Record the serial number of the computer on which you are working. Then, record the serial number for seven different application programs on the computer. Submit this information to your instructor.

LEARN HOW TO 3: **Keep Windows XP Up-to-Date**

Keeping Windows XP up-to-date is a critical part of keeping your computer in good working order. The updates made available by Microsoft for no charge over the Internet will keep errors from occurring on your computer and will ensure that all security safeguards are in place. To update Windows, complete the following steps:

1. Click the Start button on the Windows taskbar, point to All Programs, and then click Windows Update on the All Programs submenu (Figure 7-26). *A browser window will open and display the Windows Update page.*
2. Click the Express Install (Recommended) link. Your computer will be examined and then a list of recommended updates for your computer will be shown.
3. If necessary, select those updates you wish to install and then click the Install button. Be aware that some updates might take 20 minutes or more to download and install, based primarily on your Internet access speed.
4. Often, after installation of updates, you must restart your computer to allow those updates to take effect. Be sure to save any open files before restarting your computer.

FIGURE 7-26

You also can schedule automatic updates for your computer. To do so, complete the following steps:

1. Click the Start button on the Windows taskbar and then click Control Panel on the Start menu.
2. In the Control Panel window, ensure that Category view is displayed, and then click Performance and Maintenance.
3. In the Performance and Maintenance window, click System.
4. In the System Properties dialog box, click the Automatic Updates tab. *The Automatic Updates sheet is displayed in the System Properties dialog box (Figure 7-27).*
5. Select the option you want to use for Windows updates. Microsoft, together with all security and operating system experts, strongly recommends you select Automatic so updates will be installed on your computer automatically. Notice that if you select Automatic, you also should select a time when your computer will be on and be connected to the Internet. A secondary choice is to download the suggested updates and then choose when you want to install them.
6. When you have made your selection, click the OK button in the System Properties dialog box.

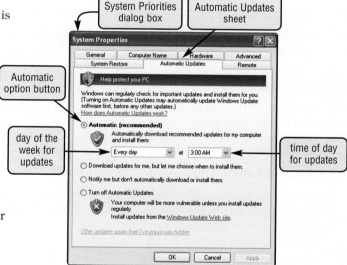

FIGURE 7-27

Updating Windows on your computer is vital to maintain security and operational integrity.

Exercise

1. Open the Windows Update window in your browser. Make a list of the recommended updates to Windows XP on the computer you are using. Add to the list the Custom Install updates that are available. If you are using your own computer, install the updates of your choice on your computer. Submit the list of updates to your instructor.
2. Optional: If you are not using your own computer, do not complete this exercise. Display the Automatic Updates sheet in the System Properties dialog box. Select the level of automatic updates you want to use. Write a report justifying your choice of automatic updates and then submit the report to your instructor.

Learn It Online

Use the Learn It Online exercises to reinforce your understanding of the chapter concepts. To access the Learn It Online exercises, visit scsite.com/dcf2e/ch7/learn.

(1) At the Movies — Windows XP Media Center Edition

To view the Windows XP Media Center Edition movie, click the number 1 button. Locate your video and click the corresponding High-Speed or Dial-Up link, depending on your Internet connection. Watch the movie and then complete the exercise by answering the questions that follow. Windows XP Media Center Edition 2004 is software that easily can enable advanced multimedia interactivity on your computer. With one touch of the remote control, you can activate your music, photographs, videos, radio shows, or television programs. Why is the Windows XP Media Center prone to viruses? How can you make sure your computer is protected from viruses?

(2) Student Edition Labs — Installing and Uninstalling Software

Click the number 2 button. When the Student Edition Labs menu appears, click *Installing and Uninstalling Software* to begin. A new browser window will open. Follow the on-screen instructions to complete the Lab. When finished, click the Exit button. If required, submit your results to your instructor.

(3) Practice Test

Click the number 3 button. Answer each question. When completed, enter your name and click the Grade Test button to submit the quiz for grading. Make a note of any missed questions. If required, submit your results to your instructor.

(4) Who Wants To Be a Computer Genius²?

Click the number 4 button to find out if you are a computer genius. Directions about how to play the game will be displayed. When you are ready to play, click the Play button. Submit your score to your instructor.

(5) Wheel of Terms

Click the number 5 button to reinforce important terms you learned in this chapter by playing the Shelly Cashman Series version of this popular game. Directions about how to play the game will be displayed. When you are ready to play, click the Play button. Submit your score to your instructor.

(6) Student Edition Labs — Working with Audio

Click the number 6 button. When the Student Edition Labs menu appears, click *Working with Audio* to begin. A new browser window will open. Follow the on-screen instructions to complete the Lab. When finished, click the Exit button. If required, submit your results to your instructor.

(7) Crossword Puzzle Challenge

Click the number 7 button. Complete the puzzle to reinforce skills you learned in this chapter. Directions about how to play the game will be displayed. When you are ready to play, click the Submit button. Submit the completed puzzle to your instructor.

(8) Lab Exercises

Click the number 8 button. When the Lab Exercises menu appears, click the exercise assigned by your instructor. A new browser window will open. Follow the on-screen instructions to complete the exercise. When finished, click the Exit button. If required, submit your results to your instructor.

(9) Chapter Discussion Forum

Select an objective from this chapter on page 249 about which you would like more information. Click the number 9 button and post a short message listing a meaningful message title accompanied by one or more questions concerning the selected objective. In two days, return to the threaded discussion by clicking the number 9 button. Submit to your instructor your original message and at least one response to your message.

Special Feature

Buyer's Guide
How to Purchase a Personal Computer

(a) desktop computer

At some point, perhaps while you are taking this course, you may decide to buy a personal computer. The decision is an important one and will require an investment of both time and money. Like many buyers, you may have little computer experience and find yourself unsure of how to proceed. You can get started by talking to your friends, coworkers, and instructors about their computers. What type of computers did they buy? Why? For what purposes do they use their computers? You also should answer the following four questions to help narrow your choices to a specific computer type, before reading this Buyer's Guide.

(b) mobile computer (notebook computer or Tablet PC)

(c) personal mobile device (smart phone or PDA)

Should I buy a desktop or mobile computer or personal mobile device?

For what purposes will I use the computer?

Should I buy a Mac or PC?

Should the computer I buy be compatible with the computers at school or work?

1 **Do you want a desktop computer, mobile computer, or personal mobile device?** A desktop computer (Figure 1a) is designed as a stationary device that sits on or below a desk or table in a location such as a home, office, or dormitory room. A desktop computer must be plugged into an electrical outlet to operate. A mobile computer, such as a notebook computer or Tablet PC (Figure 1b), is smaller than a desktop computer, more portable, and has a battery that allows you to operate it for a period without an electrical outlet. A personal mobile device (Figure 1c) runs on a battery for a longer period of time than a notebook computer or Tablet PC and can fit in your pocket.

Desktop computers are a good option if you work mostly in one place and have plenty of space in your work area. Desktop computers generally give you more performance for your money.

Increasingly, more desktop computer users are buying mobile computers to take advantage of their portability to work in the library, at school, while traveling, and at home. The past disadvantages of mobile computers, such as lower processor speeds, poor-quality monitors, weight, short battery life, and significantly higher prices, have all but disappeared when compared with desktop computers.

FIGURE 1

If you are thinking of using a mobile computer to take notes in class or in business meetings, then consider a Tablet PC with handwriting and drawing capabilities. Typically, note-taking involves writing text notes and drawing charts, schematics, and other illustrations. By allowing you to write and draw directly on the screen with a digital pen, a Tablet PC eliminates the distracting sound of the notebook keyboard tapping and allows you to capture drawings. Some notebook computers can convert to Tablet PCs.

A personal mobile device, such as a smart phone or a PDA, is ideal if you require a pocket-sized computing device as you move from place to place. Personal mobile devices provide personal organizer functions, such as a calendar, appointment book, address book, and many other applications. The small size of the processor, screen, and keyboard, however, limit a personal mobile device's capabilities when compared with a desktop or notebook computer or a Tablet PC. For this reason, most people who purchase personal mobile devices also have a desktop or notebook computer to handle heavy-duty applications.

Drawbacks of mobile computers and personal mobile devices are that they tend to have a shorter useful lifetime than desktop computers and lack the high-end capabilities. Their portability makes them susceptible to vibrations, heat or cold, and accidental drops, which can cause components such as hard disks or display devices to fail. Also, because of their size and portability, they are easy to lose and are the prime targets of thieves.

2 **For what purposes will you use the computer?** Having a general idea of the purposes for which you want to use your computer will help you decide on the type of computer to buy. At this point in your research, it is not necessary to know the exact application software titles or version numbers you might want to use. Knowing that you plan to use the computer primarily to create word processing, spreadsheet, database, and presentation documents, however, will point you in the direction of a desktop or notebook computer. If you want the portability of a smart phone or PDA, but you need more computing power, then a Tablet PC may be the best alternative. You also must consider that some application software runs only on a Mac, while others run only on a PC with the Windows operating system. Still other software may run only on a PC running the UNIX or Linux operating system.

3 **Should the computer be compatible with the computers at school or work?** If you plan to bring work home, telecommute, or take distance education courses, then you should purchase a computer that is compatible with those at school or work.

Compatibility is primarily a software issue. If your computer runs the same operating system version, such as Microsoft Windows XP, and the same application software, such as Microsoft Office, then your computer will be able to read documents created at school or work and vice versa. Incompatible hardware can become an issue if you plan to connect directly to a school or office network using a cable or wireless technology. You usually can obtain the minimum system requirements from the Information Technology department at your school or workplace.

4 **Should the computer be a Mac or PC?** If you ask a friend, coworker, or instructor, which is better — a Mac or a PC — you may be surprised by the strong opinion expressed in the response. No other topic in the computer industry causes more heated debate. The Mac has strengths, especially in the areas of graphics, movies, photos, and music. The PC, however, has become the industry standard with 95 percent of the market share. Figure 2 compares features of the Mac and PC in several different areas. Overall, the Mac and PC have more similarities than differences, and you should consider cost, compatibility, and other factors when choosing whether to purchase a Mac or PC.

Area	Comparison
Cost and availability	A Mac is priced slightly higher than a PC. Mac peripherals also are more expensive. The PC offers more available models from a wide range of vendors. You can custom build, upgrade, and expand a PC for less money than a Mac.
Exterior design	The Mac has a more distinct and stylish appearance than most PCs.
Free software	Although free software for the Mac is available on the Internet, significantly more free software applications are available for the PC.
Market share	The PC dominates the personal computer market. While the Mac sells well in education, publishing, Web design, graphics, and music, the PC is the overwhelming favorite of businesses.
Operating system	Users claim that Mac OS X provides a better all-around user experience than Microsoft Windows XP. Both the Mac and PC supports other operating systems, such as Linux and UNIX.
Program control	Both have simple and intuitive graphical user interfaces. The Mac relies more on the mouse and less on keyboard shortcuts than the PC. The mouse on the Mac has one button, whereas the mouse on a PC has a minimum of two buttons.
Software availability	The basic application software most users require, such as Microsoft Office, is available for both the Mac and PC. More specialized software, however, often is available only for PCs. Many programs are released for PCs long before they are released for Macs.
Speed	The PC provides faster processors than the Mac.
Viruses	Dramatically fewer viruses attack Macs. Mac viruses also generally are less infectious than PC viruses.

FIGURE 2 Comparison of Mac and PC features.

After evaluating the answers to these four questions, you should have a general idea of how you plan to use your computer and the type of computer you want to buy. Once you have decided on the type of computer you want, you can follow the guidelines presented in this Buyer's Guide to help you purchase a specific computer, along with software, peripherals, and other accessories.

Many of the desktop computer guidelines presented also apply to the purchase of a notebook computer, Tablet PC, and personal mobile device. Later in this Buyer's Guide, sections on purchasing a notebook computer or Tablet PC address additional considerations specific to those computer types.

This Buyer's Guide concentrates on recommendations for purchasing a desktop computer or mobile computer.

HOW TO PURCHASE A DESKTOP COMPUTER

Once you have decided that a desktop computer is most suited to your computing needs, the next step is to determine specific software, hardware, peripheral devices, and services to purchase, as well as where to buy the computer.

1 **Determine the specific software you want to use on your computer.** Before deciding to purchase software, be sure it contains the features necessary for the tasks you want to perform. Rely on the computer users in whom you have confidence to help you decide on the software to use. The minimum requirements of the software you select may determine the operating system (Microsoft Windows XP, Linux, UNIX, Mac OS X) you need. If you have decided to use a particular operating system that does not support software you want to use, you may be able to purchase similar software from other manufacturers.

Many Web sites and trade magazines, such as those listed in Figure 3, provide reviews of software products. These Web sites frequently have articles that rate computers and software on cost, performance, and support.

Your hardware requirements depend on the minimum requirements of the software you will run on your computer. Some software requires more memory and disk space than others, as well as additional input, output, and storage devices. For example, suppose you want to run software that can copy one CD's or DVD's contents directly to another CD or DVD, without first copying the data to your hard disk. To support that, you should consider a desktop computer or a high-end notebook computer, because the computer will need two CD or DVD drives: one that reads from a CD or DVD, and one that reads from and writes on a CD or DVD. If you plan to

Type of Computer	Web Site	Web Address
PC	CNET Shopper	shopper.cnet.com
	PC World Magazine	pcworld.com
	BYTE Magazine	byte.com
	PC Magazine	zdnet.com/reviews
	Yahoo! Computers	computers.yahoo.com
	MSN Shopping	eshop.msn.com
	Dave's Guide to Buying a Home Computer	css.msu.edu/PC-Guide
Mac	Macworld Magazine	macworld.com
	Apple	apple.com
	Switch to Mac Campaign	apple.com/switch

For an updated list of hardware and software reviews and their Web site addresses, visit scsite.com/dcf2e/ch7/buyers.

FIGURE 3 Hardware and software reviews.

run software that allows your computer to work as an entertainment system, then you will need a CD or DVD drive, quality speakers, and an upgraded sound card.

2 **Look for bundled software.** When you purchase a computer, it may come bundled with software. Some sellers even let you choose which software you want. Remember, however, that bundled software has value only if you would have purchased the software even if it had not come with the computer. At the very least, you probably will want word processing software and a browser to access the Internet. If you need additional applications, such as a spreadsheet, a database, or presentation graphics, consider purchasing Microsoft Works, Microsoft Office, OpenOffice.org, or Sun StarOffice, which include several programs at a reduced price.

3 **Avoid buying the least powerful computer available.** Once you know the application software you want to use, you then can consider the following important criteria about the computer's components: (1) processor speed, (2) size and types of memory (RAM) and storage, (3) types of input/output devices, (4) types of ports and adapter cards, and (5) types of communications devices. The information in Figures 4 and 5 can help you determine what system components are best for you. Figure 4 outlines considerations for specific hardware components. Figure 5 (on page 284) provides a Base Components worksheet that lists PC recommendations for each category of user discussed in this book: Home User, Small Office/Home Office User, Mobile User, Power User, and Large Business User. In the worksheet, the Home User category is divided into two groups: Application Home User and Game Home User. The Mobile User recommendations list criteria for a notebook computer, but do not include the PDA or Tablet PC options.

Computer technology changes rapidly, meaning a computer that seems powerful enough today may not serve your computing needs in a few years. In fact, studies show that many users regret not buying a more powerful computer. To avoid this, plan to buy a computer that will last you for two to three years. You can help delay obsolescence by purchasing the fastest processor, the most memory, and the largest hard disk you can afford. If you must buy a less powerful computer, be sure you can upgrade it with additional memory, components, and peripheral devices as your computer requirements grow.

CD/DVD Drives: Most computers come with a 32X to 48X speed CD-ROM drive that can read CDs. If you plan to write music, audio files, and documents on a CD, then you should consider upgrading to a CD-RW. An even better alternative is to upgrade to a DVD+RW combination drive. It allows you to read DVDs and CDs and to write data on (burn) a DVD or CD. A DVD has a capacity of at least 4.7 GB versus the 650 MB capacity of a CD.

Card Reader/Writer: A card reader/writer is useful for transferring data directly to and from a removable flash memory card, such as the ones used in your camera or music player. Make sure the card reader/writer can read from and write on the flash memory cards that you use.

Digital Camera: Consider an inexpensive point-and-shoot digital camera. They are small enough to carry around, usually operate automatically in terms of lighting and focus, and contain storage cards for storing photographs. A 2- to 4-megapixel camera with an 8 MB or 16 MB storage card is fine for creating images for use on the Web or to send via e-mail.

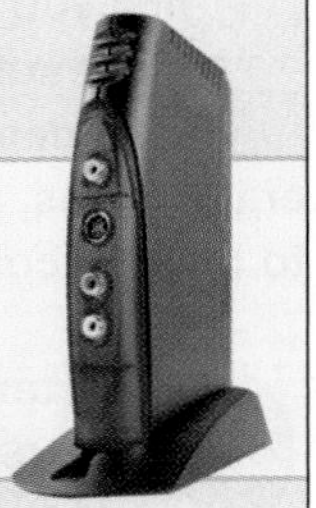

Digital Video Capture Device: A digital video capture device allows you to connect your computer to a camcorder or VCR and record, edit, manage, and then write video back on a VCR tape, a CD, or a DVD. The digital video capture device can be an external device or an adapter card. To create quality video (true 30 frames per second, full-sized TV), the digital video capture device should have a USB 2.0 or FireWire port. You will find that a standard USB port is too slow to maintain video quality. You also will need sufficient storage: an hour of data on a VCR tape takes up about 5 GB of disk storage.

Floppy Disk Drive: If you plan to use a floppy disk drive, then make sure the computer you purchase has a standard 3.5", 1.44 MB floppy disk drive. A floppy disk drive is useful for backing up and transferring files.

Hard Disk: It is recommended that you buy a computer with 40 to 60 GB if your primary interests are browsing the Web and using e-mail and Office suite-type applications; 60 to 80 GB if you also want to edit digital photographs; 80 to 100 GB if you plan to edit digital video or manipulate large audio files even occasionally; and 100 to 160 GB if you will edit digital video, movies, or photography often; store audio files and music; or consider yourself to be a power user.

Joystick/Wheel: If you use your computer to play games, then you will want to purchase a joystick or a wheel. These devices, especially the more expensive ones, provide for realistic game play with force feedback, programmable buttons, and specialized levers and wheels.

Keyboard: The keyboard is one of the more important devices used to communicate with the computer. For this reason, make sure the keyboard you purchase has 101 to 105 keys, is comfortable and easy to use, and has a USB connection. A wireless keyboard should be considered, especially if you have a small desk area.

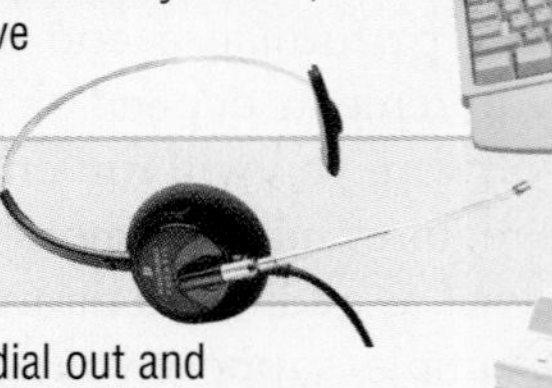

Microphone: If you plan to record audio or use speech recognition to enter text and commands, then purchase a close-talk headset with gain adjustment support.

Modem: Most computers come with a modem so that you can use your telephone line to dial out and access the Internet. Some modems also have fax capabilities. Your modem should be rated at 56 Kbps.

Monitor: The monitor is where you will view documents, read e-mail messages, and view pictures. A minimum of a 17" screen is recommended, but if you are planning to use your computer for graphic design or game playing, then you may want to purchase a 19" or 21" monitor. The LCD flat panel monitor should be considered, especially if space is an issue.

FIGURE 4 Hardware guidelines.

Mouse: As you work with your computer, you use the mouse constantly. For this reason, spend a few extra dollars, if necessary, and purchase a mouse with an optical sensor and USB connection. The optical sensor replaces the need for a mouse ball, which means you do not need a mouse pad. For a PC, make sure your mouse has a wheel, which acts as a third button in addition to the top two buttons on the left and right. An ergonomic design is also important because your hand is on the mouse most of the time when you are using your computer. A wireless mouse should be considered to eliminate the cord and allow you to work at short distances from your computer.

Network Card: If you plan to connect to a network or use broadband (cable or DSL) to connect to the Internet, then you will need to purchase a network card. Broadband connections require a 10/100 PCI Ethernet network card.

Printer: Your two basic printer choices are ink-jet and laser. Color ink-jet printers cost on average between $50 and $300. Laser printers cost from $200 to $2,000. In general, the cheaper the printer, the lower the resolution and speed, and the more often you are required to change the ink cartridge or toner. Laser printers print faster and with a higher quality than an ink-jet, and their toner on average costs less. If you want color, then go with a high-end ink-jet printer to ensure quality of print. Duty cycle (the number of pages you expect to print each month) also should be a determining factor. If your duty cycle is on the low end — hundreds of pages per month — then stay with a high-end ink-jet printer, rather than purchasing a laser printer. If you plan to print photographs taken with a digital camera, then you should purchase a photo printer. A photo printer is a dye-sublimation printer or an ink-jet printer with higher resolution and features that allow you to print quality photographs.

Processor: For a PC, a 2.8 GHz Intel or AMD processor is more than enough processor power for application home and small office/home office users. Game home, large business, and power users should upgrade to faster processors.

RAM: RAM plays a vital role in the speed of your computer. Make sure the computer you purchase has at least 512 MB of RAM. If you have extra money to invest in your computer, then consider increasing the RAM to 1 GB or more. The extra money for RAM will be well spent.

Scanner: The most popular scanner purchased with a computer today is the flatbed scanner. When evaluating a flatbed scanner, check the color depth and resolution. Do not buy anything less than a color depth of 48 bits and a resolution of 1200 x 2400 dpi. The higher the color depth, the more accurate the color. A higher resolution picks up the more subtle gradations of color.

Sound Card: Most sound cards today support the Sound Blaster and General MIDI standards and should be capable of recording and playing digital audio. If you plan to turn your computer into an entertainment system or are a game home user, then you will want to spend the extra money and upgrade from the standard sound card.

Speakers: Once you have a good sound card, quality speakers and a separate subwoofer that amplifies the bass frequencies of the speakers can turn your computer into a premium stereo system.

PC Video Camera: A PC video camera is a small camera used to capture and display live video (in some cases with sound), primarily on a Web page. You also can capture, edit, and share video and still photos. The camera sits on your monitor or desk. Recommended minimum specifications include 640 x 480 resolution, a video with a rate of 30 frames per second, and a USB 2.0 or FireWire connection.

USB Flash Drive: If you work on different computers and need access to the same data and information, then this portable miniature mobile storage device is ideal. USB flash drive capacity varies from 16 MB to 4 GB.

Video Graphics Card: Most standard video cards satisfy the monitor display needs of application home and small office users. If you are a game home user or a graphic designer, you will want to upgrade to a higher quality video card. The higher refresh rates will further enhance the display of games, graphics, and movies.

Wireless LAN Access Point: A Wireless LAN Access Point allows you to network several computers, so they can share files and access the Internet through a single cable modem or DSL connection. Each device that you connect requires a wireless card. A Wireless LAN Access Point can offer a range of operations up to several hundred feet, so be sure the device has a high-powered antenna.

Zip Drive: Consider purchasing a Zip drive to back up important files. The Zip drive, which has a capacity of up to 750 MB, is sufficient for most users. An alternative to purchasing a backup drive is to purchase a CD-RW or DVD+RW and burn backups of key files on a CD or DVD.

BASE COMPONENTS

	Application Home User	Game Home User	Small Office/Home Office User	Mobile User	Large Business User	Power User
HARDWARE						
Processor	Pentium 4 at 2.8 GHz	Pentium 4 at 3.0 GHz	Pentium 4 at 3.0 GHz	Pentium 4M at 2.4 GHz	Pentium 4 at 3.4 GHz	Multiple Itanium at 1.6 GHz
RAM	512 MB	1 GB	512 MB	512 MB	1 GB	2 GB
Cache	256 KB L2	512 KB L2	512 KB L2	512 KB L2	512 KB L2	2 MB L3
Hard Disk	80 GB	120 GB	120 GB	60 GB	160 GB	300 GB
Monitor/LCD Flat Panel	17" or 19"	21"	19" or 21"	15.7" Wide Display	19" or 21"	23"
Video Graphics Card	256 MB	512 MB	256 MB	32 MB	128 MB	256 MB
CD/DVD Bay 1	48x CD-ROM	48x CD-RW Drive	48x CD-ROM	24X CD-RW/DVD	48x CD-RW Drive	16x DVD-ROM
CD/DVD Bay 2	8x DVD+RW	12x DVD+RW	8x DVD+RW	4x DVD+RW	12x DVD+RW	8x DVD+RW
Floppy Disk Drive	3.5"	3.5"	3.5"	3.5"	3.5"	3.5"
Printer	Color Ink-Jet	Color Ink-Jet	18 ppm Laser	Portable Ink-Jet	50 ppm Laser	10 ppm Laser
PC Video Camera	Yes	Yes	Yes	Yes	Yes	Yes
Fax/Modem	Yes	Yes	Yes	Yes	Yes	Yes
Microphone	Close-Talk Headset with Gain Adjustment	Close-Talk Headset with Gain Adjustment	Close-Talk Headset with Gain Adjustment	Close-Talk Headset with Gain Adjustment	Close-Talk Headset with Gain Adjustment	Close-Talk Headset with Gain Adjustment
Speakers	Stereo	Full-Dolby Surround	Stereo	Stereo	Stereo	Full-Dolby Surround
Pointing Device	IntelliMouse or Optical Mouse	Laser Mouse and Joystick	IntelliMouse or Optical Mouse	Touchpad or Pointing Stick and Laser Mouse	IntelliMouse or Optical Mouse	IntelliMouse or Laser Mouse and Joystick
Keyboard	Yes	Yes	Yes	Built-In	Yes	Yes
Backup Disk/Tape Drive	250 MB Zip®	External or Removable Hard Disk	External or Removable Hard Disk	External or Removable Hard Disk	Tape Drive	External or Removable Hard Disk
USB Flash Drive	128 MB	256 MB	256 MB	256 MB	4 GB	2 GB
Sound Card	Sound Blaster Compatible	Sound Blaster Audigy 2	Sound Blaster Compatible	Built-In	Sound Blaster Compatible	Sound Blaster Audigy 2
Network Card	Yes	Yes	Yes	Yes	Yes	Yes
TV-Out Connector	Yes	Yes	Yes	Yes	Yes	Yes
USB Port	6	8	6	2	8	8
FireWire Port	2	2	2	1	2	2
SOFTWARE						
Operating System	Windows XP Home Edition with Service Pack 2	Windows XP Home Edition with Service Pack 2	Windows XP Professional with Service Pack 2	Windows XP Professional with Service Pack 2	Windows XP Professional with Service Pack 2	Windows XP Professional with Service Pack 2
Application Suite	Office 2003 Standard Edition	Office 2003 Standard Edition	Office 2003 Small Business Edition	Office2003 Small Business Edition	Office 2003 Professional	Office 2003 Professional
Antivirus	Yes, 12-Mo. Subscription	Yes, 12-Mo. Subscription	Yes, 12-Mo. Subscription	Yes, 12-Mo. Subscription	Yes, 12-Mo. Subscription	Yes, 12-Mo. Subscription
Internet Access	Cable, DSL, or Dial-up	Cable or DSL	Cable, DSL, or Dial-up	Wireless or Dial-up	LAN/WAN (T1/T3)	Cable or DSL
OTHER						
Surge Protector	Yes	Yes	Yes	Portable	Yes	Yes
Warranty	3-Year Limited, 1-Year Next Business Day On-Site Service	3-Year Limited, 1-Year Next Business Day On-Site Service	3-year On-Site Service	3-Year Limited, 1-Year Next Business Day On-Site Service	3-year On-Site Service	3-year On-Site Service
Other		Wheel	Postage Printer	Docking Station Carrying Case Fingerprint Scanner Portable Data Projector		Graphics Tablet Plotter or Large-Format Printer

Optional Components for All Categories	
802.11g Wireless Card	Graphics Tablet
Bluetooth Enabled	iPod Music Player
Biometric Input Device	IrDa Port
Card Reader/Writer	Mouse Pad/Wrist Rest
Digital Camera	Multifunction Peripheral
Digital Video Capture	Photo Printer
Digital Video Camera	Portable Data Projector
Dual-Monitor Support with Second Monitor	Scanner
Ergonomic Keyboard	TV/FM Tuner
External Hard Disk	Uninterruptible Power Supply

FIGURE 5 Base desktop and mobile computer components and optional components. A copy of the Base Components worksheet is on the Data Disk. To obtain a copy of the Data Disk, see the inside cover of this book for instructions.

4 **Consider upgrades to the mouse, keyboard, monitor, printer, microphone, and speakers.**
You use these peripheral devices to interact with your computer, so you should make sure they are up to your standards. Review the peripheral devices listed in Figure 4 on pages 282 and 283 and then visit both local computer dealers and large retail stores to test the computers on display. Ask the salesperson what input and output devices would be best for you and whether you should upgrade beyond what comes standard. Consider purchasing a wireless keyboard and wireless mouse to eliminate bothersome wires on your desktop. A few extra dollars spent on these components when you initially purchase a computer can extend its usefulness by years.

5 **Determine whether you want to use telephone lines or broadband (cable or DSL) to access the Internet.** If your computer has a modem, then you can access the Internet using a standard telephone line. Ordinarily, you call a local or toll-free 800 number to connect to an ISP (see Guideline 6). Using a dial-up Internet connection is relatively inexpensive but slow.

DSL and cable connections provide much faster Internet connections, which are ideal if you want faster file download speeds for software, digital photos, and music. As you would expect, they also are more expensive. DSL, which is available through local telephone companies, also may require that you subscribe to an ISP. Cable is available through your local cable television provider and some online service providers (OSPs). If you get cable, then you would not use a separate Internet service provider or online service provider.

6 **If you are using a dial-up or wireless connection to connect to the Internet, then select an ISP or OSP.** You can access the Internet via telephone lines in one of two ways: an ISP or an OSP. Both provide Internet access for a monthly fee that ranges from $6 to $25. Local ISPs offer Internet access to users in a limited geographic region, through local telephone numbers. National ISPs provide access for users nationwide (including mobile users), through local and toll-free telephone numbers and cable. Because of their size, national ISPs generally offer more services and have a larger technical support staff than local ISPs. OSPs furnish Internet access as well as members-only features for users nationwide. Figure 6 lists several national ISPs and OSPs. Before you choose an ISP or OSP, compare such features as the number of access hours, monthly fees, available services (e-mail, Web page hosting, chat), and reliability.

Company	Service	Web Address
America Online	OSP	aol.com
AT&T Worldnet	ISP	www.att.net
Comcast	OSP	comcast.net
CompuServe	OSP	compuserve.com
EarthLink	ISP	earthlink.net
Juno	OSP	juno.com
NetZero	OSP	netzero.com
MSN	OSP	msn.com
SBC Prodigy	ISP/OSP	prodigy.net

For an updated list of national ISPs and OSPs and their Web site addresses, visit scsite.com/dcf2e/ch7/buyers.

FIGURE 6 National ISPs and OSPs.

7 **Use a worksheet to compare computers, services, and other considerations.** You can use a separate sheet of paper to take notes on each vendor's computer and then summarize the information on a worksheet, such as the one shown in Figure 7. You can use Figure 7 to compare prices for either a PC or a Mac. Most companies advertise a price for a base computer that includes components housed in the system unit (processor, RAM, sound card, video card), disk drives (floppy disk, hard disk, CD-ROM, CD-RW, DVD-ROM, and DVD+RW), a keyboard, mouse, monitor, printer, speakers, and modem. Be aware, however, that some advertisements list prices for computers with only some of these components. Monitors and printers, for example, often are not included in a base computer's price. Depending on how you plan to use the computer, you may want to invest in additional or more powerful components. When you are comparing the prices of computers, make sure you are comparing identical or similar configurations.

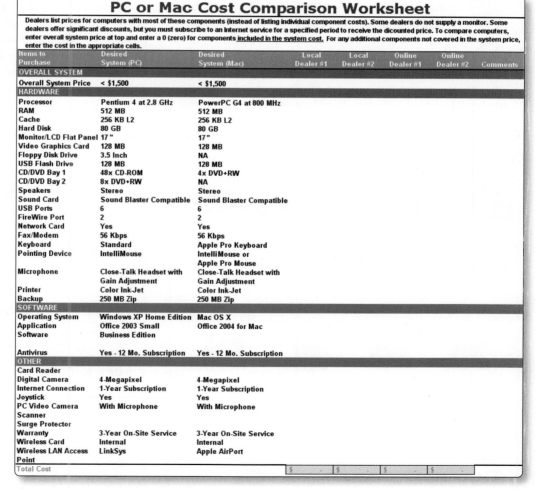

PC or Mac Cost Comparison Worksheet

Dealers list prices for computers with most of these components (instead of listing individual component costs). Some dealers do not supply a monitor. Some dealers offer significant discounts, but you must subscribe to an Internet service for a specified period to receive the dicounted price. To compare computers, enter overall system price at top and enter a 0 (zero) for components included in the system cost. For any additional components not covered in the system price, enter the cost in the appropriate cells.

Items to Purchase	Desired System (PC)	Desired System (Mac)	Local Dealer #1	Local Dealer #2	Online Dealer #1	Online Dealer #2	Comments
OVERALL SYSTEM							
Overall System Price	< $1,500	< $1,500					
HARDWARE							
Processor	Pentium 4 at 2.8 GHz	PowerPC G4 at 800 MHz					
RAM	512 MB	512 MB					
Cache	256 KB L2	256 KB L2					
Hard Disk	80 GB	80 GB					
Monitor/LCD Flat Panel	17 "	17"					
Video Graphics Card	128 MB	128 MB					
Floppy Disk Drive	3.5 Inch	NA					
USB Flash Drive	128 MB	128 MB					
CD/DVD Bay 1	48x CD-ROM	4x DVD+RW					
CD/DVD Bay 2	8x DVD+RW	NA					
Speakers	Stereo	Stereo					
Sound Card	Sound Blaster Compatible	Sound Blaster Compatible					
USB Ports	6	6					
FireWire Port	2	2					
Network Card	Yes	Yes					
Fax/Modem	56 Kbps	56 Kbps					
Keyboard	Standard	Apple Pro Keyboard					
Pointing Device	IntelliMouse	IntelliMouse or Apple Pro Mouse					
Microphone	Close-Talk Headset with Gain Adjustment	Close-Talk Headset with Gain Adjustment					
Printer	Color Ink-Jet	Color Ink-Jet					
Backup	250 MB Zip	250 MB Zip					
SOFTWARE							
Operating System	Windows XP Home Edition	Mac OS X					
Application Software	Office 2003 Small Business Edition	Office 2004 for Mac					
Antivirus	Yes - 12 Mo. Subscription	Yes - 12 Mo. Subscription					
OTHER							
Card Reader							
Digital Camera	4-Megapixel	4-Megapixel					
Internet Connection	1-Year Subscription	1-Year Subscription					
Joystick	Yes	Yes					
PC Video Camera	With Microphone	With Microphone					
Scanner							
Surge Protector							
Warranty	3-Year On-Site Service	3-Year On-Site Service					
Wireless Card	Internal	Internal					
Wireless LAN Access Point	LinkSys	Apple AirPort					
Total Cost			$.	$.	$.	$.	

FIGURE 7 A worksheet is an effective tool for summarizing and comparing components and prices of different computer vendors. A copy of the PC or Mac Cost Comparison Worksheet is on the Data Disk. To obtain a copy of the Data Disk, see the inside cover of this book for instructions.

8 **If you are buying a new computer, you have several purchasing options: buying from your school bookstore, a local computer dealer, a local large retail store, or ordering by mail via telephone or the Web.** Each purchasing option has certain advantages. Many college bookstores, for example, sign exclusive pricing agreements with computer manufacturers and, thus, can offer student discounts. Local dealers and local large retail stores, however, more easily can provide hands-on support. Mail-order companies that sell computers by telephone or online via the Web (Figure 8) often provide the lowest prices, but extend less personal service. Some major mail-order companies, however, have started to provide next-business-day, on-site services. A credit card usually is required to buy from a mail-order company. Figure 9 lists some of the more popular mail-order companies and their Web site addresses.

9 **If you are buying a used computer, stay with name brands such as Dell, Gateway, Hewlett-Packard, and Apple.** Although brand-name equipment can cost more, most brand-name computers have longer, more comprehensive warranties, are better supported, and have more authorized centers for repair services. As with new computers, you can purchase a used computer from local computer dealers, local large retail stores, or mail

order via the telephone or the Web. Classified ads and used computer sellers offer additional outlets for purchasing used computers. Figure 10 lists several major used computer brokers and their Web site addresses.

10 **If you have a computer and are upgrading to a new one, then consider selling or trading in the old one.** If you are a replacement buyer, your older computer still may have value. If you cannot sell the computer through the classified ads, via a Web site, or to a friend, then ask if the computer dealer will buy your old computer. An increasing number of companies are taking trade-ins, but do not expect too much money for your old computer. Other companies offer free disposal of your old PC.

11 **Be aware of hidden costs.** Before purchasing, be sure to consider any additional costs associated with buying a computer, such as an additional telephone line, a cable or DSL modem, an uninterruptible power supply (UPS), computer furniture, a USB flash drive, paper, and computer training classes you may want to take. Depending on where you buy your computer, the seller may be willing to include some or all of these in the computer purchase price.

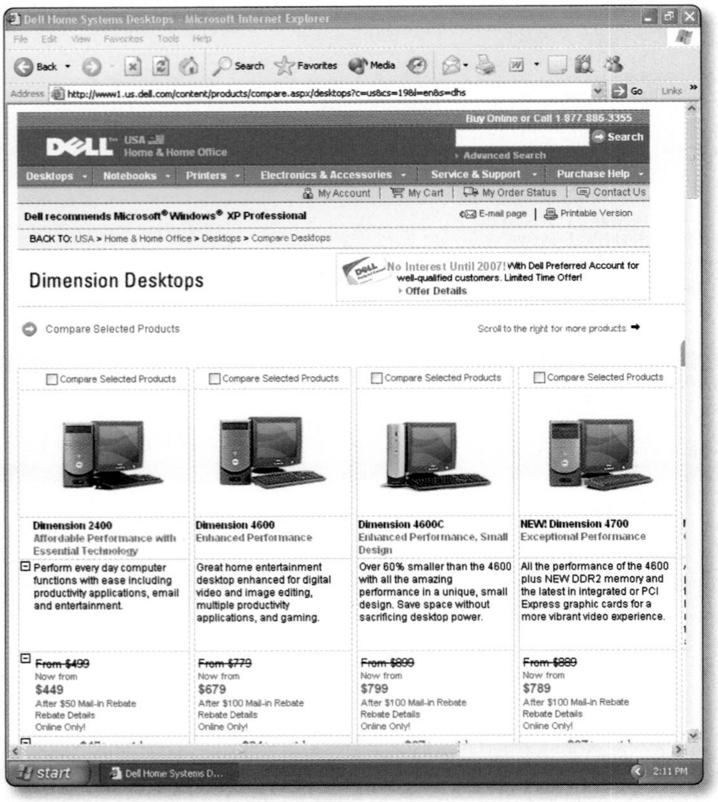

FIGURE 8 Mail-order companies, such as Dell, sell computers online.

Type of Computer	Company	Web Address
PC	CNET Shopper	shopper.cnet.com
	Hewlett-Packard	hp.com
	CompUSA	compusa.com
	Dartek	dartek.com
	Dell	dell.com
	Gateway	gateway.com
Macintosh	Apple Computer	store.apple.com
	ClubMac	clubmac.com
	MacConnection	macconnection.com
	PC & MacExchange	macx.com

For an updated list of new mail-order computer companies and their Web site addresses, visit scsite.com/dcf2e/ch7/buyers.

FIGURE 9 Computer mail-order companies.

Company	Web Address
Amazon.com	amazon.com
Off-Lease Computers	off-leasecomputers.com
American Computer Exchange	www.amcoex.com
U.S. Computer Exchange	usce.org
eBay	ebay.com

For an updated list of used computer mail-order companies and their Web site addresses, visit scsite.com/dcf2e/ch7/buyers.

FIGURE 10 Used computer mail-order companies.

12 **Consider more than just price.** The lowest-cost computer may not be the best long-term buy. Consider such intangibles as the vendor's time in business, the vendor's regard for quality, and the vendor's reputation for support. If you need to upgrade your computer often, you may want to consider a leasing arrangement, in which you pay monthly lease fees, but can upgrade or add on to your computer as your equipment needs change. No matter what type of buyer you are, insist on a 30-day, no-questions-asked return policy on your computer.

13 **Avoid restocking fees.** Some companies charge a restocking fee of 10 to 20 percent as part of their money-back return policy. In some cases, no restocking fee for hardware is applied, but it is applied for software. Ask about the existence and terms of any restocking policies before you buy.

14 **Use a credit card to purchase your new computer.** Many credit cards offer purchase protection and extended warranty benefits that cover you in case of loss of or damage to purchased goods. Paying by credit card also gives you time to install and use the computer before you have to pay for it. Finally, if you are dissatisfied with the computer and are unable to reach an agreement with the seller, paying by credit card gives you certain rights regarding withholding payment until the dispute is resolved. Check your credit card terms for specific details.

15 **Consider purchasing an extended warranty or service plan.** If you use your computer for business or require fast resolution to major computer problems, consider purchasing an extended warranty or a service plan through a local dealer or third-party company. Most extended warranties cover the repair and replacement of computer components beyond the standard warranty. Most service plans ensure that your technical support calls receive priority response from technicians. You also can purchase an on-site service plan that states that a technician will come to your home, work, or school within 24 hours. If your computer includes a warranty and service agreement for a year or less, think about extending the service for two or three years when you buy the computer.

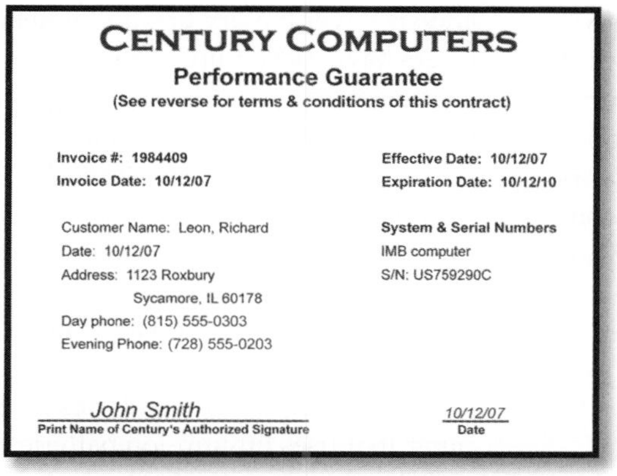

CENTURY COMPUTERS
Performance Guarantee
(See reverse for terms & conditions of this contract)

Invoice #: 1984409 | Effective Date: 10/12/07
Invoice Date: 10/12/07 | Expiration Date: 10/12/10

Customer Name: Leon, Richard | System & Serial Numbers
Date: 10/12/07 | IMB computer
Address: 1123 Roxbury | S/N: US759290C
Sycamore, IL 60178
Day phone: (815) 555-0303
Evening Phone: (728) 555-0203

John Smith
Print Name of Century's Authorized Signature

10/12/07
Date

HOW TO PURCHASE A NOTEBOOK COMPUTER

If you need computing capability when you travel or to use in lecture or meetings, you may find a notebook computer to be an appropriate choice. The guidelines mentioned in the previous section also apply to the purchase of a notebook computer. The following are additional considerations unique to notebook computers.

1 **Purchase a notebook computer with a sufficiently large active-matrix screen.**
Active-matrix screens display high-quality color that is viewable from all angles. Less expensive, passive-matrix screens sometimes are difficult to see in low-light conditions and cannot be viewed from an angle. Notebook computers typically come with a 12.1-inch, 13.3-inch, 14.1-inch, or 15.7-inch display. For most users, a 14.1-inch display is satisfactory. If you intend to use your notebook computer as a desktop computer replacement, however, you may opt for a 15.7-inch display. Notebook computers with these larger displays weigh seven to ten pounds, however, so if you travel a lot and portability is essential, you might want a lighter computer with a smaller display. The lightest notebook computers, which weigh less than 3 pounds, are equipped with a 12.1-inch display. Regardless of size, the resolution of the display should be at least 1024 x 768 pixels. To compare the monitor size on various notebook computers, visit the company Web sites in Figure 11.

Type of Notebook	Company	Web Address
PC	Acer	global.acer.com
	Dell	dell.com
	Fujitsu	fujitsu.com
	Gateway	gateway.com
	Hewlett-Packard	hp.com
	IBM	ibm.com
	NEC	nec.com
	Sony	sony.com
	Toshiba	toshiba.com
Mac	Apple	apple.com

For an updated list of companies and their Web site addresses, visit scsite.com/dcf2e/ch7/buyers.

FIGURE 11 Companies that sell notebook computers.

2 **Experiment with different keyboards and pointing devices.** Notebook computer keyboards are far less standardized than those for desktop computers. Some notebook computers, for example, have wide wrist rests, while others have none. Notebook computers also use a range of pointing devices, including pointing sticks, touchpads, and trackballs. Before you purchase a notebook computer, try various types of keyboard and pointing devices to determine which is easiest for you to use. Regardless of the pointing device you select, you also may want to purchase a regular mouse to use when you are working at a desk or other large surface.

3 **Make sure the notebook computer you purchase has a CD and/or DVD drive.** Loading and installing software, especially large Office suites, is much faster if done from a CD-ROM, CD-RW, DVD-ROM, or DVD+RW. Today, most notebook computers come with an internal or external CD-ROM drive. Some notebook computers even come with a CD-ROM drive and a CD-RW drive or a DVD-ROM drive and a CD-RW or DVD+RW drive. Although DVD drives are slightly more expensive, they allow you to play CDs and DVD movies using your notebook computer and a headset.

4 **If necessary, upgrade the processor, memory, and disk storage at the time of purchase.** As with a desktop computer, upgrading your notebook computer's memory and disk storage usually is less expensive at the time of initial purchase. Some disk storage is custom designed for notebook computer manufacturers, meaning an upgrade might not be available in the future. If you are purchasing a lightweight notebook computer, then it should include at least a 2.4 GHz processor, 512 MB RAM, and 80 GB of storage.

5 **The availability of built-in ports on a notebook computer is important.** A notebook computer does not have a lot of room to add adapter cards. If you know the purpose for which you plan to use your notebook computer, then you can determine the ports you will need. Most notebooks come with common ports, such as a mouse port, IrDA port, serial port, parallel port, video port, and USB port. If you plan to connect your notebook computer to a TV, however, then you will need a PCtoTV port. If you want to connect to networks at school or in various offices, make sure the notebook computer you purchase has a built-in network card. If your notebook computer does not come with a built-in network wireless card, then you will have to purchase an external network card that slides into an expansion slot in your notebook computer, as well as a network cable. If you expect to connect an iPod portable digital music player to your notebook computer, then you will need a FireWire port.

6 **If you plan to use your notebook computer for note-taking at school or in meetings, consider a notebook computer that converts to a Tablet PC.** Some computer manufacturers have developed convertible notebook computers that allow the screen to rotate 180 degrees on a central hinge and then fold down to cover the keyboard and become a Tablet PC (Figure 12). You then can use a stylus to enter text or drawings into the computer by writing on the screen.

FIGURE 12 The Toshiba Protégé M200 notebook computer converts to a Tablet PC.

7 **Consider purchasing a notebook computer with a built-in wireless card to connect to your home network.** Many users today are setting up wireless home networks. With a wireless home network, the desktop computer functions as the server, and your notebook computer can access the desktop computer from any location in the house to share files and hardware, such as a printer, and browse the Web. If your notebook computer does not come with a built-in wireless card, you can purchase an external one that slides into your notebook computer. Most home wireless networks allow connections from distances of 150 to 800 feet.

8 **If you are going to use your notebook computer for long periods without access to an electrical outlet, purchase a second battery.** The trend among notebook computer users today is power and size over battery life, and notebook computer manufacturers have picked up on this. Many notebook computer users today are willing to give up longer battery life for a larger screen, faster processor, and more storage. In addition, some manufacturers typically sell the notebook with the lowest capacity battery. For this reason, you need to be careful in choosing a notebook computer if you plan to use it without access to electrical outlets for long periods, such as an airplane flight. You also might want to purchase a second battery as a backup. If you anticipate running your notebook computer on batteries frequently, choose a computer that uses lithium-ion batteries, which last longer than nickel cadmium or nickel hydride batteries.

9 **Purchase a well-padded and well-designed carrying case.** An amply padded carrying case will protect your notebook computer from the bumps it will receive while traveling. A well-designed carrying case will have room for accessories such as spare floppy disks, CDs and DVDs, a user manual, pens, and paperwork (Figure 13).

FIGURE 13
A well-designed notebook computer carrying case.

10 **If you travel overseas, obtain a set of electrical and telephone adapters.** Different countries use different outlets for electrical and telephone connections. Several manufacturers sell sets of adapters that will work in most countries.

11 **If you plan to connect your notebook computer to a video projector, make sure the notebook computer is compatible with the video projector.** You should check, for example, to be sure that your notebook computer will allow you to display an image on the computer screen and projection device at the same time (Figure 14). Also, ensure that your notebook computer has the ports required to connect to the video projector.

12 **For improved security, consider a fingerprint scanner.** More than a quarter of a million notebook computers are stolen or lost each year. If you have critical information stored on your notebook computer, then consider purchasing one with a fingerprint scanner (Figure 15) to protect the data if your computer is stolen or lost. Fingerprint security offers a level of protection that extends well beyond the standard password protection.

FIGURE 15 Fingerprint scanner technology offers greater security than passwords.

FIGURE 14
A notebook computer connected to a video projector projects the image displayed on the screen.

HOW TO PURCHASE A TABLET PC

The Tablet PC (Figure 16) combines the mobility features of a traditional notebook computer with the simplicity of pencil and paper, because you can create and save Office-type documents by writing and drawing directly on the screen with a digital pen. Tablet PCs use the Windows XP Tablet PC Edition operating system, which expands on Windows XP Professional by including digital pen and speech capabilities. A notebook computer and a Tablet PC have many similarities. For this reason, if you are considering purchasing a Tablet PC, review the guidelines for purchasing a notebook computer, as well as the guidelines below.

FIGURE 16 The lightweight Tablet PC, with its handwriting capabilities, is the latest addition to the family of mobile computers.

1 **Make sure the Tablet PC fits your mobile computing needs.** The Tablet PC is not for every mobile user. If you find yourself in need of a computer in class or you are spending more time in meetings than in your office, then the Tablet PC may be the answer. Before you invest money in a Tablet PC, however, determine the programs you plan to use on it. You should not buy a Tablet PC simply because it is a new and interesting type of computer. For additional information on the Tablet PC, visit the Web sites listed in Figure 17. You may have to use the search capabilities on the home page of the companies listed to locate information about the Tablet PC.

Company	Web Address
Fujitsu	fujitsu.com
Hewlett-Packard	hp.com
Microsoft	microsoft.com/windowsxp/tabletpc
ViewSonic	viewsonic.com

For an updated list of companies and their Web site addresses, visit scsite.com/dcf2e/ch7/buyers.

FIGURE 17 Companies involved with Tablet PCs and their Web sites.

2 **Decide whether you want a convertible or pure Tablet PC.** Convertible Tablet PCs have an attached keyboard and look like a notebook computer. You rotate the screen and lay it flat against the computer for note-taking. The pure Tablet PCs are slim and lightweight, weighing less than four pounds. They have the capability of easily docking at a desktop to gain access to a large monitor, keyboard, and mouse. If you spend a lot of time attending lectures or meetings, then the pure Tablet PC is ideal. Acceptable specifications for a Tablet PC are shown in Figure 18.

TABLET PC SPECIFICATIONS

Dimensions	12" × 9" × 1.2"
Weight	Less than 4 Pounds
Processor	Pentium III processor-M at 1.33 GHz
RAM	512 MB
Hard Disk	40 GB
Display	12.1" XGA TFT
Digitizer	Electromagnetic Digitizer
Battery	4-Cell (3-Hour)
USB	2
FireWire	1
Docking Station	Grab and Go with CD-ROM, Keyboard, and Mouse
Bluetooth Port	Yes
Wireless	802.11b/g Card
Network Card	10/100 Ethernet
Modem	56 Kbps
Speakers	Internal
Microphone	Internal
Operating System	Windows XP Tablet PC Edition
Application Software	Office Small Business Edition
Antivirus Software	Yes – 12 Month Subscription
Warranty	1-Year Limited Warranty Parts and Labor

FIGURE 18 Tablet PC specifications.

3 **Be sure the weight and dimensions are conducive to portability.** The weight and dimensions of the Tablet PC are important because you carry it around like a notepad. The Tablet PC you buy should weigh four pounds or less. Its dimensions should be approximately 12 inches by 9 inches by 1.2 inches.

4 **Port availability, battery life, and durability are even more important with a Tablet PC than they are with a notebook computer.** Make sure the Tablet PC you purchase has the ports required for the applications you plan to run. As with any mobile computer, battery life is important especially if you plan to use your Tablet PC for long periods without access to an electrical outlet. A Tablet PC must be durable because if you use it the way it was designed to be used, then you will be handling it much like you handle a pad of paper.

5 **Experiment with different models of the Tablet PC to find the digital pen that works best for you.** The key to making use of the Tablet PC is to be comfortable with its handwriting capabilities and on-screen keyboard. Not only is the digital pen used to write on the screen (Figure 19), you also use it to make gestures to complete tasks, in a manner similar to the way you use a mouse. Figure 20 compares the standard point-and-click of a mouse with the gestures made with a digital pen. Other gestures with the digital pen replicate some of the commonly used keys on a keyboard.

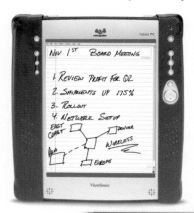

FIGURE 19 A Tablet PC lets you handwrite notes and draw on the screen using a digital pen.

Mouse	Digital Pen
Point	Point
Click	Tap
Double-click	Double-tap
Right-click	Tap and hold
Click and drag	Drag

FIGURE 20 Standard point-and-click of a mouse compared with the gestures made with a digital pen.

6 **Check out the comfort level of handwriting in different positions.** You should be able to handwrite on a Tablet PC with your hand resting on the screen. You also should be able to handwrite holding the Tablet PC in one hand, as well as with it sitting in your lap.

7 **Make sure the LCD display device has a resolution high enough to take advantage of Microsoft's ClearType technologies.** Tablet PCs use a digitizer under a standard 10.4-inch motion-sensitive LCD display to make the digital ink on the screen look like real ink on paper. To ensure you get the maximum benefits from the new ClearType technology, make sure the LCD display has a resolution of 800 × 600 in landscape mode and a 600 × 800 in portrait mode.

8 **Test the built-in Tablet PC microphone and speakers.** With many application software packages recognizing human speech, such as Microsoft Office, it is important that the Tablet PC's built-in microphone operates at an acceptable level. If the microphone is not to your liking, you may want to purchase a close-talk headset with your Tablet PC. Increasingly more users are sending information as audio files, rather than relying solely on text. For this reason, you also should check the speakers on the Tablet PC to make sure they meet your standards.

9 **Consider a Tablet PC with a built-in PC video camera.** A PC video camera adds streaming video and still photography capabilities to your Tablet PC, while still allowing you to take notes in lectures or meetings.

10 **Review the docking capabilities of the Tablet PC.** The Microsoft Windows XP Tablet PC Edition operating system supports a grab-and-go form of docking, so you can pick up and take a docked Tablet PC with you, just as you would pick up a notepad on your way to a meeting (Figure 21).

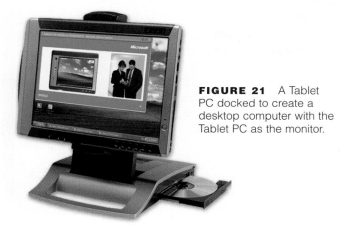

FIGURE 21 A Tablet PC docked to create a desktop computer with the Tablet PC as the monitor.

11 **Wireless access to the Internet and your e-mail is essential with a Tablet PC.** Make sure the Tablet PC has wireless networking, so you can access the Internet and your e-mail anytime and anywhere. Your Tablet PC also should include standard network connections, such as dial-up and Ethernet connections.

12 **Review available accessories to purchase with your Tablet PC.** Tablet PC accessories include docking stations, mouse units, keyboards, security cables, additional memory and storage, protective handgrips, screen protectors, and various types of digital pens.

HOW TO PURCHASE A PERSONAL MOBILE DEVICE

Whether you choose a PDA, smart phone, or smart pager depends on where, when, and how you will use the device. If you need to stay organized when you are on the go, then a PDA may be the right choice. PDAs typically are categorized by the operating system they run. If you need to stay organized and in touch when on the go, then a smart phone or smart pager may be the right choice. Just as with PDAs, smart phones, and smart pagers are categorized by the operating system they run. The six primary operating systems for these devices are the Palm OS, Windows Mobile for Pocket PC, Windows Mobile for Smartphone, Symbian OS, Blackberry, and Embedded Linux.

This section lists guidelines you should consider when purchasing a PDA, smart phone, or smart pager. You also should visit the Web sites listed in Figure 22 to gather more information about the type of personal mobile device that best suits your computing needs.

1 **Determine the programs you plan to run on your device.** All PDAs and most smart phones and smart pagers can handle basic organizer-type software such as a calendar, address book, and notepad. The availability of other software depends on the operating system you choose. The depth and breadth of software for the Palm OS is significant, with more than 20,000 basic programs and over 600 wireless programs. Devices that run Windows-based operating systems, such as Windows Mobile or Windows Smartphone, may have fewer programs available, but the operating system and application software are similar to those with which you are familiar, such as Word and Excel. Some Symbian-based smart phones also include the capability to read and/or edit Microsoft Office documents.

2 **Consider how much you want to pay.** The price of a personal mobile device can range from $100 to $800, depending on its capabilities. Some Palm OS devices are at the lower end of the cost spectrum, and Windows-based devices often are at the higher end. For the latest prices, capabilities, and accessories, visit the Web sites listed in Figure 22.

Web Site	Web Address
Hewlett-Packard	hp.com
CNET Shopper	shopper.cnet.com
palmOne	palmone.com
Microsoft	windowsmobile.com pocketpc.com microsoft.com/smartphone
PDA Buyers Guide	pdabuyersguide.com
Research in Motion	rim.com
Danger	danger.com
Symbian	symbian.com
Wireless Developer Network	wirelessdevnet.com
Sharp	myzaurus.com

For an updated list of reviews and information about personal mobile devices and their Web addresses, visit scsite.com/dcf2e/ch7/buyers.

FIGURE 22 Web site reviews and information about personal mobile devices.

3 **Determine whether you need wireless access to the Internet and e-mail or mobile telephone capabilities with your device.** Smart pagers give you access to e-mail and other data and Internet services. Smart phones typically include these features, but also include the ability to make and receive phone calls on cellular networks. Some PDAs and smart phones include wireless networking capability to allow you to connect to the Internet wirelessly. These wireless features and services allow personal mobile device users to access real-time information from anywhere to help make decisions while on the go.

4 **For wireless devices, determine how and where you will use the service.** When purchasing a wireless device, you must subscribe to a wireless service. Determine if the wireless network (carrier) you choose has service in the area where you plan to use the device. Some networks have high-speed data networks only in certain areas, such as large cities or business districts. Also, a few carriers allow you to use your device in other countries.

When purchasing a smart phone, determine if you plan to use the device more as a phone, PDA, or wireless data device. Some smart phones, such as those based on the Pocket PC Phone edition or the Palm OS, are geared more for use as a PDA and have a PDA form factor. Other smart phones, such as those based on Microsoft Smartphone or Symbian operating systems, mainly are phone devices that include robust PDA functionality. RIM Blackberry-based smart phones include robust data features that are oriented to accessing e-mail and wireless data services.

5 **Make sure your device has enough memory.** Memory (RAM) is not a major issue with low-end devices with monochrome displays and basic organizer functions. Memory is a major issue, however, for high-end devices that have color displays and wireless features. Without enough memory, the performance level of your device will drop dramatically. If you plan to purchase a high-end device running the Palm OS operating system, the device should have at least 16 MB of RAM. If you plan to purchase a high-end device running the Windows Mobile operating system, the PDA should have at least 48 MB of RAM.

6 **Practice with the touch screen, handwriting recognition, and built-in keyboard before deciding on a model.** To enter data into a PDA or smart phone, you use a pen-like stylus to handwrite on the screen or a keyboard. The keyboard either slides out or is mounted on the front of the device. With handwriting recognition, the device translates the handwriting into a computerized font. You also can use the stylus as a pointing device to select items on the screen and enter data by tapping on an on-screen keyboard. By practicing data entry before buying a device, you can learn if one device may be easier for you to use than another. You also can buy third-party software to improve a device's handwriting recognition.

7 **Decide whether you want a color display.** Pocket PC devices usually come with a color display that supports as many as 65,536 colors. Palm OS devices also have a color display, but the less expensive models display in 4 to 16 shades of gray. Symbian- and Blackberry-based devices also have the option for color displays. Having a color display does result in greater on-screen detail, but it also requires more memory and uses more power. Resolution also influences the quality of the display.

8 **Compare battery life.** Any mobile device is good only if it has the power required to run. For example, Palm OS devices with monochrome screens typically have a much longer battery life than Pocket PC devices with color screens. The use of wireless networking will shorten battery time considerably. To help alleviate this problem, most devices have incorporated rechargeable batteries that can be recharged by placing the device in a cradle or connecting it to a charger.

9 **Seriously consider the importance of ergonomics.** Will you put the device in your pocket, a carrying case, or wear it on your belt? How does it feel in your hand? Will you use it indoors or outdoors? Many screens are unreadable outdoors. Do you need extra ruggedness, such as would be required in construction, in a plant, or in a warehouse?

10 **Check out the accessories.** Determine which accessories you want for your personal mobile device. Accessories include carrying cases, portable mini- and full-sized keyboards, removable storage, modems, synchronization cradles and cables, car chargers, wireless communications, global positioning system modules, digital camera modules, expansion cards, dashboard mounts, replacement styli, hands-free headsets, and more.

11 **Decide whether you want additional functionality.** In general, off-the-shelf Microsoft operating system-based devices have broader functionality than devices with other operating systems. For example, voice-recording capability, e-book players, MP3 players, and video players are standard on most Pocket PC devices. If you are leaning towards a Palm OS device and want these additional functions, you may need to purchase additional software or expansion modules to add them later. Determine whether your employer permits devices with cameras on the premises, and if not, do not consider devices with cameras.

12 **Determine whether synchronization of data with other devices or personal computers is important.** Most devices come with a cradle that connects to the USB or serial port on your computer so you can synchronize data on your device with your desktop or notebook computer. Increasingly more devices are Bluetooth and/or wireless networking enabled, which gives them the capability of synchronizing wirelessly. Many devices today also have an infrared port that allows you to synchronize data with any device that has a similar infrared port, including desktop and notebook computers or other personal mobile devices.

CHAPTER 8

Communications and Networks

OBJECTIVES

After completing this chapter, you will be able to:

1. Discuss the components required for successful communications
2. Describe uses of computer communications
3. Differentiate among types of networks
4. Explain the purpose of communications software
5. Describe various types of lines for communications over the telephone network
6. Describe commonly used communications devices
7. Discuss different ways to set up a home network
8. Identify various physical and wireless transmission media

CONTENTS

COMMUNICATIONS

USES OF COMPUTER COMMUNICATIONS
Internet, Web, E-Mail, Instant Messaging, Chat Rooms, Newsgroups, Internet Telephony, FTP, Web Folders, Video Conferencing, and Fax
Wireless Messaging Services
Public Internet Access Points
Global Positioning System
Collaboration
Groupware
Voice Mail
Web Services

NETWORKS
LANs, MANs, and WANs
Network Architectures
Network Topologies
Intranets
Network Communications Standards

COMMUNICATIONS SOFTWARE

COMMUNICATIONS OVER THE TELEPHONE NETWORK
Dial-Up Lines
Dedicated Lines

COMMUNICATIONS DEVICES
Dial-Up Modems
ISDN and DSL Modems
Cable Modems
Wireless Modems
Network Cards
Wireless Access Points
Routers

HOME NETWORKS
Wired Home Networks
Wireless Home Networks

COMMUNICATIONS CHANNEL

PHYSICAL TRANSMISSION MEDIA
Twisted-Pair Cable
Coaxial Cable
Fiber-Optic Cable

WIRELESS TRANSMISSION MEDIA
Infrared
Broadcast Radio
Cellular Radio
Microwaves
Communications Satellite

CHAPTER SUMMARY

COMPANIES ON THE CUTTING EDGE
Cisco Systems
QUALCOMM

TECHNOLOGY TRAILBLAZERS
Robert Metcalfe
Patricia Russo

COMMUNICATIONS

Computer **communications** describes a process in which two or more computers or devices transfer data, instructions, and information. Figure 8-1 shows a sample communications system. Some communications involve cables and wires; others are sent wirelessly through the air. As illustrated in this figure, communications systems contain all types of computers and computing devices. For successful communications, you need the following:

- A **sending device** that initiates an instruction to transmit data, instructions, or information.
- A communications device that connects the sending device to a communications channel.
- A **communications channel**, or transmission media on which the data, instructions, or information travel.
- A communications device that connects the communications channel to a receiving device.
- A **receiving device** that accepts the transmission of data, instructions, or information.

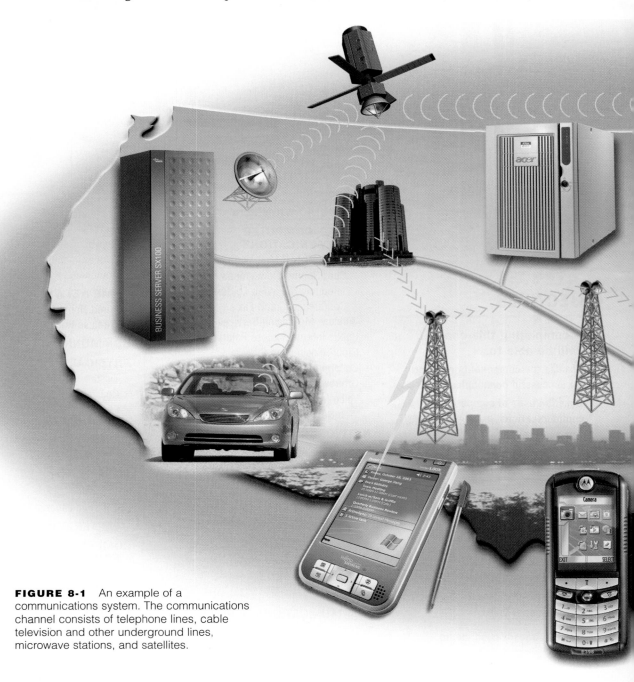

FIGURE 8-1 An example of a communications system. The communications channel consists of telephone lines, cable television and other underground lines, microwave stations, and satellites.

All types of computers and mobile devices serve as sending and receiving devices in a communications system. This includes mainframe computers, servers, desktop computers, notebook computers, Tablet PCs, smart phones, PDAs, and GPS receivers. One type of communications device that connects a communications channel to a sending or receiving device such as a computer is a modem. Two examples of communications channels are cable television lines and telephone lines.

USES OF COMPUTER COMMUNICATIONS

Computer communications are everywhere. Many require that users subscribe to an Internet access provider. With other computer communications, an organization such as a business or school provides communications services to employees, students, or customers. The following pages discuss a variety of computer communications.

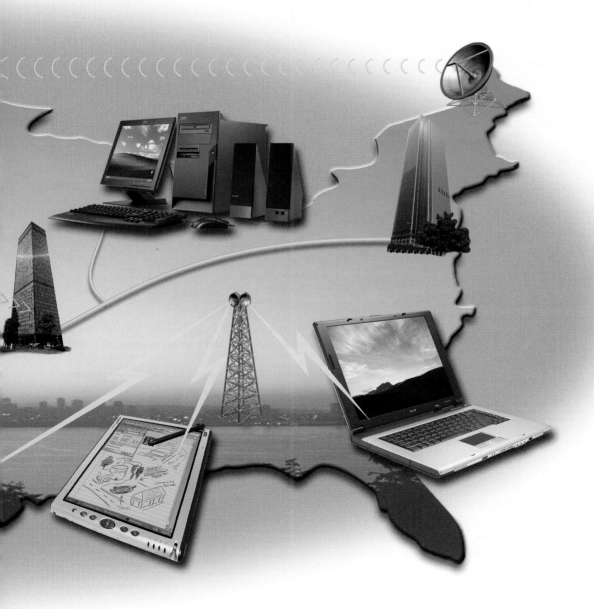

Internet, Web, E-Mail, Instant Messaging, Chat Rooms, Newsgroups, Internet Telephony, FTP, Web Folders, Video Conferencing, and Fax

Previous chapters discussed many uses of computer communications as they related to a particular topic. In the course of a day, it is likely you use, or use information generated by, one or more of the previously discussed communications technologies, which are outlined in Figure 8-2.

The following pages discuss a variety of other uses of communications that have not been discussed previously. These include wireless messaging services, public Internet access points, global positioning systems, groupware, collaboration, voice mail, and Web services.

PREVIOUSLY DISCUSSED USES OF COMMUNICATIONS

Internet   Worldwide collection of networks that links millions of businesses, government agencies, educational institutions, and individuals

Web   Worldwide collection of electronic documents on the Internet that users access through a Web browser

E-Mail   Transmission of messages and files via a computer network

Instant Messaging   Real-time Internet communications service that notifies you when one or more people are online and then allows you to exchange messages, pictures, files, audio, and video

Chat Rooms   Real-time typed conversation that takes place on a computer connected to a network that also may allow the exchange of messages, pictures, files, audio, and video

Newsgroups   Online areas in which users have written discussions about a particular subject

Internet Telephony   Conversation that takes place over the Internet using a telephone connected to a desktop computer, mobile computer, or mobile device

FTP   Internet standard that permits users to upload and download files to and from FTP servers on the Internet

Web Folders   Location on a Web server to which users publish documents and other files

Video Conferencing   Real-time meeting between two or more geographically separated people who use a network to transmit audio and video data

Fax Machine or Computer Fax/Modem   Transmits and receives documents over telephone lines

---

FIGURE 8-2   Uses of communications discussed in earlier chapters.

Wireless Messaging Services

Users can send and receive wireless messages to and from smart phones, cellular telephones, or PDAs using three techniques: text messaging, wireless instant messaging, and picture messaging (Figure 8-3).

TEXT MESSAGING   A mobile device with **text messaging**, also called SMS (short message service), capability allows users to send and receive short text messages on a smart phone or PDA. Text messaging services typically provide users with several options for sending and receiving messages:
- Mobile to Mobile: send the message from your mobile device to another mobile device
- Mobile to E-Mail: send the message from your mobile device to an e-mail address anywhere in the world
- Web to Mobile: send the message from a text messaging Web site to a mobile device

WIRELESS INSTANT MESSAGING   Wireless instant messaging (IM) is a real-time Internet communications service that allows wireless mobile devices to exchange messages with one or more mobile devices or online users. Some wireless Internet service providers partner with IM services so you can use your smart phone or PDA to send and receive wireless instant messages. With a compatible IM service, users have these IM options:
- Mobile to Mobile: use a wireless instant messenger to communicate between two mobile devices
- Mobile to Personal Computer: use a wireless instant messenger to communicate between a mobile device and a personal computer

PICTURE MESSAGING   Users can send graphics, pictures, video clips, and sound files, as well as short text messages with **picture messaging**, also called MMS (multimedia message service) to another smart phone or PDA or computer (read At Issue 8-1 for a related discussion). Picture messaging services typically provide users these options for sending and receiving messages:

- Mobile to Mobile: send the picture from your mobile device to another mobile device
- Mobile to E-Mail: send the picture from your mobile device to an e-mail address anywhere in the world

FIGURE 8-3   Users can send and receive text messages, wireless instant messages, and picture messages to and from their smart phones and other computers and devices.

AT ISSUE 8-1

High-Tech Cheating via Wireless Messaging Services

Several schools have banned student cellular telephones claiming that they disrupt classes and sometimes are used for illegal activities, such as drug sales. Now, schools may have another reason to prohibit cellular telephones and other wireless devices among students.

Once, teachers only had to watch test-takers to make sure that no one was copying from a neighbor's paper or secretly referring to notes concealed under a desk. Recently, however, students were caught using their cellular phones' messaging service to send each other answers to test questions. Others have been caught using camera-enabled cellular phones to take pictures of tests and forwarding the images to other students who were scheduled to take the test at a later time. Some teachers fear that more students soon may be using wireless devices to communicate covertly with classmates during a test, or even to receive messages from sources outside the classroom. To eliminate this high-tech method of cheating, should cellular telephones, digital cameras, notebook computers, Tablet PCs, PDAs, and other wireless devices be banned during lectures and exams? Why or why not? Short of banning these devices, what, if anything, can schools do to prevent students from using them to cheat? Should schools seek a point of compromise so that they can both embrace the new technology and control it?

Public Internet Access Points

In many public locations, people connect wirelessly to the Internet through a **public Internet access point** using mobile computers or other devices. Two types of public Internet access points are hot spots and cybercafés.

A **hot spot** is a wireless network that provides Internet connections to mobile computers and other devices. Through the hot spot, mobile users check e-mail, browse the Web, and access any service on the Internet — as long as their computers or devices have built-in wireless capability or the appropriate wireless network card or PC Card (Figure 8-4). Hot spots are appearing in airports, hotels, schools, shopping malls, bookstores, restaurants, and coffee shops. Most hot spots span from 100 to 300 feet; some can extend to 15 miles and cover entire cities.

Some hot spots provide free Internet access, some charge a per-use fee, and others require users to subscribe to a wireless Internet service provider, to which they pay per access fees, daily fees, or a monthly fee. Per access fees average $3, daily fees range from $5 to $20, and monthly fees range from $30 to $50 for unlimited access.

When mobile users travel without their notebook computer or Internet-enabled mobile device, they can visit a cybercafé to access e-mail, the Web, and other Internet services. A **cybercafé** is a coffee house or restaurant that provides personal computers with Internet access to its customers. More than 6,300 cybercafés exist in cities around the world. Although some provide free Internet access, most charge a per-hour or per-minute fee. Some cybercafés also are hot spots.

WEB LINK 8-1

Hot Spots

For more information, visit scsite.com/dcf2e/ch8/weblink and then click Hot Spots.

FIGURE 8-4   Mobile users in this hot spot access the Internet through their notebook computers. One computer uses a wireless network PC Card. The other has Intel's built-in wireless Centrino technology.

Global Positioning System

A **global positioning system** (**GPS**) is a navigation system that consists of one or more earth-based receivers that accept and analyze signals sent by satellites in order to determine the receiver's geographic location (Figure 8-5). A GPS receiver is a handheld, mountable, or embedded device that contains an antenna, a radio receiver, and a processor. Many include a screen display that shows an individual's location on a map.

Many mobile devices such as PDAs and smart phones have GPS capability built into the device or as an add-on feature. Some users carry a handheld GPS receiver; others mount a receiver to an object such as an automobile, boat, airplane, farm and construction equipment, or computer.

The first and most used application of GPS technology is to assist people with determining where they are located. The data obtained from a GPS, however, can be applied to a variety of other uses: creating a map, ascertaining the best route between two points, locating a lost person or stolen object, or monitoring the movement of a person or object. Many vehicles use GPSs to provide drivers with directions or other information.

WEB LINK 8-2

GPS

For more information, visit scsite.com/dcf2e/ch8/weblink and then click GPS.

FIGURE 8-5   HOW A GPS WORKS

Step 1:
GPS satellites orbit Earth. Every thousandth of a second, each satellite sends a signal that indicates its current position to the GPS receiver.

L O C A T E   M E

Step 2:
A GPS receiver (such as in a car, a watch, a smart phone, a handheld device, or a collar) determines its location on Earth by analyzing at least 3 separate satellite signals from the 24 satellites in orbit.

Collaboration

Many software products provide a means to **collaborate**, or work online, with other users connected to a server. With Microsoft Office, for example, users can conduct online meetings (Figure 8-6). An online meeting allows users to share documents with others in real time. That is, all participants see the document at the same time. As someone changes the document, everyone in the meeting sees the changes being made. During the online meeting, participants have the ability to open a separate window and type messages to one another.

Instead of interacting in a live meeting, many users collaborate via e-mail. For example, if users want others to review a document, they can attach a routing slip to the document and send it via e-mail to everyone on the routing slip. When the first person on the routing slip receives the document, he or she may add comments to the document. As changes are made to the document, both the original text and the changes are displayed. When subsequent persons on the routing slip receive the document via e-mail, they see all the previous users' changes and can make additional changes. Once everyone on the routing slip has reviewed the document, it automatically returns to the sender.

Groupware

Groupware is software that helps groups of people work together on projects and share information over a network. Groupware is a component of a broad concept called workgroup computing, which includes network hardware and software that enables group members to communicate, manage projects, schedule meetings, and make group decisions. To assist with these activities, most groupware provides personal information manager (PIM) functions, such as an electronic appointment calendar, an address book, and a notepad. A major feature of groupware is group scheduling, in which a group calendar tracks the schedules of multiple users and helps coordinate appointments and meeting times.

Voice Mail

Voice mail, which functions much like an answering machine, allows someone to leave a voice message for one or more people. Unlike answering machines, however, a computer in the voice mail system converts an analog voice message into digital form. Once digitized, the message is stored in a voice mailbox. A voice mailbox is a storage location on a hard disk in the voice mail system.

Web Services

Web services describe standardized software that enables programmers to create applications that communicate with other remote computers over the Internet or over an internal business network. Businesses are the primary users of Web services because this technology provides a means for departments to communicate with each other, suppliers, vendors, and with clients. For example, third-party vendors can use Web services to communicate with their online retailer's Web site to manage their inventory levels.

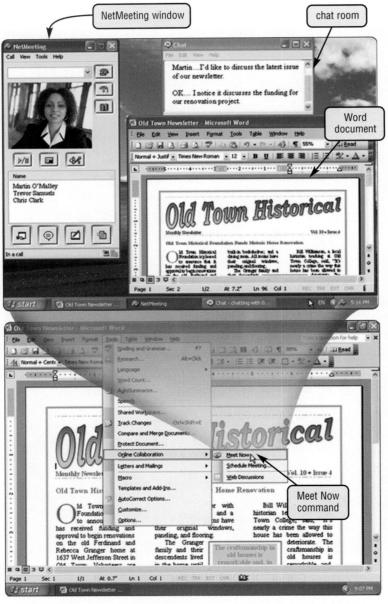

FIGURE 8-6   When you start an online meeting from a Microsoft Office product, the participants use NetMeeting to collaborate on the document.

Test your knowledge of pages 296 through 302 in Quiz Yourself 8-1.

NETWORKS

As discussed in Chapter 1, a **network** is a collection of computers and devices connected together via communications devices and transmission media. Many businesses network their computers together to facilitate communications, share hardware, share data and information, share software, and transfer funds.

A network can be internal to an organization or span the world by connecting itself to the Internet. Instead of using the Internet or an internal network, some companies hire a value-added network provider for network functions. A **value-added network** (**VAN**) is a third-party business that provides networking services for a fee.

Networks facilitate communications among users and allow users to share resources with other users. Some examples of resources are data, information, hardware, and software.

LANs, MANs, and WANs

Networks usually are classified as a local area network, metropolitan area network, or wide area network. The main differentiation among these classifications is their area of coverage, as described in the following paragraphs.

LAN A **local area network** (**LAN**) is a network that connects computers and devices in a limited geographical area such as a home, school computer laboratory, office building, or closely positioned group of buildings. Each computer or device on the network, called a node, often shares resources such as printers, large hard disks, and programs. Often, the nodes are connected via cables. A **wireless LAN** (**WLAN**) is a LAN that uses no physical wires. Very often, a WLAN communicates with a wired LAN for access to its resources (Figure 8-7).

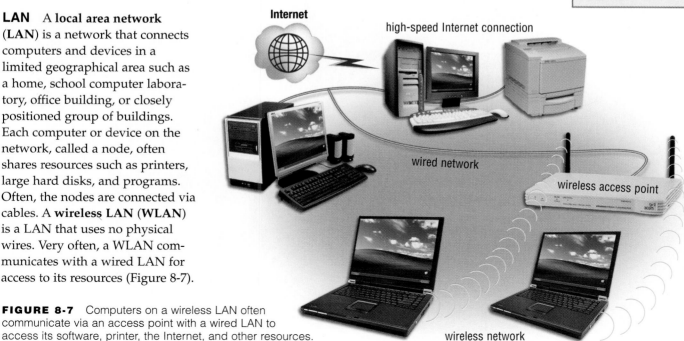

FIGURE 8-7 Computers on a wireless LAN often communicate via an access point with a wired LAN to access its software, printer, the Internet, and other resources.

MAN A **metropolitan area network** (**MAN**) is a high-speed network that connects local area networks in a metropolitan area such as a city or town and handles the bulk of communications activity across that region. A MAN typically includes one or more LANs, but covers a smaller geographic area than a WAN. The state of Pennsylvania, for example, has a MAN that connects state agencies and individual users in the region around the state capital.

A MAN usually is managed by a consortium of users or by a single network provider that sells the service to the users. Local and state governments, for example, regulate some MANs. Telephone companies, cable television operators, and other organizations provide users with connections to the MAN.

WAN A **wide area network** (**WAN**) is a network that covers a large geographic area (such as a city, country, or the world) using a communications channel that combines many types of media such as telephone lines, cables, and radio waves (Figure 8-8). A WAN can be one large network or can consist of two or more LANs connected together. The Internet is the world's largest WAN.

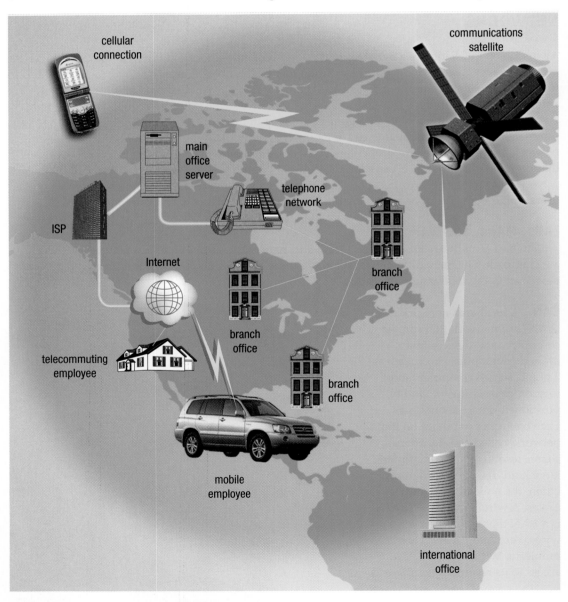

FIGURE 8-8 An example of a WAN.

Network Architectures

The design of computers, devices, and media in a network, sometimes called the network architecture, is categorized as either client/server or peer-to-peer.

CLIENT/SERVER On a **client/server network**, one or more computers act as a server; the other computers on the network request services from the server (Figure 8-9). A **server** controls access to the hardware, software, and other resources on the network and provides a centralized storage area for programs, data, and information. The **clients** are other computers and mobile devices on the network that rely on the server for its resources. For example, a server might store a database of customers. Clients on the network (company employees) access the customer database on the server.

Some servers, called dedicated servers, perform a specific task and can be placed with other dedicated servers to perform multiple tasks. For example, a file server stores and manages files. A print server manages printers and print jobs. A database server stores and provides access to a database. A network server manages network traffic (activity).

A client/server network typically provides an efficient means to connect 10 or more computers. Most client/server networks require a person to serve as a network administrator because of the large size of the network.

PEER-TO-PEER One type of **peer-to-peer network** is a simple, inexpensive network that typically connects fewer than 10 computers. Each computer, called a peer, has equal responsibilities and capabilities, sharing hardware (such as a printer), data, or information with other computers on the peer-to-peer network (Figure 8-10). Each computer stores files on its own storage devices. Thus, each computer on the network contains both the network operating system and application software. All computers on the network share any peripheral device(s) attached to any computer. For example, one computer may have a laser printer and a scanner, while another has an ink-jet printer and an external hard disk. Peer-to-peer networks are ideal for very small businesses and home users.

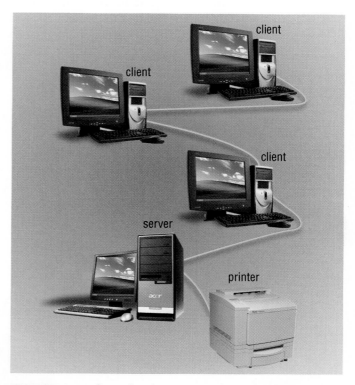

FIGURE 8-9 On a client/server network, one or more computers act as a server, and the clients access the server(s).

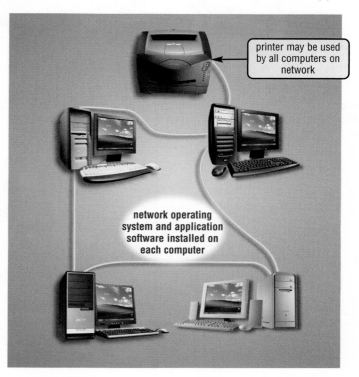

FIGURE 8-10 Each computer on a peer-to-peer network shares its hardware and software with other computers on the network.

INTERNET PEER-TO-PEER Another type of peer-to-peer, called **P2P**, describes an Internet network, on which users access each other's hard disks and exchange files directly (Figure 8-11). This type of peer-to-peer network sometimes is called a file sharing network because users with compatible software and an Internet connection copy files from someone else's hard disk to their hard disks. As more users connect to the network, each user has access to shared files on other users' hard disks. When users log off, others no longer have access to their hard disks.

Examples of networking software that support P2P are BitTorrent, Grokster, Gnutella, and Kazaa, which allow users to swap MP3 music files via the Web.

Network Topologies

A **network topology** refers to the layout of the computers and devices in a communications network. Three commonly used network topologies are bus, ring, and star. Networks usually use combinations of these topologies.

BUS NETWORK A **bus network** consists of a single central cable, to which all computers and other devices connect (Figure 8-12). The bus is the physical cable that connects the computers and other devices. The bus in a bus network transmits data, instructions, and information in both directions. When a sending device transmits data, the address of the receiving device is included with the transmission so the data is routed to the appropriate receiving device.

Bus networks are popular on LANs because they are inexpensive and easy to install. One advantage of the bus network is that computers and other devices can be attached and detached at any point on the bus without disturbing the rest of the network. Another advantage is that failure of one device usually does not affect the rest of the bus network. The greatest risk to a bus network is that the bus itself might become inoperable. If that happens, the network remains inoperative until the bus is back in working order.

FIGURE 8-11 P2P describes an Internet network on which users connect to each other's hard disks and exchange files directly.

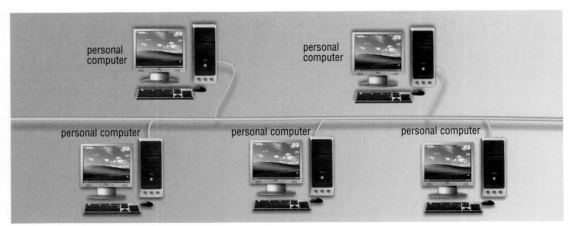

FIGURE 8-12 Devices in a bus network share a single data path.

RING NETWORK   On a **ring network**, a cable forms a closed loop (ring) with all computers and devices arranged along the ring (Figure 8-13). Data transmitted on a ring network travels from device to device around the entire ring, in one direction. When a computer or device sends data, the data travels to each computer on the ring until it reaches its destination.

If a computer or device on a ring network fails, all devices before the failed device are unaffected, but those after the failed device cannot function. A ring network can span a larger distance than a bus network, but it is more difficult to install. The ring topology primarily is used for LANs, but also is used in WANs.

STAR NETWORK   On a **star network**, all of the computers and devices (nodes) on the network connect to a central device, thus forming a star (Figure 8-14). The central device that provides a common connection point for nodes on the network is called the hub. All data that transfers from one node to another passes through the hub.

Star networks are fairly easy to install and maintain. Nodes can be added to and removed from the network with little or no disruption to the network.

On a star network, if one node fails, only that node is affected. The other nodes continue to operate normally. If the hub fails, however, the entire network is inoperable until the hub is repaired.

Intranets

Recognizing the efficiency and power of the Internet, many organizations apply Internet and Web technologies to their own internal networks. An **intranet** (intra means within) is an internal network that uses Internet technologies. Intranets generally make company information accessible to employees and facilitate working in groups.

Simple intranet applications include electronic publishing of organizational materials such as telephone directories, event calendars, procedure manuals, employee benefits information, and job postings. Additionally, an intranet typically includes a connection to the Internet. More sophisticated uses of intranets include groupware applications such as project management, chat rooms, newsgroups, group scheduling, and video conferencing.

An intranet essentially is a small version of the Internet that exists within an organization. Users update information on the intranet by creating and posting a Web page, using a method similar to that used on the Internet.

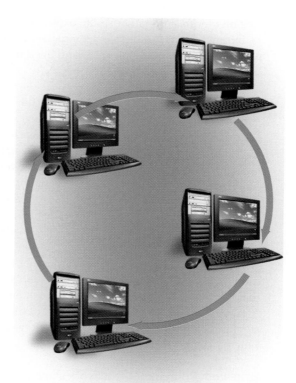

FIGURE 8-13   On a ring network, all connected devices form a continuous loop.

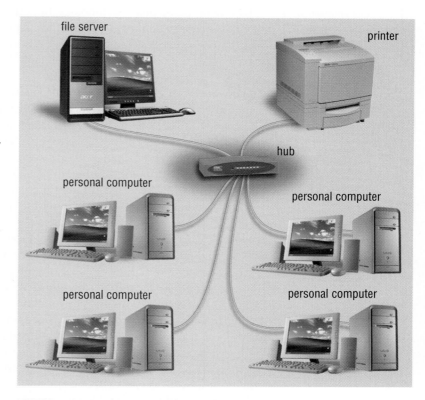

FIGURE 8-14   A star network contains a single, centralized hub through which all the devices in the network communicate.

Sometimes a company uses an extranet, which allows customers or suppliers to access part of its intranet. Package shipping companies, for example, allow customers to access their intranet to print air bills, schedule pickups, and even track shipped packages as the packages travel to their destinations.

Network Communications Standards

Today's networks connect terminals, devices, and computers from many different manufacturers across many types of networks, such as wide area, local area, and wireless. For the different devices on various types of networks to be able to communicate, the network must use similar techniques of moving data through the network from one application to another.

To alleviate the problems of incompatibility and ensure that hardware and software components can be integrated into any network, various organizations such as ANSI and IEEE (pronounced I triple E) propose, develop, and approve network standards. A **network standard** defines guidelines that specify the way computers access the medium to which they are attached, the type(s) of medium used, the speeds used on different types of networks, and the type(s) of physical cable and/or the wireless technology used. A standard that outlines characteristics of how two network devices communicate is called a protocol. Hardware and software manufacturers design their products to meet the guidelines specified in a particular standard, so their devices can communicate with the network.

The following sections discuss some of the more widely used network communications standards for both wired and wireless networks including Ethernet, token ring, TCP/IP, 802.11, Bluetooth, IrDA, RFID, and WAP.

ETHERNET   **Ethernet** is a network standard that specifies no central computer or device on the network (nodes) should control when data can be transmitted; that is, each node attempts to transmit data when it determines the network is able to receive communications. If two computers on an Ethernet network attempt to send data at the same time, a collision occurs, and the computers must attempt to send their messages again.

WEB LINK 8-4

Ethernet

For more information, visit scsite.com/dcf2e/ch8/weblink and then click Ethernet.

Ethernet is based on a bus topology, but Ethernet networks can be wired in a star pattern. The Ethernet standard defines guidelines for the physical configuration of the network, e.g., cabling, network cards, and nodes. Today, Ethernet is the most popular LAN standard because it is relatively inexpensive and easy to install and maintain. Ethernet networks often use cables to transmit data.

TOKEN RING   The second most popular network standard for LANs is token ring. The **token ring** standard specifies that computers and devices on the network share or pass a special signal, called a token, in a unidirectional manner and in a preset order. A token is a special series of bits that function like a ticket. The device with the token can transmit data over the network. Only one token exists per network. This ensures that only one computer transmits data at a time. Token ring is based on a ring topology (although it can use a star topology). The token ring standard defines guidelines for the physical configuration of a network. Some token ring networks connect up to 72 devices. Others use a special type of wiring that allows up to 260 connections.

TCP/IP   Short for Transmission Control Protocol/Internet Protocol, **TCP/IP** is a network standard, specifically a protocol, that defines how messages (data) are routed from one end of a network to the other. TCP/IP describes rules for dividing messages into small pieces, called packets; providing addresses for each packet; checking for and detecting errors; sequencing packets; and regulating the flow of messages along the network.

TCP/IP has been adopted as a network standard for Internet communications. Thus, all hosts on the Internet follow the rules defined in this standard. Internet communications also use other standards, such as the Ethernet standard, as data is routed to its destination.

When a computer sends data over the Internet, the data is divided into packets. Each packet contains the data, as well as the recipient (destination), the origin (sender), and the sequence information used to reassemble the data at the destination. Each packet travels along the fastest individual available path to the recipient's computer via communications devices called routers.

802.11   Developed by IEEE, **802.11** also known as **Wi-Fi (wireless fidelity)** and wireless Ethernet, is a series of network standards that specifies how two wireless devices communicate over the air with each other. Using Wi-Fi, wireless computers or devices communicate via radio waves with other computers or devices. The Wi-Fi standard uses techniques similar to the Ethernet standard to specify how to physically configure a wireless network.

One popular use of the Wi-Fi standard is in hot spots (discussed earlier in this chapter) that offer mobile users the ability to connect to the Internet with their wireless computers and devices. Many homes and small businesses also use Wi-Fi to network computers and devices together wirelessly.

FAQ 8-1

How prevalent are hot spots?

Very. By 2007, experts predict that more than 120,000 hot spots will exist worldwide. The United States has the most hot spots, followed by the United Kingdom, France, Germany, and Japan. In the United States, New York City has the most hot spots. For more information, visit scsite.com/dcf2e/ch8/faq and then click Hot Spots.

BLUETOOTH   **Bluetooth** is a standard, specifically a protocol, that defines how two Bluetooth devices use short-range radio waves to transmit data. To communicate with each other, Bluetooth devices often must be within about 10 meters (about 33 feet) but can be extended to 100 meters with additional equipment.

A Bluetooth device contains a small chip that allows it to communicate with other Bluetooth devices. Examples of these devices can include desktop computers, notebook computers, hand-held computers, PDAs, smart phones, headsets, microphones, digital cameras, fax machines, and printers.

IrDA   Some computers and devices use the **IrDA** specification to transmit data wirelessly to each other via infrared (IR) light waves. Infrared requires a line-of-sight transmission; that is, the sending device and the receiving device must be in line with each other so that nothing obstructs the path of the infrared light wave. Because Bluetooth does not require line-of-sight transmission, some industry experts predict that Bluetooth will replace infrared.

RFID   **RFID** (radio frequency identification) is a standard, specifically a protocol, that defines how a network uses radio signals to communicate with a tag placed in or attached to an object, an animal, or a person. The tag, called a transponder, consists of an antenna and a memory chip that contains the information to be transmitted via radio waves. Through an antenna, an RFID reader, also called a transceiver, reads the radio signals and transfers the information to a computer or computing device. Readers can be handheld or embedded in an object such as a doorway or tollbooth.

RFID tags are passive or active. An active RFID tag contains a battery that runs the chip's circuitry and broadcasts a signal to the RFID reader. A passive RFID tag does not contain a battery and thus cannot send a signal until the reader activates the tag's antenna by sending out electromagnetic waves.

WAP   The **Wireless Application Protocol (WAP)** is a standard, specifically a protocol, that specifies how some wireless mobile devices such as smart phones and PDAs can display the content of Internet services such as the Web, e-mail, chat rooms, and newsgroups. For example, to display a Web page on a smart phone, the phone must be WAP enabled and contain a micro-browser. WAP uses a client/server network. The wireless device contains the client software, which connects to the Internet service provider's server.

COMMUNICATIONS SOFTWARE

Communications software consists of programs that (1) help users establish a connection to another computer or network; (2) manage the transmission of data, instructions, and information; and (3) provide an interface for users to communicate with one another. The first two are system software and the third is application software. Chapter 3 presented a variety of examples of application software for communications: e-mail, FTP, Web browser, newsgroup/message boards, chat rooms, instant messaging, video conferencing, and Internet telephony. Read At Issue 8-2 for a discussion related to Web browser communications.

Some communications devices are preprogrammed to accomplish communications tasks. Other communications devices require separate communications software to ensure proper transmission of data. Communications software works with the network standards and protocols defined earlier to ensure data moves correctly through a network. Communications software usually is bundled with the operating system or purchased network devices.

Often, a computer has various types of communications software, each serving a different purpose. One type of communications software helps users establish a connection to the Internet using wizards, dialog boxes, and other on-screen messages. Communications software also allows home and small office users to configure wired and wireless networks and connect devices to an existing network.

COMMUNICATIONS OVER THE TELEPHONE NETWORK

The public switched telephone network (PSTN) is the worldwide telephone system that handles voice-oriented telephone calls (Figure 8-15). Nearly the entire telephone network today uses digital technology, with the exception of the final link from the local telephone company to a home, which often is analog.

AT ISSUE 8-2

Librarians Caught in Middle of Internet Censorship Battle

Most libraries offer computers that adults and children can use to connect to the Internet. To prevent children from using these computers to access obscene material on the Web, Congress enacted the Children's Internet Protection Act (CIPA). The act mandates that libraries that cater to children must install filtering software in order to receive federal funds. A group of librarians, library users, and Web site operators challenged the act, arguing that it violates the First Amendment right of free speech. In 2003, the Supreme Court upheld the law. Supporters of the decision claim that filtering software protects children. Opponents insist, however, that filtering software restricts intellectual freedom and prevents library patrons from accessing some unobjectionable sites. To control the impact of filtering software, the American Library Association has asked each manufacturer to provide a database of blocked sites that librarians can use to determine the software that best meets their needs. Yet, manufacturers are reluctant to supply the database, fearing it may be valuable to competitors. Should libraries have to use filtering software in order to receive federal funds? Why or why not? What measures, if any, should libraries be allowed to adopt instead? Is it reasonable to ask filtering software manufacturers to reveal their databases? Why?

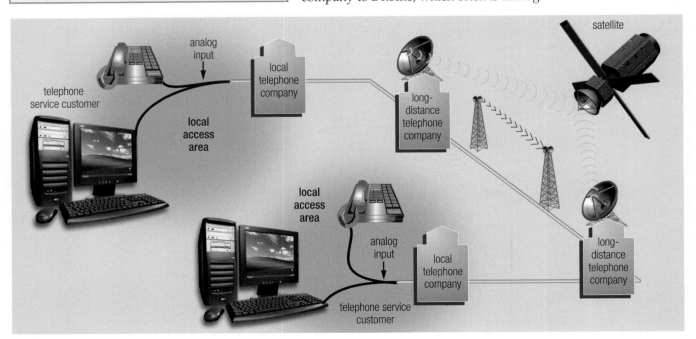

FIGURE 8-15 A sample telephone network configuration.

The telephone network is an integral part of computer communications. Data, instructions, and information are transmitted over the telephone network using dial-up lines or dedicated lines. The following sections discuss dial-up lines and the various types of dedicated lines that use the telephone network for data communications.

Dial-Up Lines

A **dial-up line** is a temporary connection that uses one or more analog telephone lines for communications. A dial-up connection is not permanent. Using a dial-up line to transmit data is similar to using the telephone to make a call. A modem at the sending end dials the telephone number of a modem at the receiving end. When the modem at the receiving end answers the call, a connection is established and data can be transmitted. When either modem hangs up, the communications end.

Using a dial-up line to connect computers costs no more than making a regular telephone call. Computers at any two locations establish an Internet or network connection using modems and the telephone network.

Dedicated Lines

A **dedicated line** is a type of always-on connection that is established between two communications devices (unlike a dial-up line where the connection is reestablished each time it is used). The quality and consistency of the connection on a dedicated line are better than a dial-up line because dedicated lines provide a constant connection.

Businesses often use dedicated lines to connect geographically distant offices. Dedicated lines can be either analog or digital. Digital lines increasingly are connecting home and business users to networks around the globe because they transmit data and information at faster rates than analog lines.

Four popular types of digital dedicated lines are ISDN lines, DSL, T-carrier lines, and ATM. Although cable television (CATV) lines and fixed wireless are not a type of standard telephone line, they are very popular ways for the home user to connect to the Internet. Fixed wireless Internet connections use an antenna on your house or business to communicate with a tower location via radio signals. Later sections in this chapter discuss the use of CATV lines and radio signals to connect to the Internet.

The table in Figure 8-16 lists the approximate monthly costs of various types of Internet connections and transfer rates (speeds), as compared with dial-up lines. The following sections discuss ISDN lines, DSL, T-carrier lines, and ATM.

ISDN LINES For the small business and home user, an ISDN line provides faster transfer rates than dial-up telephone lines. **ISDN** (Integrated Services Digital Network) is a set of standards for digital transmission of data over standard copper telephone lines. ISDN requires that both ends of the connection have an ISDN modem. The ISDN modem at your location must be within about 3.5 miles of the telephone company's ISDN modem. Thus, ISDN may not be an option for rural residents.

DSL DSL is another digital line alternative for the small business or home user. **DSL** (Digital Subscriber Line) transmits at fast speeds on existing standard copper telephone wiring. Some DSL installations include a dial tone, providing users with both voice and data communications. Others share services with an existing telephone line.

To connect to DSL, a customer must have a special network card and a DSL modem. Not all areas offer DSL service because

SPEEDS OF VARIOUS INTERNET CONNECTIONS

Type of Line	Approximate Monthly Cost	Transfer Rates
Dial-up	Local or long-distance rates	Up to 56 Kbps
ISDN	$10 to $40	Up to 128 Kbps
DSL	$30 to $80	128 Kbps to 8.45 Mbps
Cable TV (CATV)	$30 to $50	128 Kbps to 36 Mbps
Fixed Wireless	$35 to $70	256 Kbps to 10 Mbps
Fractional T1	$200 to $700	128 Kbps to 768 Kbps
T1	$500 to $1,000	1.544 Mbps
T3	$5,000 to $15,000	44.736 Mbps
ATM	$3,000 or more	155 Mbps to 622 Mbps, can reach 10 Gbps

*Kbps = thousand bits per second
Mbps = million bits per second
Gbps = billion bits per second

FIGURE 8-16 The speeds of various lines that can be used to connect to the Internet.

the local telephone company or the lines in the area may not be capable of supporting DSL technology. As with ISDN, DSL may not be an option for rural residents because the user's location (and DSL modem) and the telephone company's DSL modem must be located within about 3.5 miles of each other.

ADSL is one of the more popular types of DSLs. ADSL (asymmetric digital subscriber line) is a type of DSL that supports faster transfer rates when receiving data (the downstream rate) than when sending data (the upstream rate). ADSL is ideal for Internet access because most users download more information from the Internet than they upload.

T-Carrier Lines A **T-carrier line** is any of several types of long-distance digital telephone lines that carry multiple signals over a single communications line. T-carrier lines provide very fast data transfer rates. Only medium to large companies usually can afford the investment in T-carrier lines because these lines are so expensive.

The most popular T-carrier line is the **T1 line**. Businesses often use T1 lines to connect to the Internet. Many Internet access providers use T1 lines to connect to the Internet backbone. Home and small business users purchase fractional T1, in which they share a connection to the T1 line with other users. Fractional T1 is slower than a dedicated T1 line, but it also is less expensive.

A T3 line is equal in speed to 28 T1 lines. T3 lines are quite expensive. Main users of T3 lines include large companies, telephone companies, and Internet access providers connecting to the Internet backbone. The Internet backbone itself also uses T3 lines.

ATM **ATM** (Asynchronous Transfer Mode) is a service that carries voice, data, video, and multimedia at extremely high speeds. Telephone networks, the Internet, and other networks with large amounts of traffic use ATM. Some experts predict that ATM eventually will become the Internet standard for data transmission, replacing T3 lines.

Test your knowledge of pages 303 through 312 in Quiz Yourself 8-2.

QUIZ YOURSELF 8-2

Instructions: Find the true statement below. Then, rewrite the remaining false statements so they are true.

1. A wireless LAN is a LAN that uses physical wires.

2. An intranet is an internal network that uses video conferencing technologies.

3. Four popular types of digital dial-up lines are ISDN lines, DSL, T-carrier lines, and ATM.

4. In a client/server network, servers on the network access resources on the client.

5. P2P describes an Internet network on which users access each other's hard disks and exchange files directly over the Internet.

Quiz Yourself Online: To further check your knowledge of networks, communications software, and communications over the telephone network, visit scsite.com/dcf2e/ch8/quiz and then click Objectives 3 – 5.

COMMUNICATIONS DEVICES

A **communications device** is any type of hardware capable of transmitting data, instructions, and information between a sending device and a receiving device. One type of communications device that connects a communications channel to a sending or receiving device such as a computer is a modem. Computers process data as digital signals. Data, instructions, and information travel along a communications channel in either analog or digital form, depending on the communications channel. An analog signal consists of a continuous electrical wave. A digital signal consists of individual electrical pulses that represent bits grouped together into bytes.

For communications channels that use digital signals (such as cable television lines), the modem transfers the digital signals between the computer and the communications channel (Figure 8-17a).

If a communications channel uses analog signals (such as some telephone lines), however, the modem first converts between analog and digital signals (Figure 8-17b).

The following pages describe the following types of communications devices: dial-up modems, ISDN and DSL modems, cable modems, network cards, wireless access points, and routers.

FIGURE 8-17a   (all digital communications channel)

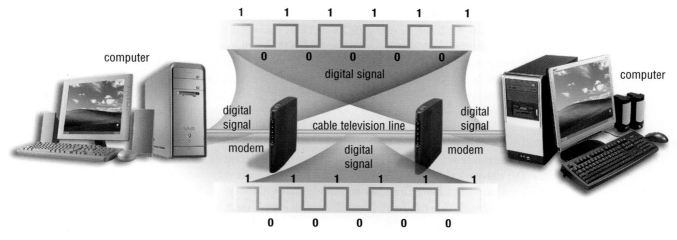

FIGURE 8-17b   (digital to analog to digital communications channel)

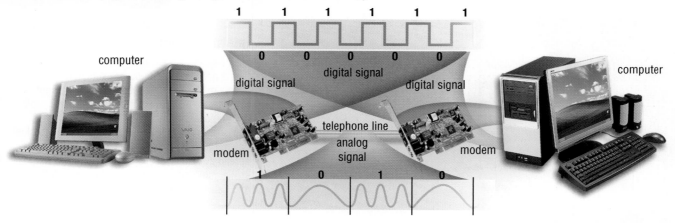

FIGURE 8-17   A modem connects a communications channel, such as a cable television line or a telephone line, to a sending or receiving device such as a computer. Depending on the type of communications channel, a modem may need to convert digital signals to analog signals (and vice versa) before transferring data, instructions, and information to or from a sending or receiving device.

Dial-Up Modems

As previously discussed, a computer's digital signals must be converted to analog signals before they are transmitted over standard telephone lines. The communications device that performs this conversion is a **modem**, sometimes called a dial-up modem. The word, modem, is derived from the combination of the words, modulate, to change into an analog signal, and demodulate, to convert an analog signal into a digital signal.

A modem usually is in the form of an adapter card that you insert in an expansion slot on a computer's motherboard (Figure 8-18). One end of a standard telephone cord attaches to a port on the modem card and the other end plugs into a telephone outlet.

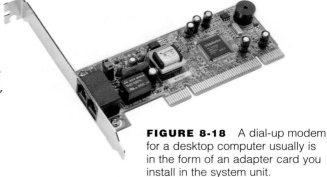

FIGURE 8-18   A dial-up modem for a desktop computer usually is in the form of an adapter card you install in the system unit.

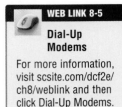
If a notebook or other mobile computer does not have built-in modem capabilities, mobile users can insert a PC Card modem in a PC Card slot on the computer. The PC Card modem attaches to a telephone outlet with a standard telephone cord. Mobile users without access to a telephone outlet also can use a special cable to attach the PC Card modem to a cellular telephone, thus enabling them to transmit data over a cellular telephone.

ISDN and DSL Modems

If you access the Internet using ISDN or DSL, you need a communications device to send and receive the digital ISDN or DSL signals. An **ISDN modem** sends digital data and information from a computer to an ISDN line and receives digital data and information from an ISDN line. A **DSL modem** sends digital data and information from a computer to a DSL line and receives digital data and information from a DSL line. ISDN and DSL modems usually are external devices, in which one end connects to the telephone line and the other end connects to a port on the system unit.

Cable Modems

A **cable modem** is a digital modem that sends and receives digital data over the cable television (CATV) network (Figure 8-19). With more than 100 million homes wired for cable television, cable modems provide a faster Internet access alternative to dial-up for the home user and have speeds similar to DSL. Cable modems currently can transmit data at speeds that are much faster than either a dial-up modem or ISDN.

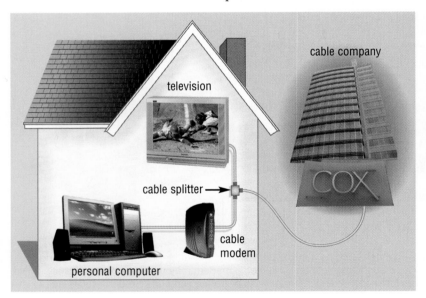

FIGURE 8-19 A typical cable modem installation.

FAQ 8-2

Which is better, DSL or cable Internet service?

Each has its own advantages. DSL uses a line that is not shared with other users in the neighborhood. With cable Internet service, by contrast, users share the node with up to 500 other cable Internet users. Simultaneous access by many users can cause the cable Internet service to slow down. Cable Internet service, however, has widespread availability. For more information, visit scsite.com/dcf2e/ch8/faq and then click DSL and Cable Internet Service.

Wireless Modems

Some mobile users have a **wireless modem** that allows access to the Web wirelessly from a notebook computer, a PDA, a smart phone, or other mobile device (Figure 8-20). Wireless modems, which have an antenna, typically use the same waves used by cellular telephones.

antenna on wireless PC Card modem communicates with wireless Internet service provider

wireless PC Card modem inserted in PC slot on notebook computer

FIGURE 8-20 Wireless modems, in the form of a PC Card or flash card, allow users to access the Internet wirelessly on their mobile computers and devices.

Network Cards

A **network card** is an adapter card, PC Card, or flash card that enables a computer or device to access a network. Personal computers on a LAN may contain a network card. The network card coordinates the transmission and receipt of data, instructions, and information to and from the computer or device containing the network card.

Network cards are available in a variety of styles (Figure 8-21). A network card for a desktop computer is an adapter card that has a port to which a cable connects. A network card for mobile computers and devices is in the form of a Type II PC Card or a flash card. Network cards that provide wireless data transmission also are available. This type of card, sometimes called a wireless network card, often has an antenna.

A network card follows the guidelines of a particular network communications standard, such as Ethernet or token ring. An Ethernet card is the most common type of network card.

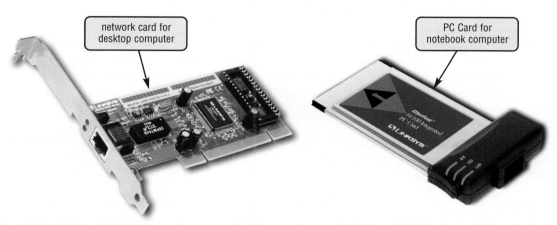

network card for desktop computer

PC Card for notebook computer

FIGURE 8-21   Network cards are available for both desktop and notebook computers.

Wireless Access Points

A **wireless access point** is a central communications device that allows computers and devices to transfer data wirelessly among themselves or to transfer data wirelessly to a wired network (Figure 8-7 on page 303). Wireless access points have high-quality antennas for optimal signals.

Routers

A **router** is a communications device that connects multiple computers or other routers together and transmits data to its correct destination on the network. A router can be used on any size of network. On the largest scale, routers along the Internet backbone forward data packets to their destination using the fastest available path. For smaller business and home networks, a router allows multiple computers to share a single high-speed Internet connection such as a cable modem or DSL modem (Figure 8-22). These routers connect from 2 to 250 computers.

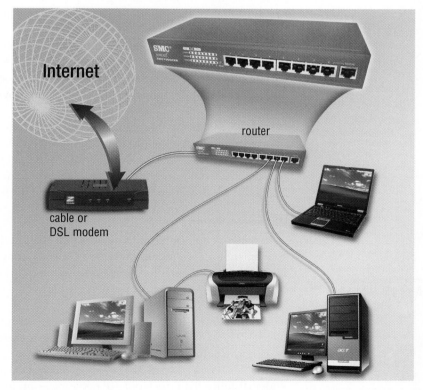

Internet

router

cable or DSL modem

FIGURE 8-22   Through a router, home and small business networks can share access to a high-speed Internet connection such as through a cable or DSL modem.

To prevent unauthorized users from accessing files and computers, many routers are protected by a built-in firewall, called a hardware firewall. Some also have built-in antivirus protection.

HOME NETWORKS

An estimated 39 million homes have more than one computer. Thus, many home users are connecting multiple computers and devices together in a **home network**. Each networked computer in the house has the following capabilities:

- Connect to the Internet at the same time
- Share a single high-speed Internet connection
- Access files and programs on the other computers in the house
- Share peripherals such as a printer, scanner, external hard disk, or DVD drive
- Play multiplayer games with players on other computers in the house

Many vendors offer home networking packages that include all the necessary hardware and software to network your home using wired or wireless techniques. Some of these packages also offer intelligent networking capabilities. An intelligent home network extends the basic home network to include features such as lighting control, thermostat adjustment, and a security system.

Wired Home Networks

As with other networks, a home network can use wires, be wireless, or use a combination of wired and wireless. Three types of wired home networks are Ethernet, powerline cable, and phoneline.

ETHERNET   Some home users have an Ethernet network. As discussed earlier in this chapter, traditional Ethernet networks require that each computer have built-in networking capabilities or contain a network card, which connects to a central network hub or similar device with a physical cable. This may involve running cable through walls, ceilings, and floors in the house. For the average home user, the hardware and software of an Ethernet network can be difficult to configure.

POWERLINE CABLE NETWORK   A home powerline cable network is a network that uses the same lines that bring electricity into the house. This network requires no additional wiring. One end of a cable plugs in the computer's parallel or USB port and the other end of the cable plugs in a wall outlet. The data transmits through the existing power lines in the house.

PHONELINE NETWORK   A phoneline network is an easy-to-install and inexpensive network that uses existing telephone lines in the home. With this network, one end of a cable connects to an adapter card or PC Card in the computer and the other end plugs in a wall telephone jack. The phoneline network does not interfere with voice and data transmissions on the telephone lines. That is, you can talk on the telephone and use the same line to connect to the Internet.

Wireless Home Networks

To network computers and devices that span multiple rooms or floors in a home, it may be more convenient to use a wireless strategy. One advantage of wireless networks is that you can take a mobile computer outside, for example in the backyard, and connect to the Internet through the home network as long as you are in the network's range. Two types of wireless home networks are HomeRF and Wi-Fi.

A HomeRF (radio frequency) network uses radio waves, instead of cables, to transmit data. A HomeRF network sends signals through the air over distances up to 150 feet. A HomeRF network usually can connect up to 10 computers.

Another home network that uses radio waves is a Wi-Fi network, which sends signals over a wider distance than the HomeRF network — up to 1,500 feet in some configurations. A Wi-Fi home

network is more expensive than a HomeRF network. Despite the higher costs, increasingly more home users set up Wi-Fi networks in their homes because they are fairly easy to configure. Each computer that accesses the network needs built-in wireless networking capabilities or a wireless network card, which communicates with a wireless access point or a combination router/wireless access point (Figure 8-23).

FIGURE 8-23 HOW TO SET UP HARDWARE FOR A WI-FI HOME NETWORK

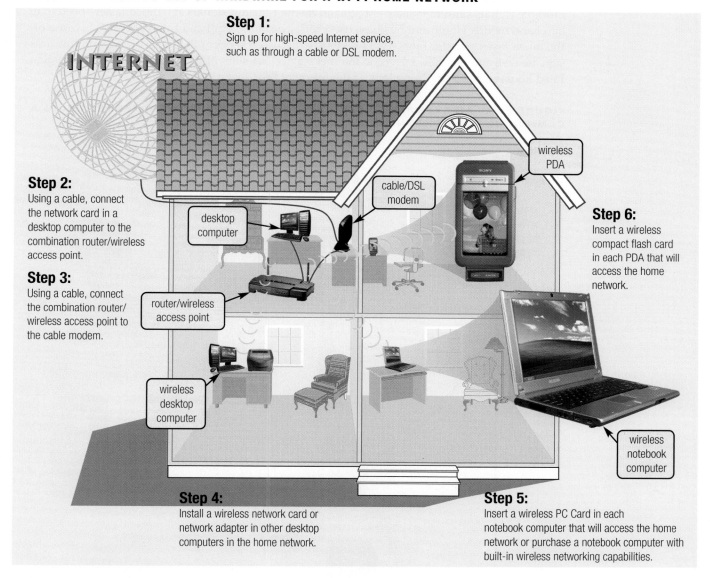

INTERNET

Step 1:
Sign up for high-speed Internet service, such as through a cable or DSL modem.

Step 2:
Using a cable, connect the network card in a desktop computer to the combination router/wireless access point.

Step 3:
Using a cable, connect the combination router/wireless access point to the cable modem.

cable/DSL modem

desktop computer

router/wireless access point

wireless desktop computer

wireless PDA

Step 6:
Insert a wireless compact flash card in each PDA that will access the home network.

wireless notebook computer

Step 4:
Install a wireless network card or network adapter in other desktop computers in the home network.

Step 5:
Insert a wireless PC Card in each notebook computer that will access the home network or purchase a notebook computer with built-in wireless networking capabilities.

COMMUNICATIONS CHANNEL

As described at the beginning of the chapter, a communications channel is the transmission media on which data, instructions, or information travel in a communications system. The amount of data, instructions, and information that can travel over a communications channel sometimes is called the **bandwidth**. The higher the bandwidth, the more the channel transmits. For example, a cable modem has more bandwidth than a dial-up modem.

For transmission of text only, a lower bandwidth is acceptable. For transmission of music, graphics, photographs, virtual reality images, or 3-D games, however, you need a higher bandwidth. When the bandwidth is too low for the application, you will notice a considerable slow-down in system performance.

A communications channel consists of one or more transmission media. **Transmission media** consists of materials or substances capable of carrying one or more signals. When you send data from a computer, the signal that carries the data may travel over various transmission media. This is especially true when the transmission spans a long distance.

Figure 8-24 illustrates a typical communications channel and shows the variety of transmission media used to complete the connection.

Baseband media transmit only one signal at a time. By contrast, **broadband** media transmit multiple signals simultaneously. Broadband media transmit signals at a much faster speed than baseband media. Home and business users today opt for broadband Internet access because of the much faster transfer rates. Two previously discussed services that offer broadband transmission are DSL and the cable television Internet service. Satellites also offer broadband transmission. Read Looking Ahead 8-1 for a look at the future of broadband.

FIGURE 8-24 AN EXAMPLE OF SENDING A REQUEST OVER THE INTERNET USING A COMMUNICATIONS CHANNEL

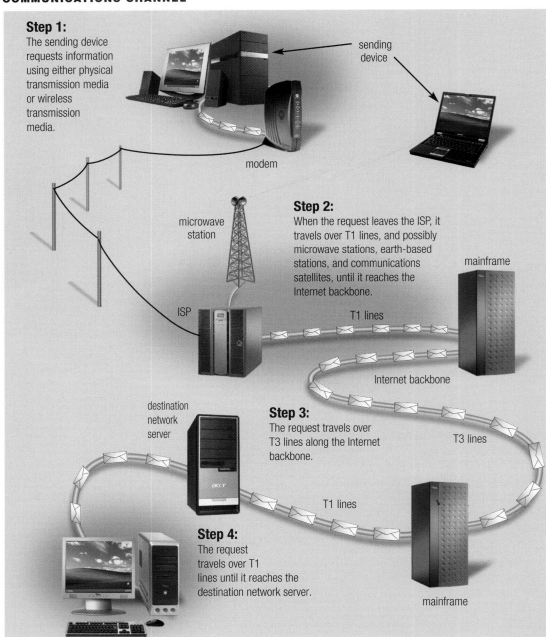

Step 1:
The sending device requests information using either physical transmission media or wireless transmission media.

sending device

modem

microwave station

Step 2:
When the request leaves the ISP, it travels over T1 lines, and possibly microwave stations, earth-based stations, and communications satellites, until it reaches the Internet backbone.

mainframe

ISP

T1 lines

Internet backbone

destination network server

Step 3:
The request travels over T3 lines along the Internet backbone.

T3 lines

T1 lines

Step 4:
The request travels over T1 lines until it reaches the destination network server.

mainframe

LOOKING AHEAD 8-1

Broadband Sparks Portal Services

When the Internet was in its infancy, many computer users were satisfied with a stable telephone connection and a variety of Web sites. With broadband becoming more commonplace, however, users are demanding superfast connection speeds and Web sites that offer easily accessible information.

Super Web portals are being developed in response to these demands. Portals offer many services in one convenient location, so a user can find a variety of related content at a single Web site. For example, yahoo.rogers.com and Sympatico.MSN.ca are media-intensive portals for people desiring to upload photos, download music, and play games.

As broadband becomes more ubiquitous, look for the convergence of the television and online communities, where viewers watch programs and simultaneously or soon afterwards find related premium content online. For more information, visit scsite.com/dcf2e/ch8/looking and then click Broadband Future.

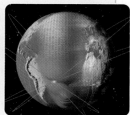

Transmission media are one of two types: physical or wireless. Physical transmission media use wire, cable, and other tangible materials to send communications signals. Wireless transmission media send communications signals through the air or space using radio, microwave, and infrared signals. The following sections discuss these types of media.

FAQ 8-3

Do many home users have a broadband Internet connection?

As shown in the chart to the right, the number of home users with a broadband Internet connection has grown to more than 75 percent. For more information, visit scsite.com/dcf2e/ch8/faq and then click Broadband Usage.

PHYSICAL TRANSMISSION MEDIA

Physical transmission media used in communications include twisted-pair cable, coaxial cable, and fiber-optic cable. These cables typically are used within or underground between buildings. Ethernet and token ring LANs often use physical transmission media.

Twisted-Pair Cable

One of the more commonly used transmission media for network cabling and telephone systems is twisted-pair cable. **Twisted-pair cable** consists of one or more twisted-pair wires bundled together (Figure 8-25). Each twisted-pair wire consists of two separate insulated copper wires that are twisted together. The wires are twisted together to reduce noise. **Noise** is an electrical disturbance that can degrade communications.

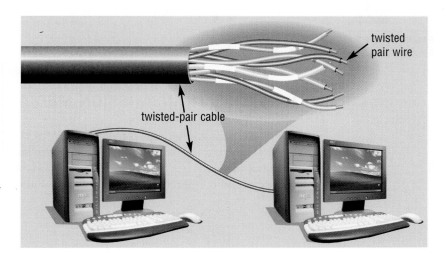

FIGURE 8-25   A twisted-pair cable consists of one or more twisted-pair wires. Each twisted-pair wire usually is color coded for identification.

Coaxial Cable

Coaxial cable, often referred to as coax (pronounced KO-ax), consists of a single copper wire surrounded by at least three layers: (1) an insulating material, (2) a woven or braided metal, and (3) a plastic outer coating (Figure 8-26).

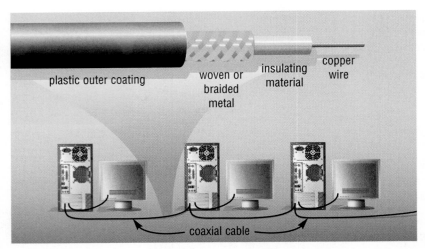

FIGURE 8-26 On a coaxial cable, data travels through a copper wire. This illustration shows computers networked together with coaxial cable.

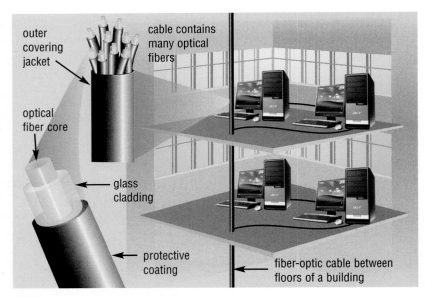

FIGURE 8-27 A fiber-optic cable consists of hair-thin strands of glass or plastic that carry data as pulses of light.

Cable television (CATV) network wiring often uses coaxial cable because it can be cabled over longer distances than twisted-pair cable. Most of today's computer networks, however, do not use coaxial cable because other transmission media such as fiber-optic cable transmit signals at faster rates.

Fiber-Optic Cable

The core of a **fiber-optic cable** consists of dozens or hundreds of thin strands of glass or plastic that use light to transmit signals. Each strand, called an optical fiber, is as thin as a human hair. Inside the fiber-optic cable, an insulating glass cladding and a protective coating surround each optical fiber (Figure 8-27).

Fiber-optic cables have the following advantages over cables that use wire, such as twisted-pair and coaxial cables:

- Capability of carrying significantly more signals than wire cables
- Faster data transmission
- Less susceptible to noise (interference) from other devices such as a copy machine
- Better security for signals during transmission because they are less susceptible to noise
- Smaller size (much thinner and lighter weight)

Disadvantages of fiber-optic cable are it costs more than twisted-pair or coaxial cable and can be difficult to install and modify. Despite these limitations, many local and long-distance telephone companies are replacing existing telephone lines with fiber-optic cables.

WIRELESS TRANSMISSION MEDIA

Many users opt for wireless transmission media because it is more convenient than installing cables. In addition, businesses use wireless transmission media in locations where it is impossible to install cables. Types of wireless transmission media used in communications include infrared, broadcast radio, cellular radio, microwaves, and communications satellites.

Infrared

As discussed earlier in the chapter, infrared (IR) is a wireless transmission medium that sends signals using infrared light waves. Mobile computers and devices, such as a mouse, printer, and smart phone, often have an IrDA port that enables the transfer of data from one device to another using infrared light waves.

Broadcast Radio

Broadcast radio is a wireless transmission medium that distributes radio signals through the air over long distances such as between cities, regions, and countries and short distances such as within an office or home. Bluetooth, HomeRF, and Wi-Fi communications technologies discussed earlier in this chapter use broadcast radio signals.

Cellular Radio

Cellular radio is a form of broadcast radio that is used widely for mobile communications, specifically wireless modems and cellular telephones. A cellular telephone is a telephone device that uses high-frequency radio waves to transmit voice and digital data messages.

Some mobile users connect their notebook computer or other mobile computer to a cellular telephone to access the Web, send and receive e-mail, enter a chat room, or connect to an office or school network while away from a standard telephone line.

Personal Communications Services (PCS) is the term used by the United States Federal Communications Commission (FCC) to identify all wireless digital communications. Devices that use PCS include cellular telephones, PDAs, pagers, and fax machines.

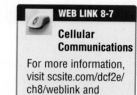

WEB LINK 8-7

Cellular Communications

For more information, visit scsite.com/dcf2e/ch8/weblink and then click Cellular Communications.

Microwaves

Microwaves are radio waves that provide a high-speed signal transmission. Microwave transmission, often called fixed wireless, involves sending signals from one microwave station to another (shown in Figure 8-15 on page 310). Microwaves can transmit data at rates up to 4,500 times faster than a dial-up modem.

A microwave station is an earth-based reflective dish that contains the antenna, transceivers, and other equipment necessary for microwave communications. Microwaves use line-of-sight transmission. To avoid possible obstructions, such as buildings or mountains, microwave stations often sit on the tops of buildings, towers, or mountains.

Microwave transmission is used in environments where installing physical transmission media is difficult or impossible and where line-of-sight transmission is available. For example, microwave transmission is used in wide-open areas such as deserts or lakes; between buildings in a close geographic area; or to communicate with a satellite. Current users of microwave transmission include universities, hospitals, city governments, cable television providers, and telephone companies. Home and small business users who do not have other high-speed Internet connections available in their area also opt for lower-cost fixed wireless plans.

Communications Satellite

A communications satellite is a space station that receives microwave signals from an earth-based station, amplifies (strengthens) the signals, and broadcasts the signals back over a wide area to any number of earth-based stations (shown in Figure 8-15 on page 310).

These earth-based stations often are microwave stations. Other devices, such as PDAs and GPS receivers, also can function as earth-based stations. Transmission from an earth-based station to a satellite is an uplink. Transmission from a satellite to an earth-based station is a downlink.

Applications such as air navigation, television and radio broadcasts, weather forecasting, video conferencing, paging, global positioning systems, and Internet connections use communications satellites. With the proper satellite dish and a satellite modem card, consumers access the Internet using satellite technology. With satellite Internet connections, however, uplink transmissions usually are slower than downlink transmissions. This difference in speeds usually is acceptable to most

Internet satellite users because they download much more data than they upload. Although a satellite Internet connection is more expensive than cable Internet or DSL connections, sometimes it is the only high-speed Internet option in remote areas. Read Looking Ahead 8-2 for a look at the next generation of satellite communications.

LOOKING AHEAD 8-2

Hear the Music on a Smart Phone

Listening to music, watching television, and using a cellular telephone probably are part of your daily life, and you soon may be able to perform all three activities on one device: your smart phone.

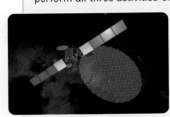

The next generation of smart phones and other pocket devices might add the capability of receiving digital terrestrial and satellite broadcasts. A satellite co-owned by Japan's Mobile Broadcasting and South Korea's TU Media beams 30 channels of audio and 7 channels of video to subscribers. The nonstop music channels feature a variety of genres and radio stations, and the video channels include news, financial information, and MTV.

The subscription service is expected to cost approximately $15 per month for audio and $23 for both audio and video. For more information, visit scsite.com/dcf2e/ch8/looking and then click Satellite Broadcasts.

Test your knowledge of pages 312 through 322 in Quiz Yourself 8-3.

QUIZ YOURSELF 8-3

Instructions: Find the true statement below. Then, rewrite the remaining false statements so they are true.

1. A cable modem converts a computer's digital signals to analog signals before they are transmitted over standard telephone lines.

2. A network card is an adapter card, PC Card, or flash card that enables the computer or device to access a network.

3. Analog signals consist of individual electrical pulses that represent bits grouped together into bytes.

4. Physical transmission media send communications signals through the air or space using radio, microwave, and infrared signals.

5. Two types of wireless home networks are HomeRF and powerline cable.

Quiz Yourself Online: To further check your knowledge of communications devices, home networks, and transmission media, visit scsite.com/dcf2e/ch8/quiz and then click Objectives 6 – 8.

CHAPTER SUMMARY

This chapter provided an overview of communications terminology and applications. It also discussed how to join computers into a network, allowing them to communicate and share resources such as hardware, software, data, and information. It also explained various types of communications devices, media, and procedures as they relate to computers.

CAREER CORNER

Network Specialist

As more companies rely on networks, the demand for network specialists will continue to grow. A **network specialist** must have a working knowledge of local area networks and their application within wide area networks. A network specialist also must be familiar with the Internet, its connectivity to LANs and WANs, and Web server management. Responsibilities of a network specialist include installing, configuring, and troubleshooting network systems. Other responsibilities may include managing system and client software, Web page integration and creation, network security measures, user accounting, and monitoring network event logs for problem resolution. A network specialist must possess good problem-solving skills and the ability to work independently. They also must have the ability to concentrate on detailed projects for long periods of time. Good oral, written, and team-oriented interpersonal skills also are beneficial.

Many institutions offer two-year network specialist programs. In addition to a college degree, industry certifications are available for further career enhancement. Two of the more notable certifications are the Novell CNA (Certified Novell Administrator) and the Cisco CCNA (Certified Cisco Networking Associate). Network specialist salaries will vary depending on education, certifications, and experience. Individuals with certifications can expect an approximate starting salary between $43,000 and $55,000. For more information, visit scsite.com/dcf2e/ch8/careers and then click Network Specialist.

Cisco Systems
Networking the Internet

As the world leader in networking equipment, Cisco Systems strives to empower the Internet generation by connecting people and networks regardless of differences in locations, time, or types of computers. The company offers a broad line of networking equipment for transporting data within a building, across a campus, or across the globe.

A group of computer scientists from Stanford University founded Cisco in 1984. From the start, the company focused on communicating over networks. Today, Cisco's Internet Protocol-based (IP) networking equipment is the basis of the Internet and most networks.

Its key products focus on the areas of home and wireless networking, network security, and communications. The company set a Guinness world record for having the highest capacity Internet router of 92 terabits (92 trillion bits per second). For more information, visit scsite.com/dcf2e/ch8/companies and then click Cisco.

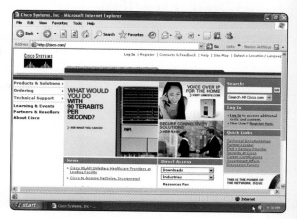

QUALCOMM
Wireless Communications Leader

When you speak into your cellular telephone, your voice is converted into digital information that is transmitted as a radio signal with a unique code. This wireless communications process is based on Code Division Multiple Access (CDMA), which QUALCOMM engineers first conceptualized in 1988.

Commercial CDMA networks were unveiled in 1995, and they provided about 10 times the capacity of analog networks. Today, QUALCOMM is the world's largest provider of 3G technology and has shipped more than 1 million chips to the 125 telecommunications equipment manufacturers using the CDMA standard.

QUALCOMM has been selected as a FORTUNE 500 company and has been named to *FORTUNE* magazine's lists of the 100 Fastest-Growing Companies in America, 100 Best Companies to Work for in America, and America's Most Admired Companies. For more information, visit scsite.com/dcf2e/ch8/companies and then click QUALCOMM.

TECHNOLOGY TRAILBLAZERS

Robert Metcalfe
Ethernet Inventor

The Internet will be filled with video within 20 years, according to Robert Metcalfe. His prediction is likely to be correct based on his visionary track record. While studying for his doctorate degree at Harvard and working at Xerox's Palo Alto Research Center (PARC), he combined hardware with a high-speed network interface and envisioned that his invention would be used widely. This network technology developed into Ethernet, today's most popular LAN technology that links millions of computers worldwide.

In 1979, Metcalfe left Xerox to found 3Com Corporation and make Ethernet the standard for computer communications. After he retired from that company, he became a columnist for *InfoWorld* magazine. He also has written three books and been a venture capitalist with Polaris Ventures. For more information, visit scsite.com/dcf2e/ch8/people and then click Robert Metcalfe.

Patricia Russo
Lucent Technologies Chairman and CEO

As captain of her high school cheerleading squad, Patricia Russo had to project a spirit of optimism, build teamwork, and solve problems. She uses these same skills in her current job as chairman and chief executive officer of Lucent Technologies, which designs and delivers communications hardware, software, and services to communications service providers worldwide.

Russo helped found Lucent in 1996 and oversaw various critical corporate functions, including global sales, strategy and business development, human resources, and public relations. She left Lucent to serve as CEO for Eastman Kodak, but nine months later Lucent asked her to return and appointed her CEO in 2002 and chairman the following year. Prior to her Lucent tenure, she headed AT&T's Business Communications System unit (now Avaya Inc.) and worked in sales and marketing at IBM. For more information, visit scsite.com/dcf2e/ch8/people and then click Patricia Russo.

Chapter Review

The Chapter Review section summarizes the concepts presented in this chapter. To obtain help from other students regarding any subject in this chapter, visit scsite.com/dcf2e/ch8/forum and post your thoughts or questions.

① What Components Are Required for Successful Communications?

Computer **communications** describes a process in which two or more computers or devices transfer data, instructions, and information. Successful communications requires a **sending device** that initiates a transmission instruction, a communications device that connects the sending device to a communications channel, a **communications channel** on which the data travels, a communications device that connects the communications channel to a receiving device, and a **receiving device** that accepts the transmission.

② How Are Computer Communications Used?

Communications technologies include the Internet, Web, e-mail, instant messaging, chat rooms, newsgroups, Internet telephony, FTP, Web folders, video conferencing, and fax machine or computer fax/modem. People also use communications for other purposes. Users send and receive wireless messages to and from smart phones, cellular telephones, or PDAs using **text messaging**, wireless instant messaging, and **picture messaging**. In many public locations, people connect wirelessly to the Internet through a **public Internet access point**, either a **hot spot** or **cybercafé**. A **global positioning system** (**GPS**) analyzes signals sent by satellites to determine an earth-based receiver's geographic location. Many software products allow users to **collaborate**, or work online, with other users connected to a server. **Groupware** is software that helps people work together and share information over a network. **Voice mail** allows someone to leave a voice message for one or more people. **Web services** describe standardized software that enables programmers to create applications that communicate with other remote computers over a network.

Visit scsite.com/dcf2e/ch8/quiz or click the Quiz Yourself button. Click Objectives 1 – 2.

③ What Are Different Types of Networks?

A **network** is a collection of computers and devices connected together via communications devices and media. Networks usually are classified as a local area network, metropolitan area network, or wide area network. A **local area network** (**LAN**) connects computers and devices in a limited geographical area or closely positioned group of buildings. A **wireless LAN** (**WLAN**) is a LAN that uses no physical wires. A **metropolitan area network** (**MAN**) connects local area networks in a metropolitan area and handles the bulk of communications activity across that region. A **wide area network** (**WAN**) covers a large geographic area using a communications channel that combines many types of media.

④ What Is the Purpose of Communications Software?

Communications software helps users establish a connection to another computer or network, manages the transmission of data, and provides an interface for users to communicate with one another.

⑤ What Are Various Types of Lines for Communications Over the Telephone Network?

The telephone network uses dial-up lines or dedicated lines. A **dial-up line** is a temporary connection that uses one or more analog telephone lines for communications. A **dedicated line** is an always-on connection established between two communications devices. Dedicated lines include ISDN lines, DSL, T-carrier lines, and ATM. **ISDN** is a set of standards for digital transmission over standard copper telephone lines. **DSL** transmits at fast speeds on existing standard copper telephone wiring. A **T-carrier line** is a long-distance digital telephone line that carries multiple signals over a single communications line. **ATM** (Asynchronous Transfer Mode) is a service that carries voice, data, video, and multimedia at extremely high speeds.

Visit scsite.com/dcf2e/ch8/quiz or click the Quiz Yourself button. Click Objectives 3 – 5.

⑥ What Are Commonly Used Communications Devices?

A **communications device** is any hardware capable of transmitting data between a sending device and a receiving device. A **modem** converts a computer's digital signals to analog signals for transmission over standard telephone lines. An

Chapter Review

ISDN modem transmits digital data to and from an ISDN line, while a **DSL modem** transmits digital data to and from a DSL line. A **cable modem** is a digital modem that sends and receives digital data over the cable television network. A **wireless modem** allows wireless access to the Web from mobile devices. A **network card** is an adapter card, PC Card, or flash card that enables a computer or device to access a network. A **wireless access point** allows computers and devices to transfer data wirelessly. A **router** connects multiple computers together and transmits data to its destination on the network.

(7) How Can a Home Network Be Set Up?

A **home network** connects multiple computers and devices in a home. An Ethernet network connects each computer to a central hub with a physical cable. A home powerline cable network uses the same lines that bring electricity into the house. A phoneline network uses existing telephone lines in a home. A HomeRF (radio frequency) network and a Wi-Fi network use radio waves, instead of cable, to transmit data.

(8) What Are Various Physical and Wireless Transmission Media?

Transmission media consists of materials or substances capable of carrying one or more signals. Physical transmission media use tangible materials to send communications signals. **Twisted-pair cable** consists of one or more twisted-pair wires bundled together. **Coaxial cable** consists of a single copper wire surrounded by at least three layers: an insulating material, a woven or braided metal, and a plastic outer coating. **Fiber-optic cable** consists of thin strands of glass or plastic that use light to transmit signals. Wireless transmission media send communications signals through the air or space. Infrared (IR) sends signals using infrared light waves. **Broadcast radio** distributes radio signals through the air over long and short distances. **Cellular radio** is a form of broadcast radio that is used widely for mobile communications. **Microwaves** are radio waves that provide a high-speed signal transmission. A **communications satellite** is a space station that receives microwave signals from an earth-based station, amplifies the signals, and broadcasts the signals back over a wide area.

 Visit scsite.com/dcf2e/ch8/quiz or click the Quiz Yourself button. Click Objectives 6 – 8.

Key Terms

You should know each key term. Use the list below to help focus your study. To further enhance your understanding of the Key Terms in this chapter, visit scsite.com/dcf2e/ch8/terms. See an example of and a definition for each term, and access current and additional information about the term from the Web.

802.11 (309)
ATM (312)
bandwidth (317)
Bluetooth (309)
broadband (318)
broadcast radio (321)
bus network (306)
cable modem (314)
cellular radio (321)
client/server network (305)
clients (305)
coaxial cable (320)
collaborate (302)
communications (296)
communications channel (296)
communications device (312)
communications satellite (321)
communications software (310)
cybercafé (300)

dedicated line (311)
dial-up line (311)
DSL (311)
DSL modem (314)
Ethernet (308)
fiber-optic cable (320)
global positioning system (GPS) (301)
groupware (302)
home network (316)
hot spot (300)
intranet (307)
IrDA (309)
ISDN (311)
ISDN modem (314)
local area network (LAN) (303)
metropolitan area network (MAN) (304)
microwaves (321)
modem (313)

network (303)
network specialist (322)
network card (315)
network standard (308)
network topology (306)
noise (319)
P2P (306)
peer-to-peer network (305)
Personal Communications Services (PCS) (321)
picture messaging (298)
public Internet access point (300)
RFID (309)
receiving device (296)
ring network (307)
router (315)
sending device (296)
server (305)
star network (307)

T1 line (312)
T-carrier line (312)
TCP/IP (308)
text messaging (298)
token ring (308)
transmission media (318)
twisted-pair cable (319)
value-added network (VAN) (303)
voice mail (302)
Web services (302)
wide area network (WAN) (304)
Wi-Fi (wireless fidelity) (309)
wireless access point (315)
Wireless Application Protocol (WAP) (309)
wireless LAN (WLAN) (303)
wireless modem (314)

Checkpoint

Use the Checkpoint exercises to check your knowledge level of the chapter.

True/False   Mark T for True and F for False. (See page numbers in parentheses.)

_____ 1. Computer communications describes a process in which two or more computers or devices transfer data, instructions, and information. (296)

_____ 2. E-mail is the transmission of messages and files via a computer network. (298)

_____ 3. Groupware is a software application that helps groups of people work together on projects and share information over a network. (302)

_____ 4. A network is a collection of computers and devices connected together via communications devices and transmission media. (303)

_____ 5. A metropolitan area network (MAN) is a network that covers a large geographic area using a communications channel that combines many types of media such as telephone lines, cables, and radio waves. (304)

_____ 6. On a ring network, all of the computers and devices on the network connect to a central device. (307)

_____ 7. An extranet is an internal network that uses Internet technologies. (307)

_____ 8. A dial-up line is a temporary connection that uses one or more analog telephone lines for communications. (311)

_____ 9. Computers process data as digital signals. (312)

_____ 10. The core of a fiber-optic cable consists of a single copper wire surrounded by an insulating material, a woven or braided metal, and a plastic outer coating. (320)

_____ 11. Microwaves are radio waves that provide a high-speed signal transmission. (321)

Multiple Choice   Select the best answer. (See page numbers in parentheses.)

1. Sending and receiving devices include _____. (297)
   a. mainframe computers and servers
   b. desktop computers and notebook computers
   c. Tablet PCs, PDAs, and smart phones
   d. all of the above

2. An online meeting allows users to _____. (302)
   a. share documents with others in real time
   b. leave voice messages for one or two people
   c. determine the receiver's geographic location
   d. print to a Web address that is associated with a particular printer

3. Because of its larger size, most _____ networks require a person to serve as a network administrator. (305)
   a. client/server   b. peer-to-peer
   c. P2P   d. all of the above

4. Today, _____ is the most popular LAN standard because it is relatively inexpensive and easy to install and maintain. (308)
   a. Bluetooth   b. WAP
   c. Ethernet   d. token ring

5. Communications software consists of programs that do all of the following, except _____. (310)
   a. help users establish a connection to another computer or network
   b. manage the transmission of data, instructions, and information
   c. provide an interface for users to communicate with one another
   d. convert a computer's analog signals into digital signals for transmission

6. The most popular T-carrier line is the _____. (312)
   a. T1 line   b. ATM
   c. T3 line   d. DSL

7. Two types of wireless home networks are _____. (316)
   a. Ethernet and powerline   b. phoneline and HomeRF
   c. Ethernet and Wi-Fi   d. HomeRF and Wi-Fi

8. Fiber-optic cables have all of the following advantages over cables that use wire, except _____. (320)
   a. lower cost   b. less susceptible to noise
   c. smaller size   d. faster data transmission

Matching   Match the terms with their definitions. (See page numbers in parentheses.)

_____ 1. public Internet access point (300)

_____ 2. collaborate (302)

_____ 3. groupware (302)

_____ 4. Ethernet (308)

_____ 5. TCP/IP (308)

a. network standard that specifies no central computer or device on a network should control when data is transmitted
b. network standard that defines how data is routed from one end of a network to another
c. a public location through which people can connect wirelessly to the Internet using mobile computers or devices
d. work online with other users connected to a server
e. online area in which users have written discussions about a subject
f. software that helps groups of people share information

Checkpoint

Short Answer

Write a brief answer to each of the following questions.

1. What is a global positioning system (GPS)? _____ What is picture messaging? _____
2. How are a local area network (LAN), a metropolitan area network (MAN), and a wide area network (WAN) different? _____ What is a wireless LAN? _____
3. What is a dedicated server? _____ How are a file server, a print server, a database server, and a network server different? _____
4. What is a network topology? _____ How are a bus network, a ring network, and a star network different? _____
5. What is bandwidth? _____ How does bandwidth affect system performance? _____

Working Together

Working in a group of your classmates, complete the following team exercise.

1. Assume you are part of a group hired as consultants to recommend a network plan for a small company of 20 employees. Using the Internet and other available resources, develop a network plan for the company. Include the following components in your plan: (1) the type of network — peer-to-peer or client/server, (2) the suggested topology, (3) the type and number of servers, (4) the peripheral devices, and (5) the communications media. Prepare a written report and a PowerPoint presentation to share with the class.

Web Research

Use the Internet-based Web Research exercises to broaden your understanding of the concepts presented in this chapter. Visit scsite.com/dcf2e/ch8/research to obtain more information pertaining to each exercise. To discuss any of the Web Research exercises in this chapter with other students, post your thoughts or questions at scsite.com/dcf2e/ch8/forum.

(1) Journaling

Respond to your readings in this chapter by writing at least one page about your reactions, evaluations, and reflections on computer communications. For example, have you visited a cybercafé? Have you used a device equipped with a global positioning system? How would you react if a classmate used a cell phone with text and picture messaging to cheat on an exam? You also can write about the new terms you learned by reading this chapter. If required, submit your journal to your instructor.

(2) Scavenger Hunt

Use one of the search engines listed in Figure 2-8 in Chapter 2 on page 58 or your own favorite search engine to find the answers to the questions below. Copy and paste the Web address from the Web page where you found the answer. Some questions may have more than one answer. If required, submit your answers to your instructor. (1) How is the IEEE 802.3 standard applied in home entertainment systems? (2) Which operating system has TCP/IP built into it? (3) What is the most common bridge used to connect two dissimilar networks? (4) What company developed the token ring protocol? What is the data transfer rate for token ring technology? (5) What is the purpose of the Bluetooth Special Interest Group? Where is the headquarters of this organization? (6) How many cybercafés are located in Paris, France? In China?

(3) Search Sleuth

Subject directories are used to find specialized topics, such as information about automobiles, travel, and real estate. Most subject directories are arranged by topic and then displayed in a series of menus. Yahoo! is one of the more popular directories. Visit this Web site and then use your word processing program to answer the following questions. Then, if required, submit your answers to your instructor. (1) Click the Shopping link in the Shop area and then click the Software link in the Computers category. What are the top three software products displayed and their prices? (2) Click your browser's Back button or press the BACKSPACE key to return to the Yahoo! home page. Click the Search text box and type "digital camera" and "5.0 megapixels" in the box. Sort the cameras by lowest price by clicking the Lowest Price link near the top of the page. Which camera is the least expensive? (3) Click your browser's Back button or press the BACKSPACE key several times to return to the Yahoo! home page. Click the College and University link in the Education area of the Web Site Directory. Click two of the links in the Site Listings area and review the articles. Write a 50-word summary of your findings.

Learn How To

Use the Learn How To exercises to learn fundamental skills when using a computer and accompanying technology. Complete the exercises and submit them to your instructor.

LEARN HOW TO 1: Set Up and Install a Wi-Fi Home Network

In this chapter you learned about home networks and their advantages (see page 316, Home Networks). Creating a Wi-Fi home network consists of four phases: 1) subscribe to a high-speed Internet connection; 2) purchase the Wi-Fi equipment; 3) connect the physical devices; and 4) create the network through the use of software.

SUBSCRIBE TO A HIGH-SPEED INTERNET CONNECTION   A high-speed Internet connection is advisable to connect all computers on the home network to the Internet. The three primary ways for home users to obtain a fast connection to the Internet are DSL, cable, and satellite. DSL is provided by telephone companies, cable is provided by cable TV companies, and satellite connections are provided by satellite TV providers. Each has its advantages and disadvantages, including the minimum and maximum speed of Internet access, cost, and availability.

Determining the optimal high-speed Internet connection depends largely on where the network will be located, local costs, and service availability. The way to obtain the best high-speed Internet connection is to research the options available in your area.

Exercise

1. Assume you live near Coeur d'Alene, Idaho. You have decided that high-speed Internet access and a Wi-Fi network would be advantageous for your at-home business. Find answers to the following questions for this Idaho town or a town specified by your instructor: What methods of high-speed Internet access are available? Which provides the best service? Which is the cheapest? Based on the information you gather, write a plan for subscribing to a high-speed Internet connection service. Submit the answers to the questions and your plan to your instructor.

PURCHASE THE WI-FI EQUIPMENT   As part of the service when you subscribe to fast access on the Internet, you receive a modem that is capable of connecting to the Internet. In most cases, the modem is not a wireless transmitter. So, in order to establish a wireless connection between the Internet and the home network, you will need a wireless router that establishes the wireless access point.

You can visit any retail electronics store and find a wide variety of wireless routers. A key to purchasing the correct router is to ensure it will work with your modem and Internet access service. Some Internet service providers support only certain brands of routers and, while it is true that other routers may work, you might be taking a risk if you purchase an unsupported router. With the popularity of wireless home networks, though, some Internet service providers now provide a wireless router as part of the subscription service, often for an additional fee. You should investigate closely the needs for the Wi-Fi router to ensure compatibility with your Internet access service.

In addition to the router, each computer that is to be part of the Wi-Fi network needs a wireless network adapter. This device allows the computers to communicate with one another. Most external wireless network adapters plug in either a PC Card slot or a USB connection. Many notebook computers have a built-in wireless network adapter.

Finally, in the better designed home networks, one computer is designated the Internet Connection Sharing (ICS) host. This is the computer that is connected directly to the wireless router, then to the modem and the Internet. Most of the time, this computer, which normally is a desktop and the most powerful computer in the network, is connected using an Ethernet network adapter and cable.

Once the Wi-Fi equipment is assembled, you are ready to connect your home network.

Exercise

1. Using your Web research skills, determine the type of IEEE 802.11 standard used by modems available from Internet service providers. What percentage use 802.11b? What percentage use 802.11g? If your modem uses 802.11b but your wireless network router is 802.11g, what happens? Based on your research, which router do you recommend? Submit your answers to your instructor.

Learn How To

CONNECT THE PHYSICAL DEVICES Once you have assembled your equipment, you can connect the devices in the network. Usually, the modem will be connected to the source of the Internet transmission (DSL, cable, or satellite). Then the modem is connected to the wireless router, which in turn is connected to the Internet Connection Sharing computer.

After these connections are completed, each of the computers that will be used in the network that do not have a built-in wireless network adapter must have the adapter attached, often by using a USB connection. Once these connections are made, the network can be created.

CREATE THE NETWORK To establish a network, operating system software must be configured based on the design of your network. To begin the process on a Windows XP computer with Service Pack 2, you should run the Wireless Network Setup Wizard by completing the following steps:

1. Click the Start button on the Windows taskbar and then click Control Panel on the Start menu.
2. In Category view, click Network and Internet Connections.
3. In the Network and Internet Connections window, click Set up a wireless network for home or small office. *The first Wireless Network Setup Wizard dialog box is displayed.*
4. Click the Next button. If the next Wireless Network Setup Wizard dialog box asks "What do you want to do?," click Set up a new wireless network and then click the Next button.
5. In the Network name (SSID) text box, type a name for the wireless network you are creating. Use a name that you will recognize as the name for the network. Make sure the Automatically assign a network key option button is selected. If your devices are so equipped, click the Use WPA encryption instead of WEP check box. This will give your network stronger security. Then, click the Next button.
6. In the next Wireless Network Setup Wizard dialog box (Figure 8-28), click Use a USB flash drive if you have a USB drive to use; otherwise, click Set up a network manually (these steps assume you have a USB drive). Click the Next button.
7. Insert your flash drive in a USB port and wait for the drive letter to appear. Click the Next button.
8. Follow the steps specified in the wizard to configure each computer in the network and then click the Next button.
9. The network has been created. Click the Finish button to close the wizard.

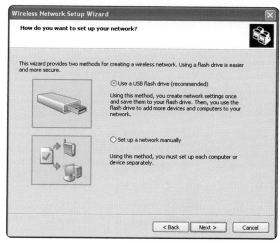

FIGURE 8-28

Next, you must run the Network Setup Wizard to configure the network by completing the following steps:

1. Open the Network and Internet Connections window in Control Panel. Click Set up or change your home or small office network. *The Network Setup Wizard is displayed (Figure 8-29).*
2. Follow the instructions in the wizard.

FIGURE 8-29

Exercise

1. Form a three-person team whose responsibility is to create a Wi-Fi network for a small business in your local area. Assign tasks to each member of the team. Write a detailed plan for creating the Wi-Fi network, including the brand and type of equipment to be purchased, costs, and a schedule for completing the work. Submit the plan to your instructor.

Learn It Online

Use the Learn It Online exercises to reinforce your understanding of the chapter concepts. To access the Learn It Online exercises, visit scsite.com/dcf2e/ch8/learn.

(1) At the Movies — Bluetooth in Action

To view the Bluetooth in Action movie, click the number 1 button. Locate your video and click the corresponding High-Speed or Dial-Up link, depending on your Internet connection. Watch the movie and then complete the exercise by answering the questions that follow. When Bluetooth works it can be a great way to optimize your personal area network (PAN). How can Bluetooth change your personal area network (PAN) into a wireless network? What are the dangers of using Bluetooth without proper security?

(2) Student Edition Labs — Networking Basics

Click the number 2 button. When the Student Edition Labs menu appears, click *Networking Basics* to begin. A new browser window will open. Follow the on-screen instructions to complete the Lab. When finished, click the Exit button. If required, submit your results to your instructor.

(3) Practice Test

Click the number 3 button. Answer each question. When completed, enter your name and click the Grade Test button to submit the quiz for grading. Make a note of any missed questions. If required, submit your results to your instructor.

(4) Who Wants To Be a Computer Genius²?

Click the number 4 button to find out if you are a computer genius. Directions about how to play the game will be displayed. When you are ready to play, click the Play button. Submit your score to your instructor.

(5) Wheel of Terms

Click the number 5 button to reinforce important terms you learned in this chapter by playing the Shelly Cashman Series version of this popular game. Directions about how to play the game will be displayed. When you are ready to play, click the Play button. Submit your score to your instructor.

(6) Student Edition Labs — Wireless Networking

Click the number 6 button. When the Student Edition Labs menu appears, click *Wireless Networking* to begin. A new browser window will open. Follow the on-screen instructions to complete the Lab. When finished, click the Exit button. If required, submit your results to your instructor.

(7) Crossword Puzzle Challenge

Click the number 7 button. Complete the puzzle to reinforce skills you learned in this chapter. Directions about how to play the game will be displayed. When you are ready to play, click the Submit button. Submit the completed puzzle to your instructor.

(8) Lab Exercises

Click the number 8 button. When the Lab Exercises menu appears, click the exercise assigned by your instructor. A new browser window will open. Follow the on-screen instructions to complete the exercise. When finished, click the Exit button. If required, submit your results to your instructor.

(9) Chapter Discussion Forum

Select an objective from this chapter on page 295 about which you would like more information. Click the number 9 button and post a short message listing a meaningful message title accompanied by one or more questions concerning the selected objective. In two days, return to the threaded discussion by clicking the number 9 button. Submit to your instructor your original message and at least one response to your message.

CHAPTER 9

Database Management

CONTENTS

OBJECTIVES

After completing this chapter, you will be able to:

1. Define the term, database
2. Identify the qualities of valuable information
3. Discuss the terms character, field, record, and file
4. Identify file maintenance techniques
5. Differentiate between a file processing system approach and the database approach
6. Discuss the functions common to most DBMSs
7. Describe characteristics of relational, object-oriented, and multidimensional databases
8. Explain how to interact with Web databases
9. Discuss the responsibilities of database analysts and administrators

DATABASES, DATA, AND INFORMATION
Data Integrity
Qualities of Valuable Information

THE HIERARCHY OF DATA
Characters
Fields
Records
Files

MAINTAINING DATA
Adding Records
Changing Records
Deleting Records
Validating Data

FILE PROCESSING VERSUS DATABASES
File Processing Systems
The Database Approach

DATABASE MANAGEMENT SYSTEMS
Data Dictionary
File Retrieval and Maintenance
Backup and Recovery
Data Security

RELATIONAL, OBJECT-ORIENTED, AND MULTIDIMENSIONAL DATABASES
Relational Databases
Object-Oriented Databases
Multidimensional Databases

WEB DATABASES

DATABASE ADMINISTRATION
Database Design Guidelines
Role of the Database Analysts and Administrators
Role of the Employee as a User

CHAPTER SUMMARY

COMPANIES ON THE CUTTING EDGE
Oracle
Sybase

TECHNOLOGY TRAILBLAZERS
E. F. Codd
Larry Ellison

DATABASES, DATA, AND INFORMATION

A database is a collection of data organized in a manner that allows access, retrieval, and use of that data. **Data** can include text, numbers, images, audio, and video. **Information** is processed data; that is, it is organized, meaningful, and useful.

Computers process data in a database into information. A database at a members-only discount warehouse, for example, contains data about members, e.g., member data, purchases data, etc. As shown in Figure 9-1, a computer at the warehouse processes new member data and then sends receipt and ID card information to the printers.

With **database software**, often called a **database management system** (**DBMS**), users create a computerized database; add, change, and delete data in the database; sort and retrieve data from the database; and create forms and reports from the data in the database. Database software includes many powerful features, as you will discover later in this chapter.

FIGURE 9-1   HOW A MEMBERS-ONLY DISCOUNT WAREHOUSE MIGHT PROCESS DATA INTO INFORMATION

Step 1:
A membership services associate uses a digital camera to take a photograph of the new member and uses a keyboard to enter other member data into the computer.

Data Integrity

Most companies realize that data is one of their more valuable assets — because data is used to generate information. Many business transactions take less time when employees have instant access to information. To ensure that data is accessible on demand, a company must manage and protect its data just as it would any other resource. Thus, it is vital that the data has integrity and is kept secure.

For a computer to produce correct information, the data that is entered into a database must have integrity. Data integrity identifies the quality of the data. An erroneous member address in a member database is an example of incorrect data. When a database contains this type of error, it loses integrity. Data integrity is very important because computers and people use information to make decisions and take actions.

Garbage in, garbage out (**GIGO**) is a computing phrase that points out the accuracy of a computer's output depends on the accuracy of the input. If you enter incorrect data into a computer (garbage in), the computer will produce incorrect information (garbage out).

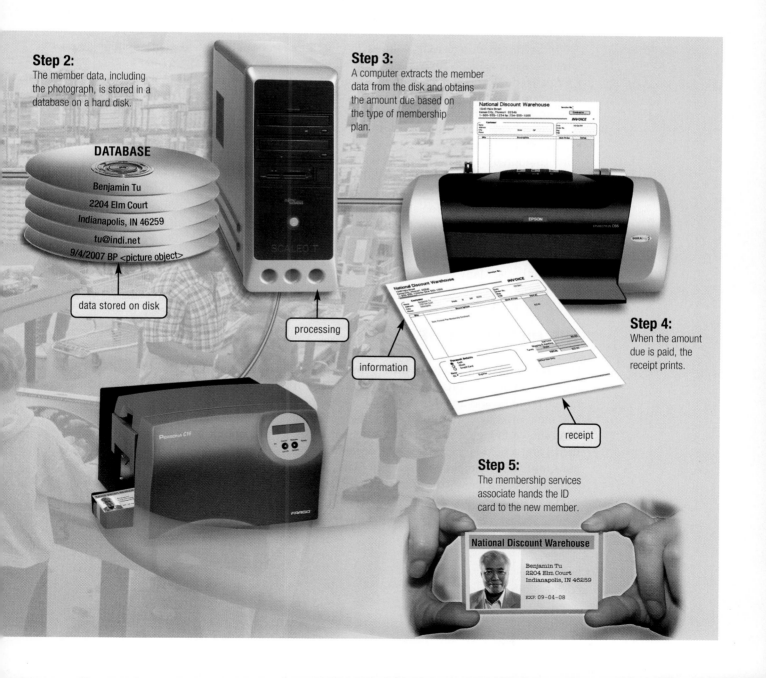

Step 2:
The member data, including the photograph, is stored in a database on a hard disk.

DATABASE

Benjamin Tu

2204 Elm Court

Indianapolis, IN 46259

tu@indi.net

9/4/2007 BP <picture object>

data stored on disk

processing

Step 3:
A computer extracts the member data from the disk and obtains the amount due based on the type of membership plan.

information

Step 4:
When the amount due is paid, the receipt prints.

receipt

Step 5:
The membership services associate hands the ID card to the new member.

National Discount Warehouse

Benjamin Tu
2204 Elm Court
Indianapolis, IN 46259

EXP. 09-04-08

Qualities of Valuable Information

The information that data generates also is an important asset. People make decisions daily using all types of information such as receipts, bank statements, pension plan summaries, stock analyses, and credit reports. In a business, managers make decisions based on sales trends, competitors' products and services, production processes, and even employee skills.

To assist with sound decision making, the information must have value. For it to be valuable, information should be accurate, verifiable, timely, organized, accessible, useful, and cost-effective.

- Accurate information is error free. Inaccurate information can lead to incorrect decisions. For example, consumers assume their credit report is accurate. If your credit report incorrectly shows past due payments, a bank may not lend you money for a car or house.
- Verifiable information can be proven as correct or incorrect. For example, a ticket agent at an airport usually requests some type of photo identification to verify that you are the person named on the ticket.
- Timely information has an age suited to its use. A decision to build additional schools in a particular district should be based on the most recent census report — not on one that is 20 years old.

    Most information loses its value with time. Some information, such as information about trends, gains value as time passes and more information is obtained.
- Organized information is arranged to suit the needs and requirements of the decision maker. Different people may need the same information presented in a different manner. For example, an inventory manager may want an inventory report to list out-of-stock items first. The purchasing agent, instead, wants the report alphabetized by vendor.
- Accessible information is available when the decision maker needs it. Having to wait for information may delay an important decision.
- Useful information has meaning to the person who receives it. Most information is important only to certain people or groups of people.
- Cost-effective information should give more value than it costs to produce. A company occasionally should review the information it produces to determine if it still is cost-effective to produce. Sometimes, it is not easy to place a value on information. For this reason, some companies create information only on demand, that is, as people request it, instead of on a regular basis. Many companies make information available online. Users then can access and print online information as they need it.

THE HIERARCHY OF DATA

Data is organized in layers. In the computer profession, data is classified in a hierarchy. Each higher level of data consists of one or more items from the lower level. For example, a member has an address, and an address consists of letters and numbers. Depending on the application and the user, different terms describe the various levels of the hierarchy.

As shown in Figure 9-2, a database contains files, a file contains records, a record contains fields, and a field is made up of one or more characters. The Discount Warehouse database contains four files: Member, Membership Plans, Member Purchases, and Products. The Member file contains records about current members. The Membership Plans file contains records identifying a type of membership and its annual fee. The Member Purchases file contains records about members' purchases at the discount warehouse, and the Products file contains records about items for sale.

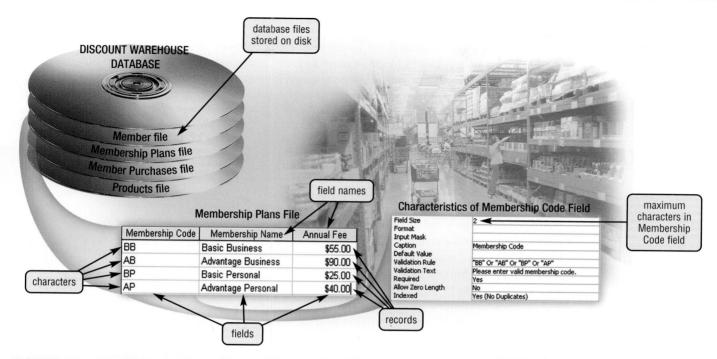

FIGURE 9-2 A sample discount warehouse database with four files: Member, Membership Plans, Member Purchases, and Products. The sample Membership Plans file contains four records. Each record contains three fields. The Membership Code field can contain a maximum of two characters (bytes).

Characters

As Chapter 4 discussed, a bit is the smallest unit of data the computer can process. Eight bits grouped together in a unit comprise a byte. In the ASCII and EBCDIC coding schemes, each byte represents a single **character**, which can be a number (4), letter (R), punctuation mark (?), or other symbol (&).

Fields

A **field** is a combination of one or more related characters or bytes and is the smallest unit of data a user accesses. A **field name** uniquely identifies each field. When searching for data in a database, you often specify the field name. Field names for the data in the Membership Plans file are Membership Code, Membership Name, and Annual Fee.

A database uses a variety of characteristics, such as field size and data type, to define each field. The **field size** defines the maximum number of characters a field can contain. For example, the Membership Code field contains two characters. Valid entries include BB (Basic Business), AB (Advantage Business), BP (Basic Personal), and AP (Advantage Personal). Thus, as shown in Figure 9-2, the Membership Code field has a field size of 2.

The type of data in a field is an important consideration. Figure 9-3 identifies the data types for fields in the Membership Plans and Member files. The **data type** specifies the kind of data a field can contain and how the field is used. Common data types include:

- Text (also called alphanumeric) — letters, numbers, or special characters
- Numeric — numbers only
- AutoNumber — unique number automatically assigned by the DBMS to each added record
- Currency — dollar and cent amounts or numbers containing decimal values
- Date — month, day, year, and sometimes time information
- Memo — lengthy text entries
- Yes/No — only the values Yes or No (or True or False)
- Hyperlink — Web address that links to a document or a Web page
- Object — photograph, audio, video, or a document created in other programs

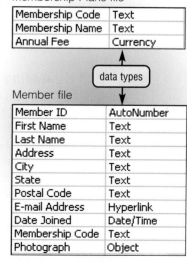

Membership Plans file

Membership Code	Text
Membership Name	Text
Annual Fee	Currency

data types

Member file

Member ID	AutoNumber
First Name	Text
Last Name	Text
Address	Text
City	Text
State	Text
Postal Code	Text
E-mail Address	Hyperlink
Date Joined	Date/Time
Membership Code	Text
Photograph	Object

FIGURE 9-3 Data types of fields in the Membership Plans and Member files.

Records

A **record** is a group of related fields. For example, a member record includes a set of fields about one member. A **key field**, or **primary key**, is a field that uniquely identifies each record in a file. The data in a key field is unique to a specific record. For example, the Member ID field uniquely identifies each member because no two members can have the same Member ID.

Files

A **data file** is a collection of related records stored on a storage medium such as a hard disk, CD, or DVD. A Member file at a discount warehouse might consist of hundreds of individual member records. Each member record in the file contains the same fields. Each field, however, contains different data. Figure 9-4 shows a small sample Member file that contains four member records, each with eleven fields.

A database includes a group of related data files. Read At Issue 9-1 for a discussion related to a use of databases.

SAMPLE MEMBER FILE

Member ID	First Name	Last Name
2295	Milton	Brewer
3876	Louella	Drake
3928	Adelbert	Ruiz
4872	Elena	Gupta

records

key field

fields

MAINTAINING DATA

File maintenance refers to the procedures that keep data current. File maintenance procedures include adding records to, changing records in, and deleting records from a file.

Adding Records

Users add new records to a file when they obtain new data. If a new member wants to join the discount warehouse club, a membership services associate adds a new record to the Member file at the discount warehouse. The process required to add this record to the file might include the following steps:

1. A membership services associate displays a Member Maintenance form that gives him or her access to the Member file. The associate then clicks the New Record button, which begins the process of adding a record to the Member file.
2. The associate fills in the fields of the member record with data (except for the Member ID, which automatically is assigned by the program).
3. The associate takes a picture of the member using a digital camera. The program stores this picture in the Member file and prints it on a member ID card.
4. The membership services associate verifies the data on the screen and then presses a key on the keyboard or clicks a button on the screen to add the new member record to the Member file. The system software determines where to write the record on the disk (Figure 9-5).

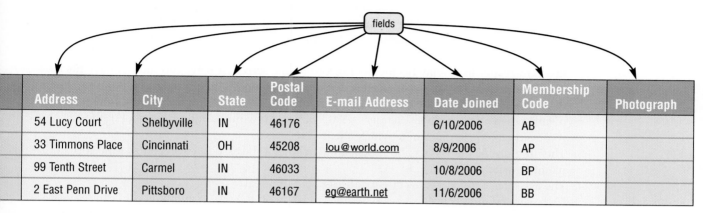

	Address	City	State	Postal Code	E-mail Address	Date Joined	Membership Code	Photograph
	54 Lucy Court	Shelbyville	IN	46176		6/10/2006	AB	
	33 Timmons Place	Cincinnati	OH	45208	lou@world.com	8/9/2006	AP	
	99 Tenth Street	Carmel	IN	46033		10/8/2006	BP	
	2 East Penn Drive	Pittsboro	IN	46167	eg@earth.net	11/6/2006	BB	

FIGURE 9-4 A sample data file, stored on a hard disk, that contains four records, each with eleven fields.

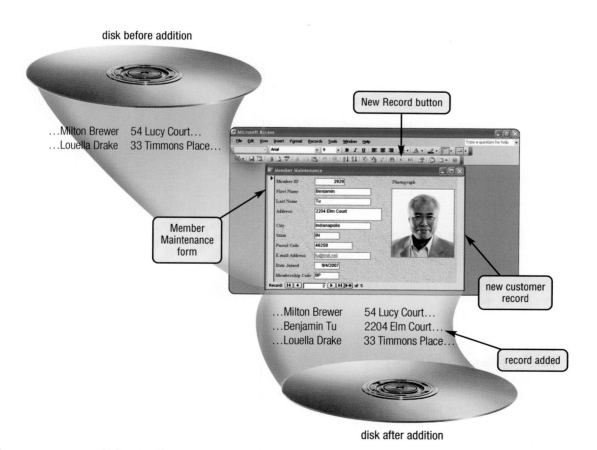

FIGURE 9-5 Using the Member Maintenance form, a membership services associate adds a new member record for Benjamin Tu. After the associate takes the photograph with the digital camera and confirms the data is correct, he or she adds the record to the database file.

Changing Records

Generally, users change a record in a file for two reasons: (1) to correct inaccurate data or (2) to update old data with new data.

Suppose, for example, that Benjamin Tu moves from 2204 Elm Court to 76 Ash Street. The process to change the address and update Benjamin Tu's record might include the following steps:

1. The membership services associate displays the Member Maintenance form.
2. Assuming Benjamin Tu is present, the services associate inserts Benjamin's member ID card in a card reader to display his member record on the screen. If Benjamin did not have his ID card or was not present, the associate could enter Benjamin's member ID — if Benjamin knew it. Otherwise, the associate could enter Tu in the Last Name field, which would retrieve all members with that same last name. The associate then would scroll through all of the retrieved records to determine which one is Benjamin's.
3. The program displays data about Benjamin Tu so that the associate can confirm the correct member record is displayed.
4. The associate enters the new street address, 76 Ash Street.
5. The membership services associate verifies the data on the screen and then clicks the Save button to change the record in the Member file. The program changes the record on the disk (Figure 9-6).

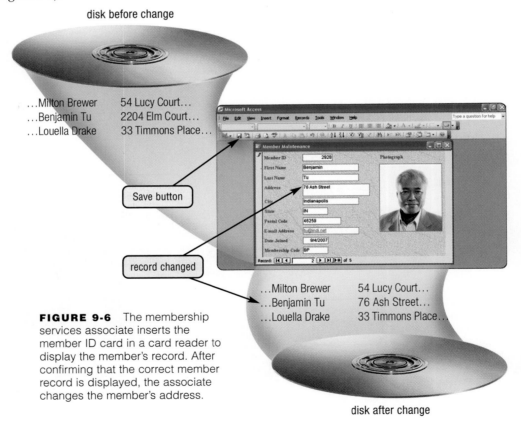

FIGURE 9-6 The membership services associate inserts the member ID card in a card reader to display the member's record. After confirming that the correct member record is displayed, the associate changes the member's address.

Deleting Records

When a record no longer is needed, a user deletes it from a file. Assume a member named Elena Gupta is moving out of the country. The process required to delete a record from a file includes the following steps:

1. The membership service associate displays the Member Maintenance form.
2. The associate displays Elena Gupta's member record on the screen.
3. The associate confirms the correct member record is displayed. Then, the associate clicks the Delete Record button to delete the record from the Member file and then clicks the Save button to save the modified file.

Programs use a variety of techniques to manage deleted records. Sometimes, the program removes the record from the file immediately. Other times, the record is flagged, or marked, so the program will not process it again. In this case, the program places an asterisk (*) or some other character at the beginning of the record (Figure 9-7).

Programs that maintain inactive data for an extended period commonly flag records. For example, a discount warehouse might flag canceled memberships. When a program flags a deleted record, the record remains physically on the disk. The record, however, is deleted logically because the program will not process it.

From time to time, users should run a utility program that removes the flagged records and reorganizes current records. For example, the discount warehouse may remove from disk any accounts that have been canceled for more than one year.

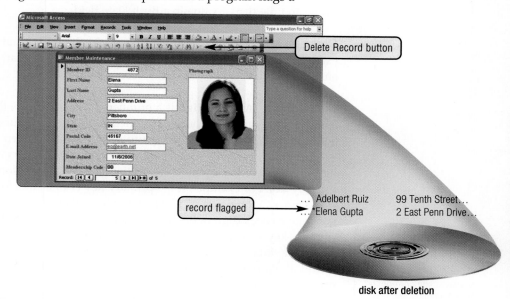

FIGURE 9-7   The membership services associate displays the member's record on the screen. After the associate verifies that the correct member record is displayed, he or she deletes the record. The program flags the member record on disk by placing an asterisk in the first position of the record.

Validating Data

Validation is the process of comparing data with a set of rules or values to find out if the data is correct. Many programs perform a validity check that analyzes entered data to help ensure that it is correct. For instance, when a membership services associate adds or changes data in a member record, the DBMS tests the entered data.

With an annual membership fee, you would expect to see numbers before and after a decimal point. For example, a valid annual membership fee is 30.00. An entry of XR.WP clearly is not correct. If the entered data fails a validity check, the computer should display an error message that instructs the user to enter the data again. Validity checks reduce data entry errors.

Various types of validity checks include alphabetic checks, numeric checks, range checks, consistency checks, and completeness checks. Check digits also validate data accuracy. The following paragraphs describe the purpose of these validity checks. The table in Figure 9-8 illustrates several of these validity checks and shows valid data that passes the check and invalid data that fails the check.

SAMPLE VALID AND INVALID DATA

Validity Check	Field Being Checked	Valid Data	Invalid Data
Alphabetic Check	First Name	Karen	Ka24n
Numeric Check	Postal Code	46322	4tr22
Range Check	Annual Fee	$30.00	$120.00
Consistency Check	Date Joined Birth Date	9/20/2006 8/27/1983	9/20/2006 8/27/2007
Completeness Check	Last Name	Tu	

FIGURE 9-8   In this table of sample valid and invalid data, the first column lists commonly used validity checks. The second column lists the name of the field that contains data being checked. The third column shows valid data that passes the validity checks. The fourth column shows invalid data that fails the validity checks.

ALPHABETIC/NUMERIC CHECK   An **alphabetic check** ensures that users enter only alphabetic data into a field. A **numeric check** ensures that users enter only numeric data into a field. For example, data in a First Name field should contain only characters from the alphabet. Data in a postal code field should contain numbers (with the exception of the special characters such as a hyphen).

RANGE CHECK   A **range check** determines whether a number is within a specified range. Assume the lowest annual membership fee at the discount warehouse is $25.00 and the highest is $90.00. A range check on the Annual Fee field ensures it is a value between $25.00 and $90.00.

CONSISTENCY CHECK   A **consistency check** tests the data in two or more associated fields to ensure that the relationship is logical. For example, the value in a Date Joined field cannot occur earlier in time than a value in a Birth Date field.

COMPLETENESS CHECK   A **completeness check** verifies that a required field contains data. For example, in many programs, you cannot leave the Last Name field blank. The completeness check ensures that data exists in the Last Name field.

CHECK DIGIT   A **check digit** is a number(s) or character(s) that is appended to or inserted in a primary key value. A check digit often confirms the accuracy of a primary key value. Bank account, credit card, and other identification numbers often include one or more check digits.

A program determines the check digit by applying a formula to the numbers in the primary key value. An oversimplified illustration of a check digit formula is to add the numbers in the primary key. For example, if the primary key is 1367, this formula would add these numbers (1 + 3 + 6 + 7) for a sum of 17. Next, the formula would add the numbers in the result (1 + 7) to generate a check digit of 8. The primary key then is 13678. This example began with the original primary key value, 1367, then the check digit, 8, was appended.

When a data entry clerk enters the primary key of 13678, for example, to look up an existing record, the program determines whether the check digit is valid. If the clerk enters an incorrect primary key, such as 13778, the check digit entered (8) will not match the computed check digit (9). In this case, the program displays an error message that instructs the user to enter the primary key value again.

WEB LINK 9-1

Check Digits

For more information, visit scsite.com/dcf2e/ch9/weblink and then click Check Digits.

Test your knowledge of pages 332 through 340 in Quiz Yourself 9-1.

QUIZ YOURSELF 9-1

Instructions: Find the true statement below. Then, rewrite the remaining false statements so they are true.

1. A database is a combination of one or more related characters or bytes and is the smallest unit of data a user accesses.

2. A record is a collection of data organized in a manner that allows access, retrieval, and use of that data.

3. Data is processed information.

4. Hierarchy of data procedures include adding records to, changing records in, and deleting records from a file.

5. To be valuable, information should be accurate, verifiable, timely, organized, accessible, useful, and cost-effective.

Quiz Yourself Online: To further check your knowledge of databases, qualities of valuable information, the hierarchy of data, and file maintenance techniques, visit scsite.com/dcf2e/ch9/quiz and then click Objectives 1 – 4.

FILE PROCESSING VERSUS DATABASES

Almost all application programs use either the file processing approach or the database approach to store and manage data. The following pages discuss these two approaches.

File Processing Systems

In the past, many organizations used file processing systems to store and manage data. In a typical **file processing system**, each department or area within an organization has its own set of files. The records in one file may not relate to the records in any other file.

Companies have used file processing systems for many years. A lot of these systems, however, have two major weaknesses: they have redundant data and they isolate data.

- Data Redundancy — Each department or area in a company has its own files in a file processing system. Thus, the same fields are stored in multiple files. If a file processing system is used at the discount warehouse, for example, the Member file and the Member Purchases file store the same members' names and addresses.

  Duplicating data in this manner wastes resources such as storage space and people's time. When new members are added or member data is changed, file maintenance tasks consume additional time because people must update multiple files that contain the same data.

  Data redundancy also can increase the chance of errors. If a member changes his or her address, for example, the discount warehouse must update the address wherever it appears. In this example, the Address field is in the Member file and also in the Member Purchases file. If the Address field is not changed in all the files where it is stored, then discrepancies among the files exist.

- Isolated Data — Often it is difficult to access data stored in separate files in different departments. Sharing data from multiple, separate files is a complicated procedure and usually requires the experience of a computer programmer.

The Database Approach

When a company uses the **database approach**, many programs and users share the data in the database. A discount warehouse's database most likely contains data about members, membership plans, member purchases, and products. As shown in Figure 9-9, various areas within the discount warehouse share and interact with the data in this database. The database does secure its data, however, so only authorized users can access certain data items.

Users can access the data in the database via application software called a DBMS. While a user is working with the database, the DBMS resides in the memory of the computer.

Programs on Computer for Checkout Lanes

Programs on Membership Services Associate's Computer

Database Management System

Member File
Membership Plans File
Member Purchases File
Products File

Discount Warehouse Database

FIGURE 9-9   In a discount warehouse that uses a database, the computer used by the membership services associate and the computer used in the checkout lane access data in a single database through the DBMS.

The database approach addresses many of the weaknesses associated with file processing systems. The following paragraphs present some strengths of the database approach.

- **Reduced Data Redundancy** — Most data items are stored in only one file, which greatly reduces duplicate data. Figure 9-10 demonstrates the differences between how a database application and a file processing application might store data.
- **Improved Data Integrity** — When users modify data in the database, they make changes to one file instead of multiple files. Thus, the database approach increases the data's integrity by reducing the possibility of introducing inconsistencies.
- **Shared Data** — The data in a database environment belongs to and is shared, usually over a network, by the entire organization. Companies that use databases typically have security settings to define who can access, add, change, and delete the data in a database.
- **Easier Access** — The database approach allows nontechnical users to access and maintain data, providing they have the necessary privileges.
- **Reduced Development Time** — It often is easier and faster to develop programs that use the database approach.

Databases have many advantages as well as some disadvantages. A database can be more complex than a file processing system. People with special training usually develop larger databases and their associated applications. Databases also require more memory, storage, and processing power than file processing systems.

Data in a database is more vulnerable than data in file processing systems. A database stores most data in a single file. Many users and programs share and depend on this data. If the database is not operating properly or is damaged or destroyed, users may not be able to perform their jobs. In some cases, certain programs may stop working. To protect their valuable database resource, individuals and companies should establish and follow security procedures. Despite these limitations, many business and home users work with databases because of their tremendous advantages.

FAQ 9-1

Can a database eliminate redundant data completely?

No, a database reduces redundant data — it does not eliminate it. Files in a database link together based on values in key fields. For example, the Member ID field will exist in any file that requires access to member data. Thus, the Member ID is duplicated (exists in many files) in the database. For more information, visit scsite.com/dcf2e/ch9/faq and then click Database Relationships.

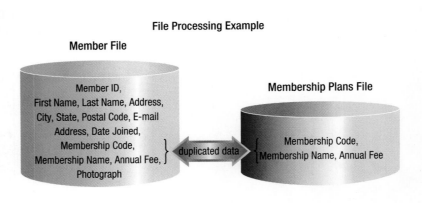

FIGURE 9-10   In the file processing environment, both files contain all membership plans data fields. In a database environment, only the Membership Plans file contains the Membership Name and Annual Fee fields. Other files, however, such as the Member file, contain the Membership Code, which links to the Membership Plans file when membership plans data is needed.

DATABASE MANAGEMENT SYSTEMS

WEB LINK 9-2

Database Management System

For more information, visit scsite.com/dcf2e/ch9/weblink and then click Database Management System.

As previously discussed, a database management system (DBMS), or database program, is software that allows you to create, access, and manage a database. DBMSs are available for many sizes and types of computers (Figure 9-11). Whether designed for a small or large computer, most DBMSs perform common functions. The following pages discuss functions common to most DBMSs.

POPULAR DATABASE MANAGEMENT SYSTEMS

Database	Manufacturer	Computer Type
Access	Microsoft Corporation	Personal computer, server, PDA
Adabas	Software AG	Midrange server, mainframe
D³	Raining Data	Personal computer, midrange server
DB2	IBM Corporation	Personal computer, midrange server, mainframe
Essbase	Hyperion Solutions Corporation	Personal computer, server
Informix	IBM Corporation	Personal computer, midrange server, mainframe
Ingres	Computer Associates International, Inc.	Personal computer, midrange server, mainframe
InterBase	Borland Software Corporation	Personal computer, server
ObjectStore	Progress Software Corporation	Personal computer, midrange server
Oracle	Oracle Corporation	Personal computer, midrange server, mainframe, PDA
SQL Server	Microsoft Corporation	Server, personal computer, PDA
Sybase	Sybase Inc.	Personal computer, midrange server, PDA
Versant	Versant Corporation	Personal computer, midrange server

FIGURE 9-11 Many database management systems run on multiple types of computers.

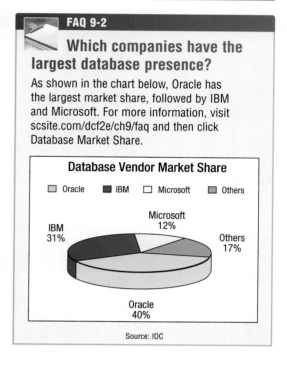

FAQ 9-2

Which companies have the largest database presence?

As shown in the chart below, Oracle has the largest market share, followed by IBM and Microsoft. For more information, visit scsite.com/dcf2e/ch9/faq and then click Database Market Share.

Database Vendor Market Share

☐ Oracle   ■ IBM   ☐ Microsoft   ▨ Others

- Microsoft 12%
- IBM 31%
- Others 17%
- Oracle 40%

Source: IDC

Data Dictionary

A **data dictionary** contains data about each file in the database and each field within those files. For each file, it stores details such as the file name, description, the file's relationship to other files, and the number of records in the file. For each field, it stores details such as the field name, description, field type, field size, default value, validation rules, and the field's relationship to other fields. Figure 9-12 shows how a data dictionary might list data for a Member file.

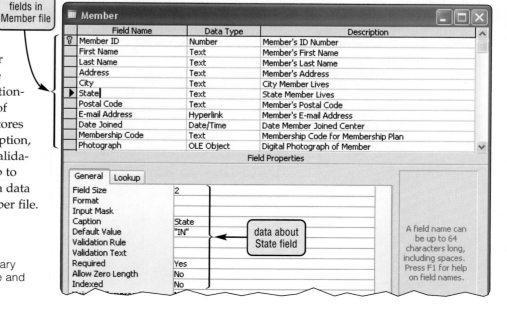

fields in Member file

Member

Field Name	Data Type	Description
Member ID	Number	Member's ID Number
First Name	Text	Member's First Name
Last Name	Text	Member's Last Name
Address	Text	Member's Address
City	Text	City Member Lives
State	Text	State Member Lives
Postal Code	Text	Member's Postal Code
E-mail Address	Hyperlink	Member's E-mail Address
Date Joined	Date/Time	Date Member Joined Center
Membership Code	Text	Membership Code for Membership Plan
Photograph	OLE Object	Digital Photograph of Member

Field Properties

General	Lookup
Field Size	2
Format	
Input Mask	
Caption	State
Default Value	"IN"
Validation Rule	
Validation Text	
Required	Yes
Allow Zero Length	No
Indexed	No

data about State field

A field name can be up to 64 characters long, including spaces. Press F1 for help on field names.

FIGURE 9-12 A sample data dictionary entry shows the fields in the Member file and the properties of the State field.

File Retrieval and Maintenance

A DBMS provides several tools that allow users and programs to retrieve and maintain data in the database. To retrieve or select data in a database, you query it. A **query** is a request for specific data from the database. Users can instruct the DBMS to display, print, or store the results of a query. The capability of querying a database is one of the more powerful database features.

A DBMS offers several methods to retrieve and maintain its data. The four more commonly used are query languages, query by example, forms, and report generators. The following paragraphs describe each of these methods.

QUERY LANGUAGE A **query language** consists of simple, English-like statements that allow users to specify the data to display, print, or store. Each query language has its own grammar and vocabulary. A person without a programming background usually can learn a query language in a short time.

To simplify the query process, many DBMSs provide wizards to guide users through the steps of creating a query. Figure 9-13 shows how to use the Simple Query Wizard in Microsoft Access to display the First Name, Last Name, and E-mail Address fields from the Member file. Instead of using the wizard, you could enter the query language statement shown in Figure 9-13 directly in the DBMS to display the results shown in Step 3. Read Looking Ahead 9-1 for a look at the next generation of query languages.

FIGURE 9-13 HOW TO USE THE SIMPLE QUERY WIZARD

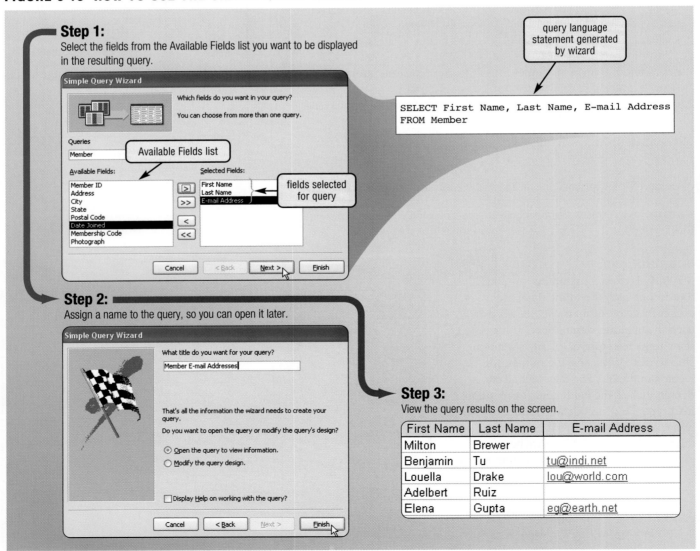

QUERY BY EXAMPLE Most DBMSs include a **query by example (QBE)** feature that has a graphical user interface to assist users with retrieving data. Figure 9-14 shows a sample QBE screen for a query that searches for and lists members on the Basic Personal plan; that is, their Membership Code field value is equal to BP.

FIGURE 9-14a (query by example screen)

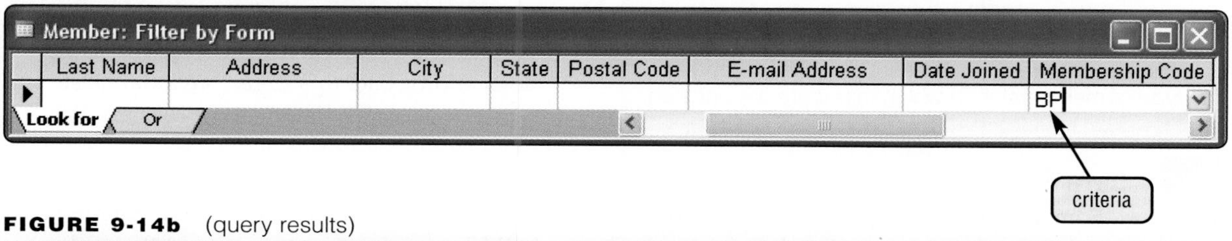

	Last Name	Address	City	State	Postal Code	E-mail Address	Date Joined	Membership Code
								BP

Member: Filter by Form

Look for / Or /

criteria

FIGURE 9-14b (query results)

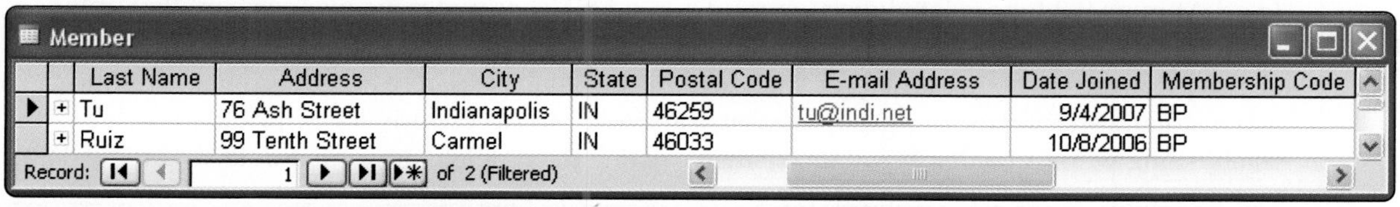

Member

		Last Name	Address	City	State	Postal Code	E-mail Address	Date Joined	Membership Code
▶	+	Tu	76 Ash Street	Indianapolis	IN	46259	tu@indi.net	9/4/2007	BP
	+	Ruiz	99 Tenth Street	Carmel	IN	46033		10/8/2006	BP

Record: ◀◀ ◀ 1 ▶ ▶▶ ▶* of 2 (Filtered)

FIGURE 9-14 Access has many QBE capabilities. One QBE technique is Filter by Form, which uses a form to show available fields. The database program retrieves records that match criteria you enter in the form fields. This example searches for members whose Membership Code is equal to BP.

FORM A **form**, sometimes called a data entry form, is a window on the screen that provides areas for entering or changing data in a database. You use forms (such as the Member Maintenance form in Figure 9-5 on page 337) to retrieve and maintain the data in a database.

To reduce data entry errors, well-designed forms should validate data as it is entered. When designing a form using a DBMS, you can make the form attractive and easy to use by incorporating color, shading, lines, boxes, and graphics; varying the fonts and font styles; and using other formatting features.

REPORT GENERATOR   A **report generator**, also called a report writer, allows users to design a report on the screen, retrieve data into the report design, and then display or print the report (Figure 9-15). Report generators usually allow you to format page numbers and dates; titles and column headings; subtotals and totals; and fonts, font sizes, color, and shading.

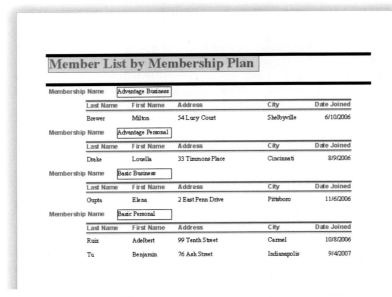

FIGURE 9-15   This report, created in Access, displays member information by the type of membership in which members are enrolled.

Backup and Recovery

Occasionally a database is damaged or destroyed because of hardware failure, a problem with the software, human error, or a catastrophe such as fire or flood. A DBMS provides a variety of techniques to restore the database to a usable form in case it is damaged or destroyed.

- A **backup**, or copy, of the entire database should be made on a regular basis. Some DBMSs have their own built-in backup utilities. Others require users to purchase a separate backup utility, or use one included with the operating system.
- More complex DBMSs maintain a **log**, which is a listing of activities that change the contents of the database.
- A DBMS that creates a log usually provides a recovery utility. A **recovery utility** uses the logs and/or backups to restore a database when it becomes damaged or destroyed.

WEB LINK 9-3

Backup and Recovery

For more information, visit scsite.com/dcf2e/ch9/weblink and then click Backup and Recovery.

Data Security

Sometimes, users accidentally delete the data from a database; others misuse the data intentionally (read At Issue 9-2 for a related discussion). Thus, a DBMS provides means to ensure that only authorized users access data at permitted times. In addition, most DBMSs allow different levels of access privileges to be identified for each field in the database. These access privileges define the actions that a specific user or group of users can perform. Access privileges for data involve establishing who can enter new data, change existing data, delete unwanted data, and view data.

AT ISSUE 9-2

Who Should Be Granted Access to Student Records?

Most database management systems specify various access privileges. When a database is created, access policies are determined. Individuals may be granted no access privileges, read-only privileges (data can be read but not changed), limited-access privileges (only certain data can be read and/or changed), or full-update privileges (all data can be read and changed). A student file, for example, contains each student's name, address, and grades, and also may contain data about ethnicity, gender, finances, family, health, activities, discipline, and so on. In a recent case, due to lax security and a simple desire to "see if it could be done," a student at a community college accessed and read all of the grades of students at the school. Being satisfied that he had done nothing wrong, the student did not alter any of the information. Using this situation as an example, what access privileges should be granted to the student, other students, faculty, administrators, financial aid officers, potential employers, and other outside groups? Explain your answers. Is it a crime to access confidential information without authorization? Why? Does it depend on the information? Does it depend on whether the information is altered? Does it depend on how the information is used? Would it be a crime for a student to access a school database of instructors' salaries? Why or why not?

Test your knowledge of pages 340 through 346 in Quiz Yourself 9-2.

QUIZ YOURSELF 9-2

Instructions: Find the true statement below. Then, rewrite the remaining false statements so they are true.

1. A DBMS is hardware that allows you to create, access, and manage an operating system.

2. A query contains data about each file in the database and each field in those files.

3. Access privileges for data involve establishing who can enter new data, change existing data, delete unwanted data, and view data.

4. Strengths of the database approach include increased data redundancy, reduced data integrity, shared data, easier access, and increased development time.

Quiz Yourself Online: To further check your knowledge of file processing systems versus databases and functions of a DBMS, visit scsite.com/dcf2e/ch9/quiz and then click Objectives 5 – 6.

RELATIONAL, OBJECT-ORIENTED, AND MULTIDIMENSIONAL DATABASES

Every database and DBMS is based on a specific data model. A **data model** consists of rules and standards that define how the database organizes data. A data model defines how users view the organization of the data. It does not define how the operating system actually arranges the data on the disk.

Three popular data models in use today are relational, object-oriented, and multidimensional. A database typically is based on one data model. Some databases, however, combine features of the relational and object-oriented data models. The following sections discuss relational, object-oriented, and multidimensional databases.

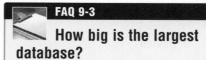

FAQ 9-3

How big is the largest database?

The world's largest database stores more than 895 TB (trillion bytes) of physics data in about 850,000 files. It requires 2,000 processors and 100 servers. More than 600 physicists and engineers contribute to the database. For more information, visit scsite.com/dcf2e/ch9/faq and then click World's Largest Database.

Relational Databases

Today, a relational database is a widely used type of database. A **relational database** is a database that stores data in tables that consist of rows and columns. Each row has a primary key and each column has a unique name.

As discussed earlier in this chapter, a file processing environment uses the terms file, record, and field to represent data. A relational database uses terms different from a file processing system. A developer of a relational database refers to a file as a **relation**, a record as a **tuple**, and a field as an **attribute**. A user of a relational database, by contrast, refers to a file as a **table**, a record as a **row**, and a field as a **column**. Figure 9-16 summarizes this varied terminology.

DATA TERMINOLOGY

File Processing Environment	Relational Database Developer	Relational Database User
File	Relation	Table
Record	Tuple	Row
Field	Attribute	Column

FIGURE 9-16 In this data terminology table, the first column identifies the terms used in a file processing environment. The second column presents the terms used by developers of a relational database. The third column indicates terms to which the users of a relational database refer.

WEB LINK 9-4

Relational Databases

For more information, visit scsite.com/dcf2e/ch9/weblink and then click Relational Databases.

In addition to storing data, a relational database also stores data relationships. A **relationship** is a connection within the data. In a relational database, you can set up a relationship between tables at any time. The tables must have a common column (field). For example, you would relate the Member table and the Membership Plans table using the Membership Code column. Figure 9-17 illustrates these relational database concepts. In a relational database, the only data redundancy (duplication) exists in the common columns (fields). The database uses these common columns for relationships.

Many businesses use relational databases for payroll, accounts receivable, accounts payable, general ledger, inventory, order entry, invoicing, and other business-related functions.

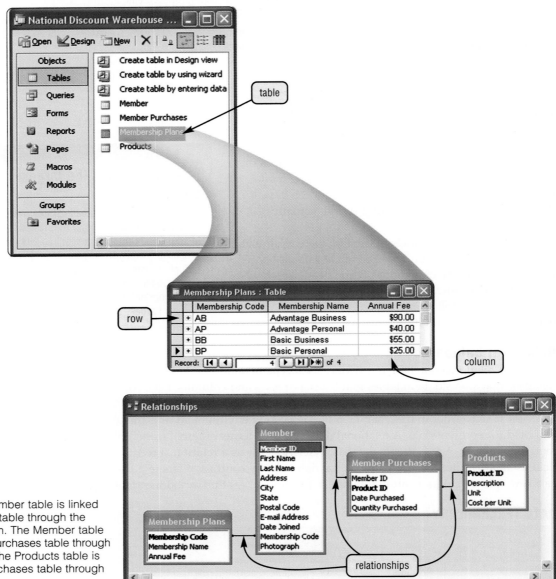

FIGURE 9-17   The Member table is linked to the Membership Plans table through the Membership Code column. The Member table is linked to the Member Purchases table through the Member ID column. The Products table is linked to the Member Purchases table through the Product ID column.

SQL   **Structured Query Language (SQL)** is a query language that allows users to manage, update, and retrieve data. SQL has special keywords and rules that users include in SQL statements. For example, the SQL statement in Figure 9-18a creates the results shown in Figure 9-18b.

Most relational database products for midrange servers and mainframes include SQL. Many personal computer databases also include SQL.

FIGURE 9-18a (SQL statement)

```
SELECT FIRST NAME, LAST NAME, ANNUAL FEE
FROM MEMBER, MEMBERSHIP PLANS
WHERE MEMBER.MEMBERSHIP CODE =
  MEMBERSHIP PLANS.MEMBERSHIP CODE
ORDER BY LAST NAME
```

FIGURE 9-18b (SQL statement results)

First Name	Last Name	Annual Fee
Milton	Brewer	$90.00
Louella	Drake	$40.00
Elena	Gupta	$55.00
Adelbert	Ruiz	$25.00
Benjamin	Tu	$25.00

FIGURE 9-18 A sample SQL statement and its results.

Object-Oriented Databases

An **object-oriented database (OODB)** stores data in objects. An **object** is an item that contains data, as well as the actions that read or process the data. A Member object, for example, might contain data about a member such as Member ID, First Name, Last Name, Address, and so on. It also could contain instructions about how to print the member record or the formula required to calculate a member's balance due.

Object-oriented databases have several advantages compared with relational databases: they can store more types of data, access this data faster, and allow programmers to reuse objects. An object-oriented database stores unstructured data more efficiently than a relational database. Unstructured data includes photographs, video clips, audio clips, and documents. When users query an object-oriented database, the results often are displayed more quickly than the same query of a relational database. If an object already exists, programmers can reuse it instead of recreating a new object — saving on program development time.

OBJECT QUERY LANGUAGE Object-oriented databases often use a query language called object query language (OQL) to manipulate and retrieve data. OQL is similar to SQL. OQL and SQL use many of the same rules, grammar, and keywords. Because OQL is a relatively new query language, not all object databases support it.

Multidimensional Databases

A **multidimensional database** stores data in dimensions. Whereas a relational database is a two-dimensional table, a multidimensional database can store more than two dimensions of data. These multiple dimensions allow users to access and analyze any view of the database data.

A Webmaster at a retailing business may want information about product sales and customer sales for each region spanning a given time. A manager at the same business may want information about product sales by department for each sales representative spanning a given time. A multidimensional database can consolidate this type of data from multiple dimensions at very high rates of speed. Nearly every multidimensional database has a dimension of time. The content of other dimensions varies depending on the subject.

No standard query language exists for multidimensional databases. Each database uses its own language. Most are similar to SQL.

DATA WAREHOUSES One application that typically uses multidimensional databases is a data warehouse. A **data warehouse** is a huge database that stores and manages the data required to analyze historical and current transactions. Through a data warehouse, managers and other users access transactions and summaries of transactions quickly and efficiently. Some major credit card companies monitor and manage customers' credit card transactions using a data warehouse. Additionally, consumers can access their own transactions in the data warehouse via the Web. A data warehouse typically has a user-friendly interface, so users easily can interact with its data.

A smaller version of a data warehouse is the data mart. A data mart contains a database that helps a specific group or department make decisions. Marketing and sales departments may have their own separate data marts. Individual groups or departments often extract data from the data warehouse to create their data marts.

WEB LINK 9-6

Object-Oriented Databases

For more information, visit scsite.com/dcf2e/ch9/weblink and then click Object-Oriented Databases.

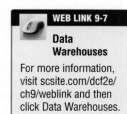

WEB LINK 9-7

Data Warehouses

For more information, visit scsite.com/dcf2e/ch9/weblink and then click Data Warehouses.

WEB DATABASES

One of the more profound features of the Web is the vast amount of information it provides. The Web offers information about jobs, travel destinations, television programming, movies and videos (Figure 9-19), local and national weather, sporting events, legislative information, and movies. You can shop for just about any product or service, buy or sell stocks, search for a job, and make airline reservations. Much of this and other information on the Web exists in databases. Read At Issue 9-3 for a related discussion.

To access data in a Web database, you fill in a form on a Web page. Many search engines such as Yahoo! use databases to store Web site descriptions. To access the database, you enter search text into the search engine. A Web database usually resides on a database server. A database server is a computer that stores and provides access to a database.

In addition to accessing information, users provide information to Web databases. Many Web sites request users to enter personal information, such as name, address, telephone number, and preferences, into an e-form (electronic form). The database then stores this personal information for future use. A company, for example, may send e-mail messages to certain groups of customers.

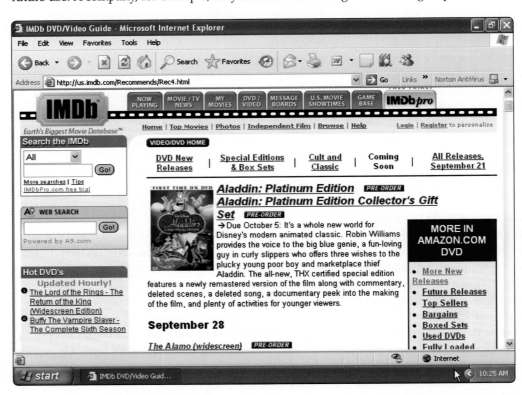

FIGURE 9-19
Through the Internet Movie Database (IMDb) Web site, users can access a huge database loaded with content about current and classic movies.

DATABASE ADMINISTRATION

> **WEB LINK 9-8**
> **Database Administrators**
> For more information, visit scsite.com/dcf2e/ch9/weblink and then click Database Administrators.

Managing a company's database requires a great deal of coordination. The role of coordinating the use of the database belongs to the database analysts and administrators. To carry out their responsibilities, these IT (information technology) professionals follow database design guidelines and need cooperation from all database users.

Database Design Guidelines

A carefully designed database makes it easier for a user to query the database, modify the data, and create reports. The guidelines shown in Figure 9-20 apply to databases of all sizes.

DATABASE DESIGN GUIDELINES

1. Determine the purpose of the database.
2. Design the tables.
   - Design tables on paper first.
   - Each table should contain data about one subject. The Member table, for example, contains data about members.
3. Design the records and fields for each table.
   - Be sure every record has a unique primary key.
   - Use separate fields for logically distinct items. For example, a name could be stored in six fields: Title (Mr., Mrs., Dr., etc.), First Name, Middle Name, Last Name, Suffix (Jr., Sr., etc.), and Nickname.
   - Do not create fields for information that can be derived from entries in other fields. For example, do not include a field for Age. Instead, store the birthdate and compute the age.
   - Allow enough space for each field.
   - Set default values for frequently entered data.
4. Determine the relationships among the tables.

FIGURE 9-20 Guidelines for developing a database.

Role of the Database Analysts and Administrators

The database analysts and administrators are responsible for managing and coordinating all database activities. The **database analyst (DA)** decides on the proper placement of fields, defines the relationships among data, and identifies users' access privileges. The **database administrator (DBA)** requires a more technical inside view of the data. The DBA creates and maintains the data dictionary, manages security of the database, monitors the performance of the database, and checks backup and recovery procedures.

In small companies, one person often is both the DA and DBA. In larger companies, the responsibilities of the DA and DBA are split among two or more people.

Role of the Employee as a User

Employees should learn how to use the data in the database effectively. The amount of information available often amazes first-time database users. Instant access to information helps employees perform their jobs more effectively. Today, employees access databases from their office desktop computers, notebook computers, or even smart phones and PDAs (Figure 9-21).

The maintenance of a database is an ongoing task that companies measure constantly against their overall goals.

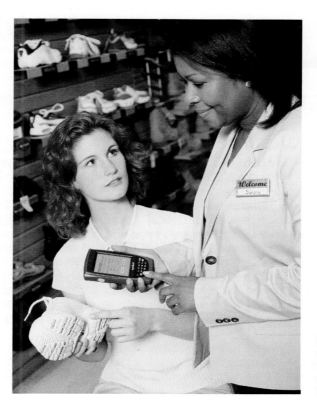

FIGURE 9-21 This sales clerk checks inventory to see if the requested shoe size is in inventory.

Test your knowledge of pages 347 through 351 in Quiz Yourself 9-3.

 QUIZ YOURSELF 9-3

Instructions: Find the true statement below. Then, rewrite the remaining false statements so they are true.

1. Object-oriented databases store data in tables.

2. Relational database users refer to a file as a table, a field as a column, and a record as a row.

3. SQL is a data modeling language that allows users to manage, update, and retrieve data.

4. The database analyst requires a more technical inside view of the data than does the database administrator.

Quiz Yourself Online: To further check your knowledge of relational, object-oriented, and multidimensional databases; Web databases; and database administration, visit scsite.com/dcf2e/ch9/quiz and then click Objectives 7 – 9.

CHAPTER SUMMARY

This chapter discussed how data and information are valuable assets to an organization (read Looking Ahead 9-2 for a look at the next generation of preserving data and information). The chapter also presented methods for maintaining high-quality data and assessing the quality of valuable information. It then discussed the advantages of organizing data in a database and described various types of databases. It also presented the roles of the database analysts and administrators.

LOOKING AHEAD 9-2

Preserving Electronic Files for Future Generations

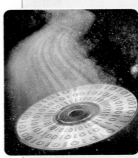

Historians and researchers are concerned that Web content and rare and unique electronic works may be lost forever because they exist only in digital form.

In an attempt to gather, organize, and preserve digital files, the United States Congress approved the National Digital Information Infrastructure & Preservation Program and commissioned The Library of Congress to supervise the project. Six digital formats have been identified: large Web sites, electronic journals, electronic books, digitally recorded sound, digital moving images, and digital television.

Library officials have partnered with industry and educational experts to discuss how to create and maintain the database. In addition, the National Science Foundation has awarded research grants to address these preservation issues. For more information, visit scsite.com/dcf2e/ch9/looking and then click Preservation.

CAREER CORNER

Database Administrator

Most businesses and organizations are built around databases. Access to timely, accurate, and relevant information is a company's lifeline. A database administrator (DBA) creates, applies, supports, and administers the policies and procedures for maintaining a company's database. Database administrators construct logical and physical descriptions of the database, establish database parameters, develop data models characterizing data elements, ensure database integrity, and coordinate database security measures including developing and implementing disaster recovery and archiving procedures. They also use query languages to obtain reports of the information in the database. With the large amounts of sensitive data generated, data integrity, backup, and security have become increasingly important aspects of the administrator's responsibilities.

Administering a database requires a great deal of mental work and the ability to focus on finite details. Database administrators must be able to read and comprehend business-related information, organize data in a logical manner, apply general rules to specific problems, identify business principles and practices, and communicate clearly with database users. Being proficient with a particular database such as Oracle, Informix, or SQL Server is an added advantage. The real key, however, is learning, understanding, and becoming an expert in database design.

Database administrators usually have a bachelor or associate degree and experience with computer programming, relational databases, query languages, and online analytical processing. Typical salaries for database administrators are between $69,000 and $95,000, depending on experience. For more information, visit scsite.com/dcf2e/ch9/careers and then click Database Administrator.

Oracle
Database Software Developer

More than half of the FORTUNE 100 companies use an Oracle product as their primary database, but Oracle's quest, according to CEO Larry Ellison, is to have its customers convert all their database applications to Oracle's software.

Ellison and two partners founded the company in 1977 with the intent of developing a commercially viable relational database. When their Oracle database was released, it was an immediate success and changed the way companies stored and managed information. For the first time, separate data tables could be connected by a common field.

The company is the world's second largest independent software company behind Microsoft. With the recent $10.3 billion acquisition of PeopleSoft, Oracle also will control 25 percent of the corporate application-software market. For more information, visit scsite.com/dcf2e/ch9/companies and then click Oracle.

Sybase
Managing Data for the Unwired Enterprise

Researchers at the University of California, Berkeley, estimate that 95 percent of the data produced by major corporations never is used after it is stored in a database because it is disorganized and inaccessible.

Sybase helps companies unlock and use this data whenever and wherever needed through its unwired enterprise. This data access solution helps mobile database users tap into corporate networks, often wirelessly. The company focuses especially on Enterprise Portal (EP) solutions, which convert stored data into information that can be used by customers, partners, and suppliers.

For more than 20 years, Sybase has produced software that links platforms, servers, databases, applications, and mobile devices. Many of its customers are part of the financial services, telecommunications, and health care professions. For more information, visit scsite.com/dcf2e/ch9/companies and then click Sybase.

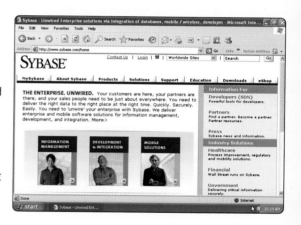

TECHNOLOGY TRAILBLAZERS

E. F. Codd
Relational Database Model Inventor

The majority of large and small databases are structured on the relational model, which is considered one of the greatest technological inventions of the 20th Century. E. F. Codd single-handedly is credited with developing and promoting that model in a series of research papers beginning with his 1969 IBM Research Report, "Derivability, Redundancy, and Consistency of Relations Stored in Large Data Banks."

Edgar F. Codd began his career in 1949 when he joined IBM as a programming mathematician after graduating from Oxford University. Throughout the 1950s he helped develop several IBM computers and then turned his attention to database management. Among his achievements is earning the prestigious A. M. Turing Award, which is the Association for Computing Machinery's highest technical achievement honor given to an individual, for his relational database theory. For more information, visit scsite.com/dcf2e/ch9/people and then click E. F. Codd.

Larry Ellison
Oracle CEO

On a visit to Kyoto, Japan, Larry Ellison became intrigued with the country's culture and the citizens' combination of confidence and humility. He says he applies these philosophical principles to his work at Oracle, where he serves as CEO.

As a young man, Ellison was interested in science and mathematics. He was inspired by E. F. Codd's relational database model and founded Oracle in 1977 under the name Software Development Laboratories with a $1,200 investment.

Under Ellison's leadership, the company doubled its sales in 11 of its first 12 years. He is known for his uncanny ability to motivate his employees and business partners toward a common goal, including a demand for a 100 percent growth in his company's software sales. For more information, visit scsite.com/dcf2e/ch9/people and then click Larry Ellison.

CHAPTER 9

Chapter Review

The Chapter Review section summarizes the concepts presented in this chapter. To obtain help from other students regarding any subject in this chapter, visit scsite.com/dcf2e/ch9/forum and post your thoughts or questions.

① What Is a Database?

A **database** is a collection of data organized in a manner that allows access, retrieval, and use of that data. **Database software**, often called a **database management system (DBMS)**, allows users to create a computerized database; add, change, and delete the data; sort and retrieve the data; and create forms and reports from the data.

② What Are the Qualities of Valuable Information?

Data can include text, numbers, images, audio, and video. **Information** is processed data; that is, it is organized, meaningful, and useful. For information to be valuable, it should be accurate, verifiable, timely, organized, accessible, useful, and cost-effective.

③ What Is Meant by Character, Field, Record, and File?

Data is classified in a hierarchy, with each level of data consisting of one or more items from the lower level. A bit is the smallest unit of data a computer can process. Eight bits grouped together in a unit form a byte, and each byte represents a single **character**. A **field** is a combination of one or more related characters and is the smallest unit of data a user accesses. A **record** is a group of related fields. A **data file** is a collection of related records stored on a storage medium.

④ How Are Files Maintained?

File maintenance refers to the procedures that keep data current. File maintenance procedures include adding records when new data is obtained, changing records to correct inaccurate data or to update old data with new data, and deleting records when they no longer are needed. **Validation** is the process of comparing data with a set of rules or values to find out if the data is correct. Many programs perform a validity check that analyzes entered data to help ensure that it is correct. Types of validity checks include an **alphabetic check**, a **numeric check**, a **range check**, a **consistency check**, a **completeness check**, and a **check digit**.

> Visit scsite.com/dcf2e/ch9/quiz or click the Quiz Yourself button. Click Objectives 1 – 4.

⑤ How Is a File Processing System Approach Different from a Database Approach?

In a **file processing system**, each department or area within an organization has its own set of data files. Two major weaknesses of file processing systems are redundant data (duplicated data) and isolated data. With a **database approach**, many programs and users share the data in a database. The database approach reduces data redundancy, improves data integrity, shares data, permits easier access, and reduces development time. A database, however, can be more complex than a file processing system, requiring special training and more computer memory, storage, and processing power. Data in a database also is more vulnerable than data in file processing systems.

⑥ What Functions Are Common to Most DBMSs?

With **database software**, often called a **database management system (DBMS)**, users can create and manipulate a computerized database. Most DBMSs perform common functions. A **data dictionary** contains data about each file in the database and each field within those files. A DBMS offers several methods to maintain and retrieve data, such as query languages, query by example, forms, and report generators. A **query language** consists of simple, English-like statements that allow users to specify the data to display, print, or store. **Query by example (QBE)** has a graphical user interface that assists users with retrieving data. A **form** is a window on the screen that provides areas for entering or changing data. A **report generator** allows users to design a report on the screen, retrieve data into the report design, and then display or print the report. To supply security, most DBMSs can identify different levels of access privileges that define the actions a specific user or group of users can perform for each field in a database. If a database is damaged or destroyed, a DBMS provides techniques to return the database to a usable form. A **backup** is a copy of the database. A **log** is a listing of activities that change the contents of the database. A **recovery utility** uses the logs and/or backups to restore the database.

> Visit scsite.com/dcf2e/ch9/quiz or click the Quiz Yourself button. Click Objectives 5 – 6.

Chapter Review

7 **What Are Characteristics of Relational, Object-Oriented, and Multidimensional Databases?**

A **data model** consists of rules and standards that define how the database organizes data. Three popular data models are relational, object-oriented, and multidimensional. A **relational database** stores data in tables that consist of rows and columns. A relational database developer refers to a file as a **relation**, a record as a **tuple**, and a field as an **attribute**. A relational database user refers to a file as a **table**, a record as a **row**, and a field as a **column**. A **relationship** is a connection within the data in a relational database. **Structured Query Language** (SQL) allows users to manage, update, and retrieve data. An **object-oriented database** (OODB) stores data in objects. An **object** is an item that contains data, as well as the actions that read or process the data. Object-oriented databases often use an object query language (OQL) to manipulate and retrieve data. A **multidimensional database** stores data in dimensions. These multiple dimensions allow users to access and analyze any view of the database data. One application that uses multidimensional databases is a **data warehouse**, which is a huge database system that stores and manages the data required to analyze historical and current transactions. No standard query language exists for multidimensional databases.

8 **How Do Web Databases Work?**

A Web database links to a form on a Web page, which is the front end to the database. To access data in a Web database, you fill in the form. A Web database usually resides on a database server, which is a computer that stores and provides access to a database.

9 **What Are the Responsibilities of Database Analysts and Administrators?**

A **database analyst** (DA) focuses on the meaning and usage of data. The DA decides on the placement of fields, defines data relationships, and identifies access privileges. A **database administrator** (DBA) requires a more technical view of the data. The DBA creates and maintains the data dictionary, manages database security, monitors database performance, and checks backup and recovery procedures.

 Visit scsite.com/dcf2e/ch9/quiz or click the Quiz Yourself button. Click Objectives 7 – 9.

Key Terms

You should know each key term. Use the list below to help focus your study. To further enhance your understanding of the Key Terms in this chapter, visit scsite.com/dcf2e/ch9/terms. See an example of and a definition for each term, and access current and additional information about the term from the Web.

alphabetic check (339)
attribute (347)
backup (346)
character (335)
check digit (340)
column (347)
completeness check (340)
consistency check (340)
data (332)
data dictionary (343)
data file (336)
data model (347)
data type (335)
data warehouse (349)
database (332)
database administrator (DBA) (351)

database analyst (DA) (351)
database approach (341)
database management system (DBMS) (332)
database software (332)
field (335)
field name (335)
field size (335)
file maintenance (336)
file processing system (341)
form (345)
garbage in, garbage out (GIGO) (333)
information (332)
key field (336)

log (346)
multidimensional database (349)
numeric check (339)
object (349)
object-oriented database (OODB) (349)
primary key (336)
query (344)
query by example (QBE) (345)
query language (344)
range check (340)
record (336)
recovery utility (346)
relation (347)
relational database (347)

relationship (348)
report generator (346)
row (347)
Structured Query Language (SQL) (348)
table (347)
tuple (347)
validation (339)

Checkpoint

Use the Checkpoint exercises to check your knowledge level of the chapter.

True/False

Mark T for True and F for False. (See page numbers in parentheses.)

_____ 1. Information is organized, meaningful, and useful data. (332)

_____ 2. Garbage in, garbage out (GIGO) is a computing phrase that points out the accuracy of a computer's output depends on the accuracy of the input. (333)

_____ 3. A data file is a group of related fields. (336)

_____ 4. Validation is the process of comparing data with a set of rules or values to find out if the data is correct. (339)

_____ 5. A range check tests the data in two or more associated fields to ensure that the relationship is logical. (340)

_____ 6. A data dictionary contains data about each file in the database and each field within those files. (343)

_____ 7. To retrieve or select data in a database, you query it. (344)

_____ 8. A multidimensional database is a database that stores data in tables that consist of rows and columns. (347)

_____ 9. A data model is a huge database that stores and manages the data required to analyze historical and current transactions. (349)

_____ 10. The database administrator (DBA) decides on the proper placement of fields and defines the relationships among data. (351)

Multiple Choice

Select the best answer. (See page numbers in parentheses.)

1. _____ information can be proven as correct or incorrect. (333)
   a. Timely
   b. Organized
   c. Cost-effective
   d. Verifiable

2. Accessible information _____. (334)
   a. is error free
   b. has an age suited to its use
   c. is available when the decision maker needs it
   d. has meaning to the person who receives it

3. A _____ is a collection of related records. (336)
   a. key field
   b. data file
   c. primary key
   d. data character

4. A _____ verifies that a required field contains data. (340)
   a. range check
   b. numeric check
   c. consistency check
   d. completeness check

5. When a company uses _____, many programs and users share the data in the database. (341)
   a. the database approach
   b. a file processing system
   c. a data model
   d. a check digit

6. All of the following are strengths of the database approach, except _____. (342)
   a. less complexity
   b. improved data integrity
   c. easier access
   d. reduced development time

7. _____ has a graphical user interface that assists users with retrieving data. (345)
   a. A query language
   b. A form
   c. A report generator
   d. A query by example (QBE) feature

8. The database analyst (DA) _____. (351)
   a. decides on the proper placement of fields
   b. creates and maintains the data dictionary
   c. monitors the performance of the database
   d. checks backup and recovery procedures

Matching

Match the terms with their definitions. (See page numbers in parentheses.)

_____ 1. field name (335)

_____ 2. field size (335)

_____ 3. data type (335)

_____ 4. key field (336)

_____ 5. query (344)

a. defines the maximum number of characters a field can contain

b. item that contains data and the actions that read or process the data

c. specifies the kind of data a field can contain and how the field is used

d. uniquely identifies each field

e. uniquely identifies each record in a file

f. request for specific data from a database

Checkpoint

Short Answer

Write a brief answer to each of the following questions.

1. What is data integrity and why is it important? _____ What does the computer phrase, garbage in, garbage out (GIGO), mean? _____

2. What is file maintenance? _____ When are records added, changed, or deleted in a file? _____

3. Why is data redundancy a weakness of file processing systems? _____ How does the database approach reduce data redundancy? _____

4. How is a query language different from query by example? _____ What is a report generator? _____

5. How is a backup different from a log? _____ What is a recovery utility? _____

Working Together

Working in a group of your classmates, complete the following team exercise.

1. Most libraries use **databases** to keep track of their collections. Have each member of your team visit a library that uses a database. Interview a librarian to find out more about the database. How many items are represented? What information does the database contain? How is the database searched? How frequently is it updated? Meet with the members of your team to discuss the results of your interviews. Use PowerPoint to create a group presentation and share your findings with the class.

Web Research

Use the Internet-based Web Research exercises to broaden your understanding of the concepts presented in this chapter. Visit scsite.com/dcf2e/ch9/research to obtain more information pertaining to each exercise. To discuss any of the Web Research exercises in this chapter with other students, post your thoughts or questions at scsite.com/dcf2e/ch9/forum.

(1) Journaling

Respond to your readings in this chapter by writing at least one page about your reactions, evaluations, and reflections on databases. For example, have you created a database to store details about your movie and music collections? Have you shopped online and accessed a merchant's database? Have you experienced problems with data integrity and tried to correct errors? Should Americans have a **national identification card**? You also can write about the new terms you learned by reading this chapter. If required, submit your journal to your instructor.

(2) Scavenger Hunt

Use one of the **search engines** listed in Figure 2-8 in Chapter 2 on page 58 or your own favorite search engine to find the answers to the questions below. Copy and paste the Web address from the Web page where you found the answer. Some questions may have more than one answer. If required, submit your answers to your instructor. (1) How does clickstream analysis examine data from Web site usage patterns? (2) What geographic information system (GIS) functions does ArcExplorer perform? (3) What company developed SQL? What is the name of the original SQL prototype developed in 1974? (4) What is the definition of data modeling? (5) What is a knowledge engineer's primary job in developing expert systems? (6) What is the object-relational divide? (7) What are the Java Data Objects (JDO) standards?

(3) Search Sleuth

Major United States newspapers helped design **Clusty** the Clustering Engine (clusty.com). One of its unique features is returning search results for Web sites, news stories, images, and shopping sites in clusters, which are categories of folders, along with a list of links. Visit this Web site and then use your word processing program to answer the following questions. Then, if required, submit your answers to your instructor. (1) Click the Web+ tab, click the Request text box, and then type "`query by example`" or `QBE` in the box. Click the Cluster button. Browse the clusters on the left side of the page and then expand the SQL cluster by clicking the + icon next to the SQL link. What are the sub-cluster categories? (2) Click the Encyclopedia tab. What is one definition retrieved and its source? (3) Click the News tab and then click the News Page link. What are two stories listed in the Top News category? (4) Click two links in the Business category and review the articles. Write a 50-word summary of your findings.

Learn How To

Use the Learn How To activities to learn fundamental skills when using a computer and accompanying technology. Complete the exercises and submit them to your instructor.

LEARN HOW TO 1: Organize and Manage Files on a Computer

Introduction   In Learn How To 1 in Chapter 3 (page 130), you learned the procedure for saving a file. In this Learn How To activity, you will learn how to manage files using folders and how to find a file if you cannot remember where you saved it.

Folders   A folder is a virtual container where you can store a file on media. When you store any file, the file must be stored in a folder. The folder symbol, together with the folder name, identifies a folder.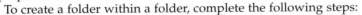

You can create folders in a variety of ways. To create a folder on the desktop, complete the following steps:

1. Right-click the desktop in a location that does not contain an icon or toolbar.
2. Point to New on the shortcut menu that is displayed (Figure 9-22).
3. Click Folder on the New submenu.
4. When the folder icon is displayed on the desktop, type the name you want to assign to the folder and then press the ENTER key. You should choose a name that identifies the contents of the folder.

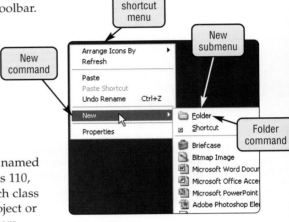

FIGURE 9-22

A folder can contain other folders. This allows you to organize your files in a hierarchical manner so that the highest level folder contains all the folders for a given subject, and lower-level folders contain more specific files and folders. For example, your highest level folder could be named Fall Semester 2006. For each class, such as Computer Information Systems 110, you could define a folder within the Fall Semester 2006 folder. Within each class folder, you could define folders for each week of the class, or for each project or assignment within the class. In this manner, you would have a set of folders, each designated for a specific use. You then would save your files in the appropriate folder.

To create a folder within a folder, complete the following steps:

1. Double-click the folder name either on the desktop or in the window or dialog box in which the folder name appears.
2. Right-click a blank space in the window that is displayed.
3. Point to New on the shortcut menu that is displayed and then click Folder on the New submenu.
4. When the folder icon is displayed, type the name you want to assign to the folder, and then press the ENTER key.

To delete a folder, complete the following steps:

1. Right-click the folder.
2. On the shortcut menu that is displayed (Figure 9-23), click Delete.
3. In the Confirm Folder Delete dialog box, click the Yes button.

When you delete a folder, all the files and folders contained in the folder you are deleting, together with all files and folders on the lower hierarchical levels, are deleted. If you accidentally delete a folder, complete the following steps:

1. Double-click the Recycle Bin icon on the desktop.
2. In the Recycle Bin window, select the folder you wish to restore.
3. Click File on the menu bar and then click Restore on the File menu.

Using folders effectively will aid you in keeping track of files you create for your classes.

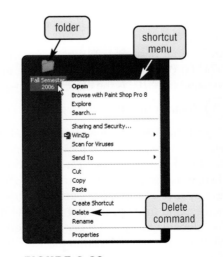

FIGURE 9-23

Learn How To

Exercise

1. Assume you are taking the following courses: Computer Information Systems 120, History 210, English 145, Marketing 221, and Business Law 120. Define the hierarchy of folders you would create for these classes. In which folder would you store an assignment from English 145 that was assigned in the sixth week of class? Submit your answers to your instructor.

LEARN HOW TO 2: Search for Files and Folders

At times, you might store a file in a folder and then forget where you stored the file. The Search Companion feature of Windows XP enables you to search storage media on a computer to find the file. To use the Search Companion, complete the following steps:

1. Click the Start button on the Windows taskbar.
2. Click Search on the Start menu.
3. Click All files and folders in the What do you want to search for balloon.
4. In the All or part of the file name text box, type the name of the file for which you are searching. If you do not know the entire file name, enter as much of the file name as you can remember. If you do not know any portion of the file name, use the other options in the balloon to provide the search criteria (Figure 9-24).
5. Click the Search button in the balloon.
6. All items containing the file name or partial file name will be displayed in the Search Results window. If the file was not found, a message to that effect is displayed.
7. To open the file you found, double-click the file name in the list. The file will be opened by the appropriate program.

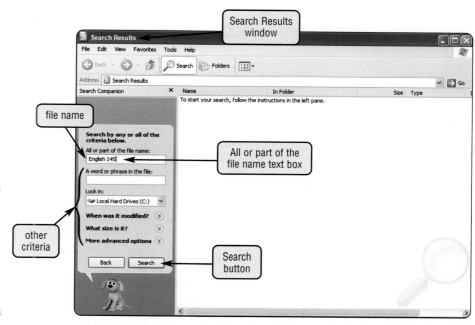

FIGURE 9-24

8. Before you close the Search Results window, make a note of the location of the file. If this is not the location where you want the file to be stored, store the file in the correct location.

Exercise

1. Using the Windows XP Search Companion, locate the file named Soap Bubbles. How many file names were returned? Which folder contains the Soap Bubbles file? Submit your answers to your instructor.
2. On the computer you are using, create a hierarchy of folders for your classes. Create a WordPad file that contains the following text: `This file will be found using Search Companion`. Save the file in one of the folders using a file name of your choice. Using Search Companion, search for the file you just created. How many files were returned from your search? Delete all folders and files you created in this exercise. Write a paragraph describing the steps you will take to organize your files for the coming semester. Submit your responses to your instructor.

Learn It Online

Use the Learn It Online exercises to reinforce your understanding of the chapter concepts. To access the Learn It Online exercises, visit scsite.com/dcf2e/ch9/learn.

 1 At the Movies — Internet Movie Database

To view the Internet Movie Database movie, click the number 1 button. Locate your video and click the corresponding High-Speed or Dial-Up link, depending on your Internet connection. Watch the movie and then complete the exercise by answering the question that follows. Using Rottentomatoes.com could help you save time and money by allowing you to view movie trailers and view customer reviews. Explain how the "tomato picker" works, and how using that feature of Rottentomatoes.com could save you time and money.

2 Student Edition Labs — Advanced Spreadsheets

Click the number 2 button. When the Student Edition Labs menu appears, click *Advanced Spreadsheets* to begin. A new browser window will open. Follow the on-screen instructions to complete the Lab. When finished, click the Exit button. If required, submit your results to your instructor.

3 Practice Test

Click the number 3 button. Answer each question. When completed, enter your name and click the Grade Test button to submit the quiz for grading. Make a note of any missed questions. If required, submit your results to your instructor.

4 Who Wants To Be a Computer Genius²?

Click the number 4 button to find out if you are a computer genius. Directions about how to play the game will be displayed. When you are ready to play, click the Play button. Submit your score to your instructor.

 5 Wheel of Terms

Click the number 5 button to reinforce important terms you learned in this chapter by playing the Shelly Cashman Series version of this popular game. Directions about how to play the game will be displayed. When you are ready to play, click the Play button. Submit your score to your instructor.

 6 Student Edition Labs — Advanced Databases

Click the number 6 button. When the Student Edition Labs menu appears, click *Advanced Databases* to begin. A new browser window will open. Follow the on-screen instructions to complete the Lab. When finished, click the Exit button. If required, submit your results to your instructor.

 7 Crossword Puzzle Challenge

Click the number 7 button. Complete the puzzle to reinforce skills you learned in this chapter. Directions about how to play the game will be displayed. When you are ready to play, click the Submit button. Submit the completed puzzle to your instructor.

 8 Lab Exercises

Click the number 8 button. When the Lab Exercises menu appears, click the exercise assigned by your instructor. A new browser window will open. Follow the on-screen instructions to complete the exercise. When finished, click the Exit button. If required, submit your results to your instructor.

9 Chapter Discussion Forum

Select an objective from this chapter on page 331 about which you would like more information. Click the number 9 button and post a short message listing a meaningful message title accompanied by one or more questions concerning the selected objective. In two days, return to the threaded discussion by clicking the number 9 button. Submit to your instructor your original message and at least one response to your message.

Computer Security, Ethics, and Privacy

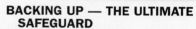

OBJECTIVES

After completing this chapter, you will be able to:

1. Identify ways to safeguard against computer viruses, worms, Trojan horses, denial of service attacks, back doors, and spoofing

2. Discuss techniques to prevent unauthorized computer access and use

3. Identify safeguards against hardware theft and vandalism

4. Explain the ways to protect against software theft and information theft

5. Discuss the types of devices available that protect computers from system failure

6. Identify risks and safeguards associated with wireless communications

7. Discuss issues surrounding information privacy

8. Discuss ways to prevent health-related disorders and injuries due to computer use

CONTENTS

COMPUTER SECURITY RISKS

INTERNET AND NETWORK ATTACKS
Computer Viruses, Worms, and Trojan Horses
Safeguards against Computer Viruses, Worms, and Trojan Horses
Denial of Service Attacks
Back Doors
Spoofing
Safeguards against DoS Attacks, Back Doors, and IP Spoofing
Firewalls
Intrusion Detection Software

UNAUTHORIZED ACCESS AND USE
Safeguards against Unauthorized Access and Use
Identifying and Authenticating Users

HARDWARE THEFT AND VANDALISM
Safeguards against Hardware Theft and Vandalism

SOFTWARE THEFT
Safeguards against Software Theft

INFORMATION THEFT
Safeguards against Information Theft
Encryption

SYSTEM FAILURE
Safeguards against System Failure

BACKING UP — THE ULTIMATE SAFEGUARD

WIRELESS SECURITY

ETHICS AND SOCIETY
Information Accuracy
Intellectual Property Rights

INFORMATION PRIVACY
Electronic Profiles
Cookies
Spyware and Adware
Phishing
Spam
Privacy Laws
Computer Forensics
Employee Monitoring
Content Filtering

HEALTH CONCERNS OF COMPUTER USE
Computers and Health Risks
Ergonomics and Workplace Design
Computer Addiction
Green Computing

CHAPTER SUMMARY

COMPANIES ON THE CUTTING EDGE
McAfee
Symantec

TECHNOLOGY TRAILBLAZERS
Donn Parker
Clifford Stoll

COMPUTER SECURITY RISKS

Today, people rely on computers to create, store, and manage critical information. Thus, it is crucial that users take measures to protect their computers and data from loss, damage, and misuse.

A **computer security risk** is any event or action that could cause a loss of or damage to computer hardware, software, data, information, or processing capability. Some breaches to computer security are accidental. Others are planned intrusions. Some intruders do no damage; they merely access data, information, or programs on the computer. Other intruders indicate some evidence of their presence either by leaving a message or by deliberately altering or damaging data.

An intentional breach of computer security often involves a deliberate act that is against the law. Any illegal act involving a computer generally is referred to as a **computer crime**. The term **cybercrime** refers to online or Internet-based illegal acts. Today, cybercrime is one of the FBI's top three priorities.

Perpetrators of cybercrime and other intrusions fall into seven basic categories: hacker, cracker, script kiddie, corporate spy, unethical employee, cyberextortionist, and cyberterrorist.

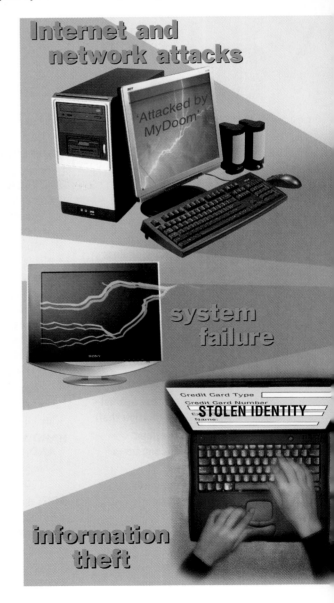

- The term **hacker**, although originally a complimentary word for a computer enthusiast, now has a derogatory meaning and refers to someone who accesses a computer or network illegally. Hackers often claim the intent of their security breaches is to improve security.

- A **cracker** also is someone who accesses a computer or network illegally but has the intent of destroying data, stealing information, or other malicious action. Both hackers and crackers have advanced computer and network skills.

- A **script kiddie** has the same intent as a cracker but does not have the technical skills and knowledge. Script kiddies often are teenagers that use prewritten hacking and cracking programs to break into computers.

- Some corporate spies have excellent computer and network skills and are hired to break into a specific computer and steal its proprietary data and information. Unscrupulous companies hire corporate spies, a practice known as corporate espionage, to gain a competitive advantage.

- Unethical employees break into their employers computers for a variety of reasons. Some simply want to exploit a security weakness. Others seek financial gains from selling confidential information. Disgruntled employees may want revenge.

- A **cyberextortionist** is someone who uses e-mail as a vehicle for extortion. These perpetrators send a company a threatening e-mail message indicating they will expose confidential information, exploit a security flaw, or launch an attack that will compromise the company's network — if they are not paid a sum of money.
- A **cyberterrorist** is someone who uses the Internet or network to destroy or damage computers for political reasons. The extensive damage might destroy the nation's air traffic control system, electricity-generating companies, or a telecommunications infrastructure. Cyberterrorism usually requires a team of highly skilled individuals, millions of dollars, and several years of planning.

Business and home users must protect, or safeguard, their computers from breaches of security and other computer security risks.

The more common computer security risks include Internet and network attacks, unauthorized access and use, hardware theft, software theft, information theft, and system failure (Figure 10-1). The following pages describe these computer security risks and also discuss safeguards users might take to minimize or prevent their consequences.

FIGURE 10-1 Computers are exposed to several types of computer security risks.

INTERNET AND NETWORK ATTACKS

Information transmitted over networks has a higher degree of security risk than information kept on a company's premises. In a business, network administrators usually take measures to protect a network from security risks. On the Internet, where no central administrator is present, the security risk is greater.

Internet and network attacks that jeopardize security include computer viruses, worms, and Trojan horses; denial of service attacks; and spoofing. The following pages address these computer security risks and suggest measures businesses and individuals can take to protect their computers while on the Internet or connected to a network.

Computer Viruses, Worms, and Trojan Horses

Every unprotected computer is susceptible to the first type of computer security risk — a computer virus, worm, and/or Trojan horse.

- A computer **virus** is a potentially damaging computer program that affects, or infects, a computer negatively by altering the way the computer works without the user's knowledge or permission. Once the virus infects the computer, it can spread throughout and may damage files and system software, including the operating system.
- A **worm** is a program that copies itself repeatedly, for example in memory or on a network, using up resources and possibly shutting down the computer or network.
- A **Trojan horse** (named after the Greek myth) is a program that hides within or looks like a legitimate program. A certain condition or action usually triggers the Trojan horse. Unlike a virus or worm, a Trojan horse does not replicate itself to other computers.

Computer viruses, worms, and Trojan horses are classified as malicious-logic programs, which are programs that act without a user's knowledge and deliberately alter the computer's operations. Unscrupulous programmers write malicious-logic programs and then test the programs to ensure they can deliver their payload. The **payload** is the destructive event or prank the program is intended to deliver. A computer infected by a virus, worm, or Trojan horse often has one or more of the following symptoms:

- Screen displays unusual message or image
- Music or unusual sound plays randomly
- Available memory is less than expected
- Existing programs and files disappear
- Files become corrupted
- Programs or files do not work properly
- Unknown programs or files mysteriously appear
- System properties change

Computer viruses, worms, and Trojan horses deliver their payload on a computer in four basic ways: when a user (1) opens an infected file, (2) runs an infected program, (3) boots the computer with an infected disk in a disk drive, or (4) connects an uprotected computer to a network. A common way computers become infected with viruses, worms, and Trojan horses is through users opening infected e-mail attachments. Figure 10-2 shows how a virus can spread from one computer to another through an infected e-mail attachment.

Currently, more than 81,000 known viruses, worms, and Trojan horse programs exist with an estimated 6 new programs discovered each day.

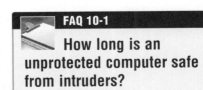

FAQ 10-1

How long is an unprotected computer safe from intruders?

One security expert maintains that an unprotected computer will be compromised by an intruder within 20 minutes. Slammer and Nimda, two devastating worms, wreaked worldwide havoc in 10 and 30 minutes, respectively. For more information, visit scsite.com/dcf2e/ch10/faq and then click Viruses and Worms.

FIGURE 10-2 HOW A VIRUS CAN SPREAD THROUGH AN E-MAIL MESSAGE

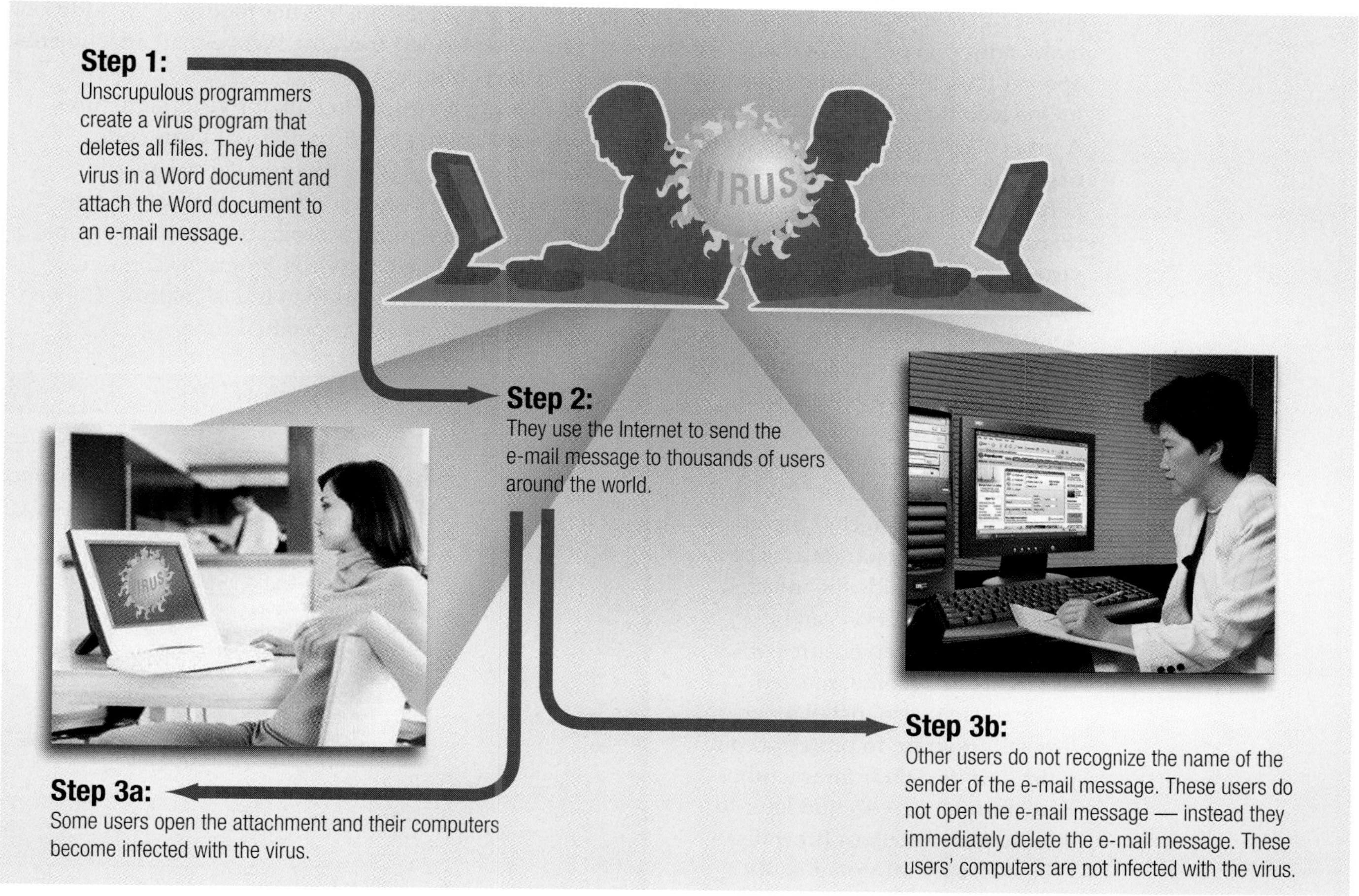

Step 1:
Unscrupulous programmers create a virus program that deletes all files. They hide the virus in a Word document and attach the Word document to an e-mail message.

Step 2:
They use the Internet to send the e-mail message to thousands of users around the world.

Step 3a:
Some users open the attachment and their computers become infected with the virus.

Step 3b:
Other users do not recognize the name of the sender of the e-mail message. These users do not open the e-mail message — instead they immediately delete the e-mail message. These users' computers are not infected with the virus.

Safeguards against Computer Viruses, Worms, and Trojan Horses

Users can take several precautions to protect their home and work computers from these malicious infections. The following paragraphs discuss these precautionary measures.

Do not start a computer with removable media, such as CDs, DVDs, and floppy disks, in the drives — unless you are certain the media is uninfected. Never open an e-mail attachment unless you are expecting the attachment *and* it is from a trusted source. If the e-mail is from an unknown source, delete the e-mail message immediately — without opening or executing any attachments. If the e-mail message is from a trusted source, but you were not expecting an attachment, verify with the source that they intended to send you an attachment — before opening it. Many e-mail programs allow users to preview an e-mail message before or without opening it. Some viruses and worms can deliver their payload when a user simply previews the message. Thus, you should turn off message preview in your e-mail program.

Some viruses are hidden in macros, which are instructions saved in an application such as a word processing or spreadsheet program. In applications that allow users to write macros, you should set the macro security level to medium. With a medium security level, the application software warns users that a document they are attempting to open contains a macro. From this warning, a user chooses to disable or enable the macro. If the document is from a trusted source, the user can enable the macro. Otherwise, it should be disabled.

Users should install an antivirus program and update it frequently. An **antivirus program** protects a computer against viruses by identifying and removing any computer viruses found in memory, on storage media, or on incoming files. Most antivirus programs also protect against worms and Trojan horses. When you purchase a new computer, it often includes antivirus software.

An antivirus program scans for programs that attempt to modify the boot program, the operating system, and other programs that normally are read from but not modified. In addition, many antivirus programs automatically scan files downloaded from the Web, e-mail attachments, opened files, and all removable media inserted in the computer.

One technique that antivirus programs use to identify a virus is to look for virus signatures. A **virus signature**, also called a **virus definition**, is a known specific pattern of virus code. Computer users should update their antivirus program's signature files regularly. Updating signature files downloads any new virus definitions that have been added since the last update (Figure 10-3). This extremely important activity allows the antivirus program to protect against viruses written since the antivirus program was released. Most antivirus programs contain an automatic update feature that regularly prompts users to download the virus signature. The vendor usually provides this service to registered users at no cost for a specified time.

If an antivirus program identifies an infected file, it attempts to remove its virus, worm, or Trojan horse. If the antivirus program cannot remove the infection, it often quarantines the infected file. A **quarantine** is a separate area of a hard disk that holds the infected file until the infection can be removed. This step ensures other files will not become infected.

Some users also install a personal firewall program to protect a computer and its data from unauthorized intrusion. A section later in this chapter discusses firewalls.

Finally, stay informed about new virus alerts and virus hoaxes. A **virus hoax** is an e-mail message that warns users of a nonexistent virus, worm, or Trojan horse. Often, these virus hoaxes are in the form of a chain letter that requests the user to send a copy of the e-mail message to as many people as possible. Instead of forwarding the message, visit a Web site that publishes a list of virus alerts and virus hoaxes.

The list in Figure 10-4 summarizes important tips for protecting your computer from virus, worm, and Trojan horse infection.

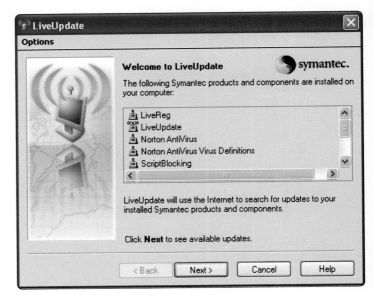

FIGURE 10-3   Many vendors of antivirus programs allow registered users to update virus signature files automatically from the Web at no cost for a specified time.

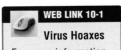
WEB LINK 10-1

Virus Hoaxes

For more information, visit scsite.com/dcf2e/ch10/weblink and then click Virus Hoaxes.

TIPS FOR PREVENTING VIRUS, WORM, AND TROJAN HORSE INFECTIONS

1. Never start a computer with removable media in the drives, unless the media is uninfected.
2. Never open an e-mail attachment unless you are expecting it *and* it is from a trusted source. Turn off message preview.
3. Set the macro security in programs so you can enable or disable macros. Enable macros only if the document is from a trusted source and you are expecting it.
4. Install an antivirus program on all of your computers. Obtain updates to the virus signature files on a regular basis.
5. Check all downloaded programs for viruses, worms, or Trojan horses. These malicious-logic programs often are placed in seemingly innocent programs, so they will affect a large number of users.
6. If the antivirus program flags an e-mail attachment as infected, delete the attachment immediately.
7. Before using any removable media, use the antivirus scan program to check the media for infection. Incorporate this procedure even for shrink-wrapped software from major developers. Some commercial software has been infected and distributed to unsuspecting users this way.
8. Install a personal firewall program.

FIGURE 10-4   With the growing number of new viruses, worms, and Trojan horses, it is crucial that users take steps to protect their computers.

Denial of Service Attacks

A **denial of service attack**, or **DoS attack**, is an assault whose purpose is to disrupt computer access to an Internet service such as the Web or e-mail. Perpetrators carry out a DoS attack in a variety of ways. For example, they may use an unsuspecting computer to send an influx of confusing data messages or useless traffic to a computer network. The victim computer network eventually jams, blocking legitimate visitors from accessing the network.

Back Doors

A **back door** is a program or set of instructions in a program that allow users to bypass security controls when accessing a program, computer, or network. Once perpetrators gain access to unsecure computers, they often install a back door or modify an existing program to include a back door, which allows them to continue to access the computer remotely without the user's knowledge.

Spoofing

Spoofing is a technique intruders use to make their network or Internet transmission appear legitimate to a victim computer or network. IP spoofing occurs when an intruder computer fools a network into believing its IP address is associated with a trusted source. Perpetrators of IP spoofing trick their victims into interacting with a phony Web site. For example, the victim may provide confidential information or download files containing viruses, worms, or other malicious programs.

Safeguards against DoS Attacks, Back Doors, and IP Spoofing

To defend against DoS attacks, improper use of back doors, and IP spoofing, users can implement firewall solutions and install intrusion detection software. The following sections discuss these safeguards.

Firewalls

A **firewall** is hardware and/or software that protects a network's resources from intrusion by users on another network such as the Internet (Figure 10-5). All networked and online computer users should implement a firewall solution.

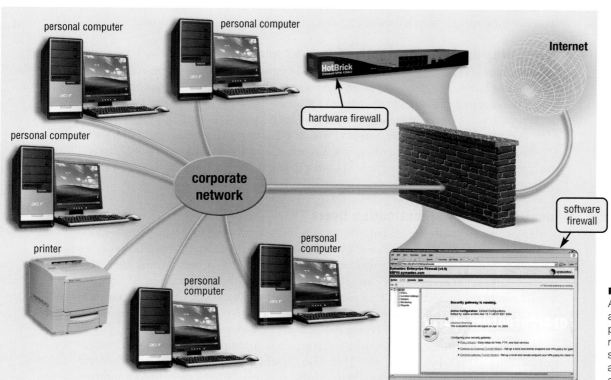

personal computer

personal computer

Internet

HotBrick

hardware firewall

personal computer

corporate network

software firewall

printer

personal computer

personal computer

Security gateway is running.

FIGURE 10-5
A firewall is hardware and/or software that protects a network's resources from intrusion by users on another network such as the Internet.

Companies use firewalls to protect network resources from outsiders and to restrict employees' access to sensitive data such as payroll or personnel records. Businesses can implement a firewall solution themselves or outsource their needs to a company specializing in providing firewall protection. Large companies often route all their communications through a proxy server, which is a component of the firewall. A proxy server is a server outside the company's network that controls which communications pass into the company's network.

Home and small office/home office users often protect their computers with a personal firewall utility. A **personal firewall utility** is a program that detects and protects a personal computer and its data from unauthorized intrusions. Some operating systems, such as Windows XP, include personal firewalls.

Some small office/home office users purchase a hardware firewall, such as a router or other device that has a built-in firewall, in addition to or instead of personal firewall software. Hardware firewalls stop intrusions before they break in your computer.

Intrusion Detection Software

WEB LINK 10-2

Intrusion Detection Software

For more information, visit scsite.com/dcf2e/ch10/weblink and then click Intrusion Detection Software.

To provide extra protection against hackers and other intruders, large companies sometimes use intrusion detection software to identify possible security breaches. **Intrusion detection software** automatically analyzes all network traffic, assesses system vulnerabilities, identifies any unauthorized access (intrusions), and notifies network administrators of suspicious behavior patterns or system breaches.

To utilize intrusion detection software requires the expertise of a network administrator because the programs are complex and difficult to use and interpret. These programs also are quite expensive.

UNAUTHORIZED ACCESS AND USE

Another type of computer security risk is unauthorized access and use. **Unauthorized access** is the use of a computer or network without permission. **Unauthorized use** is the use of a computer or its data for unapproved or possibly illegal activities. Unauthorized use includes a variety of activities: an employee using an organization's computer to send personal e-mail messages, an employee using the organization's word processing software to track his or her child's soccer league scores, or someone gaining access to a bank computer and performing an unauthorized transfer.

Safeguards against Unauthorized Access and Use

Companies take several measures to help prevent unauthorized access and use. At a minimum, they should have a written acceptable use policy (AUP) that outlines the computer activities for which the computer and network may and may not be used. A company's AUP should specify the acceptable use of computers by employees for personal reasons. Some companies prohibit such use entirely. Others allow personal use on the employee's own time such as a lunch hour.

Other measures that safeguard against unauthorized access and use include firewalls and intrusion detection software, which were discussed in the previous section, and identifying and authenticating users.

Identifying and Authenticating Users

Many companies use access controls to minimize the chance that a perpetrator intentionally may access or an employee accidentally may access confidential information on a computer. An **access control** is a security measure that defines who can access a computer, when they can access it, and what actions they can take while accessing the computer. In addition, the computer should maintain an **audit trail** that records in a file both successful and unsuccessful access attempts. An unsuccessful access attempt could result from a user mistyping his or her password, or it could result from a hacker trying thousands of passwords.

Companies should investigate unsuccessful access attempts immediately to ensure they are not intentional breaches of security. They also should review successful access for irregularities, such as use of the computer after normal working hours or from remote computers.

Many systems implement access controls using a two-phase process called identification and authentication. Identification verifies that an individual is a valid user. Authentication verifies that the individual is the person he or she claims to be. Three methods of identification and authentication include user names and passwords, possessed objects, and biometric devices. The technique(s) a company uses should correspond to the degree of risk that is associated with the unauthorized access.

USER NAMES AND PASSWORDS A **user name**, or user ID (identification), is a unique combination of characters, such as letters of the alphabet or numbers, that identifies one specific user. A **password** is a private combination of characters associated with the user name that allows access to certain computer resources.

Most multiuser (networked) operating systems require that users correctly enter a user name and a password before they can access the data, information, and programs stored on a computer or network (Figure 10-6).

Most systems require that users select their own passwords. Users typically choose an easy-to-remember word or series of characters for passwords. If your password is too obvious, however, such as your initials or birthday, others can guess it easily. Easy passwords make it simple for hackers and other intruders to break into a system. Hackers use computer automated tools to assist them with guessing passwords. Thus, you should select a password carefully. Longer passwords provide greater security than shorter ones. Each character added to a password significantly increases the number of possible combinations and the length of time it might take for someone or for a hacker's computer to guess the password (Figure 10-7).

In addition to a user name and password, some systems ask users to enter one of several pieces of personal information. Such items can include a spouse's first name, a birth date, a place of birth, or a mother's maiden name. As with a password, if the user's response does not match the information on file, the system denies access.

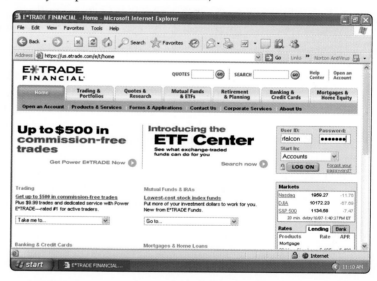

FIGURE 10-6 Many Web sites that maintain personal and confidential data require a user to enter a user name (user ID) and password.

PASSWORD PROTECTION

Number of Characters	Possible Combinations	AVERAGE TIME TO DISCOVER	
		Human	Computer
1	36	3 minutes	.000018 second
2	1,300	2 hours	.00065 second
3	47,000	3 days	.02 second
4	1,700,000	3 months	1 second
5	60,000,000	10 years	30 seconds
10	3,700,000,000,000,000	580 million years	59 years

- Possible characters include the letters A–Z and numbers 0–9
- Human discovery assumes 1 try every 10 seconds
- Computer discovery assumes 1 million tries per second
- Average time assumes the password would be discovered in approximately half the time it would take to try all possible combinations

FIGURE 10-7 This table shows the effect of increasing the length of a password that consists of letters and numbers. The longer the password, the more effort required to discover it. Long passwords, however, are more difficult for users to remember.

POSSESSED OBJECTS   A possessed object is any item that you must carry to gain access to a computer or computer facility. Examples of possessed objects are badges, cards, smart cards, and keys. The card you use in an automated teller machine (ATM) is a possessed object that allows access to your bank account.

Possessed objects often are used in combination with personal identification numbers. A **personal identification number** (**PIN**) is a numeric password, either assigned by a company or selected by a user. PINs provide an additional level of security. An ATM card typically requires a four-digit PIN. PINs are passwords. Select them carefully and protect them as you do any other password.

BIOMETRIC DEVICES   A **biometric device** authenticates a person's identity by translating a personal characteristic, such as a fingerprint, into a digital code that is then compared with a digital code stored in the computer verifying a physical or behavioral characteristic. If the digital code in the computer does not match the personal characteristic code, the computer denies access to the individual.

Biometric devices grant access to programs, computers, or rooms using computer analysis of some biometric identifier. Examples of biometric devices and systems include fingerprint scanners (Figure 10-8), hand geometry systems, face recognition systems, voice verification systems, signature verification systems, and iris recognition systems. Read Looking Ahead 10-1 for a look at the next generation of face recognition systems.

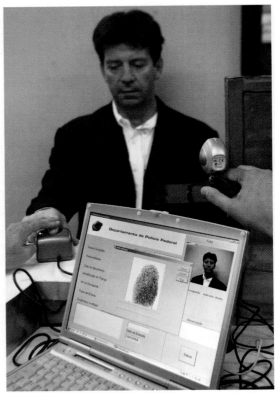

FIGURE 10-8   A fingerprint scanner verifies this traveler's identity.

LOOKING AHEAD 10-1

Three-Dimensional Facial Recognition Software — A Step Forward for Security

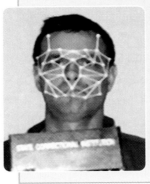

Your next passport may contain an added feature: a chip that communicates with a reader via radio frequency. The chip will contain at least one photograph of you and perhaps your fingerprints so you can be verified as the passport owner.

The facial recognition software market is expected to grow from $228 million in 2005 to $802 million in 2008 according to the International Biometric Group. Leading the way are three-dimensional systems that measure the width, height, and depth of an individual's face and then compare the dimensions to the original photographs. The software can identify an individual positively in a dark room or in a different pose than when the photographs were taken. For more information, visit scsite.com/dcf2e/ch10/looking and then click Facial Recognition.

Test your knowledge of pages 362 through 370 in Quiz Yourself 10-1.

QUIZ YOURSELF 10-1

Instructions: Find the true statement below. Then, rewrite the remaining false statements so they are true.

1. A back door attack is an assault whose purpose is to disrupt computer access to an Internet service such as the Web or e-mail.

2. All networked and online computer users should implement a firewall solution.

3. Computer viruses, worms, and Trojan horses are malicious-logic programs that act with a user's knowledge.

4. Shorter passwords provide greater security than longer ones.

5. Updating an antivirus program's quarantine protects a computer against viruses written since the antivirus program was released.

Quiz Yourself Online: To further check your knowledge of safeguards against computer viruses, worms, Trojan horses, denial of service attacks, back doors, and spoofing; and preventing unauthorized computer access and use, visit scsite.com/dcf2e/ch10/quiz and then click Objectives 1 – 2.

HARDWARE THEFT AND VANDALISM

Hardware theft and vandalism are other types of computer security risks. **Hardware theft** is the act of stealing computer equipment. **Hardware vandalism** is the act of defacing or destroying computer equipment. Hardware vandalism takes many forms, from someone cutting a computer cable to individuals breaking into a business or school computer lab and aimlessly smashing computers.

Mobile users are susceptible to hardware theft. It is estimated that more than 600,000 notebook computers are stolen each year. The size and weight of these computers make them easy to steal. Thieves often target notebook computers of company executives, so they can use the stolen computer to access confidential company information illegally.

Safeguards against Hardware Theft and Vandalism

To help reduce the chances of theft, companies and schools use a variety of security measures. Physical access controls, such as locked doors and windows, usually are adequate to protect the equipment. Many businesses, schools, and some homeowners install alarm systems for additional security. School computer labs and other areas with a large number of semifrequent users often attach additional physical security devices such as cables that lock the equipment to a desk (Figure 10-9), cabinet, or floor. Small locking devices also exist that require a key to access a hard disk or CD/DVD drive.

Mobile computer users must take special care to protect their equipment. Some users attach a physical device such as a cable to lock a mobile computer temporarily to a stationary object. Other mobile users install a mini-security system in the notebook computer. Some of these security systems shut down the computer and sound an alarm if the computer moves outside a specified distance. Others can track the location of the stolen notebook computer.

Some notebook computers use passwords, possessed objects, and biometrics as methods of security. When you boot up these computers, you must enter a password, slide a card in a card reader, or press your finger on a fingerprint scanner before the hard disk unlocks. This type of security does not prevent theft, but it renders the computer useless if it is stolen.

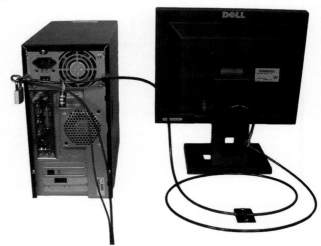

FIGURE 10-9 Using cables to lock computers can help prevent the theft of computer equipment.

SOFTWARE THEFT

Another type of computer security risk is software theft. **Software theft** occurs when someone steals software media, intentionally erases programs, or illegally copies a program. One form of software theft involves someone physically stealing the media that contain the software. Another form of software theft occurs when software is stolen from software manufacturers. This type of theft, called piracy, is by far the most common form of software theft. Software **piracy** is the unauthorized and illegal duplication of copyrighted software.

Safeguards against Software Theft

To protect software media from being stolen, owners should keep original software boxes and media in a secure location.

To protect themselves from software piracy, software manufacturers issue users license agreements. A **license agreement** is the right to use the software. That is, you do not own the software. The license agreement provides specific conditions for use of the software, which a user must accept before using the software (Figure 10-10). These terms usually are displayed when you install the software.

The most common type of license included with software purchased by individual users is a single-user license agreement, also called an end-user license agreement (EULA). A single-user license agreement typically includes many of the following conditions that specify a user's responsibility upon acceptance of the agreement.

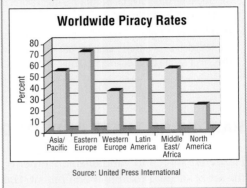

FAQ 10-2

How prevalent is software piracy?

A recent study showed that more than half of 86 countries polled had a piracy rate greater than 60 percent. The chart below outlines some of the piracy rates around the world. For more information, visit scsite.com/dcf2e/ch10/faq and then click Software Piracy.

Worldwide Piracy Rates

Source: United Press International

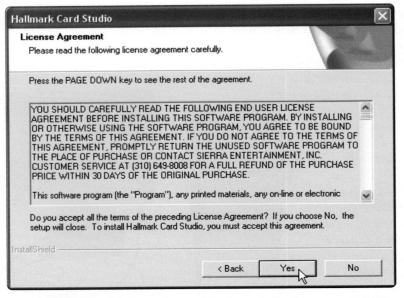

FIGURE 10-10   A user must accept the terms in the license agreement before using the software.

Users are permitted to:
- Install the software on only one computer. (Some license agreements allow users to install the software on one desktop computer and one notebook computer.)
- Make one copy of the software as a backup.
- Give or sell the software to another individual, but only if the software is removed from the user's computer first.

Users are not permitted to:
- Install the software on a network, such as a school computer lab.
- Give copies to friends and colleagues, while continuing to use the software.
- Export the software.
- Rent or lease the software.

Unless otherwise specified by a license agreement, you do not have the right to copy, loan, borrow, rent, or in any way distribute software.

Doing so is a violation of copyright law. It also is a federal crime. Despite this, some experts estimate for every authorized copy of software in use, at least one unauthorized copy exists.

In an attempt to prevent software piracy, Microsoft and other manufacturers have incorporated an activation process into many of its consumer products. During the **product activation**, which is conducted either online or by telephone, users provide the software product's 25-character identification number to receive an installation identification number unique to the computer on which the software is installed.

If you are not completely familiar with your school or employer's policies governing installation of software, check with the information technology department or your school's technology coordinator.

INFORMATION THEFT

Information theft is yet another type of computer security risk. **Information theft** occurs when someone steals personal or confidential information. An unethical company executive may steal or buy stolen information to learn about a competitor. A corrupt individual may steal credit card numbers to make fraudulent purchases.

Safeguards against Information Theft

Most companies attempt to prevent information theft by implementing the user identification and authentication controls discussed earlier in this chapter. These controls are best suited for protecting information on computers located on a company's premises. Information transmitted over networks offers a higher degree of risk because unscrupulous users can intercept it during transmission. To protect information on the Internet and networks, companies and individuals use a variety of encryption techniques.

Encryption

Encryption is the process of converting readable data into unreadable characters to prevent unauthorized access. You treat encrypted data just like any other data. That is, you can store it or send it in an e-mail message. To read the data, the recipient must **decrypt**, or decipher, it into a readable form.

In the encryption process, the unencrypted, readable data is called plaintext. The encrypted (scrambled) data is called ciphertext. To encrypt the data, the originator of the data converts the plaintext into ciphertext using an encryption key. In its simplest form, an encryption key is a programmed formula that the recipient of the data uses to decrypt ciphertext.

Many data encryption methods exist. Figure 10-11 shows examples of some simple encryption methods. An encryption key (formula) often uses more than one of these methods, such as a combination of transposition and substitution. Most organizations use available software for encryption.

WEB LINK 10-4

Encryption

For more information, visit scsite.com/dcf2e/ch10/weblink and then click Encryption.

SAMPLE ENCRYPTION METHODS

Name	Method	Plaintext	Ciphertext	Explanation
Transposition	Switch the order of characters	SOFTWARE	OSTFAWER	Adjacent characters swapped
Substitution	Replace characters with other characters	INFORMATION	WLDIMXQUWIL	Each letter replaced with another
Expansion	Insert characters between existing characters	USER	UYSYEYRY	Letter Y inserted after each character
Compaction	Remove characters and store elsewhere	ACTIVATION	ACIVTIN	Every third letter removed (T, A, O)

FIGURE 10-11   This table shows four simple methods of encryption. Most encryption programs use a combination of these four methods.

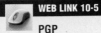

WEB LINK 10-5

PGP Encryption Software

For more information, visit scsite.com/dcf2e/ ch10/weblink and then click PGP Encryption Software.

When users send an e-mail message over the Internet, they never know who might intercept it, who might read it, or to whom it might be forwarded. If a message contains personal or confidential information, users can protect the message by encrypting it or signing it digitally. One of the more popular e-mail encryption programs is called **Pretty Good Privacy** (**PGP**). PGP is freeware for personal, noncommercial users. Home users can download PGP from the Web at no cost.

A **digital signature** is an encrypted code that a person, Web site, or company attaches to an electronic message to verify the identity of the message sender. Digital signatures often are used to ensure that an impostor is not participating in an Internet transaction. That is, digital signatures help to prevent e-mail forgery. A digital signature also can verify that the content of a message has not changed.

Many Web browsers and Web sites use encryption. A Web site that uses encryption techniques to secure its data is known as a **secure site** (Figure 10-12). Secure sites often use digital certificates. A **digital certificate** is a notice that guarantees a user or a Web site is legitimate. A **certificate authority** (CA) is an authorized person or a company that issues and verifies digital certificates. Users apply for a digital certificate from a CA. The digital certificate typically contains information such as the user's name, the issuing CA's name and signature, and the serial number of the certificate. The information in a digital certificate is encrypted.

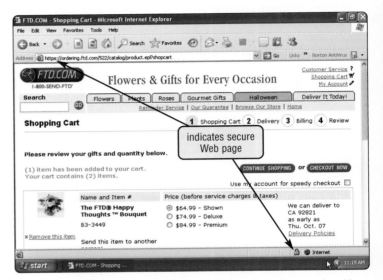

FIGURE 10-12 Web addresses of secure sites often begin with https instead of http. Secure sites also often display a lock symbol on the status bar.

SYSTEM FAILURE

System failure is yet another type of computer security risk. A **system failure** is the prolonged malfunction of a computer. System failure can cause loss of hardware, software, data, or information. A variety of causes can lead to system failure. These include aging hardware; natural disasters such as fires, floods, or hurricanes; random events such as electrical power problems; and even errors in computer programs.

One of the more common causes of system failure is an electrical power variation. Electrical power variations can cause loss of data and loss of equipment. If the computer equipment is networked, a single power disturbance can damage multiple systems.

Safeguards against System Failure

To protect against electrical power variations, use a surge protector. A **surge protector** uses special electrical components to provide a stable current flow to the computer and other electronic equipment (Figure 10-13). Sometimes resembling a power strip, the computer and other devices plug in the surge protector, which plugs in the power source.

FIGURE 10-13 Circuits inside a surge protector safeguard against overvoltages and undervoltages.

No surge protectors are 100 percent effective. Typically, the amount of protection offered by a surge protector is proportional to its cost. That is, the more expensive, the more protection the protector offers.

If your computer connects to a network or the Internet, also be sure to have protection for your modem, telephone lines, DSL lines, Internet cable lines, and network lines. Many surge protectors include plug-ins for telephone lines and other cables.

For additional electrical protection, some applications connect an uninterruptible power supply to the computer. An **uninterruptible power supply** (**UPS**) is a device that contains surge protection circuits and one or more batteries that can provide power during a loss of power (Figure 10-14). A UPS connects between your computer and a power source.

As another measure of protection, some companies use duplicate components or computers as a safeguard against system failure.

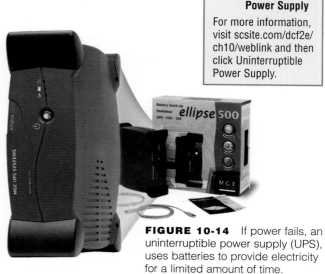

WEB LINK 10-6

Uninterruptible Power Supply

For more information, visit scsite.com/dcf2e/ch10/weblink and then click Uninterruptible Power Supply.

FIGURE 10-14 If power fails, an uninterruptible power supply (UPS), uses batteries to provide electricity for a limited amount of time.

BACKING UP — THE ULTIMATE SAFEGUARD

To prevent against data loss caused by a system failure, computer users should back up files regularly. A **backup** is a duplicate of a file, program, or disk that can be used if the original is lost, damaged, or destroyed. Thus, to **back up** a file means to make a copy of it. In the case of a system failure or the discovery of corrupted files, you **restore** the files by copying the backed up files to their original location on the computer.

You can use just about any media to store backups. A good choice for a home user might be CD-RWs or DVD+RWs. Keep backup copies in a fireproof and heatproof safe or vault, or offsite. Offsite means in a location separate from the computer site. A growing trend is to use online storage as an offsite location. Recall that online storage is a service on the Web that provides storage to computer users.

Most backup programs for the home user provide for a full backup and a selective backup. A full backup copies all of the files in the computer. With a selective backup, users choose which folders and files to include in a backup.

Some users implement a three-generation backup policy to preserve three copies of important files. The grandparent is the oldest copy of the file. The parent is the second oldest copy of the file. The child is the most recent copy of the file.

Most operating systems include a backup program. Backup devices, such as tape and removable disk drives, also include backup programs. Numerous stand-alone backup utilities exist. Many of these can be downloaded from the Web at no cost.

Some companies choose to use an online backup service to handle their backup needs. An **online backup service** is a Web site that automatically backs up files to its online location. These sites usually charge a monthly or annual fee. If the system crashes, the online backup service typically sends the company one or more CDs that contains all its backed up data.

WIRELESS SECURITY

Wireless technology has made dramatic changes in the way computer users communicate worldwide. Billions of home and business users have notebook computers, PDAs, smart phones, and other devices to access the Internet, send e-mail and instant messages, chat online, or share network connections — all without wires. Home users set up wireless home networks. Mobile users access wireless networks in hot spots at airports, hotels, schools, shopping malls, bookstores, restaurants, and coffee shops. Schools have wireless networks so students can access the school network using their mobile computers and devices as they move from building to building.

Although wireless access provides many conveniences to users, it also poses additional security risks. One study showed that about 65 percent of wireless networks have no security protection. Some perpetrators connect to other's wireless networks to gain free Internet access; others may try to access a company's confidential data.

To access the network, the perpetrator must be in range of the wireless network. Some intruders intercept and monitor communications as they transmit through the air. Others connect to a network through an unsecured wireless access point (WAP). In one technique, called **war driving**, perpetrators attempt to connect to wireless networks via their notebook computer while driving a vehicle through areas they suspect have a wireless network.

In addition to using firewalls, some safeguards that improve the security of wireless networks include reconfiguring the wireless access point and ensuring equipment uses one or more wireless security standards such as Wired Equivalent Privacy, Wi-Fi Protected Access, and 802.11i.

- A wireless access point (WAP) should be configured so it does not broadcast a network name. The WAP also should be programmed so only certain devices can access it.
- **Wired Equivalent Privacy** (WEP) is a security standard that defines how to encrypt data as it travels across wireless networks. WEP supports both 40-bit and 128-bit encryption.
- **Wi-Fi Protected Access** (WPA) is a security standard that improves on WEP by authenticating network users and providing more advanced encryption techniques.
- An **802.11i** network, the most recent network security standard, conforms to the government's security standards and uses more sophisticated encryption techniques than both WPA and WEP.

By implementing these security measures, you can help to prevent unauthorized access to wireless networks.

Test your knowledge of pages 371 through 376 in Quiz Yourself 10-2.

QUIZ YOURSELF 10-2

Instructions: Find the true statement below. Then, rewrite the remaining false statements so they are true.

1. An end-user license agreement (EULA) permits users to give copies to friends and colleagues, while continuing to use the software.
2. Encryption is a process of converting ciphertext into plaintext to prevent authorized access.
3. Mobile users are not susceptible to hardware theft.
4. Three wireless security standards are Wired Equivalent Privacy, Wi-Fi Protected Access, and 802.11i.
5. To prevent against data loss caused by a system failure, computer users should restore files regularly.

Quiz Yourself Online: To further check your knowledge of safeguards against hardware theft, software theft, information theft, protection against system failure, and wireless security, visit scsite.com/dcf2e/ch10/quiz and then click Objectives 3 – 6.

ETHICS AND SOCIETY

As with any powerful technology, computers can be used for both good and bad intentions. The standards that determine whether an action is good or bad are known as ethics.

Computer ethics are the moral guidelines that govern the use of computers and information systems. Five frequently discussed areas of computer ethics are unauthorized use of computers and networks, software theft (piracy), information accuracy, intellectual property rights, and information privacy. The questionnaire in Figure 10-15 raises issues in each of these areas.

Previous sections in this chapter discussed unauthorized use of computers and networks, and software theft (piracy). The following pages discuss issues related to information accuracy, intellectual property rights, and information privacy.

	Ethical	Unethical
1. A company requires employees to wear badges that track their whereabouts while at work.	☐	☐
2. A supervisor reads an employee's e-mail.	☐	☐
3. An employee uses his computer at work to send e-mail messages to a friend.	☐	☐
4. An employee sends an e-mail message to several coworkers and blind copies his supervisor.	☐	☐
5. An employee forwards an e-mail message to a third party without permission from the sender.	☐	☐
6. An employee uses her computer at work to complete a homework assignment for school.	☐	☐
7. The vice president of your Student Government Association (SGA) downloads a photograph from the Web and uses it in a flier recruiting SGA members.	☐	☐
8. A student copies text from the Web and uses it in a research paper for his English Composition class.	☐	☐
9. An employee sends political campaign material to individuals on her employer's mailing list.	☐	☐
10. As an employee in the registration office, you have access to student grades. You look up grades for your friends, so they do not have to wait for delivery of grade reports from the postal service.	☐	☐
11. An employee makes a copy of software and installs it on her home computer. No one uses her home computer while she is at work, and she uses her home computer only to finish projects from work.	☐	☐
12. An employee who has been laid off installs a computer virus on his employer's computer.	☐	☐
13. A person designing a Web page finds one on the Web similar to his requirements, copies it, modifies it, and publishes it as his own Web page.	☐	☐
14. A student researches using only the Web to write a report.	☐	☐
15. In a society in which all transactions occur online (a cashless society), the government tracks every transaction you make and automatically deducts taxes from your bank account.	☐	☐
16. Someone copies a well-known novel to the Web and encourages others to read it.	☐	☐

FIGURE 10-15   Indicate whether you think the situation described is ethical or unethical. Discuss your answers with your instructor and other students.

Information Accuracy

Information accuracy today is a concern because many users access information maintained by other people or companies, such as on the Internet. Do not assume that because the information is on the Web that it is correct. Users should evaluate the value of a Web page before relying on its content. Be aware that the company providing access to the information may not be the creator of the information.

In addition to concerns about the accuracy of computer input, some individuals and organizations raise questions about the ethics of using computers to alter output, primarily graphical output such as retouched photographs. Using graphics equipment and software, users easily can digitize photographs and then add, change, or remove images (Figure 10-16).

One group that completely opposes any manipulation of an image is the National Press Photographers Association. It believes that allowing even the slightest alteration could lead to misrepresentative photographs. Others believe that digital photograph retouching is acceptable as long as the significant content or meaning of the photograph does not change. Digital retouching is an area in which legal precedents so far have not been established.

FIGURE 10-16
A digitally altered photograph shows sports legend Michael Jordan (born in 1963) meeting the famous scientist Albert Einstein (who died in 1955).

Intellectual Property Rights

Intellectual property (IP) refers to unique and original works such as ideas, inventions, art, writings, processes, company and product names, and logos. **Intellectual property rights** are the rights to which creators are entitled for their work. Certain issues arise surrounding IP today because many of these works are available digitally.

A **copyright** gives authors and artists exclusive rights to duplicate, publish, and sell their materials. A copyright protects any tangible form of expression.

A common infringement of copyright is piracy. People pirate (illegally copy) software, movies, and music. Many areas are not clear-cut with respect to the law, because copyright law gives the public fair use to copyrighted material. The issues surround the phrase, fair use, which allows use for educational and critical purposes.

This vague definition is subject to widespread interpretation and raises many questions:
- Should individuals be able to download contents of your Web site, modify it, and then put it on the Web again as their own?
- Should a faculty member have the right to print material from the Web and distribute it to all members of the class for teaching purposes only?
- Should someone be able to scan photographs or pages from a book, publish them to the Web, and allow others to download them?
- Should students be able to post term papers they have written on the Web, making it tempting for other students to download and submit them as their own work?

These and many other issues are being debated strongly by members of society. Read At Issue 10-1 for a related discussion.

WEB LINK 10-7

Intellectual Property Rights

For more information, visit scsite.com/dcf2e/ ch10/weblink and then click Intellectual Property Rights.

AT ISSUE 10-1

Should Companies Be Able to Develop Software that Encourages Illegal Activity?

In 2001, the cutting-edge Napster file-sharing network was effectively shut down by courts because it contributed to the illegal sharing of copyrighted material. The main issue cited by the courts was that the service relied on a Napster-owned central database that contained the locations of files of copyrighted songs and movies. While the Napster software and service served a legitimate purpose by allowing millions of people to share legal information, the result was that most users of the service chose to engage in illegal sharing of copyrighted material.

Since then, other companies have developed similar services, but with one critical difference — the new services do not rely on a central database of the location of files. Instead, the information about the location of files is stored on many users' computers. To the dismay of the recording and motion picture industries, courts now have ruled that this technical difference in the software and services does not make the software companies liable for copyright infringement in which their users engage. Who is responsible for the enormous increase in copyright infringement: technology, software companies, or consumers? What can the recording and motion picture industries do to impede copyright infringement? Should software companies be allowed to distribute software that contributes to or encourages illegal activity?

INFORMATION PRIVACY

Information privacy refers to the right of individuals and companies to deny or restrict the collection and use of information about them. In the past, information privacy was easier to maintain because information was kept in separate locations. Each retail store had its own credit files. Each government agency maintained separate records. Doctors had their own patient files.

Today, huge databases store this data online. Much of the data is personal and confidential and should be accessible only to authorized users. Many individuals and organizations, however, question whether this data really is private.

Figure 10-17 lists measures you can take to make your personal data private. The following pages address techniques companies and employers use to collect your personal data.

HOW TO SAFEGUARD PERSONAL INFORMATION

1. Fill in only necessary information on rebate, warranty, and registration forms.

2. Do not preprint your telephone number or Social Security number on personal checks.

3. Have an unlisted or unpublished telephone number.

4. If Caller ID is available in your area, find out how to block your number from displaying on the receiver's system.

5. Do not write your telephone number on charge or credit receipts.

6. Ask merchants not to write credit card numbers, telephone numbers, Social Security numbers, and driver's license numbers on the back of your personal checks.

7. Purchase goods with cash, rather than credit or checks.

8. Avoid shopping club and buyer cards.

9. If merchants ask personal questions, find out why they want to know before releasing the information.

10. Inform merchants that you do not want them to distribute your personal information.

11. Request, in writing, to be removed from mailing lists.

12. Obtain your credit report once a year from each of the three major credit reporting agencies (Equifax, Experian, and TransUnion) and correct any errors.

13. Request a free copy of your medical records once a year from the Medical Information Bureau.

14. Limit the amount of information you provide to Web sites. Fill in only required information.

15. Install a cookie manager to filter cookies.

16. Clear your history file when you are finished browsing.

17. Set up a free e-mail account. Use this e-mail address for merchant forms.

18. Turn off file and printer sharing on your Internet connection.

19. Install a personal firewall.

20. Sign-up for e-mail filtering through your Internet service provider or use an anti-spam program such as Brightmail.

21. Do not reply to spam for any reason.

22. Surf the Web anonymously with a program such as Freedom WebSecure or through an anonymous Web site such as Anonymizer.com.

FIGURE 10-17 Techniques to keep personal data private.

Electronic Profiles

When you fill out a form such as a magazine subscription, product warranty registration card, or contest entry form, the merchant that receives the form usually enters it into a database. Likewise, every time you click an advertisement on the Web or register software online, your information and preferences enter a database. Merchants then sell the contents of their databases to national marketing firms and Internet advertising firms. By combining this data with information from public sources such as driver's licenses and vehicle registrations, these firms create an electronic profile of individuals.

Critics contend that the information in an electronic profile reveals more about an individual than anyone has a right to know. They also claim that companies should inform people if they plan to provide personal information to others. Many companies today allow people to specify whether they want their personal information distributed.

Cookies

E-commerce and other Web applications often rely on cookies to identify users. A **cookie** is a small text file that a Web server stores on your computer. Cookie files typically contain data about you, such as your user name or viewing preferences.

Many commercial Web sites send a cookie to your browser, and then your computer's hard disk stores the cookie. The next time you visit the Web site, your browser retrieves the cookie from your hard disk and sends the data in the cookie to the Web site. Figure 10-18 illustrates how Web sites work with cookies.

FIGURE 10-18   HOW COOKIES WORK

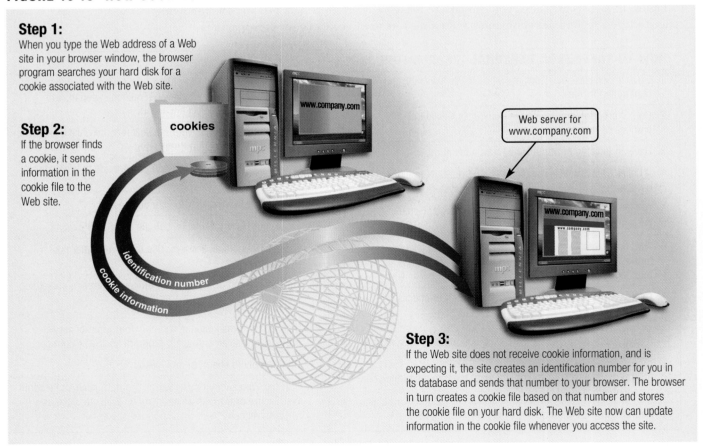

Step 1:
When you type the Web address of a Web site in your browser window, the browser program searches your hard disk for a cookie associated with the Web site.

Step 2:
If the browser finds a cookie, it sends information in the cookie file to the Web site.

Web server for www.company.com

Step 3:
If the Web site does not receive cookie information, and is expecting it, the site creates an identification number for you in its database and sends that number to your browser. The browser in turn creates a cookie file based on that number and stores the cookie file on your hard disk. The Web site now can update information in the cookie file whenever you access the site.

Web sites use cookies for a variety of purposes.

- Most Web sites that allow for personalization use cookies to track user preferences. On such sites, users may be asked to fill in a form requesting personal information, such as their name, postal code, or site preferences. A news Web site, for example, might allow users to customize their viewing preferences to display certain stock quotes. The Web site stores their preferences in a cookie on the users' hard disks.
- Some Web sites use cookies to store users' passwords, so they do not need to enter it every time they log in to the Web site.
- Online shopping sites generally use a session cookie to keep track of items in a user's shopping cart. This way, users can start an order during one Web session and finish it on another day in another session. Session cookies usually expire after a certain time, such as a week or a month.
- Some Web sites use cookies to track how regularly users visit a site and the Web pages they visit while at the site.
- Web sites may use cookies to target advertisements. These sites store a user's interests and browsing habits in the cookie.

WEB LINK 10-8

Cookies

For more information, visit scsite.com/dcf2e/ch10/weblink and then click Cookies.

You can set your browser to accept cookies automatically, prompt you if you want to accept a cookie, or disable cookie use altogether. Keep in mind if you disable cookie use, you will not be able to use many of the e-commerce Web sites.

Spyware and Adware

Spyware is a program placed on a computer without the user's knowledge that secretly collects information about the user. Spyware can enter a computer as a virus or as a result of a user installing a new program. The spyware program communicates information it collects to some outside source while you are online.

Some vendors or employers use spyware to collect information about program usage or employees. Internet advertising firms often collect information about users' Web browsing habits by hiding spyware in adware. **Adware** is a program that displays an online advertisement in a banner or pop-up window on Web pages, e-mail, or other Internet services. To remove spyware, you can purchase a special program that can detect and delete it. Read At Issue 10-2 for a related discussion.

 AT ISSUE 10-2

Should Spyware Be Legal?

Legitimate businesses and illegitimate hackers use a variety of techniques to secretly install spyware on unsecured computers. Spyware can perform a number of tasks, such as monitoring the Web sites that you visit or controlling a computer remotely. Some Web pages also have cookies that count visitors and gather basic statistical information about a visitor's location and Web browser. Online advertising agencies or Internet service providers frequently place spyware cookies as part of a promotion, sometimes without the knowledge of the Web page's sponsor. When the collected information is stored in a Web database and shared among several sites, the technology can track a visitor's travels around the Web. If a visitor completes a registration, that information also can be distributed to other advertisers. Spyware and cookies help advertisers reach their markets and refine their messages, but opponents say the technology is little more than electronic stalking. Should spyware and/or cookies be banned, or is it the right of Web page owners and advertisers to collect information about visitors? Why? Should Web page authors and/or Web page visitors be made aware of spyware and cookies? Why or why not?

Phishing

Phishing is a scam in which a perpetrator sends an official looking e-mail that attempts to obtain your personal and financial information. Some phishing e-mail messages ask you to reply with your information; others direct you to a phony Web site, or a pop-up window that looks like a Web site, that collects the information.

If you receive an e-mail that looks legitimate and requests you update credit card numbers, Social Security numbers, bank account numbers, passwords, or other private information, the FTC recommends you visit the Web site directly to determine if the request is valid.

 FAQ 10-3

What do I do if I have been caught in a phishing scam?

If you have been trapped in a phishing scam, forward the phishing e-mail message to uce@ftc.gov or call the FTC help line at 1-877-FTC-HELP. For more information, visit scsite.com/dcf2e/ch10/faq and then click Phishing Scams.

Spam

Spam is an unsolicited e-mail message or newsgroup posting sent to multiple recipients or newsgroups at once. Spam is Internet junk mail (Figure 10-19). The content of spam ranges from selling a product or service, to promoting a business opportunity, to advertising offensive material. One study indicates the average user receives more than 1,000 spam e-mail messages each year.

Users can reduce the amount of spam they receive with a number of techniques. Some e-mail programs have built-in settings that allow users to delete spam automatically. Users also can sign up for e-mail filtering from their Internet service provider. **E-mail filtering** is a service that blocks e-mail messages from designated sources. An alternative to e-mail filtering is to purchase an **anti-spam program** that attempts to remove spam before it reaches your inbox. The disadvantage of e-mail filters and anti-spam programs is that sometimes they remove valid e-mail messages.

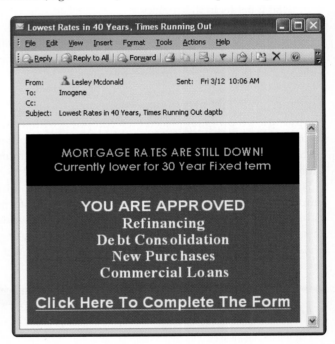

FIGURE 10-19   Spam is Internet junk mail.

Privacy Laws

The concern about privacy has led to the enactment of federal and state laws regarding the storage and disclosure of personal data (Figure 10-20).

Common points in some of these laws include the following:

1. Information collected and stored about individuals should be limited to what is necessary to carry out the function of the business or government agency collecting the data.
2. Once collected, provisions should be made to restrict access to the data to those employees within the organization who need access to it to perform their job duties.
3. Personal information should be released outside the organization collecting the data only when the person has agreed to its disclosure.
4. When information is collected about an individual, the individual should know that the data is being collected and have the opportunity to determine the accuracy of the data.

Date	Law	Purpose
2003	CAN-SPAM Act	Gives law enforcement the right to impose penalties on people using the Internet to distribute spam.
2002	Sarbanes-Oxley Act	Requires corporate officers, auditors, and attorneys of publicly-traded companies follow strict financial reporting guidelines.
2001	Children's Internet Protection Act (CIPA)	Protects minors from inappropriate content when accessing the Internet in schools and libraries.
2001	Provide Appropriate Tools Required to Intercept and Obstruct Terrorism (PATRIOT) Act	Gives law enforcement the right to monitor people's activities, including Web and e-mail habits.
1999	Gramm-Leach-Bliley Act (GLBA) or Financial Modernization Act	Protects consumers from disclosure of their personal financial information and requires institutions to alert customers of information disclosure policies.
1998	Children's Online Privacy Protection Act (COPPA)	Requires Web sites protect personal information of children under 13 years of age.
1998	Digital Millennium Copyright Act (DMCA)	Makes it illegal to circumvent antipiracy schemes in commercial software; outlaws sale of devices that copy software illegally.
1997	No Electronic Theft (NET) Act	Closes a narrow loophole in the law that allowed people to give away copyrighted material (such as software) on the Internet without legal repercussions.
1996	Health Insurance Portability and Accountability Act (HIPAA)	Protects individuals against the wrongful disclosure of their health information.
1996	National Information Infrastructure Protection Act	Penalizes theft of information across state lines, threats against networks, and computer system trespassing.
1994	Computer Abuse Amendments Act	Amends 1984 act to outlaw transmission of harmful computer code such as viruses.
1992	Cable Act	Extends the privacy of the Cable Communications Policy Act of 1984 to include cellular and other wireless services.
1991	Telephone Consumer Protection Act	Restricts activities of telemarketers.
1988	Computer Matching and Privacy Protection Act	Regulates the use of government data to determine the eligibility of individuals for federal benefits.
1988	Video Privacy Protection Act	Forbids retailers from releasing or selling video-rental records without customer consent or a court order.
1986	Electronic Communications Privacy Act (ECPA)	Provides the same right of privacy protection for the postal delivery service and telephone companies to the new forms of electronic communications, such as voice mail, e-mail, and cellular telephones.
1984	Cable Communications Policy Act	Regulates disclosure of cable television subscriber records.
1984	Computer Fraud and Abuse Act	Outlaws unauthorized access of federal government computers.
1978	Right to Financial Privacy Act	Strictly outlines procedures federal agencies must follow when looking at customer records in banks.
1974	Privacy Act	Forbids federal agencies from allowing information to be used for a reason other than that for which it was collected.
1974	Family Educational Rights and Privacy Act	Gives students and parents access to school records and limits disclosure of records to unauthorized parties.
1970	Fair Credit Reporting Act	Prohibits credit reporting agencies from releasing credit information to unauthorized people and allows consumers to review their own credit records.

FIGURE 10-20   Summary of the major U.S. government laws concerning privacy.

Computer Forensics

Computer forensics, also called digital forensics, network forensics, or cyberforensics, is the discovery, collection, and analysis of evidence found on computers and networks. Forensic analysis involves the examination of computer media, programs, data and log files on computers, servers, and networks. Many areas use computer forensics, including law enforcement, criminal prosecutors, military intelligence, insurance agencies, and information security departments in the private sector.

A computer forensics analyst must have knowledge of the law, technical experience with many types of hardware and software products, superior communication skills, familiarity with corporate structures and policies, a willingness to learn and update skills, and a knack for problem solving. For a look at the next generation of forensics, read Looking Ahead 10-2.

LOOKING AHEAD 10-2

Computer Knowledge Assessment Using Brain Fingerprinting

A powerful forensic tool may one day replace the traditional lie detector test. Brain fingerprinting examines a subset of brain waves generated involuntarily when an individual recognizes familiar information.

To conduct the test, researchers place a strap equipped with sensors on an individual's head and then present a variety of relevant and irrelevant words, pictures, and sounds. If the stimulus is familiar, the brain generates unique brain waves 300 to 800 milliseconds after receiving the stimulus.

Computers store and then analyze the series of unique brain waves to determine if the person's brain has stored critical details of a situation, such as a fraudulent or criminal act. Researchers also have determined that brain fingerprinting could help identify the onset of Alzheimer's disease. For more information, visit scsite.com/dcf2e/ch10/looking and then click Brain Fingerprinting.

Employee Monitoring

Employee monitoring involves the use of computers to observe, record, and review an employee's use of a computer, including communications such as e-mail messages, keyboard activity (used to measure productivity), and Web sites visited. Many programs exist that easily allow employers to monitor employees. Further, it is legal for employers to use these programs.

A frequently debated issue is whether an employer has the right to read employee e-mail messages. Actual policies vary widely. Some companies declare that they will review e-mail messages regularly, and others state that e-mail is private. If a company does not have a formal e-mail policy, it can read e-mail messages without employee notification. Several lawsuits have been filed against employers because many believe that such internal communications should be private.

Another controversial issue relates to the use of cameras to monitor employees, customers, and the public. Many people feel that this use of video cameras is a violation of privacy.

Content Filtering

One of the more controversial issues that surround the Internet is its widespread availability of objectionable material, such as racist literature, violence, and obscene pictures. Some believe that such materials should be banned. Others believe that the materials should be filtered, that is, restricted. **Content filtering** is the process of restricting access to certain material on the Web. Content filtering opponents argue that banning any materials violates constitutional guarantees of free speech and personal rights.

Many businesses use content filtering to limit employees' Web access. These businesses argue that employees are unproductive when visiting inappropriate or objectionable Web sites. Some schools, libraries, and parents use content filtering to restrict access to minors.

Web filtering software is a program that restricts access to specified Web sites. Some also filter sites that use specific words. Others allow you to filter e-mail messages, chat rooms, and programs. Many Internet security programs include a firewall, antivirus program, and filtering capabilities combined (Figure 10-21).

HEALTH CONCERNS OF COMPUTER USE

Users are a key component in any information system. Thus, protecting users is just as important as protecting hardware, software, and data.

The widespread use of computers has led to some important health concerns. The following sections discuss health risks and preventions, along with measures users can take to keep the environment healthy.

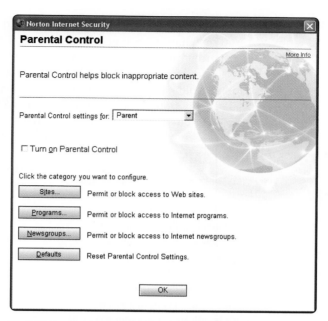

FIGURE 10-21 Many Internet security programs include content filtering capabilities, where users can block specified Web sites and applications.

Computers and Health Risks

A **repetitive strain injury (RSI)** is an injury or disorder of the muscles, nerves, tendons, ligaments, and joints. Computer-related RSIs include tendonitis and carpal tunnel syndrome. RSIs are the largest job-related injury and illness problem in the United States today.

Tendonitis is inflammation of a tendon due to some repeated motion or stress on that tendon. Carpal tunnel syndrome (CTS) is inflammation of the nerve that connects the forearm to the palm of the wrist. Repeated or forceful bending of the wrist can cause CTS or tendonitis of the wrist. Symptoms of tendonitis of the wrist include extreme pain that extends from the forearm to the hand, along with tingling in the fingers. Symptoms of CTS include burning pain when the nerve is compressed, along with numbness and tingling in the thumb and first two fingers.

Long-term computer work can lead to tendonitis or CTS. Factors that cause these disorders include prolonged typing, prolonged mouse usage, or continual shifting between the mouse and the keyboard. If untreated, these disorders can lead to permanent damage to your body.

You can take many precautions to prevent these types of injuries. Take frequent breaks during the computer session to exercise your hands and arms (Figure 10-22). To prevent injury due to typing, place a wrist rest between the keyboard and the edge of your desk. To prevent injury while using a mouse, place the mouse at least six inches from the edge of the desk. In this position, your wrist is flat on the desk. Finally, minimize the number of times you switch between the mouse and the keyboard, and avoid using the heel of your hand as a pivot point while typing or using the mouse.

HAND EXERCISES

- Spread fingers apart for several seconds while keeping wrists straight.
- Gently push back fingers and then thumb.
- Dangle arms loosely at sides and then shake arms and hands.

FIGURE 10-22 To reduce the chance of developing tendonitis or carpal tunnel syndrome, take frequent breaks during computer sessions to exercise your hands and arms.

Another type of health-related condition due to computer usage is **computer vision syndrome** (CVS). You may have CVS if you have sore, tired, burning, itching, or dry eyes; blurred or double vision; distance blurred vision after prolonged staring at a display device; headache or sore neck; difficulty shifting focus between a display device and documents; difficulty focusing on the screen image; color fringes or after-images when you look away from the display device; and increased sensitivity to light. Eyestrain associated with CVS is not thought to have serious or long-term consequences. Figure 10-23 outlines some techniques you can follow to ease eyestrain.

TECHNIQUES TO EASE EYESTRAIN

- **Every 10 to 15 minutes, take an eye break.**
  - Look into the distance and focus on an object for 20 to 30 seconds.
  - Roll your eyes in a complete circle.
  - Close your eyes and rest them for at least one minute.
- **Blink your eyes every five seconds.**
- **Place your display device about an arm's length away from your eyes with the top of the screen at eye level or below.**
- **Use large fonts.**
- **If you wear glasses, ask your doctor about computer glasses.**
- **Adjust the lighting.**

FIGURE 10-23 Following these tips may help reduce eyestrain while working on a computer.

People who spend their workday using the computer sometimes complain of lower back pain, muscle fatigue, and emotional fatigue. Lower back pain sometimes is caused from poor posture. Always sit properly in the chair while you work. Take a break every 30 to 60 minutes — stand up, walk around, or stretch. Another way to help prevent these injuries is to be sure your workplace is designed ergonomically.

Ergonomics and Workplace Design

Ergonomics is an applied science devoted to incorporating comfort, efficiency, and safety into the design of items in the workplace. Ergonomic studies have shown that using the correct type and configuration of chair, keyboard, display device, and work surface helps users work comfortably and efficiently and helps protect their health. For the computer work space, experts recommend an area of at least two feet by four feet. Figure 10-24 illustrates additional guidelines for setting up the work area.

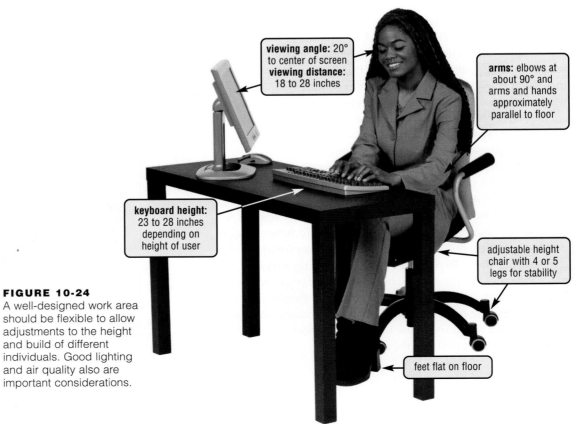

viewing angle: 20° to center of screen
viewing distance: 18 to 28 inches

arms: elbows at about 90° and arms and hands approximately parallel to floor

keyboard height: 23 to 28 inches depending on height of user

adjustable height chair with 4 or 5 legs for stability

feet flat on floor

FIGURE 10-24
A well-designed work area should be flexible to allow adjustments to the height and build of different individuals. Good lighting and air quality also are important considerations.

Computer Addiction

Computers can provide entertainment and enjoyment. Some computer users, however, become obsessed with the computer and the Internet. **Computer addiction** occurs when the computer consumes someone's entire social life. Computer addiction is a growing health problem. Symptoms of a user with computer addiction include the following:

- Craves computer time
- Overjoyed when at the computer
- Unable to stop computer activity
- Irritable when not at the computer
- Neglects family and friends
- Problems at work or school

Computer addiction is a treatable illness through therapy and support groups.

Green Computing

Green computing involves reducing the electricity and environmental waste while using a computer. People use, and often waste, resources such as electricity and paper while using a computer.

By the year 2007, experts estimate that more than 500 million personal computers will be obsolete. Because of the huge potential volumes of electronic waste, the U.S. federal government has proposed a bill that would require computer recycling across the country. Local governments are working on methods to make it easy for consumers to recycle this type of equipment.

To reduce the environmental impact of computing further, users simply can alter a few habits. Figure 10-25 lists the ways you can contribute to green computing.

GREEN COMPUTING SUGGESTIONS

1. Use computers and devices that comply with the ENERGY STAR program.
2. Do not leave the computer running overnight.
3. Turn off the monitor, printer, and other devices when not in use.
4. Use paperless methods to communicate.
5. Recycle paper.
6. Buy recycled paper.
7. Recycle toner cartridges.
8. Recycle old computers and printers.
9. Telecommute (saves gas).

FIGURE 10-25   A list of suggestions to make computing healthy for the environment.

WEB LINK 10-9

Green Computing

For more information, visit scsite.com/dcf2e/ch10/weblink and then click Green Computing.

Test your knowledge of pages 376 through 387 in Quiz Yourself 10-3.

QUIZ YOURSELF 10-3

Instructions: Find the true statement below. Then, rewrite the remaining false statements so they are true.

1. Factors that cause CVS include prolonged typing, prolonged mouse usage, or continual shifting between the mouse and the keyboard.

2. Phishing is the discovery, collection, and analysis of evidence found on computers and networks.

3. Spam is Internet junk mail.

4. Web sites use electronic profiles to track user preferences, store users' passwords, keep track of items in a user's shopping cart, and track Web site browsing habits.

5. You can assume that information on the Web is correct.

Quiz Yourself Online: To further check your knowledge of information privacy and computer-related health disorders and preventions, visit scsite.com/dcf2e/ch10/quiz and then click Objectives 7 – 8.

CHAPTER SUMMARY

This chapter identified some potential computer risks and the safeguards that schools, businesses, and individuals can implement to minimize these risks. Wireless security risks and safeguards also were discussed.

The chapter presented ethical issues surrounding information accuracy, intellectual property rights, and information privacy. The chapter ended with a discussion of computer-related health issues, their preventions, and ways to keep the environment healthy.

CAREER CORNER

Computer Forensics Specialist

Computer forensics is a rapidly growing field that involves gathering and analyzing evidence from computers and networks. It is the responsibility of the **computer forensics specialist** to carefully take several steps to identify and retrieve possible evidence that may exist on a suspect's computer. These steps include protecting the suspect's computer, discovering all files, recovering deleted files, revealing hidden files, accessing protected or encrypted files, analyzing all the data, and providing expert consultation and/or testimony as required. A computer forensics specialist must have knowledge of all aspects of the computer, from the operating system to computer architecture and hardware design.

In the past, many computer forensics specialists were self-taught computer users who may have attended computer forensics seminars, or they may have been trained in the use of one or more computer forensics tools by software vendors. The computer forensics specialist of today needs extensive training, usually from several different sources. A degree in Computer Science should be supplemented with graduate courses and university level professional development certificates.

Entry level salaries for computer forensics specialists range from $45,000 to $75,000. With experience and certifications, salaries can exceed $125,000. For more information, visit scsite.com/dcf2e/ch10/careers and then click Computer Forensics Specialist.

McAfee
Intrusion Prevention Products Developer

Researchers in sixteen countries on five continents are hard at work at McAfee laboratories trying to prevent computer intrusions. The Anti-Virus Emergency Response Team (AVERT) protects desktop computers, servers, networks, and wireless devices by collecting and then disassembling malicious-logic programs. The researchers also monitor online bulletin board systems for suspicious messages and expect to find more than 18,000 new threats each year.

More than 70 million consumers, small- and medium-sized businesses, governmental agencies, and large corporations rely on McAfee's intrusion prevention products to shield them from viruses, worms, Trojan horses, spyware and adware, and phishing schemes. In 2004, the Santa Clara, California, company sold its network analysis division and changed its name from Network Associates to improve its brand recognition. For more information, visit scsite.com/dcf2e/ch10/companies and then click McAfee.

Symantec
Computer Security Solutions Leader

Ninety percent of computer users have installed a virus protection program on their systems, but only twenty percent have a firewall to protect against malicious hackers, according to a survey conducted by Applied Marketing Research. Symantec's line of Norton products, including AntiVirus, Personal Firewall, and AntiSpam, can provide these users with peace of mind knowing that their systems are as secure as possible.

Gordon Eubank founded Symantec in 1982. Since then, more than 120 million users worldwide have used that company's products, helping it grow to one of the world's premier Internet security technology companies with operations in more than 35 countries. *Black Enterprise* magazine named Symantec's chairman and chief executive officer, John Thompson, corporate executive of the year in 2004. For more information, visit scsite.com/dcf2e/ch10/companies and then click Symantec.

TECHNOLOGY TRAILBLAZERS

Donn Parker
Cybercrime Authority

Computer criminals are troubled people, according to Donn Parker, so they violate the law in an attempt to solve their problems. In an attempt to fight cybercrime, Parker founded the International Information Integrity Institute (I-4), then interviewed hundreds of computer criminals and analyzed thousands of security crime cases during the past 30 years.

Security systems within corporations are critical, he says, but they should evolve constantly to defend against attackers. Parker says that computer criminals are unpredictable and irrational, so companies need to stay motivated to enforce their technology risk management plans.

Parker has conducted security reviews for more than 250 companies and has written 6 computer security books. For more information, visit scsite.com/dcf2e/ch10/people and then click Donn Parker.

Clifford Stoll
Computer Philosopher

Computers have become integrated in practically every phase of our lives, but Clifford Stoll wants us to think about their effect on our quality of life. He questions the benefits technology and the Internet presumably provide and the role computers play in schools.

In his books, *Silicon Snake Oil — Second Thoughts on the Information Highway* and *High Tech Heretic: Why Computers Don't Belong in the Classroom*, Stoll maintains that "life in the real world is far more interesting, far more important, far richer, than anything you'll ever find on a computer screen."

He first gained fame by tracking a hacker who was part of a spy ring selling computer secrets to the Soviet Union's KGB for money and drugs. For more information, visit scsite.com/dcf2e/ch10/people and then click Clifford Stoll.

Chapter Review

The Chapter Review section summarizes the concepts presented in this chapter. To obtain help from other students regarding any subject in this chapter, visit scsite.com/dcf2e/ch10/forum and post your thoughts or questions.

(1) How Can Users Safeguard against Computer Viruses, Worms, Trojan Horses, Denial of Service Attacks, Back Doors, and Spoofing?

A computer **virus** is a potentially damaging program that infects a computer and negatively affects the way the computer works. A **worm** is a program that copies itself repeatedly, using up resources and possibly shutting down the computer or network. A **Trojan horse** is a program that hides within or looks like a legitimate program. Users can take precautions to guard against these malicious-logic programs. Do not start a computer with removable media in the drives unless the media is uninfected. Never open an e-mail attachment unless it is from a trusted source. Disable macros in documents that are not from a trusted source. Install an **antivirus program** and a personal firewall program. Stay informed about any new virus alert or **virus hoax**. To defend against a **denial of service attack**, improper use of a **back door**, and **spoofing**, users can install a **firewall** and install **intrusion detection software**.

(2) What Are Techniques to Prevent Unauthorized Access and Use?

Unauthorized access is the use of a computer or network without permission. **Unauthorized use** is the use of a computer or its data for unapproved or illegal activities. A written acceptable use policy (AUP) outlines the activities for which the computer and network may and may not be used. Other measures include firewalls and intrusion detection software. An **access control** defines who can access a computer, when they can access it, and what actions they can take. An **audit trail** records in a file both successful and unsuccessful access attempts. Access controls include a **user name** and **password**, a possessed object, and a **biometric device**.

> Visit scsite.com/dcf2e/ch10/quiz or click the Quiz Yourself button. Click Objectives 1 – 2.

(3) What Are Safeguards against Hardware Theft and Vandalism?

Hardware theft is the act of stealing computer equipment. **Hardware vandalism** is the act of defacing or destroying computer equipment. Physical devices and practical security measures, passwords, possessed objects, and biometrics can reduce the risk of theft or render a computer useless if it is stolen.

(4) How Do Software Manufacturers Protect against Software Theft and Information Theft?

Software theft occurs when someone steals software, intentionally erases programs, or illegally copies programs. Software **piracy** is the unauthorized and illegal duplication of copyrighted software. To protect themselves from software piracy, manufacturers issue a **license agreement** that provides specific conditions for use of the software. During **product activation**, users provide the product's identification number to receive an installation identification number unique to their computer. Companies attempt to prevent **information theft** through user identification and authentication controls, **encryption**, a **digital signature**, a **digital certificate**, or a **certificate authority**.

(5) What Types of Devices Are Available to Protect Computers against System Failure?

A **system failure** is the prolonged malfunction of a computer. A common cause of system failure is an electrical disturbance. A **surge protector** uses special electrical components to provide a stable current flow to the computer. An **uninterruptible power supply** (UPS) contains surge protection circuits and one or more batteries that can provide power during a power loss.

(6) What Are Risks and Safeguards Associated with Wireless Communications?

Wireless access poses additional security risks. Intruders connect to other wireless networks to gain free Internet access or to access a company's confidential data. Some intruders intercept and monitor communications as they are transmitted. Others connect to a network through an unsecured wireless access point (WAP). Some safeguards include firewalls, reconfiguring the WAP, and ensuring equipment uses a wireless security standard, such as **Wired Equivalent Privacy**, **Wi-Fi Protected Access**, and **802.11i**.

Visit scsite.com/dcf2e/ch10/quiz or click the Quiz Yourself button. Click Objectives 3 – 6.

(7) What Are Issues Surrounding Information Privacy?

Information privacy is the right of individuals and companies to restrict the collection and use of information about them. Issues surrounding information privacy include electronic profiles, cookies, spyware and adware, spam, phishing, computer forensics, and employee monitoring. An electronic profile combines data about an individual's Web use with data from public sources. A **cookie** is a file that a Web server stores on a computer to collect data about the user. **Spyware** is a program placed on a computer that secretly collects information about the user. **Adware** is a program that displays an online advertisement in a banner or pop-up window. **Spam** is an unsolicited e-mail message or newsgroup posting sent to many recipients. **Phishing** is a scam in which a perpetrator sends an official looking e-mail that attempts to obtain a user's personal and financial information. **Computer forensics** is the discovery, collection, and analysis of evidence found on computers and networks. **Employee monitoring** uses computers to observe, record, and review an employee's computer use.

(8) How Can Health-Related Disorders and Injuries Due to Computer Use Be Prevented?

A **repetitive strain injury** (**RSI**) is an injury or disorder of the muscles, nerves, tendons, ligaments, and joints. Computer-related RSIs include tendonitis and carpal tunnel syndrome (CTS). Another health-related condition is eyestrain associated with **computer vision syndrome** (CVS). To prevent health-related disorders, take frequent breaks, use precautionary exercises and techniques, and incorporate ergonomics when planning the workplace. **Computer addiction** occurs when the computer consumes someone's entire social life. Computer addiction is a treatable illness through therapy and support groups.

 Visit scsite.com/dcf2e/ch10/quiz or click the Quiz Yourself button. Click Objectives 7 – 8.

Key Terms

You should know each key term. Use the list below to help focus your study. To further enhance your understanding of the Key Terms in this chapter, visit scsite.com/dcf2e/ch10/terms. See an example of and a definition for each term, and access current and additional information about the term from the Web.

802.11i (376)
access control (368)
adware (381)
anti-spam program (382)
antivirus program (365)
audit trail (368)
back door (367)
back up (375)
backup (375)
biometric device (370)
certificate authority (374)
computer addiction (387)
computer crime (362)
computer ethics (376)
computer forensics (384)
computer forensics specialist (388)
computer security risk (362)
computer vision syndrome (386)
content filtering (384)
cookie (380)

copyright (378)
cracker (362)
cybercrime (362)
cyberextortionist (363)
cyberterrorist (363)
decrypt (373)
denial of service attack (367)
digital certificate (374)
digital signature (374)
DoS attack (367)
e-mail filtering (382)
employee monitoring (384)
encryption (373)
firewall (367)
green computing (387)
hacker (362)
hardware theft (371)
hardware vandalism (371)
information privacy (379)
information theft (373)
intellectual property rights (378)

intrusion detection software (368)
license agreement (372)
online backup service (375)
password (369)
payload (364)
personal firewall utility (368)
personal identification number (PIN) (370)
phishing (381)
piracy (372)
Pretty Good Privacy (PGP) (374)
product activation (373)
quarantine (366)
repetitive strain injury (RSI) (385)
restore (375)
script kiddie (362)
secure site (374)
software theft (372)
spam (382)

spoofing (367)
spyware (381)
surge protector (374)
system failure (374)
Trojan horse (364)
unauthorized access (368)
unauthorized use (368)
uninterruptible power supply (UPS) (375)
user name (369)
virus (364)
virus definition (366)
virus hoax (366)
virus signature (366)
war driving (376)
Web filtering software (385)
Wired Equivalent Privacy (376)
Wi-Fi Protected Access (376)
worm (364)

Checkpoint

Use the Checkpoint exercises to check your knowledge level of the chapter.

True/False

Mark T for True and F for False. (See page numbers in parentheses.)

_____ 1. Any illegal act involving a computer generally is referred to as a cybercrime. (362)

_____ 2. A worm is a program that hides within or looks like a legitimate program. (364)

_____ 3. A firewall is hardware and/or software that allows users to bypass security controls when accessing a program, computer, or network. (367)

_____ 4. In order to prevent unauthorized access and use of its computers, a company should have an acceptable use policy (AUP). (368)

_____ 5. Software piracy occurs when someone steals software media, intentionally erases programs, or illegally copies a program. (372)

_____ 6. A digital certificate is a notice that guarantees a user or a Web site is legitimate. (374)

_____ 7. A digital signature verifies the content of a message has been changed. (374)

_____ 8. A cookie is a small text file that a Web server stores on your computer. (380)

_____ 9. Phishing is a program that allows access to specified Web sites. (385)

_____ 10. Computer addiction occurs when the computer consumes someone's entire social life. (387)

Multiple Choice

Select the best answer. (See page numbers in parentheses.)

1. The term cybercrime refers to _____. (362)
   a. events that damage computer hardware
   b. any illegal activities involving a computer
   c. online or Internet-based illegal acts
   d. destructive events or pranks

2. The _____ is the destructive event or prank that malicious-logic programs are intended to deliver. (364)
   a. payload
   b. cookie
   c. hash
   d. spam

3. _____ is a technique intruders use to make their network or Internet transmission appear legitimate. (367)
   a. Phishing
   b. Spoofing
   c. A DoS attack
   d. A back door

4. Physical access controls, such as locked doors and windows, usually are adequate to protect against _____. (371)
   a. software piracy
   b. unauthorized access
   c. hardware theft
   d. all of the above

5. Encrypted (scrambled) data is called _____. (373)
   a. hypertext
   b. ciphertext
   c. subtext
   d. plaintext

6. A _____ gives authors and artists exclusive rights to duplicate, publish, and sell their materials. (378)
   a. copyright
   b. license
   c. password
   d. firewall

7. _____ is an unsolicited e-mail message or newsgroup posting sent to multiple recipients or newsgroups at once. (382)
   a. A cookie
   b. Spam
   c. Spyware
   d. Adware

8. _____ is inflammation of the nerve that connects the forearm to the palm of the wrist. (385)
   a. Tendonitis
   b. Computer vision syndrome (CVS)
   c. Computer addiction
   d. Carpal tunnel syndrome (CTS)

Matching

Match the terms with their definitions. (See page numbers in parentheses.)

_____ 1. cracker (362)

_____ 2. quarantine (366)

_____ 3. password (369)

_____ 4. biometric device (370)

_____ 5. certificate authority (CA) (374)

a. connects a user to a computer only after the computer calls back

b. area of the hard disk that holds an infected file until the infection can be removed

c. translates a personal characteristic into digital code

d. someone who tries to access a computer or network illegally with the intent of destroying data

e. company that issues and verifies digital certificates

f. private combination of characters associated with a user name

Checkpoint

Short Answer

Write a brief answer to each of the following questions.

1. How does a hacker differ from a cracker? _____ What is a script kiddie? _____
2. How do antivirus programs detect and identify a virus? _____ What is a virus hoax? _____
3. How is identification different from authentication? _____ What are four methods of identification and authentication? _____
4. What are some examples of possessed objects? _____ What are some examples of biometric devices? _____
5. What causes a system failure? _____ What is a UPS? _____

Working Together

Working in a group of your classmates, complete the following team exercise.

1. Some schools have begun repetitive strain injury (RSI) prevention programs, but too many students still pay too little attention to ergonomic issues. How safe is your workplace? Have each member of your team compare the characteristics of his or her workplace to the ergonomic guidelines presented in this chapter. Make a sketch of the workplace indicating where it does, and does not, conform to the guidelines. Meet with the members of your team to discuss how each workplace could be improved. Then, use PowerPoint to create a group presentation and share your findings with the class.

Web Research

Use the Internet-based Web Research exercises to broaden your understanding of the concepts presented in this chapter. To discuss any of the Web Research exercises in this chapter with other students, visit scsite.com/dcf2e/ch10/forum and post your thoughts or questions.

(1) Journaling

Respond to your readings in this chapter by writing at least one page about your reactions, evaluations, and reflections on computer security, privacy, and ethics. For example, have you suffered from a **repetitive strain injury**? Does your employer monitor your computer use? Should an employer be able to read your e-mail messages? How have you tried to decrease spam? What measures have you taken to safeguard your personal information? You also can write about the new terms you learned by reading this chapter. If required, submit your journal to your instructor.

(2) Scavenger Hunt

Use one of the **search engines** listed in Figure 2-8 in Chapter 2 on page 58 or your own favorite search engine to find the answers to the questions below. Copy and paste the Web address from the Web page where you found the answer. Some questions may have more than one answer. If required, submit your answers to your instructor. (1) What is the $800 from Microsoft hoax? (2) What similarities do PGP (Pretty Good Privacy) and GPG (GNU Privacy Guard) share? (3) When did the first virus attack occur? What network was affected? (4) What company developed SSL? How does SSL differ from Secure HTTP (S-HTTP)? (5) At what university is the Computer Emergency Response Team Coordination Center (CERT/CC) located? What is one of the latest advisories or incident notes reported by this organization?

(3) Search Sleuth

Internet subject directories are used to find information on specialized topics. One of the oldest and more popular subject directories is the **WWW Virtual Library (VL)**. This Web site is administered by a group of volunteers who are experts in particular topics. Visit this Web site and then use your word processing program to answer the following questions. Then, if required, submit your answers to your instructor. (1) Click the Computing link and then click the Cryptology, PGP and Privacy link. Read two articles in the Online Documents section and then write a 50-word summary of your findings. (2) Click the Back button and then click The Virtual Museum of Computing link. When did the Museum open? What are three recent additions and events? (3) Click the Back button twice, click the Recreation link, and then click the American College Football link. Click the Official College Football Team Homepages (by State) link and then find the link for your college or a college in your state. What is a major story featured on this page?

CHAPTER 10

Learn How To

Use the Learn How To activities to learn fundamental skills when using a computer and accompanying technology. Complete the exercises and submit them to your instructor.

LEARN HOW TO 1: Backup Files on an Offsite Internet Server

Backing up files stored on your computer on another disk or computer located in a different geographical location is the ultimate safeguard for data on your computer. A good way to backup data is to use one of the services available on the Web. A leading service is found at www.IBackup.com. To subscribe to the IBackup service, complete the following steps:

1. Start a Web browser, type the Web address www.IBackup.com in the Address bar, and then press the ENTER key.
2. When the IBackup Web page is displayed, click Sign Up on the top horizontal toolbar.
3. Enter your e-mail address in the E-mail Address text box, and then click the Send Registration E-mail button.
4. In a short period, you will receive a subscription e-mail message. Because you want to subscribe to the backup service, click the backup link in the e-mail message. A form will be displayed in your browser (Figure 10-26).
5. Fill in the form. Select the plan you want in the Select a Storage Plan list. If you want to try the service for a short period of time before subscribing, select 50 MB Trial for 30 Days (Figure 10-26).
6. To continue to the next pages, you must enter credit card information. If you select the 30 day trial, your credit card will not be charged, and an automatic billing at the end of 30 days will not occur. After entering the required information, click the Continue button at the bottom of the page.
7. A message is displayed that tells you the amount charged against your credit card. Also, you can click a link to go to the login page, or enter the Web address, https://www.IBackup.com.

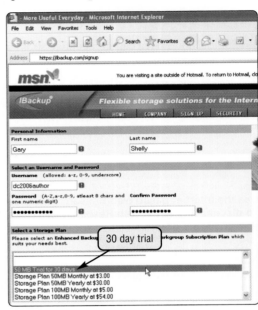

FIGURE 10-26

After establishing an account, you can use it for the time for which you subscribed. Complete the following steps to use the service:

1. Enter the Web address as noted in Step 7 above.
2. In the upper left corner of the home page, enter your user name and password, and then click the Login button. *Your file/folder page is displayed (Figure 10-27). Initially, no files will be saved in your IBackup folder.*
3. To upload a file, click the Upload button on the IBackup toolbar, click a Browse button in the window that opened, browse your computer and locate the file you wish to upload, and then click the Upload file button. The file will be placed in the IBackup folder.
4. For further activities you can accomplish on this site for backing up your files, click the links in the File/Folder area and experiment.

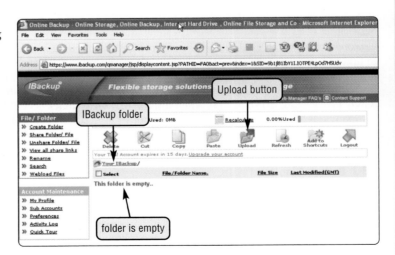

FIGURE 10-27

Exercise

1. Visit the IBackup Web site. Click IBackup Tour and then follow the screen prompts to view all the services offered by IBackup. Which service is most appropriate for your home computer? Which service is most useful for the server that is used in the computer lab at your school? If you had critical data you needed to backup, would you use a service like this? Why or why not? Submit your answers to your instructor.

2. **Optional: Perform this exercise only for your own computer. Do not perform this exercise on a school computer.** Establish an account on IBackup.com. Upload two or more files from your computer. Right-click a file you uploaded on Ibackup.com and click Save Target As on the menu. What happened? Save the file on your computer. What message(s) were displayed? Download the files you uploaded back to your computer. Is this an efficient way to backup your files? Submit your answers to your instructor.

LEARN HOW TO 2: Use the Windows XP Firewall

When you use the Internet, data is sent both from your computer to the Internet and from computers on the Internet to your computer. A firewall is a barrier that checks information coming from the Internet and either turns it away or allows it to pass through to your computer, based on your firewall settings. It also checks data being sent from your computer to the Internet to ensure your computer is not sending unsolicited messages to other computers on the Internet. A firewall can be implemented using hardware or software.

Windows XP SP2 contains a software firewall that starts automatically when you boot your computer. To control the firewall usage on your computer, complete the following steps:

1. Click the Start button on the Windows taskbar, and then click Control Panel on the Start menu.

2. In the Category view of the Control Panel, click Security Center, and then click Windows Firewall in the Windows Security Center window. *The Windows Firewall dialog box is displayed (Figure 10-28).*

3. In the Windows Firewall dialog box, select On or Off to turn on or off the Windows firewall. The firewall automatically is on when you start your computer. You should NOT turn off the firewall unless you have a compelling reason to do so.

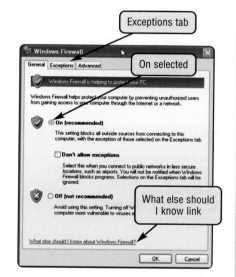

FIGURE 10-28

4. Click the Exceptions tab in the Windows Firewall dialog box. *The Exceptions sheet is displayed (Figure 10-29). The exceptions that are checked can communicate with the Internet without your clicking a link.*

5. You may want to allow programs that routinely communicate with the Internet, such as sports programs that display updated game scores, to have full access to your computer. To add a program to the Exceptions list, click the Add Program button in the Exceptions sheet. The Add a Program dialog box is displayed. Select a program and then click the OK button.

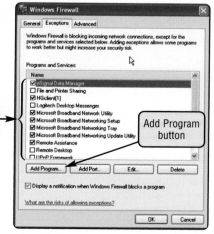

FIGURE 10-29

Exercise

1. Display the Windows Firewall dialog box. Click What else should I know about Windows Firewall in the General sheet. Read the information about Windows firewall. What did you learn that you did not know? What is a security log? How can you cause a security log to be created? Submit your answers to your instructor.

Learn It Online

Use the Learn It Online exercises to reinforce your understanding of the chapter concepts. To access the Learn It Online exercises, visit scsite.com/dcf2e/ch10/learn.

(1) At the Movies — Does Biometrics Violate Employee Privacy?

To view the Does Biometrics Violate Employee Privacy? movie, click the number 1 button. Locate your video and click the corresponding High-Speed or Dial-Up link, depending on your Internet connection. Watch the movie and then complete the exercise by answering the questions that follow. Many companies are turning to high-tech methods of identifying and tracking employees. Biometric identification methods, which include fingerprinting, iris, voice, hand, and facial scans, are gaining in popularity. These methods used to be associated with high-security facilities; but due to increased risks from terrorism, they are gaining popularity in other workplaces. Biometric identification will help employers with employee fraud and security issues. Can you think of any instances where biometric identification can be used as a safety measure for employees? Are there any circumstances under which biometric technology can be abused in the workplace?

(2) Student Edition Labs — Protecting Your Privacy Online

Click the number 2 button. When the Student Edition Labs menu appears, click *Protecting Your Privacy Online* to begin. A new browser window will open. Follow the on-screen instructions to complete the Lab. When finished, click the Exit button. If required, submit your results to your instructor.

(3) Practice Test

Click the number 3 button. Answer each question. When completed, enter your name and click the Grade Test button to submit the quiz for grading. Make a note of any missed questions. If required, submit your results to your instructor.

(4) Who Wants To Be a Computer Genius^2?

Click the number 4 button to find out if you are a computer genius. Directions about how to play the game will be displayed. When you are ready to play, click the Play button. Submit your score to your instructor.

(5) Wheel of Terms

Click the number 5 button to reinforce important terms you learned in this chapter by playing the Shelly Cashman Series version of this popular game. Directions about how to play the game will be displayed. When you are ready to play, click the Play button. Submit your score to your instructor.

(6) Student Edition Labs — Keeping Your Computer Virus Free

Click the number 6 button. When the Student Edition Labs menu appears, click *Keeping Your Computer Virus Free* to begin. A new browser window will open. Follow the on-screen instructions to complete the Lab. When finished, click the Exit button. If required, submit your results to your instructor.

(7) Crossword Puzzle Challenge

Click the number 7 button. Complete the puzzle to reinforce skills you learned in this chapter. Directions about how to play the game will be displayed. When you are ready to play, click the Submit button. Submit the completed puzzle to your instructor.

(8) Lab Exercises

Click the number 8 button. When the Lab Exercises menu appears, click the exercise assigned by your instructor. A new browser window will open. Follow the on-screen instructions to complete the exercise. When finished, click the Exit button. If required, submit your results to your instructor.

(9) Chapter Discussion Forum

Select an objective from this chapter on page 361 about which you would like more information. Click the number 9 button and post a short message listing a meaningful message title accompanied by one or more questions concerning the selected objective. In two days, return to the threaded discussion by clicking the number 9 button. Submit to your instructor your original message and at least one response to your message.

Special Feature

Digital Entertainment

The Revolution Is Underway

This feature looks at the components that comprise the world of digital entertainment. Ever since the world heard "Mary Had a Little Lamb" on Thomas Edison's newest invention — the phonograph — in 1877, the worlds of entertainment and technology began to converge. Next came mass media in the form of radio, movies, and television, followed by personal entertainment products, such as video games, CDs, and DVDs. Today, our homes have become electronic playgrounds, with powerful media center computers functioning as an interface to digital media and television tasks. Our digital world of video, audio, recording, gaming, and computing is evolving quickly, and the entertainment breakthroughs are bound to bring hours of excitement and fun to our lives.

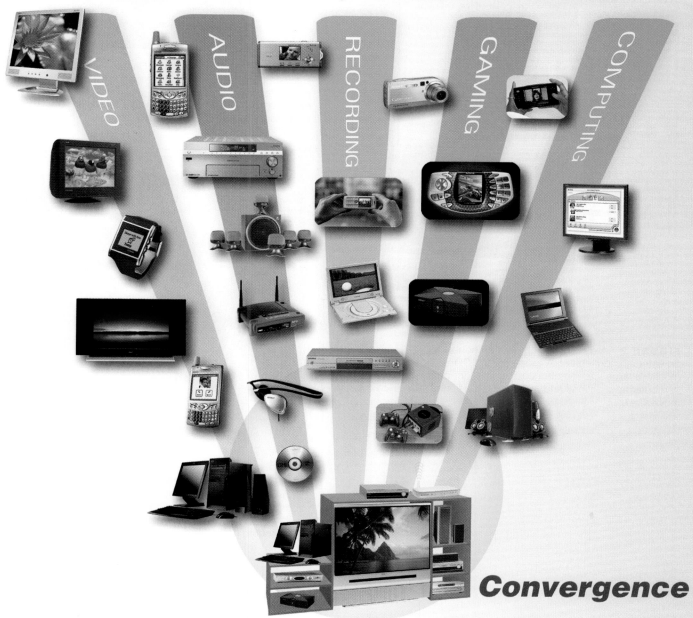

VIDEO   AUDIO   RECORDING   GAMING   COMPUTING

Convergence

The Personal Computer and Television

The personal computer and television can serve as the focal points of the entertainment system. A mid-size flat-screen CRT television delivers excellent picture quality for far less money than a plasma, LCD, or projection unit, but a plasma display gives rich, fluid image quality from a variety of viewing angles.

FIGURE 1 Microsoft's Media Center software can use wireless networking to feed programs, movies, music, and e-mail from a media center personal computer to a television in the room or elsewhere in the house.

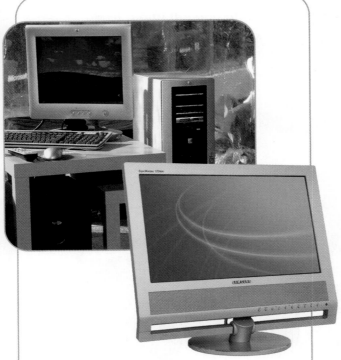

FIGURE 2 A desktop computer can double as an entertainment center. A wide-screen LCD monitor's large viewing area can be used for both computer applications and watching television or movies.

FIGURE 3 Media Center computers deliver high-definition surround sound that can bring live sports action into your media room. They have multiple TV tuners, so you can watch one program while recording another. A single remote lets you select all your television shows, music, and digital photos.

Recording Audio and Video

Whether you are in the mood for an action-packed movie or some soothing new-age music, your digital entertainment products can fulfill your needs. Burn your favorite songs to a CD and play them in your car or while you work out at the gym, burn footage recorded on your camcorder to a DVD to take to Grandma's house, or record movies and television programs on your digital video recorder when you are not at home and then play them at your convenience.

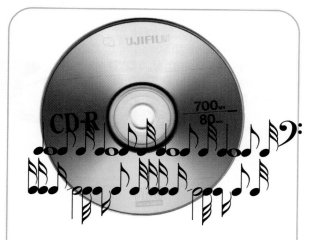

FIGURE 4 Millions of audiophiles use dedicated network audio receivers and legal music download services to hear their preferred musical bands and songs. They then record these digital audio files in MP3, WMA, and other formats and burn them to CDs.

FIGURE 5 DVD burners are considered essential peripherals and can be internally mounted in your computer or externally connected using USB or FireWire cables. Dual-format, dual-layer drives allow you to copy full DVDs without recompression, which preserves the original image quality.

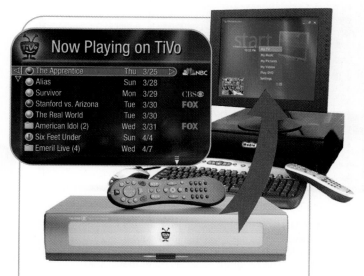

FIGURE 6 Convergence technologies have made storing and sharing video content a breeze. With digital video recorders, such as TiVo, you can record all episodes of one television show with one click, skip commercials, stream video from one unit to another, and then control recording features from a remote Web browser.

Bring Music to Your Ears

A computer now can be considered an essential component of a home entertainment system. A multimedia computer should have at least 200 GB of storage space to save thousands of CDs or digital audio files, a CD burner, a DVD drive to play multichannel audio DVDs, and several USB 2.0 ports to connect peripherals.

FIGURE 7 Music downloading services allow you to purchase individual tracks or entire albums, download the music to your computer, and then transfer the files to a portable player or burn them to a CD. Top downloading services are Apple iTunes Music Store and Microsoft's MSN Music.

FIGURE 8 Apple's creativity software, GarageBand, uses a Macintosh computer to transform any room of the house into a recording studio. The program includes more than 1,000 pieces of music and more than 50 virtual instruments to mix and edit.

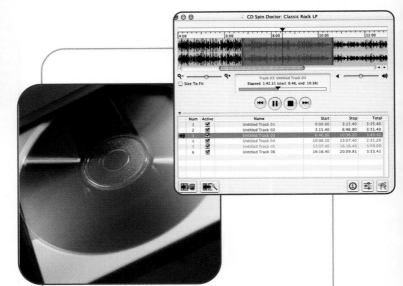

FIGURE 9 A CD-R/RW burner can be used to rip audio CDs to digital files and to burn CDs.

FIGURE 10 Manage your music with digital jukebox software, including Windows Media Player, RealPlayer, Musicmatch Jukebox, and iTunes. These programs allow you to listen to streaming audio, CDs, and downloaded files in a variety of formats. The Microsoft Windows PlaysForSure initiative assures consumers that specific devices are compatible with downloaded content.

FIGURE 11 The abundance of wireless home networks makes it easy to stream digital music stored on your computer to your stereo using devices such as Apple's AirPort Express.

FIGURE 12 iTunes jukebox software allows you to play tracks downloaded from the iTunes Music Store, create playlists, and then transfer the tunes to the trendy iPod.

All the World Is a Game

With thousands of available game titles, it is easy to quench a thirst for fun. From one-player games to serious competition with fellow gamers, it is easy to find sports, strategy, and action games to suit everyone's interests. Gaming hardware can be sorted into three categories: personal computer, console, and handheld. With a broadband connection and home network, you can compete online and tie together multiple personal computer and gaming consoles.

FIGURE 13 Millions of gamers worldwide are competing with friends living across the street or across the globe with massively multiplayer online games (MMOGs). Ultra-fast processors, enormous amounts of memory, a high-end graphics card, large monitor, superb speakers, and case fans are necessary components.

FIGURE 14 The three gaming consoles — Microsoft Xbox, Nintendo GameCube, and Sony PlayStation 2 — cost less than $150 and offer a variety of game titles.

FIGURE 15 Handheld multimedia devices weigh less than one pound and have large, high-resolution screens and incredible sound to play audio, video, and photos. Bluetooth technology allows networked gaming and syncing with other handheld units or a personal computer.

Convergence: Tying the Loose Ends Together

With wired and wireless home networking and broadband, all components are connected to provide entertainment in innovative ways. A central media hub, digital video recorder, and other devices can stream music and video files, Internet radio, and slide shows of photographs seamlessly throughout your house.

FIGURE 16 The ultimate home network requires a variety of hardware to store, share, and stream audio and video files.

The entertainment revolution has worked its way into virtually every facet of our lives. From the largest media rooms to the smallest portable media centers, we can watch our favorite television programs and movies any place at any time. We can surf the Internet, play games with partners on the other side of the world, listen to personalized music, and have fun wherever life takes us. No matter where we are, we always can have the best seat in the house for digital entertainment.

Information System Development and Programming Languages

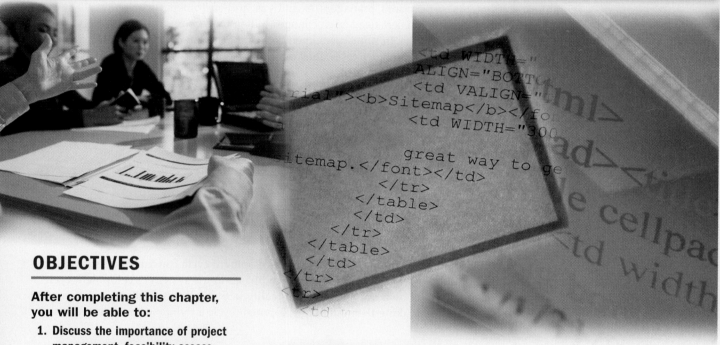

OBJECTIVES

After completing this chapter, you will be able to:

1. Discuss the importance of project management, feasibility assessment, documentation, data information gathering techniques, and information system security during system development

2. Discuss the purpose of each phase in the system development cycle

3. Differentiate between low-level languages and procedural languages

4. Identify the benefits of object-oriented and visual programming languages

5. List other programming languages and other program development tools

6. Describe various ways to develop Web pages

7. List the six steps in the program development cycle

8. Explain the basic control structures used in designing solutions to programming problems

CONTENTS

THE SYSTEM DEVELOPMENT CYCLE
Who Participates in the System Development Cycle?
Project Management
Feasibility Assessment
Documentation
Data and Information Gathering Techniques
What Initiates the System Development Cycle?
Planning Phase
Analysis Phase
Design Phase
Implementation Phase
Support Phase
Information System Security

PROGRAMMING LANGUAGES
Low-Level Languages
Procedural Languages
Object-Oriented Programming Languages
Other Programming Languages
Classic Programming Languages
Other Program Development Tools
Web Page Development
Multimedia Program Development

THE PROGRAM DEVELOPMENT CYCLE
What Initiates the Program Development Cycle?
Control Structures

CHAPTER SUMMARY

COMPANIES ON THE CUTTING EDGE
Computer Associates
Macromedia

TECHNOLOGY TRAILBLAZERS
Grace Hopper
James Gosling

THE SYSTEM DEVELOPMENT CYCLE

A system is a set of components that interact to achieve a common goal. Businesses use many types of systems. A billing system allows a company to send invoices and receive payments from customers. Through a payroll system, employees receive paychecks. A manufacturing system produces the goods that customers order. An inventory system keeps track of the items in a warehouse. Very often, these systems also are information systems.

An **information system (IS)** is a collection of hardware, software, data, people, and procedures that work together to produce quality information. An information system supports daily, short-term, and long-range activities of users. Some examples of users include store clerks, sales representatives, accountants, supervisors, managers, executives, and customers.

The type of information that users need often changes. When this occurs, the information system must meet the new requirements. In some cases, members of the system development team modify the current information system. In other cases, they develop an entirely new information system.

As a computer user in a business, you someday may participate in the modification of an existing system or the development of a new system. Thus, it is important that you understand the system development process. The **system development cycle** is a set of activities used to build an information system.

System development cycles often organize activities by grouping them into larger categories called **phases**. Most system development cycles contain five phases:

1. Planning
2. Analysis
3. Design
4. Implementation
5. Support

As shown in Figure 11-1, each phase in the system development cycle consists of a series of activities, and the phases form a loop. In theory, the five phases in the system development cycle often appear sequentially, as shown in Figure 11-1. In reality, activities within adjacent phases often interact with one another — making the system development cycle a dynamic iterative process.

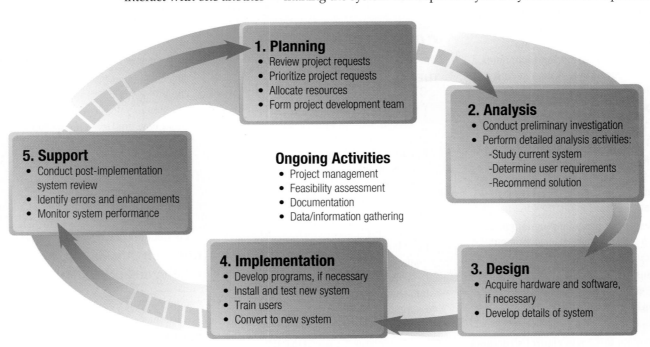

FIGURE 11-1 The system development cycle consists of five phases that form a loop. Several ongoing activities also take place throughout the entire system development cycle.

System development should follow three general guidelines: arrange activities into phases, involve the users, and develop standards.

1. The system development cycle should group activities into phases. Many system development cycles contain the five major phases shown in Figure 11-1. Others have more or fewer phases. Regardless, all system development cycles have similar activities and tasks.

2. Users must be involved throughout the entire system development cycle. **Users** include anyone for whom the system is being built. Customers, employees, data entry clerks, accountants, sales managers, and owners all are examples of users. Users are more apt to accept a new system if they contribute to its design.

3. The system development cycle should have standards clearly defined. **Standards** are sets of rules and procedures a company expects employees to accept and follow. Having standards helps people working on the same project produce consistent results.

Who Participates in the System Development Cycle?

System development should involve representatives from each department in which the proposed system will be used. This includes both nontechnical users and IT professionals. During the course of the system development cycle, the systems analyst meets and works with a variety of people (Figure 11-2). A **systems analyst** is responsible for designing and developing an information system. The systems analyst is the users' primary contact person.

FIGURE 11-2
A systems analyst meets with a variety of people during a system development project.

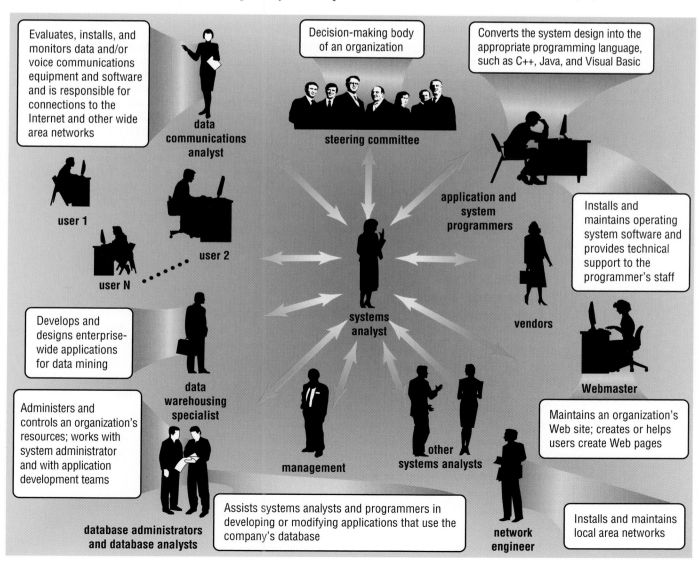

Evaluates, installs, and monitors data and/or voice communications equipment and software and is responsible for connections to the Internet and other wide area networks

data communications analyst

Decision-making body of an organization

steering committee

Converts the system design into the appropriate programming language, such as C++, Java, and Visual Basic

application and system programmers

Installs and maintains operating system software and provides technical support to the programmer's staff

user 1

user 2

user N

Develops and designs enterprise-wide applications for data mining

data warehousing specialist

Administers and controls an organization's resources; works with system administrator and with application development teams

database administrators and database analysts

management

Assists systems analysts and programmers in developing or modifying applications that use the company's database

other systems analysts

systems analyst

vendors

Webmaster

Maintains an organization's Web site; creates or helps users create Web pages

network engineer

Installs and maintains local area networks

Small companies may have one systems analyst or even one person who assumes the roles of both systems analyst and programmer. Larger companies often have multiple systems analysts. Some companies refer to a systems analyst as a **system developer**. Read Looking Ahead 11-1 for a look at the future demand for systems analysts.

Systems analysts are the liaison between the users and the IT professionals. They convert user requests into technical specifications. They must be familiar with business operations, be able to solve problems, have the ability to introduce and support change, and possess excellent communications and interpersonal skills. Systems analysts prepare many reports, drawings, and diagrams. They discuss various aspects of the development project with users, management, other analysts, database analysts, database administrators, network administrators, the Webmaster, programmers, vendors, and the steering committee. The **steering committee** is a decision-making body in a company.

For each system development project, a company usually forms a **project team** to work on the project from beginning to end. The project team consists of users, the systems analyst, and other IT professionals. One member of the team is the **project leader**, who manages and controls the budget and schedule of the project. The systems analyst may or may not be selected as the project leader of the project.

LOOKING AHEAD 11-1

Computer Systems Design and the Future

The population in the United States is expected to grow by 24 million by 2012, according to the U.S. Department of Labor. This increase will trigger a demand for goods and services in a variety of fields.

The computer systems design area and related industries are some of the fields predicted to experience continued growth. The Department of Labor expects a 54.6 percent increase in this sector, which will add more than one-third of all new jobs in the professional, scientific, and technical services areas.

Systems analysts will be needed to design and develop computer projects that are fueled by businesses' increasing reliance on information technology and the need to maintain system and network security. For more information, visit scsite.com/dcf2e/ch11/looking and then click Systems Design Future.

Project Management

Project management is the process of planning, scheduling, and then controlling the activities during the system development cycle. The goal of project management is to deliver an acceptable system to the user in an agreed-upon time frame, while maintaining costs.

To plan and schedule a project effectively, the project leader identifies the following elements for the project:

- Goal, objectives, and expectations of the project, collectively called the scope
- Required activities
- Time estimates for each activity
- Cost estimates for each activity
- Order of activities
- Activities that can take place at the same time

When these items are identified, the project leader usually records them in a project plan. A popular tool used to plan and schedule the time relationships among project activities is a Gantt chart (Figure 11-3). A Gantt chart, developed by Henry L. Gantt, is a bar chart that uses horizontal bars to show project phases or activities. The left side, or vertical axis, displays the list of required activities. A horizontal axis across the top or bottom of the chart represents time.

After a project begins, the project leader monitors and controls the project. Some activities take less time than originally planned. Others take longer. Project leaders should have good change management skills so they can recognize when a change in the project has occurred and take actions to react to the change. It is crucial that everyone is aware of and agrees on any changes made to the project plan.

WEB LINK 11-1

Project Management

For more information, visit scsite.com/dcf2e/ch11/weblink and then click Project Management.

ID	Task Name	Duration	Jan	Feb	Mar	Apr	May	Jun	Jul	Aug
1	**Planning**	2w	1/20	2/1						
2	**Analysis**	12w		2/8			5/10			
3	**Design**	12w			3/20			6/15		
4	**Implementation**	3w						6/16		8/9

FIGURE 11-3 A Gantt chart is an effective way to show the time relationships of a project's activities.

Feasibility Assessment

Feasibility is a measure of how suitable the development of a system will be to the company. A project that is feasible at one point of the system development cycle might become infeasible at a later point. Thus, systems analysts frequently reevaluate feasibility during the system development cycle.

Four tests to evaluate feasibility are:

- Operational feasibility: Measures how well the proposed information system will work. Will the users like the new system? Will they use it? Will it meet their requirements?
- Schedule feasibility: Measures whether the established deadlines for the project are reasonable. If a deadline is not reasonable, the project leader might make a new schedule. If a deadline cannot be extended, then the scope of the project might be reduced to meet the mandatory deadline.
- Technical feasibility: Measures whether the company has or can obtain the hardware, software, and people needed to deliver and then support the proposed information system.
- Economic feasibility, also called cost/benefit feasibility: Measures whether the lifetime benefits of the proposed information system will be greater than its lifetime costs.

Documentation

During the entire system development cycle, project members produce much documentation. **Documentation** is the collection and summarization of data and information. It includes reports, diagrams, programs, or any other information generated during the system development cycle.

It is important that all documentation be well written, thorough, and understandable. Maintaining up-to-date documentation should be an ongoing part of system development.

Data and Information Gathering Techniques

Systems analysts and other IT professionals use several techniques to gather data and information. They review documentation, observe, send questionnaires, interview, conduct joint-application design sessions, and do research.

* Review Documentation — By reviewing documentation such as a company's organization chart, memos, and meeting minutes, systems analysts learn about the history of a project. Documentation also provides information about the company such as its operations, weaknesses, and strengths.
* Observe — Observing people helps systems analysts understand exactly how they perform a task. Likewise, observing a machine allows you to see how it works. Read At Issue 11-1 for a related discussion.
* Questionnaire — To obtain data and information from a large number of people, systems analysts send questionnaires.
* Interview — The interview is the most important data and information gathering technique for the systems analyst. It allows the systems analyst to clarify responses and probe for face-to-face feedback.
* JAD Session — An alternative to the one-on-one interview is a joint-application design session. A **joint-application design (JAD) session** is a lengthy, structured, group meeting in which users and IT professionals work together to design or develop an application (Figure 11-4).
* Research — Newspapers, computer magazines, reference books, trade shows, and the Web are excellent sources of information. These sources can provide the systems analyst with information such as the latest hardware and software products and explanations of new processes and procedures.

FIGURE 11-4 During a JAD session, the systems analyst is the moderator, or leader, of the discussion. Another member, called the scribe, records facts and action items assigned during the session.

AT ISSUE 11-1

Do You Work Harder When Someone Is Watching?

During the data and information gathering stage of the system development cycle, employees are involved actively in the process. They complete questionnaires, participate in interviews, and are observed while performing their jobs. Many researchers suggest that during observation, employees may not exhibit everyday behavior and may perform above and beyond their normal workday activities. They base this premise on the Hawthorne Effect, which is the result of a study performed in the 1920s in the Western Electric Company plant in Hawthorne, Illinois. The study discovered that productivity improved during observation, whether the conditions were made better or worse. Researchers concluded that productivity seemed to improve whenever the workers knew they were being observed. What is your opinion of the Hawthorne Effect? Do you agree with the research? If someone is observing you at work or if you are receiving increased attention, does this cause you to alter your behavior? Why or why not? If productivity increases during observation, is observation a good data gathering technique in a system study? What precautions should be taken by the systems analyst?

What Initiates the System Development Cycle?

A user may request a new or modified information system for a variety of reasons. The most obvious reason is to correct a problem. Another reason is to improve the information system. Organizations may want to improve hardware, software, or other technology to enhance an information system.

Sometimes situations outside the control of a company require a modification to an information system. Corporate management or some other governing body may mandate a change. Competition also can lead to change. In recent years, another source of change has resulted from one company merging with or acquiring another company.

A user may request a new or modified information system verbally in a telephone conversation or written as an e-mail message (Figure 11-5a). Read At Issue 11-2 for a discussion related to e-mail writing. In larger companies, users write a formal request for a new or modified information system, which is called a request for system services or **project request** (Figure 11-5b). This project request triggers the first phase of the system development cycle: planning.

FIGURE 11-5a (informal project request)

FIGURE 11-5b (formal project request)

Web Stop Café

REQUEST FOR SYSTEM SERVICES

Form IT-102A

SUBMITTED BY: Chad Goldstein

DEPARTMENT: Marketing DATE: 12-18-2006

TYPE OF REQUEST:
New System
X Existing System Enhancement
Existing System Modification

BRIEF STATEMENT OF PROBLEM:
The staff in the marketing department is spending too much time copying and mailing materials to potential vendors.

BRIEF STATEMENT OF EXPECTED SOLUTION:
Modify our current Web site so it contains a Vendor Information Web link that displays a Vendor Information Web page. From this page, vendors could download all necessary vendor information.

ACTION (To be completed by steering committee member):
Request Approved Analyst Assigned: ______
Request Delayed Start Date: ______
Request Rejected Until: ______
Reason: ______
Signature: ______ Date: ______

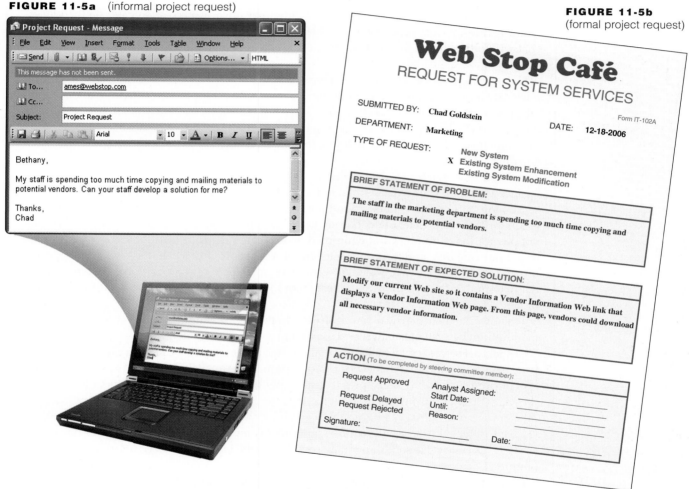

FIGURE 11-5 Sometimes users informally communicate a project request verbally or as an e-mail message. In larger companies, requests often are documented on a form such as this Request for System Services.

AT ISSUE 11-2

Is Your E-Mail Writing Up to Par?

E-mail may be today's most popular and influential method of communications. Millions of people around the world send and receive e-mail messages. E-mail links the geographically distanced, connects the economically separated, enables the physically challenged, and encourages the publicly timid. IT professionals are prolific e-mail writers because their job depends on a great deal of communication with users, management, vendors, and other departments. Because of e-mail, people are writing more than ever before — but is it good writing? The carefully crafted letters of an era gone by, handwritten in beautiful penmanship, have been replaced by e-mail messages stylistically equivalent to notes on the refrigerator. E-mail's immediacy often results in messages that are ill conceived, casually spelled, poorly worded, grammatically flawed, and tritely expressed (some trite phrases such as, in my humble opinion, are used so routinely they are replaced by abbreviations — IMHO). In general, has e-mail's impact on communications been positive or negative? Why? Should the quality of e-mail communications be a reason for concern? Why? Could someone's professional reputation be enhanced or hindered by the quality and effectiveness of his or her e-mail messages?

Web Stop Café — A Case Study

This chapter includes a case study to help you understand real-world system development applications. The case study appears shaded in blue immediately after the discussion of each phase in the system development cycle. The case is based on Web Stop Café, a fictitious cybercafé. The following paragraphs present a background about Web Stop Café.

Web Stop Café is a worldwide chain of cybercafés. With locations in 45 cities around the world, Web Stop Café is one of the more technologically advanced cybercafés on the planet. At these cafés, you can connect to the Web while drinking your favorite specialty beverage; chat with others online or send e-mail messages; and play online games or read an online book.

Through high-speed T1 lines, customers have fast Internet access. Monitors are 20 inches. Each café has a minimum of 30 computers, along with a color printer, a laser printer, a digital camera, and a scanner. All computers have popular programs such as Microsoft Office and Adobe Photoshop. The café also is a hot spot, which means customers can use their own mobile computer or mobile device to connect wirelessly to the Internet. For each beverage purchased, customers receive 30 minutes of free computer use and/or Web access. For additional time, the fee is $5.00 per hour.

Since Web Stop Café started operations in 1997, business has been thriving. The cafés serve thousands of customers around the world. Allison Popovich, chief information officer (CIO) for Web Stop Café, offers one suggestion for the company's financial success. "We do not pay for the computers and equipment in our cafés. Instead, we allow computer vendors to use our café as a storefront for their products. This provides customers with the opportunity to try out the hardware and software before making a purchase. When customers are ready to purchase computers, we direct them to the vendor's online storefront for discount pricing."

To showcase their hardware and software in the cafés, computer vendors request information from Chad Goldstein, the marketing manager. The number of these requests is rising quickly. The cost of copying and mailing this material is becoming excessive. For this reason, Chad would like this vendor information made available on the Web. Vendors could download information sheets, press releases, photographs, and other information from the Web site. Placing this information on the Web would save Chad and his staff a great deal of time and money.

Chad realizes this task will require substantial company resources. He believes a systems study is necessary. He sends an e-mail message to the vice president of information systems (Figure 11-5a on the previous page). She agrees and tells him to fill out a Request for System Services form (Figure 11-5b on the previous page) and submit it to Juanita Mendez, chair of the steering committee at Web Stop Café.

Planning Phase

The **planning phase** for a project begins when the steering committee receives a project request. This committee usually consists of five to nine people. It typically includes a mix of vice presidents, managers, nonmanagement users, and IT personnel.

During the planning phase, four major activities are performed: (1) review and approve the project requests; (2) prioritize the project requests; (3) allocate resources such as money, people, and equipment to approved projects; and (4) form a project development team for each approved project.

The projects that receive the highest priority are those mandated by management or some other governing body. These requests are given immediate attention. The steering committee evaluates the remaining project requests based on their value to the company. The steering committee approves some projects and rejects others. Of the approved projects, it is likely that only a few will begin their system development cycle immediately. Others will have to wait for additional funds or resources to become available.

Planning at Web Stop Café

After receiving the project request (Figure 11-5b on page 411) from Chad, Juanita Mendez distributes it to all members of the steering committee. They will discuss the request at their next meeting. The steering committee members of Web Stop Café are Juanita Mendez, controller and chair of the steering committee; Milan Sciranka, vice president of operations; Suzy Zhao, Webmaster; Donnell Carter, training specialist; Karl Schmidt, senior systems analyst; and Bethany Ames, vice president of information systems. Juanita also invites Chad Goldstein to the next steering committee meeting. Because he originated the project request, Chad will have the knowledge to answer questions.

During the meeting, the committee decides the project request identifies an improvement to the system, instead of a problem. They feel the nature of the improvement (to make vendor information available on the Web) could lead to considerable savings for the company. It also will provide quicker service to potential vendors.

The steering committee approves the request. Juanita points out that the company has enough funds in its budget to begin the project immediately. Thus, Bethany assembles a system development project team. She assigns Karl Schmidt, senior systems analyst, as the project leader. Karl and his team immediately begin the next phase: analysis.

Analysis Phase

The **analysis phase** consists of two major activities: (1) conduct a preliminary investigation and (2) perform detailed analysis. The following sections discuss these activities.

THE PRELIMINARY INVESTIGATION   The main purpose of the **preliminary investigation**, sometimes called the feasibility study, is to determine the exact nature of the problem or improvement and decide whether it is worth pursuing. Should the company continue to assign resources to this project? To answer this question, the systems analyst conducts a general study of the project.

The first activity in the preliminary investigation is to interview the user who submitted the project request. Depending on the nature of the request, project team members may interview other users, too.

In addition to interviewing, members of the project team may use other data gathering techniques, such as reviewing existing documentation. Often, the preliminary investigation is completed in just a few days.

Upon completion of the preliminary investigation, the systems analyst writes the feasibility report. This report presents the team's findings to the steering committee. The feasibility report contains these major sections: introduction, existing system, benefits of a new system, feasibility of a new system, and the recommendation (Figure 11-6).

In some cases, the project team may recommend not to continue the project. If the steering committee agrees, the project ends at this point. If the project team recommends continuing and the steering committee approves this recommendation, then detailed analysis begins.

Web Stop Café
MEMORANDUM

To: Steering Committee
From: Karl Schmidt, Project Leader
Date: December 29, 2006
Subject: Feasibility Study of Vendor Web System

Following is the feasibility study in response to the request for a modification to our Web site. Your approval is necessary before the next phase of the project will begin.

Introduction

The purpose of this feasibility report is to determine whether it is beneficial for Web Stop Café to continue studying the Vendor Web System. The marketing manager has indicated his staff spends a considerable amount of time duplicating and distributing materials to potential vendors. This project would affect the marketing department and customer service. Also, any person that uses the Web site would notice a change.

Existing System

Background

One of the reasons for our financial success at Web Stop Café is we do not pay for the computers and equipment in our cafés. Instead, we allow computer vendors to use our cafés as a storefront for their products. This provides customers with the opportunity to try the hardware and software before making a purchase. When customers want to purchase computers, we direct them to the vendor's online storefront for discount pricing.

To showcase their hardware and software in the cafés, computer vendors request information from our marketing manager. The number of these requests is rising quickly. The cost of copying and mailing this material is becoming excessive.

Problems

The following problems have been identified with the current information system at Web Stop Café:

- Employees spend too much time copying and duplicating vendor materials
- Potential vendors do not receive material as quickly as in the past, which possibly could cause poor relations
- Resources are wasted including employee time, equipment usage, and supplies

FEASIBILITY STUDY
Page 2

Benefits of a New System

Following is a list of benefits that could be realized if the Web site at Web Stop Café were modified:

- Potential vendors would be more satisfied, leading to possible long-term relations
- Cost of supplies would be reduced by 30 percent
- Through a more efficient use of employees' time, the company could achieve a 20 percent reduction in temporary clerks in the marketing department
- Laser printers and copy machines would last 50 percent longer, due to a much lower usage rate

Feasibility of a New System

Operational

A new system will decrease the amount of equipment use and paperwork. Vendor information will be available in an easily accessible form to any vendor. Employees will have time to complete meaningful job duties, alleviating the need to hire some temporary clerks.

Technical

Web Stop Café already has a functional Web site. To handle the increased volume of data, however, it will need to purchase a database server.

Economic

A detailed summary of the costs and benefits, including all assumptions, is available on our FTP server. The potential costs of the proposed solution could range from $15,000 to $20,000. The estimated savings in supplies and postage alone will exceed $20,000.

If you have any questions about the detailed cost/benefit summary or require further information, please contact me.

Recommendation

Based on the findings presented in this report, we recommend a continued study of the Vendor Web System.

FIGURE 11-6 A feasibility report presents the results of the preliminary investigation. The report must be prepared professionally and be well organized to be effective.

Preliminary Investigation at Web Stop Café

Karl Schmidt, senior systems analyst and project leader, meets with Chad Goldstein to discuss the project request. During the interview, Karl looks at the material that Chad's staff sends to a potential vendor. He asks Chad how many vendor requests he receives in a month. Then Karl interviews the controller, Juanita Mendez, to obtain some general cost and benefit figures for the feasibility report. He also calls a vendor. He wants to know if the material Chad's department sends is helpful.

Next, Karl prepares the feasibility report (Figure 11-6). After the project team members review it, Karl submits it to the steering committee. The report recommends proceeding to the detailed analysis phase for this project. The steering committee agrees. Karl and his team begin detailed analysis.

DETAILED ANALYSIS   Detailed analysis involves three major activities: (1) study how the current system works; (2) determine the users' wants, needs, and requirements; and (3) recommend a solution. Detailed analysis sometimes is called logical design because the systems analysts develop the proposed solution without regard to any specific hardware or software. That is, they make no attempt to identify the procedures that should be automated and those that should be manual.

During these activities, systems analysts use all of the data and information-gathering techniques. They review documentation, observe employees and machines, send questionnaires, interview employees, conduct JAD sessions, and do research.

While studying the current system and identifying user requirements, the systems analyst collects a great deal of data and information. A major task for the systems analyst is to document these findings in a way that can be understood by everyone. Systems analysts use diagrams to describe the processes that transform inputs into outputs and diagrams that graphically show the flow of data in the system. Both users and IT professionals refer to this documentation.

THE SYSTEM PROPOSAL   After the systems analyst has studied the current system and determined all user requirements, the next step is to communicate possible solutions for the project in a system proposal. The purpose of the **system proposal** is to assess the feasibility of each alternative solution and then recommend the most feasible solution for the project. The systems analyst presents the system proposal to the steering committee. If the steering committee approves a solution, the project enters the design phase.

When the steering committee discusses the system proposal and decides which alternative to pursue, it often is deciding whether to buy packaged software from an outside source, build its own custom software, or outsource some or all of its IT needs to an outside firm.

- **Packaged software** is mass-produced, copyrighted, prewritten software available for purchase. Packaged software is available for different types of computers. Chapter 3 presented many types of application software available for personal computers. These include word processing, spreadsheet, database, note taking, desktop publishing, paint/image editing, Web page authoring, personal finance, legal, tax preparation, educational/reference, e-mail, and Web browser software.

  Vendors offer two types of packaged software: horizontal and vertical. Horizontal market software meets the needs of many different types of companies. The programs discussed in Chapter 3 were horizontal. If a company has a unique way of accomplishing activities, then it also may require vertical market software. Vertical market software specifically is designed for a particular business or industry. Examples of companies that use vertical market software include banks, schools, hospitals, real estate offices, libraries, and insurance companies. Each of these industries has unique information processing requirements.

- Instead of buying packaged software, some companies write their own applications using programming languages such as Java, C++, C#, and Visual Basic. Application software developed by the user or at the user's request is called **custom software**.

  The main advantage of custom software is that it matches the company's requirements exactly. The disadvantages usually are that it is more expensive and takes longer to design and implement than packaged software.

- Companies can develop custom software in-house using their own IT personnel or **outsource** it, which means having an outside source develop it for them. Some companies outsource just the software development aspect of their IT operation. Others outsource more or all of their IT operation. Depending on a company's needs, outside firms can handle as much or as little of the IT requirements as desired. A trend that has caused much controversy relates to companies that outsource to firms located outside their homeland.

WEB LINK 11-2

Vertical Market Software

For more information, visit scsite.com/dcf2e/ ch11/weblink and then click Vertical Market Software.

Detailed Analysis at Web Stop Café

Karl and his team begin performing the activities in the detailed analysis phase of the Vendor Web System. As part of the study and requirements activities, they use several of the data and information gathering techniques available to them. They interview employees throughout the company and meet with some vendors. They observe the marketing staff copy and mail vendor information. They prepare documents that become part of the project notebook. Members of the project team refer to these documents during the remainder of the system development cycle.

After two months of studying the existing system and obtaining user requirements, Karl discusses his findings with his supervisor, Bethany Ames. Karl recommends that a link to Vendor Information be added to their current Web site. When a vendor clicks this link, a Vendor Information page will be displayed. This Web page should contain all information that the marketing department usually sends to a vendor.

Based on Karl's findings, Bethany writes a system proposal for the steering committee to review. Suzy Zhao, Webmaster at Web Stop Café, developed the current Web site. Thus, Bethany recommends that Suzy's staff modify the Web site in-house. Bethany also recommends that Web Stop Café invest in a larger database server to handle the additional vendor information.

The steering committee agrees with Bethany's proposal. Karl and his team begin the design phase of the project.

Design Phase

The **design phase** consists of two major activities: (1) if necessary, acquire hardware and software and (2) develop all of the details of the new or modified information system. The systems analyst often performs these two activities at the same time instead of sequentially.

ACQUIRING NECESSARY HARDWARE AND SOFTWARE   When the steering committee approves a solution, the systems analyst begins the activity of obtaining additional hardware or software. The systems analyst may skip this activity if the approved solution does not require new hardware or software. If this activity is required, it consists of four major tasks: (1) identify technical specifications, (2) solicit vendor proposals, (3) test and evaluate vendor proposals, and (4) make a decision.

Identifying Technical Specifications   The first step in acquiring necessary hardware and software is to identify all the hardware and software requirements of the new or modified system. To do this, the systems analysts use a variety of research techniques. They talk with other systems analysts, visit vendors' stores, and search the Web. Many trade journals, newspapers, and magazines provide some or all of their printed content as e-zines. An **e-zine** (pronounced ee-zeen), or electronic magazine, is a publication available on the Web.

After the systems analyst defines the technical requirements, the next step is to summarize these requirements for potential vendors. The systems analyst can use three basic types of documents for this purpose: an RFQ, an RFP, or an RFI. A request for quotation (RFQ) identifies the required product(s). With an RFQ, the vendor quotes a price for the listed product(s). With a request for proposal (RFP), the vendor selects the product(s) that meets specified requirements and then quotes the price(s). A request for information (RFI) is a less formal method that uses a standard form to request information about a product or service.

Soliciting Vendor Proposals   Systems analysts send the RFQ, RFP, or RFI to potential hardware and software vendors. Another source for hardware and software products is a value-added reseller. A **value-added reseller** (**VAR**) is a company that purchases products from manufacturers and then resells these products to the public — offering additional services with the product (Figure 11-7).

Instead of using vendors, some companies hire an IT consultant or a group of IT consultants. An **IT consultant** is a professional who is hired based on computer expertise, including service and advice. IT consultants often specialize in configuring hardware and software for businesses of all sizes.

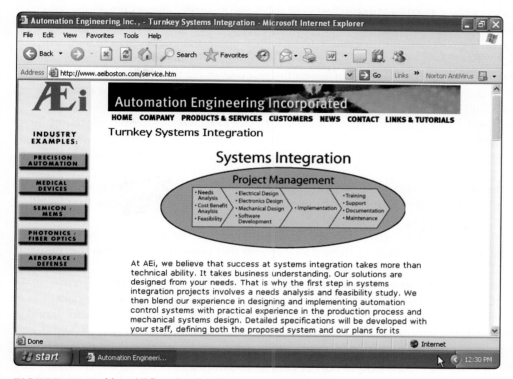

FIGURE 11-7   Many VARs advertise their services on the Web.

Testing and Evaluating Vendor Proposals   After sending RFQs and RFPs to potential vendors, the systems analyst will receive completed quotations and proposals. Evaluating the proposals and then selecting the best one often is a difficult task. It is important to be as objective as possible while evaluating each proposal.

Systems analysts use many techniques to test the various software products from vendors. They obtain a list of user references from the software vendors. They also talk to current users of the software to solicit their opinions. Some vendors will give a demonstration of the product(s) specified. Other vendors provide demonstration copies or trial versions, allowing the companies to test the software themselves.

Sometimes it is important to know whether the software can process a certain volume of transactions efficiently. In this case, the systems analyst conducts a benchmark test. A **benchmark test** measures the performance of hardware or software. For example, a benchmark test could measure the time it takes a payroll program to print 50 paychecks. Comparing the time it takes various accounting programs to print the same 50 paychecks is one way of measuring each program's performance.

Making a Decision   Having rated the proposals, the systems analyst presents a recommendation to the steering committee. The recommendation could be to award a contract to a vendor or to not make any purchases at this time.

Hardware Acquisition at Web Stop Café

Karl and his team compile a requirements list for the database server. They prepare an RFP and submit it to twelve vendors: eight through the Web and four local computer stores. Ten vendors reply within the three-week deadline.

Of the ten replies, the development team selects two to evaluate. They eliminate the other eight because these vendors did not offer adequate warranties for the database server. The project team members ask for benchmark test results for each server. In addition, they contact two current users of this database server for their opinions about its performance. After evaluating these two servers, the team selects the best one.

Karl summarizes his team's findings in a report to the steering committee. The committee gives Karl authorization to award a contract to the proposed vendor. As a courtesy and to maintain good working relationships, Karl sends a letter to all twelve vendors informing them of the commitee's decision.

DETAILED DESIGN   The next step is to develop detailed design specifications for the components in the proposed solution. The activities to be performed include developing designs for the databases, inputs, outputs, and programs.

- During database design, the systems analyst works closely with the database analysts and database administrators to identify those data elements that currently exist within the company and those that are new.

  The systems analyst also addresses user access privileges. This means that the systems analyst defines which data elements each user can access, when they can access the data elements, what actions they can perform on the data elements, and under what circumstances they can access the elements.

- During detailed design of inputs and outputs, the systems analyst carefully designs every menu, screen, and report specified in the requirements. The outputs often are designed first because they help define the requirements for the inputs. Thus, it is very important that outputs are identified correctly and that users agree to them.

  The systems analyst typically develops two types of designs for each input and output: a mockup and a layout chart. A mockup is a sample of the input or output that contains actual data (Figure 11-8). The systems analyst shows mockups to users for their approval. Because users will work with the inputs and outputs of the system, it is crucial to involve users during input and output design.

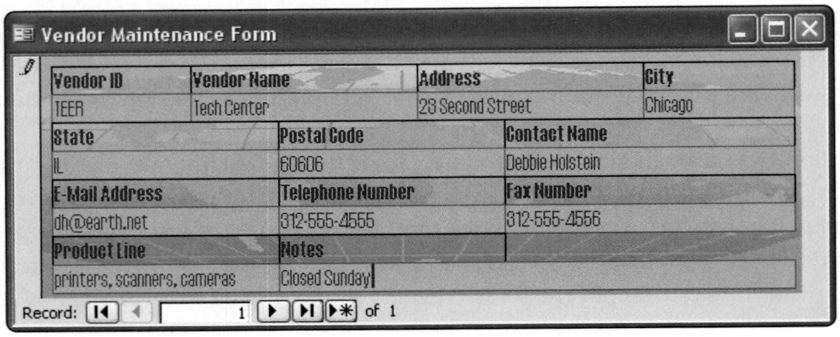

FIGURE 11-8   Users must give their approval on all inputs and outputs. This input screen is a mockup (containing actual sample data) for users to review.

After users approve the mockup, the systems analyst develops a layout chart for the programmer. A layout chart is more technical and contains programming-like notations for the data items (Figure 11-9).

Other issues that must be addressed during input and output design include the types of media to use (paper, video, audio); formats (graphical or narrative); and data entry validation techniques, which include making sure the inputted data is correct (for example, a state code has to be one of the fifty valid two-letter state abbreviations).

- During program design, the systems analyst prepares the program specification package, which identifies required programs and the relationship among each program, as well as the input, output, and database specifications.

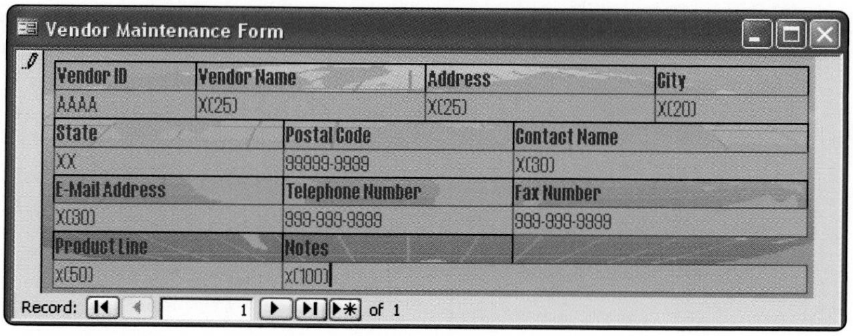

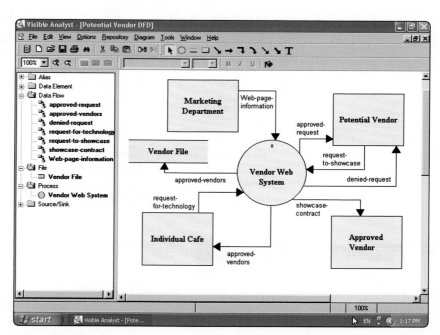

FIGURE 11-9 Once users approve a mockup, the layout chart (with technical specifications) is given to the programmer. This is the layout chart for the mockup in Figure 11-8.

PROTOTYPING   Many systems analysts today use prototypes during detailed design. A **prototype** is a working model of the proposed system. The systems analyst actually builds a functional form of the solution during design. The main advantage of a prototype is users can work with the system before it is completed — to make sure it meets their needs. As soon as users approve a prototype, system analysts can have a solution implemented more quickly than without a prototype.

CASE TOOLS   Many systems analysts use computer software to assist in system development. **Computer-aided software engineering** (CASE) software tools are designed to support one or more activities of the system development cycle (Figure 11-10).

QUALITY REVIEW TECHNIQUES   Many people should review the detailed design specifications before they are given to the programming team. Reviewers should include users, systems analysts, managers, IT staff, and members of the system development team. If the steering committee decides the project still is feasible, which usually is the case, the project enters the implementation phase.

FIGURE 11-10   Computer-aided software engineering (CASE) programs assist analysts in the development of an information system. Visible Analyst by Visible Systems Corporation enables analysts to create diagrams, as well as build the project dictionary.

Detailed Design at Web Stop Café

As approved by the steering committee, Karl and his team begin designing the Vendor Web System. After studying current vendor information and interviewing more users and vendors, the team designs changes to the company's database, Web site, and the associated programs. They prepare several documents including a mockup (Figure 11-8 on page 418) and a layout chart (Figure 11-9 on the previous page).

After completing the detailed design, Karl meets with several users and IT personnel to walk through the design. They locate two errors. He corrects the errors and then presents the design to the steering committee. The committee agrees with the design solution and consents to implement it.

Implementation Phase

The purpose of the **implementation phase** is to construct, or build, the new or modified system and then deliver it to the users. Members of the system development team perform four major activities in this phase: (1) develop programs, (2) install and test the new system, (3) train users, and (4) convert to the new system.

DEVELOP PROGRAMS   If the company purchases packaged software and no modifications to the software are required, the development team may skip this activity. For custom software or packaged software that requires modification, however, programs are developed or modified either by an outside firm or in-house. Programmers write or modify programs from the program specification package created during the analysis phase. Just as the system development cycle follows an organized set of activities, so does program development. These program development activities are known as the program development cycle.

The last sections of this chapter identify various programming languages and explain the program development cycle. The important concept to understand now is that program development is part of the implementation phase.

INSTALL AND TEST THE NEW SYSTEM   If the company acquires new hardware or software, someone must install and test it. The systems analysts should test individual programs. They also should be sure that all the programs work together in the system.

Systems analysts and users develop test data so they can perform various tests. A unit test verifies that each individual program or object works by itself. A systems test verifies that all programs in an application work together properly. An integration test verifies that an application works with other applications. An acceptance test is performed by end-users and checks the new system to ensure that it works with actual data. Read Looking Ahead 11-2 for a look at the next generation of software tests.

FAQ 11-1

How much time is spent fixing errors in programs?

One study estimates that more than 34 percent of a programmer's time is devoted to fixing program bugs. For more information, visit scsite.com/dcf2e/ch11/faq and then click Software Errors.

LOOKING AHEAD 11-2

Putting Software to the Test

Installing and testing new software are critical components of the system development cycle's implementation phase. System developers need to verify that new programs are running smoothly and that they synchronize with other programs in the system.

Companies are developing new methods of testing software in an effort to save time and money. Microsoft, for example, uses its Prefix program, which scans software for common logic errors. Sun uses its Jackpot analysis engine, created by a team of systems developers, to give programmers real-time feedback. It also uses a debugger to detect programs that have been written incorrectly. IBM's Slam and Eclipse projects analyze violations of general programming rules and encourage programmers to write code democratically. For more information, visit scsite.com/dcf2e/ch11/looking and then click Software Testing.

TRAIN USERS   Training involves showing users exactly how they will use the new hardware and software in the system. Some training takes place as one-on-one sessions or classroom-style lectures (Figure 11-11). Other companies use Web-based training, which is a self-directed, self-paced online instruction method. Whichever technique is used, it should include hands-on sessions with realistic sample data. Users should practice on the actual system during training. Users also should receive user manuals for reference. It is the systems analyst's responsibility to create user manuals, both printed and electronic.

CONVERT TO THE NEW SYSTEM   The final implementation activity is to change from the old system to the new system. This change can take place using one or more of the following conversion strategies: direct, parallel, phased, or pilot.

With **direct conversion**, the user stops using the old system and begins using the new system on a certain date. The advantage of this strategy is that it requires no transition costs and is a quick implementation technique. The disadvantage is that it is extremely risky and can disrupt operations seriously if the new system does not work correctly the first time.

Parallel conversion consists of running the old system alongside the new system for a specified time. Results from both systems are compared. The advantage of this strategy is that you can fix any problems in the new system before you terminate the old system. The disadvantage is that it is costly to operate two systems at the same time.

FIGURE 11-11   Organizations must ensure that users are trained properly on the new system. One training method uses hands-on classes to learn the new system.

Larger systems with multiple sites may use a phased conversion. In a **phased conversion**, each location converts at a separate time. For example, an accounting system might convert its accounts receivable, accounts payable, general ledger, and payroll sites in separate phases. Each site can use a direct or parallel conversion.

With a **pilot conversion**, only one location in the company uses the new system — so it can be tested. After the pilot site approves the new system, other sites convert using one of the other conversion strategies.

Implementation at Web Stop Café

Upon receiving the program specification package, Karl forms an implementation team of Suzy Zhao, Webmaster; Adam Rosen, programmer; and Stephan Davis, data modeler. The team works together to implement the Vendor Web System.

Karl works closely with the team to answer questions about the design and to check the progress of their work. When the team completes its work, they ask Karl to test it. He does and it works great!

Karl arranges a training class for the employees of the marketing and customer service departments. During the training session, he shows them how to use the new Vendor Information page on the company's Web site. Karl gives each attendee a printed user guide and indicates that he will e-mail them the electronic file. He wants to prepare everyone thoroughly for the new Web pages once they are posted. Karl also sends a letter to all existing vendors informing them when this new service will be available and how to use it.

Support Phase

The purpose of the **support phase** is to provide ongoing assistance for an information system and its users after the system is implemented. The support phase consists of four major activities: (1) conduct a post-implementation system review, (2) identify errors, (3) identify enhancements, and (4) monitor system performance.

One of the first activities the company performs in the support phase is to meet with users. The purpose of this meeting, called the post-implementation system review, is to discover whether the information system is performing according to the users' expectations. If it is not, the systems analyst must determine what must be done to satisfy the users.

In some cases, users would like the system to do more. Maybe they have additional requirements. **System enhancement** involves modifying or expanding an existing information system.

During the support phase, the systems analyst monitors performance of the new or modified information system. The purpose of performance monitoring is to determine whether the system is inefficient at any point. If so, is the inefficiency causing a problem? Is the time it takes to download vendor information reasonable? If not, the systems analyst must investigate solutions to make the download time more acceptable — back to the planning phase.

Support at Web Stop Café

During the post-implementation system review, Karl learns that the new Web page is receiving many hits. Vendors are using it and they like it. Customer service regularly receives e-mail messages from vendors that appreciate the new service. Chad says his staff is working efficiently on their primary tasks without the interruption and additional workload of making copies and sending out vendor data, now that the system has been automated.

Six months after the Vendor Web System has been in operation, Chad would like to add more information to the Vendor Information page. He sends an e-mail message to Karl requesting the change. Karl asks him to fill out a Request for System Services and puts him on the agenda of the next steering committee meeting. Back to the planning phase again!

Information System Security

Most organizations must deal with complex computer security issues. All elements of an information system — hardware, software, data, people, and procedures — must be secure from threats both inside and outside the enterprise.

Companies today often have a **chief security officer** (CSO) who is responsible for physical security of a company's property and people and also is in charge of securing computing resources. It is critical that the CSO is included in all system development projects to ensure that all projects adequately address information security. The CSO uses many of the techniques discussed in Chapter 10 to maintain confidentiality or limited access to information, ensure integrity and reliability of systems, ensure uninterrupted availability of systems, ensure compliance with laws, and cooperate with law enforcement agencies.

An important responsibility of the CSO is to develop a computer security plan. A **computer security plan** summarizes in writing all of the safeguards that are in place to protect a company's information assets. The CSO should evaluate the computer security plan annually or more frequently for major changes in information assets, such as the addition of a new computer or the implementation of a new application. In developing the plan, the CSO should recognize that some degree of risk is unavoidable; further, the more secure a system is, the more difficult it is for everyone to use. The goal of a computer security plan is to match an appropriate level of safeguards against the identified risks. Fortunately, most organizations never will experience a major information system disaster.

Test your knowledge of pages 406 through 422 in Quiz Yourself 11-1.

QUIZ YOURSELF 11-1

Instructions: Find the true statement below. Then, rewrite the remaining false statements so they are true.

1. A computer security plan summarizes in writing all of the safeguards that are in place to protect a company's information assets.

2. Feasibility is the process of planning, scheduling, and then controlling the activities during the system development cycle.

3. The five phases in most system development cycles are programming, analysis, design, sampling, and recording.

4. The purpose of the design phase is to provide ongoing assistance for an information system and its users after the system is implemented.

5. Upon completion of the preliminary investigation, the systems analyst writes the system proposal.

6. Users should not be involved throughout the system development process.

Quiz Yourself Online: To further check your knowledge of the system development cycle, visit scsite.com/dcf2e/ch11/quiz and then click Objectives 1 – 2.

PROGRAMMING LANGUAGES

The previous sections discussed the phases in the system development cycle. One activity during the implementation phase is to develop programs. Although you may never write a computer program, information you request may require a programmer to write or modify a program. Thus, you should understand how programmers develop programs to meet information requirements. A **computer program** is a series of instructions that directs a computer to perform tasks. A computer **programmer**, sometimes called a **developer**, writes and modifies computer programs.

To write a program's instructions, programmers often use a programming language. A **programming language** is a set of words, symbols, and codes that enables a programmer to communicate instructions to a computer. Programmers use a variety of programming languages and tools to write, or code, a program (Figure 11-12).

Several hundred programming languages exist today. Each language has its own rules for writing the instructions. Languages often are designed for specific purposes, such as scientific applications, business solutions, or Web page development.

FIGURE 11-12 Programmers must decide which programming languages and tools to use when they write programs.

Two types of languages are low-level and high-level. A low-level language is a programming language that is machine dependent. A machine-dependent language runs on only one particular type of computer. Each instruction in a low-level language usually equates to a single machine instruction. With a high-level language, by contrast, each instruction typically equates to multiple machine instructions. High-level languages often are machine independent. A machine-independent language can run on many different types of computers and operating systems.

The following pages discuss low-level languages, as well as several types of high-level languages.

Low-Level Languages

Two types of low-level languages are machine languages and assembly languages. **Machine language**, known as the first generation of programming languages, is the only language the computer directly recognizes (Figure 11-13). Machine language instructions use a series of binary digits (1s and 0s) or a combination of numbers and letters that represents binary digits. The binary digits correspond to the on and off electrical states. As you might imagine, coding in machine language is tedious and time-consuming.

With an **assembly language**, the second generation of programming languages, a programmer writes instructions using symbolic instruction codes (Figure 11-14). With an assembly language, a programmer writes codes such as A for addition, C for compare, L for load, and M for multiply.

					00090
000090	50E0	30B2			010B4
000094	1B44				
000096	1B77				
000098	1B55				
00009A	F273	30D6	2C81	010D8	00C83
0000A0	4F50	30D6			010D8
0000A4	F275	30D6	2C7B	010D8	00C7D
0000AA	4F70	30D6			010D8
0000AE	5070	304A			0104C
0000B2	1C47				
0000B4	5050	304E			01050
0000B8	58E0	30B2			010B4
0000BC	07FE				
					000BE
0000BE	50E0	30B6			010B8
0000C2	95F1	2C85		00C87	
0000C6	4770	20D2		000D4	
0000CA	1B55				
0000CC	5A50	35A6			015A8
0000D0	47F0	2100		00102	
0000D4	95F2	2C85		00C87	
0000D8	4770	20E4		000E6	
0000DC	1B55				
0000DE	5A50	35AA			015AC
0000E2	47F0	2100		00102	
000102	1B77				
000104	5870	304E			01050
000108	1C47				
00010A	4E50	30D6			010D8
00010E	F075	30D6	003E	010D8	0003E
000114	4F50	30D6			010D8
000118	5050	3052			01054
00011C	58E0	30B6			010B8
000120	07FE				
					00122
000122	50E0	30BA			010BC
000126	1B55				
000128	5A50	304E			01050
00012C	5B50	3052			01054
000130	5050	305A			0105C
000134	58E0	30BA			010BC
000138	07FE				

FIGURE 11-13 A sample machine language program, coded using the hexadecimal number system. A hexadecimal number system can be used to represent binary numbers using letters of the alphabet and decimal numbers.

```
*              THIS MODULE CALCULATES THE REGULAR TIME PAY
CALCSTPY EQU   *
         ST    14,SAVERTPY
         SR    4,4
         SR    7,7
         SR    5,5
         PACK  DOUBLE,RTHRSIN
         CVB   4,DOUBLE
         PACK  DOUBLE,RATEIN
         CVB   7,DOUBLE
         ST    7,RATE
         MR    4,7
         ST    5,RTPAY
         L     14,SAVERTPY
         BR    14
*              THIS MODULE CALCULATES THE OVERTIME PAY
CALCOTPY EQU   *
         ST    14,SAVEOTPY
TEST1    CLI   CODEIN,C'O'
         BH    TEST2
         SR    5,5
         A     5,=F'0'
         ST    5,OTPAY
         B     AROUND
TEST2    SR    4,4
         SR    7,7
         SR    5,5
         PACK  DOUBLE,OTHRSIN
         CVB   4,DOUBLE
         PACK  DOUBLE,RATEIN
         CVB   7,RATE
         MR    4,7
         MR    4,=F'1.5'
         ST    5,OTPAY
AROUND   L     14,SAVEOTPY
         BR    14
*              THIS MODULE CALCULATES THE GROSS PAY
CALCGPAY EQU   *
         ST    14,SAVEGPAY
         SR    5,5
         A     5,RTPAY
         A     5,OTPAY
         ST    5,GRPAY
         L     14,SAVEGPAY
         BR    14
```

FIGURE 11-14 An excerpt from an assembly language payroll program. The code shows the computations for regular time pay, overtime pay, and gross pay and the decision to evaluate the overtime hours.

Assembly languages also use symbolic addresses. A symbolic address is a meaningful name that identifies a storage location. For example, a programmer can use the name RATE to refer to the storage location that contains a pay rate.

Despite these advantages, assembly languages can be difficult to learn. In addition, programmers must convert an assembly language program into machine language before the computer can execute, or run, the program. That is, the computer cannot execute the assembly source program. A **source program** is the program that contains the language instructions, or code, to be converted to machine language. To convert the assembly language source program into machine language, programmers use a program called an assembler.

Procedural Languages

The disadvantages of machine and assembly (low-level) languages led to the development of procedural languages in the late 1950s and 1960s. In a **procedural language**, the programmer writes instructions that tell the computer what to accomplish and how to do it.

With a procedural language, often called a **third-generation language (3GL)**, a programmer uses a series of English-like words to write instructions. For example, ADD stands for addition or PRINT means to print. Many 3GLs also use arithmetic operators such as * for multiplication and + for addition. These English-like words and arithmetic symbols simplify the program development process for the programmer.

As with an assembly language program, the 3GL code (instructions) is called the source program. Programmers must convert this source program into machine language before the computer can execute the program. This translation process often is very complex, because one 3GL source program instruction translates into many machine language instructions. For 3GLs, programmers typically use either a compiler or an interpreter to perform the translation.

A **compiler** is a separate program that converts the entire source program into machine language before executing it. The machine language version that results from compiling the 3GL is called the object code or object program. The compiler stores the object code on disk for execution later.

While it is compiling the source program into object code, the compiler checks the source program for errors. The compiler then produces a program listing that contains the source code and a list of any errors. This listing helps the programmer make necessary changes to the source code and correct errors in the program. Figure 11-15 shows the process of compiling a source program.

```
*    COMPUTE REGULAR TIME PAY
     MULTIPLY REGULAR-TIME-HOURS BY HOURLY-PAY-RATE
          GIVING REGULAR-TIME-PAY.

*    COMPUTE OVERTIME PAY
     IF OVERTIME-HOURS > 0
          COMPUTE OVERTIME-PAY = OVERTIME-HOURS * 1.5 * HOURLY-PAY-RATE
     ELSE
          MOVE 0 TO OVERTIME-PAY.

*    COMPUTE GROSS PAY
     ADD REGULAR-TIME-PAY TO OVERTIME-PAY
          GIVING GROSS-PAY.

*    PRINT GROSS PAY
     MOVE GROSS-PAY TO GROSS-PAY-OUT.
     WRITE REPORT-LINE-OUT FROM DETAIL-LINE
          AFTER ADVANCING 2 LINES.
```

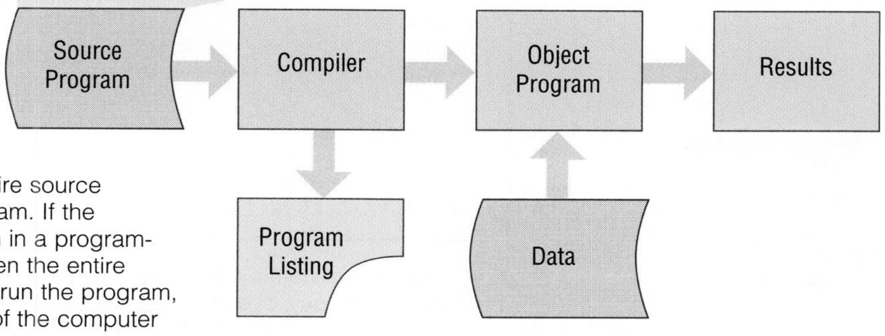

Source Program → Compiler → Object Program → Results

Compiler → Program Listing

Data → Object Program

FIGURE 11-15 A compiler converts the entire source program into a machine language object program. If the compiler encounters any errors, it records them in a program-listing file, which the programmer may print when the entire compilation is complete. When a user wants to run the program, the object program is loaded into the memory of the computer and the program instructions begin executing.

A compiler translates an entire program before executing it. An interpreter, by contrast, translates and executes one statement at a time. An **interpreter** reads a code statement, converts it to one or more machine language instructions, and then executes those machine language instructions. It does this all before moving to the next code statement in the program. Each time the source program runs, the interpreter translates and executes it, statement by statement. An interpreter does not produce an object program. Figure 11-16 shows the process of interpreting a program.

One advantage of an interpreter is that when it finds errors, it displays feedback immediately. The programmer can correct any errors before the interpreter translates the next line of code. The disadvantage is that interpreted programs do not run as fast as compiled programs.

Hundreds of procedural languages exist. Only a few, however, are used widely enough for the industry to recognize them as standards. These include COBOL and C. To illustrate the similarities and differences among these programming languages, the figures on the following pages show program code in these languages. The code solves a simple payroll problem — computing the gross pay for an employee.

The process used to compute gross pay can vary from one system to another. The examples on the following pages use a simple algorithm, or set of steps, to help you easily compare one programming language with another.

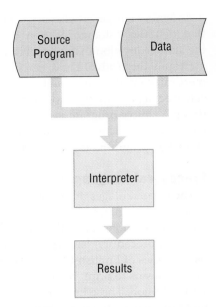

FIGURE 11-16 With an interpreter, one line of the source program at a time is converted into machine language and then immediately executed by the computer. If the interpreter encounters an error while converting a line of code, an error message immediately is displayed on the screen and the program stops.

COBOL COBOL (COmmon Business-Oriented Language) evolved out of a joint effort between the United States government, businesses, and major universities in the early 1960s. Naval officer Grace Hopper, a pioneer in computer programming, was a prime developer of COBOL.

COBOL is a programming language designed for business applications. Although COBOL programs often are lengthy, their English-like statements make the code easy to read, write, and maintain (Figure 11-17). COBOL especially is useful for processing transactions, such as payroll and billing, on mainframe computers.

```
*    COMPUTE REGULAR TIME PAY
     MULTIPLY REGULAR-TIME-HOURS BY HOURLY-PAY-RATE
         GIVING REGULAR-TIME-PAY.

*    COMPUTE OVERTIME PAY
     IF OVERTIME-HOURS > 0
         COMPUTE OVERTIME-PAY = OVERTIME-HOURS * 1.5 * HOURLY-PAY-RATE
     ELSE
         MOVE 0 TO OVERTIME-PAY.

*    COMPUTE GROSS PAY
     ADD REGULAR-TIME-PAY TO OVERTIME-PAY
         GIVING GROSS-PAY.

*    PRINT GROSS PAY
     MOVE GROSS-PAY TO GROSS-PAY-OUT.
     WRITE REPORT-LINE-OUT FROM DETAIL-LINE
         AFTER ADVANCING 2 LINES.
```

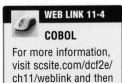

WEB LINK 11-4

COBOL

For more information, visit scsite.com/dcf2e/ch11/weblink and then click COBOL.

FIGURE 11-17 An excerpt from a COBOL payroll program. The code shows the computations for regular time pay, overtime pay, and gross pay; the decision to evaluate the overtime hours; and the output of the gross pay.

C The C programming language, developed in the early 1970s by Dennis Ritchie at Bell Laboratories, originally was designed for writing system software. Today, many software programs are written in C (Figure 11-18). C runs on almost any type of computer with any operating system, but it is used most often with the UNIX operating system.

```c
/* Compute Regular Time Pay                                    */
rt_pay = rt_hrs * pay_rate;

/* Compute Overtime Pay                                        */
if (ot_hrs > 0)
    ot_pay = ot_hrs * 1.5 * pay_rate;
else
    ot_pay = 0;

/* Compute Gross Pay                                           */
gross = rt_pay + ot_pay;

/* Print Gross Pay                                             */
printf("The gross pay is %d\n", gross);
```

FIGURE 11-18 An excerpt from a C payroll program. The code shows the computations for regular time pay, overtime pay, and gross pay; the decision to evaluate the overtime hours; and the output of the gross pay.

Object-Oriented Programming Languages

Programmers use an **object-oriented programming (OOP) language** to implement objects in a program. An object is an item that can contain both data and the procedures that read or manipulate that data. An object represents a real person, place, event, or transaction.

A major benefit of OOP is the ability to reuse and modify existing objects. For example, once a programmer creates an Employee object, it is available for use by any other existing or future program. Thus, programmers repeatedly reuse existing objects. Programs developed using the object-oriented approach have several advantages. The objects can be reused in many systems, are designed for repeated use, and become stable over time. In addition, programmers create applications faster because they design programs using existing objects. Programming languages, such as Java, C++, and C#, are complete object-oriented languages.

WEB LINK 11-5

Java

For more information, visit scsite.com/dcf2e/ch11/weblink and then click Java.

JAVA Java is an object-oriented programming language developed by Sun Microsystems. Figure 11-19 shows a portion of a Java program and the window that the program displays.

When programmers compile a Java program, the resulting object code is machine independent. Java then uses a just-in-time (JIT) compiler to convert the machine-independent code into machine-dependent code that is executed immediately. Sun's Java Development Kit (JDK) includes both the Java compiler and the JIT compiler.

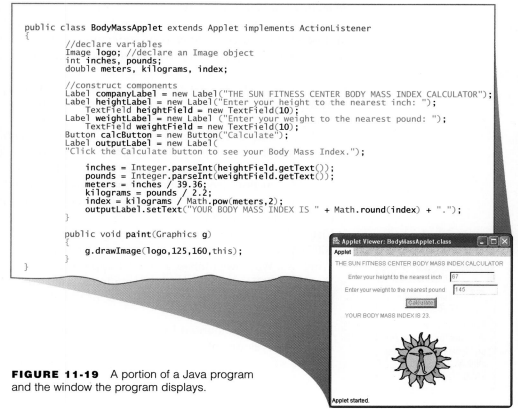

FIGURE 11-19 A portion of a Java program and the window the program displays.

C++   Developed in the 1980s by Bjarne Sroustrup at Bell Laboratories, **C++** (pronounced SEE-plus-plus) is an object-oriented programming language that is an extension of the C programming language. C++ includes all the elements of the C language (shown in Figure 11-18 on the previous page), plus it has additional features for working with objects. Programmers commonly use C++ to develop database and Web applications.

C#   Based on C++, **C#** (pronounced SEE-sharp) is an object-oriented programming language that was developed primarily by Anders Hejlsberg, Microsoft chief architect and distinguished engineer. C# has been accepted as a standard for Web applications and XML-based Web services. Many experts see C# as Java's main competition.

VISUAL PROGRAMMING LANGUAGES   A **visual programming language**, sometimes called a fifth-generation language, is a language that provides a visual or graphical interface for creating source code. The graphical interface, called a visual programming environment (VPE), allows programmers to drag and drop objects to build programs. A program that provides VPE often is characterized as a **program development tool**.

Visual programming languages often are used in a RAD environment. **RAD** (rapid application development) is a method of developing software, in which the programmer writes and implements a program in segments instead of waiting until the entire program is completed. An important concept in RAD is the use of prebuilt components. For example, programmers do not have to write code for buttons and text boxes on Windows forms because they already exist in the programming language or tools provided with the language.

The following sections discuss a variety of visual programming languages.

- **Visual Studio 2005** is the latest suite of program development tools from Microsoft that assists programmers in building programs for Windows, Windows Mobile, or any operating system that supports Microsoft's .NET architecture. The .NET (pronounced dot net) architecture is a set of technologies that allows almost any type of program to run on the Internet or an internal business network, as well as stand-alone computers.

    This latest version of Visual Studio includes enhanced support for building security and reliability into applications through its visual programming languages, RAD tools, and other resources that reduce development time. For example, Visual Studio 2005 includes **code snippets**, which are prewritten code and templates associated with common programming tasks. The following paragraphs discuss these programming languages in the Visual Studio 2005 suite: Visual Basic 2005, Visual C++ 2005, Visual C# 2005, and Visual J# 2005.

    - Visual Basic 2005 is based on the Visual Basic programming language, which was developed by Microsoft Corporation in the early 1990s. This language is easy to learn and use. Thus, Visual Basic 2005 is ideal for beginning programmers.

        The first step in building a Visual Basic 2005 program often is to design the graphical user interface using Visual Basic 2005 objects (Steps 1 and 2 in Figure 11-20). Visual Basic 2005 objects include items such as command buttons, text boxes, and labels. Next, the programmer writes instructions (code) to define any actions that should occur in response to specific events (Step 3 in Figure 11-20). Finally, the programmer generates and tests the final program (Step 4 in Figure 11-20).

    - Visual C++ 2005 is a visual programming language based on C++. Not only is Visual C++ 2005 a powerful object-oriented programming language, it enables programmers to write Windows, Windows Mobile, and .NET applications quickly and efficiently.

    - Visual C# 2005 combines the programming elements of C++ with an easier visual programming environment. The purpose of Visual C# 2005 is to take the complexity out of Visual C++ 2005.

    - Visual J# 2005 (pronounced JAY-sharp) is a visual programming language that allows Java program development in the .NET environment.

FIGURE 11-20 CREATING A VISUAL BASIC 2005 PROGRAM

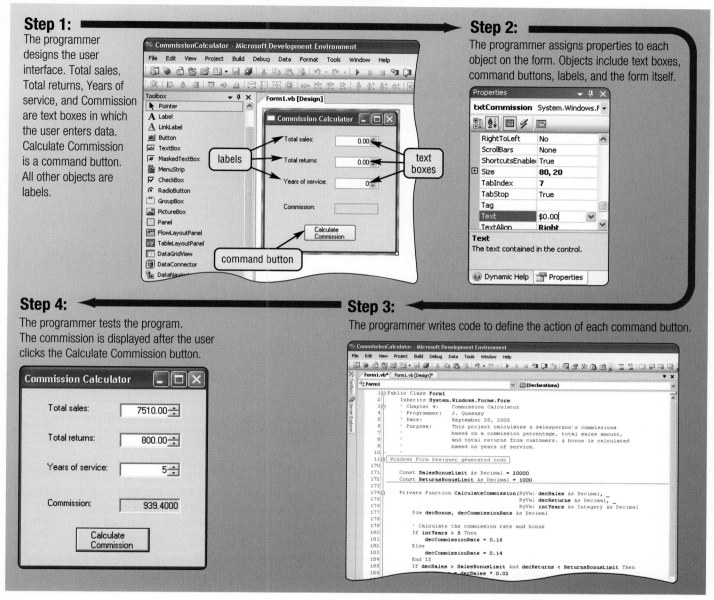

Step 1:
The programmer designs the user interface. Total sales, Total returns, Years of service, and Commission are text boxes in which the user enters data. Calculate Commission is a command button. All other objects are labels.

Step 2:
The programmer assigns properties to each object on the form. Objects include text boxes, command buttons, labels, and the form itself.

Step 4:
The programmer tests the program. The commission is displayed after the user clicks the Calculate Commission button.

Step 3:
The programmer writes code to define the action of each command button.

- Borland's **Delphi** is a powerful program development tool that is ideal for building large-scale enterprise and Web applications in a RAD enviroment. Programmers use Delphi to develop programs quickly for Windows, Linux, and .NET platforms.
- **PowerBuilder**, developed by Sybase, is another powerful program development RAD tool best suited for Web-based and large-scale enterprise object-oriented applications. Programmers also use PowerBuilder to develop small- and medium-scale client/server applications.

FAQ 11-2

What are the more popular programming languages?

According to a recent study, Java, C, and C++ are the top programming languages, with Visual Basic, Perl, Delphi, SQL, and JavaScript not far behind. For more information, visit scsite.com/dcf2e/ch11/faq and then click Popular Programming Languages.

Other Programming Languages

Two programming languages also currently used that have not yet been discussed are RPG and 4GLs. The following sections discuss these programming languages.

RPG   In the early 1960s, IBM introduced **RPG** (Report Program Generator) to assist businesses in generating reports (Figure 11-21). Today, businesses also use RPG to access and update data in databases. RPG primarily is used for application development on IBM midrange computers.

```
C* COMPUTE REGULAR TIME PAY
C           RTHRS     MULT RATE              RTPAY    72
C*
C* COMPUTE OVERTIME PAY
C           OTHRS     IFGT 0
C           RATE      MULT 1.5               OTRATE   72
C           OTRATE    MULT OTHRS             OTPAY    72
                      ELSE
C                     INZ                    OTPAY    72
C
C* COMPUTE GROSS PAY
C           RTPAY     ADD  OTPAY             GRPAY    72
C
C* PRINT GROSS PAY
C                     EXCPTDETAIL
C
C*
O* OUTPUT SPECIFICATIONS
OQPRINT  E            DETAIL
O                                    23 'THE GROSS PAY IS $'
O                     GRPAY  J       34
```

FIGURE 11-21   This figure shows an excerpt from an RPG payroll program. The code shows the computations for regular time pay, overtime pay, and gross pay; the decision to evaluate the overtime hours; and the output of the gross pay.

4GLs   A **4GL** (fourth-generation language) is a nonprocedural language that enables users and programmers to access data in a database. With a **nonprocedural language**, the programmer writes English-like instructions or interacts with a visual environment to retrieve data from files or a database.

One popular 4GL is SQL. **SQL** is a query language that allows users to manage, update, and retrieve data in a relational DBMS (Figure 11-22).

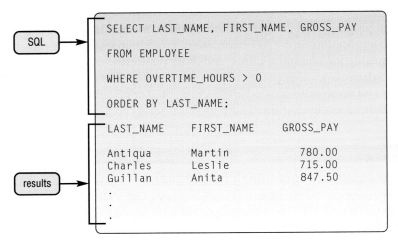

```
SELECT LAST_NAME, FIRST_NAME, GROSS_PAY

FROM EMPLOYEE

WHERE OVERTIME_HOURS > 0

ORDER BY LAST_NAME;

LAST_NAME      FIRST_NAME      GROSS_PAY

Antigua        Martin          780.00
Charles        Leslie          715.00
Guillan        Anita           847.50
  .
  .
  .
```

FIGURE 11-22   SQL is a fourth-generation language that can be used to query database tables. This query produces an alphabetical list of those employees who receive overtime pay; that is, their overtime hours are greater than 0.

Classic Programming Languages

In addition to the programming languages discussed on the previous pages, programmers sometimes use other languages (Figure 11-23). Some of the languages listed in Figure 11-23, although once popular, find little use today.

Ada	Derived from Pascal, developed by the U.S. Department of Defense, named after Augusta Ada Lovelace Byron, who is thought to be the first female computer programmer
ALGOL	ALGOrithmic Language, the first structured procedural language
APL	A Programming Language, a scientific language designed to manipulate tables of numbers
BASIC	Beginners All-purpose Symbolic Instruction Code, developed by John Kemeny and Thomas Kurtz as a simple, interactive problem-solving language
Forth	Similar to C, used for small computerized devices
Fortran	FORmula TRANslator, one of the first high-level programming languages used for scientific applications
HyperTalk	An object-oriented programming language developed by Apple to manipulate cards that can contain text, graphics, and sound
LISP	LISt Processing, a language used for artificial intelligence applications
Logo	An educational tool used to teach programming and problem-solving to children
Modula-2	A successor to Pascal used for developing systems software
Pascal	Developed to teach students structured programming concepts, named in honor of Blaise Pascal, a French mathematician who developed one of the earliest calculating machines
PILOT	Programmed Inquiry Learning Or Teaching, used to write computer-aided instruction programs
PL/1	Programming Language One, a business and scientific language that combines many features of Fortran and COBOL
Prolog	PROgramming LOGic, used for development of artificial intelligence applications
Smalltalk	Object-oriented programming language

FIGURE 11-23   Other programming languages.

Other Program Development Tools

As mentioned earlier, program development tools are user-friendly programs designed to assist both programmers and users in creating programs. In many cases, the program automatically generates the procedural instructions necessary to communicate with the computer. The visual programming languages discussed earlier in the chapter are examples of program development tools. Other program development tools include application generators and macros.

APPLICATION GENERATORS   An **application generator** is a program that creates source code or machine code from a specification of the required functionality. When using an application generator, a programmer or user works with menu-driven tools and graphical user interfaces to define the desired specifications. Application generators most often are bundled with or are included as part of a DBMS.

An application generator typically consists of a report writer, form, and menu generator. A report writer allows you to design a report on the screen, retrieve data into the report design, and then display or print the report. Figure 11-24 shows a sample form design and the resulting form it generates showing sample data a user may enter in the form. A menu generator enables you to create a menu for the application options.

FIGURE 11-24a (form design)

FIGURE 11-24b (resulting filled-in form)

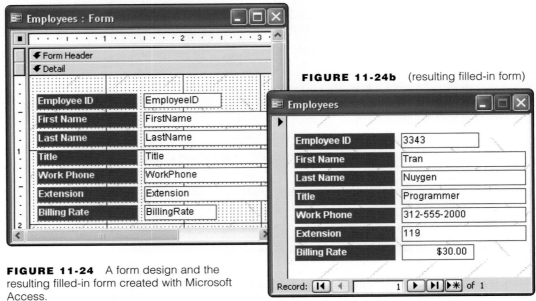

FIGURE 11-24 A form design and the resulting filled-in form created with Microsoft Access.

MACROS   A **macro** is a series of statements that instructs an application how to complete a task. Macros allow users to automate routine, repetitive, or difficult tasks in application software such as word processing, spreadsheet, or database programs. That is, users can create simple programs within the software by writing macros. You usually create a macro in one of two ways: (1) record the macro or (2) write the macro.

If you want to automate a routine or repetitive task such as formatting or editing, you would record a macro. A macro recorder is similar to a movie camera because both record all actions until turned off. To record a macro, start the macro recorder in the software. Then, perform the steps to be part of the macro, such as clicks of the mouse or keystrokes. Once the macro is recorded, you can run it anytime you want to perform that same sequence of actions. For example, if you always print three copies of certain documents, you could record the actions required to print three copies. To print three copies, you would run the macro called PrintThreeCopies.

When you become familiar with programming techniques, you can write your own macros instead of recording them. Read At Issue 11-3 for a related discussion.

AT ISSUE 11-3

Should All Students Be Required to Learn Computer Programming?

When computers were introduced in schools, instructors taught programming routinely. As time passed, however, the emphasis turned towards learning to use application software and the Internet. Many educators feel programming still should be an integral part of computer education, and some believe that all students should learn fundamental computer programming. They point out that application software often includes a programming language, such as Visual Basic for Applications (VBA), with which users can customize the software. People who have knowledge of programming can recognize more readily the kinds of problems that computers are likely to be able to solve. Many researchers claim that programming improves logical reasoning and critical thinking skills. Yet, other instructors feel that program development is irrelevant for most students and an unnecessary impediment to achieving computer literacy. How important is it to learn programming? Why? Should programming in some form be a part of computer education? Why or why not? Should everyone be taught computer programming? Why?

Web Page Development

The designers of Web pages, known as **Web page authors**, use a variety of techniques to develop Web pages. The following sections discuss these techniques.

HTML   HTML (Hypertext Markup Language) is a special formatting language that programmers use to format documents for display on the Web. You view a Web page written with HTML in a Web browser such as Internet Explorer, Netscape Navigator, Mozilla, Safari, Firefox, or Opera. Figure 11-25a shows part of the HTML code used to create the Web page shown in Figure 11-25b.

HTML is not actually a programming language. It is, however, a language that has specific rules for defining the placement and format of text, graphics, video, and audio on a Web page. HTML uses tags, which are codes that specify links to other documents and indicate how a Web page is displayed when viewed on the Web.

FIGURE 11-25a   (portion of HTML program)

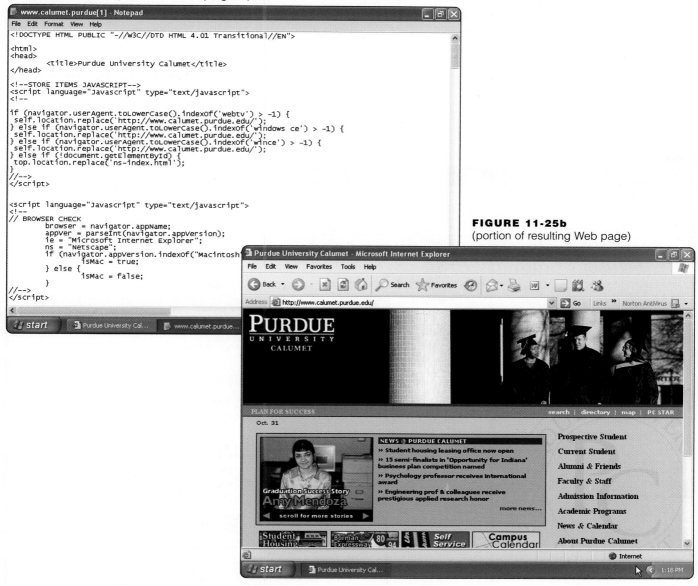

FIGURE 11-25b
(portion of resulting Web page)

FIGURE 11-25   HTML (Hypertext Markup Language) is used to create Web pages. The portion of the HTML code in the top figure generates a portion of a Web page shown in the bottom figure.

SCRIPTS, APPLETS, SERVLETS, AND ACTIVEX CONTROLS   HTML tells a browser how to display text and images, set up lists and option buttons, and establish links on a Web page. By adding dynamic content and interactive elements such as scrolling messages, animated graphics, forms, pop-up windows, and interaction, Web pages become much more interesting. To add these elements, Web page authors write small programs called scripts, applets, servlets, and ActiveX controls. These programs run inside of another program. This is different from programs discussed thus far, which are executed by the operating system. In this case, the Web browser executes these short programs.

One reason for using scripts, applets, servlets, and ActiveX controls is to add special multimedia effects to Web pages. Examples include animated graphics, scrolling messages, calendars, and advertisements. Another reason to use these programs is to include interactive capabilities on Web pages.

SCRIPTING LANGUAGES   Programmers write scripts, applets, servlets, or ActiveX controls using a variety of languages. These include some of the languages previously discussed, such as Java, C++, C#, and Visual Basic 2005. Some programmers use scripting languages. A scripting language is an interpreted language that typically is easy to learn and use. Popular scripting languages include JavaScript, Perl, Rexx, Tcl, and VBScript.

- **JavaScript** is an interpreted language that allows a programmer to add dynamic content and interactive elements to a Web page (Figure 11-26). These elements include alert messages, scrolling text, animations, drop-down menus, data input forms, pop-up windows, and interactive quizzes.

FIGURE 11-26a   (pop-up window)

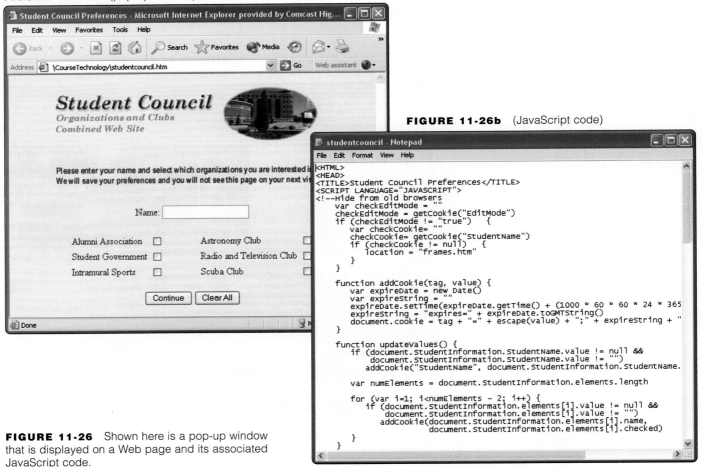

FIGURE 11-26b   (JavaScript code)

FIGURE 11-26   Shown here is a pop-up window that is displayed on a Web page and its associated JavaScript code.

- **Perl** (Practical Extraction and Report Language) originally was developed by Larry Wall at NASA's Jet Propulsion Laboratory as a procedural language similar to C and C++. The latest release of Perl, however, is an interpreted scripting language. Because Perl has powerful text processing capabilities, it has become a popular language for writing scripts.
- **Rexx** (REstructured eXtended eXecutor) was developed by Mike Cowlishaw at IBM as a procedural interpreted scripting language for both the professional programmer and the nontechnical user.
- **Tcl** (Tool Command Language) is an interpreted scripting language created by Dr. John Ousterhout and maintained by Sun Microsystems Laboratories.
- **VBScript** (Visual Basic, Scripting Edition) is a subset of the Visual Basic language that allows programmers to add intelligence and interactivity to Web pages. As with JavaScript, Web page authors embed VBScript code directly into an HTML document.

DYNAMIC HTML   Dynamic HTML (DHTML) is a newer type of HTML that allows Web page authors to include more graphical interest and interactivity in a Web page. Typically, Web pages created with DHTML are more animated and responsive to user interaction. Colors change, font sizes grow, objects appear and disappear as a user moves the mouse (Figure 11-27), and animations dance around the screen.

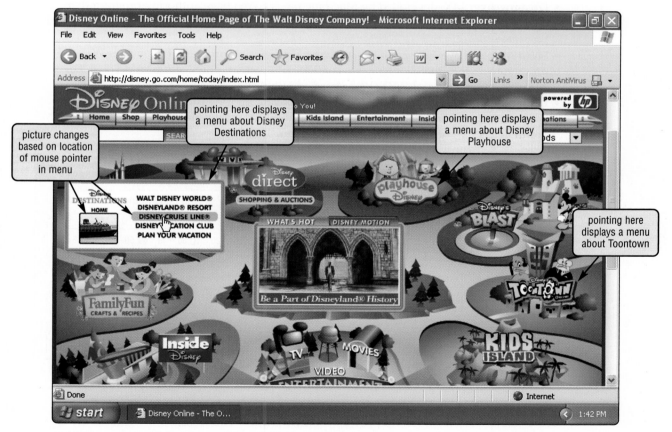

FIGURE 11-27   Web pages at Disney's Web site use DHTML. As you move the mouse around the window, a menu is displayed at the location of the mouse pointer that relates to the object to which you are pointing. As you move the mouse through menus, pictures change based on the location of the mouse pointer in the menu.

XHTML, XML, AND WML XHTML (eXtensible HTML) is a markup language that enables Web sites to be displayed more easily on microbrowsers in PDAs and smart phones. XHTML includes features of HTML and XML. **XML** (eXtensible Markup Language) is an increasingly popular format for sharing data that allows Web page authors to create customized tags, as well as use predefined tags. With XML, a server sends an entire record to the client, enabling the client to do much of the processing without going back to the server.

XML separates the Web page content from its format, allowing the Web browser to display the contents of a Web page in a form appropriate for the display device. For example, a PDA, a notebook computer, and a desktop computer all could display the same XML page.

Wireless devices use a subset of XML called WML. **WML** (wireless markup language) allows Web page authors to design pages specifically for microbrowsers. Many Internet-enabled PDAs and smart phones use WML as their markup language.

WEB PAGE AUTHORING SOFTWARE As discussed in Chapter 3, you do not need to learn HTML to develop a Web page. You can use **Web page authoring software** to create sophisticated Web pages that include graphical images, video, audio, animation, and other special effects. Web page authoring software generates HTML tags from your Web page design.

Three popular Web page authoring programs are Dreamweaver MX, Flash MX, and FrontPage.

- **Dreamweaver MX**, developed by Macromedia, is a Web page authoring program that allows Web site designers and programmers to create, maintain, and manage professional Web sites.
- **Flash MX**, also by Macromedia, is a Web page authoring program that enables Web site programmers to combine interactive content with text, graphics, audio, and video. For example, marketing and WBT (Web-based training) sites often use Flash MX.
- **FrontPage**, developed by Microsoft, is a Web page authoring program that provides nontechnical and professional users with the ability to create and manage Web sites easily. FrontPage is part of the Microsoft Office System.

WEB LINK 11-9

XML

For more information, visit scsite.com/dcf2e/ch11/weblink and then click XML.

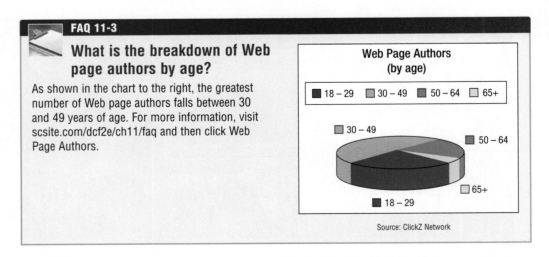

FAQ 11-3

What is the breakdown of Web page authors by age?

As shown in the chart to the right, the greatest number of Web page authors falls between 30 and 49 years of age. For more information, visit scsite.com/dcf2e/ch11/faq and then click Web Page Authors.

Web Page Authors (by age)

■ 18 – 29　■ 30 – 49　■ 50 – 64　□ 65+

30 – 49
50 – 64
65+
18 – 29

Source: ClickZ Network

Multimedia Program Development

Multimedia authoring software allows programmers to combine text, graphics, animation, audio, and video into an interactive presentation. Many developers use multimedia authoring software for computer-based training (CBT) and Web-based training (WBT). Popular software includes ToolBook, Authorware, and Director MX.

Figure 11-28 shows a sample Web application developed in ToolBook that uses DHTML. Many businesses and colleges use ToolBook to create content for distance learning courses.

FIGURE 11-28 A sample ToolBook application.

Test your knowledge of pages 423 through 437 in Quiz Yourself 11-2.

QUIZ YOURSELF 11-2

Instructions: Find the true statement below. Then, rewrite the remaining false statements so they are true.

1. COBOL and C are examples of assembly languages.
2. Delphi is an object-oriented programming language developed by Sun Microsystems.
3. Popular first-generation languages include JavaScript, Perl, Rexx, Tcl, and VBScript.
4. Three popular markup languages are Dreamweaver MX, Flash MX, and FrontPage.
5. Two types of low-level languages are machine languages and source languages.
6. Visual Studio 2005 is the latest suite of program development tools from Microsoft that assists programmers in building programs for Windows, Windows Mobile, or any operating system that supports Microsoft's .NET architecture.

Quiz Yourself Online: To further check your knowledge of programming languages, program development tools, and Web page program development, visit scsite.com/dcf2e/ch11/quiz and then click Objectives 3 – 6.

THE PROGRAM DEVELOPMENT CYCLE

The **program development cycle** is a series of steps programmers use to build computer programs. As discussed, the system development cycle guides information technology (IT) professionals through the development of an information system. Likewise, the program development cycle guides computer programmers through the development of a program. The program development cycle consists of six steps (Figure 11-29):

1. Analyze Requirements
2. Design Solution
3. Validate Design
4. Implement Design
5. Test Solution
6. Document Solution

As shown in Figure 11-29, the steps in the program development cycle form a loop. Program development is an ongoing process within system development. Each time someone identifies errors in or improvements to a program and requests program modifications, the Analyze Requirements step begins again. When programmers correct errors or add enhancements to an existing program, they are said to be **maintaining** the program. Read At Issue 11-4 for a related discussion.

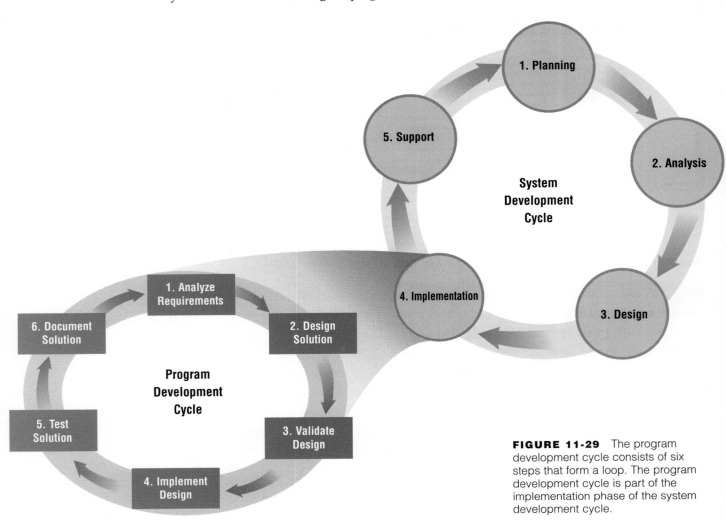

FIGURE 11-29 The program development cycle consists of six steps that form a loop. The program development cycle is part of the implementation phase of the system development cycle.

AT ISSUE 11-4

Who Is Responsible for Bugs?

The consequences of bugs, or errors, in computer programs can be staggering. An error in the code controlling a Canadian nuclear facility caused more than 3,000 gallons of radioactive water to be spilled. A bug in long-distance switching software cost AT&T more than $60 million. Users have been frustrated for years by flaws in some versions of the Windows operating system that locked up their computers and displayed the dreaded "Blue Screen of Death." Experts estimate that there are 20 to 30 bugs per 1,000 lines of code. Given that many programs contain hundreds of thousands, even millions, of code lines, bugs are not surprising. Most software licenses absolve the software creator of any responsibility for the end user getting the wrong information from a bug-riddled program. Who should be responsible for mistakes in software? Why? When you buy some software today and have trouble installing it or experience other problems, you often get charged for technical support. Should manufacturers be required to provide free technical support for a specified time? Why or why not?

What Initiates the Program Development Cycle?

As discussed, the system development cycle consists of five phases: planning, analysis, design, implementation, and support. During the analysis phase, the development team recommends how to handle software needs. Choices include purchasing packaged software, building custom software in-house, or outsourcing some or all of the IT operation.

If the company opts for in-house development, the design and implementation phases of the system development cycle become quite extensive. In the design phase, the analyst creates a detailed set of requirements for the programmers. Once the programmers receive the requirements, the implementation phase begins. At this time, the programmer analyzes the requirements of the problem to be solved. The program development cycle thus begins at the start of the implementation phase in the system development cycle.

The scope of the requirements largely determines how many programmers work on the program development. If the scope is large, a **programming team** that consists of a group of programmers may develop the programs. If the specifications are simple, a single programmer might complete all the development tasks. Whether a single programmer or a programming team, all the programmers involved must interact with users and members of the development team throughout the program development cycle.

By following the steps in the program development cycle, programmers create programs that are correct (produce accurate information) and maintainable (easy to modify). Read Looking Ahead 11-3 for a look at the next generation of programming.

LOOKING AHEAD 11-3

Robotic Vehicles Move Forward

Your morning commute will take a new turn when robotic cars, trucks, and motorcycles drive themselves without any human guidance or intervention.

This technology is emerging, in part, from the Grand Challenge contest sponsored by the Pentagon's Defense Advanced Research Projects Agency. The winning team will receive $1 million when their vehicle travels unassisted through 200 miles of the Mojave Desert's rugged terrain in less than 10 hours without human intervention.

Some of the vehicles being built for the contest have as many as 10 computers onboard, programmed to react to dozens of sensors that gather input about the race course. With assistance from a global positioning system, the computers control the steering, accelerating, and braking. For more information, visit scsite.com/dcf2e/ch11/looking and then click Robotic Vehicles.

Control Structures

When programmers are required to design the logic of a program, they typically use control structures to describe the tasks a program is to perform. A **control structure**, also known as a construct, depicts the logical order of program instructions. Three basic control structures are sequence, selection, and repetition.

SEQUENCE CONTROL STRUCTURE   A **sequence control structure** shows one or more actions following each other in order (Figure 11-30). Actions include inputs, processes, and outputs. Examples of actions are reading a record, calculating averages or totals, and printing totals.

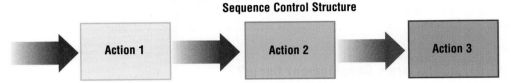

Sequence Control Structure

FIGURE 11-30   The sequence control structure shows one or more actions followed by another.

SELECTION CONTROL STRUCTURE   A **selection control structure** tells the program which action to take, based on a certain condition. Two common types of selection control structures are the if-then-else and the case.

When a program evaluates the condition in an if-then-else control structure, it yields one of two possibilities: true or false. Figure 11-31 shows the condition as a diamond symbol. If the result of the condition is true, then the program performs one action. If the result is false, the program performs a different (or possibly no) action. For example, the selection control structure can determine if an employee should receive overtime pay. A possible condition might be the following: Is Overtime Hours greater than 0? If the response is yes (true), then the action would calculate overtime pay. If the response is no (false), then the action would set overtime pay equal to 0.

With the case control structure, a condition can yield one of three or more possibilities (Figure 11-32). The size of a beverage, for example, might be one of these options: small, medium, large, or extra large. A case control structure would determine the price of the beverage based on the size purchased.

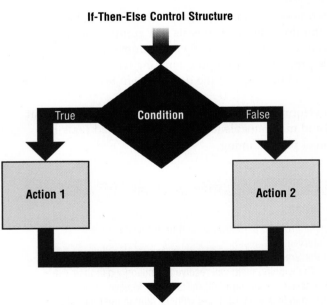

If-Then-Else Control Structure

FIGURE 11-31   The if-then-else control structure directs the program toward one course of action or another based on the evaluation of a condition.

Case Control Structure

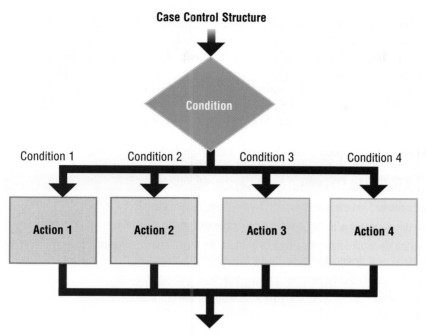

FIGURE 11-32 The case control structure allows for more than two alternatives when a condition is evaluated.

REPETITION CONTROL STRUCTURE   The **repetition control structure** enables a program to perform one or more actions repeatedly as long as a certain condition is met. Many programmers refer to this construct as a loop. Two forms of the repetition control structure are the do-while and do-until.

A do-while control structure repeats one or more times as long as a specified condition is true (Figure 11-33). This control structure tests a condition at the beginning of the loop. If the result of the condition is true, the program executes the action(s) inside the loop. Then, the program loops back and tests the condition again. If the result of the condition still is true, the program executes the action(s) inside the loop again.

This looping process continues until the condition being tested becomes false. At that time, the program stops looping and moves to another set of actions.

The do-while control structure normally is used when the occurrence of an event is not quantifiable or predictable. For example, programmers frequently use the do-while control structure to process all records in a file. A payroll program using a do-while control structure loops once for each employee. This program stops looping when it processes the last employee's record.

The do-until control structure is similar to the do-while but has two major differences: where it tests the condition and when it stops looping. First, the do-until control structure tests the condition at the end of the loop (Figure 11-34).

Do-While Control Structure

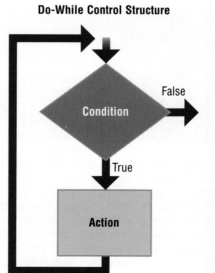

FIGURE 11-33 The do-while control structure tests the condition at the beginning of the loop. It exits the loop when the result of the condition is false.

Do-Until Control Structure

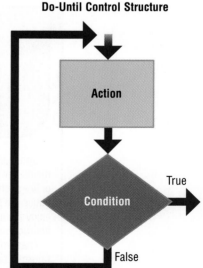

FIGURE 11-34 The do-until control structure tests the condition at the end of the loop. It exits the loop when the result of the condition is true.

The action(s) in a do-until control structure thus always will execute at least once. The loop in a do-while control structure, by contrast, might not execute at all. That is, if the condition immediately is false, the action or actions in the do-while loop never execute. Second, a do-until control structure continues looping until the condition is true — and then stops. This is different from the do-while control structure, which continues to loop while the condition is true.

An understanding of these control structures provides an insight into the steps performed by a computer when the computer is used to solve a problem or process data.

Test your knowledge of pages 438 through 442 in Quiz Yourself 11-3.

 QUIZ YOURSELF 11-3

Instructions: Find the true statement below. Then, rewrite the remaining false statements so they are true.

1. Program development is an ongoing activity within system development.

2. The program development cycle consists of these six steps: analyze requirements, design solution, validate design, implement design, test solution, and hardcode solution.

3. Three basic control structures are sequence, selection, and maintenance.

Quiz Yourself Online: To further check your knowledge of the program development cycle and basic control structures and design tools, visit scsite.com/dcf2e/ch11/quiz and then click Objectives 7 – 8.

CHAPTER SUMMARY

This chapter discussed the phases in the system development cycle. The guidelines for system development also were presented. Activities that occur during the entire system development cycle, including project management, feasibility assessment, documentation, data and information gathering, also were addressed.

This chapter also discussed various programming languages and program development tools used to write and develop computer programs. It described a variety of Web development and multimedia development tools. Finally, the chapter presented the program development cycle and the tools used in this process.

CAREER CORNER

Programmer

If you are the curious, creative type, enjoy solving puzzles, and gain satisfaction in making things work, you may want to consider a career in programming. A programmer designs, writes, and tests the code that tells computers what to do. Most programmers specialize in one of three fields: system programming, application programming, or Web development programming.

Some jobs may require that the programmer develop an entire program, while other jobs require program maintenance. Likewise, programmers can work for a small company in which they are responsible for the entire system development cycle, or for a larger company in which they are part of a team and individual duties are specialized. Projects can range from computer games to essential business applications. Programmers enjoy the achievements of working with computers to accomplish objectives as well as developing efficient instructions that tell computers how to perform specific tasks.

Academic credentials are essential for success in this career. A bachelor's degree in Computer Science or Information Technology usually is required. The key to success is familiarity with programming languages and a good foundation in programming logic. Surveys indicate that average salaries for entry level programmers are about $45,500 and can exceed $95,000 for senior programmers. For more information, visit scsite.com/dcf2e/ch11/careers and then click Programmer.

Computer Associates
Management Software Developer

Competing in today's demanding and intricate global economy requires a versatile team of managers and employees. This workforce, in turn, requires a variety of software to help adapt to the ever-changing needs and challenges. Computer Associates International, Inc. (CA) provides products to help meet these evolving business challenges.

CA's software and services range from preventing security threats to storing data intelligently. These platform-independent products help protect and optimize the operations of 95 percent of Fortune 500 companies in more than 100 countries. Charles B. Wang founded CA in 1976 with three associates, no venture capital, and one product: a sort/merge utility called CA-SORT. The company has grown to become the world's largest management software corporation. For more information, visit scsite.com/dcf2e/ch11/companies and then click Computer Associates.

Macromedia
Multimedia Software Developer

Creative interactive learning experiences and brilliant Web pages are due, in part, to Macromedia's award-winning products.

Among this software is Flash Player, which allows viewing of vivid Web content and applications. More than one million copies of this program are downloaded from the Macromedia Web site daily, which makes it the most widely Web-distributed software in history. Dreamweaver MX helps build and maintain Web sites, Shockwave permits viewing of media and 3-D Web content, and Captivate enables users to record on-screen activity to create interactive simulations and software demonstrations.

Marc Canter founded MacroMind in 1984 to supply artists with tools to create high-quality audio, video, and animation. His company merged with Paracomp and Authorware in 1992 to form Macromedia. For more information, visit scsite.com/dcf2e/ch11/companies and then click Macromedia.

TECHNOLOGY TRAILBLAZERS

Grace Hopper
COBOL Developer

Women's participation in the computer programming world was shaped by the achievements of Grace Hopper. She was one of the first software engineers, and in 1953 she perfected her best-known invention: the compiler.

After earning her Ph.D. degree from Yale University, she began teaching mathematics at Vassar College. She resigned that position in 1943 to join the Navy WAVES (Women Accepted for Voluntary Emergency Service). Her work developing compilers ultimately led to the creation of the COBOL programming language.

Although her achievements are the foundation of today's computers, she said during her lifetime that she was most proud of her service to her country. She was buried with full naval honors at Arlington National Cemetery. For more information, visit scsite.com/dcf2e/ch11/people and then click Grace Hopper.

James Gosling
Java Engineer and Architect

Known as "the Java guy," James Gosling serves as Sun Microsystems Developer Products group's chief technology officer. He is the mastermind behind Java, the network programming language running across all platforms, from servers to cellular telephones.

Gosling grew up near Calgary, Alberta, and spent much of his spare time turning spare machine parts into games. At the age of 15, he wrote software for the University of Calgary's physics department. When he was hired at Sun Microsystems, he built a multiprocessor version of UNIX, developed compilers to convert program code into machine language, engineered a window manager, and wrote a UNIX text editor.

At Sun today, he works with his research team to develop semantic modeling software that helps developers analyze an application's structure. For more information, visit scsite.com/dcf2e/ch11/people and then click James Gosling.

Chapter Review

The Chapter Review section summarizes the concepts presented in this chapter. To obtain help from other students regarding any subject in this chapter, visit scsite.com/dcf2e/ch11/forum and post your thoughts or questions.

(1) Why Are Project Management, Feasibility Assessment, Documentation, Data and Information Gathering Techniques, and Information System Security Important during System Development?

Project management is the process of planning, scheduling, and then controlling the activities during the system development cycle. **Feasibility** is a measure of how suitable the development of a system will be to the company. **Documentaton** is the collection and summarization of data and information. To gather data and information, IT professionals can review documentation, observe, send questionnaires, interview, participate in a **joint-application design (JAD) session**, and perform research. All elements of an information system must be secure from threats both inside and outside the enterprise.

(2) What Is the Purpose of Each Phase in the System Development Cycle?

Most system development cycles contain five **phases**. During the **planning phase**, a **project request** is reviewed and approved, project requests are prioritized, resources are allocated, and a project development team is formed for each approved project. During the **analysis phase**, a **preliminary investigation** is conducted to determine the exact nature of the problem or improvement, and detailed analysis is performed to study how the current system works, determine users' requirements, and recommend a solution. During the **design phase**, any necessary hardware and software is acquired, and the details of the new or modified information system are developed. In the **implementation phase**, the new or modified system is constructed and delivered to the users. During the **support phase**, ongoing assistance is provided for the information system and its users after the system is implemented.

Visit scsite.com/dcf2e/ch11/quiz or click the Quiz Yourself button. Click Objectives 1 – 2.

(3) How Are Low-Level Languages Different from Procedural Languages?

A low-level language is a programming language that runs on only one type of computer. Each instruction in a low-level language usually equates to a single machine instruction. Procedural languages are high-level languages that can run on many different types of computers and operating systems. In a **procedural language**, a programmer writes instructions that tell the computer what to accomplish and how to do it.

(4) What Are the Benefits of Object-Oriented and Visual Programming Languages?

Programmers use an **object-oriented programming (OOP) language** to implement object-oriented design. A major benefit of OOP is the ability to reuse and modify existing objects, allowing programmers to create applications faster. OOP languages include **Java**, **C++**, and **C#**.

(5) What Are Other Programming Languages and Other Program Development Tools?

Businesses use **RPG** to generate reports and access and update data in databases. A **4GL** (fourth generation language) is a **nonprocedural language** that users and programmers use to access the data in a database. An **application generator** creates source code or machine code from a specification of the required functionality. Other program development tools include an **application generator** and a **macro**.

(6) How Are Web Pages Developed?

Web page authors use a variety of techniques to develop Web pages. **HTML** (Hypertext Markup Language) is a special formatting language used to format documents for display on the Web. To add interactivity to Web pages, some

Chapter Review

programmers use a scripting language or **Dynamic HTML (DHTML)**. Other popular languages include **XHTML**, **XML**, and **WML**. Web page authors also use Web page authoring software to create sophisticated Web pages.

 Visit scsite.com/dcf2e/ch11/quiz or click the Quiz Yourself button. Click Objectives 3 – 6.

(7) **What Are the Six Steps in the Program Development Cycle?**

The **program development cycle** is a series of steps programmers use to build computer programs. The program development cycle consists of six steps: (1) analyze requirements, (2) design solution, (3) validate design, (4) implement design, (5) test solution, and (6) document solution.

(8) **What Are the Basic Control Structures Used in Designing Solutions to Programming Problems?**

A **control structure** depicts the logical order of program instructions. Three basic control structures are sequence, selection, and repetition.

 Visit scsite.com/dcf2e/ch11/quiz or click the Quiz Yourself button. Click Objectives 7 – 8.

Key Terms

You should know each key term. Use the list below to help focus your study. To further enhance your understanding of the Key Terms in this chapter, visit scsite.com/dcf2e/ch11/terms. See an example of and a definition for each term, and access current and additional information about the term from the Web.

4GL (430)
analysis phase (413)
application generator (431)
assembly language (424)
benchmark test (417)
C (427)
C# (428)
C++ (428)
chief security officer (422)
COBOL (426)
code snippets (428)
compiler (425)
computer program (423)
computer security plan (422)
computer-aided software engineering (CASE) (419)
control structure (440)
custom software (415)
Delphi (429)
design phase (416)
developer (423)
direct conversion (421)
documentation (409)
Dreamweaver MX (436)
dynamic HTML (DHTML) (435)
e-zine (416)

feasibility (409)
Flash MX (436)
FrontPage (436)
HTML (433)
implementation phase (420)
information system (IS) (406)
interpreter (426)
IT consultant (417)
Java (427)
JavaScript (434)
joint-application design (JAD) session (410)
machine language (424)
macro (432)
maintaining (438)
multimedia authoring software (437)
nonprocedural language (430)
object-oriented programming (OOP) language (427)
outsource (415)
packaged software (415)
parallel conversion (421)
Perl (435)
phased conversion (421)
phases (406)
pilot conversion (421)

planning phase (412)
PowerBuilder (409)
preliminary investigation (413)
procedural language (425)
program development cycle (438)
program development tool (428)
programmer (423)
programming language (423)
programming team (439)
project leader (408)
project management (408)
project request (411)
project team (408)
prototype (419)
RAD (428)
repetition control structure (441)
Rexx (435)
RPG (430)
selection control structure (440)
sequence control structure (440)
source program (425)
SQL (430)

standards (407)
steering committee (408)
support phase (422)
system (406)
system developer (408)
system development cycle (406)
system enhancement (422)
system proposal (415)
systems analyst (407)
Tcl (435)
third-generation language (3GL) (425)
training (421)
users (407)
value-added reseller (VAR) (417)
VBScript (435)
visual programming language (428)
Visual Studio 2005 (428)
Web page authoring software (436)
Web page authors (433)
WML (436)
XHTML (436)
XML (436)

Checkpoint

Use the Checkpoint exercises to check your knowledge level of the chapter.

True/False
Mark T for True and F for False. (See page numbers in parentheses.)

_____ 1. A Gantt chart is a bar chart that uses horizontal bars to show project phases or activities. (409)

_____ 2. Application software developed by the user or at the user's request is called packaged software. (415)

_____ 3. System enhancement involves solidifying or reducing an existing application system. (422)

_____ 4. Two types of low-level languages are procedural languages and nonprocedural languages. (424)

_____ 5. An advantage of the object-oriented approach is that objects are designed for repeated use and become stable over time. (427)

_____ 6. With a procedural language, the programmer writes English-like instructions or interacts with a visual environment. (430)

_____ 7. An application generator typically consists of a report writer, form, and menu generator. (432)

_____ 8. HTML tells a browser how to display text and images, set up lists and option buttons, and establish links on a Web page. (434)

_____ 9. Program development is an ongoing process within system development. (438)

_____ 10. The if-then-else control structure is a type of sequence control structure that can yield one of three or more possibilities. (440)

Multiple Choice
Select the best answer. (See page numbers in parentheses.)

1. The steering committee _____. (408)
   a. works on a project from beginning to end
   b. is a decision-making body in a company
   c. tests and evaluates vendor proposals
   d. all of the above

2. A _____ session is a lengthy, structured, group meeting in which users and IT professionals work together to design or develop an application. (410)
   a. request for proposal (RFP)
   b. joint-application design (JAD)
   c. request for quotation (RFQ)
   d. data flow diagram (DFD)

3. During the planning phase, the projects that receive the highest priority are those _____. (413)
   a. mandated by management or some other governing body
   b. suggested by the greatest number of users
   c. thought to be of highest value to the company
   d. proposed by the information technology (IT) department

4. The purpose of the _____ is to assess the feasibility of each alternative solution and then recommend the most feasible solution for the project. (415)
   a. project plan   b. system review
   c. project request   d. system proposal

5. With a pilot conversion, _____. (421)
   a. each location converts at a separate time
   b. users stop using the old system and begin using the new system
   c. only one location in the company uses the new system — so it can be tested
   d. the old system is run alongside the new system for a specified period

6. _____ is a popular fourth-generation query language that allows users to manage, update, and retrieve data in a relational DBMS. (430)
   a. RPG   b. ADA
   c. XML   d. SQL

7. A(n) _____ control structure repeats one or more times as long as a specified condition is true and tests a condition at the beginning of the loop. (441)
   a. do-while
   b. do-until
   c. if-then-else
   d. sequence

8. Many programmers refer to the _____ control structure as a loop. (441)
   a. sequence   b. selection
   c. case   d. repetition

Matching
Match the terms with their definitions. (See page numbers in parentheses.)

_____ 1. project request (411)

_____ 2. value-added reseller (417)

_____ 3. benchmark test (417)

_____ 4. source program (425)

_____ 5. control structure (440)

a. measures the performance of hardware or software

b. formal appeal for a new or modified information system

c. the language instructions, or code, to be converted into machine language

d. purchases products and then resells them along with additional services

e. set of rules and procedures a company expects employees to follow

f. depicts the logical order of program instructions

Checkpoint

Write a brief answer to each of the following questions.

1. What is a project leader? _____ What must a project leader identify to plan and schedule a project effectively? _____

2. What is feasibility? _____ How are operational feasibility, schedule feasibility, technical feasibility, and economic feasibility different? _____

3. How is a request for quotation (RFQ) different from a request for proposal (RFP)? _____ What is a request for information? _____

4. What are a chief security officer's responsibilities? _____ What is a computer security plan? _____

5. How is a compiler different from an interpreter? _____ What is the advantage, and disadvantage, of an interpreter? _____

Working Together Working in a group of your classmates, complete the following team exercise.

1. Choosing a programming language is an important decision. A poor choice can result in a program that is difficult, incompatible, or unproductive. Have each member of your team interview someone in the IT department of a local organization about recently developed software. What application was developed? What programming language was used? Why? What factors were important in selecting the programming language? Were other factors considered (such as the expertise of available programmers)? In hindsight, was the best language chosen? Why or why not? Meet with your team to discuss the results of your interviews. Then, create a PowerPoint presentation to share your findings with the class.

Web Research

Use the Internet-based Web Research exercises to broaden your understanding of the concepts presented in this chapter. Visit scsite.com/dcf2e/ch11/research to obtain more information pertaining to each exercise. To discuss any of the Web Research exercises in this chapter with other students, post your thoughts or questions at scsite.com/dcf2e/ch11/forum.

1 Journaling

Respond to your readings in this chapter by writing at least one page about your reactions, evaluations, and reflections on programming languages and program development. For example, would you like to be a **beta tester**? How can software be tested more accurately to eliminate the 20 to 30 errors that occur in every 1,000 lines of code? Should a software manufacturer be required to compensate a corporation when buggy software causes damages? You also can write about the new terms you learned by reading this chapter. If required, submit your journal to your instructor.

2 Scavenger Hunt

Use one of the **search engines** listed in Figure 2-8 in Chapter 2 on page 58 or your own favorite search engine to find the answers to the following questions. Copy and paste the Web address from the Web page where you found the answer. Some questions may have more than one answer. If required, submit your answers to your instructor. (1) How is recursion programming used in games such as tic-tac-toe, Connect Four, and magic squares? (2) What are three benefits of using the Document Object Model (DOM)? (3) What are some highlights from the most recent JavaOne Conference? (4) What contributions has John McCarthy made to the field of artificial intelligence? (5) How are macros used in Microsoft Office applications?

3 Search Sleuth

An international network of knowledgeable people provide the content for **About.com**, one of the top search Web sites. More than 20 million people view this resource every month to find practical advice and solutions to questions on more than 50,000 topics. Visit this Web site and then use your word processing program to answer the following questions. Then, if required, submit your answers to your instructor. (1) Click the Computing & Technology link in the Channels section. Browse the Computing & Technology Resources section. What are the latest e-mail hoaxes and virus alerts? (2) What software is reviewed in the Browse Product Reviews section? (3) Type HTML in the Search box and then click the Go button. How many results were found? What are the titles of two HTML tutorials? (4) Delete the text in the Search box, type "Visual Basic" in the Search box, and then click the Go button. Click a link that discusses Visual Basic 2005 programming for beginners and then write a 50-word summary of your findings.

Learn How To

Use the Learn How To activities to learn fundamental skills when using a computer and accompanying technology. Complete the exercises and submit them to your instructor.

LEARN HOW TO 1: Conduct an Effective Interview

As you learned in this chapter, gathering information is a critical element in the system development cycle, because without accurate facts, it is unlikely that the finished system will perform in the desired manner. An important means of gathering information is the personal interview. Interviews are used in several stages throughout the system development cycle, and they must be thorough and comprehensive.

Prior to conducting an interview, you must determine that an interview is the best means for obtaining the information you seek. You have learned a variety of ways to obtain information, and you should use each of them appropriately. Because an interview interrupts a person's work and takes time, you must be sure the information gained in the interview justifies this interruption. Once you have determined you should conduct an interview to gather information required for system development, a variety of factors become relevant.

Goal: The most important element of a successful interview is for you to determine exactly what knowledge you hope to gain as a result of the interview. If you do not have a goal, you are unlikely to emerge from the interview with much useful information.

Do Your Homework: You should complete a variety of preparatory steps that will help ensure a successful interview. These steps include the following:
1. Gather as much information as you can from the fact-gathering processes that do not require an interview. Because an interview takes a person's time and interrupts work, you must be sure the information you are seeking is not available from other sources. Additionally, if you ask someone questions to obtain information they know is available elsewhere, you will lose credibility with them during the interview process.
2. Be sure you plan to interview the best person to obtain the information you need. To do this, you must research every person you plan to interview and understand their job, their position within the department in which they work, the knowledge they should possess relative to the information you need, the culture of their work environment, how the system being developed relates to them, and an estimate of the cooperation you can expect from them. If someone is the most knowledgeable person regarding a certain subject but is unwilling to share information other than with trusted coworkers, you likely will be better served by talking to someone else.
3. Prepare the questions you want to ask prior to setting up the interview. In this way, you can have a good estimate of the time required for the interview. While other questions will occur to you as the interview proceeds, you should have a good idea of the questions you need answered to reach your goal.
4. Prior to setting an appointment for an interview, be sure the management personnel of the people you will interview have approved. Because you will be disrupting employees' work days, you must obtain management approval before even asking for an appointment.

Make an Appointment: An appointment almost always is required. By making an appointment, you ensure the person to be interviewed will be available. Normally you should request an appointment in writing, often through the use of e-mail. In this written request, you should set a time and place for the interview, inform the interviewee what you need to know, and establish an agenda with an estimated time. You must recognize that most people do not like to be interviewed, so often you will not be seen as friendly. In addition, it might be possible that the system being developed could eliminate or change the person's job, and clearly this can establish an adversarial relationship. Your task when making an appointment, then, is to establish credibility with the interviewee and set the stage for a successful interview.

Conducting the Interview: When conducting an interview, remember that you are the "intruder." Therefore, you should be polite, prompt, and attentive in the interview. Always understand the perspective of the person being interviewed and understand his or her fears, doubts, and potential hostilities. Sometimes, the interviewee might feel he or she is in conflict with you, so by listening closely and being aware of the body language, you should be able to discern the amount of truth and the amount of hedging that is occurring. Some of the details of the interview of which you should be aware are as follows:

Learn How To

1. If possible, the interview should be conducted in a quiet environment with a minimum of interruptions.
2. The demeanor should be open and friendly, but as noted you should not expect to be welcomed with open arms.
3. Your questions should directly address the goals of the interview. Do not expect the person being interviewed to provide a tutorial. Your questions must generate answers that supply your information.
4. Your questions should be thought-provoking. Do not ask questions requiring a yes or no answer. Your questions should not lead the interviewee to an answer — rather, the questions should be open-ended and allow the person to develop the answer. As an interviewer, you never should argue with the person being interviewed, you should not suggest answers or give opinions, you should ask straight-forward questions rather than compound questions, you never should assign blame for any circumstance that might come up in the interview, and you must never interrupt while the person is talking. Finally, you, as the interviewer, should not talk much. Remember, you are conducting the interview to gain information and it is the person you are interviewing who has that information. Let him or her talk.
5. Listen carefully, with both your ears and your eyes. What you hear normally is most important, but body language and other movements often convey information as well. Concentrate on the interviewee — expect that you will make much more eye contact with the person than he or she will with you. Allow silences to linger — the normal impulse in a conversation is to fill the silence quickly; in an interview, however, if you are quiet, the person being interviewed might think of additional information.
6. As you listen, concentrate on the interviewee — when points are being made, do not take notes because that will distract from what the person is saying — stay focused. When the information has been conveyed, then jot down something so you will remember.
7. Throughout the interview, offer reinforcing comments, such as, "The way I understand what you just said is …" Make sure when you leave the interview there are no misunderstandings between you and the person you interviewed.
8. Before you conclude the interview, be sure all your goals have been met. You likely will not have another opportunity to interview the person, so ensure you have nothing further to learn from the person.

Follow-Up: After the interview, it is recommended you send a follow-up letter or e-mail to the person you interviewed to review the information you learned. This document should invite the interviewee to correct any errors you made in summing up your findings. In addition, for all the people you interview, keep a log of the time and place of the interview. In this way, if any questions arise regarding the interview, you will have a log.

Exercise

1. Using the techniques in this activity, conduct interviews with three students on your campus. Your interview goal is to find out about both the most successful class and the least successful class the student has completed. Why was the class successful or unsuccessful? Discuss the instructor, textbook, subject matter, and other relevant items. After the interviews, write a one-page paper summarizing your findings and identify common elements found in successful classes and in unsuccessful classes. Submit this paper to your instructor.
2. **Optional: Conduct this exercise only with permission of your instructor.** Using the techniques you learned in this activity, conduct interviews with three instructors on your campus. The goal of your interview should be to determine the manner in which these instructors conduct and grade examinations. Find out if the instructors are happy with the process or feel improvements can be made. After the interviews, write a one-page paper summarizing your findings and identify any common complaints among the instructors. Submit this paper to your instructor.

CHAPTER 11

Learn It Online

Use the Learn It Online exercises to reinforce your understanding of the chapter concepts. To access the Learn It Online exercises, visit scsite.com/dcf2e/ch11/learn.

(1) At the Movies — VeriChip

To view the VeriChip movie, click the number 1 button. Locate your video and click the corresponding High-Speed or Dial-Up link, depending on your Internet connection. Watch the movie and then complete the exercise by answering the question that follows. In December of 2001, Applied Digital Solutions introduced the VeriChip. The chip is implanted under the skin. It is digitally inscribed with a number that, when read with a special scanner and entered into a database, will give doctors access to medical records. The company says the chip could be a lifesaver for people with illnesses that may inhibit their ability to communicate with doctors or life-squad personnel. It also could help locate Alzheimer's patients who have wandered away from home. Privacy rights experts say the chip could be used as a means of tracking people remotely who are unaware they have been implanted with the chip. What do you feel are the pros and cons of making this technology widely available?

(2) Student Edition Labs — Project Management

Click the number 2 button. When the Student Edition Labs menu appears, click *Project Management* to begin. A new browser window will open. Follow the on-screen instructions to complete the Lab. When finished, click the Exit button. If required, submit your results to your instructor.

(3) Practice Test

Click the number 3 button. Answer each question. When completed, enter your name and click the Grade Test button to submit the quiz for grading. Make a note of any missed questions. If required, submit your results to your instructor.

(4) Who Wants To Be a Computer Genius²?

Click the number 4 button to find out if you are a computer genius. Directions about how to play the game will be displayed. When you are ready to play, click the Play button. Submit your score to your instructor.

(5) Wheel of Terms

Click the number 5 button to reinforce important terms you learned in this chapter by playing the Shelly Cashman Series version of this popular game. Directions about how to play the game will be displayed. When you are ready to play, click the Play button. Submit your score to your instructor.

(6) Student Edition Labs — Visual Programming

Click the number 6 button. When the Student Edition Labs menu appears, click *Visual Programming* to begin. A new browser window will open. Follow the on-screen instructions to complete the Lab. When finished, click the Exit button. If required, submit your results to your instructor.

(7) Crossword Puzzle Challenge

Click the number 7 button. Complete the puzzle to reinforce skills you learned in this chapter. Directions about how to play the game will be displayed. When you are ready to play, click the Submit button. Submit the completed puzzle to your instructor.

(8) Lab Exercises

Click the number 8 button. When the Lab Exercises menu appears, click the exercise assigned by your instructor. A new browser window will open. Follow the on-screen instructions to complete the exercise. When finished, click the Exit button. If required, submit your results to your instructor.

(9) Chapter Discussion Forum

Select an objective from this chapter on page 397 about which you would like more information. Click the number 9 button and post a short message listing a meaningful message title accompanied by one or more questions concerning the selected objective. In two days, return to the threaded discussion by clicking the number 9 button. Submit to your instructor your original message and at least one response to your message.

Enterprise Computing

OBJECTIVES

After completing this chapter, you will be able to:

1. Discuss the special information requirements of an enterprise-sized corporation
2. Identify information systems used in the functional units of an enterprise
3. List general purpose and integrated information systems used throughout an enterprise
4. List types of technologies used throughout an enterprise
5. Describe the major types of e-commerce
6. Discuss the computer hardware needs and solutions for an enterprise
7. Determine why computer backup is important and how it is accomplished
8. Discuss the steps in a disaster recovery plan

CONTENTS

WHAT IS ENTERPRISE COMPUTING?
Organizational Structure of an Enterprise
Levels of Users
How Managers Use Information

INFORMATION SYSTEMS IN THE ENTERPRISE
Information Systems within Functional Units
General Purpose Information Systems
Integrated Information Systems

ENTERPRISE-WIDE TECHNOLOGIES
Portals
EDI
Data Warehouses
Extranets
Web Services
Workflow
Virtual Private Network

E-COMMERCE
E-Retailing
Finance
Health
Entertainment and Media

Travel
Other Business Services

ENTERPRISE HARDWARE
RAID
Network Attached Storage and Storage Area Networks
Enterprise Storage Systems
Blade Servers
High-Availability Systems
Scalability
Utility and Grid Computing
Interoperability

BACKUP PROCEDURES AND SECURITY
Disaster Recovery Plan

CHAPTER SUMMARY

COMPANIES ON THE CUTTING EDGE
SAP
IBM

TECHNOLOGY TRAILBLAZERS
Tom Siebel
Jim Clark

WHAT IS ENTERPRISE COMPUTING?

The term, enterprise, commonly describes a business or venture of any size. In this chapter, the term enterprise refers to large multinational corporations, universities, hospitals, research laboratories, and government organizations. **Enterprise computing** involves the use of computers in networks that encompass a variety of different operating systems, protocols, and network architectures. A typical enterprise consists of hundreds of individual operating entities, called functional units. The types of functional units within a typical manufacturing enterprise are accounting and finance, human resources, engineering, manufacturing, marketing, sales, distribution, customer service, and information technology. Each type of functional unit has specialized requirements for their information systems. These functional units are summarized later in this chapter.

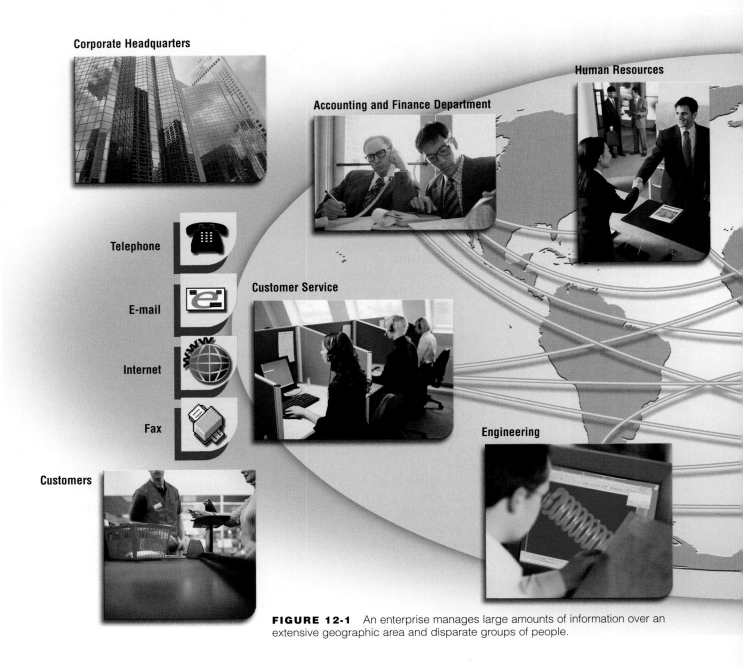

FIGURE 12-1 An enterprise manages large amounts of information over an extensive geographic area and disparate groups of people.

Enterprises produce and gather enormous volumes of information regarding customer, supplier, and employee activity. The information flows among an assortment of entities both inside and outside of the enterprise, and users consume the information during a variety of activities (Figure 12-1). Customers, suppliers, and employees interact with the enterprise in a number of ways, and computers track each interaction. Each sale of a product, purchase of a piece of equipment, or paycheck generates activity involving information systems.

Large computers connected by vast networks allow the enterprise to manage and distribute information quickly and efficiently.

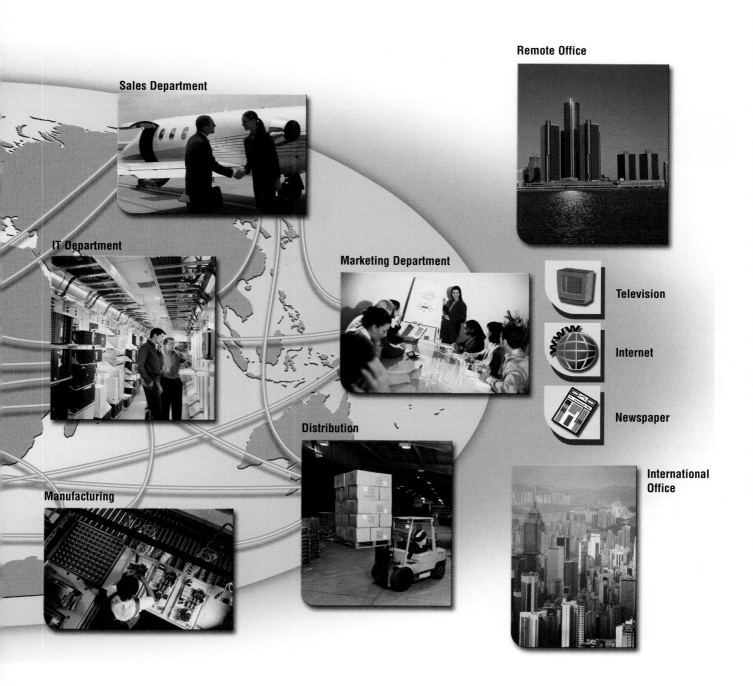

Organizational Structure of an Enterprise

Most traditional enterprises are organized in a hierarchical manner. Figure 12-2 shows an example of an organization chart of a large manufacturing company. Managers at the first two levels at the top of the chart, including the Chief Executive Officer (CEO), mainly concern themselves with strategic decisions and long-term planning. Read Looking Ahead 12-1 for a look at the changing roles of the next generation of CEOs.

In Figure 12-2, the Chief Operations Officer (COO) manages the core activities. The supporting activities include financial departments and information technology (IT) departments. The Chief Financial Officer (CFO) and the Chief Information Officer (CIO) lead these supporting roles.

Each enterprise includes its own special needs and the organizational structure of every enterprise varies. Companies may include all or some of the managers and departments shown in Figure 12-2.

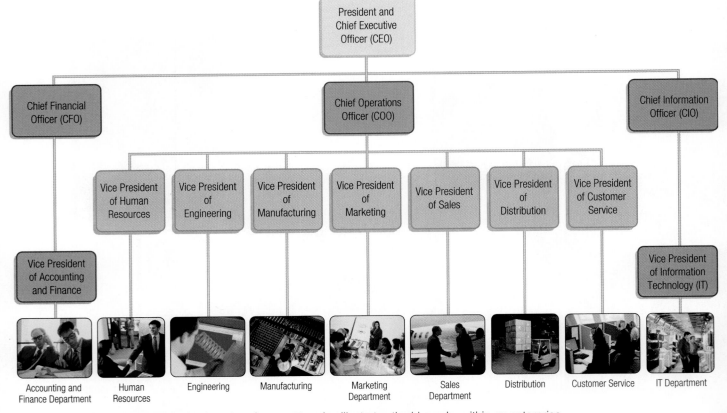

FIGURE 12-2 A typical organization chart for an enterprise illustrates the hierarchy within an enterprise.

LOOKING AHEAD 12-1

The CEO of the Future

If you can motivate people, have real-world business experience, and know about science and engineering, you have the qualities to become a successful CEO in the next generation.

According to Eric Bolland, coauthor of *Future Firms*, an upcoming CEO needs the insight to predict trends and visualize a company's growth. Collaboration skills within the company and the industry are crucial, along with courage to think in new ways and flexibility to change technological and economical strategies.

Successful next-generation CEOs will have the foresight to replace, rather than modify, the technology in older companies. They also will study the strategies of current, established businesses and envision how to increase sales and market share. For more information, visit scsite.com/dcf2e/ch12/looking and then click Future CEO.

Levels of Users

In an enterprise, users of information typically fall into one of four categories: executive management, middle management, operational management, and nonmanagement employees (Figure 12-3). The types of information that users require often depends on their employee level in the company.

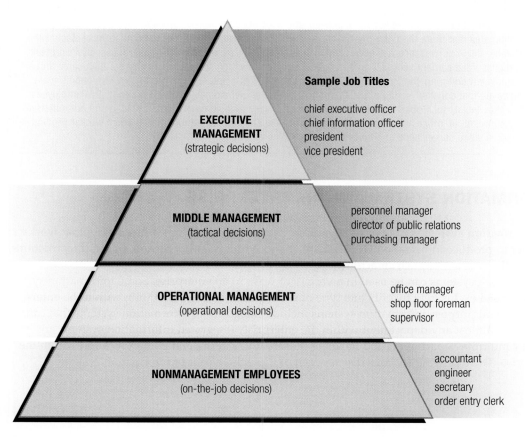

FIGURE 12-3   This pyramid illustrates the levels of users, sample job titles of each level of user, and the types of decisions these users make.

How Managers Use Information

Enterprise information is the information gathered in the ongoing operations of an enterprise-sized organization. Enterprise information begins with the day-to-day transactions that occur within a company, such as sales receipts or time cards. The company gathers and stores the information. Over time, employees collect, combine, and analyze the information. Ultimately, the role of information gathered in this way is to allow managers to make better decisions.

All employees, including managers, in a company need accurate information to perform their jobs effectively. **Managers** are responsible for coordinating and controlling an organization's resources. Resources include people, money, materials, and information. Managers coordinate these resources by performing four activities: planning, organizing, leading, and controlling (read At Issue 12-1 for a related discussion).

- Planning involves establishing goals and objectives.
- Organizing includes identifying and combining resources, such as money and people, so that the company can reach its goals and objectives.
- Leading, sometimes referred to as directing, involves communicating instructions and authorizing others to perform the necessary work.
- Controlling involves measuring performance and, if necessary, taking corrective action.

AT ISSUE 12-1

Is Video Surveillance in the Workplace Ethical?

Once, the main concern of an unproductive office worker was the informant at the next desk. Now, workers have more to worry about. Employers can use a number of products to monitor employee activity. Software can track Internet use, scrutinize keyboard activity, and even observe general office behavior. One privacy group estimates that more than one-third of today's office employees are subject to some form of electronic surveillance. Video surveillance has been used in schools, buses, parking garages, and offices. New software uses a digital video camera with real-time image recognition to watch and record all activity. Advocates argue that employee monitoring conserves office resources and makes workers more productive. Opponents maintain, however, that constant scrutiny results in uncomfortable, unimaginative, and less productive employees. Besides, they insist, such observation is an invasion of privacy. Should employers use video and computers to monitor some, or all, office activity? Why or why not? How does employee monitoring affect worker productivity? Why? Is video surveillance of employees ethical? Why or why not?

INFORMATION SYSTEMS IN THE ENTERPRISE

An **information system** is a set of hardware, software, data, people, and procedures that works together to produce information (Figure 12-4). A procedure is an instruction, or set of instructions, a user follows to accomplish an activity.

Information systems can be used in a variety of ways in an enterprise. Some information systems are used exclusively by only one type of department, or functional unit, within the enterprise. General purpose information systems include categories of information systems that can be used by almost any department within the enterprise. Integrated information systems are used by multiple departments and facilitate information sharing and communication within the enterprise. The following sections discuss each of these three uses of information systems.

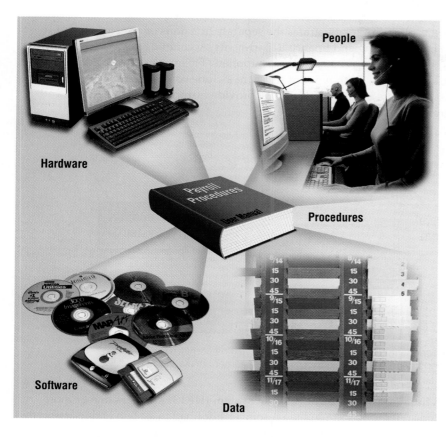

FIGURE 12-4 An information system typically contains five components: hardware, software, data, people, and procedures.

Information Systems within Functional Units

Figure 12-5 lists typical functional units and their purpose within an enterprise. The sections that follow discuss the types of information systems and software used within these units.

FUNCTIONAL UNITS WITHIN AN ENTERPRISE

Functional Unit	Description
Accounting and Finance	Responsible for managing the business's money. Accounting department tracks every financial transaction that occurs within the company. Finance department manages the business's money as efficiently as possible.
Human Resources (HR)	Responsible for recruiting and promoting employees, maintaining employee records, evaluating employees, training employees, and managing employee benefits and compensation.
Engineering or Product Development	Responsible for developing ideas into a product that can be used by customers. Ensures that the product can be manufactured effectively and designs the methods for manufacturing the product.
Manufacturing	Responsible for converting raw materials into physical products.
Marketing	Responsible for researching the market in which a business operates to determine the products and features that the business should develop. Determines the demographics to target with sales efforts and informs the target market about the company's products through advertising and education.
Sales	Responsible for selling the company's products and services.
Distribution	Responsible for delivery of products to customers.
Customer Service	Responsible for maintaining a relationship with a customer both before and after a sale has been made.
Information Technology	Responsible for designing, purchasing, implementing, testing, and maintaining information systems for the rest of the organization. Sometimes called the information services (IS) department.

FIGURE 12-5 An enterprise is composed of several functional units.

ACCOUNTING AND FINANCE   Figure 12-6 illustrates the separate functions of accounting and financial systems used by accounting and finance departments. Accounting software manages everyday transactions, such as sales and payments to suppliers. Financial software helps managers budget, forecast, and analyze. Both types of software include comprehensive and flexible reporting tools to assist managers in making decisions, provide historical documentation, and meet regulatory requirements.

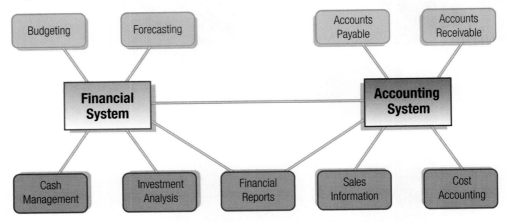

FIGURE 12-6   Accounting and financial systems perform different tasks, but share information and produce financial reports that help management make decisions.

HUMAN RESOURCES   A **human resources information system** (**HRIS**) manages one or more human resources functions (Figure 12-7). A human resources information system and its associated software help a company such as Wal-Mart maintain records on its 1.3 million employees.

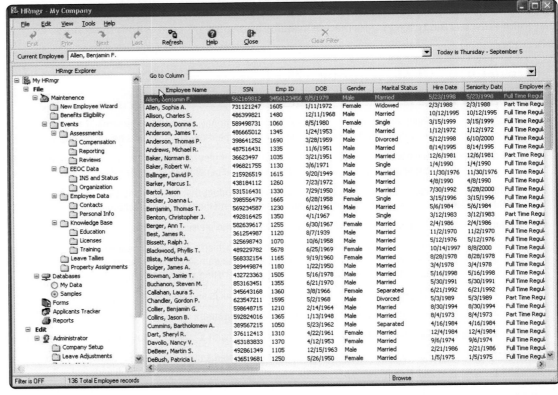

FIGURE 12-7   A human resources information system (HRIS) allows human resources personnel to manage employee information, such as benefits, personal information, performance evaluations, training, and vacation time.

An employee relationship management (ERM) system automates and manages much of the communications between employees and the business. For example, an employee may interact with employee relationship management software to gather information regarding the employee's retirement account. Most employee relationship management software includes a Web interface for the employees and the human resources personnel, allowing both to interact with the system when they are in the office or at home.

ENGINEERING OR PRODUCT DEVELOPMENT Professional workers, such as engineers, require specialized software and systems to perform their tasks. **Computer-aided design** (**CAD**) uses a computer and special software to aid in product design.

Computer-aided engineering (**CAE**) uses computers to test product designs. Using computer-aided engineering, engineers can test the design of a car or bridge before it is built. These sophisticated programs simulate the effects of wind, temperature, weight, and stress on product shapes and materials.

MANUFACTURING Manufacturing information systems and software not only assist in the actual assembly process, but also assist in scheduling and managing the inventory of parts and products. **Computer-aided manufacturing** (**CAM**) is the use of computers to control production equipment. Computer-aided manufacturing production equipment includes software-controlled drilling, lathe, welding, and milling machines.

Computer-integrated manufacturing (**CIM**) uses computers to integrate the many different operations of the manufacturing process, using such technologies as computer-aided design, computer-aided engineering, and computer-aided manufacturing (Figure 12-8).

Material Requirements Planning (**MRP**) is an approach to information management in a manufacturing environment that uses software to help monitor and control processes related to production. Material Requirements Planning focuses on issues related to inventory of parts and forecasting future demand so that materials needed for manufacturing can be on hand when they are needed.

WEB LINK 12-1

Employee Relationship Management

For more information, visit scsite.com/dcf2e/ ch12/weblink and then click Employee Relationship Management.

FIGURE 12-8 Computer-integrated manufacturing (CIM) speeds the manufacturing process and reduces product defects.

MARKETING   A **marketing information system** serves as a central repository for the tasks of the marketing functional unit. One type of marketing information system is a market research system, which stores and analyzes data gathered from demographics and surveys. Market research software assists in target marketing by allowing marketing personnel to query databases based on criteria such as income, gender, previous purchases, and favorite recreational activities.

SALES   **Sales force automation (SFA)** software equips traveling salespeople with the electronic tools they need to be more productive. Sales force automation software helps salespeople manage customer contacts, schedule customer meetings, log customer interactions, manage product information, and take orders from customers.

Sales force automation software (Figure 12-9) often runs on PDAs or notebook computers. The PDA or notebook computer may connect wirelessly to the central office, allowing the salesperson to access up-to-date corporate information in real time no matter where he or she is.

Some sales force automation programs allow the salesperson to upload information to the central office at the end of the day or end of the week. The programs also allow salespeople to download updated product and pricing information.

WEB LINK 12-2

Sales Force Automation

For more information, visit scsite.com/dcf2e/ ch12/weblink and then click Sales Force Automation.

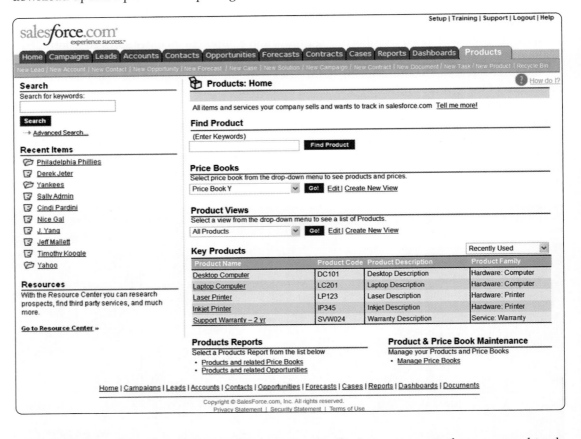

FIGURE 12-9
Sales force automation (SFA) software allows the sales force to manage customer and prospective customer relationships more effectively.

DISTRIBUTION   **Distribution systems** provide forecasting for inventory control, manage and track shipping of products, and provide information and analysis on inventory in warehouses. Some distribution systems rely on GPS and other navigation technologies to track shipping in real time.

CUSTOMER SERVICE   **Customer interaction management (CIM)** software manages the day-to-day interactions with customers, such as telephone calls, e-mail interactions, Web interactions, and instant messaging sessions. A customer interaction management program routes customer telephone calls to the most appropriate support person depending on the identity of the customer or responses the customer gives to prompts. Customer interaction management software also assists support personnel in providing the best solutions for customers.

FAQ 12-1

When should I supply personal information to a company?

Companies gather personal information about consumers for a variety of reasons. Unless you are sure you want the company to communicate with you in some way, few reasons exist to supply personal information to a company. Ask the company why it needs the information and use your judgment. Most companies can supply you with a privacy policy upon request. For more information, visit scsite.com/dcf2e/ch12/faq and then click Sharing Personal Information.

INFORMATION TECHNOLOGY The information technology department makes technology decisions for the enterprise, such as a decision whether to build or buy new customer interaction management information systems or when a computer or information system has outlived its useful life. Many companies elevate the importance of information technology by including a **chief information officer (CIO)** executive position that reports to the CEO.

General Purpose Information Systems

Some information systems in an enterprise cross the boundaries of functional units. These general purpose, or enterprise-wide, systems become necessary in an enterprise for two reasons. First, functional units within an enterprise have a significant need to share data among the units. Second, enterprise-wide systems can collect and combine data more quickly and provide executive management access to a more up-to-date and accurate view of what is happening in the organization. Advances in computing speed, storage capacity, security, and networking have made enterprise-wide systems more attractive to companies in recent years.

General purpose information systems generally fall into one of five categories: office information systems, transaction processing systems, management information systems, decision support systems, and expert systems. The following sections present each type of these general purpose information systems.

OFFICE INFORMATION SYSTEMS An **office information system (OIS)** is an information system that enables employees to perform tasks using computers and other electronic devices, instead of manually. An office information system increases employee productivity and assists with communications among employees. Some people describe an office information system as office automation.

An office information system supports many administrative activities. With this type of system, users create and distribute graphics and documents, send messages, schedule appointments, browse the Web, and publish Web pages. All levels of users utilize and benefit from the features of an office information system.

An office information system uses many common software products to support its activities. Typical software in an office information system includes word processing, spreadsheet, database, presentation graphics, e-mail, Web browser, Web page authoring, personal information management, and groupware. To send text, graphics, audio, and video to others, an office information system uses communications technology such as voice mail, fax, and video conferencing.

TRANSACTION PROCESSING SYSTEMS A **transaction processing system (TPS)** is an information system that captures and processes data from day-to-day business activities. When you make a purchase with a credit card at a store, you are interacting with a transaction processing system (Figure 12-10). A transaction is an individual business activity. Examples of transactions are deposits, payments, orders, and reservations. In a company, clerical staff typically uses computers and special software to perform activities associated with a transaction processing system.

FIGURE 12-10 When you make a purchase with a credit card, you are using a transaction processing system.

Transaction processing systems were among the first computerized systems that processed business data. Many people initially referred to the functions of a transaction processing system as data processing. The first transaction processing systems computerized an existing manual system. The intent of these transaction processing systems was to process faster, reduce clerical costs, and improve customer service.

Early TPSs mostly used batch processing. With batch processing, the computer collects data over time and processes all transactions later, as a group. As computers became more powerful, system developers created online transaction processing information systems. With online transaction processing (OLTP), the computer processes each transaction as it is entered. Today, most transaction processing systems use online transaction processing.

For example, when you register for classes, your school probably uses online transaction processing. The registration clerk enters your desired schedule. The computer immediately prints your statement of classes.

MANAGEMENT INFORMATION SYSTEMS   A **management information system (MIS)** is an information system that generates accurate, timely, and organized information, so managers and other users can make decisions, solve problems, supervise activities, and track progress.

Management information systems often are integrated with transaction processing systems. To process a sales order, the transaction processing system records the sale, updates the customer's account balance, and reduces the inventory count. Using this information, the related management information system produces reports that recap daily sales activities, summarize weekly and monthly sales activities, list customers with past due account balances, chart slow- or fast-selling products, and highlight inventory items that need reordering.

An management information system creates three basic types of reports: detailed, summary, and exception (Figure 12-11). A detailed report usually lists just transactions. For example, a Detailed Order Report lists orders taken during a given period. A summary report consolidates data usually with totals, tables, or graphs, so managers can review it quickly and easily.

An exception report identifies data outside of a normal condition. These out-of-the-ordinary conditions, called the exception criteria, define the normal activity or status range. For example, an Inventory Exception Report notifies the purchasing department of items it needs to reorder.

FIGURE 12-11a   (detailed report)

DETAILED ORDER REPORT for May 3, 2006

Part Number	Part Description	Customer	Quantity Purchased
93814	Dorm refrigerator	Union Bookstore	5
		University Supplies	2
10761	Large futon	Eddes Rentals	3
		Middleton Furnishings	6
88732	Hot plate	Union Bookstore	9
		Sam's Quick-Mart	12
		University Supplies	7
30021	Closet organizer	Eddes Rentals	3
		Lilac Imports	4

FIGURE 12-11c   (exception report)

INVENTORY EXCEPTION REPORT for May 3, 2006

Part Number	Part Description	Total Quantity on Hand	Reorder Point
93814	Dorm refrigerator	2	5
30021	Closet organizer	7	20

FIGURE 12-11b   (summary report)

SUMMARY REPORT for May 3, 2006

Part Number	Part Description	Total Quantity Sold	Supplier
93814	Dorm refrigerator	7	Van Electric
10761	Large futon	9	Carolina
88732	Hot plate	28	Chen Imports
30021	Closet organizer	7	Wilson Enterprises

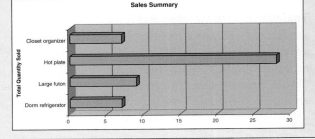

FIGURE 12-11   Three basic types of information generated in an MIS are detailed, summary, and exception.

Exception reports save managers time. Instead of searching through a detailed report, managers simply review the exception report. These reports help managers focus on situations that require immediate decisions or actions. Most information systems support all three types of reports shown in Figure 12-11.

DECISION SUPPORT SYSTEMS   A **decision support system** (**DSS**) helps users analyze data and make decisions. Often, a transaction processing system or management information system does not generate the type of report a manager needs to make a decision.

Programs that analyze data, such as those in a decision support system, sometimes are called online analytical processing (OLAP) programs. A decision support system uses data from internal and external sources. Internal sources of data might include sales orders, Material Requirements Planning results, inventory records, or financial data from accounting and financial analyses. Data from external sources could include interest rates, population trends, costs of new housing construction, or raw material pricing.

Some decision support systems include their own query languages, statistical analyses, spreadsheets, and graphics that help users retrieve data and analyze the results. Some also allow managers to create a model of the factors affecting a decision. A product manager might need to decide on a price for a new product. A simple model for finding the best price would include factors for the expected sales volume at various price levels. The model allows the user to ask what-if questions and view the expected results.

A special type of decision support system, called an executive information system (EIS), supports the strategic information needs of executive management. An executive information system presents information as charts and tables that show trends, ratios, and statistics (Figure 12-12).

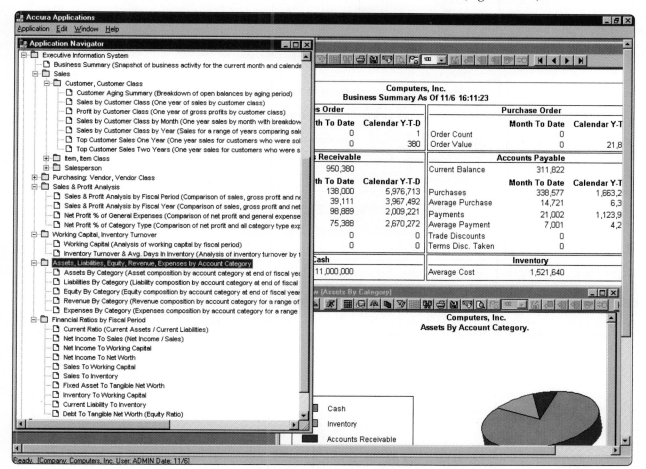

FIGURE 12-12   This executive information system (EIS) presents information to senior management in the form of graphics and reports.

EXPERT SYSTEMS   An **expert system** is an information system that captures and stores the knowledge of human experts and then imitates human reasoning and decision making. Figure 12-13 shows how one expert system assists with a medical diagnosis.

Expert systems consist of two main components: a knowledge base and inference rules. A knowledge base is the combined subject knowledge and experiences of the human experts. The inference rules are a set of logical judgments that are applied to the knowledge base each time a user describes a situation to the expert system.

FIGURE 12-13   A SAMPLE EXPERT SYSTEM

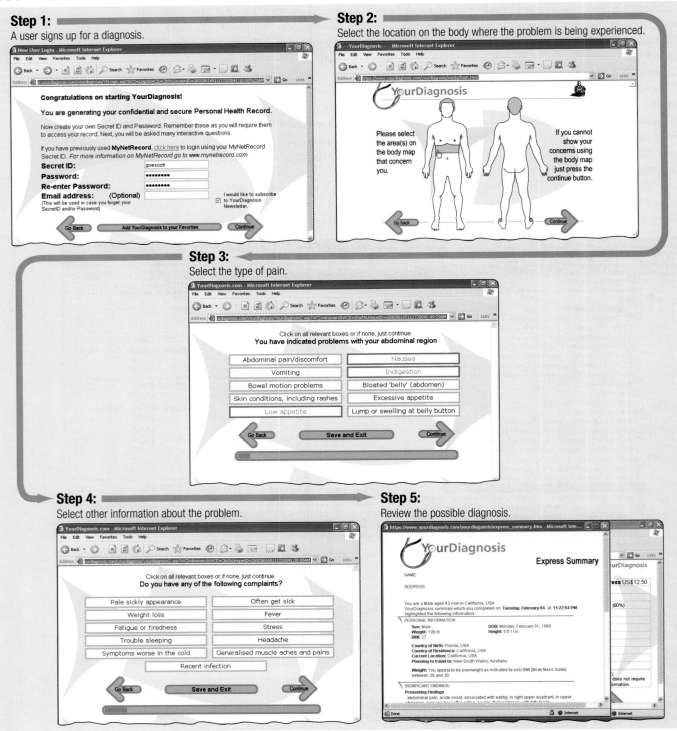

Expert systems are one aspect of an exciting branch of computer science called artificial intelligence. **Artificial intelligence (AI)** is the application of human intelligence to computers. Artificial intelligence technology senses a person's actions and, based on logical assumptions and prior experience, takes the appropriate action to complete the task. Artificial intelligence has a variety of capabilities, including speech recognition, logical reasoning, and creative responses.

Enterprises employ expert systems in a variety of roles, such as answering customer questions, training new employees, and analyzing data.

Integrated Information Systems

It often is difficult to classify an information system as belonging to only one of the five general types of information systems. Much of today's application software supports transaction processing and creates management information system reports. Other applications provide transaction processing, management information, and decision support.

ENTERPRISE RESOURCE PLANNING   **Enterprise resource planning (ERP)** provides centralized, integrated software applications to help manage and coordinate the ongoing activities of the enterprise, including manufacturing and distribution, accounting, finance, sales, product planning, and human resources. Figure 12-14 shows how enterprise resource planning fits into the operations of an enterprise.

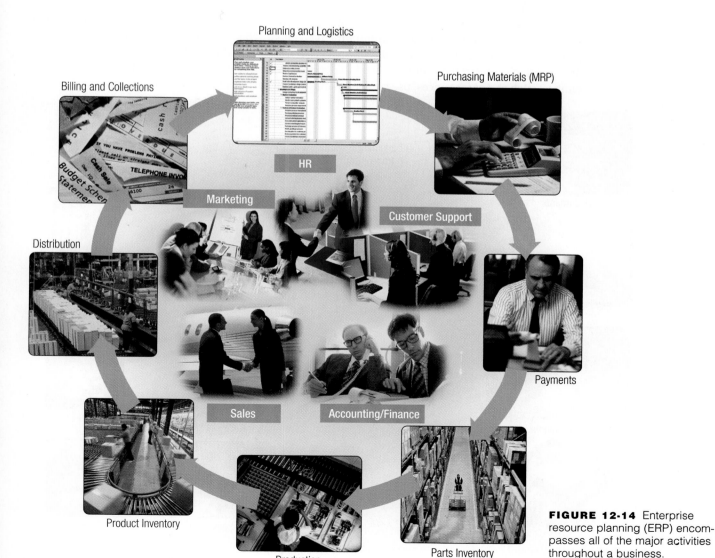

Planning and Logistics

Purchasing Materials (MRP)

Billing and Collections

HR

Marketing

Customer Support

Distribution

Payments

Sales

Accounting/Finance

Product Inventory

Parts Inventory

Production

FIGURE 12-14 Enterprise resource planning (ERP) encompasses all of the major activities throughout a business.

The enterprise resource planning system installed at each company must be customized to match the business requirements of the enterprise. At a large company, an enterprise resource planning system may take four to six years to implement and cost hundreds of millions of dollars. The company hopes to regain the investment through the advantages offered by enterprise resource planning.

Advantages of enterprise resource planning include complete integration of information systems across departments, better project management, and better customer service. Better and faster reporting of the state of the enterprise leads managers to better decisions. Enterprise resource planning also helps to better manage the global nature of many enterprises. The reliance on one information system, rather than up to several hundred systems, allows the information technology department to focus on one type of technology and simplifies relationships with information technology vendors.

CUSTOMER RELATIONSHIP MANAGEMENT   A **customer relationship management (CRM)** system manages information about customers, interactions with customers, past purchases, and interests. Customer relationship management mainly is used across sales, marketing, and customer service departments. Customer relationship management software tracks leads and inquiries from customers, stores a history of all correspondence and sales to a customer, and allows for tracking of outstanding issues with customers.

CONTENT MANAGEMENT SYSTEMS   A **content management system (CMS)** is a combination of databases, software, and procedures that organizes and allows access to various forms of documents and other files, including images and multimedia content. The content management system also provides security controls for the content, such as who is allowed to add, view, and modify content and on which content the user is allowed to perform those operations (Figure 12-15). Publishing entities, such as news services, use content management systems to keep Web sites up-to-date.

WEB LINK 12-3

Enterprise Resource Planning

For more information, visit scsite.com/dcf2e/ch12/weblink and then click Enterprise Resource Planning.

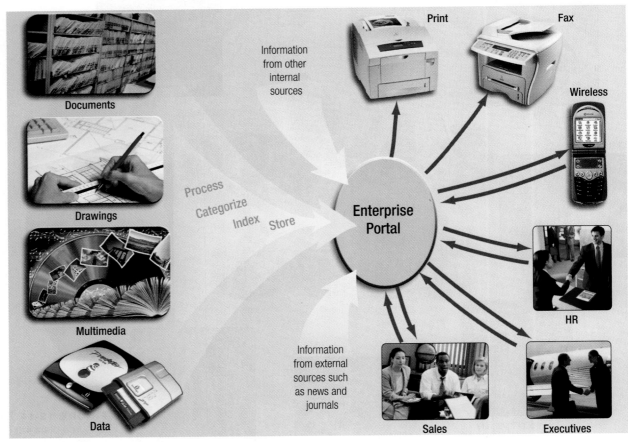

FIGURE 12-15   A content management system (CMS) helps a company classify and manage volumes of documents and media for future retrieval and use.

Test your knowledge of pages 452 through 466 in Quiz Yourself 12-1.

QUIZ YOURSELF 12-1

Instructions: Find the true statement below. Then, rewrite the remaining false statements so they are true.

1. The main task of executive managers is to make short-term, tactical decisions.

2. An information system is a set of hardware, software, and people that works together to produce information.

3. A human resources information system serves as a central repository for the tasks of the marketing functional unit.

4. Customer interaction management software manages the day-to-day interactions with customers.

5. Decision support systems capture and store the knowledge of human experts and then imitate human reasoning and decision making.

6. Enterprise resource planning is a combination of databases, software, and procedures that organizes and allows access to various forms of documents and files.

Quiz Yourself Online: To further check your knowledge of enterprise information requirements and information systems used throughout the enterprise, visit scsite.com/dc2fe/ch12/quiz and then click Objectives 1 – 3.

ENTERPRISE-WIDE TECHNOLOGIES

Several technologies adopted by enterprises allow companies flexibility and the ability to move swiftly in a business environment. Some of the common technologies used in enterprises include portals, electronic data interchange, data warehouses, extranets, Web services, workflow, and virtual private networks. The following sections discuss each of these technologies.

Portals

A **portal** is a collection of links, content, and services presented on a Web page and designed to guide users to information they likely are to find interesting for their particular job function. A portal often includes searching capabilities or a link to a search engine, such as Google. Users typically can customize the portal Web site to meet their needs.

Information from external sources included on a portal Web page can include weather, news, reference tools, and instant messaging (Figure 12-16).

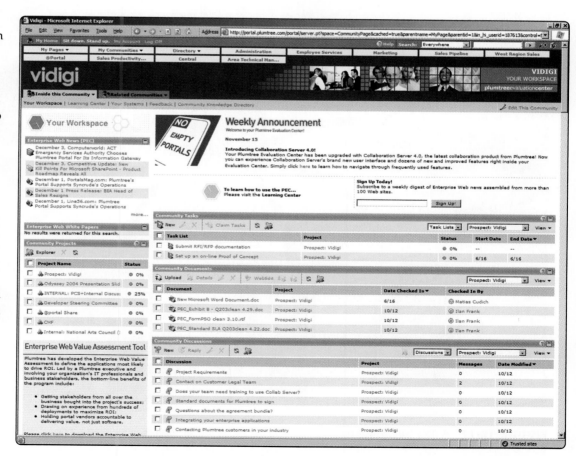

FIGURE 12-16 Portals allow users quick access to a multitude of information sources that they access on a regular basis.

EDI

EDI (electronic data interchange) is a set of standards that controls the transfer of business data and information among computers both within and among enterprises. One of the first steps in the development of e-commerce was electronic data interchange, which originally was created to eliminate paperwork and improve response time in business interactions. Today, businesses use these standards to communicate with industry partners over the Internet and telephone lines.

Data Warehouses

A **data warehouse** is a huge database that stores and manages the data required to analyze historical and current transactions. Software applications such as enterprise resource planning programs store and access data in a data warehouse.

Most data warehouses include one or more databases and one or more information systems storing data in the data warehouse. The data in the databases consists of transaction data required for decision making. This data may come from internal or external sources (Figure 12-17). Some data warehouses use Web farming for their external data. Web farming is the process of collecting data from the Internet as a source for the data warehouse.

Another growing external source of information is a click stream. A click stream is a collection of every action that users make as they move through a Web site. By analyzing visitors' click streams, companies identify consumer preferences and determine which Web pages are most attractive to visitors.

WEB LINK 12-4

Data Warehouse

For more information, visit scsite.com/dcf2e/ch12/weblink and then click Data Warehouse.

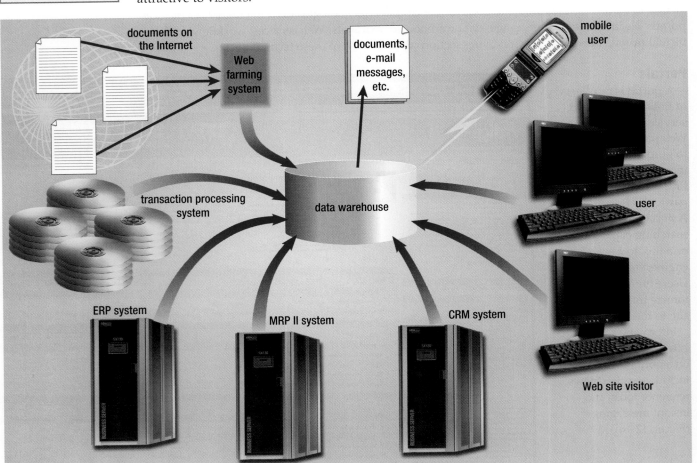

FIGURE 12-17   A data warehouse can receive data from a variety of sources, including company transactions, the Internet, and Web site visitor click streams.

The data in a data warehouse is accurate as of a moment in time. It contains snapshots of current and historical transactions. Thus, you usually do not change the content of existing data in a data warehouse. As time passes, you simply add new data. The data warehouse also contains summarizations of this data.

Extranets

An **extranet** is the portion of a company's network that allows customers or suppliers of a company to access parts of an enterprise's intranet. An extranet provides a secure, physical connection to the company's network. Customers may use the extranet to place and monitor orders electronically or to make payments. Suppliers may check inventory levels of the parts they supply to the company and receive orders and payments from the company. Extranets improve efficiency by replacing the postal service, faxes, or telephone calls as the communications medium of choice.

Web Services

Web services include a relatively new set of software technologies that allows businesses to create products and B2B (business-to-business) interactions over the Internet. Web services do not include traditional user interfaces, such as a Web page. Rather, users build their own interfaces to the Web services when necessary. Two popular platforms for building and running Web services are the Sun Microsystems J2EE platform and the Microsoft .NET platform.

For example, a company may provide inventory information as a Web service (Figure 12-18). Customers or suppliers that want to access only this information need to use an Internet connection to communicate with the Web service and request the information from the Web service. A customer may ask for a quantity of an item in stock and receive back a number from the Web service. How the customer uses that information, whether displayed to an end user or stored in a database, is up to the customer. Typically, the customer, or consumer, of the Web service must write an application to use the Web service.

Workflow

A **workflow** is a defined process that identifies the specific set of steps involved in completing a particular project or business process. A workflow may be a written set of rules or a set of rules that exists in an information system.

A **workflow application** is a program that assists in the management and tracking of all the activities in a business process from start to finish. Enterprises use workflow applications to assist in defining complex workflows.

FIGURE 12-18 HOW A WEB SERVICE MIGHT WORK

Step 1:
A user at the supplier requests inventory information from the company's Web site.

Step 2:
The company's Web page sends a request to the inventory Web service.

Step 3:
Raw inventory information is sent back to the company's Web server in XML format over the Internet.

Step 4:
The Web server formats the results as a Web page and sends the resulting Web page back to the user.

Virtual Private Network

Many companies today allow access to their company networks through a virtual private network. When a mobile user, remote office, vendor, or customer connects to a company's network using the Internet, a **virtual private network** (**VPN**) provides them with a secure connection to the company network server, as if they had a private line. Virtual private networks help to ensure that transmitted data is safe from being intercepted by unauthorized people (Figure 12-19). VPNs securely extend the company's internal network beyond the physical boundaries of the company. The secure connection created over the Internet between the user's computer and the company's network is called a VPN tunnel.

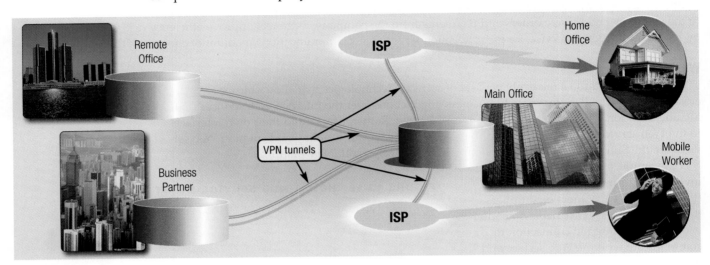

FIGURE 12-19   A virtual private network (VPN) allows a company to extend its internal network securely.

E-COMMERCE

Several market sectors have taken advantage of business opportunities on the Web. The more popular market segments include retail, finance, entertainment and media, travel, and health. The following paragraphs describe how the general public interacts with each of these types of enterprises on the Web.

E-Retailing

Retailing is one of the more visible market sectors of e-commerce. In retail, merchants sell products and services directly to a buyer. **E-retail**, also called e-tail, occurs when retailers use the Web to sell their products and services. Enterprises have adopted e-retail as a new way to reach customers. Figure 12-20 shows how an e-retail transaction might occur.

For example, a customer (consumer) visits an online business at the company's electronic storefront and adds items to a shopping cart. When ready to complete the sale, the customer proceeds to the checkout. At this time, the customer enters personal and financial data through a secure Web connection. The transaction and financial data automatically are verified at a banking Web site. Several methods are available through which a company can accept payments from a customer.

If the bank or merchant account provider approves the transaction, the customer receives a confirmation notice of the purchase. Then, the e-retailer processes the order and sends it to the fulfillment center where it is packaged and shipped. Inventory systems then are updated. The e-retailer notifies the bank of the shipment, and payment is sent via electronic channels to the e-retailer. Shipping information is posted on the Internet, so the customer can track the order. The customer typically receives the order a few days after the purchase. Read At Issue 12-2 for a related discussion.

FIGURE 12-20   HOW A BUSINESS-TO-CONSUMER (B2C) E-COMMERCE TRANSACTION TAKES PLACE

Step 1:
The customer displays the e-retailer's electronic storefront.

Step 2:
The customer collects purchases in an electronic shopping cart.

Step 3:
The customer enters payment information in a secure Web site. The e-retailer sends financial information to a bank.

Step 4:
The bank performs security checks and sends authorization back to the e-retailer.

Step 7:
While the order travels to the customer, shipping information is posted on the Web.

Step 6:
The fulfillment center packages the order, prepares it for shipment, and then sends a report to the server where records are updated.

Step 5:
The e-retailer's Web server sends confirmation to the customer, processes the order, and then sends it to the fulfillment center.

Step 8:
The order is delivered to the customer.

Finance

Financial institutions include any business that manages the circulation of money, grants credit, makes investments, or meets banking needs. These include banks, mortgage companies, brokerage firms, and insurance companies. In the past, financial institutions were strictly traditional bricks-and-mortar institutions. Today, many also conduct business on the Internet.

Online banking allows users to pay bills from their computer, that is, transfer money electronically from their account to a payee's account such as the electric company or telephone company. At anytime, online banking users also can download transactions such as cleared checks, ATM withdrawals, and deposits, which allows them to have an up-to-date bank statement.

With **online trading**, users invest in stocks, options, bonds, treasuries, certificates of deposit, money markets, annuities, mutual funds, and so on — without using a broker. Many investors prefer online stock trading because the transaction fee for each trade usually is substantially less than when trading through a broker.

FAQ 12-2

How can I tell that a financial Web site is secure?

Make sure that the Web site address begins with https:// rather than http:// whenever you are viewing or transmitting personal financial information on a Web site. Financial Web sites should include both privacy and security policies for you to read. The security policy should tell you how the information is both transmitted and then stored securely once the company has the information. For more information, visit scsite.com/dcf2e/ch12/faq and then click Web Site Security.

Health

Many Web sites provide up-to-date medical, fitness, nutrition, or exercise information. As with any other information on the Web, users should verify the legitimacy of the Web site before relying on its information.

Some of these health-related Web sites maintain databases of doctors and dentists to help individuals find the one who suits their needs. They also may have chat rooms, so people can talk to others diagnosed with similar conditions. Read At Issue 12-3 for a related discussion.

Many bricks-and-mortar pharmacies have an online counterpart that exists on the Web, allowing customers to refill prescriptions and ask pharmacists questions using customer interaction management software. Some Web sites even allow consumers to order prescription drugs online and have them delivered directly to their door.

AT ISSUE 12-3

Would You Trust an Online Medical Diagnosis?

More than 2.5 million consumers have turned to a medical-practice Web site for a diagnosis, and 35 million people claim they would be willing to try such a Web site. Most physicians' Web sites structure an online doctor's visit by having patients complete a form containing a series of questions and decision trees. Based on the responses, doctors suggest probable diagnoses and even may offer an order form that can be used, along with a credit card, to order prescribed medicines. Medical-practice Web sites provide greater access to medical information and allow doctors more time to see patients with urgent problems. Some people, though, question any medical diagnosis based on a form, worry about patient privacy, and believe obtaining prescription medicines online is unsafe. Should a physician be allowed to diagnose an ailment and/or dispense prescription medicine online? Why or why not? Does the nature of the ailment make a difference? If a problem occurs, should a medical-practice Web site be open to a malpractice lawsuit? Why? Would you trust an online medical diagnosis? Why or why not?

Entertainment and Media

The technology behind the Web has enabled entertainment and media to take many forms. Music, videos, news, sporting events, and 3-D multiplayer games are a growing part of the Web's future. Newsprint on the Web is not replacing the newspaper, but enhancing it and reaching different populations. Streaming technology currently supports live radio broadcasting, live videos, and live concerts. Users can purchase music online and download MP3 files directly to a computer hard disk, allowing them to listen to the purchased music immediately from a computer or any MP3 player.

Travel

The Web provides many travel-related services. If you need directions, you simply can enter a starting point and destination, and many Web sites provide detailed directions along with a map. Users can make airline reservations and reserve a hotel or car.

Some of these Web sites are shopping bots that save users time by doing all the investigative cost-comparison work. A **shopping bot** is a Web site that searches the Internet for the best price on a product or service in which you are interested (Figure 12-21).

WEB LINK 12-5

Online Travel

For more information, visit scsite.com/dcf2e/ch12/weblink and then click Online Travel.

FIGURE 12-21
At Priceline.com, you name the price you are willing to pay, and Priceline.com finds available commodities such as flights, hotel rooms, and car rentals that meet your budget. Priceline.com is a shopping bot.

Other Business Services

Enterprises use the Web to provide services to consumers and other businesses. Public relations, online advertising, direct mail, recruiting, credit, sales, market research, technical support, training, software consulting, and Internet access represent a few of the areas of service.

Test your knowledge of pages 467 through 473 in Quiz Yourself 12-2.

QUIZ YOURSELF 12-2

Instructions: Find the true statement below. Then, rewrite the remaining false statements so they are true.

1. A portal is the portion of a company's network that allows customers or suppliers of a company to access parts of an enterprise's intranet.

2. A data warehouse is a huge database that stores and manages the data required to analyze historical and current transactions.

3. A VPN is a server that is placed on a network with the sole purpose of providing storage to users and information systems attached to the network.

4. A workflow application helps an enterprise collect, archive, index, and retrieve its resources.

Quiz Yourself Online: To further check your knowledge of technologies used throughout the enterprise and e-commerce, visit scsite.com/dcf2e/ch12/quiz and then click Objectives 4 – 5.

ENTERPRISE HARDWARE

Enterprise hardware allows large organizations to manage and store information and data using devices geared for heavy use, maximum availability, and maximum efficiency.

One of the goals of an enterprise's hardware is to maintain a high level of availability to end users. The availability of hardware to users is a measure of how often it is online. Highly available hardware is accessible 24 hours a day, 365 days a year.

The following sections discuss a variety of enterprise hardware solutions.

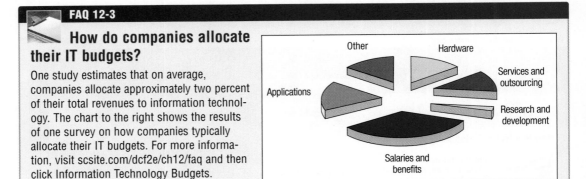

FAQ 12-3

How do companies allocate their IT budgets?

One study estimates that on average, companies allocate approximately two percent of their total revenues to information technology. The chart to the right shows the results of one survey on how companies typically allocate their IT budgets. For more information, visit scsite.com/dcf2e/ch12/faq and then click Information Technology Budgets.

Source: Information Week

RAID

For applications that depend on reliable data access, users must have the data available when they attempt to access it. Some manufacturers provide a type of hard disk system that connects several smaller disks into a single unit that acts like a single large hard disk. A group of two or more integrated hard disks is called a **RAID (redundant array of independent disks)**. Although quite expensive for large computers, RAID is more reliable than traditional hard disks (Figure 12-22). Networks and Internet servers often use RAID.

A RAID system duplicates data, instructions, and information to improve data reliability. The simplest RAID storage design, called mirroring, writes data on two disks at the same time to duplicate the data. This configuration enhances storage reliability because, if a drive should fail, a duplicate of the requested item is available elsewhere within the array of disks.

FIGURE 12-22   A group of two or more integrated hard disks, called a RAID (redundant array of independent disks), often is used with network servers. Shown here is a rack-mounted RAID chassis including the hard disks.

Network Attached Storage and Storage Area Networks

Network attached storage (**NAS**) is a server that is placed on a network with the sole purpose of providing storage to users and information systems attached to the network (Figure 12-23a). A network attached storage server often is called a storage appliance because it is a piece of equipment with only one function — to provide additional storage. Administrators quickly add storage to an existing network simply by attaching a new network attached storage server to the network.

A **storage area network (SAN)** is a high-speed network with the sole purpose of providing storage to other servers to which it is attached (Figure 12-23b). A storage area network is a network that includes only storage devices. High-speed fiber-optic cable connects other networks and servers to the storage area network, so the networks and servers have fast access to large storage capacities.

FIGURE 12-23a   (network attached storage on a LAN)

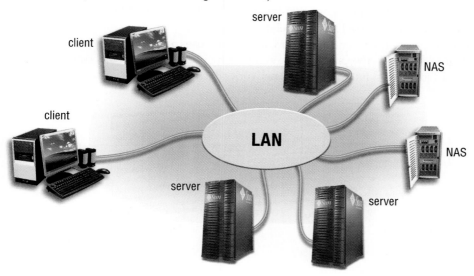

FIGURE 12-23b   (a SAN provides centralized storage for servers and networks)

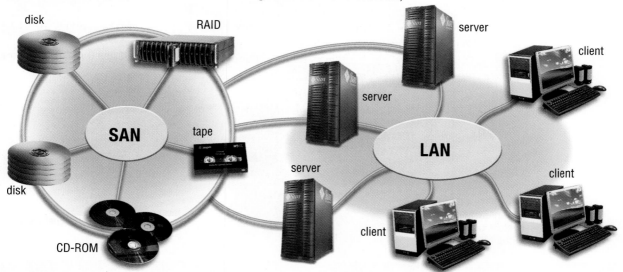

FIGURE 12-23   Network attached storage (NAS) and a storage area network (SAN) connect to existing servers and networks in different ways.

WEB LINK 12-6

NAS and SAN

For more information, visit scsite.com/dcf2e/ch12/weblink and then click NAS and SAN.

Enterprise Storage Systems

Many companies use networks. Data, information, and instructions stored on the network must be easily accessible to all authorized users. The data, information, and instructions also must be secure, so unauthorized users cannot access the network. An **enterprise storage system** is a strategy that focuses on the availability, protection, organization, and backup of storage in a company.

The goal of an enterprise storage system is to consolidate storage so operations run as efficiently as possible. Most enterprise storage systems manage extraordinary amounts of data. For example, one large retailer manages a 485-terabyte (485,000,000,000,000 bytes) storage system to store sales data. Read At Issue 12-4 for a related discussion.

To implement an enterprise storage system, a company uses a combination of techniques. As shown in Figure 12-24, an enterprise storage system may use servers, RAID, a tape library, CD-ROM and DVD-ROM jukeboxes, Internet backup, network attached storage devices, and/or a storage area network.

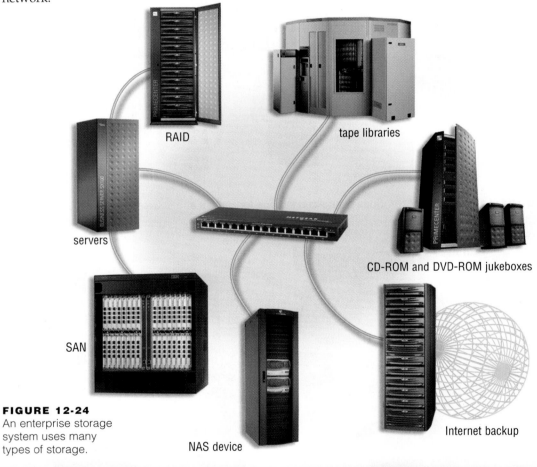

RAID

tape libraries

servers

CD-ROM and DVD-ROM jukeboxes

SAN

NAS device

Internet backup

FIGURE 12-24
An enterprise storage system uses many types of storage.

AT ISSUE 12-4

How Will Laws Requiring Retention of Business Records Affect Large Companies?

In 2002, the Sarbanes-Oxley Act was signed into law, providing a myriad of financial reporting requirements and guidelines for public companies. A main focus of the law is the retention of business records. As provisions of the law slowly have come into effect, companies have been faced with massive new data storage requirements for these records. For example, all e-mail messages within a company are considered to be business records and must be retained. Deleting stored e-mail messages constitutes a destruction of evidence infraction. Penalties include 20 years of prison for any employee who alters or destroys records or documents. IT departments are faced not only with understanding this complex law, but also with ensuring accuracy of financial data, determining policies for record retention, and building storage capacity to hold all of the data. Supporters of the law cite its need due to the recent wave of corporate scandals. Opponents say that the law is overreaching and costs too much for the added benefits. Is the Sarbanes-Oxley Act an unfair burden on companies? Why or why not? Should companies be able to engage in internal communications without the fear that those communications could be used against them later? Why or why not? How should companies go about reacting to the law?

Some companies manage an enterprise storage system in-house. Other enterprises elect to offload all (or at least the backup) storage management to an outside organization or online Web service. This practice is known as outsourcing. Some vendors focus on providing enterprise storage systems to clients. A data warehouse might seek this type of outside service.

Blade Servers

Blade servers, sometimes called ultradense servers, pack a complete computer server, such as a Web server or network server, on a single card, or blade, rather than a system unit. Each blade server includes a processor, memory, hard disk, network card, and ports on the card. The individual blades insert in a blade server chassis that can hold many blades. Using blade servers allows an organization to fit 16 or more blades in the physical space occupied by a single server. Figure 12-25 shows a blade and a chassis that holds many blades.

Besides the savings in space offered by blade servers, blade servers require less maintenance, use less energy, generate less heat, and easily are replaced or upgraded.

FIGURE 12-25 A blade server contains several very small servers, each on its own blade within the server.

High-Availability Systems

High-availability systems continue running and performing tasks for at least 99 percent of the time. Some users demand that high-availability systems be available for 99.99 percent of the time. A system that has uptime of 99.99 percent is nonfunctional for less than one hour per year. That one hour, called downtime, includes any time that the computer crashes, needs repairs, or requires installation of replacement or upgrade parts.

Telecommunications companies, such as local telephone companies, rely on high-availability systems to deliver telephone service. Emergency 911 communications centers require almost 100 percent uptime for their hardware and software applications as mandated by law. Centralized accounting or financial systems must be available to gather sales and other accounting information from locations scattered around the globe.

High-availability systems often include a feature called hot-swapping. Hot-swapping allows components, such as a RAID hard disk or power supplies, to be replaced while the rest of the system continues to perform its tasks. A high-availability system also may include redundant components. **Redundant components**, such as redundant power supplies, allow for a functioning component to take over automatically the tasks of a similar component that fails. When a component fails, the system administrator is notified, but the computer continues to perform its tasks because a redundant component has taken its place automatically in the system.

Scalability

As an enterprise grows, its information systems either must grow with it or must be replaced. **Scalability** is a measure of how well a computer hardware system, software application, or information system can grow to meet increasing performance demands. A system that is designed, built, or purchased when the company is small may be inadequate when the company doubles in size.

A company may find that its Web site is becoming overwhelmed by customers and prospective customers. If the Web site is scalable, then the Web administrator can add more Web servers to handle the additional visitors to the Web site. Similarly, an enterprise's storage needs usually grow daily, meaning that storage systems should be scalable to store the ever-growing data generated by users.

Adding additional hardware often is the easiest method to grow, or scale, an information system. Often, at some point, a system no longer scales and must be replaced with a new system.

Utility and Grid Computing

As the need for scalability increases, companies often find that using outside computing resources is more economical than building new computing capacity internally. Utility and grid computing are two new technologies that provide flexible and massive online computing power. **Utility computing**, or on demand computing, allows companies to use the processing power sitting idle in a network located somewhere else in the world. When the company uses the computing resources, they pay a fee based on the amount of computing time and other resources that they consume.

Grid computing combines many servers and/or personal computers on a network, such as the Internet, to act as one large computer. As with utility computing, a company may pay for the use of a grid based on the amount of processing time that it needs. Grid computing often is used in research environments, such as climate research and life science problems. Read Looking Ahead 12-2 for a look at the next generation of grid computing.

LOOKING AHEAD 12-2

The Future of Grid Computing

Depression, stroke, and epilepsy may be diagnosed and treated much more quickly with advances in grid computing. This same form of technology may help interpret signals from radio telescopes and discover the genetic information housed within proteins.

Near the end of this decade, scientists and engineers foresee using grid computing to study the climate and to conduct biomedical research that will end deadly diseases. In the business world, commercial applications for grid computing are expected to rake in $12 billion by 2007. For more information, visit scsite.com/dcf2e/ch12/looking and then click Grid Computing.

Interoperability

Enterprises typically build and buy a diverse set of information systems. An information system often must share information, or have **interoperability**, with other information systems within the enterprise. Information systems that more easily share information with other information systems are said to be open. Information systems that are more difficult to interoperate with other information systems are said to be closed, or proprietary. Recent open systems employ XML and Web services to allow a greater level of interoperability.

BACKUP PROCEDURES AND SECURITY

Business and home users can perform four types of backup: full, differential, incremental, or selective. A fifth type, continuous data protection, is used by large enterprises. A full backup, sometimes called an archival backup, copies all of the files in the computer. A full backup provides the best protection against data loss because it copies all program and data files. Performing a full backup can be time-consuming. A differential backup copies only the files that have changed since the last full backup. An incremental backup copies only the files that have changed since the last full or last incremental backup. A selective backup, sometimes called a partial backup, allows the user to choose specific files to back up, regardless of whether or not the files have changed since the last incremental backup. Continuous data protection (CDP), or continuous backup, is a system in which all data is backed up whenever a change is made. A continuous data protection plan keeps a journal of every transaction — reads, writes, and deletes — made to a server or servers.

Whatever backup procedures a company adopts, they should be stated clearly, documented in writing, and followed consistently.

Disaster Recovery Plan

A **disaster recovery plan** is a written plan describing the steps a company would take to restore computer operations in the event of a disaster. A disaster recovery plan contains four major components: the emergency plan, the backup plan, the recovery plan, and the test plan.

THE EMERGENCY PLAN An emergency plan specifies the steps to be taken immediately after a disaster strikes. All emergency plans should contain the following information:

1. Names and telephone numbers of people and organizations to notify (e.g., management, fire department, police department)
2. Procedures to follow with the computer equipment (e.g., equipment shutdown, power shutoff, file removal)
3. Employee evacuation procedures
4. Return procedures; that is, who can reenter the facility and what actions they are to perform

THE BACKUP PLAN Once the procedures in the emergency plan have been executed, the next step is to follow the backup plan. The backup plan specifies how a company uses backup files and equipment to resume information processing. The backup plan should specify the location of an alternate computer facility in the event the company's normal location is destroyed or unusable.

When operations are so important that a company cannot afford to lose the operations to a disaster, the company often maintains a hot site, which is a separate facility that mirrors the systems and operations of the critical site. The hot site always operates concurrently with the main site, so that if either site becomes unavailable, the other site continues to meet the company's needs.

The backup plan identifies these items:

1. The location of backup data, supplies, and equipment
2. The personnel responsible for gathering backup resources and transporting them to the alternate computer facility
3. A schedule indicating the order in which, and approximate time by which, each application should be up and running

For a backup plan to be successful, the company must back up all critical resources. Also, additional people, including possibly nonemployees, must be trained in the backup and recovery procedures because company personnel could be injured in a disaster.

FAQ 12-4

Should I have a backup plan?

Yes! Even home computers need a backup plan. You probably know someone who lost valuable personal information due to a hard disk crash or other problem. Most modern operating systems include backup software. You should familiarize yourself with the software, develop a plan, and test both backing up and recovering data. For more information, visit scsite.com/dcf2e/ch12/faq and then click Backup Software.

THE RECOVERY PLAN The recovery plan specifies the actions to be taken to restore full information processing operations. To prepare for disaster recovery, a company should establish planning committees, with each one responsible for different forms of recovery. For example, one committee is in charge of hardware replacement. Another is responsible for software replacement.

THE TEST PLAN To provide assurance that the disaster plan is complete, it should be tested. A disaster recovery test plan contains information for simulating various levels of disasters and recording an organization's ability to recover. In a simulation, all personnel follow the steps in the disaster recovery plan.

WEB LINK 12-7

Disaster Recovery

For more information, visit scsite.com/dcf2e/ ch12/weblink and then click Disaster Recovery.

Test your knowledge of pages 474 through 479 in Quiz Yourself 12-3.

QUIZ YOURSELF 12-3

Instructions: Find the true statement below. Then, rewrite the remaining false statements so they are true.

1. Network attached storage is a high-speed network with the sole purpose of providing storage to other servers to which it is attached.

2. Scalability refers to the ability of an information system to share information with other information systems.

3. A differential backup copies only the files that have changed since the last full or last incremental backup.

4. A full backup is the fastest backup method, requiring only minimal storage.

5. An emergency plan specifies how a company uses backup files and equipment to resume information processing.

6. The recovery plan specifies the actions to be taken to restore full information processing operations.

Quiz Yourself Online: To further check your knowledge of enterprise hardware, backup procedures, and a disaster recovery plan, visit scsite.com/dcf2e/ch12/quiz and then click Objectives 6 – 8.

CHAPTER SUMMARY

This chapter reviewed the special computing requirements present in an enterprise-sized organization. Various types of users within an organization require different types of information systems. Large information systems become more valuable when they communicate with each other and offer users a great deal of flexibility in interacting with the information system and other users. The chapter discussed e-retailing and the types of businesses that use e-commerce.

Enterprises manage complex hardware, including storage area networks, RAID, and blade servers. Requirements for this enterprise hardware often include high-availability, scalability, and interoperability which they meet with technologies such as grid and utility computing. The chapter also discussed the backup procedures present in a large organization.

CAREER CORNER

CIO

CIO (**chief information officer**) is the highest-ranking position in an information technology (IT) department. The CIO manages all of a company's information systems and computer resources. In large organizations, the CIO typically is a vice president and reports directly to the organization's CEO.

Depending on the organization, a CIO can be called an MIS (management information systems) manager, an IS (information systems) manager, or an IT (information technology) manager. Regardless of the title, the CIO determines an organization's information needs and provides the systems to meet those needs. The CIO sets an IT department's goals, policies, and procedures. In addition, the CIO evaluates technology, hires and supervises staff, oversees the network, directs user services, develops backup and disaster recovery plans, and manages the department budget. Perhaps most important, the CIO provides leadership, creating a vision for an IT department and helping the department deliver that vision.

Some CIOs work as consultants, providing corporate IT departments with short-term or long-term guidance. Most CIOs rise through the ranks of an organization's IT department. Generally, CIOs have a bachelor's degree or higher in computer science and at least ten years' experience in an IT department. Today, many CIOs also have an MBA. Pay reflects the importance of the CIO, with average salaries in excess of $180,000. For more information, visit scsite.com/dcf2e/ch12/careers and then click CIO.

SAP

Innovative Enterprise Software Developer

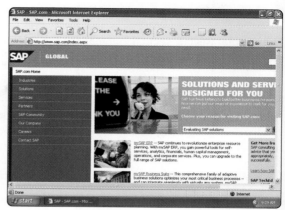

SAP wants to make innovation happen. Each employee is focused on turning new concepts into real economical and technological business benefits for customers.

Innovation was the foundation of the company. When IBM rejected an offer more than 30 years ago to develop a fully integrated software product that would support all facets of a company's operation, five of IBM's system engineers decided to form their own company in Germany to create such a product. In 1972 they founded SAP, an acronym for Systeme, Anwendugen, und Produkte in der Datenverarbeitung (Systems, Applications, and Products in Data Processing).

More than 10 million people worldwide use SAP's enterprise software products, which combine and link multiple applications to a central database and help business partners, employees, and customers work together. For more information, visit scsite.com/dcf2e/ch12/companies and then click SAP.

IBM

World's Largest Information Technology Company

In a survey of the world's 100 most powerful computers, 55 of IBM's products top the list in computing power with a total of 188 teraflops (trillions of calculations per second). But the company's products reach more than power users; IBM is the world's largest information technology corporation and works with consumers of all sizes.

IBM has a reputation for pioneering products. In 1911, three companies merged to sell a variety of business-related gadgets, including a machine that used punched cards to catalogue data. Nine years later, the company changed its name to International Business Machines (IBM). In its history of computer innovation, the company has developed the first family of computers with interchangeable software and peripherals, the personal computer with 16 KB of memory and a floppy disk drive, and the ThinkPad notebook computer. For more information, visit scsite.com/dcf2e/ch12/companies and then click IBM.

TECHNOLOGY TRAILBLAZERS

Tom Siebel
Siebel Systems CEO

Tom Siebel thought he had the talent and knowledge to run a "pretty good company." After working at Oracle, a leading database software developer, for six years, he then served as CEO for a small multimedia software company. He engineered that company's merger with Sybase, another large database software firm. In 1993, with his earnings from the merger, Siebel founded his pretty good company: Siebel Systems, Incorporated.

Siebel Systems sells customer relationship management (CRM) software, which tracks sales transactions from beginning to end. This process generally cuts costs and improves customer satisfaction. *Business Week* has recognized Siebel Systems as the world's second leading information technology company and Tom as one of the world's 25 best managers. For more information, visit scsite.com/dcf2e/ch12/people and then click Tom Siebel.

Jim Clark
Technology Innovator

When Jim Clark has an idea, people listen. As a professor at Stanford University, he developed a computer chip that processed 3-D images in real time. The high-powered chip formed the basis of Clark's first company, Silicon Graphics, and was used to create everything from suspension bridges to scenes in Hollywood movies.

Seeking more innovation opportunities, Clark contacted Marc Andreessen, creator of the Web browser, Mosaic. Together, they launched Netscape Communications Corporation, the source of one of the world's more successful Web browsers, Netscape Navigator.

Since then, Clark has started other computer-related companies: Healtheon, which links doctors, patients, and health insurance providers; MyCFO, a Web-based financial advisory firm; and Shutterfly, an online digital photo printing service. For more information, visit scsite.com/dcf2e/ch12/people and then click Jim Clark.

CHAPTER 12

Chapter Review

The Chapter Review section summarizes the concepts presented in this chapter. To obtain help from other students regarding any subject in this chapter, visit scsite.com/dcf2e/ch12/forum and post your thoughts or questions.

(1) What Are the Special Information Requirements of an Enterprise-Sized Corporation?

A large organization, or enterprise, requires special computing solutions because of its size and geographical extent. **Enterprise computing** uses computers in networks or series of interconnected networks to satisfy the information needs of an enterprise. The types of information employees require depend on their level in the company.

(2) What Information Systems Are Used in the Functional Units of an Enterprise?

An **information system** is a set of hardware, software, data, people, and procedures that works together to produce information. In an enterprise, each type of functional unit has specialized requirements for their information systems. A **human resources information system (HRIS)** manages one or more human resources functions. Accounting and financial systems manage everyday transactions and help budget. Engineers use **computer-aided design (CAD)** and **computer-aided engineering (CAE)**. **Computer-aided manufacturing (CAM)** and **computer-integrated manufacturing (CAI)** speed manufacturing. A **marketing information system** serves as a central repository for marketing tasks. **Sales force automation (SFA)** software equips salespeople with the tools they need. **Distribution systems** control inventory and manage shipping. **Customer interaction management (CIM)** software manages interactions with customers. The information technology (IT) department makes technology decisions for an enterprise.

(3) What Information Systems Are Used throughout an Enterprise?

Some general purpose information systems, or enterprise-wide systems, are used throughout an enterprise. A **transaction processing system (TPS)** captures and processes data from day-to-day business activities. A **management information system (MIS)** generates accurate, timely, and organized information, so users can make decisions, solve problems, and track progress. A **decision support system (DSS)** helps users analyze data and make decisions. **Enterprise resource planning (ERP)** provides applications to help manage and coordinate ongoing activities. **Customer relationship management (CRM)** systems manage information about customers. A **content management system (CMS)** organizes and allows access to various forms of documents and files.

Visit scsite.com/dcf2e/ch12/quiz or click the Quiz Yourself button. Click Objectives 1 – 3.

(4) What Are Types of Technologies Used throughout an Enterprise?

Technologies used throughout an enterprise include portals, electronic data interchange, data warehouses, extranets, Web services, workflow, and virtual private networks. A **portal** is a collection of links, content, and services on a Web page designed to guide users to information related to their jobs. **EDI (electronic data interchange)** controls the transfer of data and information among computers. A **data warehouse** stores and manages the data required to analyze transactions. An **extranet** allows customers or suppliers to access part of an enterprise's intranet. **Web services** allow businesses to create products and B2B interactions. A **workflow application** assists in the management and tracking of the activities in a business process. A **virtual private network (VPN)** provides users with a secure connection to a company's network server.

(5) What Are the Major Types of E-Commerce?

E-retail occurs when retailers use the Web to sell their products or services. **Online banking** allows users to pay bills from their computers, and **online trading** lets users invest without using a broker. Entertainment and media on the Web include music, videos, news, sporting events, and 3-D multiplayer games. Travel-related services on the Web include directions; airline, hotel, or car reservations; and a **shopping bot** that searches for the best price on a product or service. Many Web sites provide medical, fitness, nutrition, or exercise information.

Visit scsite.com/dcf2e/ch12/quiz or click the Quiz Yourself button. Click Objectives 4 – 5.

Chapter Review

(6) What Are the Computer Hardware Needs and Solutions for an Enterprise?

Enterprise hardware allows large organizations to manage and share information and data using devices geared for maximum availability and efficiency. A **RAID (redundant array of independent disks)** is a group of integrated disks that duplicates data, instructions, and information to improve data reliability. **Network attached storage (NAS)** is a server that provides storage for users and information systems. A **storage area network (SAN)** provides storage to other servers. An **enterprise storage system** consolidates storage so operations run efficiently. **Blade servers** pack a complete computer server on a single card. **High-availability systems** continue running and performing tasks for at least 99 percent of the time. **Utility computing** allows companies to use the processing power sitting idle in a network located elsewhere. **Grid computing** combines many servers and/or personal computers to act as one large computer.

(7) Why Is Computer Backup Important, and How Is It Accomplished?

A backup duplicates a file or program to protect an enterprise if the original is lost or damaged. A full backup copies all of the files in a computer. A differential backup copies only files that have changed since the last full backup. An incremental backup copies only files that have changed since the last full or incremental backup. A selective backup allows users to back up specific files. With continuous data protection (CDP), all data is backed up whenever a change is made.

(8) What Are the Steps in a Disaster Recovery Plan?

A **disaster recovery plan** describes the steps a company would take to restore computer operations in the event of a disaster. A disaster recovery plan contains four components. The emergency plan specifies the steps to be taken immediately after a disaster strikes. The backup plan stipulates how a company uses backup files and equipment to resume information processing. The recovery plan identifies the actions to be taken to restore full information processing operations. The test plan contains information for simulating disasters and recording an organization's ability to recover.

 Visit scsite.com/dcf2e/ch12/quiz or click the Quiz Yourself button. Click Objectives 6 – 8.

Key Terms

You should know the Key Terms. Use the list below to help focus your study. To further enhance your understanding of the Key Terms in this chapter, visit scsite.com/dcf2e/ch12/terms. See an example of and a definition for each term, and access current and additional information about the term from the Web.

artificial intelligence (AI) (465)
blade servers (477)
chief information officer (CIO) (461)
computer-aided design (CAD) (459)
computer-aided engineering (CAE) (459)
computer-aided manufacturing (CAM) (459)
computer-integrated manufacturing (CIM) (459)
content management system (CMS) (466)
customer interaction management (CIM) (460)
customer relationship management (CRM) (466)

data warehouse (468)
decision support system (DSS) (463)
disaster recovery plan (479)
distribution systems (460)
EDI (electronic data interchange) (468)
enterprise computing (452)
enterprise hardware (474)
enterprise information (456)
enterprise resource planning (ERP) (465)
enterprise storage system (476)
e-retail (470)
expert system (464)
extranet (469)
grid computing (478)
high-availability systems (477)

human resources information system (HRIS) (458)
information system (456)
interoperability (478)
management information system (MIS) (462)
managers (456)
marketing information system (460)
Material Requirements Planning (MRP) (459)
network attached storage (NAS) (474)
office information system (OIS) (461)
online banking (472)
online trading (472)
portal (467)

RAID (redundant array of independent disks) (474)
redundant components (477)
sales force automation (SFA) (460)
scalability (477)
shopping bot (472)
storage area network (SAN) (475)
transaction processing system (TPS) (461)
utility computing (478)
virtual private network (VPN) (470)
Web services (469)
workflow (469)
workflow application (469)

Checkpoint

Use the Checkpoint exercises to check your knowledge level of the chapter.

_____ 1. The term, enterprise, commonly describes a business or venture of any size. (452)

_____ 2. The Chief Operations Officer (COO) manages core activities. (454)

_____ 3. The types of information that users require seldom depend on their employee level in the company. (455)

_____ 4. An information system is a set of hardware, software, data, people, and procedures that works together to produce information. (456)

_____ 5. Computer-aided manufacturing (CAM) is the use of computers to control production equipment. (459)

_____ 6. An MIS summary report usually lists only transactions. (462)

_____ 7. Artificial intelligence is the application of human intelligence to computers. (465)

_____ 8. A RAID system duplicates data, instructions, and information to improve data reliability. (474)

_____ 9. Network attached storage is a high-speed network with the sole purpose of providing storage to other servers to which it is attached. (474)

_____10. Information systems that have interoperability and easily share information with other information systems are said to be closed, or proprietary. (478)

1. Many companies elevate the importance of information technology by including a _____ executive position that reports to the CEO. (461)
   a. chief operations officer (COO)
   b. chief financial officer (CFO)
   c. chief security officer (CSO)
   d. chief information officer (CIO)

2. An exception report _____. (462)
   a. lists all transactions during a given period
   b. consolidates data with totals, tables, or graphs
   c. identifies data outside a normal condition
   d. all of the above

3. An advantage of ERP is _____. (466)
   a. complete integration of information systems across departments
   b. better project management
   c. better customer service
   d. all of the above

4. The secure connection created between a user's computer and a company's network is called a(n) _____. (470)
   a. VPN tunnel
   b. EDI portal
   c. blade server
   d. data warehouse

5. A shopping bot is a Web site that _____. (472)
   a. allows users to pay bills from their computers
   b. guides users to information about their jobs
   c. searches the Internet for the best price on a product or service
   d. allows businesses to create products and B2B interactions

6. The _____ of hardware to users is a measure of how often it is online. (474)
   a. redundancy
   b. availability
   c. scalability
   d. interoperability

7. _____ is a system in which all data is backed up whenever a change is made. (478)
   a. Continuous data protection
   b. Full backup
   c. Differential backup
   d. Selective backup

8. A(n) _____ can be time-consuming but provides the best protection against data loss. (478)
   a. differential backup
   b. incremental backup
   c. full backup
   d. selective backup

_____ 1. MRP (459)

_____ 2. expert systems (464)

_____ 3. Web farming (468)

_____ 4. workflow (469)

_____ 5. redundant components (477)

a. process that identifies the specific set of steps involved in completing a project

b. monitors and controls processes related to production

c. process of collecting data from the Internet as a source for a data warehouse

d. allow for a functioning system component to take over if a similar component fails

e. captures and stores the knowledge of human experts and then imitates human reasoning and decision making

f. allow business to create products and B2B interactions

Checkpoint

Short Answer

Write a brief answer to each of the following questions.

1. What are managers? _____ What four activities do managers perform to coordinate resources? _____

2. In an expert system, how is the knowledge base different from the inference rules? _____ What is artificial intelligence (AI)? _____

3. What is RAID? _____ What is mirroring? _____

4. What are scalability and interoperability? _____ How is an open information system different from a closed system? _____

5. What is a disaster recovery plan? _____ What are its four major components? _____

Working Together

Working in a group of your classmates, complete the following team exercise.

1. The type of information system employed and the purpose for which it is used depend on an individual's place in an organization. Have each member of your team interview a manager and a nonmanagement employee at a local company. What type of information systems do they use? Why? How do the information systems influence their work? How were their jobs different before the information systems were introduced? Meet with the members of your team to discuss your findings. Then, create a PowerPoint presentation and share with the class how different managers and nonmanagement employees use information systems.

Web Research

Use the Internet-based Web Research exercises to broaden your understanding of the concepts presented in this chapter. Visit scsite.com/dcf2e/ch12/research to obtain more information pertaining to each exercise. To discuss any of the Web Research exercises in this chapter with other students, post your thoughts or questions at scsite.com/dcf2e/ch12/forum.

(1) Journaling

Respond to your readings in this chapter by writing at least one page about your reactions, evaluations, and reflections on enterprise computing. For example, how often do you and your employer back up computer files? Would you consider using RAID in your personal computer? What experiences have you had using e-commerce market sectors, such as finance, entertainment and media, travel, and health? You also can write about the new terms you learned by reading this chapter. If required, submit your journal to your instructor.

(2) Scavenger Hunt

Use one of the search engines listed in Figure 2-8 in Chapter 2 on page 58 or your own favorite search engine to find the answers to the questions below. Copy and paste the Web address from the Web page where you found the answer. Some questions may have more than one answer. If required, submit your answers to your instructor. (1) How does VeriSign allow consumers to transact secure online payments? (2) Using both the Orbitz (orbitz.com) and Expedia (expedia.com) Web sites, search for a 9:00 a.m. one-way flight from Chicago O'Hare airport to Los Angeles International airport. What airline offers the lowest fare? (3) Compare the products and services offered by two online banks, such as Citibank and Bank of America. What loan programs are available to finance a college education? (4) How would you make a complaint to the Federal Trade Commission about specific unsolicited commercial e-mail (spam)?

(3) Search Sleuth

One of the newer online academic research tools is **Google Scholar** (scholar.google.com). It uses newly developed algorithms to provide search results composed of books, technical reports, abstracts, peer-reviewed articles, and theses. Visit this Web site and then use your word processing program to answer the following questions. Then, if required, submit your answers to your instructor. (1) Type "enterprise computing" in the Search box and then click the Search button. How many results were found? (2) Click one of the enterprise computing links for an article. What is the article's title, and who is the author? What journal published the article? When? How many works cite this article? (3) Click your browser's Back button or press the BACKSPACE key twice to return to the Google Scholar home page. Delete the text in the Search box, type "artificial intelligence" in the Search box, and then click the Search button. Find two articles that have been cited by more than 100 other works. Write a 50-word summary of these two articles.

Learn How To

Use the Learn How To activities to learn fundamental skills when using a computer and accompanying technology. Complete the exercises and submit them to your instructor.

LEARN HOW TO 1:   Use Internet-Based Telephony — Voice over the Internet (VoIP)

Every enterprise organization depends on reliable communications. An important means of communication is voice, or telephone, communications. In most organizations today, a telephone company is the primary vendor for providing telephone communications. In the near future, however, the Internet might be the largest provider of telephone communications.

You learned in a previous chapter about Voice over Internet Protocol (VoIP), sometimes called Internet-based telephony, which provides for voice communications using the Internet instead of standard telephone connections. Two advantages claimed for VoIP are improved reliability and much lower costs. Both of these advantages are attractive to businesses, and VoIP is forecasted to become the standard voice communications method within the next 5–10 years.

VoIP also is available to individual users. One primary means to use VoIP is through the service offered by Skype, a company that offers free, unlimited calls through an Internet connection. The Skype software also is free. Using Skype, you can talk to another Skype user via the Internet anywhere in the world for no cost whatsoever. If the person you call is not a Skype user, you can use Skype to call their ordinary landline or mobile telephone quite inexpensively. For example, to call someone on a landline telephone in the United Kingdom from anywhere in the world, the cost is approximately 2 cents per minute.

The following quote indicates the potential future of VoIP and services like Skype:

"I knew it was over when I downloaded Skype," Michael Powell, chairman of the Federal Communications Commission, explained. "When the inventors of KaZaA are distributing for free a little program that you can use to talk to anybody else, and the quality is fantastic, and it's free — it's over. The world will change now inevitably."

Fortune Magazine, February 16, 2004

To download Skype, complete the following steps:

1. Start your Internet browser, type `www.skype.com` in the Address bar, and then press the ENTER key.
2. When the Skype home page is displayed, explore the Web site for information about using Skype. When you are ready, click the Download Skype now. It's free. button.
3. In the next window, the version of Skype required for your operating system is identified, along with the hardware requirements. Notice that in order to use Skype, you need, at a minimum, a sound card, speakers, and a microphone. A headset or a USB telephone provide better service. After reading the information on the screen, click the Download link.
4. When the File Download — Security Warning dialog box is displayed, click the Save button.
5. In the Save As dialog box, select the Desktop for the location of the saved file. Then, click the Save button. The Skype Setup file will download. This may take a few minutes, depending on the speed of your Internet connection, because of the large file size.
6. When the Download complete window is displayed, click the Close button. The SkypeSetup icon is displayed on the desktop.
7. Double-click the SkypeSetup icon on the desktop. If any warning dialog boxes appear, click the Run button.
8. In the Select Setup Language window, select the language you would like to use and then click the OK button.
9. If your firewall displays a message asking whether the application should have access to the Internet, grant access.
10. In the Setup — Skype window, click the Next button. Select the I accept the agreement option button in the License Agreement window and then click the Next button.
11. In the Select Destination Location window, you normally should use the default, so click the Next button.
12. In the Select Additional Tasks window, check the boxes that apply to your choices and then click the Next button. For this example, be sure to install the Skype icon on the desktop.
13. Skype will be installed on your computer. When the Completing the Skype Setup Wizard window opens, remove the check from the Launch Skype check box, and then click the Finish button.

Skype now is installed on your computer. The Skype icon should appear on your desktop. To start and use Skype, complete the following steps:

1. Double-click the Skype icon on your desktop. The first time you start Skype, the Create a new Skype account dialog box is displayed (Figure 12-26). In this dialog box, you enter your Skype name, password, and e-mail address. The Skype name is the name you will use to start Skype each time, together with the password. You can use any name and password that has not already been used on Skype. Also, be sure to check the Skype End User License Agreement check box, and then click the Next button. The Creating Account message is displayed.

2. If your Skype name and password have not been used, the Skype - User Profile dialog box is displayed (Figure 12-27). If your Skype name or password already have been used by another user, you must select another Skype name or password.

3. In the Skype - User Profile dialog box, provide as much information about yourself as you feel comfortable with, keeping in mind that this profile window will be available to other Skype users. Many users might have the same name as you, so the more details you provide, the chances are better that another Skype user will identify you as a friend or acquaintance who uses Skype. At a minimum, you should provide your full name, country, and state (if applicable) where you live. When you have entered the information, click the Update button. You can change the information in this personal profile at any time when using the Skype program.

4. The Skype program starts and opens the Skype window (Figure 12-28).

5. After installing Skype, you can make calls to other Skype users anywhere in the world for no cost. If you want to dial a telephone number for a regular landline telephone, you must subscribe to SkypeOut. This service, which costs .017 euros (about two cents in U.S. currency) to call many places in the world, can be obtained by clicking the SkypeOut:Global calling at local rates link in the Skype window.

6. To learn the techniques for calling another Skype user and for using SkypeOut, click Help on the menu bar in the Skype window, click Help on the Help menu, and then select the subject about which you want to learn.

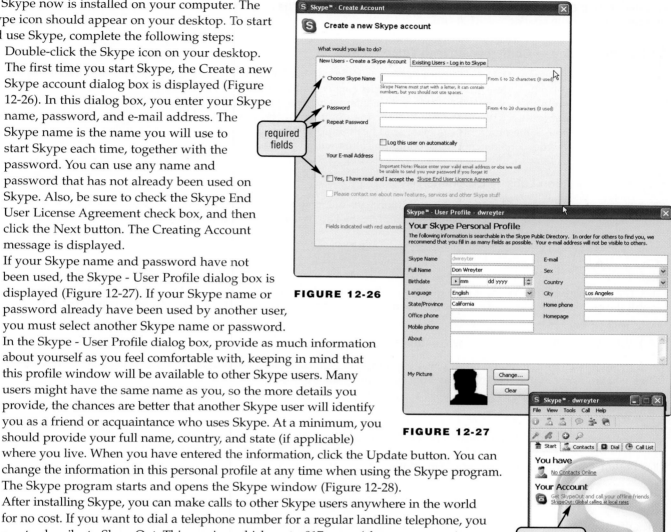

FIGURE 12-26

FIGURE 12-27

FIGURE 12-28

Exercise

1. Visit the Skype Web site. Examine the various screens and examples shown on the Web site. Do you think this type of service can be useful to you? Why? What are the advantages and disadvantages of using Skype? If you were calling a friend in Australia on a regular telephone, how much per minute would you have to pay? Submit your answers to your instructor.

2. **Optional: Perform this exercise only on your own computer. Do not perform this exercise on a school computer.** Establish an account on Skype. Call another member of your class who also has established a Skype account. What do you like about Skype? What do you not like? If you know someone in Europe or Asia who is a Skype user, call him or her. Do you like the fact the call is free anywhere in the world? As an option, subscribe to SkypeOut and then call someone somewhere else in the world on his or her regular telephone. Is the quality of the call good? What did you like or not like about the call? Submit your answers to your instructor.

Learn It Online

Use the Learn It Online exercises to reinforce your understanding of the chapter concepts. To access the Learn It Online exercises, visit scsite.com/dcf2e/ch12/learn.

(1) At the Movies — Conferencing with Video Phones

To view the Conferencing with Video Phones movie, click the number 1 button. Locate your video and click the corresponding High-Speed or Dial-Up link, depending on your Internet connection. Watch the movie and then complete the exercise by answering the question that follows. Interest in videoconferencing has surged since 9/11 as companies scramble to find a way to have face-to-face meetings without the hassles of flying. Another practical use for videoconferencing is to monitor an elderly or disabled loved one. Some programs can even send health information directly to health-care providers or create small video e-mails. How could videoconferencing make communication within your family easier?

(2) Student Edition Labs — E-Commerce

Click the number 2 button. When the Student Edition Labs menu appears, click *E-Commerce* to begin. A new browser window will open. Follow the on-screen instructions to complete the Lab. When finished, click the Exit button. If required, print a copy of your results to submit to your instructor.

(3) Practice Test

Click the number 3 button. Answer each question. When completed, enter your name and click the Grade Test button to submit the quiz for grading. Make a note of any missed questions. If required, submit your results to your instructor.

(4) Who Wants To Be a Computer Genius^2?

Click the number 4 button to find out if you are a computer genius. Directions about how to play the game will be displayed. When you are ready to play, click the Play button. Submit your score to your instructor.

(5) Wheel of Terms

Click the number 5 button to reinforce important terms you learned in this chapter by playing the Shelly Cashman Series version of this popular game. Directions about how to play the game will be displayed. When you are ready to play, click the Play button. Submit your score to your instructor.

(6) Student Edition Labs — Backing Up Your Computer

Click the number 6 button. When the Student Edition Labs menu appears, click *Backing Up Your Computer* to begin. A new browser window will open. Follow the on-screen instructions to complete the Lab. When finished, click the Exit button. If required, print a copy of your results to submit to your instructor.

(7) Crossword Puzzle Challenge

Click the number 7 button. Complete the puzzle to reinforce skills you learned in this chapter. Directions about how to play the game will be displayed. When you are ready to play, click the Submit button. Submit the completed puzzle to your instructor.

(8) Lab Exercises

Click the number 8 button. When the Lab Exercises menu appears, click the exercise assigned by your instructor. A new browser window will open. Follow the on-screen instructions to complete the exercise. When finished, click the Exit button. If required, submit your results to your instructor.

(9) Chapter Discussion Forum

Select an objective from this chapter on page 451 about which you would like more information. Click the number 9 button and post a short message listing a meaningful message title accompanied by one or more questions concerning the selected objective. In two days, return to the threaded discussion by clicking the number 9 button. Submit to your instructor your original message and at least one response to your message.

APPENDIX A

Quiz Yourself Answers

Following are possible answers to the Quiz Yourself boxes throughout the book.

Quiz Yourself 1-1

1. A computer is ~~a motorized~~an electronic device that processes ~~output~~input into ~~input~~output.
2. A storage device records (~~reads~~writes) and/or retrieves (~~writes~~reads) items to and from storage media.
3. An ~~output~~input device is any hardware component that allows you to enter data and instructions in a computer.
4. True Statement
5. Three commonly used ~~input~~output devices are a printer, a monitor, and speakers.

Quiz Yourself 1-2

1. A ~~resource~~network is a collection of computers and devices connected together via communications devices and transmission media.
2. True Statement
3. Popular ~~system~~application software includes Web browsers, word processing software, spreadsheet software, database software, and presentation graphics software.
4. The ~~Internet~~Web is one of the more popular services on the ~~Web~~Internet.
5. Two types of ~~application~~system software are the operating system and utility programs.

Quiz Yourself 1-3

1. A ~~desktop computer~~notebook computer (or laptop computer) is a portable, personal computer designed to fit on your lap.
2. True Statement
3. Each ~~large business~~home user spends time on the computer for different reasons that include budgeting and personal financial management, Web access, communications, and entertainment.
4. A ~~home~~power user requires the capabilities of a workstation or other powerful computer.
5. ~~Mainframes~~Supercomputers are the fastest, most powerful computers — and the most expensive.
6. With ~~embedded computers~~online banking, users access account balances, pay bills, and copy monthly transactions from the bank's computer right into their personal computers.

Quiz Yourself 2-1

1. True Statement
2. ~~A WISP~~An IP address (or Internet Protocol address) is a number that uniquely identifies each computer or device connected to the Internet.
3. ~~An IP address~~A domain name, such as www.google.com, is the text version of ~~a domain name~~an IP address.
4. Dial-up access takes place when the modem in your computer uses ~~the cable television network~~a standard telephone line to connect to the Internet.

Quiz Yourself 2-2

1. True Statement
2. A ~~Web browser~~subject directory classifies Web pages in an organized set of categories and related subcategories.
3. ~~Business~~Consumer-to-consumer e-commerce occurs when one consumer sells directly to another, such as in an online auction.
4. The more widely used ~~search engines~~Web browsers for personal computers are Internet Explorer, Netscape, Mozilla, Opera, and Safari.
5. To develop a Web page, you do not have to be a computer programmer.

Quiz Yourself 2-3

1. True Statement
2. An e-mail address is a combination of a user name and ~~an e-mail program~~a domain name that identifies a user so he or she can receive Internet e-mail.
3. ~~FTP~~Internet telephony uses the Internet (instead of the public switched telephone network) to connect a calling party to one or more called parties.
4. Netiquette is the code of ~~un~~acceptable behaviors while on the Internet.
5. On a newsgroup, a ~~subscription~~thread (or threaded discussion) consists of the original article and all subsequent related replies.

Quiz Yourself 3-1

1. True Statement
2. ~~Public domain~~Packaged software is mass produced, copyrighted retail software that meets the needs of a wide variety of users, not just a single user or company.
3. To use ~~system~~application software, your computer must be running ~~application~~system software.
4. When an application is started, the program's instructions load from ~~memory~~a storage medium into ~~a storage medium~~memory.

Quiz Yourself 3-2

1. ~~Enterprise computing~~Image editing software provides the capabilities of paint software and also includes the ability to modify existing images.
2. Millions of people use ~~spreadsheet~~word processing software every day to develop documents such as letters, memos, reports, fax cover sheets, mailing labels, newsletters, and Web pages.
3. Professional ~~accounting~~DTP (or desktop publishing) software is ideal for the production of high-quality color documents such as textbooks, corporate newsletters, marketing literature, product catalogs, and annual reports.
4. ~~Spreadsheet~~Presentation graphics software is application software that allows users to create visual aids for presentations to communicate ideas, messages, and other information to a group.
5. Two of the more widely used ~~CAD programs~~software suites are Microsoft Office and Sun StarOffice.
6. True Statement

Quiz Yourself 3-3

1. An ~~anti-spam~~antivirus program protects a computer against viruses by identifying and removing any computer viruses found in memory, on storage media, or in incoming files.
2. ~~Computer~~Web-based training is a type of ~~Web~~computer-based training that uses Internet technology and consists of application software on the Web.
3. True Statement
4. ~~Legal~~Personal finance software is a simplified accounting program that helps home users and small office/home office users balance their checkbooks, pay bills, track investments, and evaluate financial plans.
5. ~~Personal DTP~~Photo editing software is a popular type of image editing software that allows users to edit digital photographs.

Quiz Yourself 4-1

1. True Statement
2. Four basic operations in a machine cycle are: (1) ~~comparing~~fetching, (2) decoding, (3) executing, and, if necessary, (4) ~~pipelining~~storing.
3. Processors contain a ~~motherboard~~control unit and an arithmetic logic unit (ALU).
4. The ~~central processing unit~~motherboard, sometimes called a system board, is the main circuit board of the system unit.

5. The leading processor chip manufacturers for personal computers are ~~Microsoft~~Intel, AMD, IBM, Motorola, and Transmeta.
6. The system unit is a case that contains ~~mechanical~~ electronic components of the computer used to process data.

Quiz Yourself 4-2

1. True Statement
2. A gigabyte (GB) equals approximately 1 ~~trillion~~ billion bytes.
3. Memory cache helps speed the processes of the computer because it stores ~~seldom~~ frequently used instructions and data.
4. Most computers are ~~analog~~ digital, which means they recognize only two discrete states: on and off.
5. Most RAM ~~retains~~ loses its contents when the power is removed from the computer.
6. Read-only memory (ROM) refers to memory chips storing ~~temporary~~ permanent data and instructions.

Quiz Yourself 4-3

1. A ~~bus~~ port is the point at which a peripheral attaches to a system unit so the peripheral can send data to or receive information from the computer.
2. An ~~AC adapter~~ expansion slot is a socket on the motherboard that can hold an adapter card.
3. ~~Serial~~ USB ports can connect up to 127 different peripherals together with a single connector type.
4. The higher the bus clock speed, the ~~slower~~ faster the transmission of data.
5. True Statement

Quiz Yourself 5-1

1. A keyboard is an ~~output~~ input device that contains keys users press to enter data into a computer.
2. A ~~trackball~~ touch pad is a small, flat, rectangular pointing device commonly found on notebook computers.
3. True Statement
4. An optical mouse has no moving mechanical parts inside.
5. ~~PDAs~~ Tablet PCs use a pressure-sensitive digital pen and ~~Tablet PCs~~ PDAs use a stylus.

Quiz Yourself 5-2

1. True Statement
2. A fingerprint scanner captures curves and indentations of a ~~signature~~ fingerprint.
3. After swiping a credit card through ~~an MICR~~ a magnetic stripe card reader, it reads the information stored on the magnetic stripe on the card.
4. ~~Instant messaging~~ Voice recognition (or speech recognition) is the computer's capability of distinguishing spoken words.
5. Many smart phones today have ~~POS~~ PDA capabilities.
6. RFID is a technology that uses ~~laser~~ radio signals to communicate with a tag placed in an object, an animal, or a person.

Quiz Yourself 5-3

1. A ~~lower~~ higher resolution uses a greater number of pixels and thus provides a smoother image.
2. An output device is any type of ~~software~~ hardware component that conveys information to one or more people.
3. LCD monitors have a ~~larger~~ smaller footprint than CRT monitors.
4. True Statement

Quiz Yourself 5-4

1. A ~~laser~~ thermal printer generates images by pushing electrically heated pins against heat-sensitive paper.
2. A ~~photo~~ laser printer creates images using a laser beam and powdered ink, called toner.
3. An ink-jet printer is a type of impact printer that forms characters and graphics by spraying tiny drops of liquid ~~nitrogen~~ ink onto a piece of paper.
4. Many personal computer users add surround sound ~~printer systems~~ speakers to their computers to generate a higher-quality sound.
5. Multifunction peripherals require ~~more~~ less space than having a separate printer, scanner, copy machine, and fax machine.
6. True Statement

Quiz Yourself 6-1

1. True Statement
2. SATA is a hard disk interface that uses ~~parallel~~ serial signals to transfer data, instructions, and information.
3. ~~Storage media~~ A storage device is the computer hardware that records and/or retrieves items to and from ~~a~~ storage ~~device~~ media.
4. Three types of ~~manual~~ magnetic disks are floppy disks, Zip disks, and hard disks.

Quiz Yourself 6-2

1. A ~~CD-RW~~ CD-ROM is a type of optical disc on which users can read but not write (record) or erase.
2. A ~~DVD-RAM~~ Picture CD is a single-session disc that stores digital versions of a single roll of film using a jpg file format.
3. DVDs have ~~the same~~ much greater storage capacities ~~as~~ than CDs.
4. Optical discs are written and read by ~~mirrors~~ laser light.
5. True Statement

Quiz Yourself 6-3

1. A USB flash drive is a flash memory storage device that plugs in a ~~parallel~~ USB port on a computer or mobile device.
2. True Statement
3. Microfilm and microfiche have the ~~shortest~~ longest life of any storage media.
4. Tape storage requires ~~direct~~ sequential access, which refers to reading or writing data consecutively.

Quiz Yourself 7-1

1. A ~~buffer~~ driver is a small program that tells the operating system how to communicate with a specific device.
2. True Statement
3. A password is a ~~public~~ private combination of characters associated with the user name that allows access to certain computer resources.
4. The program you currently are using is in the ~~background~~ foreground, and the other programs running but not in use are in the ~~foreground~~ background.
5. Two types of system software are operating systems and ~~application~~ utility programs.

Quiz Yourself 7-2

1. A ~~file manager~~ personal firewall is a utility that detects and protects a personal computer from unauthorized intrusions.
2. ~~Fragmenting~~ Defragmenting a disk is the process of reorganizing it so the files are stored in contiguous sectors.
3. ~~Linux~~ Windows XP is available in five editions: Home Edition, Professional, Media Center Edition, Tablet PC Edition, and 64-bit Edition.

4. True Statement
5. ~~Windows XP~~Linux is a UNIX-type operating system that is open source software.

Quiz Yourself 7-3

1. A ~~pop-up blocker~~file compression utility shrinks the size of a file(s).
2. An ~~anti-spam~~antivirus program protects a computer against viruses.
3. True Statement
4. Pocket PCs use ~~Palm OS~~Windows Mobile as their operating system.
5. ~~Web filtering~~CD/DVD burning software writes text, graphics, audio, and video files to a recordable or rewritable CD or DVD.

Quiz Yourself 8-1

1. A ~~cybercafé~~hot spot is a wireless network that provides Internet connections to mobile computers and devices.
2. True Statement
3. ~~Receiving~~Sending devices initiate an instruction to transmit data, instructions, or information.
4. Users can send graphics, pictures, video clips, and sound files, as well as short text messages with ~~text~~picture messaging.

Quiz Yourself 8-2

1. A wireless LAN is a LAN that uses no physical wires.
2. An intranet is an internal network that uses ~~video conferencing~~Internet technologies.
3. Four popular types of digital ~~dial-up~~dedicated lines are ISDN lines, DSL, T-carrier lines, and ATM.
4. In a client/server network, ~~servers~~clients on the network access resources on the ~~client~~server.
5. True Statement

Quiz Yourself 8-3

1. A ~~cable~~dial-up modem converts a computer's digital signals to analog signals before they are transmitted over standard telephone lines.
2. True Statement
3. ~~Analog~~Digital signals consist of individual electrical pulses that represent bits grouped together into bytes.
4. ~~Physical~~Wireless transmission media send communications signals through the air or space using radio, microwave, and infrared signals.
5. Two types of wireless home networks are HomeRF and ~~powerline cable~~Wi-Fi.

Quiz Yourself 9-1

1. A ~~database~~field is a combination of one or more related characters or bytes and is the smallest unit of data a user accesses.
2. A ~~record~~database is a collection of data organized in a manner that allows access, retrieval, and use of that data.
3. ~~Data~~Information is processed ~~information~~data.
4. ~~Hierarchy of data~~File maintenance procedures include adding records to, changing records in, and deleting records from a file.
5. True Statement

Quiz Yourself 9-2

1. A DBMS is ~~hardware~~software that allows you to create, access, and manage ~~an operating system~~a database.
2. A ~~query~~data dictionary contains data about each file in the database and each field in those files.
3. True Statement
4. Strengths of the database approach include ~~increased~~reduced data redundancy, ~~reduced~~improved data integrity, shared data, easier access, and ~~increased~~reduced development time.

Quiz Yourself 9-3

1. ~~Object-oriented~~Relational databases store data in tables.
2. True Statement
3. SQL ia a ~~data modeling~~ query language that allows users to manage, update, and retrieve data.
4. The database ~~analyst~~administrator requires a more technical inside view of the data than does the ~~database administrator~~data analyst.

Quiz Yourself 10-1

1. A ~~back door~~denial of service attack is an assault whose purpose is to disrupt computer access to an Internet service such as the Web or e-mail.
2. True Statement
3. Computer viruses, worms, and Trojan horses are malicious-logic programs that act without a user's knowledge.
4. ~~Shorter~~Longer passwords provide greater security than ~~longer~~shorter ones.
5. Updating an antivirus program's ~~quarantine~~signature file protects a computer against viruses written since the antivirus program was released.

Quiz Yourself 10-2

1. An end-user license agreement (EULA) ~~permits~~does not permit users to give copies to friends and colleagues, while continuing to use the software.
2. Encryption is a process of converting ~~ciphertext~~plaintext into ~~plaintext~~ciphertext to prevent authorized access.
3. Mobile users are ~~not~~susceptible to hardware theft.
4. True Statement
5. To prevent against data loss caused by a system failure, computer users should ~~restore~~back up files regularly.

Quiz Yourself 10-3

1. Factors that cause ~~CVS~~tendonitis and CTS (carpal tunnel syndrome) include prolonged typing, prolonged mouse usage, or continual shifting between the mouse and the keyboard.
2. ~~Phishing~~Computer forensics is the discovery, collection, and analysis of evidence found on computers and networks.
3. True Statement
4. Web sites use ~~electronic profiles~~cookies to track user preferences, store users' passwords, keep track of items in a user's shopping cart, and track Web site browsing habits.
5. You can~~not~~ assume that information on the Web is correct.

Quiz Yourself 11-1

1. True Statement
2. ~~Feasibility~~Project management is the process of planning, scheduling, and then controlling the activities during the system development cycle.
3. The five phases in most system development cycles are ~~programming~~planning, analysis, design, ~~sampling~~implementation, and ~~recording~~support.
4. The purpose of the ~~design~~support phase is to provide ongoing assistance for an information system and its users after the system is implemented.
5. Upon completion of the preliminary investigation, the systems analyst writes the ~~system proposal~~feasibility report.
6. Users should ~~not~~be involved throughout the system development process.

Quiz Yourself 11-2

1. COBOL and C are examples of ~~assembly~~procedural languages.
2. ~~Delphi~~Java is an object-oriented programming language developed by Sun Microsystems.
3. Popular ~~first generation~~scripting languages include JavaScript, Perl, Rexx, Tcl, and VBScript.

4. Three popular ~~markup languages~~Web page authoring programs are Dreamweaver MX, Flash MX, and FrontPage.
5. Two types of low-level languages are machine languages and ~~source~~assembly languages.
6. True Statement

Quiz Yourself 11-3

1. True Statement
2. The program development cycle consists of these six steps: analyze requirements, design solution, validate design, implement design, test solution, and ~~hardcode~~document solution.
3. Three basic control structures are sequence, selection, and ~~maintenance~~repetition.

Quiz Yourself 12-1

1. The main task of executive managers is to make ~~short~~long-term, ~~tactical~~strategic decisions.
2. An information system is a set of hardware, software, data, procedures, and people that works together to produce information.
3. A ~~human resources~~marketing information system serves as a central repository for the tasks of the marketing functional unit.
4. True Statement
5. Decision support systems ~~capture and store the knowledge of human experts and then imitate human reasoning and decision making~~help users analyze data and make decisions.
6. Enterprise resource planning provides centralized integrated software to help manage and coordinate the ongoing activities of the functional units of an enterprise, including manufacturing and distribution, accounting, finance, sales, product planning, and human resources~~is a combination of databases, software, and procedures that organizes and allows access to various forms of documents and files~~.

Quiz Yourself 12-2

1. ~~A portal~~An extranet is the portion of a company's network that allows customers or suppliers of a company to access parts of an enterprise's intranet.
2. True Statement
3. A VPN provides mobile users, remote offices, vendors, or customers a secure connection to the company network server, as if they had a private line~~is a server that is placed on a network with the sole purpose of providing storage to users and information systems attached to the network~~.
4. A workflow application is a program that assists in the management and tracking of all the activities in a business process from start to finish~~helps an enterprise collect, archive, index, and retrieve its resources~~.

Quiz Yourself 12-3

1. ~~Network-attached storage~~A storage area network is a high-speed network with the sole purpose of providing storage to other servers to which it is attached.
2. Scalability is a measure of how well computer hardware, software, or an information system can grow to meet increasing performance demands~~refers to the ability of an information system to share information with other information systems~~.
3. A differential backup copies only the files that have changed since the last full ~~or last incremental~~backup.
4. ~~A full~~An incremental backup is the fastest backup method, requiring only minimal storage.
5. ~~An emergency~~A backup plan specifies how a company's users back up files and equipment to resume information processing.
6. True Statement

INDEX

3-D search engines, 61

3GL (third-generation language), 425. *See also* Procedural language

4GL (fourth-generation language): Fourth-generation language. Nonprocedural language that enables users and programmers to access data in a database. **430**

802.11: Series of network standards developed by IEEE that specifies how two wireless devices communicate over the air with each other. Also called wireless Ethernet standard. **309.** *See also* **Wi-Fi (wireless fidelity)**

802.11i: Network standard developed by IEEE with enhanced security for wireless communications. **376**

A+ certification, 240

AC adapter: External power supply, used by some external peripherals, that converts AC power into DC power that the peripheral requires. **152**

Acceptable use policy (AUP), 368

Acceptance test, 420

Access, unauthorized, 368–70

Access control: Security measure that defines who can access a computer, when they can access it, and what actions they can take while accessing the computer. **368–69**

Access privileges, 341, 342, 346

Access provider: Business that provides individuals and companies access to the Internet free or for a fee. **52**

Access time: Measurement of the amount of time it takes the process to read data, instructions, and information from memory. **146, 222**
hard disk, 226

Accessible information, 334

Accounting departments, 458

Accounting software: Software that helps companies record and report their financial transactions. **111,** 458

Accurate information, 334, 377–78

ActiveX, 434

ActiveX control, 434

ADA, 197. *See also* **Americans with Disabilities Act**

Ada, 431

Adapter card: Circuit board that enhances functions of a component of a system unit and/or provides connections to peripherals. 135, **147.** *See also* **Expansion card**

Addiction, computer, 387

Address
e-mail, 70
Internet Protocol, 53
mailing lists, 71
Web, 56, 57

Address (memory), 142

Address (memory cell), 142

Address book (e-mail): List of names and e-mail addresses, created and stored by a user. **70**

Address bus, 151

Adobe Acrobat Reader, 113

Adobe PDF format, 113

Adobe Systems, 125

ADSL (asymmetric digital subscriber line), 312

Advanced Micro Devices (AMD), 139, 157

Advanced transfer cache: L2 cache built directly on the processor chip. **145**

Advocacy Web site, 62

Adware: Program that displays an online advertisement in a banner or pop-up window on Web pages, e-mail, or other Internet services. **381**

AI, 465. *See also* **Artificial intelligence (AI)**

ALGOL, 431

Algorithm, 426

Alphabetic check: Validity check that ensures users enter only alphabetic data in a field. **339**

Alphanumeric, 335

AltaVista, 61

ALU, 137. *See also* **Arithmetic logic unit**

AMD, 157. *See also* Advanced Micro Devices

America Online (AOL), 52

American Standard Code for Information Interchange (ASCII), 140, 141, 335

Americans with Disabilities Act (ADA): Federal law that requires any company with 15 or more employees to make reasonable attempts to accommodate the needs of physically challenged workers. **197**

Analog formats, 214

Analysis phase: Step in the system development cycle that consists of two major activities: (1) conduct a preliminary investigation, and (2) perform detailed analysis. 406, **413–15**

Analyzing requirements, during program development, 439

Andreessen, Marc, 41

Animation: Appearance of motion created by displaying a series of still images in sequence. **64**
multimedia and, 64

Anonymous FTP, 71

Anonymous Web surfing, 379

Anti-spam program: Program that attempts to remove spam before it reaches a user's inbox. **122, 268, 382**

Anti-Virus Emergency Response Team (AVERT), 389

Antivirus program: Program that protects a computer against viruses by identifying and removing any computer viruses found in memory, on storage media, or on incoming files. 267–**268**, 365–66, 389

Antivirus protection, built into router, 316

AOL, 52. *See also* America Online

Apache, 43

APL, 431

Apple Computer, 14, 27, 38, 39, 42, 47
Macintosh processor, 139
operating system, 101. *See also* MacOSX

Applet, 434

Application generator: Program that creates source code or machine code from a specification of the required functionality. **431**

Application software: Program designed to make users more productive and/or assist them with personal tasks. **11, 100–125**
business software, 104–11
communications, 120–21
educational use, 119
graphics and, 112–14
home use, 115–20
learning aids, 122–24
memory and, 142, 144–45
multimedia and, 112–14
PDA, 110
personal use, 115–20
purchasing desktop computer and, 281
RAM and, 144–45
support tools, 122–24
system software and, 101

uninstalling, 260
Web browser as, 54

Appointment calendar, in personal information manager, 110

Archival backup, 478. *See also* Full backup

Arithmetic logic unit (ALU): Component of a processor that performs arithmetic, comparison, and other operations. **137**

Arithmetic operations, 137

ARPANET, 37, 50

Arrow keys, on keyboard, 168

Artificial intelligence (AI): The application of human intelligence to computers. **465**

Arts and literatures, Web site and, 98

ASCII, 140, 141, 335. *See also* American Standard Code for Information Interchange

Assembler, 425

Assembly language: Programming language in which a programmer writes instructions using symbolic instruction codes. **424–25**

Asymmetric digital subscriber line, 312. *See* ADSL (asymmetric digital subscriber line)

Asynchronous Transfer Mode, 312. *See* **ATM**

Attacks
Internet, 364–68
network, 364–68

AT&T WorldNet, 52

Atanasoff, John, 35

Atanasoff-Berry Computer, 35

ATM: Short for Asynchronous Transfer Mode; service that carries voice, data, video, and multimedia at very high speeds. **312.** *See also* **Asynchronous Transfer Mode**

ATM (banking), 180. *See also* **Automated teller machine**

Attribute (database): Each data element in an object. Also called a property. **347**

Audio: Music, speech, or any other sound. **64**
MIDI port and, 150
multimedia and, 64
output, 182
recording, 399
streaming, 64
on Web page, 54

Audio CD, 18
copying from, 232
using CD-ROM drive to listen to, 231

Audio editing software: Application software that allows a user to modify audio clips and produce studio-quality soundtracks. **114**

Audio input: Process of entering any sound, such as speech, music, and sound effects, into the computer. **173**

Audio output device: Component of a computer that produces music, speech, or other sounds, such as beeps. **193**

Audit trail: Computer file that records both successful and unsuccessful access attempts. **368.** *See also* **Log**

AUP, 368. *See also* Acceptable use policy (AUP)

Authentication, 368–69

Authorware, 437

Automated teller machine (ATM): Special-purpose terminal, connected to a host computer through a network that functions as a self-service banking machine. **180**

AutoNumber data type, 335

Availability, 474, 477

B2B, 68, 469. *See also* Business-to-business (B2B) e-commerce

B2C, 67. *See also* Business-to-consumer (B2C) e-commerce

Back door: Program or set of instructions in a program that allows users to bypass security controls when accessing a program, computer, or network. **367**
safeguards against, 367–68

Back pain, 386

Back up: To make a copy of a file. **261, 375**

Background, 254, 255

Backup: Duplicate or copy of a file, program, or disk that can be used if the original is lost, damaged, or destroyed. **223, 346, 375**
CD-RW used for, 232
disaster recovery and, 479
enterprise storage system and, 476
full, 375, 478
incremental, 478
Internet, 228, 476
plan, 479
procedures, 478–79
selective, 375, 478

Backup (database), 346

Backup plan, 479

Backup procedures, 478–79

Backup utility: Utility program that allows users to copy, or back up, selected files or an entire hard disk to another storage medium, which can be used if the original is lost, damaged, or destroyed. **261**

Backus, John, 36

Bandwidth: The amount of data, instructions, and information that can travel over a communications channel. **317**

Banking
e-commerce used for, 470
e-retail and, 470
MICR used by, 179
online. *See* **Online banking**

Bar chart. 108. *See also* Column chart

Bar code: Identification code consisting of vertical lines and spaces of different widths that represent a manufacturer and an item. **178**

Bar code reader: Optical reader that uses laser beams to read bar codes by using light patterns that pass through the bar code lines. Also called a barcode scanner. **178**

Bar code scanner, 178. *See* Bar code reader

Bardeen, John, 35

BASIC, 37, 431. *See also* Beginner's All-purpose Symbolic Instruction Code

Batch processing, 462

Battery
CMOS and, 146
notebook computers, 152, 288
PDAs, 293

Bay: Opening inside the system unit in which additional equipment can be installed. 135, **151**

Beginner's All-purpose Symbolic Instruction Code, 431. *See also* BASIC

Benchmark test: Test that measures the performance of hardware or software. **417**

Berners-Lee, Tim, 75, 40

Berry, Clifford, 35

Binary digit, 140, 424

Binary system: Number system used by computers that has just two unique digits, 0 and 1, called bits. **140**

Biometric device: Device that authenticates a person's identity by translating a personal characteristic, such as a finger print, into a digital code that then is compared with a digital code stored in a computer verifying a physical or behavioral characteristic. **181, 370,** 371

Biometrics: Technology of authenticating a person's identity by verifying a personal characteristic. **181**

Bit: The smallest unit of data a computer can process. Bit is short for binary digit. **140,** 141, 335
bus width and, 151

Blade, 477

Blade server chassis, 477

Blade servers: Complete computer server, such as a Web server or network server, packed on a single card. Also called ultradense servers. **477.** *See also* **Ultradense servers**

Blog: Web site that uses a regularly updated journal format to reflect the interests, opinions, and personalities of the author and sometimes site visitors. Blog is short for Web log. **63**

Bluetooth: Network standard, specifically a protocol, that defines how two Bluetooth devices use short-range radio waves to transmit data. 46, **150, 309,** 319
popularity of, 150

Blu-Ray, 233

Booting: Process of starting or restarting a computer. **252**
cold, 252
warm, 252

Borland, 429

Braille printer, 197

Brain fingerprinting, 384

Brattain, Walter, 35

Bricklin, Dan, 38, 125

Broadband: Type of media that transmits multiple signals simultaneously. **318,** 319
hackers and, 260
portals and, 319

Broadcast radio: Wireless transmission medium that distributes radio signals through the air over long distances such as between cities, regions, and countries and short distances such as within an office or home. **321**

Browser: Application software that allows users to access and view Web pages. Also called a Web browser. **54,** 55

Buffer: Segment of memory or storage in which items are placed while waiting to be transferred from an input device or to an output device. **255**

Bugs, 439

Bundled software, 281

Burning: Process of writing on an optical disc. **232**

Bus (computer): The physical cable that connects the computers and other devices in a bus network. **151**

Bus (network), 306

Bus network: Type of network topology in which a single central cable connects all computers and other devices. **306,** 308

Bus width, 151

Business services, other, 473

Business software: Application software that assists people in becoming more effective and efficient while performing their daily business activities. **104–11**

Business/marketing Web site, 62

Business-to-business (B2B) e-commerce, 67, 68

Business-to-consumer (B2C) e-commerce, 67

Button: Graphical element that is activated to cause a specific action to take place. **102–3**

Buying personal computers, 144

Buyer's guide, 279–94

Byte: Eight bits that are grouped together as a unit. A byte provides enough different combinations of 0s and 1s to represent 256 individual characters. **140,** 141, 142, 335

C: Programming language developed in the early 1970s at Bell Laboratories used for business and scientific applications. 427, **428**

C#: Object-oriented programming language based on C++ developed primarily by Anders Hejlsberg at Microsoft. 427, **428**

C++: Object-oriented programming language developed at Bell Laboratories that is an extension of the C programming language. 427, **428**

C2C, 68. *See also* Consumer-to-consumer (C2C) e-commerce

CA, 374. *See also* **Certificate authority (CA)**

Cable
coaxial, 319
fiber-optic, 320
twisted-pair, 320

Cable modem: Digital modem that sends and receives digital data over the cable television (CATV) network. Also called a broadband modem. **52, 314**
purchasing desktop computer and, 284

surge protection and, 374–75

Cable television
coaxial cable, 320
Internet access using, 314

Cache: Area of memory that stores the contents of frequently used data or instructions. **144–45**

CAD, 459. See also **Computer-aided design (CAD)**

CAD software. See **Computer-aided design (CAD) software**

CAE, 459. See also **Computer-aided engineering (CAE)**

CAI (computer-aided instruction). See **Computer-based training**

Caller ID, 379

CAM, 25, 459. See also **Computer-aided manufacturing**

Camera
digital. See **Digital camera**
digital video (DV), 176
PC video. See **PC video camera**
video, 176
Web, 176

Canter, Marc, 443

Capacity: The number of bytes (characters) a storage medium can hold. **222**
CD-ROM, 231
DVD-ROM, 233
external hard disk, 227
floppy disk, 222
hard disk, 224, 225
removable hard disk, 227
Zip disk, 223

Car computers
cyber cars, 121

Card reader/writer: Device that reads and writes data, instructions, and information stored on PC Cards or flash memory cards and transmits that data to a computer or printer through a connection to a port. **236**
purchasing desktop computer and, 282

Career
as chief information officer, 454, 461, 480
as computer engineer, 156
as computer forensics specialist, 388
as computer technician, 240
as database administrator, 351, 352
as database analyst, 351
as graphic designer/illustrator, 198
as Help Desk specialist and, 124
as network specialist, 322
as personal computer salesperson, 26
as programmer, 442

searching for, 97
as systems programmer, 270
as Web developer, 74

Carpal tunnel syndrome (CTS), 385

CASE, 419. See also **Computer-aided software engineering (CASE)**

Case control structure, 440

Cathode-ray tube (CRT), 186

CBT. See **Computer-based training**

CD. See Compact disc

CD creation software, 218

CD/DVD burner, 122

CD/DVD burning software: Stand-alone utility program that writes text, graphics, audio, and video files to a recordable or rewritable CD or DVD. **269**

CD recorder, 232. See also CD-R drive

CD-R: Multisession optical disc on which users can write, but not erase, their own items such as text, graphics, and audio. 230, **232.** See also **Compact disc-recordable**

CD-R drive: Device that can read both audio CDs and standard CD-ROM. **232.** See also **CD recorder**

CD-ROM: Type of optical disc that uses laser technology to store data, instructions, and information that users can read but not write on or erase. 230, **231.** See also **Compact disc read-only memory**

CD-ROM drive: Drive that can read CD-ROM discs and sometimes audio CDs. **231**

CD-ROM jukebox, 476

CD-RW: Erasable multisession optical disc on which users can write data, instructions, and information multiple times. See also compact disc-rewritable. 45, 230, **232.** See also **Compact disc-rewritable**
backup using, 375

CD-RW drive: Drive that can read audio CDs, standard CD-ROMs, CD-Rs, CD-RWs, and can write on, or record, CD-RWs. **232**

Celeron, 139

Cell, 107

Cellular radio: Form of broadcast radio that is used widely for mobile communications, specifically wireless modems and cellular telephones. **321**

Cellular telephone, 321
banning of, 299

camera in, 320
data transmission using, 314
sending text messages using, 175
smart. See **Smart phones**

Central processing unit (CPU): Electronic component on a computer's motherboard that interprets and carries out the basic instructions that operate the computer. Also called a processor. **7, 137–39**
comparison of, 139
components of, 137
machine cycle and, 138
purchasing, 139
RAM and, 143–45
role of, 135
system clock and, 138

Certificate authority (CA): Authorized person or company that issues and verifies digital certificates. **374**

CF, 236. See also **CompactFlash (CF)**

Changing records, in database, 338

Character: A number, letter, punctuation mark, or other symbol that is represented by a single byte in the ASCII and EBCDIC coding schemes. **335**

Chart, 64

Charting, 108

Chat: Real-time typed conversation that takes place on a computer. **71**

Chat client, 72

Chat client software, 121

Chat room: Location on an Internet server that permits users to chat with each other. **71–72**
software, 121

Check digit: Validity check consisting of a number(s) or character(s) that is appended to or inserted in a primary key value. **340**

Checks, MICR characters on, 179–80

Chief executive officer (CEO), 454
future of, 455

Chief information officer (CIO): IT executive position that reports to the CEO. 454, **461, 480**

Chief Operations Officer (COO), 454

Chief security officer (CSO): Employee responsible for physical security of a company's property and people; in charge of security computing resources. **422**

Child, 375

Children, Internet access for, 384

Chip: Small piece of semiconducting material, usually silicon, on which integrated circuits are etched. **136**
memory, 142–46
RAM. See RAM
ROM. See Read-only memory

CIM, 459. See also Computer-integrated manufacturing (CIM)

CIM, 460. See also **Customer interaction management (CIM)**

CIO, 461, 480. See also **Chief information officer (CIO)**

Ciphertext, 373

Cisco Systems, 323

Clark, Jim, 41, 481

Cleaning the computer, 155

ClearType, 291

Click: To move the mouse pointer to a button or link on the computer screen, and then to press and release the left mouse button. **57, 103**

Click stream, 468

Client: Other computers and mobile devices on a network that rely on a server for its resources. **305**

Client operating systems, 262. See also Stand-alone operating system

Client/server network: Network in which one or more computers act as a server, and the other computers on the network request services from the server. **305**
operating system for, 266

Clip art: Collection of drawings, diagrams, maps, and photographs that a user can insert in documents. **105**
presentation graphics software, 109

Clip art/image gallery: Collection of clip art and photographs that often is included in application software. **118**

Clipboard, 106

Clock
kernel maintaining, 252
system. See **System clock**

Clock cycle, 138

Clock speed: Pace of the system clock, measured by the number of ticks per second. **138**
bus, 151
needs, 139

Closed, 478. See also Proprietary

CMOS, 146. See also Complementary metal-oxide semiconductor

CMOS battery, 203

CMS, 466. *See also* **Content management system (CMS)**

Coax, 320. *See also* Coaxial cable

Coaxial cable: A single copper wire surrounded by at least three layers: (1) an insulating material, (2) a woven or braided metal, and (3) a plastic outer coating. **320.** *See also* **Coax**

COBOL: COmmon Business-Oriented Language. Programming language designed for business applications, which evolved out of a joint effort between the United States government, businesses, and major universities in the early 1960s. 36, **426.** *See also* **COmmon Business-Oriented Language**

Codd, E. F., 353

Code, 423
assembly language, 424–25
HTML, 433
JavaScript, 434
machine language, 424
object, 425
symbolic instruction, 424
VBScript, 435

Code snippets: Prewritten code and templates associated with common programming tasks. **428**

Codec, 216

Coding schemes, 140–41, 335

Cold boot: Process of turning on a computer that has been powered off completely. **252**

Collaborate: Work online with other users connected to a server. **302**

Color, 184
ink-jet printers, 189
laser printers, 190
video card and, 186

Color correction tools, 217

Colossus, 35

Column: Term used by users of relational databases for field. 108, **347**

Column chart, 108. *See also* Bar chart

COM port, 149

Command: Instruction on a menu that causes a program to perform a specific action. **103, 168**
function keys for, 168

Command-line interface: Type of user interface in which a user types commands or presses special keys on the keyboard (such as function keys or key combinations) to enter data and instructions. **253,** 262, 264, 265

COmmon Business-Oriented Language, 426. *See also* **COBOL**

Communication, and computers, 5

Communications: Process in which two or more computers or devices transfer data, instructions, and information. **296**–323
channel, 296, 317–19
devices, 312–16
home networks, 316–17
network. *See* **Network**
physical transmission media, 319–20
software, 120–21, 310
telephone network and, 310—12
wireless transmission media, 320–22

Communications channel: Transmission media on which data, instructions, or information travel. **296,** 317–19

Communications device: Any type of hardware capable of transmitting data, instructions, and information between a sending device and a receiving device. **8, 312**–16
purchasing desktop computer and, 281

Communications satellite: Space station that receives microwave signals from an earth-based station, amplifies (strengthens) the signals, and broadcasts the signals back over a wide area to any number of earth-based stations. **321**–22

Communications software: Programs that (1) help users establish a connection to another computer or network; (2) manage the transmission of data, instructions, and information; and (3) provide an interface for users to communicate with one another. **310**

Compact disc (CD), 7
audio. *See* Audio CD
burning, 232
care of, 231
direct access and, 235
USB 2.0 ports and, 149

Compact disc (CD) drive, 7
bays and, 151

Compact disc read-only memory, 231. *See also* **CD-ROM**

Compact disc-recordable, 232. *See also* **CD-R**

Compact disc-rewritable, 232. *See also* **CD-RW**

CompactFlash (CF): Type of miniature mobile storage medium that is a flash memory card capable of storing between 32 MB and 4 GB of data. **236**

Company information, system development and, 409

Compaq, Inc., 39

Comparison operations, 137

Compiler: Separate program that converts an entire source program into machine language before executing it. **425**–26, 427
just-in-time (JIT), 427

Complementary metal-oxide semiconductor (CMOS): Technology used by some RAM chips, flash memory chips, and other types of memory chips that provides high speeds and consumes little power by using battery power to retain information even when the power to a computer is off. **146**
battery, 203

Completeness check: Validity check that verifies that a required field contains data. **340**

Compress, 261

Compression, 210

Computer: Electronic device, operating under the control of instructions stored in its own memory, that can accept data, process the data according to specified rules, produce results, and store the results for future use. **3**
advantages of, 4–5
applications in society, 22–26
buyer's guide, 279–94
categories of, 13–18
cleaning of, 155
components of, 6–8
disadvantages of, 4–5
disposing of used, 387
examples of usage, 18–22
fastest, 139
fault-tolerant, 255
personal. *See* **Personal computer**
purchasing, 279–94
refurbishment of, 139
starting. *See* **Booting**
system failure and, 374–75
waste of, 139
wearable, 173

Computer addiction: Growing health problem that occurs when the computer consumes someone's entire social life. **387**

Computer Associates, 443

Computer crime: Any illegal act involving a computer. **362**

copying software, 124

Computer engineer, 156

Computer ethics: Moral guidelines that govern the use of computers and information systems. **376**–78

Computer forensics: The discovery, collection, and analysis of evidence found on computers and networks. Also called digital forensics, network forensics, or cyberforensics. **384**

Computer forensics specialist: Employee who collects and analyzes evidence found on computers and networks. **388**

Computer Fraud and Abuse Acts, 383

Computer industry
career in. *See* Career

Computer literacy: The knowledge and understanding of computers and their uses. **3,** 432

Computer Matching and Privacy Protection Act, 383

Computer output microfilm recorder, 238

Computer program: Series of instructions that directs a computer to perform tasks. **423.** *See also* **Application software; Software**

Computer security plan: Written summary of all the safeguards that are in place to protect a company's information assets. **422**

Computer security risk: Any event or action that could cause a loss of or damage to computer hardware, software, data, information, or processing capability. **362**–76

Computer service technician, 240

Computer technician: Employee who installs, maintains, and repairs hardware; installs, upgrades, and configures software; and troubleshoots hardware problems. **240**

Computer vision syndrome: Eyestrain due to prolonged computer usage. **386.** *See also* **CVS**

Computer-aided design (CAD): Software that aids in engineering, drafting, and design. **459**

Computer-aided design (CAD) software: Sophisticated type of application software that assists a professional user in creating engineering, architectural, and scientific designs. **112**

graphic designer/illustrator using, 198

Computer-aided engineering (CAE): Use of computers to test product designs. **459**

Computer-aided instruction (CAI). See **Computer-based training**

Computer-aided manufacturing (CAM): Use of computers to assist with manufacturing processes such as fabrication and assembly. **25, 459**

Computer-aided software engineering (CASE): Software tools designed to support one or more activities of the system development cycle, typically including diagrams to support both process and object modeling. **419**

Computer-based training (CBT): Type of education in which students learn by using and completing exercises with instructional software. Also called computer-aided training. **119**

multimedia authoring software for, 437

Computer-integrated manufacturing (CIM): Use of computers to integrate the many different operations of the manufacturing process. **459**

Conditions
data outside of, 463
selection control structure and, 440

Configuration information
flash memory and, 145

Connecting to Internet, 51–52

Connector: Device that joins a cable to a peripheral. **136, 149**

Consistency, and computers, 5

Consistency check: Validity check that tests the data in two or more associated fields to ensure that the relationship is logical. **340**

Construct, 440. See also Control structure

Consultant. See Computer consultant

Consumer devices
flash memory cards and, 148

Consumer-to-consumer (C2C) e-commerce, 68

Content filtering: Process of restricting access to certain material on the Web. **384–85**

Content management system (CMS): Combination of databases, software, and procedures that organizes and allows access to various

forms of documents and other files, including images and multimedia content. **466**

Continuous-form paper, 193

Contracts, legal software and, 117

Control structure: Used during program design, a depiction of the logical order of program instructions. Also called a construct. **440**. See also **Construct**

Control unit: Component of a processor that directs and coordinates most of the operations in the computer. **137**

Convertible Tablet PCs, 290

COO. See Chief Operations Officer (COO)

Cookie: Small text file that a Web server stores on a computer. **380–81**
filtering, 379

Copying
files for backup, 375
items in document, 106
optical discs, 233
software, 372–73, 378

Copyright: Exclusive rights given to authors and artists to duplicate, publish, and sell their materials. 372, **378**
Music and video and, 114

Copyrighted software, 64
freeware, 101
packaged, 101
shareware, 101

Cordless keyboard, 168

Cordless mouse, 169

Corrupt files, 260

Cost/benefit feasibility, 409. See also Economic feasibility

Cost-effective information, 334

Costs, for Internet access, 52

Cowlishaw, Mike, 435

CPU, 7, 137–39. See also **Central processing unit**

Cracker: Someone who accesses a computer or network illegally with the intent of destroying data, stealing information, or other malicious action. **362**

Create: To enter text or numbers, insert graphical images, and perform other tasks with a document using an input device such as a keyboard, mouse, microphone, or digital pen. **106**

Credit cards
POS terminals processing, 180
protecting, 379
purchasing computers using, 286, 287
smart cards, 237

theft of, 373

Credit report
reviewing, 379

CRM, 466. See also **Customer relationship management (CRM)**

Crop, 217

Cross-platform, 252

CRT, 186. See also Cathode-ray tube (CRT)

CRT monitor: Type of desktop monitor that contains a cathode-ray tube. **186**
quality of, 186
video cards and, 186

CSO, 422. See Chief security officer (CSO)

CTS, 385. See Carpal tunnel syndrome (CTS)

Currency data type, 335

Custom software: Software that performs functions specific to a business or industry, developed by a user or at a user's request. 101, 415

Customer interaction management (CIM): Software that manages the day-to-day interactions with customers, such as telephone calls, e-mail interactions, Web interactions, and instant messaging sessions. **460**

Customer relationship management (CRM): System that manages information about customers, interactions with customers, past purchases, and interest. **466, 481**

Customer service department, 466

Customers
click streams and, 468
e-mail from, 460
extranet use by, 469
instant messaging (IM) with, 460
managing interactions with, 460
managing relationships with, 21, 466, 481
virtual private network use, 470
Web services and, 469

Customer support, 353

CVS, 386. See also Computer vision syndrome

Cybercafé : Coffee house or restaurant that provides personal computers with Internet access to its customers. **300**

Cybercrime: Online or Internet-based illegal acts. **362–70, 389**

Cyberextortionist: Someone who uses e-mail as a vehicle for extortion. **363**

Cyberforensics, 384. See Computer forensics

Cyberterrorism, 363

Cyberterrorist: Someone who uses the Internet or network to destroy or damage computers for political reasons. **363**

Cylinder, 226

DA, 351. See also **Database analyst (DA)**

Data: Collection of unprocessed items, which can include text, numbers, images, audio, and video. 3, **166, 332**
accuracy of, 338
backup. See **Backup**
correct, 333, 339–40
correcting inaccurate, 338
decryption of, 373
encryption of, 258, 373
hierarchy of, 334–36
input of. See **Input; Input device**
maintaining, 336–40, 344–46, 351
organized in database, 108–9, 347
organized in worksheet, 107–8
output of. See **Output device**
privacy laws, 382–83
quality of, 334
redundant, 341, 342
relationships, 348
representation in computer, 140–41
retrieval, 344–46
security, 341, 342, 346, 351
sharing, 8, 303, 342
storage of. See **Storage; Storage medium**
traveling on Internet, 52
updating, 338
validating, 339–40

Data analysis, using decision support system (DSS), 463

Data bus, 151

Data dictionary (database): A DBMS element that contains data about each file in a database and each field in those files. Also called a repository. **343**

Data entry validation, 419

Data entry form, 345. See also Form

Data file: Collection of related records stored on a storage medium such as a hard disk, CD, or DVD. **336**

Data integrity, 333, 342

Data mart, 349

Data model: Rules and standards that define how a database organizes data. **347–49**

Data processing, 462. See also Transaction processing system

Data projector: Output device that takes the text and images displaying on a computer screen and projects them on a larger screen so an audience can see the image clearly. **195,** 289

Data type: Specifies the kind of data a field in a database can contain and how the field can be used. **335**

Data warehouse: Huge database that stores and manages the data required to analyze historical and current transactions. **349, 468–69**

Database: Collection of data organized in a manner that allows access retrieval, and use of that data. **108, 332**
administration, 351, 352
data model, 347–49
data warehouse and, 349, 468–69
design, 351, 418–19
file processing system versus, 340–42
Internet, 345
information privacy and, 379, 380
multidimensional, 347, 349
object-oriented, 347, 349
object-relational, 347
programming language for, 430
querying, 344–45, 348, 349
recovery of, 346
relational, 347–48, 353
transaction process systems, 461–62

Database administrator (DBA): Person who creates and maintains the data dictionary, manages security of a database, monitors the performance of a database, and checks backup and recovery procedures. **351, 352**

Database analyst (DA): Person who focuses on the meaning and usage of data, including proper placement of fields, defining the relationships among data, and identifying users' access privileges. Also called a data modeler. **351**

Database approach: System used to store and manage data in which many programs and users share the data in a database. **341–42**

Database management system (DBMS): Program that allows user to create a computerized database; add, change, and delete data in the database; sort and

retrieve data from the database; and create forms and reports from the data in the database. Also called database management software. **332.** See also **Database software**
backup and recovery, 346
data dictionary, 343
data model, 347–49
data security and, 346
file retrieval and maintenance, 344–46
functions of, 343–46
log, 346
popular, 343, 347
security, 341, 342, 346, 351

Database server, 305, 350

Database software: Application software used to create, access, and manage a database; add, change, and delete data in the database; sort and retrieve data from the database; and create forms and reports using the data in the database. **108, 332.** See also **Database management system (DBMS)**

Date data type, 335

DBA, 351, 352. See also **Database administrator (DBA)**

DBMS, 332. See also **Database management system (DBMS)**

Dean, Mark, 241

Decision making
data warehouse and, 468
expert systems and, 464–65
by management, 462
management information system (MIS) and, 462–63

Decision support system (DSS): Information system that helps users analyze data and make decisions. **463**

Decoding, 138

Decrypt: Process of deciphering encrypted data into a readable form. **373**

Dedicated line: Type of always-on connection that is established between two communications devices (unlike a dial-up line where the connection is reestablished each time it is used). **311–12**

Dedicated servers, 305

Default value, 343

Defragmenting: Reorganizing a disk so the files are stored in contiguous sectors, thus speeding up disk access and the performance of the entire computer. **261**

Deleting programs, 260

Deleting records, from database, 338–39

Delphi: Powerful visual programming tool that is ideal for large-scale enterprise and Web application development. **429**

Dell, Michael, 27

Dell Computer Corporation, 27

Demodulate/demodulation, 313

Denial of service attack: Assault on a computer or network whose purpose is to disrupt computer access to an Internet service such as the Web or e-mail. Also called DoS attack. **367.** See also **DoS attack**

Design phase: Phase of the system development cycle that consists of two major activities: (1) if necessary, acquire hardware and software and (2) develop all of the details of the new or modified information system. 406, **416–19**
acquiring hardware and software, 416
detailed design, 418–19
prototyping, 419
quality review techniques, 419
soliciting vendor proposals, 417
technical requirement, 416
testing and evaluating vendor proposals, 417

Desktop: On-screen work area that has a graphical user interface. **102**

Desktop computer: Computer designed so the system unit, input devices, output devices, and any other devices fit entirely on or under a desk or table. **14**
display devices, 186, 184
flat panel monitors, 184
floppy disk drive in, 223
hard disk in, 224, 225
keyboards, 167, 168,
motherboard, 136
purchasing, 279–80, 281–87
system unit, 134, 135
See also **Personal computer**

Desktop publishing (DTP) software: Application software used by professional designers to create sophisticated documents that can contain text, graphics, and many colors. **113**

Detailed analysis, 415. See also Logical design

Detailed design, 418–19

Detailed report, 462

Developer: Person who writes and modifies computer programs. Also called a programmer. **423**

Devices
kernel managing, 252

DHTML, 435. See also **Dynamic HTML**

Diagnostic utility: Utility program that compiles technical information about a computer's hardware and certain system software programs and then prepares a report outlining any identified problems. **261**

Diagrams, clip art, 105

Dialog box, 103

Dial-up access: Method of connecting to the Internet using a modem in a computer and a standard telephone line. **51**

Dial-up line: Temporary connection that uses one or more analog telephone lines for communications. **311**

Dial-up modem, 313–14. See also Modem

Differential backup, 478

Digital: Representation of data using only two discrete states: on (1) and off (0). **140**

Digital camera: Camera that stores its photographed images digitally, instead of on traditional film. 6, **175–76, 210**
attaching to PDA, 174
flash memory cards and, 148
in PDA, 174
purchasing desktop computer and, 282
quality, 175
storage media, 7
transferring pictures into computer from, 7, 118

Digital certificate: A notice that guarantees a user or a Web site is legitimate. **374**

Digital cinema, 195
projectors and, 195

Digital entertainment, 397–403

Digital Equipment Corporation (DEC), 37

Digital forensics, 384. See Computer forensics

Digital formats, 214

Digital image
converting paper documents into, 177
quality of, 175
storing, 232
See also **Digital camera**

Digital imaging technology, 210–13

Digital modem, 314

Digital movies, 195

Digital music players
flash memory cards and, 148
purchasing notebook computer and, 288

Digital pen: Input device that allows users to write or draw on the screen by pressing the pen and issue instructions to a Tablet PC by tapping on the screen. 15, **172,** 291. *See also* **Stylus**

Digital photo printer, 191. *See also* Dye-sublimation printer

Digital signature: Encrypted code that a person, Web site, or company attaches to an electronic message to verify the identity of the message sender. **374**

Digital Subscriber Line, 52, 311–12. *See also* DSL

Digital versatile disc-ROM, . *See also* **Digital video disc-ROM; DVD-ROM**

Digital video (DV) camera: Video camera that records video as digital signals instead of as analog signals. **176**

storage media for, 236

Digital video capture device, purchasing desktop computer and, 282

Digital video disc-ROM, 233. *See also* **Digital versatile disc-ROM; DVD-ROM**

Digital Video Interface port, 185. *See also* DVI.

Digital video technology, 214–18

Digital works, preserving, 352

Digital-to-analog converter (DAC), 218

Dijsktra, Edsger, 37

Dimensions, data stored in, 349

Direct access, 235

Direct conversion: Conversion strategy where the user stops using an old system and begins using a new system on a certain date. Also called abrupt cutover. **421**

Director MX, 437

Disaster recovery plan: Written plan describing the steps a company would take to restore computer operations in the event of a disaster. Contains four major components: emergency plan, backup plan, recovery plan, and test plan. **479**

Disk. *See* **Hard disk**

Disk controller: Special-purpose chip and electronic circuits that control the transfer of data, instructions, and information between a disk and the system bus and other components in a computer. **227**

Disk defragmenter: Utility that reorganizes the files and unused space on a computer's hard disk so the operating system accesses data more quickly and programs run faster. **261**

Disk Operating System, 262. *See also* **DOS**

Disk scanner: Utility that (1) detects and corrects both physical and logical problems on a hard disk and (2) searches for and removes unnecessary files. **260**

Diskette: Portable, inexpensive storage medium that consists of a thin, circular, flexible plastic Mylar film with a magnetic coating, enclosed in a square shaped plastic shell. **223.** *See also* **Floppy disk**

Display device: Output device that visually conveys text, graphics, and video information. **183–86**

CRT monitors, 186
ergonomics and, 386
eye problems and, 386
flat-panel display, 184
video cards and, 186
video content and, 187

Distribution systems: Provides forecasting for inventory control, manages and tracks shipping of products, and provides information and analysis on inventory in warehouses. **460**

DNA computer, 153

Docking station, 175
Tablet PC, 175, 291

Documentation (system development): Collection and summarization of data and information. **409**

Documents
desktop publishing, 113
scanning, 177
source, 177
word processing, 105–6

Domain name: Text version of an IP address. **53,** 54, 56

DOS: Any one of several single user operating systems that were developed in the early 1980s by Microsoft for personal computers. **262.** *See also* **Disk Operating System**

DoS attack: Assault on a computer or network whose purpose is to disrupt computer access to an Internet service such as the Web or e-mail. Also called denial of service attack. **367.** *See also* **Denial of service attack**

safeguards against, 367–68

Dot pitch, 185, 186

Dot-com, 43

Dot-matrix printer: Type of impact printer that produces printed images when tiny wire pins on a print head mechanism strike an inked ribbon. **192**

Do-until control structure, 441–43

Do-while control structure, 441

Downlink, 321

Download (camera), 175

Downloading: Process of a computer receiving information, such as a Web page, from a server on the Internet. **55**

Downstream rate, . 312

Downtime, 477

Downward compatible, 262

Dpi (dots per inch), 189

DRAM, 144. *See also* Dynamic RAM

Drawing, 64

Drawings, clip art, 105

Dreamweaver MX: Web page authoring program developed by Macromedia that allows Web site designers and programmers to create, maintain, and manage professional Web sites. **436**

Drive
CD-ROM. *See* **CD-ROM drive**
DVD. *See* DVD drive
floppy. *See* **Floppy disk drive**
hard. *See* **Hard disk drive**

Drive bays: Rectangular openings inside the system unit that typically hold disk drives. 135, **151**

Driver: Small program that tells an operating system how to communicate with a specific device. **256**
operating system and, 256

Driving directions, GPS and, 301

DRM. *See also* Digital Rights Management (DRM)

DSL: Type of digital technology that provides high-speed Internet connections using regular copper telephone lines. **52,** 311–12

DSL modem: Modem that sends digital data and information from a computer to a DSL line and receives digital data and information from a DSL line. **314**

DSS, 463. *See also* **Decision support system (DSS)**

DTP software. *See* **Desktop publishing (DTP) software**

Dubinsky, Donna: 199

DV camera, 176. *See also* **Digital video (DV) camera**

DVD (digital versatile disc or digital video disc), 7, 42, 233
care of, 231
direct access and, 235

DVD and CD mastering software, 213

DVD creation software, 218

DVD drive, 7

bays and, 151

DVD recorder, 234. *See also* DVD+RW drive

DVD/CD-RW drive, 234

DVD+R (DVD-recordable): 230, 234

DVD-R (DVD-recordable), 230, 234

DVD+RAM (DVD+random access memory), 230, 234

DVD+random access memory, 234. *See also* DVD+RAM

DVD-recordable, 234. *See also* DVD-R; DVD+R

DVD-ROM: Extremely high capacity optical disc on which users can read, but not write or erase, that is capable of storing 4.7 GB to 17 GB of data. 7, 230, **233.** *See also* **Digital versatile disc-ROM; Digital video disc-ROM**

DVD-ROM drive: Device that can read a DVD-ROM. Most DVD-ROM drives also can read audio CDs, CD-ROMs, CD-Rs, and CD-RWs. **233**

DVD-ROM jukebox, 476. *See also* DVD-ROM server

DVD+RW: Rewritable DVD format with capacities up to 4.7 GB per side that can be erased and written on, or recorded on, more than 1,000 times. 230, **234.** *See also* **DVD-RW; DVD-rewritable**

DVD-RW: Rewritable DVD format with capacities up to 4.7 GB per side that can be erased and written on, or recorded on, more than 1,000 times. 230, **234.** *See also* **DVD+RW; DVD-rewritable**

backup using, 375

DVD+RW drive, 234. *See also* DVD writer

DVD writers, 45

DVI port, 185. *See also* Digital Video Interface port

Dye-sublimation printer, 191. *See also* Digital photo printer

Dynamic HTML (DHTML): Newer type of HTML that allows Web page authors to include more graphical interest and interactivity in a Web page. **435**

Dynamic RAM (DRAM), 144

EarthLink, 52

eBay, 75

EBCDIC, 140, 335. *See also* Extended Binary Coded Decimal Interchange

e-book, 44

Eckert, J. Presper, 35

E-commerce: Short for electronic commerce, a business transaction conducted over the Web. 21, 42, 43, **67–68**
cookies and, 381
digital certificates and, 374
e-retail and, 470
finance and, 472
types of, 67–68

Economic feasibility: Measure of whether the lifetime benefits of a proposed information system will be greater than its lifetime costs. **409.** *See also* **Cost/benefit feasibility**

ECPA, 383. *See also* Electronic Communications Privacy Act

EDI (electronic data interchange): Electronic data interchange. Set of standards that controls the transfer of business data and information among computers both within and among enterprises. **468**

Edit: To make changes to the existing content of a document. **106**

Editing
audio, 114
digital images, 175
document, 106
images, 113, 118
photographs, 118
video, 114

Education
computers used in, 22–23
Web site and, 92

Educational software: Application software that teaches a particular skill. **119**

Educational use, application software for, 119

Educational Web site, 62

E-form, 350. *See also* Electronic form

EIDE (Enhanced Integrated Drive Electronics), 228

EIS, 463. *See also* Executive information system (EIS)

Electrical adapters, purchasing notebook computer and, 289

Electrical lines, home network using, 316

Electromagnetic radiation (EMR), 186

Electronic commerce. *See* **E-commerce**

Electronic Communications Privacy Act, 383. *See also* ECPA

Electronic data interchange, 468. *See also* EDI (electronic data interchange)

Electronic form, 350. *See also* E-form

Electronic magazine, 416. *See also* E-zine

Electronic mail. *See* **E-mail**

Electronic money, 237

Electronic Numerical Integrator And Computer (ENIAC), 35

Electronic profiles, 380

Electronic storefront: Online business a customer visits that contains product descriptions, graphics, and a shopping cart. **68**

Ellison, Larry, 353

E-mail: Short for electronic mail, the transmission of messages and files via a computer network. 10, 50, **69–70,** 74
collaborating via, 302
communications uses and, 298
companies monitoring, 120
impact on communications, 411
monitoring, 384
PDAs using, 293
phishing, 381–82
privacy and, 379
sending digital images via, 175, 176
spam, 379, 382
viruses spread through, 70, 268, 365, 366

E-mail address: Combination of a user name and a domain name that identifies a user so he or she can receive Internet e-mail. **70**

E-mail filtering: Service that blocks e-mail messages from designated sources. **382**

E-mail program: Software used to create, send, receive, forward, store, print, and delete e-mail messages. **69,** 121

Embedded computer: Special-purpose computer that functions as a component in a larger product. **17–18**

Embedded Linux, 267

Embedded operating system: The operating system that resides on a ROM chip inside most PDAs and small devices. **266–67**

Emergency plan, 479

Emoticons: Symbols used on the Internet to express emotion. **73**

Employee monitoring: The use of computers to observe, record, and review an employee's use of a computer, including communications such as e-mail messages, keyboard activity (used to measure productivity), and Web sites visited. 120, 381, **384,** 456

Employee relationship management (ERM) system, 458

EMR, 186. *See also* Electromagnetic radiation

Encryption: Process of converting readable data into unreadable characters to prevent unauthorized access. **258, 373**
digital signature, 374
e-mail, 374
Web browsers using, 374

Encryption key, 373

End-user license agreement (EULA), 372. *See also* Single-user license agreement

Energy, conserving, 186, 387

ENERGY STAR program: Program, developed by the U.S. Department of Energy and the U.S. Environmental Protection Agency, that encourages manufacturers of computer components to create energy-efficient devices requiring little power when they are not in use. **186,** 387

Engelbart, Douglas, 199

Engineering department, information systems used by, 459

Enhanced Integrated Drive Electronics, 228. *See also* **EIDE**

Enhanced keyboard, 168

ENIAC, 35. *See* Electronic Numerical Integrator And Computer

Enterprise, 238, 452–81
information systems in, 456–66
levels of users in, 455
organizational structure of, 454–56
technology strategy, 461

Enterprise computing: The use of computers in networks, such as LANs and WANs, or a series of interconnected networks that encompass a variety of different operating systems, protocols, and network architectures. **21,** 452–81
hardware, 474–78
software applications, 111, 456–66

Enterprise computing software, 111

Enterprise hardware: Devices geared for heavy use, maximum availability, and maximum efficiency that large organizations use to manage and store information and data. **474–78**

Enterprise information: Information gathered in the ongoing operations of an enterprise-sized organization. **456**

Enterprise resource planning (ERP): Provides centralized, integrated software to help manage and coordinate the ongoing activities of the enterprise. **465–66,** 476

Enterprise software, 456–66

Enterprise storage system: Strategy that focuses on the availability, protection, organization, and backup of storage in a company. **238, 476**

Enterprise-wide systems, 461

Enterprise-wide technologies, 467–70

Entertainment, Web and, 472

Entertainment software: Application software, such as interactive games, videos, and other programs designed to support a hobby or provide amusement and enjoyment. **120**

Entertainment Web site, 62, 84

Environment, and computers, 5, 139

Environmental Web site, 84

E-retail: Business transaction that occurs when retailers use the Web to sell their products and services. Also called e-tail. **470.** *See also* **E-tail**

Ergonomic keyboard, 168

Ergonomics: The science of incorporating comfort, efficiency, and safety into the design of the workplace. **168, 386**
PDAs and, 294

ERM system, 458. *See also* Employee relationship management (ERM) system

ERP, 465. *See also* **Enterprise resource planning (ERP)**

Errors
compiler checking for, 425
interpreter checking for, 426

E-tail, 470. *See also* E-retail

Ethernet: Network standard that specifies no central computer or device on the network should control when data can be transmitted. **308**
development of, 38
home network and, 316
inventor of, 323

Ethical issues, 376–78
copying optical discs and, 233

EULA, 372. *See also* End-user license agreement (EULA)

Ewing, Marc, 271

Exception criteria, 462

Exception report, 462–63

Execute: Process of a computer carrying out the instructions in a program. **12,** 425

Executing, 138
RAM and, 143

Executive information system (EIS), 463

Executive management, 455, 461, 463

Exercise, preventing repetitive strain injuries using, 385

Expansion bus: Bus that allows the processor to communicate with peripherals. **151**

Expansion card: Circuit board that enhances functions of a component of a system unit and/or provides connections to peripherals. **147.** *See also* **Adapter card**

Expansion slot: Socket on a motherboard that can hold an adapter card. **147**

Expert system: Information system that captures and stores the knowledge of human experts and then imitates human reasoning and decision making. **464–65**

Extended Binary Coded Decimal Interchange (EBCDIC), 140, 335

Extensible HTML, 436. *See also* XHTML

eXtensible Markup Language, 436. *See also* **XML**

External drive bay, 151

External floppy disk drive, 223

External hard disk: Separate freestanding hard disk that connects with a cable to a USB port or FireWire port on the system unit. **227**

External sources, 463, 468

Extranet: Portion of a company's network that allows customers or suppliers of a company to access parts of an enterprise's intranet. **308, 469**

Eyes
computer effect on, 386

E-zine: Publication available on the Web. Also called electronic magazine. **416.** *See also* **Electronic magazine**

Face recognition system, 181, 370

Facial recognition software, 370

Facsimile machine, 194. *See also* Fax machine

Fair Credit Reporting Act, 383

False condition, selection control structure and, 440

Fanning, Shawn, 43

FAQ (frequently asked questions): List that helps a user find answers to commonly asked questions. **4, 73**

Fault-tolerant computer: Computer that has duplicate components so it can continue to operate when one of its main components fail. **255**

Fax, 194
communications uses and, 298
sending digital images, 175

Fax machine: Output device that codes and encodes documents so they can be transmitted over telephone lines. **194.** *See also* **Facsimile machine**

Fax modem, 194

Feasibility: Measure of how suitable the development of a system will be to the company. **409**

Feasibility report, 414

Feasibility study, 413. *See also* Preliminary investigation

Fetching, 138

Fiber-optic cable: Dozens or hundreds of thin strands of glass or plastic that use light to transmit signals. **320**

Field: A combination of one or more related characters or bytes, a field is the smallest unit of data a user accesses. **108, 335**
type of data in, 335

Field name: Name that uniquely identifies each field in a database. **335**

Field size: Defines the maximum number of characters a field can contain. **335**

Fifth-generation language, 428. *See also* Visual programming language

File: Named collection of stored data, instructions, or information. **103**
adding records to, 336
backup of, 223, 227, 261, 268, 372, 375
changing records in, 338
compressing, 261, 269
conversion, 269
corrupt, 260
deleting records from, 338–39
fragmented, 261
graphics, 64
quarantining, 366
restoring, 261, 375
uncompressing, 269
virus-infected, 364, 365–66
zipped, 269

File compression utility: Utility program that shrinks the size of a file(s), so the file takes up less storage space than the original file. **122, 269**

File conversion utility: Program that transforms a file from one format to another, eliminating the need to reenter data in a new program. **122, 269**

File format, 216

File maintenance: Procedures that keep data current. **336–40, 344–46**

File management, operating system and, 257, 259

File manager: Utility that performs functions related to file and disk management. **259**

File name: Unique combination of letters of the alphabet, numbers, or other characters that identifies a file. **103**

File processing system: System used to store and manage data in which each department or area within an organization has its own set of files. **341, 347**

File retrieval, methods of, 344–46

File server, 305

File sharing, Internet connection and, 379

File sharing network, 306. *See also* **P2P**

File Transfer Protocol, 71. *See also* **FTP**

Filtering software, 310

Finance, computers used in, 23, 454, 458

Finance, Web sites and, 86

Financial departments, 454, 458

Financial planning, with personal finance software, 116

Financial transactions
accounting software tracking, 111
personal finance software and, 116

Fingerprint scanner: Biometric device that captures curves and indentations of a fingerprint and compares them with those of a stored image. **181, 289, 370, 371**

Fingerprinting, brain. *See* Brain fingerprinting

Fiorina, Carly, 27

Firewall: Hardware and/or software that protects a network's resources from intrusion by users on another network such as the Internet. **367–68**
built into router, 316
personal, 368, 379
wireless security and, 376

FireWire port: Port that can connect multiple types of devices that require faster data transmission speeds. **150**

purchasing notebook computer and, 288

Firmware: ROM chips that contain permanently written data, instructions, or information, recorded on the chips when they were manufactured. **145**

Fixed disk, 224

Fixed wireless: Microwave transmissions that send signals from one microwave station to another. **52**

Flame wars, 73

Flames, 73

Flash memory: Type of non-volatile memory that can be erased electronically and rewritten. **145**

Flash memory card: Removable flash memory device that allows users to transfer data and information from mobile devices to their desktop computers. 145, **148**
digital cameras using, 175
types of, 236,

Flash Player, 443

Flash MX: Web page authoring program developed by Macromedia that enables Web site programmers to combine interactive content with text, graphics, audio, and video. **436**

Flatbed scanner: Type of light-sensing input device that scans a document and creates a file of the document in memory instead of a paper copy. **177**

Flat-panel display, 184–85

Floppy disk: Portable, inexpensive storage medium that consists of a thin, circular, flexible plastic Mylar film with a magnetic coating, enclosed in a square shaped plastic shell. 7, 222, **223**
characteristics of, 223
direct access and, 235
formatting, 259
viruses and, 268,
See also **Diskette**

Floppy disk drive: Device that reads from and writes on a floppy disk. **223**
bays and, 151
purchasing desktop computer and, 282

Font: Name assigned to a specific design of characters. **106**

Font size: Size of the characters in a particular font. **106**

Font style: Font design, such as bold, italic, and underline, that can add emphasis to a font. **106**

Footprint, 184

Foreground, 254, 255

Form: Window on the screen that provides areas for entering or changing data in a database. Also called data entry form. **108, 345,** 432. *See also* **Data entry form**

Format: To change a document's appearance. **106**

Formatting, 259

Formula, 107

Forth, 431

Fortran, 36, 431

Fourth-generation language, 430. *See also* 4GL

Fractional T1, 312

Fragmented, 261

Frame rate, 217

Frankston, 38

Freedom WebSecure, 379

Freeware: Copyrighted software provided at no cost to a user by an individual or a company that retains all rights to the software. **101**

Frequently asked questions. *See* **FAQ**

FrontPage: Web page authoring program developed by Microsoft that provides nontechnical and professional users with the ability to create and manage Web sites easily. **436**

FTP (File Transfer Protocol): Internet standard that permits file uploading and downloading with other computers on the Internet. **71**

  software, 121

FTP server, 71

Full backup, 375, 478. *See also* Archival backup

Function, . 107

Function keys, 168

Functional units, 457–61

Games, 402

  interactive, 120

  pointing devices for, 171

Gantt, Henry L., 409

Gantt chart, 409

Garbage in, garbage out (GIGO): Computing phrase that points out the accuracy of a computer's output depends on the accuracy of the input. **333**

Gates, Bill, 27, 38

GB, 142. *See also* **Gigabyte**

General purpose information system, 461–65

Ghosting, 261

GHz, 138. *See also* **Gigahertz**

GIF, 64

Gigabyte (GB): Approximately 1 billion bytes. **142**

Gigahertz (GHz): One billion ticks of the system clock per second. **138**

GIGO, 333. *See also* **Garbage in, garbage out (GIGO)**

Global positioning system (GPS): Navigation system that consists of one or more earth-based receivers that accept and analyze signals sent by satellites in order to determine the receiver's geographic location. **301,** 320

  robots and, 439

Gnutella, 306

Google, 58, 75, 96, 467

Gosling, James, 443

Government

  computers used in, 23

  Internet structure and, 50

  personal data and, 350

  privacy laws and, 382–83

  Web site, 89

GPS, 301, 320. *See also* **Global positioning system (GPS)**

GPS receiver, 301, 320

Grandparent, 375

Graphic: Digital representation of nontext information such as a drawing, chart, or photograph. **64.** *See also* Graphical image

Graphic designer/illustrator: Employee who creates visual impressions of products and advertisements in the fields of graphics, theater, and fashion. **198**

Graphic illustrator. *See* **Graphic designer/illustrator**

Graphical image, 64. *See also* Graphic

Graphical user interface (GUI): Type of user interface that allows a user to interact with software using text, graphics, and visual images, such as icons. **10, 253,** 264, 265

  visual programming languages and, 428

Graphics, 64

  application software and, 112–14

  business software and, 104–11

  ethical issues in altering, 378

  multimedia and, 64

  output, 182

  on Web page, 54. *See also* **Clip art**

Graphics card: Adapter card that converts computer output into a video signal that travels through a cable to the monitor, which displays an image on the screen. **47.** *See also* **Video card**

Graphics chip, 186

Graphics file, viewing, 259

Graphics tablet: Flat, rectangular, electronic, plastic board that is used to create drawings and sketches. **172**

Green computing: Computer usage that reduces the electricity and environmental waste involved in using a computer. **387**

Grid computing: Technology that combines many servers and/or personal computers on a network to act as one large computer. **478**

Groupware: Software that helps groups of people work together on projects and share information over a network. **302**

GUI. *See* **Graphical user interface**

Hacker: Someone who accesses a computer or network illegally. **260, 362**

  passwords and, 369

Hand geometry system, 181, 370

Handheld computer: Computer small enough to fit in one hand. **15, 271,** 319. *See also* **Handtop computer**

  keyboards, 168

  operating systems for, 252, 266

  See also **Mobile computer; Mobile device**

Handhelds: Computers small enough to fit in one hand. See also handtop computer; handheld computer. **16**

  games, 402

Hands, carpal tunnel syndrome and, 385

Handspring, 45, 199

Handtop computer: Computer small enough to fit in one hand. **15.** *See also* **Handheld computer**

Handwriting recognition, 106, 174

Handwriting recognition software, 74

Hard disk: Type of storage device that contains one or more inflexible, circular platters that store data, instructions, and information. **7, 224–28.**

  backing up, 261, 375

  booting and, 252

  bus connection for, 151

  characteristics of, 225–26

  controller, 227–28

  defragmenting, 261

  direct access and, 235

  disk capacity, 224

  downloading from digital camera to, 175

  external, 227

  formatting, 259

  miniature, 227,

  operating system on, 251

  portable, 227

  problems on, 260

  purchasing desktop computer and, 282

  purchasing notebook computer and, 288

  removable, 227

  used for virtual memory, 255

Hard drive, Internet. *See* Internet hard drive

Hardware: Electric, electronic, and mechanical components contained in a computer. **6–8**

  acquiring in design phase, 416

  communications, 312–16

  diagnostic utility, 261

  disposing of used, 387

  drivers, 256

  electrical problems, 374–75

  enterprise, 474–78

  identifying requirements, 416

  input device. *See* **Input device**

  operating system coordinating, 251

  output device. *See* **Output device**

  performance monitoring, 257

  purchasing notebook computer and, 288

  scalability, 477

  storage. *See* **Storage; Storage media**

  system failure and, 374

  system unit. *See* **System unit**

  theft, 371

  vandalism, 371

  vendors, 417

Hardware theft: The act of stealing computer equipment. **371**

Hardware vandalism: The act of defacing or destroying computer equipment. **371**

Hawthorne Effect, 410

Hayes, 39

Head crash, 226

Head-mounted pointer, 197

Headphone port, on CD drives, 229

Headset: Audio output device that fits over a user's ears and generates sound only the user can hear. **194**

  sound card and, 147

Health care, computers used in, 23–24

Health information, storing on smart cards, 237

Health issues, 385–87

  CRT monitors, 186

  disadvantage in computers, 5

  keyboards, 168

  radiation, 186

Health Web sites, 95, 473

Hearing impaired users, output devices for, 197

Help

application software and, 122–23

Online. *See* **Online Help**

Web-based, 122–23

Help desk specialist: Employee who answers hardware, software, or networking questions in person, over the telephone, and/or in a chat room. **124**

Hertz, 138

Hewlett-Packard (HP), 27, 39, 199

Hibernate, 252

High-availability systems: Systems that continue running and performing tasks for at least 99 percent of the time. **477**

High-level language, 424

History file, clearing, 379

Hits, 60

Hoff, Ted, 38

Home design/landscaping software: Application software that assists users with the design, remodeling, or improvement of a home, deck, or landscape. **119**

Home network: Network consisting of multiple devices and computers connected together in a home. **316–17**

wireless, 316–17, 317

Home page: First page that a Web site displays. **55**

Home user: User who spends time on a computer at home. **18–19**

application software for, 115–20

backup and, 375, 479

input devices, 196

output devices, 190, 196

printers, 190

processor selection, 139, 154

RAM needs, 144

storage and, 220, 221, 239

Web cams, 176

wireless security and, 375

HomeRF (radio frequency) network, 316–17

Hopper, Grace, 36, 426, 443

Horizontal market software, 415

Host: Any computer that provides services and connections to other computers on a network. **50**

Hot site, 479

Hot spot: Wireless network that provides Internet connections to mobile computers and other devices. **300**

number of, 309

Hot-swapping, 477

HRIS, 458. *See also* **Human Resources Information Systems**

HTML: Hypertext Markup Language. Special formatting language that programmers use to format documents for display on the Web. **433**–34. *See also* **Hypertext Markup Language**

Dynamic, 435

Extensible, 436

http: A set of rules that defines how pages transfer on the Internet. See also Hypertext Transfer Protocol. **56.** *See also* **Hypertext Transfer Protocol**

Human experts, expert systems and, 464–65

Human Resources Information Systems (HRIS): Information system that manages one or more human resources function(s). **458**

Hyperlink: Built-in connection to another related Web page or part of a Web page. **57.** *See also* **Link**

Hyperlink data type, in database, 335

HyperTalk, 431

Hypertext Markup Language, 433. *See also* **HTML**

Hypertext Transfer Protocol, 56. *See also* **http**

IBM (International Business Machines), 36, 37, 38, 481

Eclipse, 420

grid computing,

Millipede storage device,

Slam, 420

Icon: Miniature image displayed on a computer screen that represents a program, an instruction, a document, or some other object. 10, **102**

Identification, 369, 373

Identity theft, 379–82

IEEE 1394 port, 150. *See also* FireWire port

If-then-else control structure, 440

Illustration software, 113. *See also* Paint software

IM, 72–73. *See also* **Instant messaging**

iMac, 42

Image editing software: Application software that provides the capabilities of paint software and also includes the capability to enhance and modify existing

images and pictures. **113, 212**

personal, 118

professional, 113

Image viewer: Utility program that allows users to display, copy, and print the contents of a graphics file. **259**

Images, 64, 65

as links, 57

personal DTP software, 118

See also Graphics; **Video**

Impact printer: Type of printer that forms characters and graphics on a piece of paper by striking a mechanism against an inked ribbon that physically contacts the paper. **192–93**

Implementation phase: Phase of the system development cycle during which the new or modified system is constructed, or built, and then delivered to the users. Four major activities performed include: (1) develop programs, (2) install and test the new system, (3) train users, and (4) convert to the new system. 406, **420**–21

Import: To bring graphics into a document. **117**

Incremental backup, 478

Industry, computers used in, 25

Inference rules, 464

Information: Processed data that conveys meaning and is useful to people. **3, 332**

accuracy of, 5, 377–78

downloading, 55

enterprise, 456

gathering for system development, 410

memory processing, 142

personal, 379–82

RAM and, 144

reading. *See* **Reading**

ROM and, 145

searching for on the Web, 57–61

sharing, 8, 303

storage of. *See* **Storage; Storage media**

theft of, 373–74

valuable, 334

writing. *See* **Writing**

Information privacy: Right of individuals and companies to deny or restrict the collection and use of information about them. **379–85**

encryption and, 373

laws, 382–83

Information processing cycle: Series of input, process, output, and storage activities performed by a computer. **5**

Information system (IS): Collection of hardware, software, data, people, and procedures that work together to produce quality information. **406, 456–66**

closed, 478

converting to new, 421

development of. *See* System development; **System development cycle**

enterprise-wide, 466–70

executive, 463

expert, 464–65

functional units using, 457–61

general purpose, 461–65

installing and testing, 420

integrated, 465–66

management, 462–63

open, 478

prototype of, 419

security, 422

Information technology (IT) department, 454

outsourcing functions of, 415

Information theft: Computer security risk that occurs when someone steals personal or confidential information. **373–74**

Informational Web site, 62

Infrared (IR), 150, 309, 321

cordless keyboards using, 168

See also **IrDA**

Ink-jet printer: Type of nonimpact printer that forms characters and graphics by spraying tiny drops of liquid ink on a piece of paper. **189–90**

cost of cartridges, 190

refilling cartridges, 190

Input: Any data and instructions entered into the memory of a computer. **166–81**

accuracy of, 377–78

audio, 173

biometric, 181

designing, 418–19

device. *See also* **Input device**

digital cameras, 175

storage devices as source of, 222

terminals, 180

video, 176

voice, 173

Input device: Any hardware component that allows users to enter data and instructions into a computer. **6, 166–81**

biometric, 181

keyboard, 167–68, 180, 197

mobile computers and devices, 172, 174–75

pointing. *See also* **Pointing device**

purchasing desktop computer and, 281

scanners, 177–80
video, 176
voice, 173
Installing
new information system, 420
Installing (software): Process of setting up software to work with the computer, printer, and other hardware components. **12,** 252
Instant messaging (IM): Real-time Internet communications service that notifies a user when one or more people are online and then allows the user to exchange messages or files or join a private chat room with those people. **72–73**
customer support using, 460
live images added to, 176
software for, 73, 121
wireless, 298
Instant messenger, 73, 121
Instructions, 4, 166
cache and, 144
input of, 166
memory processing, 142, 145, 255
operating system allocating to memory, 255
reading. See **Reading**
ROM and, 145
storage of. See **Storage; Storage media**
writing. See **Writing**
Integrated circuit, 136
invention of, 36, 157
Integrated Services Digital Network, 311. See also **ISDN**
Integration test, 420
Intel, 40, 42, 44, 45, 157
processors, 139
Intel-compatible processors, 139
Intellectual property (IP), 378
Intellectual property rights: Rights to which creators are entitled for their work. **378**
Intelligent agents, 57
Intelligent home network, 316
Interactive applications, creating using multimedia authoring software, 114
Interface
disk controller as, 227
EIDE, 228
SCSI, 228
Internal drive bay, 151
Internal sources, 463, 468
International Business Machines, 481. See also IBM (International Business Machines)
International Information Integrity Institute (I-4), 389
Internet: Worldwide collection of networks that connects millions of businesses, government agencies,

educational institutions, and individuals. Also called the Net. **8–10,** **50–75**
backup using, 476
broadcasting images over, 176
chat rooms on, 71–72
content filtering, 384–85
control of, 51
cybercafé connection, 300
data traveling on, 52
e-form and, 350
e-mail using, 69–70
file and printer sharing and, 379
high-speed access, 52
history of, 50
how it works, 51–54
information accuracy and, 377–78
instant messaging on, 121
mailing lists and, 71
Netiquette and, 73
newsgroups on, 71
objectionable material on, 384
pirated software on, 373, 378
public Internet access point, 300
search engines, 57, 58, 60–61
security and, 389
spyware and, 381
surge protector and, 374–75
telephone calls over, 73, 176
video conference using, 176
virtual private network and, 470
Web farming and, 468
World Wide Web and. See **World Wide Web**
Internet access, 50, 51–52
car, 121
PDAs, 293
purchasing desktop computer and, 284, 285
Tablet PCs, 292
Internet access provider. See **Access provider**
Internet attacks, 364–68
Internet backbone: Major carriers of network traffic on the Internet. **52**
Internet connection, 51–52
cable television network and, 314
dedicated lines and, 311–12
dial-up line and, 311
wireless, 300
Internet backup, 476
Internet databases, 345
Internet etiquette, 73. See also **Netiquette**
Internet Explorer. See Microsoft Internet Explorer
Internet filters, 268
anti-spam programs, 268
pop-up blockers, 269
Web filters, 268
Internet Protocol address, 53. See also **IP address**
Internet service provider. See **ISP**

Internet telephony: Technology that allows users to speak to other users over the Internet using their desktop computer, mobile computer, or mobile device. Also called Voice over IP. **73, 194**
Internet-enabled: Technology that allows mobile devices to connect to the Internet wirelessly. **15, 21**
Internet-enabled devices, 52
Internet2, 57
Interoperability: Sharing information with other information systems within an enterprise. **478**
Interpreter: Program used to convert a source program into machine language and then executes the machine language instructions. **426**
Interview
for system development, 410
Intranet: An internal network that uses Internet technologies. **307–8**
Intrusion detection software: Program that automatically analyzes all network traffic, assesses system vulnerabilities, identifies any unauthorized intrusions, and notifies network administrators of suspicious behavior patterns or system breaches. **368**
Inventory
distribution systems, 460
e-retail and, 470
extranet and, 469
scheduling and managing, 459
Investing
online. See **Online investing**
Iomega Corporation, 223
IP, 378. See also Intellectual property
IP address: A number that uniquely identifies each computer or device connected to the Internet. **53** See also **Internet Protocol address**
iPod music player, purchasing notebook computer and, 288
IR, 321. See also **Infrared (IR)**
IrDA: Network standard used to transmit data wirelessly via infrared (IR) light waves. **309**
IrDA port: Port that uses infrared light waves to transmit signals between a wireless device and a computer. **150**
Iris recognition system: Biometric device that uses iris recognition technology

to read patterns in the iris of the eye. **181**
Iris scanner, 370
IS, 406. See also **Information system**
ISDN (Integrated Services Digital Network): Short for Integrated Services Digital Network; Set of standards for digital transmission of data over standard copper telephone lines. **311**
ISDN modem: Modem that sends digital data and information from a computer to an ISDN line and receives digital data and information from an ISDN line. **314**
ISP (Internet service provider): Regional or national Internet access provider. **52**
e-mail filtering and, 382
subscribing to, 285
IT consultant: Employee, typically hired based on computer expertise, who provides computer services to his or her clients. **417**
IT department. See **Information technology (IT) department**
Itanium, 139
iTunes, 401

J2EE, 469
Jack: Term sometimes used to identify an audio or video port. **148**
JAD session, 410. See also **Joint-application design (JAD) session**
Java: Object-oriented programming language developed by Sun Microsystems. **427,** 443
creation of, 41
JavaScript: Interpreted language that allows a programmer to add dynamic content and interactive elements to a Web page. **434**
Jewel box, 230
JIT compiler, 427. See also Just-in-time (JIT) compiler
Job: Operation that the processor manages. **255–56**
Joint-application design (JAD) session: Lengthy, structured, group meeting in which users and IT professionals work together to design or develop an application. **410**
Joystick: Pointing device used for games or flight and driving simulations that is a vertical lever mounted on a base. **171**
purchasing desktop computer and, 282
JPEG, 64, 211

Picture CD using, 232
JPEG 2000, 195
Just-in-time (JIT) compiler, 427

K, 142. *See also* **Kilobyte**
Kay, Alan, 271
Kazaa, 306
KB, 142. *See also* **Kilobyte**
Kemeny, John, 37
Kernel, 252
Key field: Field in a database that uniquely identifies each record in a file. Also called primary key. **336.** *See also* **Primary key**
Keyboard: Input device that contains keys users press to enter data and instructions into a computer. 6, **168**
connections, 168
ergonomics, 168, 386
health issues, 168, 385
on-screen, 174, 197
PDAs, 293
purchasing desktop computer and, 282, 284
purchasing notebook computer and, 288
terminal, 180
Keyboard monitoring software, 384
Keywords, 60–61,
Kilby, Jack, 36, 157
Kilobyte (KB or K): Exactly 1,024 bytes. **142**
Kiosk, 171
Knowledge base, 464
Kodak, Picture CD and, 232

L1 cache: A type of memory cache that is built directly into the processor chip, with a capacity of 8 KB to 16 KB. **145**
L2 cache: A type of memory cache that is slightly slower than L1 cache, but has a much larger capacity, ranging from 64 KB to 16 MB. **145**
Label, 107
Labor force, in computers, 5
LAN, 303. *See also* **Local area network**
Laptop computer: 14. *See* **Notebook computer**
Large business user: Computer user working for a business that has hundreds or thousands of employees in offices across a region, the country, or the world. 18, **21–22**
input devices, 196
operating systems for, 266
output devices, 190, 196
printers, 190
processor selection and, 154
storage and, 220, 221, 239
Large-format printer: Printer that creates photo-realistic quality color prints, used

mainly by graphic artists. **192**
Large-scale integration (LSI), 37
Laser printer: Type of high-speed, high-quality nonimpact printer that creates images using a laser beam and powdered ink called toner. 190–91
Layers, 218
Layout chart, 418–19
LCD, 185. *See also* **Liquid crystal display**
LCD monitor: Desktop monitor that uses a liquid crystal display instead of a cathode-ray tube to produce images on a screen, resulting in a sharp, flicker-free display. Also called flat-panel monitor. 47, **184**
ports and, 185
quality of, 185
on mobile computers and devices, 184
Leading, 456
Learning
computer-based training and, 119
computers used in, 22–23
educational software for, 119
Legal issues
copyright. *See* **Copyright**
employee monitoring, 384
intellectual property, 378
Internet access, 384
privacy, 382–83
software theft, 372–73, 378
Legal software: Application software that assists in the preparation of legal documents and provides legal information to individuals, families, and small businesses. **117**
Libraries
content filtering used by, 384
Internet access from, 310
License agreement: An agreement issued by a software manufacturer that gives the user the right to use the software. 372–73
Light pen: Handheld input device that can detect the presence of light. **171**
Line chart, 108
Line printer: Type of high-speed impact printer that prints an entire line at a time. **193**
Line-of-sight transmission, 309, 321
Link: Built-in connection to another related Web page or part of a Web page. Short for hyperlink. **57**
animation, 64
portal providing, 467
search engine and, 60, 96

subject directories and, 58
Linux: Popular, multitasking UNIX-type operating system. 41, 43, 47, **265**, 266, 271
future of, 265
Liquid crystal display (LCD): Type of display that uses a liquid compound to present information on a display device. **185**
for Tablet PCs, 291
LISP, 431
Lithium-ion batteries, 288
Loads, 12, 101, 103
Local area network (LAN): Network that connects computers and devices in a limited geographical area such as a home, school computer laboratory, office building, or closely positioned group of buildings. **303**
bus network, 306
Ethernet, 308
first, 38
ring network, 307
Log (database): Listing of activities that change the contents of a database. **346**
Log on: To access a computer or network as a user. **258**
Logical design, 415. *See also* Detailed analysis
Logitech, 199
Logo, 431
Longhorn, 263
LookSmart, 57
Loop, 441
Lotus, 39
Lotus 1–2–3, 39
Low-level language, 424–25
LSI. *See* Large-scale integration
Lycos, 57

Mac OS, 14
Mac OS X: Multitasking operating system that is the latest version of the Macintosh operating system. 101, **264**
Machine cycle, 138
Machine language: The only language a computer directly recognizes, using a series of binary digits or a combination of numbers and letters that represent binary digits. **424**, 426
Machine-dependent language, 424
Machine-independent language, 424
Macintosh, purchasing, 280–81
Macintosh operating system: Operating system for Apple's Macintosh computer. 14, 39, 101, **264**
Macro (application program): Series of statements that instructs an application how to complete a task. **365, 432**
Macro recorder, 432

Macromedia, 443
Magazines
online, 25
Magnetic disks: Storage medium that uses magnetic particles to store items such as data, instructions, and information on a disk's surface. **222–28**
hard disk, 224–28
floppy disk, 223
types of, 222
Zip disk, 223
Magnetic-ink character recognition. *See* MICR
Magnetic stripe card reader: Reading device that reads the magnetic stripe on the back of credit, entertainment, bank, and other similar cards. See also magstripe reader. **179.** *See also* **Magstripe reader**
Magnetic Tape/Selectric Typewriter (MT/ST), 37
Magnetoresistive RAM (MRAM), 144
Magstripe reader, 179, 180 *See also* Magnetic stripe card reader
Mailing list: Group of e-mail names and addresses given a single name. **71**
Main memory, 143. *See also* RAM
Mainframe: Large, expensive, powerful computer that can handle hundreds or thousands of connected users simultaneously, storing tremendous amounts of data, instructions, and information. **17**
Maintaining
data, 336–40, 344–46, 351
database, 344–46, 351
Maintaining (program): Act of correct errors or adding enhancements to an existing program. **438**
Malicious-logic programs, 364
MAN, 304. *See also* **Metropolitan area network (MAN)**
Management information system (MIS): Information system that generates accurate, timely, and organized information, so managers and other users can make decisions, solve problems, supervise activities, and track progress. **462–63**
Management information systems (MIS) manager, 480
Managers: Employees responsible for coordinating and controlling an organization's resources. **456**

decision making by, 456, 462–63
levels of, 454
Manufacturers
processors, 139
ROM chips, 145
Manufacturing enterprise functional units in, 457
information systems used by, 459
Manufacturing information systems, 459
Maps
clip art, 105
GPS and, 301
Margins, 105
Market research system, 460
Marketing information system: Information system that serves as a central repository for the tasks of the marketing functional unit. **460**
Massively multiplayer online games (MMOGs), 402
Master, 218
Material Requirements Planning (MRP): Approach to information management in a manufacturing environment that uses software to help monitor and control processes related to production. **459**
Mauchley, John, 35
Maxtor, 241
MB, 142. *See also* **Megabyte**
McAfee VirusScan, 268
Mechanical mouse: Mouse that has a rubber or metal ball on its underside. **169**
Media, Web and, 472
Media card, printing photos using, 190
Medical Information Bureau, medical records from, 239, 379
Meeting
online, 302
using video conference, 176
Megabyte (MB): Approximately 1 million bytes. **142**
Megahertz, access time stated in, 146
Megapixels (MP), 210
Memo data type, 335
Memory: Electronic components in a computer that store instructions waiting to be executed and data needed by those instructions. **7, 142–46**
access times, 146, 222
address, 142
address bus, 151
application software in, 103
buffer, 255
cache, 144–45
CMOS, 146
creating document and, 106

flash, 145
nonvolatile, 142, 145
operating system files loaded into, 101
operating system managing, 255
PDAs, 293
program loading into, 12, 101, 103
purchasing desktop computer and, 281–82
purchasing notebook computer and, 288
RAM. *See* **RAM**
read-only. *See* **Read-only memory**
role of, 135
ROM. *See* **Read-only memory**
sizes, 142
types of, 142
virtual, 255
volatile, 142, 144
Memory cache: Cache that helps speed the processes of a computer by storing frequently used instructions and data. **144–45**
Memory cards, 7
Memory management: Operating system activity that optimizes the use of random access memory (RAM). **255**
Memory module: Small circuit board that houses RAM chips and is held in a memory slot on the motherboard. **144**
Memory resident, 252, 253
Memory slots: Slots on the motherboard that hold memory modules. **144**
Memory Stick: Type of miniature mobile storage medium that is a flash memory card capable of storing between 256 MB and 2 GB of data. **236**
digital cameras using, 175
Menu: Item on the computer screen that contains a list of commands from which a user can make selections. **103, 168**
sub-, 103
Menu generator, 432
Menu-driven interface, 262
Menu-driven tools, application generator and, 431
Message board: Popular Web-based type of discussion group that does not require a newsreader. **71, 121**
Messaging
instant. *See* **Instant messaging**
short. *See* Short message service (SMS)
Metcalfe, Robert M., 38, 323

Metropolitan area network (MAN): High-speed network that connects local area networks in a metropolitan area such as a city or town and handles the bulk of communications activity across that region. **304**
MICR (magnetic-ink character recognition): Technology that reads text printed with magnetized ink. **179.** *See also* **Magnetic-ink character recognition**
MICR reader: Reading device that converts MICR characters into a form that a computer can process. **179, 180**
Microfiche: A small sheet of film, usually about 4 inches by 6 inches in size, on which microscopic images of documents are stored. **238**
Microfilm: A roll of film, usually 100 to 215 feet long, on which microscopic images of documents are stored. **238**
Microphone, 6
input using, 173
purchasing desktop computer and, 282, 284
purchasing Tablet PC and, 291
sound card and, 147
video conference using, 176
Microprocessor: Term used by some computer and chip manufacturers to refer to a processor chip for a personal computer. **137.** *See also* **Processor**
invention of, 38
Microsoft, 27, 38, 39, 40, 41, 42, 44, 46, 47, 48, 125
ActiveX, 434
ClearType technologies, 291
legal problems, 43, 45
MS-DOS, 38, 262
.NET architecture, 428
operating system, 11, 101. *See also* **Windows XP**
Prefix, 420
Microsoft Media Center, 398
Microsoft Network (MSN), 52
online meetings using, 302
Microsoft Word, 104
Microwave station: Earth-based reflective dish that contains the antenna, transceivers, and other equipment necessary for microwave communications. **321**
Microwaves: Radio waves that can provide a high-speed signal transmission. **321**
Middle management, 455

MIDI, 150, 173. *See also* Musical Instrument Digital Interface
MIDI port: Special type of serial port that connects the system unit to a musical instrument, such as an electronic keyboard. **150**
Midrange server: Server that is more powerful and larger than a workstation computer, typically supporting several hundred and sometimes up to a few thousand connected computers at the same time. **16**
Millipede, 224
Miniature hard disk, 227
Miniature mobile storage media, 235–37
Mini disc, digital cameras using, 175
Mirroring, 474
MIS, 462. *See also* **Management information system (MIS)**
MIS (management information system) manager, 480
MITS, Inc., 38
MMOG. *See* Massively multiplayer online game
MMS, 298. *See also* Multimedia message service
Mobile computer: Personal computer that a user can carry from place to place. **14–15**
purchasing, 279–80, 292–93
Mobile device: Computing device small enough for a user to hold in his or her hand. **14, 15–16, 152–53**
display device, 183
flash memory and, 145, 148
GPS capability, 301
input devices, 172, 174–75
Internet access, 309
LCD screens, 184
operating system, 251
PC Card modem, 314
PDA. *See* **PDA (personal digital assistant)**
purchasing, 292–94
storage media for, 235–37, 239
system unit, 135
theft of, 371
touch screens, 172
Internet access and, 52, 436
Mobile printer: Small, lightweight, battery-powered printer used by a mobile user to print from a notebook computer, Tablet PC, PDA, or smart phone while traveling. **192**
Mobile users: Users who work on a computer while away from a main office or school. **18, 20**
input devices, 196

Internet access by, 52
output devices, 183, 184, 192, 196
processor selection, 154
sales force, 460
storage and, 235–37, 239
system unit, 152–53
virtual private network use, 470
wireless security and, 375
Moblogs, 63
Mockup, 418–19
Models, decision support system (DSS) using, 463
Modem: Communications device that converts a computer's digital signals to analog signals. Also called a dial-up modem. 8, 297, **313–16**
cable, 52, 314
dial-up, 313–14
digital, 312, 314
DSL, 311–12, 314
fax, 194
Internet access using, 51, 53
ISDN, 311, 314
PC Card, 314
port, 149
purchasing desktop computer and, 282
surge protection and, 375
wireless, 52, 314
Modula-2, 431
Modulate/modulation, 313
Monitor: Display device that is packaged as a separate peripheral. 7, **183–86**
CRT. See CRT monitor
flat-panel, 184
gas plasma, 185
purchasing desktop computer and, 282, 284
purchasing notebook computer and, 287
Monochrome, 184
Moore, Gordon, 157
Moore's Law, 157
Morphing, 217
Motherboard: Main circuit board of the system unit, which has some electronic components attached to it and others built into it. See also system board. 7, 135, **136**. See also **System board**
memory slots on, 144
Motorola processor, 139
Mouse: Pointing device that fits comfortably under the palm of a user's hand. 6, **169**
connections, 169
creator of, 199
manufacturer, 199
operations, 240
purchasing desktop computer and, 283, 284
repetitive strain injuries and, 385
types, 169
using, 103, 169

Mouse operations, 240
Mouse pad: Rectangular rubber or foam pad that provides traction for a mechanical mouse. **169**
Mouse pointer, 169
Movies, digital, 195
Moving Pictures Experts Group (MPEG), 65
Mozilla, 48
MP, 175
MP3: Format that reduces an audio file to about one-tenth of its original size, while preserving much of the original quality of the sound. **64**
downloading files, 472
swapping files via the Web and, 306
MP3 players
flash memory and, 145
storage capacity, 145
USB 2.0 ports and, 149
See also Digital music players
MPEG, 65. See also Moving Pictures Experts Group
MPEG-4: Current version of a popular video compression standard. **65**
MRAM, 144. See also Magnetoresistive RAM
MRP, 459. See also **Material Requirements Planning (MRP)**
MS-DOS, 262
MSN. See Microsoft Network, The
MSBlast worm, 46
MT/ST. See Magnetic Tape/Selectric Typewriter
Multidimensional database: Database that stores data in dimensions. 347, **349**
Multifunction peripheral: Output device that looks like a copy machine but provides the functionality of a printer, scanner, copy machine, and perhaps a fax machine. See also all-in-one device. **194**
Multimedia: Any application that combines text, graphics, audio, and video. 21, **64–66**
adding to Web pages, 434
application software and, 112–14
RAM needs, 144
Multimedia authoring software: Software that allows users to combine text, graphics, audio, video, and animation in an interactive application and that often is used for computer-based training and Web-based presentations. **114, 437**
Multimedia message service (MMS), 298. See also **Picture messaging**

Multiprocessing, 255
Multipurpose operating system, 266
Music, 64
computers and, 400
downloading, 64, 400
input, 173
MIDI port and, 150
See also **Audio; MIDI; MP3**
Multisession disc, 232
Multitasking operating system, 253, 264, 267
Multiuser, 255
Muscle fatigue, 386
Music
downloading from Web, 472
purchasing online, 472
swapping, 306, 378
Music players, storage media for, 236
Musical Instrument Digital Interface (MIDI), 150, 173

Name
file. See File name
field. See **Field name**
Names
mailing lists, 71
user, 70
Nanosecond (ns): One billionth of a second. **146**
Napster, 43
NAS, 474. See also **Network attached storage (NAS)**
National Digital Information Infrastructure & Preservation Program, 352
National ISP, 52
National Press Photographers Association, 378
Navigation, using GPS. See **Global positioning system (GPS)**
Net: Worldwide collection of networks that links millions of businesses, government agencies, educational institutions, and individuals. **50.** See also **Internet**
.NET, 45, 428, 469
Netiquette: Short for Internet etiquette, the code of acceptable behaviors users should follow while on the Internet. **73**
Netscape Navigator, 41
Netscape Communications Corporation, 41, 57
NetWare, 266
Network: Collection of computers and devices connected together via communications devices and transmission media, allowing computers to share resources. 8–10, **303–9**
access control, 371
attacks, 364–68
bus, 306
business, 8
cable television, 314

cellular telephone, 321
client/server, 305
communications standards, 308–9
cyberterrorism and, 363
data accessibility on, 476
extranet and, 469
file sharing, 306
firewalls, 367–68
groupware and, 302
home, 316–17,
host, 50
Internet. See **Internet**
intranet, 307
local area. See **Local area network (LAN)**
metropolitan area (MAN), 304
.NET architecture and. See .NET
peer-to-peer, 305–6
purchasing notebook computer and, 288
ring, 307
security, 258
star, 307
storage area (SAN), 475, 476
telephone, 310–12
topologies, 306–7
value-added (VAN), 303
virtual private (VPN), 470
wide area (WAN), 304
wireless LAN, 303
Network administrator: Employee who installs, configures, and maintains LANs, WANs, intranets, and Internet systems; identifies and resolves connectivity issues. **257**
intrusion detection and, 368
security and, 258, 368,
Network architecture, 305–6
Network attached storage (NAS): Server that is placed on a network with the sole purpose of providing storage to users and information systems attached to the network. **474**, 476
Network attacks, 364–68
Network card: Adapter card, PC Card, or flash card that enables the computer or device to access a network. Also called a network interface card (NIC). **315**
purchasing desktop computer and, 283
purchasing notebook computer and, 288
Network forensics, 384. See Computer forensics
Network operating system (NOS): Operating system that organizes and coordinates how multiple users access and share resources on a network. **257**, 266. See also **Network OS**

Network OS: 257. *See also* **Network operating system**
peer-to-peer network, 305
user access and, 369
Network server, 305
Network specialist: Person who installs, configures, and troubleshoots network systems; manages system and client software, Web page integration and creation, network security measures, and user accounting; and monitors network event logs for problem resolution. **322**
Network standard: Guidelines that specify the way computers access the medium to which they are attached, the type(s) of medium used, the speeds used on different types of networks, and the type(s) of physical cable and/or the wireless technology used. **308**
Network topology: Layout of computers and devices in a communications network. **306–7**
News, Web and, 472
News Web site, 61, 91
Newsgroup: Online area in which users have written discussions about a particular subject. **71,** 121
communications uses and, 298
spam and, 382
Newspapers, online, 25
Newsreaders, 71, 121
Nit, 185
Node, 303, 307
Noise: Electrical disturbance that can degrade communications. **319**
Nonimpact printer: Type of printer that forms characters and graphics on a piece of paper without actually striking the paper. **189–92**
Nonmanagement employees, 455
Nonprocedural language: Type of programming language in which a programmer writes English-like instructions or interacts with a visual environment to retrieve data from files or a database. **430**
Nonresident, 252
Nonvolatile memory: Type of memory that does not lose its contents when a computer's power is turned off. **142,** 145
Norton AntiVirus, 268
Norton SystemWorks, 270
Notebook computer: Portable,

personal computer designed to fit on a user's lap. **14**–15, 21
converting to Tablet PC, 288
display device, 184
floppy disk drive in, 223
hard disk in, 224
keyboards, 168
PC Cards, 235
pointing stick, 170
power supply, 152
printing from, 192
processors, 139
purchasing, 279–80, 287–89
sales force using, 460
storage media, 223, 236
system unit, 134
theft of, 371
touchpads, 170
Notepad, in personal information manager, 110
Note taking software: Application software that enables users to enter typed text, handwritten comments, drawings, or sketches anywhere on a page. **110**
Noyce, Robert, 157
NS, 146. *See also* **Nanosecond**
Number systems, coding systems and, 140–41
Numbers
check digit, 340
input of, 168
range check, 340
used in worksheets, 107
Numeric check: Validity check that ensures users enter only numeric data in a field. **339**
Numeric data type, 335
Numeric keypad, 168

Object, 427
possessed, 370, 371
Object (database): Database item that contains data, as well as the actions that read or process the data. **349**
Object code: *See* Object program
Object data type, 335
Object program, 425
Object query language (OQL), 384
Object-oriented database (OODB): Database that stores data in objects. 347, **349**
Object-oriented programming (OOP) language: Programming language used to implement an object-oriented design. **427–29**
Object-relational databases, 347
Obscenity, Internet and, 384
Observation, system development and, 410

OCR, 177. *See also* **Optical character recognition**
OCR devices: Optical character recognition devices that include small optical scanners for reading characters and sophisticated software to analyze what is read. **177**
Office automation. *See* **Office information system (OIS)**
Office information system (OIS): Information system that enables employees to perform tasks using computers and other electronic devices, instead of manually. Also called office automation. **461**
Offsite, 375
OIS, 461. *See also* **Office information system (OIS)**
OLTP, 462. *See also* Online transaction processing (OLTP)
OMR, 177. *See also* **Optical mark recognition**
Online: Describes the state of a computer when it is connected to a network. **8**
Online auction: E-commerce method that allows consumers to bid on an item being sold by someone else. **68,** 88
Online backup service: Web site that automatically backs up files to its online location, usually charging a monthly or annual fee. **375**
Online banking: Online connection to a bank's computer to access account balances, pay bills, and copy monthly transactions to a user's computer. **23, 116,** 472
Online dating, 19
Online Help: Electronic equivalent of a user manual that usually is integrated in a program. **122–23**
Online investing: Use of a computer to buy and sell stocks and bonds online, without using a broker. **23,** 472
Online meeting, 302
Online service provider (OSP): Company that provides Internet access as well as many members-only features. **52**
subscribing to, 285
Online shopping, 90, 381, 470
Online storage: Service on the Web that provides hard disk storage to computer users, usually for a minimal monthly fee. **228,** 261, 375. *See also* **Internet hard drive**

Online trading: Online connection that allows users to invest in stocks, options, bonds, treasuries, certificates of deposit, money markets, annuities, mutual fund, and so on — without using a broker. **472**
Online transaction processing (OLTP), 462
On-screen keyboard, 174, 197
OODB, 349. *See also* **Object-oriented database (OODB)**
OOP language, 427. *See also* **Object-oriented programming (OOP) language**
Open (Information Systems), 478
Open Source Code software, 43
Open source software: Software provided for use, modification, and redistribution. **101, 265, 267,** 271
Opening Adobe PDF files, 113
Operating system (OS): Set of programs that coordinates all the activities among computer hardware devices. **11,** 251–71
application software and, 101, 252
booting and, 252
client, 262
device configuration, 256
embedded, 266
file management, 257, 259
functions of, 251, 252–58
handheld computers, 252, 266
Internet connection and, 256
job scheduling, 255–56
managing programs, 253–55
memory and, 142, 143
multiprocessing, 255
multipurpose, 266
multitasking, 253, 264, 265, 266
multiuser, 255
network, 257, 266, 305
PDAs, 266, 292
performance monitoring, 257
personal firewall and, 260, 368
purchasing desktop computer and, 281
RAM and, 143
security and, 257, 258
stand-alone, 262–65
types of, 14, 262–65
user interface and, 253
utility programs, 250, 259–61
See also **Platform**
Operational feasibility, 409
Operational management, 455
Optical character recognition (OCR): Optical reader technology that involves reading typewritten, computer-printed, or hand-

printed characters from ordinary documents and translating the images to a form that a computer can process. **177**

Optical discs: Type of storage medium that consists of a flat, round, portable disc made of metal, plastic, and lacquer that is written on and read by a laser. **229–34**
characteristics of, 229
cleaning, 231
paper disks, 233
Optical fiber, 320

Optical mark recognition (OMR): Optical reader technology that reads hand-drawn marks such as small circles or rectangles. **177**

Optical mouse: Mouse that uses devices, such as optical sensors or lasers, that emit and sense light to detect the mouse's movement. **169**
Optical reader, 177
Optical scanner, 177. *See also* **Scanner**
Optical storage medium. *See* CD (compact disc); DVD (digital versatile disc or digital video disc)
OQO handheld computer, 48
Oracle Corporation, 353
Organizational structure, of an enterprise, 454–56
Organized information, 334
Organizing, 456

OS, 251. *See also* **Operating system (OS)**
OSP. *See* **Online service provider**
Ousterhout, John, 435
Outlook, 69
Outlook Express, 69

Output: Data that has been processed into a useful form. **182**, 183–99
design, 418–19
ethics of altering, 378
voice, 194
See also **Output device**

Output device: Any hardware component that conveys information to one or more people. **7**, 183–96
audio, 193
data projector, 195, 289
display. *See* **Display device**
fax machine, 194
headsets, 194
multifunction peripheral, 194
physically challenged users, 197
printers, 187–93
purchasing desktop computer and, 281
speakers, 193

Outsource (software development): Having a source

outside a company develop software for the company. Some companies outsource just the software development aspect of their IT operation, while others outsource more or all of their IT operation. **415**
Outsourcing (storage), 477

P2P: Type of peer-to-peer network on which users access each other's hard disks and exchange files directly over the Internet. **306**. *See also* **File sharing network**

Packaged software: Mass-produced, copyrighted, prewritten software available for purchase. **101, 415**
Packets, 308
Paging, 255
Paint program, starting, 102, 103

Paint software: Application software that allows users to draw pictures, shapes, and other graphical images with various onscreen tools. **113**. *See also* **Illustration software**
personal, 118
professional, 113
starting, 102, 103
Palm, 199
palmOne, 199
PalmPilot, 41
Palm OS, 266, 292, 293
Paper
ink-jet printer, 189
laser printer, 190
wasting, 387

Parallel conversion: Conversion strategy where the old system runs alongside the new system for a specified time. **421**

Parallel port: Type of interface that connects devices to the system unit by transferring more than one bit at a time. **149**
Parent, 375
Parents, content filtering by, 384
Parker, Donn, 389
Partial backup, 478. *See also* **Selective backup**
Pascal, 431

Password: Private combination of characters associated with a user name that allows access to certain computer resources. **258, 369**
cookies and, 381
encrypted data and, 373
guidelines, 258
hackers and, 369
notebook computers and, 371
Pasting, 106

Payload: Destructive event or prank a malicious-logic program is intended to deliver. **364**
Payments
online banking used to make, 472
PC camera, 176. *See also* **PC video camera**

PC Card: Thin, credit-card-sized device that adds memory, storage, sound, fax/modem, network, and other capabilities to mobile computers. **147, 235**
PC Card modem, 314

PC Card slot: Special type of expansion slot in notebook and other mobile computers that can hold a PC Card. **147**

PC video camera: Type of digital video camera that enables a home or small business user to capture video and still images, send e-mail messages with video attachments, add live images to instant messages, broadcast live images over the Internet, and make video telephone calls. 6, **176**
purchasing desktop computer and, 283
purchasing Tablet PC and, 291
PC-compatible, 14
PC-DOS, 262
PCMCIA, 147. *See also* Personal Computer Memory Card International Association
PCS, 321. *See also* **Personal Communications Services (PCS)**
PC-to-TV port, 288

PDA (personal digital assistant): One of the more popular lightweight mobile devices in use today, providing personal organizer functions such as a calendar, appointment book, address book, calculator, and notepad. **15**, 41. *See also* **Personal digital assistant**
flash memory cards, 148
input, 172, 174
Internet access, 52, 436
operating system, 266, 292
Palm devices, 199
picture messaging using, 298
printing from, 192
purchasing, 279–80, 292–94
sales force using, 460
screens, 184
software for, 110
storage media for, 236
stylus, 172, 174
system unit, 135
text messaging using, 298

Peer, 305

Peer-to-peer network: Simple, inexpensive network that typically connects fewer than 10 computers. **305–6**
Pen drive, 236. *See also* **USB flash drive**

Pen input: Input device used by mobile users to write, draw, and tap on a flat surface to enter input. **172**
Pentium, 40, 42, 44, 45, 139

Performance monitor (operating system): Operating system program that assesses and reports information about various computer resources and devices. **257**
Performance monitoring (system development), 422

Peripheral: Device that connects to a system unit and is controlled by the processor in the computer. **147**

Perl: Practical Extraction and Report Language. Scripting language developed at NASA's Jet Propulsion Laboratory as a procedural language similar to C and C++. **435**

Personal Communications Services (PCS): Term used by the U.S. Federal Communications Commission (FCC) to identify all wireless digital communications. **321**

Personal computer: Computer that can perform all of its input, processing, output, and storage activities by itself and contains a processor, memory, one or more input and output devices, and storage devices. **14**
buying, 144
cache, 144–45
desktop. *See* **Desktop computer**
entertainment and, 398
notebook. *See* **Notebook computer**
price of, 144
processor, 139
purchasing, 144, 279–81
transferring information between PDA and, 110
transferring pictures from digital camera into, 118

Personal computer maintenance utility: Utility program that identifies and fixes operating system problems, detects and repairs disk problems, and includes the capability of improving a computer's performance. 122, **270**

Personal Computer Memory Card International Association (PCMCIA), 147
Personal computer salesperson, 26
Personal digital assistant, 15. *See also* **PDA**
Personal DTP (desktop publishing) software: Application software that helps home and small office/ home office users create newsletters, brochures, advertisements, postcards, greeting cards, letterhead, business cards, banners, calendars, logos, and Web pages. **117**
Personal finance software: Simplified accounting program that helps home users or small office/home office users manage finances. **116**
Personal firewall utility: Program that detects and protects a personal computer and its data from unauthorized intrusions. **260, 368,** 379
Personal identification number (PIN), ATM, 180
Personal identification number (PIN), user: Numeric password, either assigned by a company or selected by a user. **370**
Personal identity, theft of, 379–82
Personal information, safeguarding, 379
Personal information manager (PIM): Application software that includes features to help users organize personal information. **110**
Personal paint/image editing software: Application software that provides an easy-to-use interface, usually with more simplified capabilities that allows users to draw pictures, shapes, and other images. **118**
Personal use, software for, 115–20
Personal Web site, 63
PGP, 374. *See also* Pretty Good Privacy (PGP)
Pharmacies, online, 473
Phased conversion: Conversion strategy used by larger systems with multiple sites where each location converts at a separate time. **421**
Phases: Categories into which system development activities are grouped: (1) planning phase, (2) analysis

phase, (3) design phase, (4) implementation phase, and (5) support phase. **406–22**
Phishing: Scam in which a perpetrator sends an official looking e-mail that attempts to obtain your personal and financial information. 48, **381–82**
Phoneline network, 316
Photo community, 175, 177
Photo editing software: Popular type of image editing software that allows users to edit digital photographs and create electronic photo albums. **118,** 175
Photo printer: Type of nonimpact color printer that produces photo-lab-quality pictures. **190**
storage media for, 236
Photographs, 64
altering, 378
clip art, 105
editing, 118
personal DTP software, 117
Picture CDs and, 232
Physical transmission media, 319–20
Physically challenged users input devices for, 197
output devices for, 197
Picture CD: Single-session CD-ROM that stores digital versions of a single roll of film using a jpg file format. **232**
Picture messaging: Service that allows users to send graphics, pictures, video clips, and sound files, as well as short text messages to another smart phone, PDA, or computer. **298.** *See also* **Multimedia message service (MMS).**
Pictures
scanning, 177
Pie chart, 108
PILOT, 431
Pilot conversion: Conversion strategy where only one location in a company uses a new system – so it can be tested. **421**
PIM. *See* **Personal information manager**
PIN, 180, 370. *See also* **Personal identification number (PIN)**
Piracy: Unauthorized and illegal duplication of copyrighted material. **372**
software, 372, 378
Pixel: The smallest element in an electronic image. Short for picture element. **175,** 185
CRT monitor, 186
digital camera and, 175
distance between, 185

Pixel pitch, 185
Pixilated, 212
PKZIP, 269
Plaintext, 373
Planning, 456
project management and, 408–9
Planning phase: Step in the system development cycle that begins when a steering committee receives a project request. 406, 411, **412–13,** 422
Plasma monitor: Display device that uses gas plasma technology, which sandwiches a layer of gas between two glass plates. **185**
Platform, 252
Platter, 224, 225, 226
Player: Software used by a person to listen to an audio file on a computer. **64**
PL/1, 431
Plotters: Sophisticated printers that produce high-quality drawings such as blueprints, maps, and circuit diagrams using a row of charged wires (called styli) to draw an electrostatic pattern on specially coated paper and then fuse toner to the pattern. **192**
Plug and Play: Technology that gives a computer the capability to configure adapter cards and other peripherals automatically as a user installs them. **256**
Plug-in: Program that extends the capability of a browser; often used to enhance multimedia. **66**
Pocket PC, 266
Point, 106
Point of sale (POS), 180
Pointer: Small symbol displayed on a computer screen whose location and shape changes as a user moves a pointing device. **103, 167,** 197
Pointing device: Input device that allows a user to control a pointer on the screen. **167–72**
digital pen, 172, 175
joystick, 171
light pen, 171
mouse, 169
physically-challenged users, 197
pointing stick, 170
purchasing notebook computer and, 288
stylus, 172, 174
touch screen, 171
touchpad, 170

trackball, 170
wheel, 171
Pointing stick: Pressure-sensitive pointing device shaped like a pencil eraser that is positioned between keys on a keyboard and moved by pushing the pointing stick with a finger. **170**
Policy
acceptable use. *See* **Acceptable use policy (AUP)**
employee monitoring, 384
software installation and use, 372
Pop-up blocker: Filtering program that stops pop-up ads from displaying on Web pages. 122, **269**
Port: Point at which a peripheral attaches to a system unit so it can send data to or receive information from the computer. 136, **148–50**
Bluetooth, 150
COM, 149
FireWire, 150
IrDA, 150
LCD monitor, 185
MIDI, 150
parallel, 149, 150
purchasing desktop computer and, 281
purchasing notebook computer and, 288
SCSI, 150
serial, 149, 150
USB, 149–50
Portable (storage medium), 222
Portable computer. *See* **Notebook computer**
Portal: Web site that offers a variety of Internet services from a single, convenient location. **61, 467**
broadband and, 319
POS, 180. *See also* **Point of sale**
POS terminal: Terminal used by retail stores to record purchases, process credit or debit cards, and update inventory. **180**
Possessed object, 370, 371
Post-implementation system review, 422
Posture, 386
Power
flat-panel monitor use of, 185
problems with, 374–75
saving, 387
PowerBuilder: Powerful program development tool developed by Sybase that is best suited for Web-based and large-scale enterprise object-oriented applications. **429**

Power Macintosh, processor in, 139

Power supply: Component of the system unit that converts wall outlet AC power to the DC power that is used by a computer. 136, **152**
CMOS, 146
notebook computers, 152
RAM and, 143, 144

Power user: User who requires the capabilities of a workstation or other powerful computer, typically working with multimedia applications and using industry-specific software. 18, **21**
input devices for, 196
output devices, 192, 196
printers, 192
processor selection, 154
storage and, 220–21, 239
UNIX and, 264

Powerline cable network, 316
PowerPC G4, 139
PowerPC G5, 139

Practical Extraction and Report Language, 435. *See also* **Perl**

Preliminary investigation: Investigation that determines the exact nature of a problem or improvement and decides whether it is worth pursuing. Also called feasibility study. **413–14.** *See also* **Feasibility study**

Presentation graphics software: Application software that allows a user to create visual aids for presentations to communicate ideas, messages, and other information to a group. 11, **109**

Presentations
developing using presentation graphics software, 109
multimedia, 114

Pretty Good Privacy (PGP): Popular e-mail encryption program that is free for personal, noncommercial use. **374**

Price
of personal computers, 144
scanned items and, 178

Primary key: Field in a database that uniquely identifies each record in a file. Also called key field. **336.** *See also* **Key field**

Print: Placing the copy of a document on paper or some other medium. **106**
Print server, 305
Print spooler, 256

Printer: Output device that produces text and graphics on a physical medium such

as paper or transparency film. 7, **187–93**
dot-matrix, 192
impact, 192–93
ink-jet, 189–90
large-format, 192
laser, 190–91
line, 193
mobile, 192
nonimpact, 189–92
parallel ports, 149
photo, 190
plotters, 192
purchasing desktop computer and, 283, 284
storage media for, 236
thermal, 191

Printer sharing, Internet connection and, 379

Printing
database report, 346
digital images, 175
pictures from Picture CD, 232
process of, 106
screen display and, 103
spooling and, 256

Privacy
brain fingerprinting and, 384
disadvantage in computers, 5
consumer, 461
employee monitoring and, 120, 384
information, 379–85
laws, 382–83
medical records and, 239

Procedural language: Type of programming language in which a programmer writes instructions that tell the computer what to accomplish and how to do it using a series of English-like words to write instructions. Often called a third-generation language (3GL). **425–26.** *See also* **Third-generation language (3GL)**

Procedure, 456
backup, 478
Process (enterprise), workflow and, 469

Processing
batch, 462
electronic data interchange (EDI) and, 468
grid computing and, 478
multi-, 255
online transaction (OLTP), 462

Processor: Electronic component on a computer's motherboard that interprets and carries out the basic instructions that operate the computer. Also called CPU or central processing unit. **7, 137–39.** *See also* **Central processing unit (CPU)**
purchasing desktop computer and, 281, 283

purchasing notebook computer and, 288

Product activation: Process that attempts to prevent software piracy by requiring users to provide a software product's 25-character identification number in order to receive an installation identification number. **373**

Product design, software for, 459

Production, manufacturing enterprise and, 459

Profile, electronic, 380

Program: Series of instructions that tells a computer what to do and how to do it. Also called software. **10**
background, 254, 255
backup of, 223, 374–75
designing, 419
development tools, 431–32
foreground, 254–255
kernel managing, 252

Program development cycle: Series of steps programmers use to build computer programs, consisting of six steps: (1) analyze requirements, (2) design solution, (3) validate design, (4) implement design, (5) test solution, and (6) document solution. 420, **438–42**

Program development tools: Program that provides a VPE or user-friendly environment for building programs. **428–32**

Program specification package, 419

Programmer: Person who writes and modifies computer programs. Also called a developer. **12, 423, 442**
career as, 442
layout chart for, 419
program development cycle and, 438–39

Programming
learning, 432

Programming language: Set of words, symbols, and codes that enables a programmer to communicate instructions to a computer. **423–37**
low-level, 424–25
machine-dependent, 424
object-oriented, 427–29
other, 430–31
procedural, 425–26
visual, 428–29

Programming team: A group of programmers that may develop programs during the program development cycle. **439**

Project leader: Member of a

project team who manages and controls the budget and schedule of the project. **408**

Project management: Process of planning, scheduling, and then controlling the activities during the system development cycle. **408–9**

Project management software (users): Application software that allows a user to plan, schedule, track, and analyze the events, resources, and costs of a project. **111**

Project plan, 409

Project request: Written, formal request for a new or modified system. Also called a request for system services. **411.** *See also* Request for system services

Project team: Group of people that consists of users, the systems analyst, and other IT professionals. **408**
preliminary investigation and, 414

Projector, data, 195, 289

Prolog, 431

Proprietary (Information systems), 478. *See also* Closed (Information systems)

Protocol, Internet address, 53, 54

Prototype: Working model of a proposed system. **419**

Proxy server, 368

Pruning, 217

PSTN, 310. *See also* Public switched telephone network (PSTN)

Public Internet access point: Location where people can connect wirelessly to the Internet using mobile computers or other devices. **300**

Public switched telephone network (PSTN), 310

Public-domain software: Free software that has been donated for public use and has no copyright restrictions. **101**

Publishing entities, content management systems and, 466

Publishing, computers used in, 25

Publish, 10

Purchasing
desktop computer, 281–87
mobile device, 292–94
notebook computer, 287–89
personal computer, 279–81
processors, 139
tablet PC, 290–91
Pure Tablet PCs, 290

QBE, 345. *See also* **Query by example**

QUALCOMM, 323

Quality review, 419

Quarantine: Separate area of a hard disk that holds the infected file until a virus can be removed. **366**

Queue: Lineup of multiple print jobs within a buffer. **256**

Query: Request for specific data from a database. **109, 344,** 348, 349

Query by example (QBE): DBMS feature that has a graphical user interface to assist users with retrieving data. **345**

Query language: Language used with databases that consists of simple, English-like statements that allows users to specify the data to display, print, or store. **344,** 348, 349, 430

Questionnaire, for system development, 410

RAD: Rapid application development. Method of developing software in which a programmer writes and implements a program in segments instead of waiting until an entire program is finished. **428,** 429. *See also* **Rapid application development**

Radiation, display devices and, 186

Radio, broadcast, 321

Radio frequency identification, 178–79, 309. *See also* **RFID**

Radio waves
  Bluetooth and, 309
  microwave, 321

RAID (redundant array of independent disks): Redundant array of independent disks. Group of two or more integrated hard disks that acts like a single large hard disk. **474**

RAM (random access memory): Type of memory that can be read from and written to by the processor and other devices. Programs and data are loaded into RAM from storage devices such as a hard disk and remain in RAM as long as the computer has continuous power. 142, **143–45.** *See also* **Main memory; Primary storage**
  access times, 146
  booting computer and, 252

operating system managing, 255
  purchasing desktop computer and, 281, 283
  system files loaded into, 252
  types of, 144

Random access memory (RAM), 143–45. *See also* **RAM**

Range check: Validity check that determines whether a number is within a specified range. **340**

Rapid application development, 428. *See also* **RAD**

Reading: Process of transferring data, instructions, and information from a storage medium into memory. **222**
  CD-R, 232
  CD-ROM, 231
  CD-RW, 232
  direct access and, 235
  floppy disk, 223,
  hard disk, 224

Read-only memory (ROM): Type of nonvolatile memory that is used to store permanent data and instructions. **145**
  access times, 146

Read/write head, 224, 225, 226
  hard disk, 224, 225, 226

Real time: Describes users and the people with whom they are conversing being online at the same time. **71**

RealOne Player, 64

Recalculation, in spreadsheets, 108

Receiving device: Device that accepts the transmission of data, instructions, or information. **296,** 306

Record: Group of related fields in a database . **108, 336**
  adding, 336
  changing, 338
  deleting, 338–9

Recording, audio and video, 399

Recording Industry of America (RIAA), 46

Recovery disk (boot), 268. *See also* Boot disk

Recovery plan, 479

Recovery utility: DBMS feature that uses logs and/or backups to restore a database when it becomes damaged or destroyed. **346**

Recycling
  computer equipment, 387
  toner cartridges, 191

Red Hat, 271

Redundancy, 477

Redundant array of independent disks, 474. *See*

also **RAID (redundant array of independent disks)**

Redundant components: Components used so that a functioning computer can take over automatically the tasks of a similar component that fails. **477**

Redundant data, 341, 342

Reference software: Application software that provides valuable and thorough information for all individuals. **119**

Refresh rate, 186
  CRT monitor, 186

Regional ISP, 52

Relation: Term used by developers of relational databases for file. **347**

Relational database: Database that stores data in tables that consist of rows and columns, with each row having a primary key and each column having a unique name. **347–48,** 353

Relationship: Connection within data in a database. **348**
  logical, 340

Reliability of computers, 5

Removable disk drives, backup using, 375

Removable hard disk: Hard disk that can be inserted and removed from either a dock or drive. **227.** *See also* **Disk cartridge**

Repetition control structure: Type of control structure that enables a program to perform one or more actions repeatedly as long as a certain condition is met. Also called a loop. **441–42**

Repetitive strain injury (RSI): Injury or disorder of the muscles, nerves, tendons, ligaments, and joints. 168, **385**
  government standards and, 169

Replace, 105

Report
  database, 108, 346
  decision support system and, 463
  feasibility, 414
  management information system and, 462–63

Report generator: DBMS feature that allows users to design a report on the screen, retrieve data into the report design, and then display or print the report. Also called a report writer. **346.** *See also* **Report writer**

Report Program Generator, 430. *See also* **RPG**

Report writer, 346, 432. *See also* **Report generator**

Request for information (RFI), 16, 417

Request for proposal (RFP), 416, 417

Request for quotation (RFQ), 416, 417

Request for system services, 411. *See also* Project request

Requirements analysis, during program development, 439

Research
  in design phase, 416
  market, 460
  for system development, 410
  Web site, 96

Reset button, restarting computer using, 252

Resolution: The number of horizontal and vertical pixels in a display device. **175**
  CRT monitor, 186
  ink-jet printers, 189
  LCD displays, 185

Resources, 8
  Web site, 87

Resources (enterprise) coordinating and controlling, 456

Response time, 185

Restarting a computer, 252

Restore: To copy backed up files by copying them to their original location on the computer. **375**

Restore program: Program that reverses the backup process and returns backed up files to their original form. **261**

REstructured eXtended eXecutor, 435. *See* **Rexx**

Retailers
  See also **E-tail**

Review, post-implementation system, 422

Revolutions per minute (rpm), 226

Rexx: REstructured eXtended eXecutor. Procedural interpreted scripting language for both professional programmers and nontechnical users. **435.** *See also* **REstructured eXtended eXecutor**

RFI, 416, 417. *See* Request for information (RFI)

RFID: Short for radio frequency identification; standard, specifically a protocol, that defines how a network uses radio signals to communicate with a tag placed in or attached to an object, an animal, or a person. 178–79, **309.** *See also*

Radio frequency identification

RFID reader: Reading device that reads information on an RFID tag via radio waves. **178**

RFID tags, 47

RFP, 416, 417. *See* Request for proposal (RFP)

RFQ, 416, 417. *See* Request for quotation (RFQ)

RIAA. *See* Recording Industry of America

Ring network: Type of network topology in which a cable forms a closed loop (ring) with all computers and devices arranged along the ring. **307**

Ripping, 232

Ritchie, Dennis, 427

Robots,22, 439

ROM, 145. *See also* **Read-only memory**

Router: Communications device that connects multiple computers or other routers together and transmits data to its correct destination on a network. **315–16**

Routing slip, collaboration and, 302

Row (database): Term used by users of relational databases for record. 108, **347**

Row (spreadsheet), 107

RPG: Report Program Generator. Developed by IBM in the early 1960s to assist businesses in generating reports. **430.** *See also* **Report Program Generator**

Rpm, 226. *See also* Revolutions per minute (rpm)

RSI, 385. *See also* **Repetitive strain injury (RSI)**

Run: Process of using software. **12**

Russo, Patricia, 323

Safeguards, 363

Sales force automation (SFA): Software that equips traveling salespeople with the electronic tools they need to be more productive. **460**

SAN, 475. *See also* **Storage area network (SAN)**

SanDisk Corporation, 241

SAP, 481

SATA, 228. *See also* Serial Advanced Technology Attachment

Satellite communications, 321–22

GPS and, 301

microwave and, 321

Satellite companies Internet structure and, 51

wireless Internet access, 52

Satellite modem: Internet connection that communicates with a satellite dish to provide high-speed Internet connections via satellite. **52**

Save: To transfer a document from a computer's memory to a storage medium. **106**

Scalability: Measure of how well computer hardware, software, or an information system can grow to meeting increasing performance demands. **477**

Scanner: Light-sending input device that reads printed text and graphics and then translates the results into a form the computer can process. 6, **177**–80. *See also* Optical scanner

bar code, 178

fingerprint, 181

flatbed, 177

optical, 177

purchasing desktop computer and, 283

Scanner fraud, 178

Scenes, 217

Schedule feasibility, 409

School connecting to Internet through, 51

content filtering used by, 384

Science, computers used in, 24

Web site, 93

Screen, 186

Screen saver: Utility program that causes a display device's screen to show a moving image or blank screen if no mouse activity occurs for a specified time. **261**

Scope, 408

Script,434

Script kiddie: Someone who accesses a computer or network illegally with the intent of destroying data, stealing information, or other malicious action but does not have the technical skills and knowledge. **362**

Scripting language, 434–35

Scrolling: Process of moving different portions of a document on the computer's screen into view. **105**

SCSI interface, 228

SCSI port: Special high-speed parallel port to which peripherals, such as disk drives and printers, can be attached. **150**

SD, 236. *See also* **Secure Digital**

Search engine: Program that

finds Web sites and Web pages. **57, 58, 60**–61

3-D, 61

databases and, 350

popular search sites and, 58

portal link to, 467

using, 57, 58, 60–61, 96

Search sites, popular, 58

Search text: Word or phrase entered in a search engine's text box to find information on a Web page. **60**–61. *See also* **Keywords**

Search tools, 96

Secondary storage, 221. *See also* **Storage medium**

Sectors, 222

floppy disk, 223

storing data and, 261

Secure Digital (SD): Type of miniature mobile storage medium that is a flash memory card capable of storing between 16 MB and 1 GB of data. **236**

Secure site: Web site that uses encryption techniques to secure its data. **374**

Security, 362–76, 389

backup and, 375, 478

biometric devices and, 181

database, 341, 342, 346, 351

developing plan, 479

disaster recovery plan and, 479

enterprise storage system and, 476

enterprise-wide, 479

ethics and, 376–78

financial Web sites, 472

hardware vandalism and theft, 371

information privacy, 379–85

information system, 422

information theft, 373–74

Internet and, 389

online shopping, 471

operating system and, 258

passwords and, 258

personal data and, 350

screen savers for, 261

software theft, 372–73, 378

system failure, 374–75

unauthorized access, 368–70

unauthorized use, 368–70

virtual private network and, 470

Selection control structure: Type of control structure that tells the program which action to take, based on a certain condition. **440**

Selective backup, 375, 478. *See also* Partial backup

Sending device: Device that initiates instructions to transmit data, instructions, or information. **296,** 297, 306

Sequence control structure: Type of control structure

that shows one or more actions following each other in order. **440**

Sequential access, 235

Serial Advanced Technology Attachment, 228. *See* SATA

Serial port: Type of interface that connects a device to the system unit by transmitting data one bit at a time. **149,** 150

Server: Computer that controls access to the hardware, software, and other resources on a network and provides a centralized storage area for programs, data, and information. **50, 305.** *See also* **Host**

blade, 477

database, 305, 350

dedicated, 305

file, 305

FTP, 71

midrange, 16

network, 305

network attached storage, 474

network operating system on, 266

print, 305

processors, 139

proxy, 368

Web, 54

Service plan, purchasing computer and, 287

Servlet, 434

Session cookie, 381

SFA, 460. *See also* **Sales force automation (SFA)**

Shareware: Copyrighted software that is distributed at no cost for a trial period. **101**

Sharing copyrighted music, 114

copyrighted videos, 114

resources, 8

Shipping, distribution systems and, 460

Shockley, William, 35

Shockwave, 443

Shopping e-commerce used for, 68

Shopping bot: Web site that searches the Internet for the best price on a product or service. **472**

Shopping cart: Element of an electronic storefront that allows a customer to collect purchases. **68,** 470

cookies and, 381

Short message service (SMS), 298

Shugart, Al, 37, 38, 241

Siebel, Tom, 481

Siebel Systems, Inc., 481

Signature verification system, 181, 370

Single user/multitasking, 253
Single user/single tasking, 253
Single-session disc, 231
Picture CD, 232
Single-user license agreement, 372. *See also* End-user license agreement (EULA)
Slide show, 109
Small office/home office (SOHO): Describes any company with fewer than 50 employees, as well as the self-employed who work from home. 18, **20**
  input devices, 196
  output devices, 190, 196
  printer, 190
  processor selection, 154
  storage and, 239
  Web cam, 176
Smalltalk, 431
Smart card: Card, similar in size to a credit card or ATM card, that stores data on a thin microprocessor embedded in the card. 181, **237**
Smart card (biometric): Card that stores personal biometric data on a thin microprocessor embedded in the card. **181**
Smart dust, 179
Smart Media: Type of miniature mobile storage medium that is a flash memory card capable of storing between 32 MB and 128 MB of data. **236**
Smart phone: Internet-enabled telephone that usually also provides PDA capabilities. **16**, 48
  flash memory and, 145, 148
  mobile users, 21
  operating system for, 266
  picture messaging and, 298
  screen on, 184
  storage media for, 225
  text messaging and, 298
  Web access and, 436
  wireless service provider and, 52
Smart watch: Internet-enabled watch. **16**
SMS (short message service). 298. *See also* **Text messaging**
SoBig virus, 46
Social security number, protecting, 379
Society
  computer applications in, 22–26
  ethics and, 376–78
Software: Series of instructions that tells a computer what to do and how to do it. Also called a program. **10–13**
  acquiring in design phase, 416
  bundled, 281

communications, 310
compatibility, 280
copyrighted, 378
custom, 101, 415
development of, 12
enterprise, 456–66
filtering, 310
illegal copying of, 124
installing new, 252
license agreement, 372–73
open source, 265, 267, 271
packaged, 101, 415
purchasing desktop computer and, 281
suite, 116
system, 10–11
system failure and, 374–75
testing, 417
vendors, 417
Software piracy, 372, 378
Software suite: Collection of individual programs sold as a single package. Business software suites typically include word processing, spreadsheet, e-mail, and presentation graphics software. **110**, 116, 281
Software theft: Computer security risk that occurs when someone (1) steals software media, (2) intentionally erases programs, or (3) illegally copies a program. **372–73**, 378
SOHO, 20. *See also* **Small office/home office**
Solaris, 266
Son, Masayoshi, 125
Sound, 64, 173. *See also* **Audio; Microphone; Music; Sound card; Speakers**
Sound card: Adapter card that enhances the sound generating capabilities of a personal computer by allowing sound to be input through a microphone and output through external speakers or headset. 135, **147**
  MIDI standard, 150
  purchasing desktop computer and, 283
Source document, 177
Source program: Program that contains the language instructions, or code, to be converted to machine language. **425–26**
Spam: Unsolicited e-mail message or newsgroups posting sent to many recipients or newsgroups at once. 48, **73**, **268**, 379, **382**
Speakers: Audio output devices that generate sound. 7, **193**
  purchasing desktop computer and, 283, 284
  purchasing Tablet PC and, 291

Special-purpose terminal, 180
Speech, 64
Speech recognition: Computer's capability of distinguishing spoken words. Also called voice recognition. **173**
Speed
  advantage in computers, 5
  access times, 146
  bus, 151
  bus width, 151
  cache, 144–45
  processor, 139
  RAM, 144–45
  of storage devices and memory, 222
  system clock influence on, 139
Spelling checker, 106
Splitting, 217
Spoiler, 73
Spoofing: Technique intruders use to make their network or Internet transmission appear legitimate to a victim computer or network. **367**
  safeguards against, 367–68
Spooling: Operating system process that sends print jobs to a buffer instead of sending them immediately to the printer. The buffer then holds the information waiting to print while the printer prints from the buffer at its own rate of speed. **256**
Sports, Web site and, 91
Spreadsheet software: Application software that allows a user to organize data in rows and columns and to perform calculations on the data. 11, **107–8**
Spyware: Program placed on a computer without the user's knowledge that secretly collects information about the user. 48, **381**
Spyware remover: Program that detects and deletes spyware on a user's computer. 122, **268**
SQL: Query language that allows users to manage, update, and retrieve data in a relational DBMS. **348, 430.** *See also* **Structured Query Language**
SRAM, 144. *See also* Static RAM
Stand By, 252
Stand-alone operating system: Complete operating system that works on a desktop computer, notebook computer, or mobile computing device and that also works

in conjunction with a network operating system. **262–65.** *See also* **Client operating system**
Stand-alone utility programs, 122, 259, 267–70
Standards: Sets of rules and procedures a company expects employees to accept and follow. **407**
Star network: Type of network topology in which all computers and devices on the network connect to a central device, thus forming a star. **307**
Start button (Windows XP), starting application using, 103
Starting
  application software, 102, 103
  See also **Booting**
Startup instructions, flash memory holding, 145
Static RAM (SRAM), 144
Steering committee: Decision-making body in a company. **408**
  approval by, and, 418
  implementation phase and, 419
  planning phase and, 412
  preliminary investigation and, 414
  system proposal and, 415
Stock trading, online, 472
Stoll, Clifford, 389
Storage, 142, 220–41
  advantage in computers, 5
  back up and, 261
  buffer, 255
  clipboard used for, 106
  compressed files, 261
  digital cameras using, 175
  file manager functions, 259
  grid computing and, 478
  network attached (NAS), 474, 476
  online, 375
  RAID and, 474
  saving document and, 106
  scalability, 477
  storage area network (SAN), 475, 476
  swapping data between memory and, 255
  terms, 222
Storage appliance, 474
Storage area network (SAN): High-speed network with the sole purpose of providing storage to other servers to which it is attached. **475**, 476
Storage device: Hardware used to record (write and/or read) items to and from storage media. 7, **222**
  size of, 142
Storage media: The physical

material on which a computer keeps data, instructions, and information. 7, **221**
access times, 222
capacity, 222
CD, 232
CD-ROM, 231
CD-RW, 232
DVD, 233
DVD+RW, 234
DVD-RW, 234
DVD-ROM, 233
floppy disk, 222, 223
hard disk, 224–28
microfiche, 238
microfilm, 238
miniature mobile, 235–37
online storage, 228
optical discs, 229–34
PC Card, 235
Picture CD, 232
tape, 235–35
Zip disk, 223
Stored program concept, 142
Storing, 138. *See also* **Storage**
Strategic decisions, 463
Streaming: Process of transferring data in a continuous and even flow. **64,** 472
Streaming audio, 64
Streaming video, 65
Structured Query Language (SQL): Query language used with databases that allows users to manage, update, and retrieve data. **348, 430**
Stylus: Small metal or plastic device that looks like a ballpoint pen, but uses pressure instead of ink to write, draw, or make selections. **15, 172,** 174, 293. *See also* **Digital pen**
Subject directory: Search tool that classifies Web pages in an organized set of categories and subcategories. **57,** 58, 96
popular search sites and, 96
using, 96
Submenu, 103
Subscribe (mailing list): Process of a user adding his or her e-mail name and address to a mailing list. **71**
Subwoofer, 193
Summary report, 462
Sun, 266
J2EE platform, 469
Jackpot, 420
Java and, 41, 443
JavaScript, 434
Sun StarOffice, 110
Supercomputer: Fastest, most powerful, and most expensive computer, capable of processing more than 100 trillion instructions in a single second. **17**

Support phase: Phase of the system development cycle that consists of four major activities: (1) conduct a post-implementation system review, (2) identify errors, (3) identify enhancements, and (4) monitor system performance. 406, **422**
Support tools, for application software, 122–24
Surfing the Web: Activity of using links to explore the Web. **57**
anonymously, 379
Surge protector: Device that uses special electrical components to smooth out minor noise, provide a stable current flow, and keep an overvoltage from reaching the computer and other electronic equipment. Also called a surge suppressor. **374–75**
S-video, 215
Sybase, 353, 429
Symantec, 389
Symbian, 271
Symbian OS, 267
Symbolic address, 425
Symbolic instruction codes, 424
Synthesizer, 150
System: Set of components that interact to achieve a common goal. **406**
System board, 136. *See also* Motherboard
System bus: Bus that is part of the motherboard and connects the processor to main memory. **151**
System clock: Small quartz crystal circuit that is used by the processor to control the timing of all computer operations. **138**
System developer: Person responsible for designing and developing an information system. Also called a systems analyst. **408**
System development guidelines, 407
project team, 408
System development cycle: Set of activities used to build an information system, including planning, analysis, design, implementation, and support. **406**–22, 438–39
analysis phase, 406, 413–15
design phase, 406, 416–19
feasibility assessment, 409
implementation phase, 406, 420–21
loop, 406
planning phase, 406, 412–13, 422

project management, 408–9
support phase, 406, 422
System enhancement: Support phase activity that involves modifying or expending an existing information system. **422**
System failure: Prolonged malfunction of a computer. **374–75**
System files
uninstalling programs and, 260
System proposal: Document that assesses the feasibility of each alternative solution and then recommends the most feasible solution for a project. **415**
System software: Programs that control or maintain the operations of a computer and its devices. **10–11, 101, 250–71**
memory and, 142
role of, 101
System unit: Case that contains the electronic components of a computer that are used to process data. **7, 134–36**
adapter cards, 147–48
bays, 151
buses, 151
cleaning, 155
connectors, 148–50
data representation and, 140–41
expansion slots, 147
hard disk in, 224
memory and, 142–46
mobile computers and devices, 152–53
motherboard, 136
ports, 148–50
power supply, 152
processor. *See* **Processor**
Systems analysis
preliminary investigation and, 413–14
Systems analyst: Person responsible for designing and developing an information system. Also called a system developer. **407**
need for, 408
preliminary investigation and, 413–14
program development and, 439
role of, 407–8
system proposal and, 415
testing software, 417
user and, 407
Systems programmer: Person who evaluates, installs, and maintains system software and provides technical support to the programming staff. **270**
Systems test, 420

T1 line: The most popular T-carrier line. **312**
T3 line, 312
Table: Term used by users of relational databases for file. **347**
Tablet PC: Special type of notebook computer that resembles a letter-sized slate, which allows a user to write on the screen using a digital pen. **5,** 135, 153
Tags, 433
XML, 436
Tape: Magnetic Magnetically coated ribbon of plastic capable of storing large amounts of data and information at a low cost. **234–35,** 375
Tape cartridge, 234
Tape drive: Device used to read and write data and information on tape. **234**
bays and, 151
Tape library, 234, 476
Tax preparation software: Application software that is used to guide individuals, families, or small businesses through the process of filing federal taxes. **117**
TB, 142. *See also* **Terabyte.**
T-carrier line: Any of several types of long-distance digital telephone lines that carry multiple signals over a single communications line. **312**
Tcl: Tool Command Language. Interpreted scripting language maintained by Sun Microsystems Laboratories. **435.** *See also* **Tool Command Language**
TCP/IP: Short for Transmission Control Protocol/Internet Protocol; network standard, specifically a protocol, that defines how messages (data) are routed from one end of a network to the other, ensuring the data arrives correctly. **308**
Technical feasibility, 409
Technical support, 353
Technology
access to, 22
enterprise strategy, 461
Telecommuting: Work arrangement in which employees work away from a company's standard workplace and often communicate with the office through the computer. **22,** 42

Telemedicine: Form of long-distance health care where health-care professionals in separate locations conduct live conferences on the computer. **24,** 44

Telephone
cellular. *See* Cellular telephone
smart. *See* **Smart phone**
twisted-pair cable, 319

Telephone adapters, purchasing notebook computer and, 289

Telephone companies, Internet structure and, 51

Telephone line
connecting to Internet through, 51–52
home network using, 316
surge protection and, 375

Telephone network, communications over, 310–12

Telephone number, unlisted, 379

Television
connecting computer to, 288
entertainment and, 398

Template, 118

Tendonitis: Inflammation of a tendon due to some repeated motion or stress on that tendon. **385**

Terabyte (TB): Approximately one trillion bytes. **142**

Terminal: Device that consists of a keyboard, a monitor, a video card, and memory, which often all are housed in a single unit. 17, **180**

Test
benchmark, 417
disaster recovery plan, 479
feasibility, 409
new information system, 420
product designs, 459
software and hardware, 417

Test plan, 479

Text
editing in word processing document, 106
input, 177
links, 57
optical character recognition and, 177
output, 182
search, 60–61
Web page, 53, 57
worksheet, 107

Text data type, 335

Text messaging: Service that allows users to send and receive short text messages on a smart phone or PDA. **298** *See also* Short message service (SMS)

Theft
hardware. *See* **Hardware theft**
identity. *See* **Identity theft**
information. *See* **Information theft**

software. *See* **Software theft**

Thermal printer: Type of nonimpact printer that generates images by pushing electrically heated pins against heat-sensitive paper. **191**

Third-generation language (3GL): Type of programming language in which a programmer writes instructions that tell the computer what to accomplish and how to do it using a series of English-like words to write instructions. Also called a procedural language. **425.** *See also* **Procedural language**

Thrashing, 255

Three-generation backup policy, 375

Thumbnail: Small version of a larger graphic. **64**
image viewer and, 259

Time schedules, for system development, 408–9

TIFF, 211

Timely information, 334

Title bar: Horizontal space, located at the top of a window, that contains the window's name. **103**

T-Mobile, 52

Token, 308

Token ring: Network standard in which computers and devices on the network share or pass a special signal, called a token, in a unidirectional manner and in a preset order. **308**

Toner, 191
disposing of, 191

Tool Command Language, 435. *See* **Tcl**

ToolBook, 437

Top-level domain: Identifies the type of organization associated with the domain. **54**

Topology. *See* **Network topology**

Torvalds, Linus, 41, 271

Touch screen: Touch-sensitive display device with which users interact by touching areas of the screen. **171**

Touchpad: Small, flat, rectangular pointing device that is sensitive to pressure and motion. **170**

Tower, 14

TPS, 461–62. *See also* **Transaction processing system (TPS)**

Track, 222
floppy disk, 223
hard disk, 225, 226

Trackball: Stationary pointing device with a ball on its top

or side. **170**

Tracking, GPS used for, 301

Traffic, 52

Training
computer-based. *See* **Computer-based training**
Web-based, 123

Training (system development): Showing users exactly how they will use new hardware and software in a system. **421**

Transaction, 461

Transaction processing system (TPS): Information system that captures and processes data from day-to-day business activities. **461–62** *See also* **Data processing**

Transfer rate
telephone line, 312

Transistor, 136, 157
history of, 35

Transitions, 218

Transmission Control Protocol/Internet Protocol, 308. *See also* **TCP/IP**

Transmission media: Materials or substances capable of carrying one or more signals in a communications channel. **318**

Travel, computers used in, 25

Travel Web sites, 85, 473

Trojan horse: Malicious-logic program named after the Greek myth that hides within or looks like a legitimate program. **267, 364–66**
safeguards against, 365–66

True condition, selection control structure and, 440

Trusted source, 365

Tuple: Term used by developers of relational databases for record. **347**

Turing, Alan, 35

Turnaround document: Document that a user returns to the company that has created and sent it. **177**

Twisted-pair cable: Transmission media that consists of one or more twisted-pair wires bundled together. **319**

Twisted-pair wire, 319

Typing, repetitive strain injuries and, 385

Ultradense servers, 477. *See also* Blade servers

Unauthorized access: Use of a computer or network without permission. **368–70**

Unauthorized use: Use of a computer or its data for unapproved or possibly illegal activities. **368–70**

Uncompress: To restore a com-

pressed, or zipped, file to its original form. *See also* unzip. **269.** *See also* **Unzip**

Uniform Resource Locator, 56. *See also* **URL; Web address**

Uninstaller: Utility program that removes a program, as well as any associated entries in the system files. **260**

Uninstalling programs, 260

Uninterruptible power supply (UPS): Device that contains surge protection circuits and one or more batteries that can provide power during a temporary or permanent loss of power. 286, **375**

Unit test, 420

UNIVAC 1, 35. *See* Universal Automatic Computer

Universal Automatic Computer (UNIVAC 1), 35

Universal serial bus port: Port that can connect up to 127 different peripherals with a single connector type. **149–50.** *See also* **USB port**

UNIX: Multitasking operating system that now is available for most computers of all sizes. **264,** 265, 266, 427

Unsubscribe: Process of a user removing his or her e-mail name and address from a mailing list. **71**

Unzip, 269. *See also* **Uncompress**

Updating
antivirus programs, 365
data, 338

Upgrade, 262

Uplink, 321

Uploading: Process of transferring documents, graphics, and other objects from a computer to a server on the Internet. **71**
compressed files, 269

UPS, 375. *See also* **Uninterruptible power supply (UPS)**

Upstream rate, 312

Upward compatible, 262

URL (Uniform Resource Locator): Unique address for a Web page. Also called a Web address. **56**

U.S. Robotics, 41

USB 2.0, 149

USB flash drive: Flash memory storage device that plugs in a USB port on a computer or portable device. 7, 47, **148,** 236. *See also* **Pen drive**

USB hub: Device that plugs in a USB port on the system unit and contains multiple USB ports in which cables from USB devices can be plugged. **149**–50

USB port: Port that can connect up to 127 different peripherals with a single connector type. **149**–50
keyboards with, 168
Use, unauthorized, 368–70
Useful information, 334

User: Anyone who communicates with a computer or utilizes the information it generates. **4**

User ID: Unique combination of characters, such as letters of the alphabet or numbers, that identifies one specific user. Also called user name. **258, 369.** *See also* **User name**

User interface: The portion of software that defines how a user interacts with a computer, including how the user enters data and instructions and how information is displayed on the screen. 10, **253**
command-line, 253, 262, 264, 265
graphical. *See* **Graphical user interface (GUI)**
menu-driven, 262

User name: Unique combination of characters, such as letters of the alphabet and/or numbers, that identifies a specific user. **70, 258, 369.** *See also* **User ID**

Users
access controls, 368–69, 373
authenticating using biometric devices, 181
authorized, 341, 346
commands issued by, 167
employee as, 351
hardware availability for, 474, 477
health concerns, 385–87
interacting with DBMS, 341–42
levels of, in enterprise, 455
names, 70
number on Internet, 50
passwords, 369
physically challenged. *See also* Physically challenged users
program development and, 431, 439
spyware collecting information about, 381
types of, 18–22
Web services and, 469

Users (system development): 407

Utility: Type of system software that allows a user to perform maintenance-type tasks, usually related to managing a computer, its devices, or its programs.

259–61. *See also* **Utility program**

Utility computing: Technology that allows companies to use the processing power sitting idle in a network located somewhere else in the world. Also called on demand computing. **478**

Utility program: Type of system software that allows a user to perform maintenance-type tasks usually related to managing a computer, its devices, or its programs. **11,** 250, **259**–61. *See also* **Utility**
anti-spam, 122
antivirus, 122, 267–68
backup, 261, 375
CD/DVD burning, 122, 269
diagnostic, 261
disk defragmenter, 261
disk scanner, 260
file compression, 122, 269
file conversion, 122, 269
file manager, 259
image viewer, 259
Internet filters, 268–69
operating system, 251, 259–61
personal computer maintenance, 122, 270
personal firewall, 260
pop-up blocker, 122
screen saver, 261
stand-alone, 259, 267–70
spyware remover, 122
uninstaller, 260
Web filter, 122
See also **Utility**

Validation: Process of comparing data with a set of rules or values to find out if the data is correct. **339**–40
Validity check, 339–40. *See also* Validation rules
Value, 107

Value-added network (VAN): Third-party business that provides networking services such as secure data and information transfer, storage, e-mail, and management reports. **303**

Value-added reseller (VAR): Company that purchases products from manufacturers and then resells these products to the public – offering additional services with the product. **417**

VAN, 303. *See also* **Value-added network (VAN)**
Vandalism, hardware, 371
VAR, 417. *See* **Value-added reseller (VAR)**
VBA, 432. *See* Visual Basic for Applications (VBA)

VBScript: Visual Basic, Scripting Edition. Subset of

the Visual Basic language that allows programmers to add intelligence and interactivity to Web pages. **435.** *See also* Visual Basic, Scripting Edition

Vendors
packaged software, 415
purchasing computers from, 286, 287
soliciting proposals from, 417
testing and evaluating proposals of, 417
virtual private network use, 470
See also Manufacturers
Verifiable information, 334
Vertical market software, 415

Video: Full-motion images that are played back at various speeds. **65**
entertainment software and, 120
multimedia and, 64
output, 182
processors and, 139
recording, 399
on Web page, 54
Video camera. *See* PC video camera

Video card: Adapter card that converts computer output to a video signal that travels through a cable to a monitor, which displays an image on the screen. 135, **147, 186.** *See also* **Graphics card**
purchasing desktop computer and, 283
terminal and, 180
See also **Graphics card**
Video CD, 218
Video chats, 72

Video conference: Meeting between two or more geographically separated people who use a network or the Internet to transmit audio and video data. **176**
software for, 121

Video editing software: Application software that allows a user to modify a segment of video, called a clip. **114**

Video input: Process of capturing full-motion images and storing them on a computer's storage medium. **176**
Video projector
connecting notebook computer to, 289

Video telephone call: Telephone call made using a PC video camera that allows both parties to see each other as they communicate over the Internet. **176**
Viewable size, 186

Virtual memory: A portion of a storage medium, usually the hard disk, that the operating system allocates to function as additional RAM. **255**

Virtual private network (VPN): Network that provides a mobile user with a secure connection to a company network server, as if the user has a private line. **470**

Virtual reality (VR): Computers used to simulate a real or imagined environment that appears as a three dimensional (3-D) space. **65**
multimedia and, 64

Virus: Potentially damaging computer program that affects, or infects, a computer negatively by altering the way the computer works without a user's knowledge or permission. **70, 122, 267**–68, **364**–66
first, 38
payload, 364
protection from, 267–68
safeguards against, 365–66
spyware as, 381
types of, 364–66
Virus author, 267

Virus definition: Known specific pattern of virus code. Also called virus signature. **366.** *See also* **Virus signature**

Virus hoax: E-mail message that warns users of a nonexistent virus, worm, or Trojan horse. **366**

Virus signature: Known specific pattern of virus code. Also called virus definition. **366.** *See also* **Virus definition**
VisiCalc, 38
Visual Basic for Applications (VBA), 432
Visual Basic 2005, 428

Visual Basic, Scripting Edition, 435. *See also* **VBScript**
Visual C# 2005, 428
Visual C++ 2005, 428
Visual J# 2005, 428
Visual programming environment (VPE), 428

Visual programming language: Programming language that provides a visual or graphical interface for creating source code. Sometimes called a fifth-generation language. **428**–29. *See also* **Fifth-generation language**

Visual Studio 2005: Latest suite of program development tools from Microsoft that assists programmers in building programs for Windows, Windows Mobile, or operating systems that support Microsoft's .NET architecture. 48, **428**–29

Visually impaired users, output devices for, 197

Voice chats, 72

Voice commands, querying database using, 345

Voice input: Process of entering data by speaking into a microphone. **173**

Voice mail: Service that functions much like an answering machine, allowing a user to leave a voice message for one or more people. **302**

Voice mailbox, 302

Voice output: Audio output that occurs when a user hears a person's voice or when a computer talks to the user through the speakers on the computer. **194**

Voice over IP: Technology that allows users to speak to other users over the Internet using their desktop computer, mobile computer, or mobile device. See also Internet telephony. **73**

Voice recognition: Computer's capability of distinguishing spoken words. Also called speech recognition. 106, **173**
RAM needed for, 144
See also **Speech recognition**

Voice verification system, 181, 370

VoiceXML (eXtensible Markup Language), 345

Volatile memory: Type of memory that loses its contents when a computer's power is turned off. **142,** 144

Volume control, for optical disc drives, 229

von Neumann, John, 35

VPE, 428. *See also* Visual programming environment

VPN, 470. *See also* **Virtual private network (VPN)**

VPN tunnel, 470

VR. *See* Virtual reality

W3C, 51. *See also* **World Wide Web Consortium**

Wall, Larry, 435

WAN, 304. *See also* **Wide area network (WAN)**

WAP, 309, 376. *See also* **Wireless Application Protocol (WAP)**

War driving: Intrusion technique in which a perpetrator attempts to connect to

wireless networks via their notebook computer while driving a vehicle through areas they suspect have a wireless network. **376**

Warm boot: Process of using the operating system to restart a computer. **252**

Warranty, purchasing computer and, 287

WBT, 123. *See also* **Web-based training**

Weather, Web site and, 91

Web: Worldwide collection of electronic documents called Web pages, the Web is one of the more popular services on the Internet. Also called the World Wide Web. **10,** 50, **54**–68
addresses, 56
browsing. *See* **Web browser**
communications uses and, 298
cookies and, 380–81
creator of, 75
denial of service attacks and, 367
e-commerce on, 67–68
freeware on, 101
information privacy and, 379–82
multimedia on, 64–66
navigating, 57
processors and, 139
public-domain software on, 101
publishing Web pages on. *See* Web publishing
searching for information on, 57–61
shareware on, 101
surfing, 57
surfing anonymously, 379
types of Web sites, 61–63
See also **Internet**

Web address: Unique address for a Web page. Also called a URL (Uniform Resource Locator). **56**

Web browser: Application software that allows users to access and view Web pages. Also called a browser. **54**
cookies and, 380, 381
encryption used by, 374
home page, 55,
online service provider, 52
software, 11, 121

Web cam: Video camera that displays its output on a Web page. **176**

Web database, 350

Web developer, 74

Web farming, 468

Web filtering software: Program that restricts access to certain material on the Web. **268, 385**

Web filter, 122

Web folders, communications uses and, 298

Web log, 63. *See also* **blog**
mobile, 63

Web page: Electronic document on the Web, which can contain text, graphics, audio, and video and often has built-in connections to other documents, graphics, Web pages, or Web sites. **10, 54**
downloading, 55
multimedia on, 64
number of visits per month, 56
portal, 467
searching for, 57–61

Web page authoring software: Software used to create Web pages that include graphical images, video, audio, animation, and other special effects with interactive content. **114, 436**

Web page authors: Designers of Web pages. **433**

Web publishing: Development and maintenance of Web pages. 66–67

Web server: Computer that delivers requested Web pages to a computer. **54**

Web services: Web applications created with any programming language or with any operating system to communicate and share data seamlessly. **302, 469**

Web site: Collection of related Web pages and associated items, such as documents and pictures, stored on a Web server. 10, 21, **54**
arts and literature, 98
auctions, 88
careers, 97
click stream and, 468
creating, 66, 67
deploying, 66, 67
directories, 59
entertainment, 84, 472
evaluating, 63, 377
environment, 94
finance, 86
government, 89
guide to, 83–98
health, 95, 473
home page, 55
learning, 92
maintaining, 66, 67
news, 91
planning, 66, 67
posting photographs on, 175
research and, 96
resources and, 87
scalability, 477
science and, 93
shopping, 90
sports, 91
travel, 85, 472

types of, 61–63, 83–98
weather, 91

Web-based Help, 122–23

Web-based training (WBT): Computer-based training that uses Internet technology and consists of application software on the Web. **23**

WEP, 376. *See also* **Wired Equivalent Privacy**

Wheel: Steering-wheel-type input device that is used to simulate driving a vehicle. **171**

Wheel, purchasing a computer and, 282

White House, Web site, 40

Whitman, Meg, 75

Wide area network (WAN): Network that covers a large geographic area (such as a city, country, or the world) using a communications channel that combines many types of media such as telephone lines, cables, and radio waves. **304**

Wi-Fi (wireless fidelity): Short for wireless fidelity; term for any network based on the 802.11 series of standards. 46, **309.** *See also* **802.11**

Wi-Fi Protected Access (WEP): Security standard that improves on WEP by authenticating network users and providing more advanced encryption techniques. **376**

Winchester hard drive, 38

Window: Rectangular area of a computer screen that displays data or information. **103**

Windows CE, 266

Windows operating system, 11

Windows 2000 Server, 266

Windows Explorer, 259

Windows Future Storage, 263. *See* WinFS

Windows Media Player, 64

Windows NT Server, 266

Windows Media Player, 401

Windows Mobile, 266, 292, 293

Windows Picture and Fax Viewer, 259

Windows Server 2003, 266

Windows XP: The latest version of the Windows operating system, which is Microsoft's fastest, most reliable Windows operating system. 11, 44, 48, **262**–63
date and time and, 146
desktop, 102
disk defragmenter, 261
features of, 262–63
file manager, 259
Internet connection, 256

personal firewall and, 260, 368

role of, 101

security, 257

Windows XP 64-bit Edition: 263

Windows XP Home Edition, 263

Windows XP Media Center Edition, 48, 263

Windows XP Professional, 263

Windows XP Tablet PC Edition, 263

WinFS, 263. *See also* Windows Future Storage

WinZip, 269

Wired Equivalent Privacy (WEP): Security standard that defines how to encrypt data as it travels across wireless networks. **376**

Wired home networks, 316

Wireless access point: Central communications device that allows computers and devices to transfer data wirelessly among themselves or to transfer data wirelessly to a wired network. **315**

wireless security and, 376

Wireless Application Protocol (WAP): Network standard, specifically a protocol, that specifies how some wireless mobile devices such as smart phones and PDAs can display the content of Internet services such as the Web, e-mail, chat rooms, and newsgroups. **309**

Web, 436

Wireless computer, 46

Wireless Ethernet, 309. *See* 802.11

Wireless fidelity, 309. *See also* Wi-Fi (wireless fidelity)

Wireless home networks, 316–17

Wireless instant messaging, 298

Wireless Internet access, 52, 292, 293, 300, 309, 314

Wireless Internet service provider (WISP): Type of Internet service provider that provides wireless Internet access to comput-

ers with wireless modems or access devices or to Internet-enabled mobile computers or devices. **52, 300**

Wireless keyboard *See also* Cordless keyboard

Wireless LAN (WLAN): Local area network that uses no physical wires. **303**

Wireless LAN Access Point, 283

Wireless markup language, 436. *See also* **WML**

Wireless messaging services, 298–99

cheating and, 299

Wireless modem: Modem that allows access to the Web wirelessly from a notebook computer, PDA, smart phone, or other mobile device. **314**

Wireless mouse. *See also* Cordless mouse

Wireless network

home, 288

purchasing notebook computer and, 288

Wireless port, 150

Wireless security, 375–76

firewalls and, 376

home users and, 375

mobile users and, 375

Wireless transmission media, 319, 320–22

WISP, 52, 300. *See also* **Wireless Internet service provider (WISP)**

WLAN, 303. *See also* **Wireless LAN (WLAN)**

WML: Wireless markup language. Subset of XML that allows Web page authors to design pages specifically for microbrowsers. **436.** *See also* **Wireless markup language**

Word processing software: One of the more widely used types of application software; allows a user to create and manipulate documents containing mostly text and sometimes graphics. 11, **105**–6. *See also* **Word processor**

developing document using, 106

See also **Word processor**

Word processor, 105–6. *See also* **Word processing software**

Wordwrap, 105

Workflow: Defined process that identifies the specific set of steps involved in completing a particular project or business process. **469**

Workflow application: Program that assists in the management and tracking of all the activities in a business process from start to finish. **469**

Workgroup computing, 302

Worksheet: Rows and columns used to organize data in a spreadsheet. **107**

Workspace, ergonomics and, 386

World Wide Web (WWW): Worldwide collection of electronic documents. **54**–68. *See also* **Web**

creation of, 40

World Wide Web Consortium (W3C): Consortium of more than 350 organizations from around the world that oversees research and sets standards and guidelines for many areas of the Internet. 40, **51,** 75

accessibility guidelines and, 197

Worm: Malicious-logic program that copies itself repeatedly, using up system resources and possibly shutting down the system. **267,** 364–66

WPA, 376. *See also* **Wi-Fi Protected Access**

Wrist rest, 385

Write-protect notch: Small opening on a floppy disk that has a tab a user can slide to cover or expose the notch. **223**

Write-protected recovery disk, 268

Writing: Process of transferring data, instructions, and information from memory to a storage medium. **222**

CD-R, 232

CD-ROMs, 231

CD-RW, 232

direct access and, 235

DVD+RW, 234

floppy disk, 222, 223

hard disk, 224

WWW, 54. *See also* **World Wide Web**

WYSIWYG (what you see is what you get), 103

xD Picture Card: Type of miniature mobile storage media that is a flash memory card capable of storing between 64 MB and 512 MB of data. **236**

Xeon, 139

XHTML: eXtensible HTML. Markup language that enables Web sites to be displayed more easily on microbrowsers in PDAs and smart phones. **436.** *See also* **Extensible HTML**

XML: eXtensible Markup Language. Format for sharing data that allows Web page authors to create customized tags, as well as use predefined tags. **436.** *See also* **eXtensible Markup Language**

Y2K (Year 2000), 43

Y2K bug, 43

Yahoo!, 61, 75

Yes/No data type, 335

Young, Bob, 271

Zip disk: Type of portable magnetic media that can store from 100 MB to 750 MB of data. **223**

direct access and, 235

Zip drive: Type of high-capacity disk drive, developed by Iomega Corporation, that can read from and write on a Zip disk. **223**

bay and, 151

purchasing desktop computer and, 283

Zipped files: Type of compressed files that usually have a .zip extension. **269**

PHOTO CREDITS